THE VIKING PORTABLE LIBRARY

Poets of the English Language

VOLUME I: LANGLAND TO SPENSER

The Viking Portable Library

POETS OF THE ENGLISH LANGUAGE

Edited by

W. H. AUDEN

and

NORMAN HOLMES PEARSON

VOLUME I: LANGLAND TO SPENSER

VOLUME II: MARLOWE TO MARVELL

VOLUME III: MILTON TO GOLDSMITH

VOLUME IV: BLAKE TO POE

VOLUME V: TENNYSON TO YEATS

POETS
OF THE
ENGLISH
LANGUAGE

I

Langland to Spenser

With *emendations of texts, and glosses, by*
E. TALBOT DONALDSON

NEW YORK
The Viking Press
1950

Grateful acknowledgment is made to the following
for permission to reprint selections. Houghton Mif-
flin Company, Boston, excerpt from F. N. Robin-
son's text of *The Romance of the Rose* and from
Troilus and Criseide and *The Canterbury Tales*,
Works of Geoffrey Chaucer, edited by F. N. Robin-
son; Harvard University Press, Cambridge, and
Routledge and Kegan Paul, Ltd., London, excerpts
from *The Collected Poems of Sir Thomas Wyatt*,
edited by Kenneth Muir.

General Principles

SELECTION

Literary judgment is neither completely conditioned by history nor completely autonomous. On the one hand, critical opinion as to which are the great masterpieces or upon the division between major and minor work remains substantially the same at all times: for example, *The Iliad, The Divine Comedy, Anthony and Cleopatra, War and Peace,* are great for every generation; on the other hand, the particular aspects of any great poet which elicit attention and the relative positions of writers of the second rank are always varying slightly. Tennyson enjoyed a period of great glory, then was for a time ignored, and now is once again admired. The same variation is exhibited by individual taste in any one period; while all agree that Shakespeare is a great dramatist, many differ as to which is his greatest play.

Although an anthology may be regarded as a public treasury, it can never include the total sum of poetical resources, or, invariably, the particular preferences of individuals. The creation of an anthology involves choice, and choice in turn involves the personalities of the editors. Impersonality is as dull in a book of this sort as it is in human beings. Nevertheless, a primary concern with the themes and craft of poetry in English serves as a controlling check against vagrant idiosyncrasy. What we have tried to give is a picture of the poetical tradition from Langland to the beginning of World War I. Langland has been chosen as a beginning, not because the tradition began with him, but because the language of earlier periods communicates directly only to those with scholarly training. We have ended the selections when we did because the practice of poetry from that time on is a matter of the present. *Poets of the English Language* is a presentation of our tradition, and should be received as such.

ARRANGEMENT

In general the poets have been presented in their historical order, but since there is no absolute value inherent in such a scheme we have departed from strict chronology whenever another kind of order seemed usefully suggestive. What is true of the arrangement of poets is also true of the arrangement of individual selections from the work of a single poet. Subsequent revisions of a poem destroy much of the significance of the original sequence of composition. We remember most poets in terms of the finally achieved body of their poetry rather than of its development. We have simply tried to present the poets and their poems at their best.

The divisions between individual volumes have inevitably been influenced by the number of pages available to us for each, but each volume represents a grouping which seems reasonable and natural. They are not, however, inevitable. The poetry of Edmund Spenser, for example, may be considered with equal justice to have ended one broad period of English poetry, or to have begun another. For the sake of those who are accustomed to regard Spenser's poetry as the beginning of what we call the English literary renaissance, we can say only that we have taken the point of view which sees it as the culmination of the use of allegory, which in this volume begins with Langland and *The Romance of the Rose*. We do so without quarreling with the second point of view and without any conviction that there is real justice in dichotomizing poetical tradition. For we hope that the reader of one volume will go on to the following ones with no more significant gap than will occur within his reading of any one of them. This is one reason why the separate volumes of *Poets of the*

English Language have not been given categorizing titles, and why we prefer to think of the series as a unit. For the spirit of most groups is to be found latent in an earlier period and lingering on into the next. This is the way in which the consciousness of poets works.

TEXTS

The tendency of editors has been to present the poetry of earlier ages in modern spelling, punctuation, and capitalization. But this frequently does violence to both the meaning and the poetic effect of the lines. In using the contemporary appearance of poems we have followed the reasoning that important evidence has thus been retained as to pronunciation, syllabic values, emphasis, and breath pauses, as well as to the unit of phrasing. The following modifications have, however, been made:

(1) Letters which have fallen out of use have been replaced by their nearest equivalents in the standard alphabet.

(2) Where the spelling of a word in the original text seemed definitely confusing and could be altered without affecting either the meter or the pronunciation, we have altered it.

(3) Where the original punctuation seemed to nullify or badly obscure the meaning to the modern reader, we have changed it.

SUPPLEMENTARY DATA

We have not tried to supply biographical data on the poets, although the dates of their births and deaths will be found with the poems, and those of their principal works in the charts which are a supplement to each volume. The amount of biographical data which could have been supplied within the volumes would in actuality have been meaningless. For such study there are published biographies which it would have been folly to attempt to summarize in a few lines. We have preferred to print more poems.

If there is anything in the nature of biography in the various volumes, it is the autobiography of the poetical imagination and fancy as it has been expressed in poems. Comments on this autobiography occur in the introductions to each volume, which are meant not to be definitive but to suggest as freshly as possible the problems with which poetry has coped. Instead of biographical data for each poet, therefore, we have drawn up tables in which, on one side, is given the direct course of poetry and, on the other, are to be found certain of the cultural and societal events which had formative effect. These will be of some help, we trust, toward seeing the course of poetry in historical perspective.

Contents

Introduction to Volume I

LANGUAGE

Though the difficulties of appreciating Langland and Chaucer without special study of Middle English have perhaps been exaggerated by scholars, the reader will encounter in the poems at the beginning of this volume a language definitely different from his own. By the time he reaches the end, however, the language of the poets —of Sidney, for example—is in all essentials the one he reads and speaks himself. First, the question of what is to be regarded as standard English and what as dialect has been settled in favor of Southeast Midland or London English as the literary standard; second, with the disappearance of the þ and the ȝ the alphabet has become the one we now employ; and, third, the modern forms of the singular and plural of nouns and verbs, of the present and past participle, and of the personal and relative pronouns have been established.

The scholars are, of course, right in saying that for *complete* understanding linguistic study is required. The first thing that the average reader requires, however, is a conviction that the poetry deserves such trouble, and this conviction he can obtain, not simply by trusting the authority of others, but by reading for himself without worrying too much if he fails to understand every word. Once he has learned to like the poems, he will want to understand them fully.

The development of English out of an inflected language into an uninflected is already far advanced by the

time Chaucer wrote, but there are enough inflections left
to indicate some of the musical advantages which a language like Italian or German still possesses, and which
every English song writer and composer of vocal music
must envy. The writer of verses also may often envy an
inflected language its greater richness in rhymes, for the
few inflections remaining in English seem to have been
left simply to annoy him. What poet has not at some
time or other lost his temper over the unfortunate fact
that the addition of *s* makes nouns plural but verbs singular? On the whole, however, the paucity of rhymes in
English has not proved a disadvantage, for it has dis-
couraged or at least instantaneously revealed the wrong
kind of facility.

The real poetic advantage of an inflected language is
of another kind. An inflected language implies that the
nature of a thing is determined by its relations to other
things, so that a change in its relations causes a change
in its nature. In so far as poetry is concerned with emotions, this seems a more natural poetic attitude than that
implied by an uninflected language, for I certainly feel
myself to be a different person when I am kicking from
the one I am when I am being kicked. Further, since the
form of a word itself expresses its syntactical relations, it
is possible for the poet by his choice of word order to
obtain a double set of relations, those of syntax and those
of neighborhood.

Every English poet must regret that his language
makes it impossible for him to secure effects such as
these of Horace:

> *Nunc et campus et areae*
> *lenesque sub noctem sussuri*
> *composita repetantur hora*

.   .   .

nunc et latentis proditor intumo
gratus puellae risus ab angulo
pignusque dereptur lacertis
aut digito male pertinaci

There is a peculiar illusion that crops up from time to time on both sides of the English Channel that the English poets are nature's children "warbling their wood-notes wild" and that the others, the French for instance, care about the rules of art. "Formless," cries the one party; "Artificial," cries the other.

This of course is bosh: there is no such animal as a natural poet. The difference, if any, between English poetry and that of the rest of Europe is due to the former language's being a mongrel tongue containing elements of Anglo-Saxon, Scandinavian, French, and Latin.

This has two consequences. First, it makes for a large vocabulary. Where English has two words for two meanings, French, for instance, often has only one and must express the difference by two idiomatic constructions, with the result that the single word tends to become generalized in meaning, so that it is not altogether unfair to say that English is a more concrete language than French. This does not necessarily imply a better poetry, only a different kind. Neither a Shakespeare nor a Racine is translatable into the language of the other.

Second, a mongrel language inherits from its various ancestors their various metrical traditions. It is not true that the English poets have been less careful craftsmen than their European colleagues, but their tradition is perhaps more flexible. It is to be noted that when a French poet becomes dissatisfied with the classical French pros-ody, he is more likely than is an English poet in the same position to throw it over entirely and write prose poetry.

This volume illustrates both the establishment of a standard language, and the settling down of English prosody into a norm which is still valid. To demonstrate what this norm is, a few general statements may not be out of place:

1. Nearly all poetry in the West has been written in verse, that is, in lines constructed out of a regular pattern of metrical units.

2. Each metrical unit, or foot, consists of an emphatic nuclear syllable and one or more unemphatic satellite syllables.

3. The criterion of emphasis can be (*a*) the length of the syllable, (*b*) the degree of vocal accentuation or (*c*) a mixture of both.

(*a*) In classical Greek and Latin poetry, the nucleus is a long syllable, which contains either a long vowel or a short vowel followed by more than one consonant, and the satellites are short syllables.

Cēnā|bĭs bĕnĕ: | nam tŭ|ī Că|tŭllī
Catullus

or

Āll cŏm|pōsed ĭn ă | mētrĕ | ōf Că|tŭllŭs
Tennyson

Such verse is called quantitative.

(*b*) In most English verse, the nucleus is an accented syllable and the satellites are unaccented syllables. Such verse is called qualitative. Compare a qualitative hexameter:

This is the | forest pri|meval, the | murmuring | pines and
the | hemlocks

> Longfellow

with a quantitative

Wouldst thou | know who | here visi|teth, dwelleth | and
singeth | also

> Bridges

(c) In Anglo-Saxon verse, the emphatic element or
lift is either a long accented syllable or a short accented
syllable plus a short unaccented one.

It has been suggested, not implausibly, that a quantitative metric has its origin in song and dance, that is,
in actions of ritual or play, and a qualitative metric in
actions of work.

4. A quantitative metric was imposed on classical
Latin poetry by Greek models, but in late Latin verse
an accentual element reappeared. At first accent and
length coincided.

Crās āmet qui nūmquam amāvit quique amāvit crās āmet

which scans the same by either rule. But in medieval
Latin the quantitative element began to weaken, and a
line like

> *Nobis datus, nobis natus, ex intacta virgine*
> Aquinas

can be scanned only accentually, as in English.

Lonely | in the | Regent | Palace, | sipping | a ba|nana | blush

> Betjeman

If accent tended to supersede length in Latin verse, it
was all the more certain to do so in English with its in-
herited accentual tradition from Anglo-Saxon and—as

it lost its inflections—its predominance of consonants, which makes so many short syllables long by position. From time to time experiments in quantitative English verse have been attempted, but the difficulties are so great that the experiments have remained curiosities or *tours de force*.

5. There are two opposite metrical extremes possible in English:

(*a*) To count only the accents in the line and to ignore the number of unaccented syllables, so that, with its three accents,

> A pied and peeled May

is regarded as equivalent to

> Of his sodden with its sorrowing heart
>
> Hopkins

(*b*) To count only the number of syllables in the line and to ignore their accented or unaccented quality, so that, with its fifteen syllables,

> I recall their magnificence, now not more magnificent

is regarded as equivalent to

> Wedge-shaped, slate-grey marks on their forelegs and the resolute tail
>
> Marianne Moore

The bulk of English verse is written in a way that lies between these extremes, i.e., equivalent lines contain the same number of syllables and the same underlying regular pattern of metrical feet scanned qualitatively. But the musical art of the poet depends on his capacity to vary from this pattern without the sense of the pattern being lost:

> In tyme of trewe, on hawkyng wolde 'he ride
> Or elles honte boor, bere, or lyoun;

The smale bestes leet he gon biside.
And whan that he com ridyng into town,
Ful ofte his lady from hire wyndow down,
As fresshe as faucon comen out of muwe,
Ful redy was hym goodly to saluwe.

Chaucer

The metrical base in all of these lines is the same—that is, each has five iambic feet, but only a child in the classroom would, in reading line 3, accent *leet*, or in line 4 accent *he* and *in*, so that only four accents are actually insisted on in the former, and only three in the latter.

The smă|lĕ bēs|tĕs leet | hĕ gŏn | bĭsīde.

Ănd whān | thăt hĕ | cŏm rĭ|dўng ĭn|tŏ tōwn.

The commonest kinds of feet in English verse are the iamb (◡-) and the trochee (-◡). Single dactyls (- ◡ ◡) and anapests (◡ ◡ -) often appear through an inversion of an iamb or a trochee, but as a metrical base they have played only a minor role.

What variations are possible depends on the poet's ear. The only rule seems to be an empirical and negative one, namely, that two successive accents cannot be suppressed or displaced without destroying the underlying pattern. Thus:

Ĭ wānt | tŏ bĕ | ă gĕ|nuīne | sŭccēss

or

Gīve mĕ | yŏur hānd; | prŏmĭse | yŏu'll stīll | bĕ trūe

will pass as iambic pentameters.
But

Ĭ wānt | tŏ bĕ | ĭn ăn | ĕxcīt|ĕd stāte

or

Lāy yŏur | knīfe ănd | yŏur fōrk | ăcrōss | yŏur plāte

will not.

6. The tradition of Anglo-Saxon continued, particularly in the north, well into the fifteenth century, and shows itself not only in poems definitely written in alliterative meter but also in the elaborate alliteration of poems written on French metrical models. If it was unable to hold its own, one of the reasons is that the writers of alliterative verse had lost a sense of what the original meter actually was, so that their verse represents a decadence without a development.

Compare

Hīe dȳgel lond
warigeath wulfhleothu,   windige næssas,
frēcne fengelād,   thaer fyrgenstrēam
under næssa genipu   nither gewiteth,
flōd under foldan.

Beowulf

with

> Thay bowen by bonkes wher bowes ar bare,
> Thay clomben by cliffes wher clenges the colde.
> The heven was up halt, bot ugly ther-under;
> Mist muged on the mor, malt on the mounte,
> Uch hille hade a hatte, a mist-hakel huge.
> *Sir Gawain and the Green Knight*

The rule that there be no alliteration in the last lift has been forgotten, a dactylic rhythm is no longer avoided, and no efforts are taken to counterpoint line structure and sentence structure. The meter has thus lost the gravity and subtlety of the original and actually increased the great drawback of all alliterative verse, a tendency to artificial diction.

THE MIDDLE AGES

Apart from any linguistic difficulties, the modern reader, particularly if his previous knowledge of poetry begins with the Romantic poets, may be puzzled by the content of medieval poetry. We are so accustomed to a culture in which poetry is the highbrow medium, to be employed only for communicating the most intense and subtle experiences, while the natural medium for every-day use is prose, that it is difficult for us to imagine a society in which the relative positions were the other way round, a time when verse was the popular medium for instruction and entertainment, and prose, mostly in Latin, the specialized medium for the intercourse of scholars.

If this anthology were being compiled by a contem-porary of the poets themselves, the selection would cer-tainly be very different and the impression we should get would be that they were very "impure" poets, al-ways forsaking the poetry for moralizing or teaching. It is easier for us to understand the practical reasons why this should have been so—how, for instance, among a people without books and dependent on the oral trans-mission of culture, rhyme is a useful mnemonic device— than to appreciate it aesthetically.

Curiously enough, the lowbrow often has a much less inhibited attitude to *verse* than, shall we say, the middle-brow, as is evidenced by the popularity of limericks and those little moral and consolatory verses which are syn-dicated in newspapers. The highbrow may be right in purifying the poetry he himself writes from every "prosy" element, but one should, I think, have serious doubts of his poetic gift if he gets no personal pleasure from such poems as

> And masculine is found to be
> Hadria the Adriatic Sea

or

> Minus times minus equals plus;
> The reason for this we need not discuss.

It must be admitted that, to our taste, the medieval poets are frequently prolix and formless, but this is rather because they were too ambitious for their talents than because of any fault in their goal itself—too many average poets set out to write as all-embracing a masterpiece as *The Divine Comedy*. After the Middle Ages no one, not even Shakespeare or Milton, really attempts such a thing.

Allegory is so typical of medieval thinking and so untypical of ours—or, rather, when we are using allegory we are unconscious of the fact and believe we are thinking logically—that many people have difficulty in understanding medieval poetry because they do not grasp the principles of mythological and allegorical thought. Here are a few of them:

1. If an emotion or a concept is thought of as being absolute or given, that is, as being its own cause for being, then it may be represented as an immortal god or goddess.

2. If *A* is the logical ground of *B*—if *A*, for instance, is the general case of which B is the special case—*A* is represented as the parent of *B* (Aphrodite and Eros).

3. If *A* is the cause of *B*, *A* is represented as the social superior of *B*.

4. If *A* and *B* are equal and distinct but generally associated with each other, they are represented as having a sexual relation. If their association is considered socially desirable, this relation is one of marriage (Cupid and Psyche); if it is considered socially undesirable, it is one of adultery (Venus and Mars).

5. Consciousness or will is masculine.

6. Potentiality is young (the Future); actuality is old (Fate).

7. Moral goods and the goals of desire are physically beautiful. Moral evils and the objects of aversion are physically ugly. If the desire and the aversion are evil, then the beauty and the ugliness are enchanted simulacra.

8. Animal features indicate that what is represented cannot be fully grasped by consciousness.

9. Nature is heavy; the spirit is light. Therefore, to obey gravity is to follow natural desires; to climb or fly is to follow spiritual aspirations.

Anglo-Saxon poetry is the poetry of a tribe; Elizabethan poetry is the poetry of a nation; the poetry in this volume represents that portion of the poetry of Christendom which was written in English. Christendom was not a unity which grew out of the preceding unity of the Roman Empire, but a new structure created by the Papal Revolution of 1000–1200. The term "dark ages" has a real meaning in the sense that for more than five hundred years after the collapse of the Roman Empire there was no common Western culture, only scattered and isolated outposts of civilization, such as the Benedictine monasteries.

The Papal Revolution established once and for all that a man may have two loyalties, a local loyalty to the region where he is born, lives, and dies, and a universal loyalty to the truth which is the same for all. Whenever scientists and artists of different countries exchange periodicals they are enjoying a right won for them by the popes of the eleventh and twelfth centuries; whenever a national state keeps scientific discoveries secret or censors artistic creations for reasons of national security or public order, it is attempting to undo the revolutionary accomplishment of the Middle Ages. It is right and proper that the setting of *The Canterbury Tales* should be a pilgrimage in which all sorts and conditions of men are brought together away from their homes in a common intention to pay homage to one of the martyrs of that revolution, Thomas à Becket.

It would probably be a good thing if the word Renaissance were to disappear forever from our vocabulary, for few words have caused more popular misunderstanding. If our own experience is not untypical, the impression retained from the classroom is something like this: Modern Man was born around 1450, probably through the efforts of Greek refugees from Constantinople. Before that time there was Medieval Man, who dared not think for himself, did not look out objectively at the world of nature or consider his body with respect, but only looked inward to worry about the state of his soul. Suddenly, in the middle of the fifteenth century, the dreamer awoke and began to see reality for the first time, and to become an individual.

This is not only untrue in itself but diverts attention from the real revolutionary events, namely, the publication of Luther's ninety-five Theses in 1517, of Machiavelli's *Prince* in 1513, and of Descartes' *Discours de la Methode* in 1637. With these end five centuries of uninterrupted humanism, during which the energies of European civilization were directed toward making the whole of reality universally visible to the physical eye or the eye of reason, on the assumption that there was no truth, however mysterious, that could not be objectified in an image or a syllogism. This humanistic period begins with Anselm's ontological proof of the existence of God; it receives a temporary check with the condemnation of Abelard through the efforts of St. Bernard; it is seriously challenged by the Cathar Movement with its doctrine that matter was incapable of salvation. But after

the crusade against the Albigenses in 1226, the ortho-
doxy of Christian humanism remains secure until Luther.
Its dramatic dates are 1215, when the mystery of the
Mass was intellectually defined at the Council in Lat-
eran; 1233, when it asserts its conviction of its rightness
by establishing the Inquisition (whenever and wherever
an individual denies what is held to be demonstrable, his
denial is bound to be regarded as malice or lunacy, and
persecution, however genteel its form, is inevitable); and
1264, when it shows its conscious awareness of its nature
by the establishment of the feast of Corpus Christi. Its
typical literary expressions are Courtly Love as a subject
and Allegory as a form. It is not true that the literature
of the Middle Ages is unconcerned with the individual;
but it defines the individual not as a "character" but as
a soul. All souls are equal in the sight of God; conse-
quently, more than any before or since, medieval literature is democratic. Everyman is not a type, that is, a
projection of a passion, but a complete individual who
lives with others and dies alone; at the same time what
he suffers is what we all suffer, whatever our differences
in temperament, intelligence, and social situation. Troilus is an individual, but Chaucer's main concern is not
with the way in which Troilus is peculiar as a lover but
with how an individual falls in love.

One literary consequence of the conviction of the
Middle Ages that everything could be made explicit is
that, in their poetry, the treatment of the invisible sin
of pride is perfunctory; in fact it is never pride itself
that is described but only the visible and less serious sin
of vanity. It is only after 1517 that the poets (Shakespeare, for example) study pride profoundly. It is significant that Dante and Milton are each strongest where
the other is weakest: Satan is the least convincing figure

in *The Divine Comedy;* God the least convincing figure in *Paradise Lost.*

It is to the end of the Middle Ages, not to the beginning of the next, that the Italian painters of the *quattrocento* and the poets in this volume belong. It is not a new vision that they offer but illustrations of the *Summa.*

What happened was not the appearance of a new humanism—that was always there—but a fading away of its Christian base. The symptoms of the real break with the past appear with tragedy as a literary form, and baroque as an architectural style. Spenser, though he was not born till 1552 and was in belief an ardent Protestant, as an artist exhibits the old sensibility and is much nearer in spirit to the *Romaunt de la Rose* than he is to his contemporary, Fulke-Greville. Again one has only to compare the love poetry of Wyatt with that of the Provençal poets four centuries earlier and with that of Donne less than a century later to see the continuity with the former and the radical break before the latter.

The Middle Ages believed that an ultimate and intelligible unity embraced all the diversity of existence.

Within its depths, I saw ingathered, bound by love into one volume, the scattered leaves of the universe;
Substance and accidents and their relations, as though together fused, after such fashion that what I tell of is one simple flame.

Dante, *Paradiso,* canto xxxiii, lines 85–90

Faith in this unity, or rather faith in its intelligibility, was shattered in the sixteenth century. The causes of this breakdown were, as always, various: moral—the arrogance of the visible church in which, in the eyes of many thoughtful and thoughtless people, the corpus seemed to be smothering the Christus; economic—the dislocation of the traditional structure of society after the Black Death in 1381; and intellectual—the characteristic medieval method of demonstrating the unity of particulars and the relation of the invisible to the visible by *analogy* began to seem too easy to be true.

It is nonsense to say that the men of the Middle Ages did not observe nature, or cared only about their own souls, ignoring social relations: indeed it would be truer to say that their intellectual weakness was an oversimple faith in the direct evidence of their senses and the immediate data of consciousness, an oversimplification of the relation between the objective and subjective world. Believing that the individual soul was a microcosm of the universe and that all visible things were signs of spiritual truths, they thought that to demonstrate this, it was enough simply to use one's eyes and one's powers of reflection to perceive analogies. For example:

As the soul aspires to God, *so* the stone of the Gothic arch soars.

As individuals and armies fight for territory, *so* the virtues and vices struggle for the possession of the soul.

As indulgence money is a gift, *so* pardon is a gift.

As a noble man and woman love each other, *so* is the love that moves the sun and stars.

When Bacon defines science as putting nature to the question—that is, the torture—he is rebuking this trust in direct observation, for he implies that nature is secretive and must be compelled against her will to reveal the truth. Modern science begins when, instead of asking what a thing is like, for which simple observation is enough, one asks how long it is or how heavy, questions which cannot be answered without performing experiments. When the break came it was drastic. Luther denied any intelligible relation between Faith and Works, Machiavelli any intelligible relation between private and public morality, and Descartes any intelligible relation between Matter and Mind. Allegory became impossible as a literary form, and the human Amor seemed no longer a parable of the Divine Love but its blasphemous parody.

There has been no time since its own when the literature of the Middle Ages could appeal to readers as greatly as it can today, when the dualism inaugurated by Luther, Machiavelli, and Descartes has brought us to the end of our tether and we know that either we must discover a unity which can repair the fissures that separate the individual from society, feeling from intellect, and conscience from both, or we shall surely die by spiritual despair and physical annihilation.

The interest of modern poets in myths and symbols as devices for making their private and personal experiences public and typical, the tendency of modern novelists to take as their hero not the exceptional character, but the individual Everyman, Mr. Earwicker, or K, are literary evidences of our search for a kind of unity similar to that which Christendom believed it had found. We must not, however, be nostalgic. Luther and Descartes, to whatever brink of disaster we may have allowed them to push us, stand, like the angels about Eden, barring the way back from an unintelligible dualism to any simple one-to-one relation. That way lies, not the Earthly Paradise, but a totalitarian hell.

Note on the Middle English Selections

BY E. TALBOT DONALDSON

In preparing these selections for the use of readers who are not specialists in Middle English the principal aim has been to enhance readability while retaining in so far as possible the form and appearance of the original. Where no phonetic considerations are involved, spelling has been altered to conform with modern usage: that is, throughout the selections obsolete letters have been changed to their present equivalents, and such conventional scribal alternates as *y* and *i, u* and *v, i* and *j,* etc., have been sorted out according to the practice of today. In addition to these constant revisions a number of lesser alterations in spelling have been made in order to give to individual pieces an inner consistency which makes possible a reduction in the number of glosses. The amount of editing of this sort has been determined by the special problems presented by each selection and therefore varies from piece to piece. In accordance with the ideal of readability the editor has, in preparing some of the less settled texts, frequently borrowed an emendation or made one of his own without notifying the reader. It goes without saying that this practice, along with the alterations in spelling, renders the texts unsatisfactory for the serious scholar, who should consult the various excellent and well-known editions of the works represented. What is printed in this volume are selections edited for the nonspecialist reader who wishes, without too much difficulty, to sample our earlier literature.

The principle of readability has also governed the glossing, although it is recognized that no system of glossing will prove universally pleasing, since each reader has his own kind of imagination, his own particular method and experience in reading; and even within the same reader varying moods may impede or expedite his powers of comprehension. The glossing herein has been done as far as possible according to contextual sense: that is, if recognition of a word seems encouraged by its context—for instance, the name of a flower in the description of a garden—no gloss has been given, but if the same word appears in an unexpected context, it has been glossed. It is hoped that the result, while statistically inconsistent, will prove intellectually satisfactory. The tendency in general has been to overgloss rather than to undergloss—a practice which may of course be as discouraging to the reader with superior linguistic equipment as its opposite is to the novice. But it is better to have too much than too little, and since the presence of the glosses is not advertised by insistent footnote numbers within the text itself, the advanced reader may proceed without distraction, ignoring the explanations at the bottom of the page. Some readers will no doubt at times disagree with the shades of meaning suggested by the glosses; it is hoped, however, that such disagreements will result more often from the difference between one person's poetic sensibility and another's than from a conviction that the explanation is seriously in error. The exact sense of Middle English is often difficult to determine, as is attested in this book by the number of question marks preceding glosses. Each of these represents a guess on the part of the editor, who hereby disclaims any unwavering faith in the rectitude of his guesses.

NOTES ON THE LANGUAGE

The term "Middle English," unlike the term "Modern Standard English," actually describes, not a single homogeneous language, but a number of separate dialects, each of which possesses many idiosyncrasies of form, spelling, and vocabulary. It is this fact that renders the reading of a wide variety of pieces in Middle English

difficult. In order to simplify the following notes, Middle English, as illustrated by the selections in this book, has been arbitrarily—and, to be sure, from the point of view of the linguist incorrectly—divided into two types, that of the English Midlands and that of northern England and Scotland. The Midland type may be said to be represented in its most characteristic form by Chaucer; the Northern type by Richard Rolle. Of the remaining selections, Gower, who shows a few Kentish forms that will not be considered, and Langland, who shows a number of Southwestern forms, are perhaps most nearly related to the dialect of Chaucer; the majority of the remainder are either mixed or North Midland, which means that they partake of a number of Northernisms while preserving also a number of Midland characteristics. The beginner in Middle English is advised to start with a selection from Chaucer and then move on to Richard Rolle; this will ground him in the two chief dialects, and enable him thereafter to handle the dialect mixtures. In the following notes forms that are either Midland or common Middle English are unlabeled; Northern forms are labeled N; Southwestern forms S.

Personal Pronouns

SUBJECTIVE CASE	OBJECTIVE CASE	POSSESSIVE CASE
I: *I, ich*	me: *me*	my: *my, min(e)*
you (sing.): *thou*	you (sing.): *thee*	your (sing.): *thy, thin(e)*
he: *he*	him: *him*	his: *his; hus* S
she: *she; he* S; *s(c)he, s(c)ho* N	her: *hir(e), her(e)*	her: *hir(e), her(e)*
it: *hit, it*	it: *hit, it*	its: *his*
we: *we*	us: *us*	our: *our(e)*
you (plu.): *ye* (not *you*)	you (plu.): *you*	your (plu.): *your(e)*
they: *they; hi(i)* S; *thay* N	them: *hem; the(i)-m; tha(i)m* N	their: *her(e), the(i)r(e), hir(e); tha(i)r(e)* N

Nouns

Nouns are ordinarily inflected with *-es* (or *-us; -is* N)
for the genitive, and the same for the plural. Irregular
forms are glossed.

Adjectives

Adjectives are sometimes formed from nouns by adding *-lich(e)* or the reduced form *-ly:* compare Modern
English *lovely.*

Adverbs

Adverbs are formed from adjectives by adding final *-e*
(in which case they are ordinarily glossed), by adding
-lich(e) (also used in forming adjectives from nouns),
or by adding the reduced form *-ly* as in Modern English.
Such simple adverbs as *tho,* "then," should be mastered
immediately.

Verbs

Verbs are either strong or weak. Strong verbs show
stem-vowel variation and do not take *-(e)d* in the preterite or past participle: for example, Modern English
ride, rode, ridden. Middle English strong verbs differ
from their Modern English counterparts frequently by
having two different vowels in the preterite, one for the
indicative singular, the other for the indicative plural
and the subjunctive: for example, in Chaucer "I rode"
is *I rōd,* but "we rode" is *we rĭde(n).* Sometimes, as
here, the second vowel is the same as that of the past
participle (Midland *yrĭde(n),* Modern English *ridden*).
Sometimes both vowels of the preterite are different
from Modern English, which has replaced them from
the past participle: for example, "I bore," *I băr,* "we
bore," *we bēre(n).* Moreover, very commonly the same

Middle English text will show several alternates. In most cases where confusion might arise, these forms have been glossed.

Weak verbs show no stem-vowel variation and form their preterite and past participle by adding -(e)d: for example, Modern English *love, loved, loved,* Middle English *love, loved(e), loved* (N often *lovit*). With verbs ending in the present in -t the -d of the past is coalesced with the -t, as in Modern English *hit, hit, hit.*

1. The endings of the present indicative, weak and strong, are:

I ride: *I ride; rides, -is* N

you (sing.) ride: *thou ridest; rides, -is* N

he, etc., rides: *he rideth;*[1] *rides, -is* N

we, etc., ride: *we ride(n); rideth* S; *rides, -is* N

2. The endings of the preterite indicative, strong, are:
I rode: *I rod*

you (sing.) rode: *thou rod* or *ride* (not N)

he, etc., rode: *he rod*

we, etc., rode: *we riden; rod* N

3. The endings of the preterite indicative, weak, are:
I loved: *I loved(e)*

you (sing.) loved: *thou lovedest; loved(e)* N

he, etc., loved: *he loved(e)*

we, etc., loved: *we lovede(n); loved* (generally N)

4. The endings of the subjunctive, which is far commoner in Middle English than in Modern, for both strong and weak verbs are -e for the singular, -e(n) for the plural, in both tenses. In strong verbs the preterite subjunctive singular is generally formed on the stem of the preterite indicative plural.

---

[1] Or *rit:* with verbs whose stem ends in -t or -d the third singular indicative often shows contraction.

5. The endings of the imperative are (*-e*) for the singular, *-eth* (*-es* N) for the plural. Uninflected plural imperatives also occur.

6. The infinitive ends in *-e(n)*; N never with *-n*, and frequently without *e*.

7. The present participle ends in *-ing(e)*; *-and(e)* N; *-ende* Gower. The past participle strong is *ywrite, write, ywriten,* or *writen* (N always the last). Initial *y-* is generally a sign of the past participle.

Conjunctions, etc.

But, frequently written *bot(e)*, sometimes has the meaning "unless," as does the phrase *but if. An(d)* frequently means "if." *There* frequently appears for Modern English *where,* as does *that* for Modern English *what* in relative uses.

Negatives

The negatives are *not, nat, nought* (which may have the force either of an adverb or a noun), and *ne*. Negatives do not cancel out; multiple negatives merely intensify.

General

Short *o* is very commonly used for short *u* in Middle English; thus *bot(e)* may appear for *but,* as *love* still does for *luve.* If perplexed by a word with *o,* try *u.*

The letter which appears as initial *g-* in Modern English and in Northern Middle English frequently appears in the Midlands as *y-*: *yive,* N *give,* "give."

The Northern texts show a number of differences in form and spelling from those of the Midland. Readers of Burns will not have much trouble with these, but for convenience the chief difficulties are listed here:

1. Long *a* very commonly appears for Modern English *o* or *oa*: *bald,* "bold"; *hare,* "hoar."

2. Long *u* very commonly appears for Modern English *oo*: *gude,* "good"; *buke,* "book."

3. An *f* very commonly appears for Modern English *v*: *gif,* "give"; *luf,* "love."

4. The verb "is" very commonly appears as *es;* "are" as *er;* "was" as *wes;* "were" as *war(e);* "has" as *hes;* "there" as *thar(e),* etc.

5. Initial *qwh-* very commonly appears for Modern English *wh-*.

6. The preposition *till* does duty for Modern English "to" in expressions of place, and *into* does duty for "in."

7. An *i* is added after long vowels to indicate length: *maik,* "make"; *qwheil,* "wheel"; *noine,* "noon"; *guid,* "good," etc. In later texts the diphthongs *ai* and *oi* fall together in sound with long *a* and *o* respectively, producing a number of apparently illogical spellings: *maid,* "maid" or "made"; *made,* "made" or "maid"; *noise,* "noise" or "nose"; *nose,* "nose" or "noise." The reader must exercise his ingenuity in reading these texts.

Pronunciation

No rules for pronunciation will cover texts of such different dialects and different dates. The following highly simplified suggestions are based on Chaucer's language, and are, even roughly, applicable only to selections dated before 1400. Many readers will find, however, that the attempt to pronounce selections according to this system will increase their comprehension, even though such pronunciation will not approximate closely the actual sound of many of the selections.

Long *a*	*a*	in *father*	"m**a**ken," make
Short *a*	*a*	in German *mann*	"**a**sken," ask
Long *e* (close: Mod. Eng. spelling *ee*)	*a*	in *name*	"w**e**pen," weep
Long *e* (open: Mod. Eng. spelling *ea*)	*ai*	in *air*	"t**e**chen," teach
Short *e*	*e*	in *set*	"s**e**tten," set
Unstressed *e*	*a*	in *sofa*	"mak**e**," make
Long *i*	*i*	in *machine*	"wr**i**ten," write
Short *i*	*i*	in *sit*	"y**i**ven," give
Long *o* (close: Mod. Eng. spelling *oo*)	*o*	in *note*	"g**o**de," good
Long *o* (open: Mod. Eng. spelling *o, oa*)	*oa*	in *broad*	"n**o**se," nose
Short *o*	*o*	in *pod*	"G**o**d," God
Long *u*	*u*	in *pure*	"vert**u**," virtue
Short *u* (frequently spelled *o*)	*u*	in *full*	"c**u**ppe, s**o**nne," cup, sun

Diphthongs: *ai, ay* and *ei, ey* are pronounced with a sound between the *ai* in *aisle* and the *ay* in *day; au* is pronounced like the *ou* in *house; eu, ew* like the *u* in *pure; oi, oy* like the *oy* in *toy; ou, ow* like their Modern English equivalent in words having the sound in Modern English of *ow* in *grow; ou, ow* like the *oo* in *boot* in words having in Modern English either the same sound or the sound of *ou* in *house.*

Double vowels indicate length, but many single vowels are long. The Modern English equivalent, when one exists, is usually a safe determinant of length.

All consonants are pronounced except for *g* in the combination *gn*: observe *k-night, k-ne*, etc. The combination *gh* is sounded like *ch* in Scottish *loch.*

The easiest rule for final unstressed *-e* is to pronounce it where it fits metrically and to ignore it elsewhere. It is rather rarely pronounced in the Northern texts.

A Calendar of British
and American Poetry

GENERAL BACKGROUND	DATE	DIRECT HISTORY
Pope Innocent III installed	1198	
	c.1200	Layamon's *Brut:* first rendering in English of Arthurian legend
Fourth Lateran Council: transubstantiation, compulsory confession	1215	
Magna Charta		
Founding of Cambridge University	c.1217	
Francis of Assisi, *Il cantico di frate sole*	1225	
Thomas Aquinas	c.1227–74	
Guillaume de Lorris, *Roman de la rose*	c. 1237	
	c.1255	*Havelok the Dane* *King Horn* *The Owl and the Nightingale*
Bracton, *De legibus et consuetudinibus Angliae*	a.1257	
Feast of Corpus Christi instituted	1264	
Aquinas, *Summa Theologica*	1265–73	
Marco Polo begins embassy from the Pope to Kublai, Grand Khan of Tartary	1271	
Introduction of duple time in music	1275	
Dante begins *Divina commedia*	1300	
	c.1300–49	Richard Rolle of Hampole
Papal bull *Unam sanctam:* extreme assertion of papal supremacy over states and lay rulers	1302	
Giotto's frescoes of the Life of Christ for Arena Chapel, Padua	1305	
John Wycliffe	1320–84	
Introduction of *fauxbourdon* as a result of papal decrees against descant	1322	

GENERAL BACKGROUND	DATE	DIRECT HISTORY
Petrarch, *Rime*	c.1327–30	
Outbreak of the Hundred Years' War	1337	
The York Mysteries	c.1340–50	
Machaut's ballades: secular musical compositions	c.1350	
Boccaccio, *Decameron*	c.1353	
Travels of Sir John Mandeville	1355–66	
	c.1360	Alliterative *Morte Arthure*
	c.1362	Chaucer, translation of *Romance of the Rose*
		Langland, *Piers Plowman* (the A-text)
	1369	Chaucer, *Book of the Duchess*
John Dunstable, foundations of polyphonic composition	1370?–1453	
	1375	Barbour, *The Bruce*
		Sir Gawain and the Green Knight
		The Pearl
York Pater Noster play: first morality play	1378	
First Navigation Act: regulation of foreign trade	1381	
	c.1383	Chaucer, *Troilus and Criseide*
	c.1387	Chaucer, *The Canterbury Tales* begun
	1390–92	Gower, *Confessio Amantis*
Wycliffe's revised Bible	c.1395	
De haeretico comburendo: English statute authorizing the burning of witches	1401	
	c.1412	Hoccleve, *The Regimen of Princes*
Prince Henry the Navigator sends out first expedition	1418	
	c.1420	Lydgate, *Troy Book*
	c.1424	James I of Scotland, *The King's Quair*
	c.1425	*The Castle of Perseverance:* a morality
	1450–1500	*Second Shepherds' Play* (supposed date of ms.)
Fall of Constantinople	1453	
Surrender of Bordeaux to the French: end of the Hundred Years' War		
Gutenberg, first Bible printed from movable type	1453–55	
The Wars of the Roses	1455–85	

GENERAL BACKGROUND	DATE	DIRECT HISTORY
Caxton, printing of Chaucer's *Canterbury Tales*	1478	
Caxton, printing of Malory's *Morte d'Arthur*	1485	
Columbus discovers America	1492	
	c.1499	Skelton, *Bouge of Court*
Erasmus, *Adagia*	1500	
	c.1503	Dunbar, *The Golden Targe*
	1505–08	Hawes, *Pastime of Pleasure*
	c.1508	Skelton, *Philip Sparrow*
Michelangelo's Last Judgment frescoes for Sistine Chapel	1508–12	
Erasmus, *Moriae encomium*	1509	Barclay's rendering from the Dutch of *The Ship of Fools*
	c.1510–19	*The Summoning of Every Man* printed
Erasmus, *De duplici copia verborum ac rerum commentarii*	1511	
	1512–13	Douglas, *The Aeneid*, translated into Scottish metre; printed 1553
	1512–16	Medwall, *Fulgens and Lucrece*, first secular play, printed; acted Christmas 1497
Erasmus, *Parabolae sive similia*	1513	
Machiavelli, *Il Principe*		
Agricola, *De inventione dialectica*	1515	
	c.1515–16	*Hycke Scorner*, first moral interlude, printed
Ariosto, *Orlando Furioso*	1516	
More, *Utopia*		
Luther posts his 95 theses	1517	
Cortés begins conquest of Mexico	1519	
First circumnavigation of the globe	1519–22	
Melanchthon, *Institutiones rhetoricae*	1521	
Luther's marriage	1525	
Tyndale's translation of the New Testament		
	1525–27	Rastell, *The Nature of the Four Elements*: an interlude
Castiglione, *Il Libro del Cortegiano*	1528	
	c.1530	Terence, *Andria*, first English translation printed

GENERAL BACKGROUND	DATE	DIRECT HISTORY
Elyot, *The Book named the Governour*	1531	
Erasmus, *Apophthegmata*		
	1532	Henryson, *The Testament of Cresseid*
Udall, *Floures for Latine Spekynge*	1533	John Heywood, *The Play of the Wether*
Act of Supremacy: King of England head of English church	1534	
Founding of Jesuit Order		
Luther's Bible		
Execution of Sir Thomas More	1535	
Publication of Tyndale-Coverdale English Bible		
Calvin, *Christianae religionis institutio*	1536	
Dissolution of English monasteries	1536–39	
Elyot, *Dictionary*: Latin-English	1538	
Colloquy of Ratisbon: abortive attempt to reconcile the Catholic and the Reformed churches	1541	
Copernicus, *De revolutionibus orbium coelestium*	1543	
More, *History of Richard III*		
Ramus, *Dialecticae partitiones*		
Vesalius, *De humani corporis fabrica*		
Baldwin, *Treatise of Moral Phylosophie*	1547	Sternhold and Hopkins, *Psalms*
Ignatius de Loyola, *Ejercicios espirituales*	1548	
Book of Common Prayer	1549	Baldwin, *The Canticles of Solomon in Englysh Metres*
The Laborious Journey and Search of John Leylande for England's Antiquities: rediscovery of Old English literature		
Robynson, first English translation of More's *Utopia*	1551	Wyatt, *Certayne Psalmes drawn into English Meter*
Wilson, *The Art of Rhetoric*	1553	
Temporary reconciliation of England to Rome under Mary	1554	
Index Expurgatorius drawn up by the Council of Trent	1557	*The Book of Songs and Sonnets* ("Tottel's Miscellany"): including lyrics by Wyatt, Surrey, Vaux, etc.
		Surrey, *Certain Books* [2nd

GENERAL BACKGROUND	DATE	DIRECT HISTORY
	1557	and 4th] *of Virgil's Aeneid:* first English blank verse
John Knox returns to Scotland Matthew Parker made Archbishop of Canterbury	1559	Baldwin, ed., *A Mirror for Magistrates* Jasper Heywood, *Troas:* first English translation of Seneca
Hoby, *The Courtyer,* translation of Castiglione	1561	
	1562	Broke, *History of Romeus and Juliet*
End of the Council of Trent Foxe, *Actes and Monuments* ("Book of Martyrs")	1563	Googe, *Eclogs, Epitaphs and Sonnets* Sackville, *The Complaint of Henrie Duke of Buckinghame*
Fabricius, *De re poetica*	1565	Norton and Sackville, *Gorboduc:* first blank-verse tragedy, printed
	1566	Udall, *Ralph Roister Doister;* written 1553
Painter, *The Palace of Pleasure:* collection of *novelle*	1566–67	Golding, *The XV Books of P. Ovidius Naso's Work entitled Metamorphoses*
Bishops' Bible	1568	
	1569	Ingelend, *The Disobedient Child:* "prodigal son" play
Ascham, *The Scholemaster* Euclid's *Elements of Geometry* first translated into English	1570	
Latimer, *Frutefull Sermons*	1571–75	Edwards, *Damon and Pithias:* earliest extant court drama
Massacre of St. Bartholomew	1572	
	1573	Gascoigne, *A Hundreth Sundrie Flowres:* experiments in versification *Jocasta:* translation of Italian translation of Euripides, first Greek tragedy in English *The Masque for Lord Montacute:* first printed masque
Gascoigne, *The Noble Arte of Venerie or Hunting*	1575	Breton, *Small Handful of Fragrant Flowers* Gascoigne, *Certain Notes of Instruction concerning the Making of Verse or Rime in English*
The first Blackfriars built: first private theater Pettie, *A Petite Pallace of Pettie his Pleasure*	1576	Gascoigne, *The Steel Glass:* first original poem in blank verse

GENERAL BACKGROUND	DATE	DIRECT HISTORY
The Theatre built: first public theater	1576	
Holinshed, *Chronicles*	1577	
Peacham, *The Garden of Eloquence*		
Lyly, *Euphues, the Anatomy of Wit*	1578	
Frampton, translation of travels of Marco Polo	1579	Spenser, *The Shepheardes Calender*
Lodge, *A Defence of Poetry, Music, and Stage Plays*		
North, translation of Plutarch's *Lives*		
Lyly, *Euphues and his England*	1580	
Montaigne, *Essais*		
Tasso, *Gerusalemme liberata* published	1581	
Mulcaster, *Right Writing of our English Tongue*	1582	Stanyhurst, *The First Four Books of Virgil His Aeneid*
Lyly, *Alexander and Campaspe; Sapho and Phao*	1584	Peele, *The Arraignment of Paris*
Camden, *Britannia*	1586	Webbe, *A Discourse of English Poetrie*: prosody
Historia vom D. Johann Fausten	1587	Turberville, *Tragical Tales*: chiefly from Boccaccio
	1588	Byrd, *Psalms, Sonnets, and Songs*
Greene, *Menaphon*	1589	Puttenham, *The Arte of English Poesie*
Hakluyt, *Voyages*	1589–1600	
Galileo, *Sermones de motu gravium*, date of ms.	1590	Marlowe, *Tamburlaine the Great*
Lodge, *Rosalynde*		Spenser, *The Faerie Queene*, books I–III
Sidney, *Arcadia*		
Janssen's invention of the microscope	c.1590	
Harington, translation of Ariosto's *Orlando Furioso*	1591	Sidney, *Astrophel and Stella*
		The Troublesome Reign of King John: first historical drama
Establishment of Presbyterianism in Scotland	1592	Constable, *Diana*
		Daniel, *Delia*
Greene, *Groatsworth of Witte bought with a Million of Repentance; A Disputation between a hee Conny-Catcher and a she Conny-Catcher*		Kyd, *The Spanish Tragedy*
		The Lamentable and True Tragedy of M. Arden of Feversham in Kent: first domestic drama
	1593	Drayton, *Idea*
	1593	*Sir Thomas More*

GENERAL BACKGROUND	DATE	DIRECT HISTORY
		The Phoenix Nest: including lyrics by Dyer, Ralegh, Lodge, Peele, Breton, etc.
		Shakespeare, *Venus and Adonis*
Fairfax, *Godfrey of Bulloigne,* translation of Tasso's *Gerusalemme liberata*	1594	Barnfield, *The Affectionate Shepherd*
		Chapman, *The Shadow of Night*
		Daniel, *Cleopatra*
		Greene, *Friar Bacon and Friar Bungay*
		Greene and Lodge, *A Looking Glass for London and England*
		Lodge, *The Wounds of Civil War*
		Marlowe, *Edward the Second*
		Morley, *Madrigals to Four Voices*
		Shakespeare, *The Rape of Lucrece; Titus Andronicus*
Richard Hooker, *Of the Lawes of Ecclesiasticall Politie*	1594–97	
	1595	Barnes, *A Divine Century of Spiritual Sonnets*
		Sidney, *The Defence of Poesie;* written about 1583
		Southwell, *Moeoniae*
		Spenser, *Amoretti; Ephithalamion*
Carew, *The Excellence of the English Tongue*	1595–96	
Ralegh, *The Discoverie of Guiana*	1596	Davies, *Orchestra*
		Griffin, *Fidessa*
		Spenser, *The Faerie Queene,* books IV–VI
Bacon, *Essayes* Gabriel Harvey, *The Trimming of Thomas Nashe*	1597	Dowland, *The First Book of Songs*
		Drayton, *England's Heroical Epistles*
		Shakespeare, *Romeo and Juliet; Richard III*
Florio, *A Worlde of Wordes:* Italian-English dictionary Meres, *Palladis Tamia, Wits Treasury*	1598	Breton, *A Solemn Passion of the Soul's Love*
		Marlowe, *Hero and Leander*
		A Most Pleasant Comedy of Mucedorus; 12 editions before 1640
		Shakespeare, *Love's Labour's Lost*
Blundeville, *The Art of Logike* Opening of Globe Playhouse	1599	Daniel, *Musophilus*
		Davies, *Nosce Teipsum*
		Peele, *David and Bethsabe*

THE VIKING PORTABLE LIBRARY

Poets of the English Language

VOLUME I: LANGLAND TO SPENSER

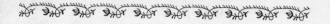

William Langland

(1330?–1390?)

FROM *Piers Plowman*

[*The Field of Folk*]

In a somer seson, whan soft was the sonne,
I shope me into shroudes, as I a shepe were;
In habite as an heremite unholy of workes
Went wide in this world, wondres to here.
Ac on a May morninge on Malverne hulles   5
Me bifel a ferly, of fairy me thoughte:
I was wery forwandred and went me to reste
Under a brode banke by a bornes side,
And as I lay and lened and loked on the waters,
I slombred in a sleping, it sweyed so merye.   10
Thanne gan I to meten a merveilouse swevene,
That I was in a wildernesse, wist I never where.
As I bihelde into the est, an hiegh to the sonne,
I seigh a towre on a toft, trielich ymaked,
A depe dale binethe, a dongeon thereinne,   15
With depe diches and derke, and dredful of sight.
A faire felde ful of folke fonde I there bitwene,

2 *shope me into,* clad myself in; *shepe,* shepherd   4 *here,* hear
5 *ac,* but; *hulles,* hills
6 *me bifel a ferly,* there befell me a marvel
7 *wery forwandred,* weary from wandering   8 *bornes,* brook's
9 *lened,* rested   10 *sweyed,* sounded
11 *gan I to meten,* began I to dream; *swevene,* dream
12 *wist,* knew   13 *an heigh,* on high
14 *seigh,* saw; *toft,* knoll; *trielich ymaked,* finely made
17 *fonde,* found

1

Of alle maner of men, the mene and the riche,
Worching and wandring as the worlde asketh.
Some putten hem to the plow, pleyed ful selde,   20
In setting and in sowing swonken ful harde,
And wonnen that this wastours with glotonye
    destruyeth.
And some putten hem to pruide, apparailed hem there-
    after,
In contenaunce of clothing comen disgised.
In prayers and penances putten hem manye,   25
Al for love of oure Lorde liveden ful streite,
In hope for to have heveneriche blisse:
As ancres and heremites that holden hem in here celles,
And coveiten nought in contré to cairen aboute,
For no likerous liflode her likam to plese.   30
And somme chosen chaffare: they cheveden the bettere,
As it semeth to oure sight that suche men thriveth.
And somme murthes to make, as minstralles conneth,
And geten gold with here glee, sinneles, I leve.
Ac japers and jangelers, Judas childeren,   35
Feinen hem fantasies and foles hem maketh,
And han here witte at wille to worche yif they wolde:
That Poule precheth of hem, I nel nought preve it
    here—

18 *mene*, poor   19 *worching*, working
20 *putten hem*, applied themselves; *selde*, seldom
21 *swonken*, worked   22 *that this*, what these
23 *pruide*, pride; *hem*, themselves
24 *contenaunce*, appearance; *disgised*, i.e., decked out
25 *putten hem manye*, many devoted themselves
26 *streite*, rigorously   27 *heveneriche*, the kingdom of heaven's
28 *ancres*, anchorites; *hem*, themselves; *here*, their
29 *coveiten nought*, do not desire; *cairen*, wander
30 *likerous liflode*, tasty victuals; *her likam*, their body
31 *chaffare*, trade; *cheveden*, prospered
33 *conneth*, know how to do
34 *here glee*, their music; *leve*, believe   35 *ac*, but
36: i.e., pretend to be suffering from hallucinations and make fools of
    themselves   37 *worche*, work; *yif*, if
38 *nel nought preve*, will not demonstrate

Qui turpiloquium loquitur is Luciferes hine.

Bidders and beggeres fast aboute yede   40
With here belies and here bagges bretful ycrammed,
Faiteden for here fode, foughten atte ale;
In glotonye, God wote, gon hii to bedde,
And risen with ribaudye, tho Roberdes knaves:
Slepe and sory sleuthe seweth hem evre.   45
Pilgrimes and palmers plighted hem togidere
To seke Seint James and seintes in Rome;
They went forth in here wey with many wise tales,
And hadden leve to lie al here lif after.
I seigh somme that seiden they had ysought seintes: 50
To eche a tale that they tolde here tonge was tempred
    to lie
More than to sey soth, it semed by here speche.
Heremites on an heep with hoked staves
Wenten to Walsingham, and here wenches after;
Grete lobies and longe that loth were to swinke   55
Clotheden hem in copis to ben knowen fram othere,
And shopen hem heremites, here ese to have.
I fonde there freris, alle the foure ordres,
Prechinge the peple for profit of the wombe,
Glosed the Gospel as hem good liked,   60
For coveitise of copis construed it as they wolde.
Many of this maistres freris mowe clothen hem at liking,
For here money and marchandise marchen togideres;

39 *hine,* servant   40 *yede,* walked
41 *bretful,* brimful
42 *faiteden,* begged under false pretenses; *atte ale,* i.e., at alehouses
43 *wote,* knows; *hii,* they
44 *ribaudye,* lechery; *tho Roberdes knaves,* those marauding vagabonds
45 *sleuthe,* sloth; *seweth,* pursue   48 *in here wey,* on their way
50 *seigh,* saw   53 *on an heep,* in droves
54 *here wenches after,* their wenches behind them
55 *lobies,* louts; *swinke,* work   56 *copis,* copes
57 *shopen hem,* clothed themselves as
58 *freris,* friars   59 *wombe,* belly
60 *glosed,* interpreted; *as hem . . . liked,* as they pleased
61 *coveitise,* avarice   62 *this,* these; *mowe,* may; *liking,* pleasure

For sith charité hath be chapman and chief to shrive
      lordes,
Many ferlys han fallen in a fewe yeris: 65
But holychirche and hii holde better togideres
The moste mischief on molde is mounting wel faste.
There preched a pardonere as he a prest were,
Broughte forth a bulle with bishopes seles,
And seide that himself mighte assoilen hem alle   70
Of falsnesse of fasting, of vowes ybroken.
Lewed men leved him wel and liked his wordes,
Comen up kneling to kissen his bulles;
He bonched hem with his brevet and blered here eyes,
And raughte with his ragman ringes and broches.   75
Thus they geven here golde glotones to kepe,
And leneth it loseles that lecherye haunten.
Were the bischop yblissed and worth bothe his eres,
His seel shoulde nought be sent to deceive the peple.
Ac it is naught by the bischop that the boy precheth, 80
For the parisch prest and the pardonere parten the
      silver
That the poraille of the parisch sholde have yif they
      nere.
Persones and parisch prestes pleined hem to the bischop
That here parisshes were pore sith the pestilence time,
To have a licence and leve at London to dwelle,   85
And singen there for simonye, for silver is swete.
Bischopes and bachelers, bothe maistres and doctours,

---

64 *sith*, since; *chapman*, peddler; *chief*, foremost
65 *ferlys*, marvels; *fallen*, occurred   66 *but*, unless; *hii*, they
67 *molde*, earth   70 *assoilen*, pardon
72 *lewed*, ignorant; *leved*, believed
74 *bonched hem*, thumped them; *brevet*, letter of indulgence
75 *raughte*, raked in; *ragman*, rolled-up letter of indulgence
76 *geven*, give   77 *leneth it*, bestow it on; *loseles*, scoundrels
78 *yblissed*, worthy of reverence   80 *ac*, but
81 *parten*, divide
82 *poraille*, poor; *yif they nere*, if it weren't for them
83 *persones*, parsons; *pleined hem*, complained
84 *sith*, since   87 *bachelers*, divinity students

That han cure under Criste, and crowning in tokne
And signe that they sholden shriven here paroschienes,
Prechen and prey for hem, and the pore fede, 90
Liggen in London in Lenten an elles.
Some serven the king and his silver tellen,
In cheker and in chancerye chalengen his dettes
Of wardes and wardmotes, weives and streives. . . .
Yit hoved there an hondreth in houves of selke, 95
Serjaunts it semed that serveden atte barre,
Pleddeden for penies and poundes the lawe,
And nought for love of oure Lorde unlese here lippes
    onis:
Thou mightest better mete miste on Malverne hulles
Than gete a momme of here mouthe til money were
    shewed. 100
Barones and burgeis and bondemen als
I seigh in this assemblé, as ye shul here after.
Baxsteres and brewesteres and bocheres manye,
Wollewebsteres and weveres of linnen,
Taillours and tinkeres and tolleres in marketes, 105
Masons and minours and many other craftes—
Of alkin libbing laboreres lopen forth somme,
As dikers and delveres that doth here dedes ille,
And driven forth the longe day with "Dieu vous save,
    Dame Emme."
Cokes and here knaves crieden "Hote pies, hote! 110

88 *crowning*, the tonsure   89 *paroschienes*, parishioners
91 *liggen*, lie out; *an elles*, and at other times   92 *tellen*, count
93 *cheker*, exchequer; *chalengen*, assert the king's claim to
94 *wardmotes*, ward-meetings; *weives and streives*, waifs and strays
95 *hoved*, waited; *hondreth*, hundred; *houves of selke*, silk skull-caps
96 *serjaunts*, sergeants of law; *atte*, at the
97 *unlese*, unfasten   99 *mete*, measure
100 *momme*, sound   101 *burgeis*, burgesses; *als*, also
102 *seigh*, saw   103 *baxsteres and brewesteres*, bakers and brewers
104 *wollewebsteres*, wool-weavers   105 *tolleres*, toll-collectors
107 *alkin*, all kinds of; *libbing*, living; *lopen*, leapt
108 *here dedes*, their deeds
109 *Dieu . . . Emme*, probably a popular song   110 *hote*, hot

Gode gris and gees, go we dine, go we!"
Taverners until hem tolde the same,
"White win of Oseye and red win of Gascoigne,
Of the Rine and of the Rochel, the roste to defye."
Al this seigh I sleping, and sevene sithes more. 115

> (B-Text, Prologue, lines 1–94, 210–30. These
> lines parallel in general the complete Prologue
> of the earliest version [A-Text] of the poem.)

111 *gris*, pork   112 *until*, to
113 *Oseye*, ? Alsace   114 *defye*, digest   115 *sithes*, times

[*The Incarnation*]

For treuthe telleth that love is triacle to abate sinne
And most sovereine salve for saule and for body.
Love is plonte of pees, most precious of vertues,
For hevene holde hit ne mighte, so hevy hit semede,
Til hit hadde of erthe y-yoten hitselve.   5
Was nevere lef upon linde lighter therafter
As whanne hit hadde of the folde flesch and blode ytake.
Tho was hit portatif and persaunt as the point of a
        nelde:
May none armure hit lette, ne none hye walles.

> (C-Text, II, lines 147–55)

1 *triacle*, medicine   3 *plonte of pees*, plant of peace
4 *holde . . . mighte*, could not hold it
5 *hit*, it; *of*, with; *y-yoten*, alloyed   6 *linde*, tree
7 *folde*, earth
8 *tho*, then; *portatif and persaunt*, mobile and penetrating; *nelde*,
    needle   9 *lette*, obstruct

[*The Poor*]

The most needy aren oure neighebores, and we nime
        good hede,
As prisones in puttes and poure folke in cotes,

1 *and*, if; *nime*, take   2 *prisones in puttes*, prisoners in pits

Charged with children and chef-lordes rente.
That they with spinninge may spare, spenen hit on
    hous-hire,
Bothe in milk and in mele to make with papelotes   5
To aglotye with here gurles that greden after fode.
And hemselve also suffren muche hunger,
And wo in winter-time, and wakinge on nightes,
To rise to the ruel, to rocke the cradel,
Bothe to carde and to cembe, to clouten and to
    wasche,   10
To ribbe and to rele, russhes to pilye,
That reuthe is to rede othere in rime rime shewe
The wo of these women that wonieth in cotes,
And of meny other men that muche wo suffren,
Bothe afingrede and afurst, to turne the faire out-
    warde,   15
And beth abasshed for to begge, and wolle nat be aknowe
What hem needeth at here neighebores at non and at
    even.   *(C-Text, X, lines 71-87)*

3 *charged*, burdened; *chef-lordes*, landlord's
4 *spare*, save; *spenen hit*, spend it   5 *papelotes*, porridge
6 *aglotye*, glut; *here gurles*, their children; *greden*, cry
7 *hemselve*, themselves
                                 9 *ruel*, bedside
10 *cembe*, comb (wool); *clouten*, patch
11 *ribbe*, scrape (flax); *rele*, reel (yarn); *pilye*, peel
12 *reuthe*, pity; *othere*, or   13 *wonieth*, dwell
15 *afingrede and afurst*, hungry and thirsty; *to turne . . . outwarde*,
i.e., to put on the best appearance
16 *wolle . . . aknowe*, will not let it be known
17 *here*, their; *non*, noon

[A Vision of Nature]

And ich bowede my body and bihelde al aboute,
And seigh the sonne and the see and the sand after,
And wher that briddes and bestes by here makes they
    yeden,

1 *ich*, I   2 *seigh*, saw   3 *here makes*, their mates; *yeden*, walked

Wilde wormes in wodes and wonderful fowles
With fleckede fetheres and of fele colours.   5
Man and hus make ich mighte see bothe,
Poverté and plenté, bothe pees and werre;
Blisse and bale, bothe ich seigh at ones,
And how that men mede token and mercy refuseden.
Reson ich seigh sothliche suwen alle bestes   10
In etinge and drinking, in engendrure of kinde.
After cours of concepcion non tok kepe of other,
And when they hadde ruteyed, anon they resten after.
Males drowen hem to males on morweninge by hemself,
And femeles to femeles ferdide and drow.   15
Ther ne was cow ne cow-kinde that conceived hadde
That wolde bere after bole, ne bor after sowe.
Ther ne was no kinne kinde that conceived hadde
That ne lees the likinge of lust of flesch, as hit were,
Save man and hus make. And therof me wondrede,   20
For out of reson they ride and rechelesliche token on,
As in durne dedes, bothe in drinkinge and elles.
Briddes ich bihelde in bosshes maden nestes:
Hadde nevere weye wit to worche the leste.
Ich hadde wonder at wham and wher that the pie   25
Lernede to legge stickes that leyen on here neste:
There is no wright as ich wene sholde worche here nest
     to paye;

If eny mason made a molde therto, muche wonder me
    thinketh.

And yut me mervaillede more, menye of the briddes
Hudden and heleden here egges durneliche   30
For no fowl sholde it finde bote hus fere and himself.
And some treden, ich tok kepe, and on trees bredden,
And broughten forth here briddes al above the grounde.
In mareis and in mores, in mires and in wateres
Dompinges diveden. "Deere God," ich saide,   35
"Where hadden these wilde suche wit, and at what
    scole?"
And how the pocock caukede, therof took ich kepe,
How uncorteisliche the cok hus kinde forth strenede,
And ferliede of hus fairnesse and of hus foule ledene.
And sitthe ich loked on the see, and so forth on the
    sterres,   40
Meny selcouthes ich seigh aren nought to seggen
    nouthe;
Ne what on flowres in felde, and of here faire coloures,
And how of greot and of gras growe so meny huwes,
And somme soure and somme swete, selcouth me
    thoughte;
Of here kinde and of here colours to carpen hit were
    to longe.   45

(*C-Text, XIV, lines* 134–79)

29 *yut,* yet
30 *hudden and heleden,* hid and concealed; *durneliche,* secretly
31 *for,* so that; *bote,* except; *fere,* mate
34 *mareis,* marshes; *mores,* swamps   35 *dompinges,* dabchicks
37 *pocock,* peacock; *caukede,* trod
38 *kinde forth strenede,* begot his progeny
39 *ferliede,* I wondered; *ledene,* voice
40 *sitthe,* afterwards; *sterres,* stars
41 *selcouthes,* marvels; *seggen nouthe,* speak of now
42 *ne what on,* i.e., nor what I saw of   43 *greot,* soil
45 *kinde,* nature; *carpen,* speak

[*The Descent into Hell*]

A vois loude in that light to Lucifer seide,
"Princes of this place, prest undo this yates,
For here cometh with coroune the Kinge of alle glorye."
Thenne sighede Satan and seide to Helle,
"Suche a light ayeins our leve Lazar hit fette: 5
Care and combraunce is come to us alle.
If this king come in, mankinde wol he fecche,
And leden hit ther Lazar is, and lightliche me binde.
Patriarkes and prophetes han parled herof longe,
That suche a lorde and a light shal leden hem alle
        hennes.   10
Ac aris up, Ragamoffin, and areche me alle the barres
That Belial thy belsire bet with thy damme,
And ich shal lette this lorde and hus light stoppe.
Ar we thorgh brightnesse be blent, go barre we the
        yates,
Cheke we and cheine we, and eche a chine stoppe,   15
That no light lepe in at lover ne at loupe.
Astrot, hot out and have oute oure knaves,
Colting and al hus kinne, the care to save.
Brinston boilaunt brenning outcasteth hit
Al hot on here hedes that entren ny the walles.   20
Setteth bowes of brake and brasene gonnes,

1 *vois*, voice   2 *prest*, quickly; *this yates*, these gates
3 *coroune*, crown
5 *ayeins*, against; *Lazar hit fette*, i.e., fetched Lazarus
6 *combraunce*, trouble   7 *wol*, will
8 *hit*, it; *ther*, where; *lightliche*, easily   9 *parled*, spoken
10 *hem*, them; *hennes*, hence   11 *ac*, but; *areche*, hand
12 *belsire*, grandfather; *bet . . . damme*, beat your dam with
13 *ich*, I; *lette*, hinder; *hus*, his   14 *ar*, ere; *blent*, blinded
15 *cheke we*, let us stop up (the walls); *chine*, chink
16 *lover*, chimney-hole; *loupe*, loophole   17 *hot*, call
18 *Colting*, one of the devils; *care*, i.e., what is in our charge
19 i.e., cast out boiling, burning brimstone   20 *here*, their
21 *setteth*, emplace; *bowes of brake*, large crossbows; *gonnes*, guns

And sheteth out shot ynough hus shultrom to blende.

Sette Mahon at the mangonel and mullestones throweth;

With crokes and calketrappes acloye we hem ech one!"

"Lusteneth," quath Lucifer, "for ich this lord knowe, 25

Bothe this lord and this light is longe gon ich knew him.

May no deth this lord dere, ne no develes queintise,

And wher he wole, is hus wey—ac war him of the
       periles:

If he reve me of my right, he robbeth me of his mais-
       trye.

For by right and by reson the renkes that ben here 30

Body and soule beth mine, bothe good and ille.

For himself seide hit that sire is of Hevene,

That Adam and Eve and al hus issue

Sholden deye with doel and here dwelle evere

If that they touchede a tre other toke therof an appel. 35

Thus this lord of light suche a lawe made,

And sutthe he is so leel a lorde, ich leve that he wol nat

Reven us of oure right, sutthe reson hem dampned.

And sutthe we han be sesed sevene thousand winter,

And nevere was therayein, and now wolde biginne, 40

Then were he unwrast of hus worde, that witnesse is
      of treuthe."

"That is soth," seide Satan, "bote ich me sore doute,

For thou gete hem with gile and hus gardin breke,

---

22 *sheteth*, shoot; *shultrom*, troops; *blende*, cast into confusion
23 *mangonel*, catapult; *mullestones*, millstones
24 *crokes and calketrappes*, grappling hooks and caltrops; *acloye*, lame
25 *lusteneth*, listen
26 *is longe . . . him*, I have known him for a long time
27 *dere*, harm; *queintise*, cunning
28 *wole*, i.e., will go; *ac war him*, but warn him
29 *reve*, deprive; *of his maistrye*, by force   30 *renkes*, men
34 *doel*, grief   35 *other*, or
37 *sutthe*, since; *leel*, just; *leve*, believe   38 *dampned*, damned
39 *be sesed*, been in possession
40 *and never was therayein*, i.e., and he never disputed it
41 *unwrast*, untrustworthy   42 *bote*, but
43 *for thou gete*, because you got; *breke*, violated

Agein hus love and hus leve on hus londe yedest,

Nat in forme of a fende, bote in forme of an addre,   45

And entisedest Eve to ete by here on, *Vae soli!*

And bihightest here and him after to knowe

As two godes with God bothe good and ille:

Thus with treison and trecherye thou troiledest hem
    bothe,

And dudest hem breke here buxomnesse thorgh false
    bihestes;   50

And so haddest hem oute and hider atte last.

Hit is nat greithly getin ther gile is the rote."

"For God wol nat be bigiled," quath Gobelin, "ne bi-
    japed.

We have no treue title to hem, for thy treison hit
    maketh."

"Forthy ich drede me," quath the Devel, "lest Treuthe
    wol hem fecche,   55

And as thou bigiledest Godes image in goinge of an
    addre,

So hath God bigiled us alle in goinge of a wye."

"For God hath go," quath Gobelin, "in a gome liknesse

This thritty winter, as ich wene, and went aboute and
    prechede.

Ich have asailid him with sinne, and som time ich
    askede   60

Wher he were God other Godes sone—he gaf me short
    answere.

44 *yedest*, walked   46 *by here on*, by herself
47 *bihightest here*, promised her   48 *godes*, gods
49 *troiledest*, deceived
50 *dudest*, made; *here buxomnesse*, their obedience; *bihestes*, promises
51 *hider*, hither
52 *hit*, it; *greithly getin*, properly acquired; *ther*, i.e., in cases where;
    rote, root   53 *bijaped*, tricked
54 *hit maketh*, i.e., causes our possession   55 *forthy*, therefore
56 *goinge*, i.e., guise   57 *wye*, man
58 *gome*, man's   59 *wene*, think
61 *wher*, whether; *gaf*, gave

Thus hath he trolled forth like a tidy man this two and
    thritty wintere,

And whenne ich seigh hit was so, ich sotelide how ich
    mighte

Lette hem that lovede him nat, lest they wolde him
    martrye.

Ich wolde have lengthed hus lif, for ich levede if he
    deyede, 65

That if hus soule huder come, hit shulde shende us alle.

The body, whiles hit on bones yede, aboute was hit
    evere

To lere men to be leel, and eche man to loven other.

The whiche lif and lawe, be hit longe y-used,

Hit shal undon us develes, and down bringe us alle. 70

And now I se wher hus soule cometh seilinge hider-
    wardes

With glorye and with gret light—God hit is, ich wot
    wel."

"Ich rede we fle," quath the Fend, "faste alle hennes,

For us were betere nat be than abide in hus sighte.

For thy lesinges, Lucifer, we loste furst our joye, 75

And out of Hevene hider thy prude made us falle.

For we levede on thy lesinges ther losten we oure blisse,

And now for a later lesinge that thou lowe til Eve

We han lost our lordshep, a londe and in Helle."

    Nunc princeps huius mundi eiecetur foras.

(Sutthe that Satan missaide thus foule 80

Lucifer for hus lesinges, leve ich non other

---

62 *trolled*, walked; *tidy*, worthy
64 *lette*, prevent
66 *huder*, hither; *shende*, destroy
68 *lere*, teach; *leel*, just
73 *rede*, advise; *hennes*, hence
76 *prude*, pride
78 *lowe*, lied; *til*, to
80 *missaide*, abused

63 *seigh*, saw; *sotelide*, schemed
65 *levede*, believed
67 *yede*, walked
72 *wot*, know
75 *lesinges*, lies
77 *for*, because; *levede on*, believed
79 *a londe*, on earth
81 *leve*, believe

Bote oure Lord atte laste lieres here rebuke

And wite hem al the wrecchednesse that wrought is
    here on erthe.

Be ware, ye wise clerkes and ye witty men of lawe,

That ye beleiye nat this lewed men, for atte laste
    David   85

Witnesseth in hus writinge what is lieres mede:

   Odisti omnes qui operantur iniquitatem, et perdes
     omnes qui loquuntur mendacium.

A litel ich overlep, for lesinges sake,

That ich ne segge nat as ich seigh, suinge my teme.)

For eft that light bad unlouke, and Lucifer answerede.

"What lord art thou?" quath Lucifer. A vois aloud
    seide,   90

"The lord of might and of main, that made alle thinges:

Dukes of this dimme place, anon undo the yates,

That Crist mowe comen in, the Kinges Sone of Hevene."

And with that breth Helle brake, with alle Beliales
    barres;

For eny wye other warde wide open the gates.   95

Patriarkes and prophetes, *populus in tenebris,*

Songen with seint Johan *Ecce Agnus Dei.*

Lucifer loke ne mighte, so light him ablente,

And tho that oure Lord lovede forth with that light
    flowen.

"Lo me her," quath oure Lorde, "lif and soule bothe, 100

For alle sinful soules to save our bothe right.

---

82 *lieres here rebuke,* will rebuke liars here
83 *wite him,* blame them for
85 *beleiye,* calumniate; *this lewed,* these ignorant; *atte,* at the
86 *mede,* reward   87 *overlep,* digress
88 *that,* with the result that; *segge,* say; *seigh,* saw; *suinge my teme,*
    pursuing my theme   89 *eft,* again; *unlouke,* unlock
93 *mowe,* may
95 *for eny . . . warde,* despite any soldier or sentinel
97 *songen,* sang   98 *ablente,* blinded
99 *tho,* those; *flowen,* flew   100 *lo me her,* behold me here; *lif,* body
101: i.e., to maintain the right both of myself and of all sinful souls

Mine they were and of me, ich may the beter hem
    cleime.

Althaugh reson recorde and right of myselve

That if they eten the appel alle sholden they deye,

Ich bihighte hem nat here Helle for evere. 105

For the dedliche sinne that they duden thy deceite hit
    made;

With gile thou hem gete agein alle reson:

For in my paleis Paradis in persone of an addere

Falsliche fettest there that me bifel to loke,

Biglosedest hem and bigiledest hem, and my gardin
    breke, 110

Ayeins my love and my leve. The olde lawe techeth

That gilours be bigilid and in here gile falle,

And ho so hitteth out a mannes eye other elles hus for-
    teth,

Othere eny manere membre maimeth other hurteth,

The same sore shal he have, that eny so smiteth: 115

    Dentem pro dente, et oculum pro oculo.

So lif shal lif lete ther lif hath lif aniented,

So that lif quite lif, the olde lawe hit asketh.

Ergo, soule shal soule quite, and sinne to sinne
    wende,

And al that man misdude ich, man, to amenden hit,

And that deth fordude, my deth to releven, 120

And bothe quikye and quite that queint was thorgh
    sinne,

And gile be bigiled thorgh grace atte laste:

    Ars ut artem falleret, etc.

---

105 *bihighte,* promised   106 *duden,* did; *hit made,* caused it
106 *gete,* got
109 *fettest,* you fetched; *that me bifel to loke,* whom it fell to me to
care for   110 *biglosedest,* deceived
112 *be bigilid,* shall be beguiled   113 *ho so,* whoso; *other,* or
116: i.e., so shall a body lose its own life when a body has destroyed
life   117 *quite,* requite
119 *misdude,* misdid   120 *that,* what; *fordude,* brought to ruin
121 *quikye,* revive; *queint,* quenched

So lef hit nat, Lucifer, ayeins the lawe ich fecche

Here eny sinful soule sovereinliche by maistrye,

Bot thorgh right and thorgh reson raunson here mine
    lige: 125

   Non veni solvere legem, sed adimplere.

So that thorgh gile was geten, thorgh grace is now
    ywonne,

And as Adam and alle thorgh a tre deyden,

Adam and alle thorgh a tre shal turne to live.

And now biginneth thy gile again on thee to turne,

And my grace to growe ay widder and widder.   130

The biternesse that thou hast browe, now brouk hit
    thyself—

That art doctour of deth—drink that thou madest.

For ich that am lord of lif, love is my drinke,

And for that drinke todaye ich deyede, as hit semede.

Ac ich wol drinke of no disshe, ne of no dep
    cleregye,   135

Bote of comune coppes, alle Cristene soules;

Ac thy drinke worth deth, and dep Helle thy bolle.

Ich faught so, me fursteth yut, for mannes soule sake:

   Sicio.

May no piement ne pomade ne preciouse drinkes

Moiste me to the fulle ne my furst slake   140

Til the vendage falle in the Vale of Josaphat,

And drinke right ripe most, *resurrectio mortuorum*.

And then shal ich come as king, with coroune and with
    angeles,

123 *lef*, believe   124 *sovereinliche*, principally
125 *lige*, vassals   126 *that*, what; *geten*, procured
130 *widder*, wider   131 *browe*, brewed; *brouk*, enjoy
135 *ac*, but; *disshe*, vessel; *dep cleregye*, subtle science
136 *coppes*, cups   137 *worth*, shall be; *dep*, deep; *bolle*, bowl
138 *me fursteth yut*, I thirst still
139 *piement*, spiced wine; *pomade*, cider   140 *furst*, thirst
141 *vendage falle*, vintage-time occur
142 *drinke . . . most*, I shall drink mellow new wine
143 *coroune*, crown

And have out of Helle alle menne soules.

Fendes and fendekenes bifor me shullen stande,   145

And be at my bidding, at blisse other at peine.

Ac to be merciable to man thenne my kinde asketh,

For we beth bretheren of blod, ac nat in baptisme alle.

Ac alle that beth mine hole-bretheren, in blod and in
      baptisme,

Shal nevere in Helle eft come, be he ones oute: 150

   Tibi soli peccavi, et malum coram te feci, etc.

Hit is nat used on erthe to honge eny felones

Ofter than ones, thaugh they weren treitours;

And if the king of the kingdom come in the time

Ther a thef tholy sholde deth other juwise,

Lawe wolde he yeve him lif, and he lokede on him.   155

And ich that am kinge over kinges shal come suche a
      time

Ther that dom to the deth dampneth alle wickede,

And if lawe wol ich loke on hem, hit lith in my grace

Whether they deye other deye nat, dude they nevere
      so ille.

Be hit eny thing abought, the boldness of here
      sinne,   160

Ich may do mercy of my rightwisnesse and alle mine
      wordes trewe.

For Holy Writ wole that ich be wreke of hem that
      wroughte ille:

   *Nullum malum impunitum, et nullum bonum irre-
      muneratum.*

144 *menne,* men's   145 *fendekenes,* fiendkins
147 *ac,* but; *merciable,* merciful; *kinde,* nature
149 *hole-bretheren,* full brothers   150 *eft,* again
151 *hit . . . erthe,* the custom on earth is not
154 *tholy,* suffer; *juwise,* penalty
155 *wolde,* requires; *yeve,* give; *and,* if
157 *dom,* sentence; *dampneth,* condemns   158 *wol,* wills; *lith,* lies
159 *dude,* did
160: i.e., if the boldness of their sin has in any way been redeemed
162 *wreke,* avenged

And so of alle wickede ich wolle here take venjaunce,

Ac yut my kinde in my kene ire shal constreine my
wil—

*Domine, ne in furore tuo arguas me, neque in ira tua
corripias me—*

To be merciable to menye of my half-brethren.   165

For blod may se blood bothe afurst and acale,

Ac blod may nat se blod blede bote him rewe:

Audivi arcana verba quae non licet homini loqui.

Ac my rightwisnesse and right shal regnen in Helle,

And mercy and mankinde bifor me in Hevene.

For ich were an unkinde kinge bote ich my kin
holpe,   170

And nameliche at suche a nede that nedes help asketh:

Non intres in iudicium cum servo tuo, Domine.

Thus by lawe," quath oure Lord, "lede ich wol fro
hennes

Alle that ich lovye and levede in my cominge.

Ac for the lesinge that thou lowe, Lucifer, til Eve,

Thou shalt abigge bitere," quath God, and bond him
with cheines.   175

Astrot and alle othere hudden hem in hernes:

They dorst nat loken on oure Lorde, the leste of hem
alle,

Bote leten Him leden forth which Him luste and leve
which Him likede.

Mony hundrede of aungelis harpeden tho and songen,

Culpat caro, purgat caro, regnat Deus Dei caro.

164 *kinde,* nature
166 *blod,* i.e., kin; *afurst and acale,* thirsty and cold
167 *bote him rewe,* without his grieving
170 *bote,* unless; *holpe,* helped   171 *nameliche,* especially
173: i.e., all those that I loved and all those who believed in my
coming   174 *ac,* but; *lesinge,* lie; *lowe,* lied
175 *abigge bitere,* pay for it bitterly
176 *hudden,* hid; *hernes,* corners   177 *leste,* least
178 *which Him luste, which Him likede,* whom He pleased
179 *tho,* then; *songen,* sang

Thenne pipede Pees of poetes a note: 180
  Clarior est solito post maxima nebula phoebus:
  Post inimicitias clarior est et amor.
"After sharpest showres," quath Pees, "most sheene is
    the sonne;
Is no weder warmer than after watery cloudes,
Ne no love levere, ne levere frendes,
Than after werre and wrake, whanne Love and Pees
    ben maistres. 185
Was nevere werre in this worlde, ne wickeder envye,
That Love, and him luste, to laughinge hit ne broughte,
And Pees thorgh pacience alle pereles stoppede."
"Treuwes," quath Treuthe, "thou tellest us soth, by
    Jesus!
Cluppe we in covenaunt, and ech of us kusse other!" 190
"And leet no peuple," quath Pees, "parceive that we
    chide!
For impossible is no thing to Him that is almighty."
"Thou seist soth," quath Rightwisnesse, and reverent-
    liche heo kuste
Pees, and Pees here, *per saecula saeculorum.*
  Misericordia et veritas obviaverunt sibi; iustitia et pax
  osculatae sunt.
Treuthe trompede tho, and song *Te Deum Lauda-*
    mus. 195
And then lutede Love in a loud note,
  Ecce quam bonum et quam iocundum est habitare
  fratres in unum.
Til the day dawede these damseles carolede,

183 *sheene,* bright   184 *levere,* dearer
185 *werre and wrake,* war and trouble
187 *and him luste,* if he pleased   188 *pereles,* perils
189 *Treuwes,* i.e., peace   190 *cluppe,* embrace; *kusse,* kiss
193 *heo,* she   194 *here,* (kissed) her
195 *trompede,* blew the trumpet; *tho,* then
196 *lutede,* played the lute
197 *dawede,* dawned; *carolede,* danced

That men rang to the Resurreccioun; and right with that
    ich wakede,
And callid Kitte my wif and Calote my doughter:
"Aris and go reverence Godes resurreccioun,   200
And crep to the Cros on knes and kusse hit for a juwel,
And rightfullokest a relic, non riccher on erthe.
For Godes blesside body hit bar for oure bote,
And hit afereth the Fende, for such is the mighte,
May no grisliche gost glide ther hit shadeweth."   205

(C-Text, XXI, lines 273–479)

---

201 *crep,* creep   203 *hit bar,* it bore; *bote,* redemption
204 *afereth,* frightens
205 *ther hit shadeweth,* where it casts its shadow

Anonymous Lyrics

(Thirteenth–Fifteenth Centuries)

Now sprinkes the spray

Now sprinkes the spray,
Al for love ich am so seek
That slepen I ne may.

Als I me rode this endre day
  O my playinge,   5
Seigh I whar a litel may
  Bigan to singe,
    "The clot him clinge!
    Way es him i love-longinge
Sal libben ay!"   10

Son ich herde that mirye note,
  Thider I drogh.
I fonde hire in an herber swot
  Under a bogh,
  With joye ynogh.   15
  Son I asked, "Thou mirye may,
Why sinkestou ay?"

---

1 *sprinkes,* springs   2 *ich,* I; *seek,* sick
3 *ne may,* cannot   4 *als,* as; *this endre,* the other
5 *o,* on   6 *seigh,* saw; *may,* maid
8: i.e., may the earth (in his grave) cling to him
9 *way es,* woe is; *i,* in   10 *sal libben,* shall live
11 *son,* as soon as   12: i.e., thither I drew
13 *fonde,* found; *herber swot,* arbor sweet
17 *sinkestou,* do you sing

Than answerde that maiden swote
   Mid wordes fewe,
"My lemman me haves bihot   20
   Of love trewe:
   He chaunges anewe.
   Yif I may, it shal him rewe,
By this day."

19 *mid,* with   20 *lemman,* lover; *haves bihot,* has promised
23 *yif,* if

Spring Song

Lenten is come with love to towne,
With blosmen and with briddes roune,
   That al this blisse bringeth.
Dayeseyes in this dales,
Notes swete of nightegales,   5
   Uch fowl song singeth.
The threstelcok him threteth oo,
Away is huere winter wo,
   When woderove springeth.
This fowles singeth ferly fele,   10
Ant wliteth on huere winne wele,
   That al the wode ringeth.

The rose raileth hire rode,
The leves on the lighte wode
   Waxen al with wille.   15

2 *briddes roune,* birds' voice   4 *this,* these   6 *uch,* each
7: i.e., The song-thrush chides constantly   8 *huere,* their
9 *woderove,* woodruff   10 *ferly fele,* wondrous many
11: i.e., ? and warble on their wealth of joy
13 *raileth hire rode,* puts on her hue   15 *wille,* delight

The mone mandeth hire bleo,
The lilye is lossom to seo,
   The fenil and the fille.
Wowes this wilde drakes:
Males murgeth huere makes,   20
   On strem that striketh stille.
Mody meneth, so doth mo:
Ichot ich am on of tho
   For love that likes ille.

The mone mandeth hire light;   25
So doth the semly sonne bright,
   When briddes singeth breme.
Deawes donketh the downes;
Deores whisperes dernes rounes,
   Domes for te deme;   30
Wormes woweth under cloude;
Wimmen waxeth wounder proude,
   So wel hit wol hem seme.
Yef me shal wonte wille of on,
This wunne wele I wol forgon,   35
   Ant wight in wode be fleme.

16 *mandeth hire bleo,* sends forth her radiance
17 *lossom to seo,* lovely to see   19 *wowes,* woo; *this,* these
20 *males,* ms: *miles; murgeth huere makes,* gladden their mates
21 *on,* ms: *ase; striketh,* flows
22: i.e., passionate (lovers) complain, so do others
23 *ichot,* I know; *ich,* I; *tho,* those   24 *likes ille,* i.e., are troubled
27 *breme,* clearly   28 *donketh,* moisten
29: i.e., animals whisper dark secrets; *whisperes,* ms: *with huere*
30: i.e., in order to settle their affairs
31 *woweth,* woo; *cloude,* ground   32 *wounder,* wondrous
33: i.e., ? so well it (their pride) will suit them
34: i.e., if I must do without my delight in one of them
35 *wunne wele,* wealth of joy; *wol,* will
36 *wight,* creature; *fleme,* fugitive

Alisoun

Bitwene Mersh and Averil,
    When spray biginneth to springe,
The lutel fowl hath hire wil
    On hire lud to singe.
    Ich libbe in love-longinge   5
For semlokest of alle thinge;
He may me blisse bringe:
    Ich am in hire baundoun.
An hendy hap ichabbe yhent;
Ichot from hevene it is me sent,   10
From alle wimmen my love is lent,
    And light on Alisoun.

On heu hire her is fair ynogh,
    Hire browe browne, hire eye blake;
With lossum chere he on me logh,   15
    With middel smal and wel ymake.
Bote he me wolle to hire take,
For te buen hire owen make,
Longe to liven ichulle forsake,
    And feye fallen adown.   20

Nightes when I wende and wake,
    Forthy min wonges waxeth won;

---

3 *lutel*, little; *hire wil*, her delight   4 *on hire lud*, ? in her language
5 *ich libbe*, I live
                         6 *semlokest*, fairest
7 *he*, she
                    8 *in hire baundoun*, in her control
9: i.e., a lucky chance I have received   10 *ichot*, I know
11 *lent*, taken away
                        12 *light*, (has) alighted
13 *hire her*, her hair
15 *lossum chere*, lovely face; *he*, she; *logh*, smiled
16 *ymake*, made
                    17 *bote he*, unless she; *hire*, her
18: i.e., for to be her own mate
                    19 *ichulle*, I will
20 *feye*, dead
                    21 *wende*, turn
22 *forthy*, therefore; *min wonges*, my cheeks; *won*, wan

Levedy, al for thine sake
    Longinge is ylent me on.
    In world nis non so witer mon   25
    That al hire bounte telle con;
    Hire swire is whittore then the swon,
        And feirest may in towne.

Ich am for wowing al forwake,
    Wery so water in wore,   30
Lest eny reve me my make;
    Ichabbe y-yirned yore:
    Betere is tholien while sore
    Then mournen evermore.
    Geinest under gore,   35
        Herkne to my roun:
An hendy hap ichabbe yhent;
Ichot from hevene it is me sent;
From alle wimmen my love is lent,
        And light on Alisoun.   40

23 *levedy*, lady   24 *ylent me on*, come upon me
25 *nis non*, is none; *witer mon*, clever man   26 *con*, can
27 *swire*, neck; *swon*, swan   28 *may*, maid
29 *wowing*, wooing; *forwake*, i.e., sleepless   30 *so*, as; *wore*, ? weir
31 *reve me*, deprive me of   32: i.e., I've yearned since long ago
33 *tholien while sore*, suffer pain for a time
35: i.e., most gracious under gown   36 *roun*, voice

Ich am of Irlonde

Ich am of Irlonde,
    Ant of the holy londe
      Of Irlonde.

1 *ich*, I   2 *ant*, and

Gode sire, pray ich thee,
For of sainte charite,   5
Come ant dance wit me,
In Irlonde.

5 *for of,* for the sake of   6 *wit,* with

Maiden in the mor

Maiden in the mor lay,
    In the mor lay,
Sevenist fulle, sevenist fulle,
Maiden in the mor lay,
    In the mor lay,   5
Sevenistes fulle ant a day.

Welle was hire mete.
    Wat was hire mete?
The primerole ant the—
The primerole ant the—   10
Welle was hire mete.
    Wat was hire mete?
The primerole ant the violet.

Welle was hire dring.
    Wat was hire dring?   15
The chelde water of the—
The chelde water of the—
Welle was hire dring.
    Wat was hire dring?
The chelde water of the welle-spring.   20

3 *sevenist,* seven-night
6 *ant,* and   7 *welle,* good; *hire mete,* her meat
9 *primerole,* cowslip; *ant the,* and the   14 *dring,* drink
16 *chelde,* cold

Welle was hire bowr.
　　Wat was hire bowr?
The rede rose an te—
The rede rose an te—
Welle was hire bowr.　　　　　　　　25
　　Wat was hire bowr?
The rede rose an te lilye flowr.

23 *an te,* and the

Adam lay yboundin

O Felix Culpa!

Adam lay yboundin, boundin in a bond,
Foure thousand winter thought he not to long.
And al was for an appil, an appil that he took,
As clerkes findin wretin in here book.
Ne hadde the appil take ben, the appil taken ben,　　5
Ne hadde never our Lady a ben hevene quen.
Blissed be the time that appil take was,
Therfore we mown singin *Deo Gratias.*

4 *wretin,* written; *here,* their
5 *ne hadde,* had not
7 *blissed,* blessed
6 *a,* have
8 *mown,* may

I have a yong suster

I have a yong suster
　　Fer beyondin the se;
Many be the drouryis
　　That sche sente me.

2 *fer,* far
3 *drouryis,* love tokens

Sche sente me the cherye,   5
    Withoutin ony ston,
And so sche dede the dove,
    Withoutin ony bon.

Sche sente me the brere,
    Withoutin ony rinde,   10
Sche bad me love my lemman
    Withoutin longing.

How schulde ony cherye
    Be withoute ston?
And how schulde ony dove   15
    Ben withoute bon?

How schulde any brere
    Ben withoute rinde?
How schulde I love my lemman
    Without longing?   20

Qwan the cherye was a flowr,
    Than hadde it non ston;
Qwan the dove was an ey,
    Than hadde it non bon.

Qwan the brere was onbred,   25
    Than hadde it no rind;
Qwan the maiden has that sche lovith,
    Sche is without longing.

---

7 *dede*, did   9 *brere*, briar
10 *rinde*, bark   11 *lemman*, beloved
21 *qwan*, when   23 *ey*, egg
25 *onbred*, ungrown   27 *that*, what

I sing of a maiden

I sing of a maiden
    That is makeles;
King of alle kinges
    To here sone che ches.

He cam also stille   5
    Ther his moder was,
As dew in Aprille
    That fallith on the gras.

He cam also stille
    To his moderes bowr,   10
As dew in Aprille
    That fallith on the flowr.

He cam also stille
    Ther his moder lay,
As dew in Aprille   15
    That fallith on the spray.

Moder and maiden
    Was never non but che;
Wel may swich a lady
    Godes moder be.   20

2 *makeles,* matchless
5 *also,* as
18 *che,* she

4 *che ches,* she chose
6 *moder,* mother
19 *swich,* such

Quia Amore Langueo

I

In the vaile of restless mind
   I sought in mountein and in mede,
Trusting a treulofe for to find:
   Upon an hill than toke I hede;
   A voise I herd (and nere I yede)   5
      In gret dolour complaining tho,
  "See, dere soule, my sides blede
      Quia amore langueo."

Upon this mount I fand a tree;
   Undir this tree a man sitting;   10
From hede to fote woundid was he,
   His hert blode I saw bleding;
   A semely man to be a king,
      A graciose face to loke unto.
I askid him how he had paining,   15
      He said, "*Quia amore langueo.*

"I am treulove that fals was never;
   My sistur, mannis soule, I loved hir thus;
By-cause I wold on no wise dissevere,
   I left my kingdome gloriouse;   20
   I purveyd hir a place full preciouse;
      She flitt, I folowid, I luffed her soo
That I suffred these paines piteuouse
      Quia amore langueo.

---

1 *vaile,* valley   3 *treulofe,* truelove, a four-leaf clover
5 *yede,* went   6 *tho,* then
9 *fand,* found   21 *purveyd,* prepared
22 *flitt,* i.e., fled; *luffed,* loved

"My faire love and my spouse bright,   25
   I saved hir fro beting, and she hath me bett;
I clothed hir in grace and hevenly light,
   This blody surcote she hath on me sett;
   For langing love I will not lett;
      Swete strokis be thes, loo;   30
   I haf loved ever als I hett,
     Quia amore langueo.

"I crownid hir with blisse and she me with thorne,
   I led hir to chambre and she me to die;
I brought hir to worship and she me to scorne,   35
   I did hir reverence and she me velanye.
To love that loveth is no maistrye,
   Hir hate made never my love hir foo;
Ask than no moo questions whye,
    But *Quia amore langueo.*   40

II

"Loke unto min handis, man!
   Thes gloves were geven me whan I hir sought;
They be nat white, but rede and wan,
   Embrodred with blode my spouse them brought;
They will not of, I lefe them nought,   45
      I wowe hir with them where ever she goo;
Thes handes full frendly for hir fought,
    Quia amore langueo.

"Marvell not, man, thof I sitt still,
   My love hath shod me wondir straite;   50
She boklid my fete as was hir will

---

26 *beting*, beating; *bett*, beaten   29 *langing*, longing; *lett*, cease
31 *als*, as; *hett*, promised   36 *velanye*, discourtesy
37: i.e., no force can constrain true love   42 *geven*, given
43 *wan*, discolored   45 *of*, i.e., come off; *lefe*, leave
46 *wowe*, woo   49 *thof*, though
50 *straite*, tight

With sharp nailes, loo thou mayst waite!
In my love was never dissaite,
    For all my membres I haf opind hir to;
My body I made hir hertis baite,   55
    Quia amore langueo.

"In my side I haf made hir nest,
    Loke, in me how wide a wound is here!
This is hir chambre, here shall she rest,
    That she and I may slepe in fere.   60
    Here may she wasshe, if any filth were;
        Here is socour for all hir woo;
    Cum if she will, she shall haf chere,
        Quia amore langueo.

"I will abide till she be redy,   65
    I will to hir send if she sey nay;
If she be rechelesse I will be gredy,
    If she be daungerouse I will hir pray.
    If she do wepe, than bid I nay;
        Min armes ben spred to clipp hir to;   70
    Crye onis, 'I cum!' now, soule, assaye!
        Quia amore langueo.

"I sitt on an hille for to se farre,
    I loke to the vaile, my spouse I see;
Now rinneth she awayward, now cummith she
        narre,   75
    Yet fro min eyesight she may nat be;
    Sum waite ther pray, to make hir flee,
        I rinne tofore to chastise hir foo;

---

52 *waite*, look   53 *dissaite*, deceit
55 *baite*, allurement   60 *in fere*, together
67 *rechelesse*, heedless; *gredy*, importunate
68 *daungerouse*, disdainful
71 *assaye*, make trial   70 *clipp*, embrace
77 *waite*, lie in wait for   75 *rinneth*, runs; *narre*, nearer

Recover, my soule, againe to me,
    Quia amore langueo.   80

III

"My swete spouse, will we goo play?
    Apples ben ripe in my gardine;
I shall clothe thee in new array,
    Thy mete shall be milk, honye, and wine;
    Now, dere soule, latt us go dine,   85
        Thy sustenance is in my scripp, loo!
    Tary not now, faire spouse mine,
        Quia amore langueo.

"If thou be foule, I shall make thee clene,
    If thou be seke, I shall thee hele;   90
If thou ought morne, I shall be-mene;
    Spouse, why will thou nought with me dele?
    Thou foundist never love so lele;
        What wilt thou, soule, that I shall do?
    I may of unkindnes thee appele,   95
        Quia amore langueo.

"What shall I do now with my spouse?
    Abide I will hire jantilnesse;
Wold she loke onis out of hir house
    Of flesshely affeccions and unclennesse;   100
    Hir bed is made, hir bolstar is blisse,
        Hir chambre is chosen, suche ar no moo;
    Loke out at the windows of kindnesse,
        Quia amore langueo.

"Long and love thou never so high,   105
    Yit is my love more than thin may be;

79 *recover,* return	86 *scripp,* wallet
90 *seke,* sick	91 *morne,* mourn; *be-mene,* lament
92 *dele,* treat	93 *lele,* true
95 *appele,* accuse	98 *jantilnesse,* gentleness
102 *suche ar no moo,* there are no others like it	106 *thin,* thine

Thou gladdist, thou wepist, I sitt thee bygh.
   Yit might thou, spouse, loke onis at me!
Spouse, shuld I alway fede thee
     With childis mete? nay, love, nat so!   110
I preve thee, love, with adversite,
    Quia amore langueo.

"My spouse is in chambre, hald youre pease!
   Make no noise, but lat hir slepe;
My babe shall sofre noo disease,   115
   I may not here my dere childe wepe,
For with my pappe I shall hir kepe;
   No wondir though I tend hir to,
This hoole in my side had never been so depe,
   But *Quia amore langueo.*   120

"Wax not wery, min owne dere wife!
   What mede is aye to liffe in comfort?
For in tribulacion, I rin more rife
   Ofter times than in disport;
In welth, in woo, ever I support;   125
   Than, dere soule, go never me fro!
Thy mede is markid, whan thou art mort,
   In blisse; *Quia amore langueo.*"

---

107 *thee bygh,* by thee   111 *preve,* prove
115 *disease,* disturbance   122 *mede,* reward; *liffe,* live
123 *rin more rife,* run more often   127 *markid,* destined; *mort,* dead

Richard Rolle

(1300–1349)

A Song of the Love of Jesus

Luf es lif that lastes ay, thar it in Criste es feste;
For wele ne wa it chaunge may, als writen has men
   wiseste.
The night it tournes intil the day, thy travel intil reste:
If thou wil luf thus as I say, thou may be with the beste.

Lufe es thoght with grete desire of a faire loving;   5
Lufe I liken til a fire that sloken may na thing;
Lufe us clenses of oure sin; luf us bote sall bring;
Lufe the Kinges hert may win; lufe of joy may sing.

The settel of lufe es lift hee, for intil heven it ranne;
Me think in erth it es sle, that makes men pale and
   wanne;   10
The bed of bliss it gase ful nee, I tel thee as I canne;
Thof us think the way be dregh, luf copuls God and
   manne.

Lufe es hatter then the cole; lufe may nane beswike;
The flaume of lufe wha might it thole, if it war ay ylike?

1 *luf,* love; *lif,* life; *thar,* there, i.e., where; *es feste,* is fastened
2 *wa,* woe; *als,* as   3 *intil,* into
5 *loving,* i.e., beloved   6 *til,* to; *sloken,* extinguish
7 *bote,* redress; *sall,* shall   9 *settel,* throne; *lift hee,* raised high
10 *sle,* elusive   11 *gase,* goes; *nee,* nigh; *canne,* know
12 *thof,* though; *dregh,* tedious
13 *hatter,* hotter; *nane beswike,* none cheat
14 *thole,* endure

Luf us comfortes, and mase in quart, and liftes til
   hevenrike;   15
Luf ravisches Criste intil our hert; I wate na lust it like.

Lere to luf if thou wil life when thou sall hethen fare;
All thy thoght til Him thou gif that may thee kepe fra
   care;
Loke thy hert fra Him noght twin, if thou in wandreth
   ware;
Sa thou may Him welde and win, and luf Him ever-
   mare.   20

Jesu that me life has lent, intil Thy lufe me bring;
Take til Thee al mine entent, that Thou be my yerning.
Wa fra me away war went, and comne war my
   covaiting,
If that my saule had herd and hent the sang of Thy
   loving.

Thy lufe es ay lastand, fra that we may it fele;   25
Tharein make me birnand, that na thing gar it kele.
My thoght take into Thy hand, and stabil it ilk a dele,
That I be noght heldand to luf this worldes wele.

If I luf any erthly thing that payes to my will,
And settes my joy and my liking when it may comm me
   till,   30
I may drede of parting, that will be hate and ill,

15 *mase in quart*, puts in health; *hevenrike*, kingdom of heaven
16 *wate*, know; *na*, no   17 *lere*, learn; *hethen*, hence
18 *gif*, give; *fra*, from
19 *twin*, separate; *wandreth*, trouble; *ware*, were
20 *sa*, so; *welde*, possess
22 *yerning*, i.e., what I yearn for   23 *war*, were; *covaiting*, desire
24 *saule*, soul; *hent*, grasped; *loving*, praise
25 *lastand*, lasting; *fra that*, from the time that
26 *birnand*, burning; *gar it kele*, make it cool
27 *ilk a dele*, entirely   28 *heldand*, inclined
29 *payes*, is pleasing   30 *liking*, pleasure; *me till*, to me
31 *hate*, bitter

For al my welth es bot weping when pine my saule sal
    spill.

The joy that men has sene es lickend til the haye,
That now es faire and grene, and now wites awaye:
Swilk es this worlde, I wene, and bees til Domes-
    daye,   35
All in travel and tene, fle that na man it maye.

If thou luf in all thy thoght and hate the filth of sin,
And gif Him thy saule that it boght, that He thee dwell
    within,
Als Crist thy saule hase soght and therof walde noght
    blin,
Sa thou sal to blis be broght and heven won within.   40

The kind of luf es this, thar it es traist and trew,
To stande still in stabilnes and chaunge it for na new.
The life that lufe might find, or ever in hert it knew,
Fra care it turnes that kind and lendes in mirth and
    glew.

For now lufe thou, I rede, Criste, as I thee tell,   45
And with aungels take thy stede—that joy loke thou
    noght sell!
In erth thou hate, I rede, all that thy lufe may fell,
For luf es stalworth as the dede, luf es hard as hell.

Luf es a light birthen; lufe gladdes yong and alde;
Lufe es withouten pine, as lofers has me talde;   50

32 *bot*, but; *pine*, torment; *spille*, destroy   33 *lickend*, likened
34 *wites*, fades   35 *swilk*, such; *wene*, think; *bees*, is
36 *tene*, grief
39 *als*, as; *hase*, has; *walde . . . blin*, would not cease
40 *won*, dwell   41 *kind*, nature; *traist*, faithful
42 *still*, constantly   43 *life*, i.e., man
44 *that kind*, i.e., his nature; *lendes*, brings (it); *glew*, glee
45 *rede*, advise   46 *stede*, place
47 *rede*, advise; *fell*, destroy   48 *the dede*, death; *hard*, strong
49 *birthen*, burden; *alde*, old   50 *lofers*, lovers

Lufe es a gastly wine that makes men bigge and balde;
Of lufe sal he na thing tine that hit in hert will halde.

Lufe es the swettest thing that man in erth has tane;
Lufe es Goddes derling; lufe bindes blode and bane.
In lufe be oure liking, I ne wate na better wane,   55
For me and my lufing lufe makes bath be ane.

Bot fleschly lufe sal fare as dose the flowre in May,
And lastand be na mare than ane houre of a day,
And sithen sighe ful sare thar lust, thar pride, thar play,
When thay er casten in care til pine that lastes ay.   60

When thair bodis lise in sin, thair sauls may quake and
     drede,
For up sal rise al men and answer for thair dede:
If thay be fonden in sin, als now thair life thay lede,
Thay sal sitt hell within and mirknes hafe to mede.

Riche men thair hend sal wring, and wicked werkes sal
     by   65
In flaume of fire, bath knight and king, with sorow
     schamfully.
If thou wil lufe than may thou sing til Crist in melody;
The lufe of Him overcomes al thing—tharto thou traiste
     treuly.

I sigh and sob bath day and night for ane sa faire of
     hew.
Thar es na thing my hert may light bot lufe that es ay
     new.   70

51 *gastly*, spiritual; *balde*, bold   52 *tine*, lose; *hit*, it
53 *swettest*, sweetest; *tane*, taken   54 *bane*, bone
55 *liking*, pleasure; *wate*, know; *wane*, ? dwelling
56 *bath be ane*, both be one   58 *lastand*, lasting; *mare*, more
59 *sithen*, afterwards; *sare*, sore; *thar*, their   60 *pine*, torment
61 *lise*, lie   62 *dede*, deed
63 *fonden*, found; *als*, as
64 *mirknes*, darkness; *to mede*, for reward
65 *hend*, hands; *by*, pay for   68 *traiste*, trust

Wha sa had Him in his sight or in his hert Him knew,
His mourning turned til joy ful bright, his sang intil glew.

In mirth he lifes night and day that lufes that swete
childe;
It es Jesu, forsoth I say, of al mekest and milde;
Wreth fra him walde al away, thof he wer never sa
wilde, 75
He that in hert lufed Him that day fra evel He wil him
schilde.

Of Jesu mast list me speke, that al my bale may bete;
Me think my hert may al tobreke when I think on that
swete;
In lufe lacid He has my thoght, that I sal never forgete;
Ful dere me think He hase me boght with blody hende
and fete. 80

For luf my hert es boune to brest when I that faire
behalde;
Lufe es fair thare it es fest, that never will be calde;
Lufe us reves the night-rest, in grace it makes us balde;
Of al warkes luf es the best, als haly men me talde.

Na wonder gif I sighand be and sithen in sorow be
sette: 85
Jesu was nailed apon the tre and al blody forbette.
To think on Him es grete pité, how tenderly he grette:
This hase He sufferde, man, for thee, if that thou sin
will lette.

72 *sang*, song; *glew*, music
75 *wreth*, wrath; *thof*, though; *wilde*, self-willed
76 *schilde*, shield
77 *mast*, most; *list me*, it pleases me to; *bale may bete*, ill may as-
suage   78 *tobreke*, break
79 *lacid*, ensnared   80 *hende*, hands
81 *boune*, ready; *brest*, break; *behalde*, behold   82 *calde*, cold
83 *balde*, bold   84 *warkes*, works; *haly*, holy
85 *gif*, if; *sighand*, sighing; *sithen*, then   86 *forbette*, beaten
87 *grette*, cried   88 *hase*, has; *lette*, leave

Thare es na tonge in erth may tell of lufe the swetnesse;

That stedfastly in lufe can dwell, his joy es endlesse; 90

God schilde that he sulde til hell, that lufes and langand es,

Or ever his enmys sulde him quell or make his luf be lesse.

Jesu es lufe that lastes ay, til Him es oure langing;

Jesu the night turnes to the day, the dawing intil spring.

Jesu, think on us now and ay, for Thee we halde oure king;   95

Jesu, gif us grace as Thou wel may to luf Thee withouten ending.

---

91 *schilde,* forbid; *sulde,* i.e., should go; *langand,* longing
92 *quell,* kill   94 *dawing intil spring,* dawn into sunrise
96 *gif,* give

Anonymous

(Fourteenth Century)

FROM Morte Arthur

[Sir Gawain Encounters Sir Priamus]

Now ferkes to the firthe thees fresche men of armes,
To the fell so fawe, thees frescliche bernes,
Thorowe hopes and hemlande, hillis and other,
Holtis and hare-wodes with heslin schawes,
Thorowe marasse and mosse and montes so heghe,   5
And in the misty morninge on a mede falles,
Mawen and unmade, mainoirede bot littil,
In swathes sweppen down, full of swete flowres.
Thare unbridils thees bolde, and baites theire horses,
To the gringinge of the daye, that birdes gan singe.   10
Whills the surs of the sonne, that sonde es of Criste,
That solaces all synfull, that sighte has in erthe.
Thane wendes out the wardaine, sir Wawaine
    himselfen,
Als he that wise was and wighte, wondirs to seke.

1 *ferkes,* hasten; *firthe,* woodland
2 *fell so fawe,* moor so many-colored; *frescliche bernes,* vigorous warriors   3 *hopes,* dales; *hemlande,* ? land bordering a forest
4 *hare-wodes,* hoar-woods; *heslin schawes,* hazel thickets
5 *marasse and mosse,* swampland and bog; *heghe,* high
6 *falles,* i.e., they come
7 *mawen,* mowed; *unmade,* not tedded and turned; *mainoirede,* cultivated   8 *sweppen,* cut
9 *bolde,* i.e., bold men; *baites,* pasture
10 *to,* until; *gringinge,* dawning
11 *whills,* until; *surs,* rising; *sonde es,* gift is
13 *wardaine,* warden; *Wawaine,* Gawain   14 *als,* as; *wighte,* bold

41

Than was he ware of a wye wondire wele armide,   15
Baitand on a watire banke by the wode-eves,
Buskede in brenies brighte to behalde,
Enbrassede a brode schelde, on a blonke riche,
Withouten ony berne, bot a boye one
Hoves by him on a blonke and his spere holdes.   20
He bare glessenande in golde thre grayhondes of sable,
With chapes and cheines of chalke-white silver,
A charebocle in the cheefe, chaungande of hewes,
And a cheefe anterous, chalange who likes.

Sir Gawaine gliftes on the gome with a glade will,   25
A grete spere fro his grome he gripes in hondes,
Girdes even overe the streme on a stede riche.
To that sterin in stour on strenghe thare he hovis,
Egerly on Inglisce, "Arthure!" he ascries.

The tother irouslye answers him sone   30
On the launge of Lorraine with a loude steven,
That ledes mighte listen the lenghe of a mile:
"Whedir prickes thou, pilour, that profers so large?
Here pikes thou no praye—profire when thee likes!
Bot thou in this perel put of thee bettire   35
Thou sall be my presonere, for all thy proude lates!"
"Sir," says sir Gawaine, "so me God helpe,
Siche glaverande gomes greves me bot littil.

---

15 *wye,* warrior
16 *baitand,* resting his horse; *wode-eves,* edge of a wood
17 *buskede,* dressed; *brenies,* mail-armor   18 *blonke,* horse
19 *berne,* man; *one,* only   20 *hoves,* waits
21 *glessenande,* glistening (on his shield)   22 *chapes,* plating
23 *charebocle,* carbuncle; *cheefe,* upper third of the shield
24 *cheefe,* leader; *anterous,* daring   25 *gliftes,* looks; *gome,* man
26 *grome,* groom   27 *girdes even,* springs straight
28 *sterin in stour,* bold one in battle; *thare he hovis,* where he waits
29 *Inglisce,* English; *ascries,* shouts as a challenge
30 *irouslye,* angrily   31 *launge,* language; *steven,* voice
32 *ledes,* people; *listen,* hear
33 *whedir prickes,* whither ride; *pilour,* thief   34 *pikes,* steal
35 *bot,* unless; *put of thee,* account for yourself
36 *lates,* behavior
38 *siche . . . gomes,* such flattering fellows; *bot,* but

Bot if thou graithe thy gere, thee will grefe happen
Or thou go of this greve, for all thy grete wordes." 40
Than theire launces they lachen, thes lordliche bernes,
Laggen with longe speres on liarde stedes,
Coupen at auntere be craftes of armes,
Till bothe the crouel speres brousten at ones.
Thorowe scheldis they schotte, and scherde thorowe
 mailes, 45
Bothe scherde thorowe schoulders a schaft-monde large.
Thus worthilye thes wyes wondede ere bothen:
Or they wreke them of wrethe awaye will they never.
Than they raughte in the reine and againe rides,
Redely thees rathe men rusches out swerdes, 50
Hittes on helmes full herteliche dintis,
Hewes appon hauberkes with full harde wapins.
Full stoutly they strike, thire sterin knightes,
Stokes at the stomake with stelin pointes,
Feghten and floresche with flaumande swerdes. 55
Till the flawes of fire flaumes on theire helmes.
Thane sir Gawaine was grevede and grichide full sore:
With Galuthe his gude swerde grimlye he strikes,
Clefe the knightes schelde clenliche in sondre.
Who lukes to the lefte side, when his horse launches, 60
With the lighte of the sonne men mighte see his livere.
Thane granes the gome for greefe of his wondis

39 *bot if,* unless; *graithe,* prepare   40 *or,* ere; *greve,* thicket
41 *lachen,* grasp; *lordliche,* lordly 42 *laggen,* ? thrust; *liarde,* gray
43 *coupen,* tilt; *at auntere,* recklessly; *be craftes,* by might
44 *brousten,* break   45 *scherde,* cut
46 *schaft-monde,* spearhead-width
47 *wyes,* warriors; *wondede,* wounded; *ere,* are
48 *or,* ere; *wreke,* avenge; *wrethe,* injury 49 *raughte,* drew
50 *rathe,* reckless; *rusches,* pull 51 *herteliche,* hearty
52 *wapins,* weapons   53 *thire,* these; *sterin,* bold
54 *stokes,* stab; *stelin,* steely 55 *feghten,* fight; *flaumande,* flaming
56 *flawes,* sparks   57 *grichide,* complained
58 *gude,* good   59 *clefe,* cleft; *clenliche,* cleanly
60 *lukes,* looks; *launches,* lunges
62 *granes,* groans

And girdis at sir Gawaine as he by glentis,
And awkewarde egerly sore he him smites;
An alet enamelde he oches in sondire,　　　　　65
Bristes the rerebrace with the bronde riche,
Cerves of at the coutere with the clene egge,
Aventis the avaumbrace, vailede with silver.
Thorowe a double vesture of velvet riche
With the venimous swerde a vaine has he touchede,　70
That voides so violently that all his witte changede:
The vesere, the aventaile, his vesturis riche,
With the valiant blode was verrede all over.

(*Lines 2501–73*)

63 *girdis,* strikes; *by glentis,* darts by
64 *awkewarde,* with a back stroke; *egerly,* fiercely
65 *alet,* shoulder-plate; *oches,* lops
66 *bristes,* breaks; *rerebrace,* upper-arm guard; *bronde,* sword
67 *cerves of,* cuts it off; *coutere,* elbow guard; *egge,* edge
68 *aventis,* lays open; *avaumbrace,* arm plate; *vailede,* covered
71 *voides,* drains　　　　　　　　　　　　　72 *vesere,* vizor
73 *verrede,* spattered

Anonymous

(Fourteenth Century)

FROM Sir Gawain and the Green Knight

[*The Passage of a Year*]

A yere yernes ful yerne, and yeldes never like:
The forme to the finisment foldes ful selden.
Forthy this Yol overyede, and the yere after,
And uche sesoun serlepes sued after other.
After Cristenmasse com the crabbed Lentoun   5
That fraistes flesch with the fische and fode more simple.
Bot thenne the weder of the worlde with winter hit
      threpes:
Colde clenges adown, cloudes upliften,
Schire schedes the rain in schowres ful warme,
Falles upon faire flat, flowres there schewen,   10
Bothe groundes and the greves grene are her wedes;
Briddes busken to bilde, and bremlich singen
For solace of the softe somer that sues therafter
    By bonk.
    And blossumes bolne to blowe   15
    By rawes rich and ronk;

1 *yernes,* runs; *yerne,* quickly
2 *forme,* beginning; *finisment,* end; *foldes,* accords
3 *forthy,* therefore; *Yol,* Yuletide; *overyede,* passed by
4 *uche,* each; *serlepes,* in turn; *sued,* followed   6 *fraistes,* tests
7 *weder,* weather; *hit,* it; *threpes,* quarrels   8 *clenges,* shrinks
9 *schire,* bright; *schedes,* falls   10 *flat,* meadow
11 *greves,* thickets; *her,* their   12 *busken,* prepare; *bremlich,* clearly
13 *solace,* delight   14 *bonk,* hillside
15 *bolne to blowe,* swell to bloom
16 *rawes,* hedge-rows; *ronk,* luxuriant

45

Then notes noble innowe
Ar herde in wod so wlonk.

After, the sesoun of somer with the soft windes,
When Zeferus sifles himself on sedes and erbes; 20
Wela-winne is the wort that waxes theroute,
When the donkande dewe dropes of the leves,
To bide a blisful blusch of the bright sunne.
Bot then highes hervest, and hardenes him sone,
Warnes him for the winter to wax ful ripe; 25
He drives with droght the dust for to rise,
Fro the face of the folde to flighe ful highe.
Wrothe winde of the welkin wrasteles with the sunne,
The leves laucen fro the linde and lighten on the
        grounde,
And al grayes the gres that grene was ere: 30
Thenne al ripes and rotes that ros upon first.
And thus yernes the yere in yisterdayes mony,
And winter windes ayain, as the worlde askes.

(Lines *498–530*)

17 *innowe,* enough   18 *wlonk,* glorious
20 *sifles,* blows   21 *wela-winne,* very joyful; *wort,* plant
22 *donkande,* moistening   23 *blusch,* beam
24 *highes,* hastens; *hervest,* autumn; *hardenes him,* ? matures him (the
     plant)   27 *folde,* earth
28 *wrasteles,* wrestles   29 *laucen,* fall; *linde,* tree
30 *gres,* grass   31 *rotes,* rots
33 *windes,* returns

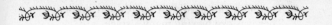

TRANSLATED BY
Geoffrey Chaucer

FROM *The Romance of the Rose*

[*The Garden of Amour*]

The gardin was, by mesuring,
Right evene and square in compassing;
It as long was as it was large.
Of fruit hadde every tree his charge,
But it were any hidous tree,   5
Of which ther were two or three.
There were, and that wot I full well,
Of pome-garnettis a full gret dell;
That is a fruit full well to like,
Namely to folk whanne they ben sike.   10
And trees there were, gret foisoun,
That baren notes in her sesoun,
Such as men notemigges calle,
That swote of savour ben withalle.
And alemandres gret plente,   15
Figes, and many a date-tree
There wexen, if men hadde nede,

2 *evene*, level; *compassing*, design   3 *large*, wide
5 *but if*, unless   7 *wot*, know
8 *pome-garnettis*, pomegranates; *dell*, portion   9 *well to like*, pleasing
10 *namely*, especially   11 *foisoun*, quantity
12 *baren*, bore; *notes*, nuts; *her*, their   13 *notemigges*, nutmegs
14 *swote*, sweet   15 *alemandres*, almond trees
17 *wexen*, grew

47

Thorough the gardin in length and brede.
Ther was eke wexing many a spice,
As clowe-gelofre, and licorice,   20
Gingevre, and grein de paris,
Canell, and setewale of pris,
And many a spice delitable
To eten whan men rise fro table.
And many homly trees ther were   25
That peches, coines, and apples beere,
Medlers, ploumes, peris, chesteines,
Cherys, of which many oon fain is,
Notes, aleys, and bolas,
That for to seen it was solas.   30
With many high lorer and pin
Was renged clene all that gardin,
With cipres and with oliveres,
Of which that nigh no plente heere is.
There were elmes grete and stronge,   35
Maples, assh, ok, asp, planes longe,
Fin ew, popler, and lindes faire,
And othere trees full many a paire.
    What shulde I tel you more of it?
There were so many trees yit,   40
That I shulde al encombred be
Er I had rekened every tree.
    These trees were set, that I devise,

18 *brede*, breadth   20 *clowe-gelofre*, clove
21 *gingevre*, ginger; *grein de paris*, grain of Paradise, a spice
22 *canell*, cinnamon; *setewale*, setwall, a spice; *pris*, value
23 *delitable*, delectable   26 *coines*, quinces
27 *ploumes*, plums; *peris*, pears; *chesteines*, chestnuts
28 *fain*, eager
29 *aleys*, fruit of the wild service tree; *bolas*, wild plums
30 *solas*, delight   31 *lorer*, laurel
32 *renged*, ringed   33 *oliveres*, olive trees
34 *nigh no plente*, almost no supply   36 *planes*, plane trees
37 *ew*, yew; *lindes*, lime trees   39 *what*, why
40 *yit*, yet, i.e., in addition
43 *devise*, describe

Oon from another, in assise,
Five fadome or sixe, I trowe so;   45
But they were hye and great also,
And for to kepe out wel the sonne,
The croppes were so thicke yronne,
And every braunche in other knet,
And ful of grene leves set,   50
That sonne might there non discende,
Lest it the tender grasses shende.
There might men does and roes yse,
And of squirels ful great plente
From bowe to bowe alway lepinge.   55
Conies there were also playinge,
That comin out of her clapers,
Of sondrye colours and manners,
And maden many a tourneying
Upon the fresshe grass springing.   60

In places saw I welles there,
In whiche there no frogges were,
And fair in shadowe was every welle.
But I ne can the nombre telle
Of stremis smal that by devis   65
Mirthe had don come through condis,
Of whiche the water, in renning,
Gan make a noise ful liking.

About the brinkes of these welles,
And by the stremes overal elles,   70
Sprang up the grass, as thicke yset
And softe as any veluët,

44 *assise,* position   45 *fadome,* armsbreadths; *trowe,* think
48 *croppes,* top branches; *yronne,* i.e., grown   49 *knet,* intertwined
52 *shende,* destroy   53 *yse,* see
57 *clapers,* burrows   58 *maners,* sorts
59 *tourneying,* game   61 *welles,* springs
65 *devis,* contrivances
66 *Mirthe,* i.e., one of the characters in the allegory; *don,* made;
   condis, conduits   67 *renning,* running
68 *gan,* did; *liking,* pleasing   70 *overal,* everywhere

On which men might his lemman leye,
As on a fetherbed, to pleye;
For the erthe was ful softe and swete.   75
Through moisture of the welle wete
Sprong up the sote grene gras
As faire, as thicke, as mister was.
But moche amended it the place,
That th'erthe was of such a grace   80
That it of flowres hath plente,
That bothe in somer and winter be.

Ther sprang the violet al newe,
And fressh pervinke, riche of hewe,
And flowres yelowe, white, and rede;   85
Such plente grew there never in mede.
Ful gay was al the ground, and queint,
And powdred, as men had it peint,
With many a fressh and sondry flowr,
That casten up ful good savour.   90

I wol nat longe holde you in fable
Of al this garden dilectable.
I mot my tonge stinten nede,
For I ne may, withouten drede,
Naught tellen you the beaute al,   95
Ne half the bounte therewithal.

I went on right hond and on left
About the place; it was nat left,
Til I had in al the garden ben,
In the estres that men mighte sen.   100

And thus while I wente in my play,
The God of Love me folowed ay,
Right as an hunter can abide

73 *lemman,* mistress   77 *sote,* sweet
78 *mister,* need   79 *amended,* improved further
84 *pervinke,* periwinkle   93 *mot,* must; *stinten nede,* needs stop
94 *drede,* doubt   98 *left,* quitted
100 *estres,* inner parts

The beest, til he seeth his tide
To shoten at good mes to the der,   105
Whan that him nedeth go no ner.
   And so befil, I rested me
Besides a wel, under a tree,
Which tree in Fraunce men cal a pin.
But sithe the time of king Pepin,   110
Ne grew there tree in mannes sighte
So fair, ne so wel woxe in highte;
In al that yard so high was non.
And springing in a marble ston
Had Nature set, the sothe to telle,   115
Under that pin-tree a welle.
And on the border, al withoute,
Was written in the ston aboute,
Letters smal, that saiden thus,
"Here starf the faire Narcisus."   120
   Narcisus was a bacheler,
That Love had caught in his danger,
And in his net gan him so straine,
And did him so to wepe and plaine,
That nede him must his lif forgo.   125
For a fair lady, that hight Echo,
Him loved over any creature,
And gan for him such paine endure
That on a time she him tolde
That if he her loven nolde,   130
That her behoved nedes die,
There laye non other remedye.

---

104 *tide,* time	105 *mes,* advantage
106 *ner,* nearer	107 *bifil,* befell
108 *wel,* spring	110 *sithe,* since
112 *woxe,* grown	114 *springing,* gushing
120 *starf,* died	122 *danger,* power
123 *gan,* did; *straine,* bind	124 *did,* caused; *plaine,* lament
126 *hight,* was called	130 *nolde,* would not
131 *her behoved nedes,* she needs must	

But natheles, for his beaute,
So feirs and daungerous was he,
That he nolde graunten hir asking,   135
For weping ne for fair praying;
And whanne she herde him werne her soo,
She hadde in herte so gret woo,
And took it in so gret dispit,
That she, withoute more respit,   140
Was deed anoon. But er she deide,
Full pitously to God she preyde
That proude-hertid Narcisus,
That was in love so daungerous,
Might on a day ben hampred so   145
For love, and ben so hoot for woo,
That never he might to joye atteine;
Than shulde he feele in every veine
What sorowe trewe lovers maken,
That ben so vilainsly forsaken.   150
    This prayer was but resonable;
Therfore God held it ferme and stable.
For Narcisus, shortly to telle,
By aventure com to that welle
To reste him in the shadowing   155
A day whanne he com fro hunting.
This Narcisus hadde suffred paines
For renning alday in the plaines,
And was for thurst in gret distresse
Of heet, and of his werinesse   160
That hadde his breth almost binomen.
Whanne he was to that welle ycomen,
That shadowid was with braunches grene,

133 *natheles,* nevertheless   134 *feirs,* proud; *daungerous,* disdainful
137 *werne,* refuse   146 *hoot,* hot
154 *aventure,* chance
158 *renning,* running
161 *binomen,* taken away

He thoughte of thilke water shene
To drinke, and fresshe him wel withalle;   165
And down on knees he gan to falle,
And forth his heed and necke out-straughte
To drinken of that welle a draugthe.
And in the water anoon was seene
His nose, his mouth, his ÿen sheene,   170
And he therof was all abasshed;
His owne shadowe had him bitrasshed.
For well wende he the forme see
Of a child of gret beaute.
Well couthe Love him wreke thoo   175
Of daunger and of pride also,
That Narcisus somtime him beer.
He quitte him well his guerdoun ther;
For he musede so in the welle
That, shortly all the sothe to telle,   180
He lovede his owne shadowe soo,
That atte laste he starf for woo.
For whanne he saugh that he his wille
Might in no maner wey fulfille,
And that he was so faste caught   185
That he him couthe comfort nought,
He loste his wit right in that place,
And diede withinne a litel space.
And thus his warisoun he took
For the lady that he forsook.   190
    Ladies, I preye ensample takith,
Ye that ageins youre love mistakith;

164 *thoughte*, intended; *thilke*, the same; *shene*, clear
165 *fresshe*, refresh
167 *out-straughte*, stretched out
170 *ÿen*, eyes; *sheene*, bright
172 *bitrasshed*, entrapped
173 *wende*, supposed   175 *couthe*, could; *wreke*, avenge; *thoo*, then
176 *daunger*, disdainfulness
177 *him beer*, displayed to him
178 *guerdoun*, reward
182 *starf*, died
183 *saugh*, saw
189 *warisoun*, reward
192 *mistakith*, offend

For if her deth be you to wite,
God can ful well youre while quite.
    Whanne that this lettre, of which I telle,   195
Hadde taught me that it was the welle
Of Narcisus in his beaute,
I gan anoon withdrawe me,
Whanne it fel in my remembraunce
That him bitidde such mischaunce.   200
But at the laste thanne thought I
That scatheles, full sikerly,
I might unto the welle goo.
Wherof shulde I abasshen soo?
Unto the welle than wente I me,   205
And down I loutede for to see
The clere water in the stoon,
And eke the gravell, which that shoon
Down in the botme as silver fin;
For of the well this is the fin,   210
In world is noon so cler of hewe.
The water is evere fresh and newe,
That welmeth up with wawis brighte
The mountance of two finger highte.
Abouten it is gras springing,   215
For moiste so thikke and wel liking,
That it ne may in winter die,
No more than may the see be drye.
    Down at the botme set saw I
Two cristall stonis craftely   220
In thilke freshe and faire welle.
But o thing sothly dar I telle,

193 *her,* their; *wite,* blame
194 *youre while quite,* repay your trouble
202 *scatheles,* without harm; *sikerly,* securely   206 *loutede,* stooped
210 *fin,* end, i.e., the whole truth
213 *welmeth,* bubbles; *wawis,* ripples   214 *mountance,* distance
216 *moiste,* moisture; *liking,* pleasing   221 *thilke,* the same
222 *o,* one

That ye wole holde a gret mervaile
Whanne it is told, withouten faile.
For whanne the sonne, cler in sighte,   225
Cast in that well his bemis brighte,
And that the heete descendid is,
Thanne taketh the cristall stoon, ywis,
Again the sonne an hundrid hewis,
Blew, yelow, and red, that fresh and newe is.   230
Yitt hath the merveilous cristall
Such strengthe that the place overall,
Bothe flowr, and tree, and leves grene,
And all the yerd in it is seene.
And for to don you to undirstonde,   235
To make ensample wole I fonde.
Right as a mirrour openly
Shewith all thing that stondith therby,
As well the colour as the figure,
Withouten ony coverture;   240
Right so the cristall stoon, shining,
Withouten ony disseiving,
The estrees of the yerd accusith
To him that in the water musith.
For evere, in which half that he be,   245
He may well half the gardin se;
And if he turne, he may right well
Sen the remenaunt everydell.
For ther is noon so litil thing
So hid, ne closid with shitting,   250
That it ne is sene, as though it were
Peintid in the cristall there.
    This is the mirrour perilous,

228 *ywis*, indeed   229 *again*, facing
235 *don*, make   236 *fonde*, try
240 *coverture*, falsification   242 *disseiving*, distortion
243 *estrees*, inner parts; *accusith*, discloses   248 *everydell*, every bit
250 *shitting*, obstacle

In which the proude Narcisus
Saw all his face fair and bright, 255
That made him sithe to ligge upright.
For whoso loketh in that mirrour,
Ther may nothing ben his socour
That he ne shall there sen somthing
That shal him lede into loving. 260
Full many a worthy man hath it
Yblent, for folk of grettist wit
Ben soone caught heere and awaited;
Withouten respit ben they baited.
Heere comth to folk of-newe rage; 265
Heere chaungith many wight corage;
Heere lith no red ne wit therto;
For Venus sone, daun Cupido,
Hath sowen there of love the seed,
That help ne lith there noon, ne red, 270
So cerclith it the welle aboute.
His ginnes hath he sette withoute,
Right for to cacche in his panters
These damoisels and bachelers.
Love will noon other briddes cacche, 275
Though he sette oither net or lacche.
And for the seed that heere was sowen,
This welle is clepid, as well is knowen,
The Welle of Love, of verray right,
Of which ther hath ful many a wight 280
Spoken in bookis diversely.
But they shull never so verily

256 *sithe*, afterwards; *ligge upright*, lie flat   262 *yblent*, blinded
263 *awaited*, waylaid   264 *baited*, harassed
264 *of-newe*, for the second time; *rage*, passion
266 *wight*, creature; *corage*, mood
267 *lith*, lies; *red*, remedy; *wit*, device   268 *daun*, master
272 *ginnes*, snares   273 *panters*, nets
276 *oither*, either; *lacche*, trap   278 *clepid*, called
279 *of verray right*, with perfect propriety

Descripcioun of the welle heere,
Ne eke the sothe of this matere,
As ye shull, whanne I have undo   285
The craft that hir bilongith too.

Allway me liked for to dwelle,
To sen the cristall in the welle,
That shewide me full openly
A thousand thinges faste by.   290
But I may say, in sory houre
Stode I to loken or to poure;
For sithen have I sore siked;
That mirrour hath me now entriked.
But hadde I first knowen in my wit   295
The vertu and the strengthe of it,
I nolde not have mused there.
Me hadde bet ben elliswhere;
For in the snare I fell anoon,
That hath bitrasshed many oon.   300

In thilke mirrour saw I tho,
Among a thousand thinges mo,
A roser chargid full of rosis,
That with an hegge aboute enclos is.
Tho had I sich lust and envye,   305
That for Paris ne for Pavie
Nolde I have left to goon and see
There grettist hep of roses be.
Whanne I was with this rage hent,
That caught hath many a man and shent,   310
Toward the roser gan I go;

284 *sothe*, truth   285 *undo*, explained
286 *craft*, power   290 *faste*, close
293 *sithen*, since; *siked*, sighed   294 *entriked*, beguiled
298 *me hadde bet ben*, I should have been better
300 *bitrasshed*, entrapped   301 *thilke*, the same; *tho*, then
302 *mo*, more   303 *roser*, rosebush
304 *enclos*, enclosed   305 *tho*, then; *lust*, desire; *envye*, longing
307 *nolde I*, I should not   308 *there*, i.e., the place where
309 *rage*, passion; *hent*, seized   310 *shent*, destroyed

And whanne I was not fer therfro,
The savour of the roses swote
Me smot right to the herte-rote,
As I hadde all enbaumed be.   315
And if I ne hadde endouted me
To have ben hatid or assailed,
My thankis, wolde I not have failed
To pulle a rose of all that route
To beren in min hond aboute,   320
And smellen to it where I wente;
But ever I dredde me to repente,
And lest it grevede or forthoughte
The lord that thilke gardin wroughte.
Of roses ther were gret won;   325
So faire waxe never in ron.
Of knoppes clos some sawe I there;
And some wel beter woxen were;
And some ther ben of other moisoun,
That drowe nigh to her sesoun,   330
And spedde hem faste for to sprede.
I love well sich roses rede,
For brode roses and open also
Ben passed in a day or two;
But knoppes wille al freshe be   335
Two dayes, atte leest, or thre.
The knoppes gretly liked me,
For fairer may ther no man se.
Whoso might have oon of alle,

---

312 *fer,* far
315 *enbaumed,* embalmed
318 *my thankis,* willingly
323 *forthoughte,* displeased
325 *won,* quantity
327 *knoppes clos,* closed buds
329 *moisoun,* size
332 *sich,* such
336 *atte,* at the

313 *swote,* sweet
316 *endouted me,* feared
319 *route,* crowd
324 *thilke,* the same
326 *ron,* ? thicket
328 *woxen,* grown
330 *drowe,* drew
333 *brode,* full-bloomed
337 *liked,* pleased

It ought him ben full lief withalle.   340
Might I a gerlond of hem geten,
For no richesse I wolde it leten.
Among the knoppes I ches oon
So fair, that of the remenaunt noon
Ne preise I half so well as it,   345
Whanne I avise it in my wit.
For it so well was enlumined
With colour reed, and as well fined
As nature couthe it make faire.
And it hath leves wel foure paire,   350
That Kinde hath sett, thorough his knowing,
Aboute the rede Rose springing.
The stalke was as rishe right,
And theron stod the knoppe upright,
That it ne bowide upon no side.   355
The swote smelle sprong so wide
That it dide all the place aboute—

(*From the French of Guillaume de Lorris, lines 1349–1705*)

---

340 *lief,* glad   342 *leten,* leave
343 *ches,* chose   346 *avise,* consider
347 *enlumined,* adorned   348 *fined,* furbished
349 *couthe,* could   351 *Kinde,* Nature
353 *rishe,* rush; *right,* straight   356 *swote,* sweet
357 With this line the fragment ends abruptly.

John Gower

(1330?–1408)

FROM *Confessio Amantis*

[*The Parting of Venus and Old Age*]

I

Whanne I this Supplicacioun
With good deliberacioun,
In such a wise as ye now wite,
Hadde after min entente write
Unto Cupide and to Venus,   5
This Prest which highte Genius
It tok on honde to presente,
On my message and forth he wente
To Venus, forto wite hire wille.
And I bod in the place stille,   10
And was there bot a litel while,
Noght full the montance of a mile,
Whan I behield and sodeinly
I sigh wher Venus stod me by.
So as I mighte, under a tre   15
To grounde I fell upon my kne,
And preyde hire forto do me grace.
Sche caste hire chiere upon my face,
And as it were halvinge a-game

3 *wite*, know   6 *prest*, priest; *highte*, is called
8 *message*, errand; *and* should be read before *on*   10 *bod*, remained
12 *montance*, distance (it takes to go)   13 *behield*, beheld
14 *sigh*, saw   18 *chiere*, look
19 *halvinge a-game*, half in sport

Sche axeth me what is my name.   20
"Ma dame," I seide, "John Gower."
"Now, John," quod sche, "in my power
Thou most as of thy love stonde;
For I thy bille have understonde,
In which to Cupide and to me   25
Somdiel thou hast compleigned thee,
And somdiel to Nature also.
Bot that schal stonde among you two,
For therof have I noght to done;
For Nature is under the mone   30
Maistresse of every lives kinde,
Bot if so be that sche may finde
Som holy man that wol withdrawe
His kindly lust ayein hir lawe;
Bot sielde whanne it falleth so,   35
For fewe men ther ben of tho,
Bot of these othre ynowe be,
Whiche of here oghne nicete
Ayein Nature and hire office
Deliten hem in sondry vice,   40
Whereof that sche ful ofte hath pleigned,
And ek my Court it hath desdeigned
And evere schal; for it receiveth
Non such that kinde so deceiveth.
For al onliche of gentil love   45
My court stant alle courts above

---

20 *axeth,* asks   22 *quod,* quoth
23 *most,* must; *as of,* in regard to   24 *bille,* i.e., petition
26 *somdiel,* partly   28: i.e., but that issue is between you and Nature
30 *mone,* moon   31 *lives kinde,* living thing
32 *bot if,* unless   33 *withdrawe,* restrain
34 *kindly,* natural; *ayein,* against   35 *sielde whanne,* rarely
36 *tho,* those   37 *ynowe,* enough
38 *here oghne nicete,* their own folly   40 *deliten hem,* take delight
41 *pleigned,* complained   42 *it hath desdeigned,* has scorned it
44 *kinde,* nature   45 *al onliche,* exclusively
46 *stant,* stands

And takth noght into retenue
Bot thing which is to kinde due,
For elles it schal be refused.
Wherof I holde thee excused, 50
For it is manye dayes gon,
That thou amonges hem were on
Which of my court hast ben witholde;
So that the more I am beholde
Of thy desese to commune, 55
And to remue that fortune
Which manye dayes hath thee grieved.
Bot if my conseil may be lieved,
Thou schalt ben esed er thou go
Of thilke unsely jolif wo, 60
Whereof thou seist thin herte is fired.
Bot as of that thou hast desired
After the sentence of thy bille,
Thou most therof don at my wille,
And I therof me wole avise. 65
For be thou hol, it schal suffise:
My medicine is noght to sieke
For thee and for suche olde sieke,
Noght al perchance as ye it wolden,
Bot so as ye be reson scholden, 70
Acordant unto loves kinde.
For in the plit which I thee finde,
So as my court it hath awarded,
Thou schalt be duely rewarded;

48 *kinde,* nature   52 *hem,* them; *on,* one
53: i.e., who have been maintained by my court   54 *beholde,* obliged
55 *desease,* trouble; *commune,* confer   56 *remue,* remove
58 *lieved,* trusted   60: i.e., of this same unlucky lustful woe
61 *seist,* say   63 *sentence,* purport
64 *most,* must   65 *me wole avise,* will take thought
66 *be thou hol,* i.e., once you are cured
67 *is noght to sieke,* i.e., is not deficient   68 *sieke,* sickly men
70 *be,* by   71 *acordant,* according; *kinde,* nature
72 *plit,* plight

And if thou woldest more crave,   75
It is no right that thou it have."
    Venus, which stant withoute lawe
In non certein, bot as men drawe
Of Rageman upon the chance,
Sche leith no peis in the balance,   80
Bot as hir liketh forto weye;
The trewe man ful ofte aweye
Sche put, which hath hir grace bede,
And set an untrewe in his stede.
Lo, thus blindly the world sche diemeth   85
In loves cause, as to me siemeth:
I not what othre men wol seyn,
Bot I algate am so besein,
And stonde as on amonges alle
Which am out of hir grace falle: 90
It nedeth take no witnesse,
For sche which seid is the goddesse,
To whether part of love it wende,
Hath sett me for a final ende,
The point wherto that I schal holde.   95
For whan sche hath me wel beholde,
Halvinge of scorn, sche seide thus:
"Thou wost wel that I am Venus,
Which al only my lustes seche;
And wel I wot, thogh thou beseche   100
My love, lustes ben ther none,
Whiche I may take in thy persone;

---

77 *stant*, stands   78 *non certein*, nothing secure
79 *Rageman*, a game of chance
80 *leith no peis*, lays no weight; *balance*, scales
81 *hir liketh*, she pleases   83 *put*, puts; *bede*, prayed for
84 *set*, sets   85 *diemeth*, judges
87 *not*, know not   88 *algate*, at any rate; *besein*, situated
89 *on*, one   92 *seid is*, is called
93 *whether*, whichever; *wende*, go   94 *ende*, settlement
97 *halvinge of scorn*, half in scorn   98 *wost*, know
99: i.e., who seek only my own pleasure   101 *lustes*, pleasures

For loves lust and lockes hore
In chambre acorden neveremore,
And thogh thou feigne a yong corage,   105
It scheweth wel be the visage
That olde grisel is no fole:
Ther ben ful manye yeeres stole
With thee and with suche othre mo,
That outward feignen youthe so   110
And ben withinne of pore assay.
'Min herte wolde and I ne may'
Is noght beloved nowadayes;
Er thou make eny such assayes
To love, and faile upon the fet,   115
Betre is to make a beau retret;
For thogh thou mightest love atteigne,
Yit were it bot an idel peine,
Whan that thou art noght sufficant
To holde love his covenant.   120
Forthy tak hom thin herte ayein,
That thou travaile noght in vein,
Whereof my Court may be deceived.
I wot and have it wel conceived,
How that thy will is good ynough;   125
Bot mor behoveth to the plough,
Wherof thee lacketh, as I trowe:
So sitte it wel that thou beknowe
Thy fieble astat, er thou beginne
Thing wher thou might non ende winne.   130
What bargain scholde a man assaye,

105 *corage*, heart   106 *be*, by
107: i.e., the old gray horse is no colt   108 *stole*, stolen by
109 *mo*, more   112: i.e., my heart would and I cannot
115 *fet*, act   116 *beau retret*, graceful retreat
117 *atteigne*, attain   118 *idel peine*, vain trouble
119 *sufficant*, sufficient   121 *forthy*, therefore
122 *travaile*, labor   124 *wot*, know
126 *behoveth*, is needful   127 *trowe*, believe
128 *sitte*, let it sit; *beknowe*, acknowledge   129 *astat*, condition

Whan that him lacketh forto paye?
My sone, if thou be wel bethoght,
This toucheth thee; foryet it noght:
The thing is torned into was;   135
That which was whilom grene gras,
Is welked hey at time now.
Forthy my conseil is that thou
Remembre wel how thou art old."

    Whan Venus hath hir tale told,   140
And I bethoght was al aboute,
Tho wiste I wel withoute doute
That ther was no recoverir;
And as a man the blase of fir
With water quencheth, so ferd I;   145
A cold me caughte sodeinly,
For sorwe that min herte made,
My dedly face pale and fade
Becam, and swoune I fell to grounde.

(Book VIII, lines 2301–2449)

134 *foryet,* forget
135 *torned into was,* become a matter of has-been
136 *whilom,* formerly   137 *welked,* withered
138 *forthy,* therefore   141: And I had taken thought on all issues
142 *tho,* then; *wiste,* knew   143 *recoverir,* recovery
144 *blase,* blaze   145 *ferd,* fared
148 *dedly,* deathlike; *fade,* faded   149 *swoune,* swooning

II

    Cupido, which may hurte and hele
In loves cause, as for min hele
Upon the point which him was preyd
Cam with Venus, wher I was leid
Swounende upon the grene gras.   5

2 *as for min hele,* i.e., in order to give me satisfaction
3 *preyd,* prayed   5 *swounende,* swooning

And, as methoghte, anon ther was
On every side so gret presse,
That every lif began to presse,
I wot noght wel how many score,
Suche as I spak of now tofore,   10
Lovers, that comen to beholde,
Bot most of hem that weren olde:
They stoden there at thilke tide,
To se what ende schal betide
Upon the cure of my sotye.   15
Tho mighte I hiere gret partye
Spekende, and ech his oghne avis
Hath told, on that, another this:
Bot among alle this I herde,
They weren wo that I so ferde,   20
And seiden that for no riote
An old man scholde noght assote;
For as they tolden redely,
Ther is in him no cause why,
Bot if he wolde himself benice   25
So were he wel the more nice.
And thus desputen some of tho,
And some seiden nothing so,
Bot that the wilde loves rage
In mannes lif forberth non age;   30
Whil ther is oile forto fire,
The lampe is lightly set afire,
And is ful hard er it be queint,

---

7 *presse*, throng   8 *every lif*, everybody
9 *wot*, know   12 *hem*, them
13 *thilke tide*, the same time   15 *sotye*, folly
16 *tho*, then   16–17 *gret partye spekende*, i.e., many speakers on
  various sides of the question   17 *oghne avis*, own opinion
18 *on*, one   20 *ferde*, fared
21 *riote*, dissipation   22 *assote*, act like a fool
25 *bot if*, unless; *benice*, besot
27 *tho*, those   26 *nice*, foolish
                                            30 *forberth*, spares
32 *lightly*, readily   33: i.e., and it is difficult to put it out

Bot only if it be som seint,
Which God preserveth of His grace.   35
And thus methoghte, in sondry place
Of hem that walken up and down
Ther was diverse opinioun:
And for a while so it laste,
Til that Cupide to the laste,   40
Forth with his moder full avised
Hath determined and devised
Unto what point he wol descende.
And al this time I was liggende
Upon the ground tofore his yghen,   45
And they that my desese sighen
Supposen noght I scholde live:
Bot he, which wolde thanne yive
His grace, so as it may be,
This blinde god which may noght se,   50
Hath groped til that he me fond;
And as he pitte forth his hond
Upon my body, wher I lay,
Methoghte a firy lancegay,
Which whilom thurgh min herte he caste,   55
He pulleth oute, and also faste
As this was do, Cupide nam
His weye, I not where he becam,
And so dede al the remenant
Which unto him was entendant,   60
Of hem that in avision

34 *bot only if,* unless
41 *moder,* mother; *full advised,* having taken full counsel
44 *liggende,* lying   45 *tofore,* before; *yghen,* eyes
46 *sighen,* saw   48 *yive,* give
49 *fond,* found   52 *pitte,* put
54 *lancegay,* lance   55 *whilom,* previously
56 *also,* as   57 *nam,* took
58 *I . . . becam,* i.e., I don't know where he went
59 *dede,* did   60 *entendant,* attending
61 *hem,* them; *avision,* dream

I hadde a revelacion,
So as I tolde now tofore.

    Bot Venus wente noghte therfore,
Ne Genius, whiche thilke time   65
Abiden bothe faste by me.
And sche which may the hertes binde
In loves cause and ek unbinde,
Er I out of my trance aros,
Venus, which hield a boiste clos,   70
And wolde noght I scholde deye,
Tok out—mor cold than eny keye—
An oignement, and in such point
Sche hath my wounded herte enoignt,
My temples and my reins also.   75
And forth withal sche tok me tho
A wonder mirour forto holde,
In whiche sche bad me to beholde
And taken hiede of that I sighe;
Wherinne anon min hertes yghe   80
I caste, and sigh my colour fade,
Min yghen dimme and al unglade,
My chiekes thinne, and al my face
With elde I mighte se deface,
So riveled and so wo-besein,   85
That ther was nothing full ne plein;
I sigh also min heres hore.
My will was tho to se no more
Outwith, for ther was no plesance;
And thanne into my remembrance   90

---

65 *thilke*, the same   70 *hield*, held; *boiste clos*, closed box
71 *wolde*, willed   74 *enoignt*, anointed
75 *reins*, loins   76 *tok me tho*, gave me then
79 *that*, what; *sighe*, should see   80 *yghe*, eye
81 *fade*, dull   84 *elde*, old age; *deface*, defaced
85 *riveled*, wrinkled; *wo-besein*, sorry-looking   86 *plein*, rounded
87 *sigh*, saw; *heres*, hairs   88 *tho*, then
89 *outwith*, beyond

I drough min olde dayes passed,
And as reson it hath compassed,
I made a liknesse of myselve
Unto the sondry monthes twelve,
Wherof the yeer in his astat   95
Is mad, and stant upon debat,
That lich til other non acordeth.
For who the times wel recordeth,
And thanne at Marche if he beginne,
Whan that the lusty yeer comth inne,   100
Til Augst be passed and Septembre,
The mighty youthe he may remembre
In which the yeer hath his deduit
Of gras, of lef, of flowr, of fruit,
Of corn and of the winy grape.   105
And afterward the time is schape
To frost, to snow, to wind, to rein,
Til eft that Mars be come ayein:
The winter wol no somer knowe,
The grene lef is overthrowe,   110
The clothed erthe is thanne bare,
Despuiled is the somer fare,
That erst was hete is thanne chele.
And thus thenkende thoghtes fele,
I was out of my swoune affrayed,   115
Wherof I sigh my wittes strayed,
And gan to clepe hem hom ayein.
And whan Resoun it herde seyn
That loves rage was aweye,

---

91 *drough*, drew   92 *compassed*, contrived
96 *mad*, made; *stant upon debat*, consists in variation
97 *lich til*, like to   98 *recordeth*, considers
103 *deduit*, pleasure
106 *schape*, destined
108 *eft*, again   112 *despuiled*, despoiled
113 *erst*, formerly; *chele*, cold 114 *thenkende*, thinking; *fele*, many
115 *affrayed*, disturbed
116 *sigh*, saw
117 *gan*, began; *clepe*, call   118 *seyn*, said

He cam to me the righte weye   120
And hath remued the sotye
Of thilke unwise fantasye,
Wherof that I was wont to pleigne,
So that of thilke firy peine
I was mad sobre and hol ynough.   125
     Venus behield me than and lough,
And axeth, as it were in game,
What love was: and I for schame
Ne wiste what I scholde answere;
And natheles I gan to swere   130
That be my trouthe I knew him noght;
So ferr it was out of my thoght,
Right as it hadde nevere be.
"My goode sone," tho quod sche,
"Now at this time I lieve it wel,   135
So goth the fortune of my whiel;
Forthy my conseil is thou leve."
     "Ma dame," I seide, "be your leve,
Ye witen wel, and so wot I,
That I am unbehovely   140
Your Court fro this day forth to serve:
And for I may no thonk deserve,
And also for I am refused,
I preye you to ben excused.
And natheles as for the laste,   145
Whil that my wittes with me laste,

120 *the righte weye,* directly
121 *remued the sotye,* removed the folly   122 *thilke,* the same
123 *pleigne,* complain   125 *mad,* made; *hol,* whole
126 *lough,* laughed   127 *axeth,* asks
129 *wiste,* knew   130 *natheles,* nevertheless
131 *be,* by   132 *ferr,* far
134 *tho,* then   135 *lieve,* believe
136 *whiel,* wheel
137: i.e., therefore my advice is that you leave off (love)
138 *be,* by   139 *witen, wot,* know
140 *unbehovely,* unsuitable   142 *for,* because; *thonk,* favor

Touchende my confession
I axe an absolucioun
Of Genius, er that I go."
The prest anon was redy tho,   150
And seide, "Sone, as of thy schrifte
Thou hast ful pardoun and foryifte;
Foryet it thou, and so wol I."
"Min holy fader, grant mercy,"
Quod I to him, and to the queene   155
I fell on knes upon the grene,
And tok my leve forto wende.
Bot sche, that wolde make an ende,
As therto which I was most able,
A peire of bedes blak as sable   160
Sche tok and heng my necke aboute;
Upon the gaudes al withoute
Was write of gold, *Por Reposer.*
"Lo," thus sche seide, "John Gower,
Now thou art ate laste cast,   165
This have I for thin ese cast,
That thou no more of love sieche.
Bot my will is that thou besieche
And preye hierafter for thee pes,
And that thou make a plein reles   170
To love, which takth litel hiede
Of olde men upon the nede,
Whan that the lustes ben aweye:
Forthy to thee nis bot o weye,
In which let reson be thy guide;   175

147 *touchende,* concerning   152 *foryifte,* forgiveness
153 *foryet,* forget   154 *grant mercy,* many thanks
158 *ende,* settlement
159: i.e., something for which I was most suited
160 *peire of bedes,* i.e., a rosary   161 *heng,* hung
162 *gaudes,* larger beads   163 *Por Reposer,* i.e., For Quiet Heart
165 *ate laste cast,* at the final extremity   166 *cast,* devised
167 *sieche,* seek   170 *plein reles,* full remission
171 *hiede,* heed   174: i.e., therefore there is but one way for you

For he may sone himself misguide
That seth noght the peril tofore.
My sone, be wel war therfore,
And kep the sentence of my lore,
And tarye thou my Court no more,   180
Bot go ther vertu moral dwelleth,
Wher ben thy bokes, as men telleth,
Whiche of long time thou hast write.
For this I do thee wel to wite,
If thou thin hele wolt pourchace,   185
Thou might noght make suite and chace,
Wher that the game is noght pernable;
It were a thing unresonable,
A man to be so overseye.

Forthy tak hiede of that I seye;   190
For in the lawe of my comune
We be noght schape to comune,
Thyselfe and I, nevere after this.
Now have I seid al that ther is
Of love as for thy final ende: 195
Adieu, for I mot fro thee wende."
And with that word al sodeinly,
Enclosed in a sterred sky,
Venus, which is the queene of love,
Was take into hire place above,   200
More wist I noght wher sche becam.
And thus my leve of hire I nam,
And forth withal the same tide
Hire prest, which wolde noght abide,

177 *seth,* sees   179: i.e., and hold to the purport of my teaching
180 *tarye,* linger in   181 *ther,* where
184 *do,* cause; *wite,* know   185 *hele,* recovery
186 *suite,* pursuit   187 *pernable,* to be caught
189 *overseye,* mistaken   191 *comune,* commonwealth
192 *schape,* destined   196 *mot,* must
197 *sterred,* starry   201: i.e., I knew no more of where she went
202 *nam,* took   203 *tide,* time
204 *prest,* priest

Or be me lief or be me loth, 205
Out of my sighte forth he goth,
And I was left withouten helpe.
So wiste I noght wherof to yelpe,
But only that I hadde lore
My time, and was sory therfore. 210
And thus bewhaped in my thoght.
Whan al was turned into noght,
I stod amased for a while,
And in myself I gan to smile
Thenkende upon the bedes blake, 215
And how they weren me betake,
For that I schulde bidde and preye.
And whanne I sigh no othre weye,
Bot only that I was refused,
Unto the lif which I hadde used 220
I thoghte nevere torne ayein:
And in this wise, soth to sein,
Homward a softe pas I wente.

(*Book VIII, lines 2745–2967*)

205: i.e., whether I liked it or lumped it   208 *yelpe,* boast
209 *lore,* wasted   211 *bewhaped,* bewildered
215 *thenkende,* thinking   216 *me betake,* commended to me
218 *sigh,* saw   223 *a softe pas,* slowly

Geoffrey Chaucer

(1340?–1400)

FROM *Troilus and Criseide*

[*The Wooing of Criseide*]

Incipit prohemium tertii libri.

O blisful light, of which the bemes clere
Adorneth al the thridde heven faire!
O sonnes lief, O Joves doughter deere,
Plesance of love, O goodly debonaire,
In gentil hertes ay redy to repaire!   5
O veray cause of heele and of gladnesse,
Yheried be thy might and thy goodnesse!

In hevene and helle, in erthe and salte see
Is felt thy might, if that I wel descerne;
As man, brid, best, fissh, herbe, and grene tree   10
Thee fele in times with vapour eterne.
God loveth, and to love wol nought werne;
And in this world no lives creature
Withouten love is worth, or may endure.

Ye Joves first to thilk effectes glade,   15
Thorugh which that thinges liven alle and be,

1 *light*, i.e., the planet Venus
3 *sonnes lief*, beloved of the sun
7 *yheried*, praised
12 *werne*, refuse
14 *worth*, worthy
2 *thridde*, third
6 *heele*, welfare
11 *vapour*, exhalation
13 *lives*, living
15 *Joves*, Jove (object of *comeveden*); *thilk*, the same

74

Comeveden, and amorous him made
On mortal thing, and as you list, ay ye
Yeve him in love ese or adversitee;
And in a thousand formes down him sente   20
For love in erthe, and whom you liste, he hente.

Ye fierse Mars apaisen of his ire,
And as you list, ye maken hertes digne;
Algates hem that ye wol sette a-fire,
They dreden shame, and vices they resigne;   25
Ye do hem corteis be, fresshe and benigne;
And heighe or lowe, after a wight entendeth,
The joyes that he hath, youre might him sendeth.

Ye holden regne and hous in unitee;
Ye sothfast cause of frendshipe ben also;   30
Ye knowe al thilke covered qualitee
Of thinges, which that folk on wondren so,
Whan they can nought construe how it may jo,
She loveth him, or why he loveth here,
As why this fissh, and naught that, comth to were. 35

Ye folk a lawe han set in universe,
And this knowe I by hem that lovers be,
That whoso striveth with you hath the werse.
Now, lady bright, for thy benignite,
At reverence of hem that serven thee,   40
Whos clerk I am, so techeth me devise
Som joye of that is felt in thy servise.

17 *comeveden*, excited	18 *list*, please
19 *yeve*, give	21 *hente*, seized
22 *apaisen*, appease	23 *digne*, worthy
24 *algates*, at all times; *hem*, them	26 *do*, make
27 *after*, according as; *wight*, creature	31 *thilke covered*, that secret
32 *on wondren*, wonder about	33 *jo*, ? come about
34 *here*, her	35 *were*, wier
36 *folk*, i.e., for folk	40 *at*, in
41 *devise*, describe	

Ye in my naked herte sentement
Inhielde, and do me shewe of thy swetnesse.—
Caliope, thy vois be now present,   45
For now is nede; sestou not my destresse,
How I mot telle anonright the gladnesse
Of Troilus, to Venus heryinge?
To which gladnesse, who nede hath, God him bringe!

Explicit prohemium tertii libri.
Incipit liber tertius.

Lay al this mene while Troilus,   50
Recording his lesson in this manere,
"Mafay!" thoughte he, "thus wol I sey, and thus;
Thus wol I pleine unto my lady dere;
That word is good, and this shal be my cheere;
This nil I nought foryeten in no wise."   55
God leve him werken as he can devise!

And Lord, so that his herte gan to quappe,
Hering hire come, and shorte for to sike!
And Pandarus, that ledde hire by the lappe,
Com ner, and gan in at the curtin pike,   60
And seide, "God do boot on alle sike!
Se who is here you comen to visite;
Lo, here is she that is youre deth to wite."

Therwith it semed as he wepte almost.
"Ha, a," quod Troilus so reufully,   65
"Wher me be wo, O mighty God, thou woost!

---

44 *inhielde,* infuse; *do,* make   46 *sestou,* do you see
47 *mot,* must   48 *to Venus heryinge,* for Venus' glory
52 *mafay,* my faith   53 *pleine,* complain
55 *nil I,* will I not; *foryeten,* forget   56 *leve,* let; *werken,* work
57 *gan,* began; *quappe,* palpitate
58 *hire,* her; *shorte . . . sike,* to pant   59 *lappe,* fold of a garment
60 *pike,* peek   61 *boot on,* good to; *sike,* sick
63 *youre . . . wite,* to blame for your death
66 *wher,* whether; *woost,* know

Who is ther? I se nought trewely."
"Sire," quod Criseide, "it is Pandare and I."
"Ye, swete herte? allas, I may nought rise,
To knele and do you honour in som wise."   70

    And dressed him upward, and she right tho
Gan bothe hire hondes softe upon him leye.
"O, for the love of God, do ye nought so
To me," quod she, "I! what is this to seye?
Sire, comen am I to you for causes tweye;   75
First, you to thonke, and of your lordshipe eke
Continuaunce I wolde you biseke."

    This Troilus, that herde his lady preye
Of lordshipe him, wex neither quik ne ded,
Ne mighte o word for shame to it seye,   80
Although men sholde smiten of his hed.
But Lord, so he wex sodeinliche red,
And sire, his lessoun, that he wende conne,
To preyen hire, is thorugh his wit yronne.

    Criseide al this aspied wel ynough,   85
For she was wis, and loved him nevere the lasse,
Al nere he malapert, or made it tough,
Or was to bold, to singe a fool a masse.
But whan his shame gan somwhat to passe,
His resons, as I may my rimes holde,   90
I wol you telle, as techen bokes olde.

    In chaunged vois, right for his verray drede,
Which vois ek quook, and therto his manere

71 *dressed,* raised; *tho,* then   72 *gan,* did
75 *tweye,* two   77 *biseke,* beseech
79 *wex,* grew   80 *o,* one
83 *wende conne,* thought he knew   84 *yronne,* run out
86 *lasse,* less
87 *al nere he,* even if he was not; *malapert,* forward; *or made it tough,*
    nor behaved boldly   88 *or,* i.e., nor; *to,* too
90 *resons,* speeches   93 *quook,* quaked

Goodly abaist, and now his hewes rede,
Now pale, unto Criseide, his lady dere,   95
With look down cast and humble yyolden chere,
Lo, the alderfirste word that him asterte
Was, twies, "Mercy, mercy, swete herte!"

And stinte a while, and whan he mighte out bringe,
The nexte word was, "God woot, for I have,   100
As ferforthly as I have had conninge,
Ben youres al, God so my soule save,
And shal, til that I, woful wight, be grave!
And though I dar, ne can, unto you pleine,
Ywis, I suffre nought the lasse peine.   105

"Thus muche as now, O wommanliche wif,
I may outbringe, and if this you displese,
That shal I wreke upon min owen lif
Right soone, I trowe, and do youre herte an ese,
If with my deth youre wreththe I may apese.   110
But sin that ye han herd me somwhat seye,
Now recche I nevere how soone that I deye."

Therwith his manly sorwe to biholde,
It mighte han mad an herte of stoon to rewe;
And Pandare wep as he to water wolde,   115
And poked evere his nece new and newe,
And seide, "Wo bigon ben hertes trewe!
For love of God, make of this thing an ende,
Or sle us both at ones, er ye wende."

94 *abaist*, abashed; *rede*, red
96 *humble . . . chere*, submissive expression
97 *alderfirste*, very first; *asterte*, escaped   99 *stinte*, paused
101 *ferforthly*, completely   103 *shal*, i.e., shall be; *grave*, buried
104 *pleine*, complain   105 *ywis*, indeed
108 *wreke*, avenge   110 *wreththe*, wrath
111 *sin*, since   112 *recche*, care
115 *wep*, wept; *wolde*, i.e., would turn   119 *sle*, slay

"I! what?" quod she, "by God and by my trouthe,   120
I not nat what ye wilne that I seye."
"I! what?" quod he, "that ye han on him routhe,
For Goddes love, and doth him nought to deye."
"Now thanne thus," quod she, "I wolde him preye
To telle me the fin of his entente.   125
Yet wist I nevere wel what that he mente."

"What that I mene, O swete herte deere?"
Quod Troilus, "O goodly, fresshe free,
That with the stremes of youre eyen cleere
Ye wolde somtime frendly on me see,   130
And thanne agreen that I may ben he,
Withouten braunche of vice on any wise,
In trouthe alwey to don you my servise,

"As to my lady right and chief resort,
With al my wit and al my diligence;   135
And I to han, right as you list, comfort,
Under youre yerde, egal to min offence,
As deth, if that I breke youre defence;
And that ye deigne me so muche honoure,
Me to comanden aught in any houre;   140

"And I to ben youre verray, humble, trewe,
Secret, and in my paines pacient,
And evere mo desiren fresshly newe
To serve, and ben ay ylike diligent,
And with good herte al holly youre talent   145
Receiven wel, how sore that me smerte,—
Lo, this mene I, min owen swete herte."

120 *trouthe,* troth   121 *not,* know not; *wilne,* wish
122 *routhe,* pity   123 *doth,* cause
125 *fin,* end   126 *wist,* knew
128 *free,* generous one   129 *stremes,* beams
130 *see,* look   136 *han,* have
137 *yerde,* rod; *egal,* equal   138 *defence,* prohibition
143 *mo,* more   145 *al holly,* entirely; *talent,* desire
146 *me smerte,* I smart

Quod Pandarus, "Lo, here an hard requeste,
And resonable, a lady for to werne!
Now, nece min, by natal Joves feste,   150
Were I a god, ye sholden sterve as yerne,
That heren wel, this man wol nothing yerne
But youre honour, and sen him almost sterve,
And ben so loth to suffren him you serve."

With that she gan hire eyen on him caste   155
Ful esily and ful debonairly,
Avising hire, and hied nought to faste
With nevere a word, but seide him softely,
"Min honour sauf, I wol wel trewely,
And in swich forme as he gan now devise,   160
Receiven him fully to my servise,

"Biseching him, for Goddes love, that he
Wolde, in honour of trouthe and gentilesse,
As I wel mene, eke menen wel to me,
And min honour with wit and bisinesse   165
Ay kepe; and if I may don him gladnesse,
From hennesforth, ywis, I nil nought feine.
Now beth al hool, no lenger ye ne pleine.

"But natheles, this warne I you," quod she,
"A kinges sone although ye be, ywis,   170
Ye shal namore han sovereignete
Of me in love, than right in that cas is;
N'I nil forbere, if that ye don amis,

149 *werne,* refuse   150 *feste,* feast
151 *sterve as yerne,* die as quickly   152 *yerne,* desire
153 *sen,* see   155 *gan,* did
157 *avising hire,* pondering   159 *sauf,* safe
160 *gan devise,* did describe
167 *ywis,* indeed; *nil nought feine,* will not shirk
168 *hool,* hale; *lenger,* longer; *pleine,* complain
169 *natheles,* nevertheless
173 *n'I nil,* nor will I

To wratthe you; and whil that ye me serve,
Chericen you right after ye disserve.   175

"And shortly, deere herte and al my knight,
Beth glad, and draweth you to lustinesse,
And I shal trewely, with al my might,
Youre bittre tornen al into swetenesse;
If I be she that may you do gladnesse,   180
For every wo ye shal recovere a blisse."
And him in armes took, and gan him kisse.

Fil Pandarus on knees, and up his eyen
To heven threw, and held his hondes highe,
"Immortal god," quod he, "that mayst nought deyen, 185
Cupid I mene, of this mayst glorifye;
And Venus, thou mayst maken melodye!
Withouten hond, me semeth that in towne,
For this merveille, ich here ech belle sowne.

"But ho! namore as now of this matere;   190
For-why this folk wol comen up anon,
That han the lettre red; lo, I hem here.
But I conjure thee, Criseide, and oon,
And two, thou Troilus, whan thou mayst goon,
That at min hous ye ben at my warninge,   195
For I ful well shal shape youre cominge;

"And eseth there youre hertes right ynough;
And lat se which of you shal bere the belle,
To speke of love aright!"—therwith he lough—
"For ther have ye a leiser for to telle."   200
Quod Troilus, "How longe shal I dwelle,
Er this be don?" Quod he, "Whan thou mayst rise,
This thing shal be right as I you devise."

175 *chericen,* cherish   179 *tornen,* turn
183 *fil,* fell   188 *withouten hond,* i.e., spontaneously
189 *ich,* I; *sowne,* ring   191 *for-why,* because
194 *goon,* walk   196 *shape,* manage
198 *lat,* let   199 *lough,* laughed

With that Eleine and also Deiphebus
Tho comen upward, right at the steires ende;   205
And Lord, so thanne gan gronen Troilus,
His brother and his suster for to blende.
Quod Pandarus, "It time is that we wende.
Tak, nece min, youre leve at alle thre,
And lat hem speke, and cometh forth with me."   210

She took hire leve at hem ful thriftily,
As she wel coude, and they hire reverence
Unto the fulle diden, hardily,
And wonder wel speken, in hire absence,
Of hire, in preising of hire excellence,   215
Hire governaunce, hire wit; and hire manere
Comendeden, it joye was to here.

Now lat hire wende unto hire owen place,
And torne we to Troilus ayein,
That gan ful lightly of the lettre pace   220
That Deiphebus hadde in the gardin sein;
And of Eleine and him he wolde fein
Delivered ben, and seide that him leste
To slepe, and after tales have reste.

Eleine him kiste, and took hire leve blive,   225
Deiphebus ek, and hom wente every wight;
And Pandarus, as faste as he may drive,
To Troilus tho com, as line right,
And on a paillet al that glade night
By Troilus he lay, with mery chere,   230
To tale; and wel was hem they were yfeere.

205 *tho,* then   207 *blende,* deceive
211 *thriftily,* properly   213 *hardily,* frankly
215 *hire,* her   220 *gan pace,* did páss over
221 *sein,* seen   223 *leste,* pleased
224 *tales,* conversation   225 *blive,* straightway
228 *tho,* then; *line right,* straight line
231 *to tale,* for conversation; *yfeere,* together

Whan every wight was voided but they two,
And alle the dores weren faste yshette,
To telle in short, withouten wordes mo,
This Pandarus, withouten any lette,   235
Up roos, and on his beddes side him sette,
And gan to speken in a sobre wise
To Troilus, as I shal you devise:

"Min alderlevest lord, and brother deere,
God woot, and thou, that it sat me so soore,   240
When I thee saugh so languisshing to-yere
For love, of which thy wo wax alwey moore,
That I, with al my might and al my loore,
Have evere sithen don my bisinesse
To bringe thee to joye out of distresse,   245

"And have it brought to swich plit as thou woost,
So that thorugh me thou stondest now in weye
To faren wel; I sey it for no bost,
And wostou why? for shame it is to seye:
For thee have I bigonne a gamen pleye,   250
Which that I nevere do shal eft for other,
Although he were a thousand fold my brother.

"That is to seye, for thee am I bicomen,
Bitwixen game and ernest, swich a meene
As maken wommen unto men to comen;   255
Al sey I nought, thou wost wel what I meene.
For thee have I my nece, of vices cleene,
So fully maad thy gentilesse triste,
That al shal ben right as thyselven liste.

232 *voided,* withdrawn   233 *yshette,* shut
234 *mo,* more   235 *lette,* delay
239 *alderlevest,* dearest   240 *woot,* knows
241 *saugh,* saw; *to-yere,* this year   244 *sithen,* since
246 *plit,* situation   249 *wostou,* do you know
251 *eft,* again   254 *game,* sport
258 *triste,* trust

"But God, that al woot, take I to witnesse,   260
That nevere I this for coveitise wroughte,
But oonly for t'abregge that distresse
For which wel neigh thou deidest, as me thoughte.
But, goode brother, do now as thee oughte,
For Goddes love, and kep hire out of blame,   265
Sin thou art wis, and save alwey hire name.

"For wel thou woost, the name as yet of here
Among the peeple, as who seith, halwed is;
For that man is unbore, I dar wel swere,
That evere wiste that she dide amis.   270
But wo is me, that I, that cause al this,
May thinken that she is my nece deere,
And I hire em, and traitour eke yfeere!

"And were it wist that I, thorugh min engin,
Hadde in my nece yput this fantasye,   275
To doon thy lust and holly to ben thin,
Why, al the world upon it wolde crye,
And seyn that I the werste trecherye
Dide in this cas, that evere was bigonne,
And she forlost, and thou right nought ywonne.   280

"Wherfore, er I wol ferther gon a pas,
Yet eft I thee biseche and fully seye,
That privete go with us in this cas,
That is to seyn, that thou us nevere wreye;
And be nought wroth, though I thee ofte preye   285
To holden secree swich an heigh matere,
For skilfull is, thou woost wel, my prayere.

261 *coveitise*, avarice	262 *abregge*, lessen
265 *hire*, her	266 *sin*, since
267 *here*, her	268 *halwed*, held sacred
269 *unbore*, unborn	270 *wiste*, knew
273 *em*, uncle; *yfeere*, together	274 *engin*, devising
276 *holly*, wholly; *thin*, thine	280 *forlost*, utterly lost
281 *gon a pas*, proceed	282 *eft*, again
283 *privete*, secrecy	284 *wreye*, disclose
287 *skilfull*, reasonable	

"And think what wo ther hath bitid er this,
For making of avantes, as men rede;
And what meschaunce in this world yet ther is,   290
Fro day to day, right for that wicked dede;
For which thise wise clerkes that ben dede
Han evere thus proverbed to us yonge,
That 'firste vertu is to kepe tonge.'

"And nere it that I wilne as now t'abregge   295
Diffusioun of speche, I coude almoost
A thousand olde stories thee allegge
Of wommen lost through fals and foles bost.
Proverbes canst thyself ynowe and woost,
Ayeins that vice, for to ben a labbe,   300
Al seide men soth as often as they gabbe.

"O tonge, allas! so often here-biforn
Hath mad ful many a lady bright of hewe
Seid 'weilaway, the day that I was born!'
And many a maides sorwe for to newe;   305
And for the more part, al is untrewe
That men of yelpe, and it were brought to preve.
Of kinde non avauntour is to leve.

"Avauntour and a liere, al is on;
As thus: I pose, a womman graunte me   310
Hire love, and seith that other wol she non,
And I am sworn to holden it secree,
And after I go telle it two or thre;
Ywis, I am avauntour at the leeste,
And liere, for I breke my biheste.   315

289 *avantes*, boasts   295 *nere it*, were it not; *abregge*, cut short
297 *allegge*, adduce   298 *foles*, fools'
299 *canst*, *woost*, know; *ynowe*, enough   300 *labbe*, blabbermouth
301 *al*, even if; *gabbe*, lie   303 *mad*, made
305 *newe*, to be renewed   307 *of yelpe*, boast of; *and*, if; *preve*, trial
308: i.e., it's a rule of nature not to believe a braggart
310 *pose*, put the case   311 *wol*, desires
314 *ywis*, indeed; *leeste*, least   315 *biheste*, promise

"Now loke thanne, if they be nought to blame,
Swich manere folk—what shal I clepe hem? what?—
That hem avaunte of wommen, and by name,
That nevere yet bihighte hem this ne that,
Ne knewe hem more than min olde hat! 320
No wonder is, so God me sende hele,
Though wommen dreden with us men to dele.

"I sey nought this for no mistrust of you,
Ne for no wise men, but for foles nice,
And for the harm that in the werld is now, 325
As wel for folye ofte as for malice;
For wel woot I, in wise folk that vice
No womman drat, if she be wel avised;
For wise ben by foles harm chastised.

"But now to purpos; leve brother deere, 330
Have al this thing that I have seid in minde,
And kep thee clos, and be now of good cheere,
For at thy day thou shalt me trewe finde.
I shal thy proces set in swich a kinde,
And God toforn, that it shal thee suffise, 335
For it shal be right as thou wolt devise.

"For wel I woot, thou menest wel, parde;
Therfore I dar this fully undertake.
Thou woost ek what thy lady graunted thee,
And day is set, the chartres up to make. 340
Have now good night, I may no lenger wake;
And bid for me, sin thou art now in blisse,
That God me sende deth or soone lisse."

317 *swich manere,* such sorts of; *clepe,* call   318 *hem avaunte,* boast
319 *bihighte,* promised   321 *hele,* salvation
324 *nice,* silly   328 *drat,* dreads
330 *leve,* beloved
334 *proces,* cause; *set . . . kinde,* arrange in such a way
335 *God toforn,* before God   341 *lenger,* longer
342 *bid,* pray; *sin,* since   343 *lisse,* comfort

Who mighte tellen half the joye or feste
Which that the soule of Troilus tho felte,   345
Hering th'effect of Pandarus biheste?
His olde wo, that made his herte swelte,
Gan tho for joye wasten and tomelte,
And al the richesse of his sikes sore
At ones fledde; he felte of hem namore.   350

But right so as thise holtes and thise hayis,
That han in winter dede ben and dreye,
Revesten hem in grene, when that May is,
Whan every lusty liketh best to pleye;
Right in that selve wise, soth to seye.   355
Wax sodeinliche his herte ful of joye,
That gladder was ther nevere man in Troye.

And gan his look on Pandarus up caste
Ful sobrely, and frendly for to se,
And seide, "Frend, in Aperil the laste,—   360
As wel thou woost, if it remembre thee—
How neigh the deth for wo thou founde me,
And how thou dedest al thy bisinesse
To knowe of me the cause of my destresse.

"Thou woost how longe ich it forbar to seye   365
To thee, that art the man that I best triste;
And peril non was it to thee biwreye,
That wist I wel, but telle me, if thee liste,
Sith I so loth was that thyself it wiste,
How dorst I mo tellen of this matere,   370
That quake now, and no wight may us here?

---

344 *feste,* festiveness   345 *tho,* then
346 *biheste,* promise   347 *swelte,* faint
348 *tomelt,* dissolve 349 *the richesse . . . sikes,* his wealth of sighs
351 *hayes,* hedges   354 *lusty,* i.e., lusty heart
363 *dedest,* did   366 *triste,* trust
367 *biwreye,* disclose   369 *sith,* since; *wiste,* should have known
370 *mo,* others

"But natheles, by that God I thee swere,
That, as him list, may al this world governe,—
And, if I lie, Achilles with his spere
Min herte cleve, al were my lif eterne,   375
As I am mortal, if I late or yerne
Wolde it bewreye, or dorst, or sholde conne,
For al the good that God made under sonne—

"That rather deye I wolde, and determine,
As thinketh me, now stocked in prisoun,   380
In wrecchidnesse, in filthe, and in vermine,
Caitif to cruel king Agamenoun;
And this in all the temples of this town
Upon the goddes alle, I wol thee swere
To-morwe day, if that it like thee here.   385

"And that thou hast so muche ydo for me
That I ne may it nevere more diserve,
This know I wel, al mighte I now for thee
A thousand times on a morwe sterve.
I can namore, but that I wol thee serve   390
Right as thy sclave, whider so thou wende,
For evere more, unto my lives ende.

"But here, with al min herte, I thee biseche
That nevere in me thou deme swich folye
As I shal seyn; me thoughte by thy speche   395
That this which thou me dost for compaignye,
I sholde wene it were a bauderye.
I am nought wood, al if I lewed be!
It is nought so, that woot I wel, parde!

372 *natheles*, nevertheless   376 *yerne*, soon
377 *conne*, know how   379 *determine*, come to end
380 *stocked*, put in the stocks   382 *caitif*, captive
385 *like*, please; *here*, hear   387 *diserve*, requite
389 *morwe*, morning; *sterve*, die   391 *sclave*, slave; *whider*, whither
394 *deme*, suspect   397 *wene*, suppose
398 *wood*, insane; *lewed*, ignorant

"But he that gooth, for gold or for ricchesse,   400
On swich message, calle him what thee list;
And this that thou doost, calle it gentilesse,
Compassioun, and felawship, and trist.
Departe it so, for wide-wher is wist,
How that ther is diversite requered   405
Bitwixen thinges like, as I have lered.

"And, that thou knowe I thinke nought, ne wene,
That this servise a shame be or jape,
I have my faire suster Polixene,
Cassandre, Eleine, or any of the frape,   410
Be she nevere so fair or wel yshape,
Telle me which thou wilt of everichone,
To han for thin, and lat me thanne allone.

"But sith thou hast ydon me this servise,
My life to save, and for non hope of mede,   415
So, for the love of God, this grete emprise
Perfourme it out, for now is moste nede;
For heigh and lough, withouten any drede,
I wol alwey thin hestes alle kepe.
Have now good night, and lat us bothe slepe."   420

Thus held him ech of other wel apayed,
That al the world ne mighte it bet amende;
And on the morwe, whan they were arayed,
Ech to his owen nedes gan entende.
But Troilus, though as the fir he brende   425

401 *message,* errand   403 *trist,* trust
404 *departe it so,* make this distinction; *wide-wher,* far and wide;
  wist, known   405 *requered,* necessitated
406 *lered,* learned   407 *wene,* suppose
408 *jape,* trick   410 *frape,* company
412 *everichone,* each one   413 *thin,* thine
414 *sith,* since   415 *mede,* reward
416 *emprise,* enterprise   418 *lough,* low; *drede,* doubt
419 *hestes,* commands   421 *apayed,* satisfied
422 *bet,* better   424 *entende,* attend
425 *brende,* burned

For sharp desir of hope and of plesaunce,
He nought forgat his goode governaunce.

But in himself with manhod gan restreine
Ech racle dede and ech unbridled cheere,
That alle tho that liven, soth to seyne,   430
Ne sholde han wist, by word or by manere,
What that he mente, as touching this matere.
From every wight as fer as is the cloude
He was, so wel dissimulen he coude.

And al the while which that I you devise,   435
This was his lif; with all his fulle might,
By day, he was in Martes heigh servise,
This is to seyn, in armes as a knight;
And for the more part, the longe night
He lay and thoughte how that he mighte serve   440
His lady best, hire thonk for to deserve.

Nil I naught swere, although he lay ful softe,
That in his thought he nas somwhat disesed,
Ne that he torned on his pilwes ofte,
And wold of that him missed han ben sesed.   445
But in swich cas man is nought alwey plesed,
For aught I woot, namore than was he;
That can I deme of possibilitee.

But certein is, to purpos for to go,
That in this while, as writen is in geeste,   450
He say his lady somtime, and also
She with him spak, whan that she dorst and leste;

427 *governaunce,* self-control
429 *racle,* rash; *cheere,* look
433 *fer,* far
441 *thonk,* gratitude
443 *nas,* was not; *disesed,* troubled
450 *geeste,* story
452 *leste,* pleased

428 *gan,* did
430 *tho,* those
434 *dissimulen,* dissemble
442 *nil I,* will I not
445 *sesed,* possessed
451 *say,* saw

And by hire bothe avis, as was the beste,
Apointeden full warly in this nede,
So as they durste, how they wolde procede.   455

But it was spoken in so short a wise,
In swich await alwey, and in swich feere,
Lest any wight devinen or devise
Wolde of hem two, or to it laye an ere,
That al this world so leef to hem ne were   460
As that Cupide wolde hem grace sende
To maken of hire speche aright an ende.

But thilke litel that they spake or wroughte,
His wise goost took ay of al swich heede,
It semed hire he wiste what she thoughte   465
Withouten word, so that it was no nede
To bidde him ought to doon, or ought forbeede;
For which she thought that love, al come it late,
Of alle joye hadde opned hire the yate.

And shortly of this proces for to pace,   470
So wel his werk and wordes he bisette,
That he so ful stood in his lady grace,
That twenty thousand times, er she lette,
She thonked God that evere she with him mette.
So coude he him governe in swich servise,   475
That al the world ne might it bet devise.

For-why she fond him so discret in al,
So secret, and of swich obëisaunce,

453 *hire bothe avis,* mutual consent   454 *warly,* cautiously
457 *await,* watchfulness   458 *devinen,* guess; *devise,* imagine
460 *leef,* dear   462: i.e., to bring their plans to consummation
463 *thilke litel,* the little   464 *goost,* spirit
465 *hire,* her; *wiste,* knew   467 *forbeede,* forbid
469 *yate,* gate   470: i.e., and to make short of this business
471 *bisette,* applied   472 *lady,* lady's
473 *lette,* ceased   476 *bet,* better
477 *for-why,* wherefore
478 *obeisaunce,* courtesy

That wel she felte he was to hire a wal
Of stiel, and sheld from every displesaunce;   480
That to ben in his goode governaunce,
So wis he was, she was namore afered,—
I mene, as fer as oughte ben requered.

And Pandarus, to quike alwey the fir,
Was evere ylike prest and diligent;   485
To ese his frend was set al his desir.
He shof ay on, he to and fro was sent;
He lettres bar whan Troilus was absent;
That nevere man, as in his frendes nede,
Ne bar him bet than he, withouten drede.   490

But now, paraunter, som man waiten wolde
That every word, or soonde, or look, or cheere
Of Troilus that I rehercen sholde,
In al this while unto his lady deere.
I trowe it were a long thing for to here;   495
Or of what wight that stant in swich disjointe,
His wordes alle, or every look, to pointe.

For sothe, I have naught herd it don er this
In story non, ne no man here, I wene;
And though I wolde, I coude nought, ywis;   500
For ther was som epistel hem bitwene,
That wolde, as seith min autour, wel contene
Neigh half this book, of which him liste nought write.
How sholde I thanne a line of it endite?

But to the grete effect. Than sey I thus,   505
That stonding in concord and in quiete,

483 *fer*, far; *requered*, necessary   484 *quike*, quicken
485 *prest*, prompt   487 *shof*, pushed
488 *bar*, bore   490 *bet*, better; *drede*, doubt
491 *paraunter*, perchance; *waiten*, expect
492 *soonde*, message; *cheere*, glance   495 *trowe*, think
496 *stant*, stands; *disjointe*, predicament   497 *pointe*, list
499 *wene*, suppose   500 *ywis*, indeed

Thise ilke two, Criseide and Troilus,
As I have told, and in this time swete,—
Save only often mighte they nought mete,
Ne leiser have hire speches to fulfelle,—   510
That it bifel right as I shal you telle,

That Pandarus, that evere dide his might
Right for the fin that I shal speke of here,
As for to bringen to his hous som night
His faire nece and Troilus yfere,   515
Wheras at leiser al this heighe matere,
Touching here love, were at the fulle upbounde,
Hadde out of doute a time to it founde.

For he with gret deliberacioun
Hadde every thing that herto might availle   520
Forncast and put in execucioun,
And neither left for cost ne for travaile.
Come if hem list, hem sholde no thing faille;
And for to ben in ought aspied there,
That, wiste he wel, an impossible were.   525

Dredeles, it cler was in the wind
From every pie and every lette-game;
Now al is wel, for al the world is blind
In this matere, bothe fremed and tame.
This timbur is al redy up to frame;   530
Us lakketh nought but that we witen wolde
A certein houre, in which she comen sholde.

And Troilus, that al this purveiaunce
Knew at the fulle, and waited on it ay,

507 *ilke*, same   510 *fulfelle*, fulfil
513 *fin*, end   515 *yfere*, together
521 *forncast*, provided for   522 *left*, left off
524 *in ought aspied*, in any way detected
525 *impossible*, impossibility   526 *dredeles*, doubtless; *cler*, free
527 *pie*, i.e., tell-tale bird; *lette-game*, spoilsport   529 *fremed*, wild
530 *up to frame*, to be erected   531 *witen*, know
533 *purveiaunce*, preparation

Hadde hereupon ek mad gret ordinaunce,   535
And found his cause, and therto his aray,
If that he were missed, night or day,
Ther-while he was aboute this servise,
That he was gon to don his sacrifise,

And moste at swich a temple allone wake,   540
Answered of Apollo for to be;
And first to sen the holy laurer quake,
Er that Apollo spake out of the tree,
To telle him next whan Grekes sholde flee,—
And forthy lette him no man, God forbede,   545
But prey Apollo helpen in this nede.

Now is ther litel more for to doone,
But Pandare up, and shortly for to seyne,
Right sone upon the chaunginge of the moone,
Whan lightles is the world a night or tweine,   550
And that the wolken shop him for to reine,
He streght o morwe unto his nece wente;
Ye han wel herd the fin of his entente.

Whan he was com, he gan anon to pleye
As he was wont, and of himself to jape;   555
And finaly he swor and gan hire seye,
By this and that, she sholde him nought escape,
Ne lenger don him after hire to cape;
But certeinly she moste, by hire leve,
Come soupen in his hous with him at eve.   560

535 *ordinaunce,* arrangements
536 *cause,* plan of action; *array,* i.e., pretext   538 *ther-while,* while
540 *moste,* must
542 *laurer quake,* laurel shake (in oracular response)
545 *forthy,* therefore; *lette,* let hinder   548 *up,* i.e., was ready
551 *wolken shape him,* sky was getting ready
552 *o morwe,* in the morning   553 *fin,* end
555 *jape,* joke   556 *gan,* did
558 *don,* make; *cape,* gape   559 *moste,* must
560 *soupen,* sup

At which she lough, and gan hire faste excuse,
And seide, "It reineth; lo, how sholde I gon?"
"Lat be," quod he, "ne stant nought thus to muse.
This moot be don! Ye shal be ther anon."
So at the laste herof they fille aton,   565
Or elles, softe he swor hire in hire ere,
He nolde nevere comen ther she were.

Soone after this, she gan to him to roune,
And axed him if Troilus were there.
He swor hire nay, for he was out of towne,   570
And seide, "Nece, I pose that he were;
You thurste nevere han the more fere;
For rather than men mighte him ther aspye,
Me were levere a thousand fold to die."

Nought list min auctour fully to declare   575
What that she thoughte whan he seide so,
That Troilus was out of towne yfare,
As if he seide therof soth or no;
But that, withouten await, with him to go,
She graunted him, sith he hire that bisoughte,   580
And, as his nece, obeyed as hire oughte.

But natheles, yet gan she him biseche,
Although with him to gon it was no fere,
For to ben war of goosish poeples speche,
That dremen thinges whiche that nevere were,   585
And wel avise him whom he broughte there;
And seide him, "Em, sin I most on you triste,
Loke al be wel, and do now as you liste."

561 *lough,* laughed   563 *stant,* stand
564 *moot,* must   565 *fille aton,* fell into agreement
568 *roune,* whisper   569 *axed,* asked
571 *I pose,* i.e., even supposing   572 *thurste,* need
575 *nought list,* it does not please   577 *yfare,* gone
579 *await,* watchfulness   580 *sith,* since
582 *natheles,* nevertheless   583 *fere,* fear
584 *goosish,* gooselike
587 *em,* uncle; *sin,* since; *most,* must; *triste,* trust

He swor hire yis, by stockes and by stones,
And by the goddes that in hevene dwelle,　　　590
Or elles were him levere, soule and bones,
With Pluto king as depe ben in helle
As Tantalus!—what sholde I more telle?
Whan al was wel, he roos and took his leve,
And she to soper com, whan it was eve,　　　595

With a certein of hire owen men,
And with hire faire nece Antigone,
And other of hire wommen nine or ten.
But who was glad now, who, as trowe ye,
But Troilus, that stood and might it se　　　600
Thoroughout a litel window in a stewe,
Ther he bishet sin midnight was in mewe,

Unwist of every wight but of Pandare?
But to the point; now whan that she was come,
With alle joye and alle frendes fare,　　　605
Hire em anon in armes hath hire nome,
And after to the soper, alle and some,
Whan time was, ful softe they hem sette.
God woot, ther was no deinte for to fette!

And after soper gonnen they to rise,　　　610
At ese wel, with hertes fresshe and glade,
And wel was him that coude best devise
To liken hire, or that hire laughen made.
He song; she pleyde; he tolde tale of Wade.
But at the laste, as every thing hath ende,　　　615
She took hire leve, and nedes wolde wende.

589 *yis*, yes　　　　　　　596 *certein*, certain number
601 *stewe*, closet
602 *bishet*, shut up; *sin*, since; *in mewe*, i.e., as in a coop
603 *unwist*, unknown　　　　　　605 *fare*, company
606 *nome*, taken　　　607 *alle and some*, all and sundry
609 *to fette*, to fetch, i.e., lacking　　　610 *gonnen*, began
612 *devise*, contrive　　　　613 *liken hire*, please her

But O Fortune, executrice of wirdes,
O influences of thise hevenes hye!
Soth is, that under God ye ben oure hierdes,
Though to us bestes ben the causes wrye.   620
This mene I now, for she gan homward hie,
But execut was al biside hire leve
The goddes wil; for which she moste bleve.

The bente moone with hire hornes pale,
Saturne, and Jove, in Cancro joined were,   625
That swich a rein from heven gan avale,
That every maner womman that was there
Hadde of that smoky rein a verray feere;
At which Pandare tho lough, and seide thenne,
"Now were it time a lady to gon henne!   630

"But goode nece, if I mighte evere plese
You any thing, than prey ich you," quod he,
"To don min herte as now so gret an ese
As for to dwelle here al this night with me,
For-why this is youre owen hous, parde.   635
For, by my trouthe, I sey it nought a-game,
To wende as now, it were to me a shame."

Criseide, which that coude as muche good
As half a world, took hede of his preyere;
And sin it ron, and al was on a flod,   640
She thoughte, "As good chep may I dwellen here,
And graunte it gladly with a frendes chere,
And have a thonk, as grucche and thanne abide;
For hom to gon, it may nought wel bitide."

617 *wirdes*, destinies   619 *hierdes*, herdsmen
620 *bestes*, beasts; *wrye*, hidden
622 *execut*, executed; *biside*, contrary to
623 *moste bleve*, must remain   624 *bente*, curved
626 *avale*, fall   628 *smoky*, misty
629 *tho lough*, then laughed   630 *henne*, hence
635 *for-why*, because   636 *a-game*, in sport
638 *coude*, knew   640 *sin it ron*, since it was raining
641 *as good chep*, as easily   643 *grucche*, complain

"I wol," quod she, "min uncle lief and deere;   645
Sin that you list, it skile is to be so.
I am right glad with you to dwellen here:
I seide but a-game, I wolde go."
"Ywis, graunt mercy, nece," quod he tho,
"Were it a game or no, soth for to telle,   650
Now am I glad, sin that you list to dwelle."

Thus al is wel; but tho bigan aright
The newe joye and al the feste again.
But Pandarus, if goodly hadde he might,
He wolde han hied hire to bedde fain,   655
And seide, "Lord, this is an huge rain!
This were a weder for to slepen inne;
And that I rede us soone to biginne.

"And, nece, woot ye wher I wol you leye,
For that we shul nat liggen far asonder,   660
And for ye neither shullen, dar I seye,
Heren noise of reines nor of thonder?
By God, right in my litel closet yonder.
And I wol in that outer hous allone
Be wardein of youre wommen everichone.   665

"And in this middel chaumbre that ye se
Shul youre wommen slepen, wel and softe;
And there I seide shal yourselven be;
And if ye liggen wel to-night, com ofte,
And careth nought what weder is alofte.   670
The win anon, and whan so that you leste,
So go we slepe; I trowe it be the beste."

645 *lief*, beloved   646 *sin*, since; *skile*, reason
649 *ywis*, indeed; *graunt mercy*, many thanks; *tho*, then
655: i.e., he gladly would have hastened her to bed
657 *weder*, weather   658 *rede*, advise
660 *liggen*, lie   665 *wardein*, guardian; *everichone*, all
671 *leste*, please

Ther nis no more, but hereafter soone,
The voide dronke, and travers drawe anon,
Gan every wight, that hadde nought to done   675
More in the place, out of the chaumbre gon.
And evere mo so sterneliche it ron,
And blew therwith so wondirliche loude,
That wel neigh no man heren other coude.

Tho Pandarus, hire em, right as him oughte,   680
With wommen swiche as were hire most aboute,
Ful glad unto hire beddes side hire broughte,
And took his leve, and gan ful lowe loute,
And seide, "Here at this closet dore withoute,
Right overthwart, youre wommen liggen alle,   685
That, whom you list of hem, ye may here calle."

So whan that she was in the closet leid,
And alle hire wommen forth by ordinaunce
Abedde weren, ther as I have seid,
There was nomore to skippen nor to traunce,   690
But boden go to bedde, with meschaunce,
If any wight was stering anywhere,
And lat hem slepen that abedde were.

But Pandarus, that wel coude ech a deel
The olde daunce, and every point therinne,   695
Whan that he sey that alle thing was wel,
He thought he wolde upon his werk biginne,
And gan the stuwe doore al softe unpinne,
And stille as stoon, withouten lenger lette,
By Troilus adown right he him sette.   700

673 *nis no,* is no   674 *voide,* loving-cup; *travers,* curtains
677 *mo,* more; *sterneliche,* violently; *ron,* rained
678 *wondirliche,* wonderfully
680 *em,* uncle   683 *loute,* bow
685 *overthwart,* opposite   690 *traunce,* tramp about
691 *boden,* commanded   692 *stering,* stirring
694–695 *coude . . . daunce,* i.e., knew all the tricks of the trade
696 *sey,* saw   698 *stuwe,* closet
699 *lenger lette,* further delay

And, shortly to the point right for to gon,
Of al this werk he tolde him word and ende,
And seide "Make thee redy right anon,
For thou shalt into hevene blisse wende."
"Now, blisful Venus, thou me grace sende!"   705
Quod Troilus, "For nevere yet no nede
Hadde ich er now, ne halvendel the drede."

Quod Pandarus, "Ne drede thee nevere a deel,
For it shal be right as thou wolt desire;
So thrive I, this night shal I make it weel,   710
Or casten al the gruwel in the fire."
"Yet, blisful Venus, this night thou me enspire,"
Quod Troilus, "As wis as I thee serve,
And evere bet and bet shal, til I sterve.

"And if ich hadde, O Venus ful of mirthe,   715
Aspectes badde of Mars or of Saturne,
Or thou combust or let were in my birthe,
Thy fader prey al thilke harm disturne
Of grace, and that I glad ayein may turne,
For love of him thou lovedest in the shawe,   720
I meene Adoun, that with the boor was slawe.

"O Jove ek, for the love of faire Europe,
The which in forme of bole awey thou fette,
Now help! O Mars, thou with thy blody cope,
For love of Cipris, thou me nought ne lette!   725
O Phebus, think whan Dane hireselven shette
Under the bark, and laurer wax for drede,
Yet for hire love, O help now at this nede!

707 *ich,* I; *halvendel,* half   708 *deel,* bit
710 *weel,* well   711 *gruwel,* gruel
713 *wis,* surely   714 *bet,* better; *sterve,* die
717 *combust or let,* quenched or hindered
718 *thilke,* that same; *disturne,* turn aside   720 *shawe,* wood
721 *Adoun,* Adonis; *slawe,* slain   723 *bole,* bull; *fette,* carried
724 *cope,* cloak   725 *lette,* hinder
726 *shette,* shut   727 *laurer wax,* turned to laurel

"Mercurye, for the love of Hierse eke,
For which Pallas was with Aglauros wroth,   730
Now help! and ek Diane, I thee biseke,
That this viage be nought to thee looth.
O fatal sustren, which, er any cloth
Me shapen was, by destine me sponne,
So helpeth to this werk that is bigonne!"   735

Quod Pandarus, "Thou wrecched mouses herte,
Artou agast so that she wol thee bite?
Why, don this furred cloke upon thy sherte,
And folwe me, for I wol have the wite.
But bid, and lat me gon biforn a lite."   740
And with that word he gan undon a trappe,
And Troilus he brought in by the lappe.

The sterne wind so loude gan to route
That no wight oother noise mighte heere;
And they that layen at the dore withoute,   745
Ful sikerly they slepten alle yfere;
And Pandarus, with a ful sobre cheere,
Goth to the dore anon, withouten lette,
There as they laye, and softely it shette.

And as he com ayeinward prively,   750
His nece awook, and axed, "Who goth there?"
"My dere nece," quod he, "it am I.
Ne wondreth nought, ne have of it no fere."
And ner he com, and seide hire in hire ere,
"No word, for love of God, I you biseche!   755
Lat no wight risen and heren of oure speche."

731 *biseke,* beseech   732 *viage,* expedition
733 *sustren,* sisters   739 *wite,* blame
740 *bid,* wait; *lite,* little   741 *trappe,* trapdoor
742 *lappe,* fold of a garment   743 *route,* roar
746 *sikerly,* confidently; *yfere,* together   747 *cheere,* countenance
748 *lette,* delay   749 *shette,* shut
751 *axed,* asked

"What! which wey be ye comen, *benedicite?*"
Quod she, "and how thus unwist of hem alle?"
"Here at this secre trappe-dore," quod he.
Quod tho Criseide, "Lat me som wight calle!"　　760
"I! God forbede that it sholde falle,"
Quod Pandarus, "that ye swich folye wroughte!
They mighte demen thing they nevere er thoughte.

"It is nought good a sleping hound to wake,
Ne yeve a wight a cause to devine.　　765
Youre wommen slepen alle, I undertake,
So that, for hem, the hous men mighte mine,
And slepen wollen til the sonne shine.
And whan my tale brought is to an ende,
Unwist, right as I com, so wol I wende.　　770

"Now, nece min, ye shul wel understonde,"
Quod he, "so as ye wommen demen alle,
That for to holde in love a man in honde,
And him hire lief and deere herte calle,
And maken him an houve above a calle,　　775
I meene, as love another in this while,
She doth hireself a shame, and him a gile.

"Now, wherby that I telle you al this:
Ye woot youreself, as wel as any wight,
How that youre love al fully graunted is　　780
To Troilus, the worthieste knight,
Oon of this world, and therto trouthe yplight,
That, but it were on him along, ye nolde
Him nevere falsen while ye liven sholde.

---

758 *unwist,* unknown　　　　　　　　　760 *tho,* then
763 *demen,* suspect　　　　　765 *yeve,* give; *devine,* imagine
766 *undertake,* warrant　　　　　　　772 *demen,* believe
773: i.e., that to pretend to love a man　　774 *lief,* beloved
775: and make him a hood over a cap, i.e., deceive him
782 *oon of this world,* i.e., unique
783 *on him along,* through his fault; *nolde,* would not
784 *falsen,* play false to

"Now stant it thus, that sith I fro you wente,   785
This Troilus, right platly for to seyn,
Is thorough a goter, by a prive wente,
Into my chaumbre come in al this rein,
Unwist of every manere wight, certein,
Save of myself, as wisly have I joye,   790
And by that feith I shal Priam of Troye.

"And he is come in swich peine and distresse
That, but he be al fully wood by this,
He sodeinly mot falle into wodnesse,
But if God helpe; and cause why this is,   795
He seith him told is of a frend of his,
How that ye sholde loven oon that hatte Horaste;
For sorwe of which this night shal ben his laste."

Criseide, which that al this wonder herde,
Gan sodeinly aboute hire herte colde,   800
And with a sik she sorwfully answerde,
"Allas! I wende, whoso tales tolde,
My deere herte wolde me nought holde
So lightly fals! Allas! conceites wronge,
What harm they don, for now live I to longe!   805

"Horaste! allas, and falsen Troilus?
I knowe him nought, God helpe me so," quod she.
"Allas, what wicked spirit tolde him thus?
Now certes, em, tomorwe, and I him se,
I shal therof as ful excusen me,   810
As evere dide womman, if him like."
And with that word she gan ful soore sike.

785 *stant*, stands; *sith*, since   786 *platly*, flatly
787 *goter*, gutter; *prive wente*, secret passage   789 *unwist*, unknown
790 *wisly*, surely   791 *shal*, owe
793 *but*, unless; *wood*, insane; *this*, i.e., this time
794 *mot*, must; *wodnesse*, madness
797 *hatte*, is named   800 *colde*, to chill
801 *sik*, sigh   802 *wende*, thought
809 *and*, if   811 *like*, it pleases
812 *sike*, to sigh

"O God!" quod she, "so worldly selinesse,
Which clerkes callen fals felicitee,
Ymedled is with many a bitternesse!   815
Ful anguissous than is, God woot," quod she,
"Condicioun of vein prosperitee;
For either joyes comen nought yfeere,
Or elles no wight hath hem alwey here.

"O brotel wele of mannes joye unstable!   820
With what wight so thou be, or how thou pleye,
Either he woot that thou, joye, art muable,
Or woot it nought; it mot ben oon of tweye.
Now if he woot it nought, how may he seye
That he hath verray joye and selinesse,   825
That is of ignoraunce ay in derknesse?

"Now if he woot that joye is transitorye,
As every joye of worldly thing mot flee,
Than every time he that hath in memorye,
The drede of lesing maketh him that he   830
May in no perfit selinesse be;
And if to lese his joye he sette a mite,
Than semeth it that joye is worth ful lite.

"Wherfore I wol diffine in this matere,
That trewely, for aught I can espye,   835
Ther is no verray weele in this world heere.
But O thou wicked serpent, jalousye,
Thou misbileved and envious folye,
Why hastou Troilus mad to me untriste,
That nevere yet agilt him, that I wiste?"   840

813 *selinesse*, happiness   815 *ymedled*, mingled
816 *anguissous*, anguished   818 *yfeere*, together
820 *brotel*, brittle; *wele*, weal   822 *muable*, mutable
823 *mot*, must; *tweye*, two   830 *lesing*, loss
831 *perfit*, perfect   832 *lese*, lose; *sette a mite*, i.e., cares at all
833 *lite*, little   834 *diffine*, state definitely
839 *mad*, made; *untriste*, distrustful   840 *agilt*, wronged

Quod Pandarus, "Thus fallen is this cas—"
"Why, uncle min," quod she, "who tolde him this?
Why doth my deere herte thus, allas?"
"Ye woot, ye, nece min," quod he, "what is.
I hope al shal be wel that is amis;   845
For ye may quenche al this, if that you leste.
And doth right so, for I holde it the beste."

"So shal I do to-morwe, ywis," quod she,
"And God toforn, so that it shal suffise."
"To-morwe? allas, that were a fair!" quod he.   850
"Nay, nay, it may nat stonden in this wise.
For, nece min, thus writen clerkes wise,
That peril is with drecching in ydrawe;
Nay, swiche abodes ben nought worth an hawe.

"Nece, alle thing hath time, I dar avowe,   855
For whan a chaumbre afire is, or an halle,
Wel more nede is, it sodeinly rescoue
Than to dispute and axe amonges alle
How this candele in the strawe is falle.
A, *benedicite!* for al among that fare   860
The harm is don, and fare-wel feldefare!

"And nece min, ne take it naught agrief,
If that ye suffre him al night in this wo,
God help me so, ye hadde him nevere lief,—
That dar I seyn, now ther is but we two.   865
But wel I woot that ye wol nat do so;
Ye ben to wis to doon so gret folye,
To putte his lif al night in jupertye."

846 *leste,* please   849 *God toforn,* before God
850 *a fair,* i.e., a fine thing
853 *with drecching in ydrawe,* increased by procrastination
854 *abodes,* delays   857 *sodeinly,* straightway; *rescoue,* rescue
858 *axe,* ask   860 *al among that fare,* while that is going on
861 *fare-wel feldefare,* i.e., the bird has flown   862 *agrief,* amiss
864 *hadde,* held; *lief,* beloved   868 *jupertye,* jeopardy

"Hadde I him nevere lief? by God, I weene
Ye hadde nevere thing so lief!" quod she.   870
"Now by my thrift," quod he, "that shal be seene!
For sin ye make this ensaumple of me,
If ich al night wolde him in sorwe se,
For al the tresour in the town of Troye,
I bidde God I nevere mote have joye.   875

"Now loke thanne, if ye that ben his love
Shul putte his lif al night in jupertye
For thing of nought, now, by that God above,
Naught oonly this delay comth of folye,
But of malice, if that I shal naught lie.   880
What! platly, and ye suffre him in destresse,
Ye neither bounte don ne gentilesse."

Quod tho Criseide, "Wol ye don o thing,
And ye therwith shal stinte al his disese?
Have heere, and bereth him this blewe ring,   885
For ther is nothing mighte him bettre plese,
Save I myself, ne more his herte apese;
And sey my deere herte, that his sorwe
Is causeles, that shal be sene to-morwe."

"A ring?" quod he, "ye, haselwodes shaken!   890
Ye, nece min, that ring moste han a stoon
That mighte dede men alive maken;
And swich a ring trowe I that ye have non.
Discrecioun out of youre hed is gon;
That fele I now," quod he, "and that is routhe.   895
O time ylost, wel maystou corsen slouthe!

---

869 *weene*, think
872 *sin*, since
875 *bidde*, pray to; *mote*, may
883 *tho*, then; *o*, one
885 *have*, i.e., take
895 *routhe*, a pity

871 *thrift*, welfare
873 *ich*, I
881 *platly*, flatly; *and*, if
884 *stinte*, stop; *disese*, trouble
891 *moste*, must
896 *corsen*, curse; *slouthe*, sloth

"Woot ye not wel that noble and heigh corage
Ne sorweth nought, ne stinteth ek, for lite?
But if a fool were in a jalous rage,
I nolde setten at his sorwe a mite,   900
But feffe him with a fewe wordes white
Anothir day, whan that I mighte him finde;
But this thing stant al in another kinde.

"This is so gentil and so tendre of herte,
That with his deth he wol his sorwes wreke;   905
For trusteth wel, how sore that him smerte,
He wol to you no jalous wordes speke.
And forthy, nece, er that his herte breke,
So speke youreself to him of this matere;
For with o word ye may his herte stere.   910

"Now have I told what peril he is inne,
And his cominge unwist is to every wight;
Ne, parde, harm may ther be non, ne sinne;
I wol myself be with you al this night.
Ye knowe ek how it is youre owen knight,   915
And that by right ye moste upon him triste,
And I al prest to fecche him whan you liste."

This accident so pitous was to here,
And ek so like a sooth, at prime face,
And Troilus hire knight to hir so deere,   920
His prive coming, and the siker place,
That, though that she did him as thanne a grace,
Considered alle thinges as they stoode,
No wonder is, sin she did al for goode.

897 *corage,* heart   898 *lite,* little
900: i.e., I would not account his sorrow of any importance
901 *feffe,* endow; *white,* i.e., plausible   902 *stant,* stands
905 *wreke,* banish   908 *forthy,* therefore
910 *o,* one; *stere,* control   912 *unwist,* unknown
916 *moste,* must; *triste,* trust   917 *prest,* ready
921 *siker,* secure   924 *sin,* since

Criseide answerde, "As wisly God at reste   925
My soule bringe, as me is for him wo!
And, em, ywis, fain wolde I don the beste,
If that ich hadde grace to do so.
But whether that ye dwelle or for him go
I am, til God me bettre minde sende,   930
At dulcarnoun, right at my wittes ende."

Quod Pandarus, "Yee, nece, wol ye here?
Dulcarnoun called is 'fleming of wrecches.'
It semeth hard, for wrecches wol nought lere,
For verray slouthe or other wilfull tecches;   935
This seid by hem that ben nought worth two fecches.
But ye ben wis, and that we han on honde
Nis neither hard, ne skilful to withstonde."

"Than em," quod she, "doth herof as you list.
But er he com, I wil up first arise,   940
And, for the love of God, sin al my trist
Is on you two, and ye ben bothe wise,
So werketh now in so discret a wise
That I honour may have, and he plesaunce;
For I am here al in youre governaunce."   945

"That is wel seid," quod he, "my nece deere.
Ther good thrift on that wise gentil herte!
But liggeth stille, and taketh him right here;
It nedeth nought no ferther for him sterte.
And ech of you ese otheres sorwes smerte,   950
For love of God; and Venus, I thee herye;
For soone hope I we shul ben alle merye."

925 *wisly,* surely   931 *at dulcarnoun,* i.e., at an impasse
933 *fleming of wrecches,* Lat. *fuga miserorum,* the name for a diffi-
     cult proposition in geometry   934 *lere,* learn
935 *tecches,* defects   936 *this,* i.e., this is; *fecches,* beans
938 *nis neither,* is neither; *skilful,* reasonable
947: i.e., may prosperity come to that wise gentle heart
948 *liggeth,* lie   949 *sterte,* move
951 *herye,* praise

This Troilus ful soone on knees him sette
Ful sobrely, right be hire beddes hed,
And in his beste wise his lady grette.   955
But, Lord, so she wex sodeinliche red!
Ne though men sholde smiten of hire hed,
She couthe nought a word aright out bringe
So sodeinly, for his sodein cominge.

But Pandarus, that so wel coude feele   960
In every thing, to pleye anon bigan,
And seide, "Nece, se how this lord can knele!
Now, for youre trouthe, se this gentil man!"
And with that word he for a quisshen ran,
And seide, "Kneleth now, while that you leste,   965
There God youre hertes bringe soone at reste!"

Can I naught seyn, for she bad him nought rise,
If sorwe it putte out of hire remembraunce,
Or elles that she took it in the wise
Of dewete, as for his observaunce;   970
But wel finde I she dede him this plesaunce,
That she him kiste, although she siked sore,
And bad him sitte adown withouten more.

Quod Pandarus, "Now wol ye wel biginne.
Now doth him sitte, goode nece deere,   975
Upon youre beddes side al ther withinne,
That ech of you the bet may other heere."
And with that word he drow him to the feere,
And took a light, and fond his contenaunce,
As for to looke upon an old romaunce.   980

Criseide, that was Troilus lady right,
And cler stood on a ground of sikernesse,

955 *grette,* greeted   964 *quisshen,* cushion
970 *dewete,* duty   971 *dede,* did
972 *siked,* sighed   975 *doth,* make
977 *bet,* better   978 *drow him,* withdrew; *feere,* fire
979 *fond his contenance,* assumed an attitude   982 *sikernesse,* security

Al thoughte she hire servant and hire knight
Ne sholde of right non untrouthe in hire gesse,
Yet natheles, considered his distresse,   985
And that love is in cause of swich folye,
Thus to him spak she of his jalousye:

"Lo, herte min, as wolde the excellence
Of love, ayeins the which that no man may
Ne oughte ek goodly make resistence;   990
And ek bicause I felte wel and say
Youre grete trouthe and servise every day,
And that youre herte al min was, soth to seyne,
This drof me for to rewe upon youre peine.

"And youre goodnesse have I founde alwey yit,   995
Of which, my deere herte and al my knight,
I thonke it you, as fer as I have wit,
Al can I nought as muche as it were right;
And I, emforth my conning and my might,
Have and ay shal, how sore that me smerte,   1000
Ben to you trewe and hool with al min herte;

"And dredeles, that shal be founde at preve.
But, herte min, what al this is to seyne
Shal wel be told, so that ye nought you greve,
Though I to you right on yourself compleine.   1005
For therwith mene I finaly the peine
That halt youre herte and min in hevinesse
Fully to slen, and every wrong redresse.

"My goode min, noot I for-why ne how
That jalousye, allas! that wicked wivere,   1010

983 *al*, although   991 *say*, saw
994 *drof*, drove   995 *yit*, still
999 *emforth*, according to   1001 *hool*, whole
1002 *dredeles*, doubtless; *preve*, proof   1007 *halt*, holds
1008 *slen*, slay   1009 *min*, mine; *noot*, know not
1010 *wivere*, snake

Thus causeles is cropen into you,
The harm of which I wolde fain delivere.
Allas, that he, al hool, or of him slivere,
Shuld han his refut in so digne a place,
Ther Jove him soone out of youre herte arace!   1015

"But O, thou Jove, O auctour of nature,
Is this an honour to thy deite,
That folk ungiltif suffren hire injure,
And who that giltif is, al quit goth he?
O, were it leful for to plein on thee,   1020
That undeserved suffrest jalousye,
Of that I wolde upon thee pleine and crye!

"Ek al my wo is this, that folk now usen
To seyn right thus, 'Ye, jalousye is love!'
And wolde a busshel venim al excusen,   1025
For that o grein of love is on it shove.
But that woot heighe God that sit above,
If it be likkere love, or hate, or grame;
And after that, it oughte bere his name.

"But certein is, som manere jalousye   1030
Is excusable more than som, ywis;
As whan cause is, and som swich fantasye
With piete so wel repressed is
That it unnethe doth or seith amis,
But goodly drinketh up al his distresse;   1035
And that excuse I, for the gentilesse.

1011 *cropen*, crept   1013 *hool*, whole; *slivere*, part
1014 *refut*, refuge; *digne*, honorable
1015 *ther*, i.e., may; *arace*, pluck   1018 *ungiltif*, guiltless; *hire*, their
1019 *quit*, unpunished   1020 *leful*, lawful; *pleine*, complain
1021: i.e., that permit unwarranted jealousy to exist
1023 *usen*, are accustomed   1026 *o*, one; *shove*, i.e., laid
1028 *likkere*, more like; *grame*, wrath   1033 *piete*, pity
1034 *unnethe*, scarcely

"And som so ful of furye is and despit
That it sourmounteth his repressioun.
But, herte min, ye be nat in that plit,
That thonke I God; for which youre passioun   1040
I wol nought calle it but illusioun,
Of habundaunce of love and besy cure,
That doth youre herte this disese endure.

"Of which I am right sory, but nought wroth;
But, for my devoir and youre hertes reste,   1045
Wherso you list, by ordal or by oth,
By sort, or in what wise so you leste,
For love of God, lat preve it for the beste;
And if that I be giltif, do me deye!
Allas, what might I more don or seye?"   1050

With that a fewe brighte teris newe
Out of hire eighen fille, and thus she seide,
"Now God, thou woost, in thought ne dede untrewe
To Troilus was nevere yet Criseide."
With that here heed down in the bed she leide,   1055
And with the sheete it wreigh, and sighte soore,
And held hire pees; nought o word spak she more.

But now help God to quenchen al this sorwe!
So hope I that he shal, for he best may.
For I have sein, of a ful misty morwe   1060
Folowen ful ofte a mirye someris day;
And after winter foloweth grene May.
Men sen alday, and reden ek in stories,
That after sharpe showres ben victories.

1039 *plit*, plight   1042 *cure*, care
1043 *doth*, makes   1045 *devoir*, duty
1046 *ordal*, ordeal   1047 *sort*, lot; *leste*, please
1048 *preve*, prove   1049 *do me deye*, put me to death
1052 *fille*, fell   1056 *wreigh*, covered; *sighte*, sighed
1060 *sein*, seen; *morwe*, morning   1063 *alday*, constantly
1064 *showres*, battles

This Troilus, whan he hire wordes herde,   1065
Have ye no care, him liste nought to slepe;
For it thought him no strokes of a yerde
To heere or seen Criseide, his lady, wepe;
But wel he felt aboute his herte crepe,
For every tere which that Criseide asterte,   1070
The crampe of deth, to streine him by the herte.

And in his minde he gan the time acorse
That he com there, and that he was born;
For now is wicke torned into worse,
And al that labour he hath don biforn,   1075
He wende it lost; he thoughte he nas but lorn.
"O Pandarus," thoughte he, "allas, thy wile
Serveth of nought, so weilaway the while!"

And therwithal he heng adown the heed,
And fil on knees, and sorwfully he sighte.   1080
What mighte he seyn? He felte he nas but deed,
For wroth was she that sholde his sorwes lighte.
But natheles, whan that he speken mighte,
Than seide he thus, "God woot that of this game,
Whan al is wist, than am I nought to blame."   1085

Therwith the sorwe so his herte shette,
That from his eyen fil ther nought a tere,
And every spirit his vigour in knette,
So they astoned or oppressed were.
The feling of his sorwe, or of his fere,   1090
Or of aught elles, fled was out of towne;
And down he fel al sodeinly a-swoune.

1067 *it thought him,* he thought it; *yerde,* rod
1070 *asterte,* escaped from   1072 *acorse,* accurse
1074 *wicke,* evil   1076 *wende,* thought; *nas but lorn,* was lost
1079 *heng,* hung   1080 *fil,* fell
1081 *nas but deed,* was dead   1086 *shette,* closed off
1088: i.e., and each of his vital spirits contracted its vigor
1089 *astoned,* stunned   1092 *a-swoune,* swooning

This was no litel sorwe for to se;
But al was hust, and Pandare up as faste,
"O nece, pes, or we be lost!" quod he,   1095
"Beth naught agast!" But certein, at the laste,
For this or that, he into bed him caste,
And seide, "O thef, is this a mannes herte?"
And of he rente al to his bare sherte;

And seide, "Nece, but ye helpe us now,   1100
Allas, youre owen Troilus is lorn!"
"Ywis, so wolde I, and I wiste how,
Ful fain!" quod she, "Allas, that I was born!"
"Yee, nece, wol ye pullen out the thorn
That stiketh in his herte," quod Pandare,   1105
"Sey 'al foryeve,' and stint is al this fare!"

"Ye, that to me," quod she, "ful levere were
Than al the good the sonne aboute gooth."
And therwithal she swor him in his ere,
"Ywis, my deere herte, I am nought wroth,   1110
Have here my trouthe!" and many an other oth;
"Now speke to me, for it am I, Criseide!"
But al for nought; yit might he nought abreide.

Therwith his pous and paumes of his hondes
They gan to frote, and wete his temples tweine;   1115
And to deliveren him fro bittre bondes,
She ofte him kiste; and shortly for to seyne,
Him to revoken she did al hire peine.
And at the laste, he gan his breth to drawe,
And of his swough sone after that adawe,   1120

1094 *hust*, hushed   1099 *of*, off
1101 *lorn*, lost   1102 *and*, if
1106 *al foryeve*, all is forgiven; *stint*, ended
1113 *abreide*, come to his senses   1114 *pous*, pulse; *paumes*, palms
1115 *frote*, rub   1118 *revoken*, recall to his senses
1120 *swough*, swoon; *adawe*, awake

And gan bet minde and reson to him take,
But wonder soore he was abaist, ywis.
And with a sik, whan he gan bet awake,
He seide, "O mercy, God, what thing is this?"
"Why do ye with youreselven thus amis?"   1125
Quod tho Criseide. "Is this a mannes game?
What, Troilus, wol ye do thus for shame?"

And therwithal hire arm over him she leide,
And al foryaf, and ofte time him keste.
He thonked hire, and to hire spak, and seide   1130
As fil to purpos for his hertes reste;
And she to that answerde him as hire leste,
And with hire goodly wordes him disporte
She gan, and ofte his sorwes to comforte.

Quod Pandarus, "For aught I can aspyen,   1135
This light, nor I, ne serven here of nought.
Light is nought good for sike folkes yën!
But, for the love of God, sin ye ben brought
In thus good plit, lat now no hevy thought
Ben hanging in the hertes of you tweye"—   1140
And bar the candele to the chimeneye.

Soone after this, though it no nede were,
Whan she swiche othes as hire leste devise
Hadde of him take, hire thoughte tho no fere,
Ne cause ek non, to bidde him thennes rise.   1145
Yet lasse thing than othes may suffise
In many a cas; for every wight, I gesse,
That loveth wel, meneth but gentilesse.

1121 *bet*, better   1122 *abaist*, abashed
1123 *sik*, sigh   1129 *foryaf*, forgave; *keste*, kissed
1131 *fil*, fell   1133 *disporte*, cheer
1137 *sike*, sick; *yen*, eyes   1140 *tweye*, two
1141 *bar*, bore; *chimeneye*, fireplace

But in effect she wolde wit anon
Of what man, and ek wheer, and also why   1150
He jalous was, sin ther was cause non;
And ek the signe that he took it by,
She badde him that to telle hire bisily;
Or elles, certein, she bar him on honde
That this was done of malice, hire to fonde.   1155

Withouten more, shortly for to seyne,
He most obeye unto his lady heste;
And for the lasse harm, he moste feine.
He seide hire, whan she was at swich a feste,
She might on him han loked at the leste,—   1160
Noot I nought what, al deere ynough a risshe,
As he that nedes most a cause fisshe.

And she answerde, "Swete, al were it so,
What harm was that, sin I non ivel mene?
For, by that God that bought us bothe two,   1165
In alle thing is min entente cleene.
Swiche argumentes ne ben naught worth a beene.
Wol ye the childissh jalous contrefete?
Now were it worthy that ye were ybete."

Tho Troilus gan sorwfully to sike;   1170
Lest she be wroth, him thoughte his herte deide;
And seide, "Allas, upon my sorwes sike
Have mercy, swete herte min, Criseide!
And if that in tho wordes that I seide
Be any wrong, I wol no more trespace.   1175
Doth what you list, I am al in youre grace."

1149 *wolde wit,* would have knowledge
1154 *bar him on honde,* accused him   1155 *fonde,* test
1157 *heste,* command   1158 *feine,* pretend
1161 *noot I,* I don't know; *al deere . . . risshe,* i.e., of no importance
1164 *ivel,* evil   1168 *contrefete,* imitate
1169 *ybete,* beaten   1170 *sike,* sigh
1172 *sike,* sickly

And she answerde, "Of gilt misericorde!
That is to seyn, that I foryeve al this.
And evere more on this night you recorde,
And beth wel war ye do namore amis."   1180
"Nay, dere herte min," quod he, "ywis!"
"And now," quod she, "that I have don you smerte,
Foryeve it me, min owene swete herte."

This Troilus, with blisse of that supprised,
Putte al in Goddes hand, as he that mente   1185
Nothing but wel; and sodeinly avised,
He hire in armes faste to him hente.
And Pandarus, with a ful good entente,
Leide him to slepe, and seide, "If ye be wise,
Swouneth nought now, lest more folk arise!"   1190

What mighte or may the sely larke seye,
Whan that the sperhawk hath it in his foot?
I can namore, but of thise ilke tweye,—
To whom this tale sucre be or soot,—
Though that I tarye a yer, somtime I moot,   1195
After min auctour, tellen hire gladnesse,
As wel as I have told hire hevinesse.

Criseide, which that felte hire thus ytake,
As writen clerkes in hire bokes olde,
Right as an aspes leef she gan to quake,   1200
Whan she him felte hire in his armes folde.
But Troilus, al hool of cares colde,
Gan thanken tho the blisful goddes sevene.
Thus sondry peines bringen folk to hevene.

1177 *of gilt misericorde*, i.e., mercy exists for guilt
1179 *you recorde*, remember
1186 *avised*, i.e., clear-headed
1190 *swouneth*, swoon
1192 *sperhawk*, sparrowhawk
1194 *sucre*, sugar
1198 *hire*, herself
1200 *aspes*, aspen
1182 *don*, made
1187 *hente*, took
1191 *sely*, poor
1193 *ilke tweye*, same two
1195 *moot*, must
1199 *hire*, their
1202 *hool*, well

This Troilus in armes gan hire streine,　　　　　1205
And seide, "O swete, as evere mot I gon,
Now be ye caught, now is ther but we tweine!
Now yeldeth you, for other bote is non!"
To that Criseide answerde thus anon,
"Ne hadde I er now, my swete herte deere,　　　1210
Ben yold, ywis, I were now nought heere!"

O, sooth is seid, that heled for to be
As of a fevre, or other gret siknesse,
Men moste drinke, as men may ofte se,
Ful bittre drinke; and for to han gladnesse,　　1215
Men drinken ofte peine and gret distresse;
I mene it here, as for this aventure,
That thorugh a peine hath founden al his cure.

And now swetnesse semeth more swete,
That bitternesse assayed was biforn;　　　　　　1220
For out of wo in blisse now they flete;
Non swich they felten sin that they were born.
Now is this bet than bothe two be lorn.
For love of God, take every womman heede
To werken thus, if it comth to the neede.　　　　1225

Criseide, al quit from every drede and tene,
As she that juste cause hadde him to triste,
Made him swich feste, it joye was to seene,
Whan she his trouthe and clene entente wiste;
And as aboute a tree, with many a twiste,　　　1230
Bitrent and writh the swote wodebinde,
Gan ech of hem in armes other winde.

1205 *streine*, press
1206 *mot I gon*, may I walk
1208 *bote*, remedy
1211 *yold*, yielded
1220 *that*, because
1221 *flete*, float
1223 *bet*, better; *lorn*, lost
1226 *tene*, grief
1227 *triste*, trust
1231 *bitrent*, encircles; *writh*, twines

And as the newe abaised nightingale,
That stinteth first whan she biginneth to singe,
Whan that she hereth any herde tale, 1235
Or in the hegges any wight stiringe,
And after siker doth hire vois out ringe,
Right so Criseide, whan hire drede stente,
Opned hire herte, and tolde him hire entente.

And right as he that seth his deth yshapen, 1240
And dien mot, in ought that he may gesse,
And sodeinly rescous doth him escapen,
And from his deth is brought in sikernesse,
For al this world, in swich present gladnesse
Was Troilus, and hath his lady swete. 1245
With worse hap God lat us nevere mete!

Hire armes smale, hire streghte bak and softe,
Hire sides longe, flesshly, smothe, and white
He gan to stroke, and good thrift bad ful ofte
Hire snowisshe throte, hire brestes rounde and lite: 1250
Thus in this hevene he gan him to delite,
And therwithal a thousand time hire kiste,
That what to don, for joye unnethe he wiste.

Than seide he thus, "O Love, O Charite!
Thy moder ek, Cytherea the swete, 1255
After thyself next heried be she,
Venus mene I, the wel-willy planete!
And next that, Ymeneus, I thee grete;
For nevere man was to you goddes holde
As I, which ye han brought fro cares colde. 1260

1233 *newe abaised*, suddenly shy	1234 *stinteth*, pauses
1235 *herde tale*, shepherd speak	1237 *siker*, confident
1238 *stente*, ended	1240 *seth*, sees
1241 *mot*, must	1242 *rescous doth*, rescue causes
1243 *sikernesse*, safety	1249 *good thrift bad*, i.e., blessed
1250 *lite*, small	1253 *unnethe he wiste*, he scarcely knew
1256 *heried*, praised	1257 *wel-willy*, propitious
1259 *holde*, beholden	

"Benigne Love, thou holy bond of thinges,
Whoso wol grace, and list thee nought honouren,
Lo, his desir wol fle withouten winges.
For noldestou of bounte hem socouren
That serven best and most alwey labouren,   1265
Yet were al lost, that dar I wel seyn certes,
But if thy grace passed oure desertes.

"And for thou me, that leest coude disserve
Of hem that noumbred ben unto thy grace,
Hast holpen, ther I likly was to sterve,   1270
And me bistowed in so heigh a place
That thilke boundes may no blisse pace,
I can namore; but laude and reverence
Be to thy bounte and thin excellence!"

And therwithal Criseide anon he kiste,   1275
Of which certein she felte no disese.
And thus seide he, "Now wolde God I wiste,
Min herte swete, how I you might plese!
What man," quod he, "was evere thus at ese
As I, on which the faireste and the beste   1280
That evere I say, deineth hire herte reste?

"Here may men seen that mercy passeth right;
Th'experience of that is felt in me,
That am unworthy to so swete a wight.
But herte min, of youre benignite,   1285
So thinketh, though that I unworthy be,
Yet mot I nede amenden in some wise,
Right thorugh the vertu of youre heigh servise.

1262 *wol*, wants   1264 *noldestou*, if you would not
1267 *but if*, unless   1268 *for*, because
1270 *sterve*, die   1272 *pace*, surpass
1276 *disese*, displeasure   1281 *say*, saw
1287 *mot*, must

"And for the love of God, my lady deere,
Sin God hath wrought me for I shall you serve,— 1290
As thus I mene, he wol ye be my steere,
To do me live, if that you liste, or sterve,—
So techeth me how that I may disserve
Youre thonk, so that I thorugh min ignoraunce,
Ne do no thing that you be displesaunce.   1295

"For certes, fresshe wommanliche wif,
This dar I seye, that trouth and diligence,
That shal ye finden in me al my lif;
N'I wol nat, certein, breken youre defence;
And if I do, present or in absence,   1300
For love of God, lat sle me with the dede,
If that it like unto youre wommanhede."

"Ywis," quod she, "min owen hertes list,
My ground of ese, and al min herte deere,
Gramercy, for on that is al my trist!   1305
But lat us falle awey fro this matere,
For it suffiseth, this that seid is heere,
And at o word, withouten repentaunce,
Welcome, my knight, my pees, my suffisaunce!"

Of hire delit, or joyes oon the leeste,   1310
Were impossible to my wit to seye;
But juggeth ye that han ben at the feste
Of swich gladnesse, if that hem liste pleye!
I can namore, but thus thise ilke tweye,
That night, bitwixen drede and sikernesse,   1315
Felten in love the grete worthinesse.

1291 *he wol . . . steere,* he wants you to be my guide
1292 *do,* make   1299 *defence,* prohibition
1300 *sle,* slay   1303 *list,* desire
1305 *trist,* trust   1310 *hire,* their; *oon the leeste,* the least one
1315 *sikernesse,* certainty

O blisful night, of hem so longe ysought,
How blithe unto hem bothe two thou weere!
Why nad I swich oon with my soule ybought,
Ye, or the leeste joye that was theere?   1320
Awey, thou foule daunger and thou feere,
And lat hem in this hevene blisse dwelle,
That is so heigh that al ne can I telle!

But soth is, though I can nat tellen al,
As can min auctour, of his excellence,   1325
Yet have I seid, and God toforn, and shal
In every thing, al holy his sentence;
And if that ich, at Loves reverence,
Have any word in eched for the beste,
Doth therwithal right as youreselven leste.   1330

For mine wordes, heere and every part,
I speke hem alle under correccioun
Of you that feling han in loves art,
And putte it al in youre discrecioun
To encresse or maken diminucioun   1335
Of my langage, and that I you biseche.
But now to purpos of my rather speche.

Thise ilke two, that ben in armes laft,
So loth to hem asonder gon it were,
That ech from other wenden ben biraft,   1340
Or elles, lo, this was hir mooste feere,
That al this thing but nice dremes were;
For which ful ofte ech of hem seide, "O swete,
Clippe ich you thus, or elles I it meete?"

1319 *nad*, had not   1321 *daunger*, disdain
1327 *holy*, wholly; *sentence*, meaning   1328 *ich*, I
1329 *in eched*, added   1330 *leste*, please
1337 *rather speche*, former topic   1338 *laft*, left
1340 *wenden*, thought to   1341 *mooste feere*, greatest fear
1342 *nice*, empty   1344 *clippe*, embrace; *meete*, dream

And Lord! so he gan goodly on hire se,   1345
That nevere his look ne bleinte from hire face,
And seide, "O deere herte, may it be
That it be soth, that ye ben in this place?"
"Yee, herte min, God thank I of his grace,"
Quod tho Criseide, and therwithal him kiste,   1350
That where his spirit was, for joye he niste.

This Troilus ful ofte hire eyen two
Gan for to kisse, and seide, "O eyen clere,
It weren ye that wroughte me swich wo,
Ye humble nettes of my lady deere!   1355
Though ther be mercy writen in youre cheere,
God woot, the text ful hard is, soth, to finde!
How coude ye withouten bond me binde?"

Therwith he gan hire faste in armes take,
And wel an hondred times gan he sike,   1360
Naught swiche sorwfull sikes as men make
For wo, or elles when that folk ben sike,
But esy sikes, swiche as ben to like,
That shewed his affeccioun withinne;
Of swiche sikes coude he nought bilinne.   1365

Soone after this they spake of sondry thinges,
As fel to purpos of this aventure,
And pleyinge, entrechaungeden hire ringes,
Of whiche I can nought tellen no scripture;
But wel I woot, a broche, gold and asure,   1370
In which a ruby set was lik an herte,
Criseide him yaf, and stak it on his sherte.

1345 *se,* look
1351 *niste,* knew not
1360 *sike,* sigh
1362 *sike,* sick
1365 *bilinne,* cease
1372 *yaf,* gave; *stak,* pinned

1346 *bleinte,* turned aside
1356 *cheere,* expression
1361 *sikes,* sighs
1363 *to like,* pleasing
1369 *scripture,* motto

Lord, trowe ye a coveitous or a wrecche,
That blameth love, and halt of it despit,
That of tho pens that he can mokre and crecche   1375
Was evere yit yyeven him swich delit
As is in love, in o point, in som plit?
Nay, douteles, for also God me save,
So perfit joye may no nigard have.

They wol seyn "yis," but Lord! so that they lie,   1380
Tho besy wrecches, ful of wo and drede!
They callen love a woodnesse or folye,
But it shall falle hem as I shal you rede;
They shal forgon the white and ek the rede,
And live in wo, ther God yeve hem meschaunce,   1385
And every lovere in his trouthe avaunce!

As wolde God tho wrecches that dispise
Servise of love hadde eris also longe
As hadde Mida, ful of coveitise,
And therto dronken hadde as hoot and stronge   1390
As Crassus dide for his affectis wronge,
To techen hem that they ben in the vice,
And loveres nought, although they holde hem nice.

Thise ilke two, of whom that I you seye,
Whan that hire hertes wel assured were,   1395
Tho gonne they to speken and to pleye,
And ek rehercen how, and whan, and where
They knewe hem first, and every wo and feere
That passed was; but al swich hevinesse,
I thank it God, was torned to gladnesse.   1400

1373 *trowe ye*, do you think; *a coveitous*, a miser
1374 *halt . . . despit*, holds it in despite
1375 *tho pens*, those pennies; *mokre*, hoard; *crecche*, scrape together
1376 *yit*, yet; *yyeven*, given   1377 *o*, one
1378 *also*, so   1379 *perfit*, perfect
1380 *yis*, yes   1382 *woodnesse*, madness
1383 *rede*, declare   1385 *yeve*, give
1388 *eris*, ears; *also*, as   1389 *coveitise*, avarice
1391 *affectis*, desires   1393 *nice*, foolish

And evere mo, when that hem fel to speke
Of any wo of swich a time agoon,
With kissing al that tale sholde breke,
And fallen in a newe joye anoon;
And diden al hire might, sin they were oon,   1405
For to recoveren blisse and ben at eise,
And passed wo with joye contrepeise.

Resoun wol nought that I speke of slep,
For it acordeth nought to my matere.
God woot, they took of that ful litel kep!   1410
But lest this night, that was to hem so deere,
Ne sholde in vein escape in no manere,
It was biset in joye and bisinesse
Of al that souneth into gentilesse.

But whan the cok, comune astrologer,   1415
Gan on his brest to bete and after crowe,
And Lucifer, the dayes messager,
Gan for to rise, and out hire bemes throwe,
And estward roos, to him that coude it knowe,
Fortuna Major, that anoon Criseide,   1420
With herte soor, to Troilus thus seide:

"Min hertes lif, my trist, and my plesaunce,
That I was born, allas, what me is wo,
That day of us moot make disseveraunce!
For time it is to rise and hennes go,   1425
Or ellis I am lost for evere mo!
O night, allas! why niltou over us hove,
As longe as whan Almena lay by Jove?

1402 *agoon,* gone by   1403 *breke,* interrupt
1407 *contrepeise,* counterbalance   1408 *wol,* wills
1410 *kep,* heed   1413 *biset,* employed
1414 *souneth into,* relates to   1422 *trist,* trust
1424 *moot,* must   1425 *hennes,* hence
1427 *niltou hove,* will you not linger

"O blake night, as folk in bokes rede,
That shapen art by God this world to hide   1430
At certein times with thy derke wede,
That under that men mighte in reste abide,
Wel oughten bestes pleine, and folk thee chide,
That there as day with labour wolde us breste,
That thou thus fleest, and deinest us nought reste.   1435

"Thou doost, allas, to shortly thin office,
Thou rakle night, ther God, maker of kinde,
Thee, for thin haste and thin unkinde vice,
So faste ay to oure hemisperye binde,
That nevere more under the ground thou winde!   1440
For now, for thou so hiest out of Troye,
Have I forgon thus hastily my joye!"

This Troilus, that with tho wordes felte,
As thoughte him tho, for piëtous distresse,
The blody teris from his herte melte,   1445
As he that nevere yet swich hevinesse
Assayed hadde, out of so gret gladnesse,
Gan therwithal Criseide, his lady deere,
In armes streine, and seide in this manere:

"O cruel day, accusour of the joye   1450
That night and love han stole and faste ywrien,
Acorsed be thy coming into Troye,
For every bore hath oon of thy brighte yën!
Envious day, what list thee so to spyen?
What hastou lost, why sekestou this place?   1455
Ther God thy light so quenche, for his grace.

1433 *bestes,* beasts; *pleine,* complain   1434 *breste,* afflict
1437 *rakle,* hasty; *ther,* i.e., may; *kinde,* nature
1439 *hemisperye,* hemisphere   1440 *winde,* return
1441 *for,* because   1443 *tho,* those
1444 *tho,* then; *pietous,* piteous   1450 *accusour,* betrayer
1451 *ywrien,* hidden   1453 *bore,* chink
1456 *ther,* i.e., may

"Allas! what have thise loveris thee agilt,
Dispitous day? Thin be the peine of helle!
For many a lovere hastou slain, and wilt;
Thy pouringe in wol nowher lat hem dwelle. 1460
What profrestou thy light here for to selle?
Go selle it hem that smale selis grave;
We wol thee nought, us nedeth no day have."

And ek the sonne, Titan, gan he chide,
And seide, "O fool, wel may men thee dispise, 1465
That hast the dawing al night by thy side,
And suffrest hire so soone up fro thee rise,
For to disese loveris in this wise.
What! holde youre bed ther, thou, and ek thy Morwe!
I bidde God, so yeve you bothe sorwe!" 1470

Therwith ful soore he sighte, and thus he seide:
"My lady right, and of my wele or wo
The welle and roote, O goodly min, Criseide,
And shal I rise, allas, and shal I so?
Now fele I that min herte moot a-two. 1475
For how sholde I my lif an houre save,
Sin that with you is al the lif ich have?

"What shal I don? For, certes, I not how,
Ne whan, allas! I shal the time see
That in this plit I may ben eft with you. 1480
And of my lif, God woot how that shall be,
Sin that desir right now so biteth me,
That I am ded anon, but I retourne.
How sholde I longe, allas, fro you sojourne?

1457 *agilt*, wronged   1458 *thin*, thine
1462 *selis*, seals; *grave*, engrave 1463 *wol*, want
1466 *dawing*, dawn   1468 *disese*, discomfit
1470 *bidde*, pray to; *yeve*, give 1471 *sighte*, sighed
1473 *min*, mine   1475 *moot*, i.e., must break
1478 *not*, know not   1480 *eft*, again
1483 *but*, unless

"But natheles, min owen lady bright,   1485
Yit were it so that I wiste outrely
That I, youre humble servant and youre knight,
Were in youre herte yset as fermely
As ye in min, the which thing, trewely,
Me levere were than thise worldes tweine,   1490
Yet sholde I bet enduren al my peine."

To that Criseide answerde right anon,
And with a sik she seide, "O herte deere,
The game, ywis, so forferth now is gon,
That first shal Phebus fallen fro his spere,   1495
And everich egle ben the douves feere,
And every roche out of his place sterte,
Er Troilus out of Criseides herte.

"Ye ben so depe in-with min herte grave,
That, though I wolde it torne out of my thought, 1500
As wisly verray God my soule save,
To dien in the peine, I coude nought.
And, for the love of God that us hath wrought,
Lat in youre brain non other fantasye
So crepe, that it cause me to die!   1505

"And that ye me wolde han as faste in minde
As I have you, that wolde I you biseche;
And if I wiste sothly that to finde,
God mighte nought a point my joyes eche.
But herte min, withouten more speche,   1510
Beth to me trewe, or ellis were it routhe;
For I am thin, by God and by my trouthe!

1486 *outrely*, absolutely   1491 *bet*, better
1493 *sik*, sigh   1494 *forferth*, far
1495 *spere*, sphere   1496 *douves*, dove's; *fere*, mate
1497 *roche*, rock; *sterte*, start   1499 *grave*, buried
1501 *wisly*, surely   1502 *the peine*, torture
1509 *eche*, increase   1512 *thin*, thine

"Beth glad, forthy, and live in sikernesse!
Thus seide I nevere er this, ne shal to mo;
And if to you it were a gret gladnesse   1515
To torne ayein soone after that ye go,
As fain wolde I as ye that it were so,
As wisly God min herte bringe at reste!"
And him in armes tok, and ofte keste.

Agains his wil, sith it mot nedes be,   1520
This Troilus up ros, and faste him cledde,
And in his armes took his lady free
An hondred time, and on his wey him spedde;
And with swiche vois as though his herte bledde,
He seide, "Farewel, dere herte swete,   1525
Ther God us graunte sounde and soone to mete!"

To which no word for sorwe she answerde,
So soore gan his parting hire distreine;
And Troilus unto his paleis ferde,
As wo-bigon as she was, soth to seyne.   1530
So harde him wrong of sharp desir the peine,
For to ben eft there he was in plesaunce,
That it may nevere out of his remembraunce.

Retorned to his real paleis soone,
He softe into his bed gan for to slinke,   1535
To slepe longe, as he was wont to doone.
But al for nought; he may wel ligge and winke,
But slep ne may ther in his herte sinke,
Thinking how she, for whom desir him brende,
A thousand fold was worth more than he wende.   1540

1513 *forthy*, therefore; *sikernesse*, confidence   1514 *mo*, others
1516 *torne*, return   1519 *keste*, kissed
1520 *mot*, must   1521 *cledde*, clad
1526 *ther*, i.e., may   1528 *distreine*, distress
1529 *ferde*, went   1531 *wrong*, wrung
1532 *eft*, again   1534 *real*, royal
1537 *ligge*, lie   1539 *brende*, burned
1540 *wende*, supposed

And in his thought gan up and down to winde
Hire wordes alle, and every countenaunce,
And fermely impressen in his minde
The leeste point that to him was plesaunce;
And verraylich, of thilke remembraunce,   1545
Desir al newe him brende, and lust to brede
Gan more than erst, and yet took he non hede.

Criseide also, right in the same wise,
Of Troilus gan in hire herte shette
His worthinesse, his lust, his dedes wise,   1550
His gentilesse, and how she with him mette,
Thonkinge Love he so wel hire bisette;
Desiring eft to han hire herte deere
In swich a plit, she dorste make him cheere.

Pandare, o-morwe which that comen was   1555
Unto his nece, and gan hire faire grete,
Seide, "Al this night so reined it, allas,
That al my drede is that ye, nece swete,
Han litel laiser had to slepe and mete.
Al night," quod he, "hath rein so do me wake,   1560
That som of us, I trowe, hire hedes ake."

And ner he com, and seide, "How stant it now
This mury morwe? Nece, how can ye fare?"
Criseide answerde, "Nevere the bet for you,
Fox that ye ben! God yeve youre herte care!   1565
God help me so, ye caused al this fare,
Trowe I," quod she, "for al youre wordes white.
O, whoso seeth you, knoweth you ful lite."

1545 *verraylich,* verily   1546–47 *lust . . . gan,* desire began to rise
1547 *erst,* before   1549 *shette,* shut
1552 *bisette,* employed   1555 *o-morwe,* in the morning
1559 *mete,* dream   1560 *do,* made
1562 *stant,* stands   1563 *can,* i.e., do
1564 *bet,* better   1565 *yeve,* give
1567 *white,* i.e., specious   1568, *lite,* little

With that she gan hire face for to wrye
With the shete, and wax for shame al reed;   1570
And Pandarus gan under for to prye,
And seide, "Nece, if that I shal be ded,
Have here a swerd and smiteth of min hed!"
With that his arm al sodeinly he thriste
Under hire necke, and at the laste hire kiste.   1575

I passe al that which chargeth nought to seye.
What! God foryaf his deth, and she al so
Foryaf, and with here uncle gan to pleye,
For other cause was ther noon than so.
But of this thing right to the effect to go,   1580
Whan time was, hom to here hous she wente,
And Pandarus hath fully his entente.

Now torne we ayein to Troilus,
That resteles ful longe abedde lay,
And prively sente after Pandarus,   1585
To him to com in al the haste he may.
He com anon, nought ones seide he nay;
And Troilus ful soberly he grette,
And down upon his beddes side him sette.

This Troilus, with al th'affeccioun   1590
Of frendes love that herte may devise,
To Pandarus on knowes fil adown,
And er that he wolde of the place arise,
He gan him thonken in his beste wise
An hondred sithe, and gan the time blesse   1595
That he was born, to bringe him fro destresse.

He seide, "O frend of frendes the alderbeste
That evere was, the sothe for to telle,

1569 *wrye,* cover   1570 *reed,* red
1574 *thriste,* thrust   1576 *chargeth nought,* is of no importance
1577 *foryaf,* forgave   1588 *grette,* greeted
1592 *knowes,* knees; *fil,* fell   1595 *sithe,* times
1597 *alderbeste,* best of all

Thou hast in hevene ybought my soule at reste
Fro Flegetoun, the fery flood of helle;   1600
That, though I might a thousand times selle,
Upon a day, my lif in thy servise,
It mighte naught a moote in that suffise.

"The sonne, which that al the world may se,
Saugh nevere yet my lif, that dar I leye,   1605
So inly fair and goodly as is she,
Whos I am al, and shal, til that I deye.
And that I thus am hires, dar I seye,
That thanked be the heighe worthinesse
Of Love, and ek thy kinde bisinesse.   1610

"Thus hastou me no litel thing yyive,
For which to thee obliged be for ay
My lif, and why? For thorugh thin help I live,
Or elles ded hadde I ben many a day."
And with that word down in his bed he lay,   1615
And Pandarus ful sobrely him herde
Til al was seid, and than he thus answerde:

"My deere frend, if I have don for thee
In any cas, God wot, it is me lief;
And am as glad as man may of it be,   1620
God help me so; but tak it nat a-grief
That I shal seyn, be war of this meschief,
That, there as thou now brought art in thy blisse,
That thou thyself ne cause it nat to misse.

"For of fortunes sharpe adversitee   1625
The worste kinde of infortune is this,
A man to han ben in prosperitee,

1600 *Flegetoun*, Phlegethon; *fery*, fiery
1605 *saugh*, saw; *leye*, bet
1608 *hires*, hers
1619 *it is me lief*, I am glad of it
1626 *infortune*, misfortune

1603 *moote*, mote
1607 *shal*, i.e., shall be
1611 *yyive*, given
1621 *a-grief*, amiss

And it remembren, whan it passed is.
Th'art wis ynough, forthy do nat amis:
Be naught to rakel, theigh thou sitte warme;   1630
For if thou be, certein, it wol thee harme.

"Thou art at ese, and hold thee wel therinne;
For also seur as reed is every fir,
As gret a craft is kepe wel as winne.
Bridle alwey wel thy speche and thy desir,   1635
For worldly joye halt nought but by a wir.
That preveth wel it brest alday so ofte;
Forthy nede is to werken with it softe."

Quod Troilus, "I hope, and God toforn,
My deere frend, that I shal so me beere,   1640
That in my gilt ther shal nothing be lorn,
N'I nil nought rakle as for to greven heere.
It nedeth naught this matere ofte stere;
For wistestou min herte wel, Pandare,
God woot, of this thou woldest litel care."   1645

Tho gan he telle him of his glade night,
And wherof first his herte dred, and how,
And seide, "Frend, as I am trewe knight,
And by that feith I shal to God and you,
I hadde it nevere half so hote as now;   1650
And ay the more that desir me biteth
To love hire best, the more it me deliteth.

"I not myself naught wisly what it is;
But now I feele a newe qualitee,
Yee, al another than I dide er this."   1655

1629 *forthy,* therefore   1630 *rakel,* rash; *theigh,* though
1633 *also seur,* as surely; *reed,* red   1636 *halt,* holds; *wir,* wire
1637 *preveth,* proves; *brest,* breaks; *alday,* constantly
1640 *me beere,* behave   1641 *in,* through; *lorn,* lost
1642 *n'I nil,* nor will I; *rakle,* behave rashly; *heere,* her
1643 *stere,* bring up   1644 *wistestou,* if you knew
1649 *shal,* owe   1653 *not,* know not; *wisly,* surely

Pandare answerd, and seide thus, that "he
That ones may in hevene blisse be,
He feleth other weyes, dar I leye,
Than thilke time he first herde of it seye."

This is o word for al; this Troilus   1660
Was nevere ful to speke of this matere,
And for to preisen unto Pandarus
The bounte of his righte lady deere,
And Pandarus to thanke and maken cheere.
This tale was ay span-newe to biginne,   1665
Til that the night departed hem atwinne.

Soon after this, for that Fortune it wolde,
Ycomen was the blisful time swete
That Troilus was warned that he sholde,
There he was erst, Criseide his lady mete;   1670
For which he felte his herte in joye flete,
And feithfully gan alle the goddes herye;
And lat se now if that he can be merye!

And holden was the forme and all the wise
Of hire comming, and eek of his also,   1675
As it was erst, which nedeth nought devise.
But pleinly to th'effect right for to go,
In joye and suerte Pandarus hem two
Abedde brought, whan that hem bothe leste,
And thus they ben in quiete and in reste.   1680

Nought nedeth it to you, sin they been met,
To axe at me if that they blithe were;
For if it erst was wel, tho was it bet

1658 *leye*, wager   1659 *seye*, spoken
1661 *ful*, i.e., too full   1665 *span-newe*, brand-new
1666 *departed hem atwinne*, separated them   1667 *wolde*, willed
1670 *erst*, before   1671 *flete*, float
1672 *herye*, praise   1678 *suerte*, security
1682 *axe*, ask   1683 *tho*, then; *bet*, better

A thousand fold; this nedeth nought enquere.
Agon was every sorwe and every feere;   1685
And bothe, ywis, they hadde, and so they wende,
As muche joye as herte may comprende.

This is no litel thing of for to seye;
This passeth every wit for to devise;
For ech of hem gan otheres lust obeye.   1690
Felicite, which that thise clerkes wise
Comenden so, ne may nought here suffise;
This joye may nought writen be with inke;
This passeth al that herte may bithinke.

But cruel day, so wailaway the stounde!   1695
Gan for t'aproche, as they by signes knewe;
For which hem thoughte feelen dethis wounde.
So wo was hem that changen gan hire hewe,
And day they gonnen to despise al newe,
Calling it traitour, envious, and worse,   1700
And bitterly the dayes light they corse.

Quod Troilus, "Allas, now am I war
That Pirous and tho swifte steedes thre,
Which that drawen forth the sonnes char,
Han gon som bi-path in dispit of me;   1705
That maketh it so soone day to be;
And, for the sonne him hasteth thus to rise,
Ne shal I nevere don him sacrifise."

But nedes day departe hem moste soone,
And whan hire speche don was and hire cheere,   1710
They twinne anon, as they were wont to doone,

1685 *agon,* passed   1686 *wende,* thought
1688 *seye,* speak   1695 *stounde,* time
1699 *gonnen,* began   1701 *corse,* curse
1704 *char,* chariot   1707 *for,* because
1709 *departe,* separate; *moste,* must   1711 *twinne,* part

And setten time of meting eft yfeere.
And many a night they wroughte in this manere,
And thus Fortune a time ledde in joye
Criseide, and ek this kinges sone of Troye.   1715

In suffisaunce, in blisse, and in singinges,
This Troilus gan al his lif to lede.
He spendeth, jousteth, maketh festeinges;
He yeveth frely ofte, and chaungeth wede,
And held aboute him alwey, out of drede,   1720
A world of folk, as com him wel of kinde,
The fresshest and the beste he coude finde;

That swich a vois was of him and a stevene
Thorughout the world, of honour and largesse,
That it up rong unto the yate of hevene.   1725
And, as in love, he was in swich gladnesse,
That in his herte he demed, as I gesse,
That ther nis lovere in this world at ese
So wel as he; and thus gan love him plese.

The goodlihede or beaute which that kinde   1730
In any other lady hadde yset
Can nought the montance of a knotte unbinde,
Aboute his herte, of al Criseides net.
He was so narwe ymasked and yknet,
That it undon on any manere side,   1735
That nil naught ben, for aught that may bitide.

And by the hond ful ofte he wolde take
This Pandarus, and into gardin lede,

1712 *eft yfeere*, again together   1718 *festeinges*, feastings
1719 *yeveth frely*, gives generously; *wede*, clothes   1720 *held*, kept
1721 *as com . . . kinde*, such as naturally became him
1723 *vois, stevene*, report   1725 *rong*, rang; *yate*, gate
1728 *nis*, is no   1729 *gan*, did
1730 *kinde*, nature   1732 *montance*, extent
1734 *ymaked and yknet*, enmeshed and snared   1735 *nil*, will not

And swich a feste and swich a proces make
Him of Criseide, and of hire womanhede,   1740
And of hire beaute, that, withouten drede,
It was an hevene his wordes for to here;
And thanne he wolde singe in this manere:

"Love, that of erthe and se hath governaunce,
Love, that his hestes hath in hevenes hye,   1745
Love, that with an holsom alliaunce
Halt peples joined, as him lest hem gye,
Love, that knetteth lawe of compaignye,
And couples doth in vertu for to dwelle,
Bind this acord, that I have told and telle.   1750

"That that the world with feith, which that is stable,
Diverseth so his stoundes concordinge,
That elements that ben so discordable
Holden a bond perpetuely duringe,
That Phebus mote his rosy day forth bringe,   1755
And that the mone hath lordshipe over the nightes,—
Al this doth Love, ay heried be his mightes!

"That that the se, that gredy is to flowen,
Constreineth to a certein ende so
His flodes that so fiersly they ne growen   1760
To drenchen erthe and al for evere mo;
And if that Love aught lete his bridel go,
Al that now loveth asondre sholde lepe,
And lost were al that Love halt now to-hepe.

1739 *proces,* story   1741 *drede,* doubt
1745 *hestes,* commands   1746 *holsom,* wholesome
1747 *halt,* holds; *as him . . . gye,* as it pleases him to govern them
1748 *knetteth,* weaves   1749 *doth,* makes
1751 *that that,* the fact that   1752: Varies so its harmonious seasons
1753–54: i.e., the fact that elements that are so discordant share a
  perpetually enduring bond   1755 *mote,* may
1757 *doth Love,* Love causes; *heried,* praised   1758 *gredy,* anxious
1762 *aught,* in any way   1764 *halt,* holds; *to-hepe,* together

"So wolde God, that auctour is of kinde,   1765
That with his bond Love of his vertu liste
To cerclen hertes alle, and faste binde,
That from his bond no wight the wey out wiste;
And hertes colde, hem wolde I that he twiste
To make hem love, and that hem liste ay rewe   1770
On hertes sore, and kepe hem that ben trewe!"—

In alle nedes, for the townes werre,
He was, and ay, the first in armes dight,
And certeinly, but if that bokes erre,
Save Ector most ydred of any wight;   1775
And this encrees of hardinesse and might
Com him of love, his ladies thank to winne,
That altered his spirit so withinne.

In time of trewe, on hawking wolde he ride,
Or elles honte boor, beer, or lioun;   1780
The smale bestes leet he gon biside.
And whan that he com riding into town,
Ful ofte his lady from hire window down,
As fressh as faukoun comen out of muwe,
Ful redy was him goodly to saluwe.   1785

And moost of love and vertu was his speche,
And in despit hadde alle wrecchednesse;
And douteles, no nede was him biseche
To honouren hem that hadde worthinesse,
And esen hem that weren in destresse.   1790
And glad was he if any wight wel ferde,
That lovere was, whan he it wiste or herde.

1765 *kinde,* nature
1766–67: that it might please Love by his power with his bond to
          encircle all hearts and bind them fast   1768 *wiste,* should know
1769 *twiste,* would twist   1771 *kepe hem,* guard those
1772 *werre,* war   1773 *dight,* clad
1779 *trewe,* truce   1780 *honte,* hunt
1781 *leet,* let   1784 *muwe,* coop
1785 *saluwe,* salute   1791 *ferde,* fared

For, soth to seyne, he lost held every wight,
But if he were in Loves heigh servise,
I mene folk that oughte it ben of right.   1795
And over al this, so wel coude he devise,
Of sentement and in so uncouth wise,
Al his array, that every lovere thoughte
That al was wel, what so he seide or wroughte.

And though that he be come of blood royal,   1800
Him liste of pride at no wight for to chace;
Benigne he was to ech in general,
For which he gat him thank in every place.
Thus wolde Love, yheried be his grace,
That Pride, Envye, and Ire, and Avarice   1805
He gan to fle, and everich other vice.

Thou lady bright, the doughter to Dione,
Thy blinde and winged sone ek, daun Cupide,
Yee sustren nine ek, that by Elicone
In hil Pernaso listen for t'abide,   1810
That ye thus fer han deined me to gide,
I can namore, but sin that ye wol wende,
Ye heried ben for ay withouten ende!

Thorugh you have I seid fully in my song
Th'effect and joye of Troilus servise,   1815
Al be that ther was som disese among,
As to min auctour listeth to devise.
My thridde bok now ende ich in this wise,
And Troilus in lust and in quiete
Is with Criseide, his owen herte swete.   1820

(BOOK III, ENTIRE)

1794 *but if*, unless   1796 *devise*, arrange
1797 *of sentement*, ? i.e., with regard for the tender emotions; **uncouth,**
  unusual   1801 *chace*, harass
1803 *gat him*, got for himself   1804 *yheried*, praised
1808 *daun*, master   1809 *sustren*, sisters
1810 *listen*, are pleased   1816 *among*, as well   1819 *lust*, pleasure

[*The Sorrow of Troilus*]

LITERA TROILI

"Right fresshe flowr, whos I ben have and shal,
Withouten part of elleswhere servise,
With herte, body, lif, lust, thought, and al,
I, woful wight, in everich humble wise
That tonge telle or herte may devise,   5
As ofte as matere occupieth place,
Me recomaunde unto youre noble grace.

"Liketh you to witen, swete herte,
As ye wel knowe, how longe time agon
That ye me lefte in aspre peines smerte,   10
Whan that ye wente, of which yit boote non
Have I non had, but evere wors bigon
Fro day to day am I, and so mot dwelle,
While it you list, of wele and wo my welle.

"For which to you, with dredful herte trewe,   15
I write, as he that sorwe drifth to write,
My wo, that everich houre encresseth newe,
Compleining as I dar or can endite.
And that defaced is, that may ye wite
The teris which that fro min eyen reine,   20
That wolden speke, if that they coude, and pleine.

"You first biseche I, that youre eyen clere,
To loke on this, defouled ye nat holde;
And over al this, that ye, my lady deere,

2: i.e., without sharing my service elsewhere   4 *everich,* every
8 *liketh . . . witen,* may it please you to know   10 *aspre,* bitter
11 *yit,* yet; *boote,* remedy   12 *wors bigon,* worse off
13 *mot,* must   14 *list,* pleases; *wele,* weal
16 *drifth,* drives   19 *that,* the part that; *wite,* blame upon
21 *pleine,* complain

Wol vouchesauf this lettre to biholde. 25
And by the cause ek of my cares colde,
That sleth my wit, if aught amis m'asterte,
Foryeve it me, min owen swete herte!

"If any servant dorste or oughte of right
Upon his lady pitously compleine, 30
Thanne wene I that ich oughte be that wight,
Considered this, that ye thise monthes tweine
Han taried, ther ye seiden, soth to seyne,
But dayes ten ye nolde in oost sojourne,—
But in two monthes yet ye nat retourne. 35

"But for as muche as me moot nedes like
Al that you liste, I dar nat pleine moore,
But humblely, with sorwful sikes sike,
You write ich min unresty sorwes soore,
Fro day to day desiring evere moore 40
To knowen fully, if youre wille it weere,
How ye han ferd and don whil ye be theere;

"The whos welfare and hele ek God encresse
In honour swich, that upward in degree
It growe alwey, so that it nevere cesse. 45
Right as youre herte ay can, my lady free,
Devise, I prey to God so moot it be,
And graunte it that ye soone upon me rewe,
As wisly as in al I am you trewe.

"And if you liketh knowen of the fare 50
Of me, whos wo ther may no wit discrive,

26 *by the cause,* because   27 *sleth,* slays; *m'asterte,* escape from me
28 *foryeve,* forgive   31 *wene,* think; *ich,* I
34 *nolde,* would not; *oost,* (the Greek) host
36–37 *me moot . . . you liste,* I must be pleased by whatever pleases
you   38 *sikes sike,* sickly sighs
40 *unresty,* unabating   42 *ferd,* fared
44 *hele,* health   47 *moot,* may
49 *wisly,* surely   51 *discrive,* describe

I can namore but, chiste of every care,
At writing of this lettre I was on-live,
Al redy out my woful gost to drive;
Which I delaye, and holde him yet in honde,   55
Upon the sighte of matere of youre sonde.

"Min eyen two, in vein with which I se,
Of sorwful teris salte arn woxen welles;
My song, in pleinte of min adversitee;
My good, in harm; min ese ek woxen helle is;   60
My joye, in wo; I can sey you naught ellis,
But torned is, for which my lif I warye,
Everich joye or ese in his contrarye.

"Which with youre coming hom ayein to Troye
Ye may redresse, and more a thousand sithe   65
Than evere ich hadde, encressen in me joye.
For was ther nevere herte yet so blithe
To han his lif as I shal ben as swithe
As I you se; and though no manere routhe
Commeve you, yet thinketh on youre trouthe.   70

"And if so be my gilt hath deth deserved.
Or if you list namore upon me se,
In guerdoun yet of that I have you served,
Biseche I you, min hertes lady free,
That hereupon ye wolden write me,   75
For love of God, my righte lode-sterre,
That deth may make an ende of al my werre.

52 *chiste,* receptacle   54 *gost,* spirit
56 *upon,* i.e., in expectation of; *sonde,* sending
58 *woxen,* grown into
59 *pleinte,* complaint   62 *torned,* turned; *warye,* curse
65 *sithe,* times   68 *swithe,* soon
70 *commeve,* excite; *trouthe,* oath   72 *se,* look
73 *guerdoun,* reward   76 *righte lode-sterre,* true lode-star
77 *werre,* war

"If other cause aught doth you for to dwelle,
That with youre lettre ye me recomforte;
For though to me youre absence is an helle, 80
With pacience I wol my wo comporte,
And with youre lettre of hope I wol desporte.
Now writeth, swete, and lat me thus nat pleine;
With hope, or deth, delivereth me fro peine.

"Ywis, mine owene deere herte trewe, 85
I woot that, whan ye next upon me se,
So lost have I min hele and ek min hewe,
Criseide shal nought conne knowen me.
Ywis, min hertes day, my lady free,
So thursteth ay min herte to biholde 90
Youre beute, that my lif unnethe I holde.

"I say namore, al have I for to seye
To you wel more than I telle may.
But wheither that ye do me live or deye,
Yet praye I God, so yeve you right good day! 95
And fareth wel, goodly, faire, fresshe may,
As ye that lif or deth may me comande!
And to youre trouthe ay I me recomande

"With hele swich that, but ye yeven me
The same hele, I shal non hele have. 100
In you lith, whan you liste that it so be,
The day in which me clothen shal my grave;
In you my lif, in you might for to save

78 *doth*, makes   79 *recomforte*, comfort
81 *comporte*, endure   83 *lat*, let
85 *ywis*, indeed   86 *woot*, know
87 *hele*, health; *hewe*, color   88 *conne knowen*, be able to recognize
91 *unnethe*, with difficulty   92 *al*, although
94 *do*, make   95 *yeve*, give
96 *may*, maid
98 *recomande*, commend   99 *but*, unless; *yeven*, give
100 There is a play on the two shades of meaning of *hele*, health and
    salutation   101 *lith*, lies

Me fro disese of alle peines smerte;
And far now wel, min owen swete herte!   105
        le vostre T."

This lettre forth was sent unto Criseide,
Of which hire answere in effect was this:
Ful pitously she wroot ayein, and seide,
That also sone as that she mighte, ywis,
She wolde come, and mende al that was mis.   110
And finaly she wroot and seide him thenne,
She wolde come, ye, but she niste whenne.

But in hire lettre made she swich festes
That wonder was, and swerth she loveth him best;
Of which he fond but botmeles bihestes.   115
But Troilus, thou mayst now, est or west,
Pipe in an ivy lef, if that thee lest!
Thus goth the world. God shilde us fro meschaunce,
And every wight that meneth trouthe avaunce!

Encressen gan the wo fro day to night   120
Of Troilus, for tarying of Criseide;
And lessen gan his hope and ek his might,
For which al down he in his bed him leide.
He ne eet, ne dronk, ne slep, ne no word seide,
Imagining ay that she was unkinde;   125
For which wel neigh he wex out of his minde.

This drem, of which I told have ek biforn,
May nevere come out of his remembraunce.
He thought ay wel he hadde his lady lorn,
And that Joves, of his purveiaunce,   130

105 *far,* fare   109 *also,* as
110 *mis,* amiss   112 *niste,* did not know
113 *festes,* i.e., endearments   114 *swerth,* swears
115 *fond,* found; *botmeles bihestes,* baseless promises
117 *pipe . . . lef,* i.e., go whistle; *lest,* pleases   118 *shilde,* shield
119 *avaunce,* prosper   126 *wex,* i.e., went
129 *lorn,* lost   130 *Joves,* Jove; *purveiaunce,* foresight

Him shewed hadde in slep the signifiaunce
Of hire untrouthe and his disaventure,
And that the boor was shewed him in figure.

For which he for Sibylle his suster sente,
That called was Cassandre ek al aboute,   135
And al his drem he tolde hire er he stente,
And hire bisoughte assoilen him the doute
Of the stronge boor with tuskes stoute;
And finaly, withinne a litel stounde,
Casandre him gan right thus his drem expounde.   140

She gan first smile, and seide, "O brother deere,
If thou a soth of this desirest knowe,
Thou most a fewe of olde stories heere,
To purpos, how that Fortune overthrowe
Hath lordes olde; thorugh which, withinne a
          throwe,   145
Thou wel this boor shalt knowe, and of what kinde
He comen is, as men in bokes finde.

"Diane, which that wroth was and in ire
For Grekis nolde don hire sacrifise,
Ne encens upon hire auter sette afire,   150
She, for that Grekis gonne hire so despise,
Wrak hire in a wonder cruel wise;
For with a boor as gret as ox in stalle
She made up frete hire corn and vines alle.

"To sle this boor was al the contre raised,   155
Amonges which ther com, this boor to se,
A maide, oon of this world the beste ypreised;

133 *boor,* boar; *in figure,* i.e., as a symbol
137 *assoilen,* resolve
142 *a soth,* the truth
145 *throwe,* little time
151 *gonne,* did
154 *up frete,* be eaten up

136 *stente,* ceased
139 *stounde,* time
143 *most,* must
149 *nolde,* would not
152 *wrak hire,* avenged herself

And Meleagre, lord of that contree,
He loved so this fresshe maiden free,
That with his manhod, er he wolde stente,   160
This boor he slough, and hire the hed he sente;

"Of which, as olde bokes tellen us,
Ther ros a contek and a gret envye;
And of this lord descended Tydeus
By ligne, or ellis olde bookes lie.   165
But how this Meleagre gan to die
Thorugh his moder, wol I you naught telle,
For al to longe it were for to dwelle."

She tolde ek how Tydeus, er she stente,
Unto the stronge citee of Thebes,   170
To cleimen kingdom of the citee, wente,
For his felawe, daun Polymites,
Of which the brother, daun Ethiocles,
Ful wrongfully of Thebes held the strengthe;
This tolde she by proces, al by lengthe.   175

She tolde ek how Hemonides asterte,
Whan Tydeus slough fifty knightes stoute.
She tolde ek alle the prophecies by herte,
And how that seven kinges with hire route
Bisegeden the citee al aboute;   180
And of the holy serpent, and the welle,
And of the furies, al she gan him telle;

Of Archimoris burying and the pleyes,
And how Amphiorax fil thorugh the grounde,
How Tydeus was slein, lord of Argeyes,   185

160 *stente*, cease
163 *contek*, strife
167 *moder*, mother
175 *by proces*, in due course
179 *route*, company
184 *fil*, fell

161 *slough*, slew
165 *ligne*, line
172 *daun*, master
176 *asterte*, escaped
183 *pleyes*, games

And how Ipomedoun in litel stounde
Was dreint, and ded Parthonope of wounde;
And also how Capaneus the proude
With thonder-dint was slain, that cride loude.

She gan ek telle him how that either brother, 190
Ethiocles and Polymite also,
At a scarmuche ech of hem slough other,
And of Argives wepinge and hire wo;
And how the town was brent, she tolde ek tho.
And so descendeth down from gestes olde 195
To Diomede, and thus she spak and tolde.

"This ilke boor bitokneth Diomede,
Tydeüs sone, that down descended is
Fro Meleagre, that made the boor to blede.
And thy lady, wherso she be, ywis, 200
This Diomede hire herte hath, and she his.
Wep if thou wolt, or lef! For, out of doute,
This Diomede is inne, and thou art oute."

"Thou seyst nat soth," quod he, "thou sorceresse.
With al thy false goost of prophecye! 205
Thou wenest ben a gret devineresse!
Now sestou nat this fool of fantasye
Peineth hire on ladys for to lie?
Awey!" quod he, "ther Joves yeve thee sorwe!
Thou shalt be fals, peraunter, yet tomorwe! 210

---

186 *stounde,* time
187 *dreint,* drowned; *ded . . . wounde,* and Parthenope dead of
wounds   192 *scarmuche,* skirmish
193 *hire,* their   194 *brent,* burned; *tho,* then
195 *gestes,* stories   202 *or lef,* i.e., or don't (weep)
205 *goost,* spirit   206 *wenest ben,* think to be
207 *sestou,* do you see   208 *peineth hire,* takes pains
209 *ther,* i.e., may; *yeve,* give
210 *fals,* i.e., proved false; *peraunter,* by chance

"As wel thou mightest lien on Alceste,
That was of creatures, but men lie,
That evere weren, kindest and the beste!
For whan hire housbonde was in jupertye
To die himself, but if she wolde die, 215
She ches for him to die and gon to helle,
And starf anon, as us the bokes telle."

Cassandre goth, and he with cruel herte
Foryat his wo, for angre of hire speche;
And from his bed al sodeinly he sterte, 220
As though al hool him hadde ymad a leche.
And day by day he gan enquere and seche
A sooth of this with al his fulle cure;
And thus he drieth forth his aventure.

Fortune, which that permutacioun 225
Of thinges hath, as it is hire comitted
Thorugh purveiaunce and disposicioun
Of heighe Jove, as regnes shal be flitted
Fro folk in folk, or when they shal be smitted,
Gan pulle awey the fetheres brighte of Troye 230
Fro day to day, til they ben bare of joye.

Among al this, the fin of the parodye
Of Ector gan aprochen wonder blive.
The fate wolde his soule sholde unbodye,
And shapen hadde a mene it out to drive, 235
Ayeins which fate him helpeth nat to strive;

211 *lien on,* lie about
212 *but,* unless
214 *jupertye,* jeopardy
215 *but if,* unless
216 *ches,* chose
217 *starf,* died
219 *foryat,* forgot
220 *sterte,* leaped
221 *hool,* well; *leche,* physician
222 *seche,* inquire
223 *cure,* care
224 *drieth forth,* endures
227 *purveiaunce,* foresight
228 *flitted,* shifted
229 *in,* to; *smitted,* disgraced
232 *fin . . . parodye,* end of the period
233 *blive,* quickly
235 *mene,* means

But on a day to fighten gan he wende,
At which, allas! he caught his lives ende.

For which me thinketh every manere wight
That haunteth armes oughte to biwaille   240
The deth of him that was so noble a knight;
For as he drough a king by th'aventaille,
Unwar of this, Achilles thorugh the maille
And thorugh the body gan him for to rive;
And thus this worthy knight was brought of live.   245

For whom, as olde bokes tellen us,
Was mad swich wo, that tonge it may nat telle;
And namely, the sorwe of Troilus,
That next him was of worthinesse welle.
And in this wo gan Troilus to dwelle,   250
That, what for sorwe, and love, and for unreste,
Ful ofte a day he bad his herte breste.

But natheles, though he gan him dispaire,
And dradde ay that his lady was untrewe,
Yet ay on hire his herte gan repaire.   255
And as thise loveres don, he soughte ay newe
To gete ayein Criseide, brighte of hewe;
And in his herte he wente hire excusinge,
That Calkas caused al hire taryinge.

And ofte time he was in purpos grete   260
Himselven lik a pilgrim to desgise,
To seen hire; but he may nat contrefete
To ben unknowen of folk that weren wise,

240 *haunteth*, practices
242 *drough*, dragged; *aventaille*, mouthpiece of a helmet
245 *of*, out of   247 *mad*, made
248 *namely*, especially   249 *welle*, the source
252 *breste*, break   253 *natheles*, nevertheless
254 *dradde*, dreaded   255 *hire*, her; *repaire*, return
262 *contrefete*, i.e., counterfeit in such a way as

Ne finde excuse aright that may suffise,
If he among the Grekis knowen were;   265
For which he wep ful ofte and many a tere.

To hire he wroot yet ofte time al newe
Ful pitously,—he lefte it nought for slouthe,—
Biseching hire, sin that he was trewe,
That she wol come ayein and holde hire trouthe.   270
For which Criseide upon a day, for routhe,—
I take it so,—touching al this matere,
Wrot him ayein, and seide as ye may here:

LITERA CRISEIDIS

"Cupides sone, ensample of goodliheede,
O swerd of knighthod, sours of gentilesse,   275
How might a wight in torment and in drede
And heleles, you sende as yet gladnesse?
I herteles, I sik, I in destresse!
Sin ye with me, nor I with you, may dele,
You neither sende ich herte may nor hele.   280

"Youre lettres ful, the papir al ypleinted,
Conceived hath min hertes pietee.
I have ek sein with teris al depeinted
Youre lettre, and how that ye requeren me
To come ayein, which yet ne may nat be   285
But why, lest that this lettre founden were,
No mencioun ne make I now, for feere.

"Grevous to me, God woot, is youre unreste,
Youre haste, and that the goddes ordinaunce,

265 *knowen*, recognized   266 *wep*, wept
268 *slouthe*, negligence   269 *sin*, since
274 *goodliheede*, excellence   275 *swerd*, sword; *sours*, source
277 *heleles*, comfortless   279 *sin*, since
280 *ich*, I; *hele*, health
281 *ypleinted*, i.e., bearing signs of your grief
282: i.e., my heart's pity has comprehended
283 *sein*, seen, *depeinted*, stained

It semeth nat ye take it for the beste. 290
Nor other thing nis in youre remembraunce,
As thinketh me, but only youre plesaunce;
But beth nat wroth, and that I you biseche;
For that I tarye is al for wikked speche.

"For I have herd wel moore than I wende, 295
Touching us two, how thinges han ystonde;
Which I shal with dissimuling amende.
And beth nat wroth, I have ek understonde
How ye ne do but holden me in honde.
But now no force, I can nat in you gesse 300
But alle trouthe and alle gentilesse.

"Come I wole; but yet in swich disjointe
I stonde as now, that what yer or what day
That this shal be, that can I naught apointe.
But in effect I pray you, as I may, 305
Of youre good word and of youre frendship ay.
For trewely, while that my lif may dure,
As for a frend ye may in me assure.

"Yet preye ich you, on ivel ye ne take
That it is short which that I to you write; 310
I dar nat, ther I am, wel lettres make,
Ne nevere yet ne coude I wel endite.
Ek gret effect men write in place lite;
Th'entente is al, and nat the lettres space.
And fareth now wel, God have you in his grace!
                    La vostre C." 315

291 *nis,* is not   295 *wende,* supposed
296 *ystonde,* stood   297 *dissimuling,* dissembling
299: i.e., how all you do is deceive me   300 *force,* matter
302 *disjointe,* predicament   307 *dure,* last
308 *assure,* have confidence   309 *ivel,* evil
313 *gret effect,* matters of great moment; *lite,* small

This Troilus this lettre thoughte al straunge,
Whan he it saugh, and sorwfullich he sighte.
Him thoughte it lik a calendes of chaunge.
But finaly, he ful ne trowen mighte
That she ne wolde him holden that she highte;   320
For with ful ivel wille list him to leve,
That loveth wel, in swich cas, though him greve.

But natheles, men seyen that at the laste,
For any thing, men shal the soothe se.
And swich a cas bitidde, and that as faste,   325
That Troilus wel understod that she
Nas nought so kinde as that hire oughte be.
And finaly, he woot now, out of doute,
That al is lost that he hath ben aboute.

Stood on a day in his malencolye   330
This Troilus, and in suspecioun
Of hire for whom he wende for to die.
And so bifel that thoroughout Troye town,
As was the gise, yborn was up and down
A manere cote-armure, as seith the storye,   335
Biforn Deiphebe, in signe of his victorye;

The whiche cote, as telleth Lollius,
Deiphebe it hadde rent fro Diomede
The same day. And whan this Troilus
It saugh, he gan to taken of it hede,   340
Avising of the lengthe and of the brede,
And al the werk; but as he gan biholde,
Ful sodeinly his herte gan to colde,

317 *saugh,* saw; *sorwfullich,* sorrowfully; *sighte,* sighed
319 *ful,* fully; *trowen,* believe   320 *highte,* promised
321–22: i.e., for in such cases, even though he is in distress the true
    lover is reluctant to believe   323 *natheles,* nevertheless
327 *nas nought,* was not   332 *wende,* thought
334 *gise,* fashion   335 *manere,* sort of
339 *rent,* stripped   341 *brede,* breadth
343 *colde,* grow cold

As he that on the coler fond withinne
A broche, that he Criseide yaf that morwe   345
That she from Troye moste nedes twinne,
In remembraunce of him and of his sorwe.
And she him leide ayein hire feith to borwe
To kepe it ay! But now ful wel he wiste,
His lady nas no lenger on to triste.   350

He goth him hom, and gan ful soone sende
For Pandarus; and al this newe chaunce,
And of this broche, he tolde him word and ende,
Compleining of hire hertes variaunce,
His longe love, his trouthe, and his penaunce.   355
And after deth, withouten wordes moore,
Ful faste he cride, his reste him to restore.

Than spak he thus, "O lady min, Criseide,
Where is youre feith, and where is youre biheste?
Where is youre love? where is youre trouthe?" he
seide.   360
"Of Diomede have ye now al this feeste!
Allas! I wolde han trowed atte leeste
That, sin ye nolde in trouthe to me stonde,
That ye thus nolde han holden me in honde!

"Who shal now trowe on any othes mo?   365
Allas! I nevere wolde han wend, er this,
That ye, Criseide, coude han chaunged so;
Ne, but I hadde agilt and don amis,

344 *coler*, collar; *fond*, found   345 *yaf*, gave; *morwe*, morning
346 *twinne*, depart   348: i.e., and she in answer pledged her faith
349 *wiste*, knew   350: i.e., his lady was no longer to be trusted
355 *penaunce*, distress   359 *biheste*, promise
361 *feeste*, i.e., joy   362 *leeste*, least
363 *sin*, since; *nolde*, would not
364 *holden . . . honde*, deceived me (by lying)
365 *othes mo*, other oaths   366 *wend*, thought
368 *but*, unless; *agilt*, done wrong

So cruel wende I nought youre herte, ywis,
To sle me thus! Allas, youre name of trouthe   370
Is now fordon, and that is al my routhe.

"Was ther non other broche you liste lete
To feffe with youre newe love," quod he,
"But thilke broch that I, with teris wete,
You yaf, as for a remembraunce of me?   375
Non other cause, allas, ne hadde ye
But for despit, and ek for that ye mente
Al outrely to shewen youre entente.

"Thorough which I se that clene out of youre minde
Ye han me cast; and I ne can nor may,   380
For al this world, withinne min herte finde
To unloven you a quarter of a day!
In corsed time I born was, weilaway,
That you, that doon me al this wo endure,
Yet love I best of any creature!   385

"Now God," quod he, "me sende yet the grace
That I may meten with this Diomede!
And trewely, if I have might and space,
Yet shal I make, I hope, his sides blede.
O God," quod he, "that oughtest taken heede   390
To fortheren trouthe, and wronges to punice,
Why niltou don a vengeaunce of this vice?

"O Pandarus, that in dremes for to triste
Me blamed hast, and wont art oft upbreide,
Now maystou se thyself, if that thee liste,   395

370 *sle*, slay   371 *fordon*, ruined; *routhe*, grief
372 *you liste lete*, it pleased you to let go
373 *feffe with*, present to   374 *thilke*, the same
375 *yaf*, gave   378 *al outrely*, unequivocally
383 *corsed*, cursed   385 *doon*, make
391 *fortheren*, further; *punice*, punish   392 *niltou*, will you not
393 *triste*, trust

How trewe is now thy nece, bright Criseide!
In sondry formes, God it woot," he seide,
"The goddes shewen bothe joye and tene
In slep, and by my drem it is now sene.

"And certeinly, withouten moore speche,   400
From hennesforth, as ferforth as I may,
Min owen deth in armes wol I seche.
I recche nat how soone be the day!
But trewely, Criseide, swete may,
Whom I have ay with al my might yserved,   405
That ye thus doon, I have it nat deserved."

This Pandarus, that al thise thinges herde,
And wiste wel he seide a soth of this,
He nought a word ayein to him answerde;
For sory of his frendes sorwe he is,   410
And shamed for his nece hath don amis,
And stant, astoned of thise causes tweye,
As stille as ston; a word ne coude he seye.

But at the laste thus he spak, and seide:
"My brother deer, I may do thee namore.   415
What sholde I seyen? I hate, ywis, Criseide;
And, God woot, I wol hate hire evermore!
And that thou me bisoughtest don of yoore,
Having unto min honour ne my reste
Right no reward, I dide al that thee leste.   420

"If I dide aught that mighte liken thee,
It is me lief; and of this tresoun now,
God woot that it a sorwe is unto me!

398 *tene,* grief   401 *ferforth,* far
402 *seche,* seek   403 *recche,* care
404 *may,* maid   411 *for,* because
412 *stant,* stands; *astoned,* astonished 420 *leste,* pleased
421 *liken,* please   422 *it is me lief,* I am glad of it

And dredeles, for hertes ese of you,
Right fain I wolde amende it, wiste I how.   425
And fro this world, almighty God I preye
Delivere hire soon! I can namore seye."

Gret was the sorwe and pleinte of Troilus;
But forth hire cours Fortune ay gan to holde.
Criseide loveth the sone of Tydeüs,   430
And Troilus moot wepe in cares colde.
Swich is this world, whoso it can biholde:
In ech estat is litel hertes reste.
God leve us for to take it for the beste!

In many cruel bataille, out of drede,   435
Of Troilus, this ilke noble knight,
As men may in thise olde bokes rede,
Was seen his knighthod and his grete might.
And dredeles, his ire, day and night,
Ful cruwely the Grekis ay aboughte;   440
And alwey moost this Diomede he soughte.

And ofte time, I finde that they mette
With blody strokes and with wordes grete,
Assayinge how hire speres weren whette;
And, God it woot, with many a cruel hete   445
Gan Troilus upon his helm to bete!
But natheles, Fortune it naught ne wolde,
Of oothers hond that either deyen sholde.

And if I hadde ytaken for to write
The armes of this ilke worthy man,   450
Than wolde ich of his batailles endite;

424 *dredeles*, doubtless   425 *wiste I*, if I knew
428 *pleinte*, complaint   431 *moot*, must
434 *leve*, grant   435 *drede*, doubt
440 *aboughte*, paid for   441 *moost*, most
444 *hire*, their   445 *hete*, bout

But for that I to writen first bigan
Of his love, I have seid as I can,—
His worthy dedes, whoso list hem heere,
Rede Dares, he can telle hem alle yfeere— 455

Biseching every lady bright of hewe,
And every gentil womman, what she be,
That al be that Criseide was untrewe,
That for that gilt she be nat wroth with me.
Ye may hire giltes in other bokes se; 460
And gladlier I wol write, yif you leste,
Penelopeës trouthe and good Alceste.

N'I sey nat this al oonly for thise men,
But moost for wommen that bitraised be
Thorough false folk; God yeve hem sorwe, amen! 465
That with hire grete wit and subtilte
Bitraise you! And this commeveth me
To speke, and in effect you alle I preye,
Beth war of men, and herkneth what I seye!—

Go, litel bok, go, litel min tragedye, 470
Ther God thy makere yet, er that he die,
So sende might to make in som comedye!
But litel book, no making thou n'envye,
But subgit be to alle poesye;
And kis the steppes, where as thou seest pace 475
Virgile, Ovide, Omer, Lucan, and Stace.

And for ther is so gret diversite
In Englissh and in writing of oure tonge,
So prey I God that non miswrite thee,

455 *yfeere,* together
463 *n'I sey nat,* nor do I say
465 *yeve,* give
471 *ther,* i.e., may
472: i.e., grant (thy maker) power to write some comedy
473 *making,* poetry
479 *miswrite,* miscopy
461 *yif you leste,* if it pleases you
464 *bitraised,* betrayed
467 *commeveth,* moves
474 *subgit,* subject

Ne thee mismetre for defaute of tonge.   480
And red wherso thou be, or elles songe,
That thou be understonde, God I biseche!
But yet to purpos of my rather speche.—

The wrath, as I bigan you for to seye,
Of Troilus the Grekis boughten deere.   485
For thousandes his hondes maden deye,
As he that was withouten any peere,
Save Ector, in his time, as I can heere.
But weilawey, save only Goddes wille!
Despitously him slough the fierse Achille.   490

And whan that he was slain in this manere,
His lighte goost ful blisfully is went
Up to the holughnesse of the eighthe spere,
In convers leting everich element;
And ther he saugh, with ful avisement,   495
The erratic sterres, herkening armonye
With sounes ful of hevenissh melodye.

And down from thennes faste he gan avise
This litel spot of erthe, that with the se
Embraced is, and fully gan despise   500
This wrecched world, and held al vanite
To respect of the plein felicite
That is in hevene above; and at the laste,
Ther he was slain, his loking down he caste.
And in himself he lough right at the wo   505

480 *mismetre*, scan wrongly; *defaute of tonge*, ignorance of language
481 *red*, read; *songe*, sung   482 *understonde*, understood
483 *rather*, earlier   490 *slough*, slew
492 *lighte goost*, insubstantial spirit
493 *holughnesse*, concave; *spere*, sphere
494: i.e., leaving behind him every (other) sphere
495 *saugh*, saw; *avisement*, consideration
496 *erratic sterres*, wandering stars; *herkening*, hearing
497 *sounes*, sounds; *hevenissh*, heavenly
498 *avise*, consider   502 *to respect of*, in comparison with; *plein*, full
504 *loking*, look   505 *lough*, laughed

Of hem that wepten for his deth so faste;
And dampned al oure werk that foloweth so
The blinde lust, the which that may nat laste,
And sholden al oure herte on heven caste.
And forth he wente, shortly for to telle,   510
Ther as Mercurye sorted him to dwelle.

Swich fin hath, lo, this Troilus for love!
Swich fin hath al his grete worthinesse!
Swich fin hath his estat real above,
Swich fin his lust, swich fin hath his noblesse!   515
Swich fin hath false worldes brotelnesse!
And thus bigan his loving of Criseide,
As I have told, and in this wise he deide.

O yonge, fresshe folkes, he or she,
In which that love up groweth with youre age,   520
Repeireth hom fro worldly vanite,
And of youre herte up casteth the visage
To thilke God that after his image
You made, and thinketh al nis but a faire
This world, that passeth soone as flowres faire.   525

And loveth Him, the which that right for love
Upon a crois, oure soules for to beye,
First starf, and roos, and sit in hevene above;
For He nil falsen no wight, dar I seye,
That wol his herte al holly on Him leye.   530
And sin He best to love is, and most meke,
What nedeth feinede loves for to seke?

(Book V, lines 1317–1848)

507 *dampned,* condemned	511 *sorted,* allotted
512 *fin,* end	514 *real,* royal
516 *brotelnesse,* brittleness	524 *nis but,* is but
527 *beye,* buy	528 *starf,* died
529 *nil falsen no,* will betray no	530 *holly,* wholly
531 *sin,* since	532 *feinede,* feigned

FROM *The Canterbury Tales*

THE PROLOGUE
TO THE WIFE OF BATH'S TALE

"Experience, though noon auctoritee
Were in this world, is right ynogh for me
To speke of wo that is in mariage;
For, lordinges, sith I twelve yeer was of age,
Thonked be God that is eterne on live,   5
Housbondes at chirche dore I have had five,—
If I so ofte mighte have ywedded bee,—
And alle were worthy men in hir degree.
But me was toold, certein, nat longe agoon is,
That sith that Crist ne wente nevere but onis   10
To wedding, in the Cane of Galilee,
That by the same ensample taughte he me
That I ne sholde wedded be but ones.
Herkne eek, lo, which a sharp word for the nones,
Biside a welle, Jesus, God and man,   15
Spak in repreeve of the Samaritan:
'Thou hast yhad five housbondes,' quod he,
'And that ilke man that now hath thee
Is noght thin housbonde,' thus seide he certein.
What that he mente therby, I can nat seyn;   20
But that I axe, why that the fifthe man
Was noon housbonde to the Samaritan?
How manye mighte she have in mariage?
Yet herde I nevere tellen in min age

4 *lordinges*, gentlemen; *sith*, since   14 *for the nones*, to the purpose
16 *repreeve*, reproof   18 *ilke*, same
21 *axe*, ask

Upon this nombre diffinicioun.   25
Men may devine and glosen, up and down,
But wel I woot, expres, withoute lie,
God bad us for to wexe and multiplye;
That gentil text can I wel understonde.
Eek wel I woot, he seide min housbonde   30
Sholde lete fader and mooder, and take to me.
But of no nombre mencion made he,
Of bigamye, or of octogamye;
Why sholde men thanne speke of it vileinye?

Lo, heere the wise king, daun Salomon;   35
I trowe he hadde wives mo than oon.
As wolde God it were leveful unto me
To be refresshed half so ofte as he!
Which yifte of God hadde he for alle his wivis!
No man hath swich that in this world alive is.   40
God woot, this noble king, as to my wit,
The firste night had many a mirye fit
With ech of hem, so wel was him on live.
Yblessed be God that I have wedded five!
Welcome the sixte, whan that evere he shal.   45
For sothe, I wol nat kepe me chaast in al.
Whan min housbonde is fro the world ygon,
Som Cristen man shal wedde me anon,
For thanne, th'apostle seith that I am free
To wedde, a Goddes half, where it liketh me.   50
He seith that to be wedded is no sinne;
Bet is to be wedded than to brinne.
What rekketh me, thogh folk seye vileinye

25 *diffinicioun,* definition	26 *devine,* guess; *glosen,* interpret
27 *woot,* know	31 *lete,* leave
35 *daun,* master	36 *trowe,* believe; *mo,* more
37 *leveful,* permissible	39 *yifte,* gift
40 *swich,* such	42 *fit,* experience
45 *shal,* i.e., shall come	50 *a,* on
52 *bet,* better; *brinne,* burn	53 *rekketh me,* care I

Of shrewed Lameth and his bigamye?
I woot wel Abraham was an hooly man,   55
And Jacob eek, as ferforth as I can;
And ech of hem hadde wives mo than two,
And many another holy man also.
Wher can ye seye, in any manere age,
That hye God defended mariage   60
Be expres word? I pray you, telleth me.
Or where comanded he virginitee?
I woot as wel as ye, it is no drede,
Th'apostel, whan he speketh of maidenhede,
He seide that precept therof hadde he noon.   65
Men may conseille a womman to been oon,
But conseilling is no comandement.
He putte it in oure owene juggement;
For hadde God comanded maidenhede,
Thanne hadde he dampned wedding with the dede. 70
And certes, if ther were no seed ysowe,
Virginitee, thanne wherof sholde it growe?
Poul dorste nat comanden, atte leeste,
A thing of which his maister yaf noon heeste.
The dart is set up for virginitee: 75
Cacche whoso may, who renneth best lat see.
    But this word is nat taken of every wight,
But ther as God lust give it of his might.
I woot wel that th'apostel was a maide;
But nathelees, thogh that he wroot and saide   80
He wolde that every wight were swich as he,

54 *shrewed*, cursed   56 *forforth as I can*, far as I know
57 *mo*, more   60 *defended*, forbade
63 *drede*, doubt   66 *oon*, single
70 *dampned*, condemned   71 *certes*, certainly
73 *atte leeste*, at any rate   74 *yaf*, gave; *heeste*, commandment
75 *dart*, i.e., a prize   76 *renneth*, runs; *lat*, let
77 *taken*, understood; *wight*, creature   78 *lust*, it pleases
79 *maide*, virgin   80 *nathelees*, nevertheless
81 *swich*, such

Al nis but conseil to virginitee.
And for to been a wif he yaf me leve
Of indulgence; so nis it no repreve
To wedde me, if that my make die,   85
Withouten excepcion of bigamye.
Al were it good no womman for to touche,—
He mente as in his bed or in his couche;
For peril is bothe fir and tow t'assemble:
Ye knowe what this ensample may resemble.   90
This is al and som, he heeld virginitee
Moore parfit than wedding in freletee.
Freletee clepe I, but if that he and she
Wolde leden al hir lif in chastitee.

  I graunte it wel, I have noon envye,   95
Thogh maidenhede preferre bigamye.
It liketh hem to be clene, body and goost;
Of min estaat I nil nat make no boost.
For wel ye knowe, a lord in his houshold,
He nath nat every vessel al of gold;   100
Somme been of tree, and doon hir lord servise.
God clepeth folk to him in sondry wise,
And everich hath of God a propre yifte,
Som this, som that, as him liketh shifte.

  Virginitee is greet perfeccion,   105
And continence eek with devocion,
But Crist, that of perfeccion is welle,
Bad nat every wight he sholde go selle
Al that he hadde, and give it to the poore

---

82 *nis,* i.e., is nothing   84 *nis,* is not; *repreeve,* disgrace
85 *to wedde me,* i.e., for me to marry; *make,* mate
86: i.e., there being no objection to remarriage
91 *al and som,* i.e., all there is to it
92 *parfit,* perfect; *freletee,* frailty   93 *clepe,* call; *but if,* unless
96 *preferre,* excel; *bigamye,* remarriage
97 *liketh hem,* pleases them; *goost,* spirit   98 *nil,* will not
100 *nath,* has not   101 *tree,* wood
103 *everich,* each one; *yifte,* gift   104 *shifte,* ordain

And in swich wise folwe him and his foore.　　110
He spak to hem that wolde live parfitly;
And lordinges, by youre leve, that am nat I.
I wol bistowe the flowr of al min age
In the actes and in fruit of mariage.

Telle me also, to what conclusion　　115
Were membres maad of generacion,
And for what profit was a wight ywroght?
Trusteth right wel, they were nat maad for noght.
Glose whoso wole, and seye bothe up and down,
That they were maked for purgacioun　　120
Of urine, and oure bothe thinges smale
Were eek to knowe a femele from a male,
And for noon oother cause,—sey ye no?
The experience woot wel it is noght so.
So that the clerkes be nat with me wrothe,　　125
I sey this, that they maked ben for bothe,
This is to seye, for office, and for ese
Of engendrure, ther we nat God displese.
Why sholde men elles in hir bookes sette
That man shal yelde to his wif hire dette?　　130
Now wherwith sholde he make his payement,
If he ne used his sely instrument?
Thanne were they maad upon a creature
To purge urine, and eek for engendrure.

But I seye noght that every wight is holde,　　135
That hath swich harneis as I to you tolde,
To goon and usen hem in engendrure.
Thanne sholde men take of chastitee no cure.
Crist was a maide, and shapen as a man,
And many a seint, sith that the world bigan;　　140

110 *foore,* footsteps	111 *parfitly,* perfectly
115 *conclusion,* end	129 *hir,* their
130 *yelde,* pay; *hire,* her	132 *sely,* innocent
135 *holde,* bound	136 *harneis,* equipment
138 *cure,* heed	139 *maide,* virgin
140 *sith,* since	

Yet lived they evere in parfit chastitee.
I nil envye no virginitee.
Lat hem be breed of pured whete-seed,
And lat us wives hoten barly-breed;
And yet with barly-breed, Mark telle can,   145
Oure Lord Jesu refresshed many a man.
In swich estaat as God hath cleped us
I wol persevere; I nam nat precius.
In wifhod I wol use min instrument
As frely as my Makere hath it sent.   150
If I be daungerous, God yeve me sorwe!
Min housbonde shal it have bothe eve and morwe,
Whan that him list come forth and paye his dette.
An housbonde I wol have, I wol nat lette,
Which shal be bothe my dettour and my thral,   155
And have his tribulacion withal
Upon his flessh, whil that I am his wif.
I have the power duringe al my lif
Upon his propre body, and noght he.
Right thus the Apostel tolde it unto me;   160
And bad oure housbondes for to love us weel.
Al this sentence me liketh every deel"—
      Up stirte the Pardoner, and that anon:
"Now, dame," quod he, "by God and by seint John!
Ye been a noble prechour in this cas.   165
I was aboute to wedde a wif; allas!
What sholde I bye it on my flessh so deere?
Yet hadde I levere wedde no wif to-yeere!"
      "Abide!" quod she, "my tale is nat bigonne.
Nay, thou shalt drinken of another tonne,   170

142 *nil,* will not   143 *breed,* bread; *pured,* refined
144 *hoten,* be called   145 *can,* did
147 *cleped,* called   148 *nam,* am not; *precius,* fastidious
151 *daungerous,* standoffish; *yeve,* give   154 *lette,* withhold myself
159 *propre,* own   162 *deel,* bit
163 *stirte,* started   167 *what,* why
169 *to-yeere,* this year (or ever)   170 *tonne,* tun

Er that I go, shal savoure wors than ale.
And whan that I have toold thee forth my tale
Of tribulacion in mariage,
Of which I am expert in al min age,
This is to seyn, myself have been the whippe,—   175
Than maystou chese wheither thou wolt sippe
Of thilke tonne that I shal abroche.
Be war of it, er thou to ny approche;
For I shal telle ensamples mo than ten.
'Whoso that nil be war by othere men,   180
By him shul othere men corrected be.'
The same wordes writeth Ptholomee;
Rede in his Almageste, and take it there."

    "Dame, I wolde praye you, if youre wil it were,"
Seide this Pardoner, "as ye bigan,   185
Telle forth youre tale, spareth for no man,
And teche us yonge men of youre practike."

    "Gladly," quod she, "sith it may you like;
But that I praye to al this compaignye,
If that I speke after my fantasye,   190
As taketh not agrief of that I seye;
For min entente is nat but for to pleye.

    Now, sires, now wol I telle forth my tale.—
As evere moote I drinken win or ale,
I shal seye sooth, tho housbondes that I hadde,   195
As thre of hem were goode, and two were badde.
The thre were goode men, and riche, and olde;
Unnethe mighte they the statut holde
In which that they were bounden unto me.
Ye woot wel what I meene of this, pardee!   200
As help me God, I laughe whan I thinke

176 *chese*, choose   177 *thilke*, the same; *abroche*, broach
179 *mo*, more   180 *nil*, will not
187 *practike*, mode of operation   188 *sith*, since
191 *agrief*, amiss   194 *moote*, might
195 *tho*, those   198 *unnethe*, with difficulty
201 *as*, so

How pitously a-night I made hem swinke!
And, by my fey, I tolde of it no stoor.
They had me yeven hir lond and hir tresoor;
Me neded nat do lenger diligence   205
To winne hir love, or doon hem reverence.
They loved me so wel, by God above,
That I ne tolde no deintee of hir love!
A wis womman wol bisye hire evere in oon
To gete hire love, ther as she hath noon.   210
But sith I hadde hem hoolly in min hond,
And sith they hadde me yeven al hir lond,
What sholde I taken keep hem for to plese,
But it were for my profit and min ese?
I sette hem so a-werke, by my fey,   215
That many a night they songen 'weilawey!'
The bacon was nat fet for hem, I trowe,
That som men han in Essex at Dunmowe.
I governed hem so wel, after my lawe,
That ech of hem ful blisful was and fawe   220
To bringe me gaye thinges fro the faire.
They were ful glad whan I spak to hem faire;
For, God it woot, I chidde hem spitously.

　　Now herkneth how I baar me proprely,
Ye wise wives, that can understonde.   225

　　Thus shulde ye speke and bere hem wrong on honde;
For half so boldely can ther no man
Swere and lien, as a womman can.
I sey nat this by wives that been wise,
But if it be whan they hem misavise.   230

202 *swinke,* work 203 *fey,* faith; *tolde . . . stoor,* set no store by it
204 *yeven,* given; *hir,* their   205 *lenger,* longer
208 *tolde no deintee,* held in no esteem
209 *bisye,* employ; *in oon,* on one thing
211 *sith,* since; *holly,* wholly   213 *what,* why; *keep,* care
214 *but,* unless   217 *fet,* brought back
218 *trowe,* believe   220 *fawe,* glad
223 *spitously,* cruelly 226 *bere . . . honde,* accuse them wrongfully
230 *hem misavise,* act unwisely

A wis wif shal, if that she can hir good,
Bere him on honde that the cow is wood,
And take witnesse of hir owene maide
Of hir assent; but herkneth how I saide:

'Sire olde cainard, is this thin array?   235
Why is my neighebores wif so gay?
She is honoured over al ther she gooth;
I sitte at hoom, I have no thrifty clooth.
What dostou at my neighebores hous?
Is she so fair? artou so amorous?   240
What roune ye with oure maide? *Benedicite!*
Sire olde lecchour, lat thy japes be!
And if I have a gossib or a freend,
Withouten gilt, thou chidest as a feend,
If that I walke or pleye unto his hous!   245
Thou comest hoom as dronken as a mous,
And prechest on thy bench, with ivel preef!
Thou seist to me it is a greet meschief
To wedde a poure womman, for costage;
And if that she be riche, of heigh parage,   250
Thanne seistou that it is a tormentrye
To soffre hire pride and hire malencolye.
And if that she be fair, thou verray knave,
Thou seist that every holour wol hire have;
She may no while in chastitee abide,   255
That is assailled upon ech a side.

Thou seist som folk desiren us for richesse,
Somme for oure shap, and somme for oure fairnesse,
And som for she can outher singe or daunce,

---

231 *can hir good,* knows what's good for her
232: i.e., maintain to him that the chough (a guardian bird tradi-
tionally set to watch over wives by suspicious husbands) is crazy
234 *of hir assent,* (who is) of her party   235 *cainard,* sluggard
238 *thrifty,* decent   241 *roune,* whisper
247 *ivel preef,* bad result   249 *costage,* expense
250 *parage,* descent   254 *holour,* whoremonger
259 *outher,* either

And som for gentillesse and daliaunce; 260
Som for hir handes and hir armes smale:
Thus goth al to the devel, by thy tale.
Thou seist men may nat kepe a castel wal,
It may so longe assailled been over al.

And if that she be foul, thou seist that she 265
Coveiteth every man that she may se,
For as a spainel she wol on him lepe,
Til that she finde som man hire to chepe.
Ne noon so grey goos gooth ther in the lake
As, seistou, wol been withoute make. 270
And seist it is an hard thing for to welde
A thing that no man wole, his thankes, helde.
Thus seistou, lorel, whan thou goost to bedde;
And that no wis man nedeth for to wedde,
Ne no man that entendeth unto hevene. 275
With wilde thonder-dint and firy levene
Moote thy welked nekke be tobroke!

Thou seist that dropping houses, and eek smoke,
And chiding wives maken men to flee
Out of hir owene hous; a! *benedicitee!* 280
What eileth swich an old man for to chide?

Thou seist we wives wol oure vices hide
Til we be fast, and thanne we wol hem shewe,—
Wel, may that be a proverbe of a shrewe!

Thou seist that oxen, asses, hors, and houndes, 285
They been assayed at diverse stoundes;
Bacins, lavours, er that men hem bye,
Spoones and stooles, and al swich housbondrye,
And so been pottes, clothes, and array;

---

268 *chepe,* buy   270 *make,* mate
271 *welde,* possess   272 *his thankes,* willingly; *helde,* hold
273 *lorel,* rogue   276 *levene,* lightning
277 *moote,* may; *welked,* withered; *tobroke,* broken
278 *dropping,* leaky   284 *shrewe,* villain
286 *stoundes,* times   287 *lavours,* wash basins

But folk of wives maken noon assay,   290
Til they be wedded; olde dotard shrewe!
And thanne, seistou, we wol oure vices shewe.

Thou seist also that it displeseth me
But if that thou wolt preise my beautee,
And but thou poure alwey upon my face,   295
And clepe me "faire dame" in every place.
And but thou make a feeste on thilke day
That I was born, and make me fressh and gay;
And but thou do to my norice honour,
And to my chamberere withinne my bowr,   300
And to my fadres folk and his allies,—
Thus seistou, olde barel-ful of lies!

And yet of oure apprentice Janekin,
For his crispe heer, shininge as gold so fin,
And for he squiereth me bothe up and down,   305
Yet hastou caught a fals suspecioun.
I wol him noght, thogh thou were deed tomorwe!

But tel me this: why hidestou, with sorwe,
The keyes of thy cheste awey fro me?
It is my good as wel as thin, pardee!   310
What, wenestou make an idiot of oure dame?
Now by that lord that called is Seint Jame,
Thou shalt nat bothe, thogh thou were wood,
Be maister of my body and of my good;
That oon thou shalt forgo, maugree thine ÿen.   315
What helpith it of me to enquere or spyen?
I trowe thou woldest loke me in thy chiste!
Thou sholdest seye, "Wif, go wher thee liste;
Taak youre disport, I wol nat leve no talis.

---

294 *but if,* unless   296 *clepe,* call
297 *thilke,* that same   299 *norice,* nurse
300 *chamberere,* chambermaid   307 *wol,* want
311 *wenestou,* do you think to   313 *wood,* furious
315 *maugree,* despite; *ÿen,* eyes   317 *trowe,* believe; *loke,* lock
319 *leve,* believe

I knowe you for a trewe wif, dame Alis."   320
We love no man that taketh kep or charge
Wher that we goon; we wol ben at oure large.

   Of alle men yblessed moot he be,
The wise astrologien, daun Ptholome,
That seith this proverbe in his Almageste: 325
"Of alle men his wisdom is the hyeste
That rekketh nevere who hath the world in honde."
By this proverbe thou shalt understonde,
Have thou ynogh, what thar thee recche or care
How mirily that othere folkes fare?   330
For, certein, olde dotard, by youre leve,
Ye shul have queinte right ynogh at eve.
He is to greet a nigard that wolde werne
A man to lighte a candle at his lanterne;
He shal have never the lasse light, pardee.   335
Have thou ynogh, thee thar nat pleine thee.

   Thou seist also, that if we make us gay
With clothing, and with precious array,
That it is peril of oure chastitee;
And yet, with sorwe! thou most enforce thee,   340
And seye thise wordes in the Apostles name:
"In habit maad with chastitee and shame
Ye wommen shul apparaille you," quod he,
"And noght in tressed heer and gay perree,
As perles, ne with gold, ne clothes riche."   345
After thy text, ne after thy rubriche,
I wol nat wirche as muchel as a gnat.

   Thou seidest this, that I was lik a cat;
For whoso wolde senge a cattes skin,

---

321 *kep*, notice; *charge*, trouble   323 *moot*, may
327 *in honde*, at his disposal   329 *thar*, need; *recche*, reck
332 *queinte*, pudendum   333 *werne*, refuse
335 *lasse*, less   336 *pleine thee*, complain
340 *most*, must   344 *heer*, hair; *perree*, jewelry
346 *rubriche*, rubric   347 *muchel*, much
349 *senge*, singe

Thanne wolde the cat wel dwellen in his in;   350
And if the cattes skin be slik and gay,
She wol nat dwelle in house half a day,
But forth she wole, er any day be dawed,
To shewe hir skin, and goon a-caterwawed.
This is to seye, if I be gay, sire shrewe,   355
I wol renne out, my borel for to shewe.

Sire olde fool, what helpeth thee to spyen?
Thogh thou preye Argus with his hundred ÿen
To be my warde-cors, as he can best,
In feith, he shal nat kepe me but me lest;   360
Yet coude I make his berd, so moot I thee!

Thou seidest eek that ther been thinges thre,
The whiche thinges troublen al this erthe,
And that no wight may endure the ferthe.
O leeve sire shrewe, Jesu shorte thy lif!   365
Yet prechestou and seist an hateful wif
Yrekened is for oon of thise meschances.
Been ther none othere maner resemblances
That ye may likne youre parables to,
But if a sely wif be oon of tho?   370

Thou liknest eek wommenes love to helle,
To bareine lond, ther water may nat dwelle.
Thou liknest it also to wilde fir;
The moore it brenneth, the moore it hath desir
To consume every thing that brent wole be.   375
Thou seyest, right as wormes shende a tree,
Right so a wif destroyeth hire housbonde;

351 *slik,* sleek   353 *dawed,* dawned
354 *a-caterwawed,* caterwauling   356 *renne,* run; *borel,* clothing
358 *ÿen,* eyes   359 *warde-cors,* bodyguard
360 *but me lest,* unless I please
361 *make his berd,* outwit him; *moot I thee,* may I thrive
364 *ferthe,* fourth   365 *leeve,* dear
367 *yrekened,* reckoned   370 *sely,* innocent; *tho,* those
374 *brenneth,* burns   375 *brent,* burnt
376 *shende,* destroy

This knowe they that been to wives bonde.'

   Lordinges, right thus, as ye have understonde,
Baar I stifly mine olde housbondes on honde   380
That thus they seiden in hir dronkenesse;
And al was fals, but that I took witnesse
On Janekin, and on my nece also.
O Lord! the peine I dide hem and the wo,
Ful giltelees, by Goddes sweete pine!   385
For as an hors I coude bite and whine.
I coude pleine, and yit was in the gilt,
Or elles often time hadde I been spilt.
Whoso that first to mille comth, first grint;
I pleined first, so was oure werre ystint.   390
They were ful glade to excuse hem blive
Of thing of which they nevere agilte hir live.

   Of wenches wolde I beren him on honde,
Whan that for sik unnethes mighte he stonde.
Yet tikled it his herte, for that he   395
Wende that I hadde of him so greet chiertee!
I swoor that al my walkinge out by nighte
Was for t'espye wenches that he dighte;
Under that colour hadde I many a mirthe.
For al swich wit is yeven us in oure birthe;   400
Deceite, weping, spinning God hath yive
To wommen kindely, whil that they may live.
And thus of o thing I avaunte me,
Atte ende I hadde the bettre in ech degree,

380 *baar I stifly on honde*, I stoutly accused   385 *pine*, suffering
387 *pleine*, complain   388 *spilt*, brought to ruin
389 *grint*, grinds   390 *werre*, war; *ystint*, ended
391 *blive*, quickly
392 *of which . . . agilte*, in which they had never sinned; *hir live*,
   during their lives   393 *beren hym on honde*, accuse him
394 *for sik*, for sickness; *unnethes*, hardly
396 *wende*, supposed; *chiertee*, affection
398 *dighte*, had intercourse with   400 *yeven*, given
401 *yive*, given   402 *kindely*, naturally
403 *o*, one; *avaunte me*, boast   404 *atte*, at the

By sleighte, or force, or by som maner thing,　405
As by continueel murmur or grucching.
Namely abedde hadden they meschaunce:
Ther wolde I chide, and do hem no plesaunce;
I wolde no lenger in the bed abide,
If that I felte his arm over my side,　410
Til he had maad his raunson unto me;
Thanne wolde I suffre him do his nicetee.
And therfore every man this tale I telle,
Winne whoso may, for al is for to selle;
With empty hand men may none hawkes lure.　415
For winning wolde I al his lust endure,
And make me a feined appetit;
And yet in bacon hadde I nevere delit;
That made me that evere I wolde hem chide.
For thogh the pope hadde seten hem biside,　420
I wolde nat spare hem at hir owene bord;
For, by my trouthe, I quitte hem word for word.
As helpe me verray God omnipotent,
Though I right now sholde make my testament,
I ne owe hem nat a word that it nis quit.　425
I broghte it so aboute by my wit
That they moste yeve it up, as for the beste,
Or elles hadde we nevere been in reste.
For thogh he looked as a wood leon,
Yet sholde he faille of his conclusion.　430
　　Thanne wolde I seye, 'Goode lief, taak keep
How mekely looketh Wilkin, oure sheep!
Com neer, my spouse, lat me ba thy cheke!

406 *grucching*, grumbling
411 *raunson*, ransom
418 *bacon*, i.e., old meat; *delit*, delight
425 *nis quit*, is not repaid
429 *wood*, fierce
431 *lief*, friend; *keep*, notice
407 *namely*, especially
412 *nicetee*, lust
422 *trouthe*, troth
427 *yeve*, give
430 *conclusion*, object
433 *ba*, kiss

Ye sholde been al pacient and meke,
And han a sweete spiced conscience,   435
Sith ye so preche of Jobes pacience.
Suffreth alwey, sin ye so wel can preche;
And but ye do, certein we shal you teche
That it is fair to have a wif in pees.
Oon of us two moste bowen, doutelees;   440
And sith a man is moore resonable
Than womman is, ye moste been suffrable.
What eileth you to grucche thus and grone?
Is it for ye wolde have my queinte allone?
Wy, taak it al! lo, have it every deel!   445
Peter! I shrewe you, but ye love it weel;
For if I wolde selle my *bele chose*,
I coude walke as fressh as is a rose;
But I wol kepe it for youre owene tooth.
Ye be to blame, by God! I sey you sooth.'   450
    Swiche manere wordes hadde we on honde.
Now wol I speken of my fourthe housbonde.
    My fourthe housbonde was a revelour;
This is to seyn, he hadde a paramour;
And I was yong and ful of ragerye,   455
Stibourn and strong, and joly as a pie.
How coude I daunce to an harpe smale,
And singe, ywis, as any nightingale,
Whan I had dronke a draughte of sweete win!
Metellius, the foule cherl, the swin,   460
That with a staf birafte his wif hir lif,
For she drank win, thogh I hadde been his wif,

435 *spiced,* scrupulous	436 *sith,* since
437 *sin,* since	438 *but,* unless
442 *suffrable,* patient	443 *grucche,* grumble
444 *queinte,* pudendum	445 *deel,* bit
446 *shrewe,* curse	455 *ragerye,* wantonness
456 *pie,* magpie	458 *ywis,* indeed
461 *birafte,* deprived	462 *for,* because

He sholde nat han daunted me fro drinke!
And after win on Venus moste I thinke,
For al so siker as cold engendreth hail,   465
A likerous mouth moste han a likerous tail.
In wommen vinolent is no defence,—
This knowen lecchours by experience.

But, Lord Crist! whan that it remembreth me
Upon my youthe, and on my jolitee,   470
It tikleth me aboute min herte roote.
Unto this day it dooth min herte boote
That I have had my world as in my time.
But age, allas! that al wole envenime,
Hath me biraft my beautee and my pith.   475
Lat go, farewel! the devel go therwith!
The flour is goon, ther is namoore to telle;
The bren, as I best can, now moste I selle;
But yet to be right mirye wol I fonde.
Now wol I tellen of my fourthe housbonde.   480

I seye, I hadde in herte greet despit
That he of any oother had delit.
But he was quit, by God and by Seint Joce!
I made him of the same wode a croce;
Nat of my body, in no foul manere,   485
But certeinly, I made folk swich cheere
That in his owene grece I made him frye
For angre, and for verray jalousye.
By God! in erthe I was his purgatorye,
For which I hope his soule be in glorye.   490
For, God it woot, he sat ful ofte and song,
Whan that his shoo ful bitterly him wrong.

---

464 *moste*, must
466 *likerous*, (1) greedy, (2) lecherous
472 *boote*, good
478 *bren*, husks
483 *quit*, repaid
491 *song*, sang

465 *silker*, sure
467 *vinolent*, bibulous
474 *evenime*, poison
479 *fonde*, try
484 *croce*, staff
492 *wrong*, pinched

Ther was no wight, save God and he, that wiste,
In many wise, how soore I him twiste.
He deide whan I cam fro Jerusalem,   495
And lith ygrave under the roode beem,
Al is his tombe noght so curius
As was the sepulcre of him Darius,
Which that Appelles wroghte subtilly;
It nis but wast to burye him preciously.   500
Lat him fare wel, God yeve his soul reste!
He is now in his grave and in his cheste.

   Now of my fifthe housbonde wol I telle.
God lete his soule nevere come in helle!
And yet was he to me the mooste shrew;   505
That feele I on my ribbes al by rewe,
And evere shal unto min ending day.
But in oure bed he was so fressh and gay,
And therwithal so wel coude he me glose,
Whan that he wolde han my *bele chose,*   510
That thogh he hadde me bete on every bon,
He coude winne again my love anon.
I trowe I loved him best, for that he
Was of his love daungerous to me.
We wommen han, if that I shal nat lie,   515
In this matere a queinte fantasye;
Waite what thing we may nat lightly have,
Therafter wol we crye al day and crave.
Forbede us thing, and that desiren we;
Preesse on us faste, and thanne wol we fle.   520
With daunger oute we al oure chaffare;

---

493 *wiste,* knew
496 *lith,* lies; *ygrave,* buried; *roode beam,* rood-beam of a church
497 *al,* albeit   500 *nis,* i.e., is nothing
501 *yeve,* give   505 *moste shrewe,* greatest villain
506 *by rewe,* in order   509 *glose,* wheedle
513 *trowe,* think   514 *daungerous,* standoffish
517 *waite,* observe; *lightly,* easily
521 *daunger,* coyness; *oute,* expose; *chaffare,* wares

Greet prees at market maketh deere ware,
And to greet cheep is holde at litel pris:
This knoweth every womman that is wis.

My fifthe housbonde, God his soule blesse! 525
Which that I took for love, and no richesse,
He som time was a clerk of Oxenford,
And hadde left scole, and wente at hom to bord
With my gossib, dwellinge in oure town;
God have hir soule! hir name was Alisoun. 530
She knew min herte, and eek my privetee,
Bet than oure parisshe preest, so moot I thee!
To hire biwreyed I my conseil al.
For hadde min housbonde pissed on a wal,
Or doon a thing that sholde han cost his lif, 535
To hire, and to another worthy wif,
And to my nece, which that I loved weel,
I wolde han toold his conseil every deel.
And so I dide ful often, God it woot,
That made his face ful often reed and hoot 540
For verray shame, and blamed himself for he
Had toold to me so greet a privetee.

And so bifel that ones in a Lente—
So often times I to my gossib wente,
For evere yet I loved to be gay, 545
And for to walke in March, Averill, and May,
Fro hous to hous, to heere sondry talis—
That Jankin clerk, and my gossib dame Alis,
And I myself, into the feeldes wente.
Min housbonde was at Londoun al that Lente; 550
I hadde the bettre leiser for to pleye,
And for to se, and eek for to be seye

522 *prees*, crowds
523 *to greet cheep*, too much merchandise; *pris*, value
532 *bet*, better; *moot I thee*, may I thrive
533 *biwreyed*, disclosed; *conseil*, secrets   536 *hire*, her
538 *deel*, bit   540 *reed and hoot*, red and hot
552 *seye*, seen

Of lusty folk. What wiste I wher my grace
Was shapen for to be, or in what place?
Therfore I made my visitaciouns   555
To vigilies and to processiouns,
To preching eek, and to thise pilgrimages,
To pleyes of miracles, and to mariages,
And wered upon my gaye scarlet gites.
Thise wormes, ne thise motthes, ne thise mites,   560
Upon my peril, frete hem never a deel;
And wostou why? for they were used weel.
    Now wol I tellen forth what happed me.
I seye that in the feeldes walked we,
Til trewely we hadde swich daliance,   565
This clerk and I, that of my purveiance
I spak to him and seide him how that he,
If I were widwe, sholde wedde me.
For certeinly, I sey for no bobance,
Yet was I nevere withouten purveiance   570
Of mariage, n'of othere thinges eek.
I holde a mouses herte nat worth a leek
That hath but oon hole for to sterte to,
And if that faille, thanne is al ydo.
    I bar him on honde he hadde enchanted me,—   575
My dame taughte me that soutiltee.
And eek I seide I mette of him al night,
He wolde han slain me as I lay upright,
And al my bed was ful of verray blood;
But yet I hope that he shal do me good,   580
For blood bitokeneth gold, as me was taught.
And al was fals; I dremed of it right naught,

553 *wiste*, knew; *grace*, luck   554 *shapen*, destined
559 *wered upon*, wore; *gites*, gown   561 *frete*, ate
562 *wostou*, do you know   566 *purveiance*, foresight
569 *bobance*, boast   573 *sterte*, escape
575 *bar him on honde*, pretended to him   576 *soutiltee*, subtlety
577 *mette*, dreamed   578 *upright*, supine

But as I folwed ay my dames loore,
As wel of this as of othere thinges moore.

    But now, sire, lat me se, what I shal seyn?   585
A ha! by God, I have my tale agein.

    Whan that my fourthe housbonde was on beere,
I weep algate, and made sory cheere,
As wives mooten, for it is usage,
And with my coverchief covered my visage.   590
But for that I was purveyed of a make,
I wepte but smal, and that I undertake.

    To chirche was min housbonde born a-morwe
With neighebores, that for him maden sorwe;
And Jankin, oure clerk, was oon of tho.   595
As help me God! whan that I saugh him go
After the beere, me thoughte he hadde a paire
Of legges and of feet so clene and faire
That al min herte I yaf unto his hoold.
He was, I trowe, a twenty winter oold,   600
And I was fourty, if I shal seye sooth;
But yet I hadde alwey a coltes tooth.
Gat-tothed I was, and that bicam me weel;
I hadde the prente of seinte Venus seel.
As help me God! I was a lusty oon,   605
And faire, and riche, and yong, and wel bigon;
And trewely, as mine housbondes tolde me,
I hadde the beste *quoniam* mighte be.
For certes, I am al Venerien
In feelinge, and min herte is Marcien.   610
Venus me yaf my lust, my likerousnesse,
And Mars yaf me my sturdy hardinesse;

588 *algate,* anyhow   589 *mooten,* must
591 *purveyed,* provided in advance; *make,* mate
592 *undertake,* guarantee   593 *a-morwe,* in the morning
595 *tho,* those   596 *saugh,* saw
599 *yaf,* gave; *hoold,* possession   603 *gat-tothed,* gap-toothed
604 *prente,* print   606 *bigon,* situated
611 *likerousnesse,* lecherousness

Min ascendent was Taur, and Mars therinne.
Allas! allas! that evere love was sinne!
I folwed ay min inclinacioun   615
By vertu of my constellacioun;
That made me I coude noght withdrawe
My chambre of Venus from a good felawe.
Yet have I Martes mark upon my face,
And also in another privee place.   620
For God so wis be my savacioun,
I ne loved nevere by no discrecioun,
But evere folwede min appetit,
Al were he short, or long, or blak or whit;
I took no kep, so that he liked me,   625
How poore he was, ne eek of what degree.

What sholde I seye? but, at the monthes ende,
This joly clerk, Jankin, that was so hende,
Hath wedded me with greet solempnitee;
And to him yaf I al the lond and fee   630
That evere was me yeven therbifoore.
But afterward repented me ful soore;
He nolde suffre nothing of my list.
By God! he smoot me ones on the list,
For that I rente out of his book a leef,   635
That of the strook min ere wax al deef.
Stibourn I was as is a leonesse,
And of my tonge a verray jangleresse,
And walke I wolde, as I had doon biforn,
From hous to hous, although he had it sworn;   640
For which he often times wolde preche,
And me of olde Romain geestes teche;

613 *Taur,* Taurus   619 *Martes,* Mars's
621 *wis,* surely   625 *kep,* heed; *liked,* pleased
628 *hende,* attractive   630 *yaf,* gave; *fee,* property
631 *yeven,* given   633 *nodde,* would not; *list,* pleasure
634 *list,* ear   640 *sworn,* i.e., sworn the contrary
642 *geestes,* stories

How he Simplicius Gallus lefte his wif,
And hire forsook for terme of al his lif,
Noght but for open-heveded he hir say   645
Lookinge out at his dore upon a day.

Another Romain tolde he me by name,
That, for his wif was at a someres game
Withouten his witing, he forsook hire eke.
And thanne wolde he upon his Bible seke   650
That ilke proverbe of Ecclesiaste
Where he comandeth, and forbedeth faste,
Man shal nat suffre his wif go roule aboute.
Thanne wolde he seye right thus, withouten doute:

    'Whoso that buildeth his hous al of salwes,   655
And priketh his blinde hors over the falwes,
And suffreth his wif to go seken halwes,
Is worthy to been hanged on the galwes!'
But al for noght, I sette noght an hawe
Of his proverbes n'of his olde sawe,   660
Ne I wolde nat of him corrected be.
I hate him that my vices telleth me,
And so doo mo, God woot, of us than I.
This made him with me wood al outrely;
I nolde noght forbere him in no cas.   665

    Now wol I seye you sooth, by seint Thomas,
Why that I rente out of his book a leef,
For which he smoot me so that I was deef.

    He hadde a book that gladly, night and day,
For his desport he wolde rede alway;   670
He cleped it Valerie and Theofraste,
At which book he lough alwey ful faste.

---

645 *open-heveded,* bare-headed; *say,* saw   649 *witing,* knowledge
651 *ilke,* same   653 *roule,* roam
655 *salwes,* osiers   656 *priketh,* rides; *falwes,* plowed land
657 *seken halwes,* seek shrines, i.e., go on pilgrimages
659 *sette . . . hawe,* i.e., paid no attention   663 *mo,* more
664 *wood,* furious; *al outrely,* altogether   665 *forbere,* submit to
672 *lough,* laughed

And eek ther was somtime a clerk at Rome,
A cardinal, that highte Seint Jerome,
That made a book again Jovinian;   675
In which book eek ther was Tertulan,
Crisippus, Trotula, and Helowis,
That was abbesse nat fer fro Paris;
And eek the Parables of Salomon,
Ovides Art, and bookes many on,   680
And alle thise were bounden in o volume.
And every night and day was his custume,
Whan he hadde leiser and vacacioun
From oother worldly occupacioun,
To reden on this book of wicked wives,   685
He knew of hem mo legendes and lives
Than been of goode wives in the Bible.
For trusteth wel, it is an impossible
That any clerk wol speke good of wives,
But if it be of hooly seintes lives,   690
Ne of noon oother womman never the mo.
Who peintede the leon, tel me who?
By God! if wommen hadde writen stories,
As clerkes han withinne hire oratories,
They wolde han writen of men moore wickednesse   695
Than al the mark of Adam may redresse.
The children of Mercurye and of Venus
Been in hir wirking ful contrarius;
Mercurye loveth wisdam and science,
And Venus loveth riot and dispence.   700
And, for hire diverse disposicioun,
Ech falleth in otheres exaltacioun.
And thus, God woot, Mercurye is desolat
In Pisces, wher Venus is exaltat;

674 *highte,* was named   675 *again,* against
677 *Helowis,* Eloise   681 *o,* one
686 *mo,* more   688 *impossible,* impossibility
700 *dispence,* expenditure   701 *exaltat,* exalted

And Venus falleth ther Mercurye is reised.   705
Therfore no womman of no clerk is preised.
The clerk, whan he is oold, and may noght do
Of Venus werkes worth his olde sho,
Thanne sit he down, and writ in his dotage
That wommen can nat kepe hir mariage!   710
     But now to purpos, why I tolde thee
That I was beten for a book, pardee!
Upon a night Jankin, that was oure sire,
Redde on his book, as he sat by the fire,
Of Eva first, that for hir wickednesse   715
Was al mankinde broght to wrecchednesse,
For which that Jesu Crist himself was slain,
That boghte us with his herte blood again.
Lo, heere expres of womman may ye finde,
That womman was the los of al mankinde.   720
     Tho redde he me how Sampson loste his heres:
Slepinge, his lemman kitte it with hir sheres;
Thurgh which treson loste he bothe his ÿen.
     Tho redde he me, if that I shal nat lien,
Of Hercules and of his Dianire,   725
That caused him to sette himself afire.
     No thing forgat he the care and the wo
That Socrates hadde with his wives two;
How Xantippa caste pisse upon his heed.
This sely man sat stille as he were deed;   730
He wiped his heed, namoore dorste he seyn,
But 'Er that thonder stinte, comth a rein!'
     Of Phasipha, that was the queene of Crete,
For shrewednesse, him thoughte the tale swete;
Fy! spek namoore—it is a grisly thing—   735

---

713 *oure sire*, i.e., my husband   720 *los*, ruin
721 *tho*, then   722 *lemman*, mistress; *kitte*, cut
723 *ÿen*, eyes   730 *sely*, poor
732 *stinte*, stop   734 *shrewedness*, malice

Of hire horrible lust and hir liking.

Of Clytermistra, for hire lecherye,
That falsly made hire housbonde for to die,
He redde it with ful good devocioun.

He tolde me eek for what occasioun   740
Amphiorax at Thebes loste his lif.
Min housbonde hadde a legende of his wif,
Eriphylem, that for an ouche of gold
Hath prively unto the Grekes told
Wher that hir housbonde hidde him in a place,   745
For which he hadde at Thebes sory grace.

Of Livia tolde he me, and of Lucye:
They bothe made hir housbondes for to die;
That oon for love, that oother was for hate.
Livia hir housbonde, on an even late,   750
Empoisoned hath, for that she was his fo.
Lucia, likerous, loved hire housbonde so
That, for he sholde alwey upon hire thinke,
She yaf him swich a manere love-drinke
That he was deed er it were by the morwe;   755
And thus algates housbondes han sorwe.

Thanne tolde he me how oon Latumius
Compleined unto his felawe Arrius
That in his gardin growed swich a tree
On which he seide how that his wives thre   760
Hanged hemself for herte despitus.
'O leeve brother,' quod this Arrius,
'Yif me a plante of thilke blissed tree,
And in my gardin planted shal it bee.'

Of latter date, of wives hath he red   765
That somme han slain hir housbondes in hir bed,

743 *ouche*, piece of jewelry   752 *likerous*, lecherous
754 *yaf*, gave   756 *algates*, continually
761 *for herte despitus*, i.e., for sheer malevolence of heart
762 *leeve*, dear; *quod*, said   763 *yif*, give; *thilke*, this same

And lete hir lecchour dighte hire al the night,
Whan that the corps lay in the floor upright.
And somme han drive nailes in hir brain,
Whil that they slepte, and thus they han hem slain. 770
Somme han hem yeve poisoun in hire drinke.
He spak moore harm than herte may bithinke;
And therwithal he knew of mo proverbes
Than in this world ther growen gras or herbes.
'Bet is,' quod he, 'thin habitacioun   775
Be with a leon or a foul dragoun,
Than with a womman usinge for to chide.'
'Bet is,' quod he, 'hye in the roof abide,
Than with an angry wif down in the hous;
They been so wicked and contrarious,   780
They haten that hir housbondes loven ay.'
He seide, a 'womman cast hir shame away,
Whan she cast of hir smok;' and forthermo,
'A fair womman, but she be chaast also,
Is lik a gold ring in a sowes nose.'   785
Who wolde wene, or who wolde suppose,
The wo that in min herte was, and pine?
    And whan I saugh he wolde nevere fine
To reden on this cursed book al night,
Al sodeinly thre leves have I plight   790
Out of his book, right as he radde, and eke
I with my fest so took him on the cheke
That in oure fir he fil bakward adown.
And he up stirte as dooth a wood leoun,

767 *dighte*, have intercourse with   768 *upright*, flat
771 *yeve*, given   773 *mo*, more
775 *bet*, better   777 *usinge*, accustomed
784 *but*, unless   786 *wene*, think
787 *pine*, torment   788 *saugh*, saw; *fine*, cease
790 *plight*, snatched   791 *radde*, read
792 *fest*, fist   793 *fil*, fell
794 *stirte*, started; *wood*, maddened

And with his fest he smoot me on the heed,   795
That in the floor I lay as I were deed.
And whan he saugh how stille that I lay,
He was agast, and wolde han fled his way,
Til atte laste out of my swogh I breide.
'O! hastou slain me, false theef?' I seide,   800
'And for my land thus hastou mordred me?
Er I be deed, yet wol I kisse thee.'

    And neer he cam, and kneled faire adown,
And seide, 'Deere suster Alisoun,
As help me God! I shal thee nevere smite.   805
That I have doon, it is thyself to wite.
Foryeve it me, and that I thee biseke!'
And yet eftsoones I hitte him on the cheke,
And seide, 'Theef, thus muchel am I wreke;
Now wol I die, I may no lenger speke.'   810
But atte laste, with muchel care and wo,
We fille acorded by us selven two.
He yaf me al the bridel in min hond,
To han the governance of hous and lond,
And of his tonge, and of his hond also;   815
And made him brenne his book anon right tho.
And whan that I hadde geten unto me,
By maistrye, al the soverainetee,
And that he seide, 'Min owene trewe wif,
Do as thee lust the terme of al thy lif;   820
Keep thin honour, and keep eek min estaat'—
After that day we hadden never debaat.
God helpe me so, I was to him as kinde
As any wif from Denmark unto Inde,

---

799 *atte*, at the; *swogh*, swoon; *breide*, started   806 *wite*, blame
807 *foryeve*, forgive; *biseke*, beseech   808 *eftsoones*, afterwards
809 *muchel*, much; *wreke*, avenged   812 *fille*, fell, i.e., became
813 *yaf*, gave   816 *brenne*, burn; *tho*, then
818 *maistrye*, skill   820 *lust*, it pleases

And also trewe, and so was he to me.   825
I prey to God, that sit in magestee,
So blesse his soule for his mercy deere.
Now wol I seye my tale, if ye wol heere."

(Fragment III, lines 1–828)

826 *sit*, sits

THE PARDONER'S TALE

In Flaundres whilom was a compaignye
Of yonge folk that haunteden folye,
As riot, hasard, stiwes, and tavernes,
Where as with harpes, lutes, and giternes,
They daunce and pleyen at dees bothe day and night,   5
And eten also and drinken over hir might,
Thurgh which they doon the devel sacrifise
Withinne that develes temple, in cursed wise,
By superfluitee abhominable.
Hir othes been so grete and so dampnable   10
That it is grisly for to heere hem swere.
Oure blissed Lordes body they totere,—
Hem thoughte that Jewes rente him noght ynough;
And ech of hem at otheres sinne lough.
And right anon thanne comen tombesteres   15
Fetis and smale, and yonge frutesteres,
Singeres with harpes, bawdes, wafereres,
Whiche been the verray develes officeres
To kindle and blowe the fir of lecherye,

1 *whilom*, once upon a time   2 *haunteden*, practiced
3 *hasard*, dicing; *stiwes*, brothels   4 *giternes*, guitars   5 *dees*, dice
10 *hir*, their; *dampnable*, damnable   11 *hem*, them
12 *totere*, tear apart   14 *lough*, laughed
15 *tombesteres*, dancers
16 *fetis*, shapely; *frutesteres*, female fruit venders
17 *wafereres*, cake venders   18 *verray*, veritable

That is annexed unto glotonye.   20
The Hooly Writ take I to my witnesse
That luxurye is in win and dronkenesse.

Lo, how that dronken Looth, unkindely,
Lay by his doghtres two, unwitingly;
So dronke he was, he niste what he wroghte.   25

Herodes, whoso wel the stories soghte,
Whan he of win was repleet at his feeste,
Right at his owene table he yaf his heeste
To sleen the Baptist John, ful giltelees.

Senec seith a good word doutelees;   30
He seith he can no difference finde
Bitwix a man that is out of his minde
And a man which that is dronkelewe,
But that woodnesse, yfallen in a shrewe,
Persevereth lenger than dooth dronkenesse.   35
O glotonye, ful of cursednesse!
O cause first of oure confusioun!
O original of oure dampnacioun,
Til Crist hadde boght us with his blood again!
Lo, how deere, shortly for to sayn,   40
Aboght was thilke cursed vileinye!
Corrupt was al this world for glotonye.

Adam oure fader, and his wif also,
Fro Paradis to labour and to wo
Were driven for that vice, it is no drede.   45
For whil that Adam fasted, as I rede,
He was in Paradis; and whan that he
Eet of the fruit deffended on the tree,
Anon he was out cast to wo and peine.

22 *luxurye,* lust   23 *Looth,* Lot; *unkindely,* unnaturally
25 *niste,* did not know   28 *yaf,* gave; *heeste,* command
33 *dronkelaw,* drunken
34 *woodnesse,* madness; *yfallen,* i.e., occurring; *shrewe,* villain
35 *lenger,* longer   41 *aboght,* paid for; *thilke,* the same
45 *drede,* doubt   48 *deffended,* forbidden

O glotonye, on thee wel oghte us pleine!   50
O, wiste a man how manye maladies
Folwen of excesse and of glotonies,
He wolde been the moore mesurable
Of his diete, sittinge at his table.
Allas! the shorte throte, the tendre mouth,   55
Maketh that est and west and north and south,
In erthe, in eir, in water, men to swinke
To gete a glotoun deintee mete and drinke!
Of this matiere, o Paul, wel canstou trete:
"Mete unto wombe, and wombe eek unto mete,   60
Shal God destroyen bothe," as Paulus seith.
Allas! a foul thing is it, by my feith,
To seye this word, and fouler is the dede,
Whan man so drinketh of the white and rede
That of his throte he maketh his privee,   65
Thurgh thilke cursed superfluitee.

The apostel weping seith ful pitously,
"Ther walken manye of whiche you toold have I—
I seye it now weping, with pitous vois—
That they been enemys of Cristes crois,   70
Of whiche the ende is deeth, wombe is hir god!"
O wombe! O bely! O stinking cod,
Fulfilled of dong and of corrupcioun!
At either ende of thee foul is the soun.
How greet labour and cost is thee to finde!   75
Thise cookes, how they stampe, and streine, and grinde,
And turnen substaunce into accident,
To fulfille al thy likerous talent!
Out of the harde bones knokke they

50 *pleine,* complain
51 *wiste,* knew
53 *mesurable,* moderate
57 *swinke,* toil
60 *wombe,* belly
64 *white and rede,* i.e., wines
69 *vois,* voice
70 *crois,* cross
72 *cod,* bag
73 *fulfilled,* filled full
74 *soun,* sound
75 *finde,* provide for
78 *likerous talent,* dainty appetite

The mary, for they caste noght awey   80
That may go thurgh the golet softe and swoote.
Of spicerye of leef, and bark, and roote
Shal been his sauce ymaked by delit,
To make him yet a newer appetit.
But, certes, he that haunteth swiche delices   85
Is deed, whil that he liveth in tho vices.

    A lecherous thing is win, and dronkenesse
Is ful of striving and of wrecchednesse.
O dronke man, disfigured is thy face,
Sour is thy breeth, foul artou to embrace,   90
And thurgh thy dronke nose semeth the soun
As though thou seidest ay "Sampsoun, Sampsoun!"
And yet, God woot, Sampsoun drank nevere no win.
Thou fallest as it were a stiked swin;
Thy tonge is lost, and al thin honeste cure;   95
For dronkenesse is verray sepulture
Of mannes wit and his discrecioun.
In whom that drinke hath dominacioun
He can no conseil kepe, it is no drede.
Now kepe you fro the white and fro the rede,   100
And namely fro the white win of Lepe,
That is to selle in Fisshstrete or in Chepe.
This win of Spaigne crepeth subtilly
In othere wines, growinge faste by,
Of which ther riseth swich fumositee   105
That whan a man hath dronken draughtes thre,
And weneth that he be at hoom in Chepe,
He is in Spaigne, right at the towne of Lepe,—

80 *mary,* marrow   81 *swoote,* sweet
82 *spicerye,* spices   83 *delit,* delight
85 *certes,* surely; *delices,* pleasures   86 *deed,* dead; *tho,* those
93 *woot,* knows   94 *stiked swin,* stuck pig
95 *honeste cure,* concern for honor   96 *sepulture,* burial
99 *drede,* doubt   101 *namely,* particularly; *Lepe,* a town in Spain
102 *Chepe,* Cheapside in London
105 *swich fumositee,* such heady fumes   106 *weneth,* thinks

Nat at the Rochele, ne at Burdeux town;
And thanne wol he seye "Sampsoun, Sampsoun!" 110

But herkneth, lordinges, o word, I you preye,
That alle the soverein actes, dar I seye,
Of victories in the Olde Testament,
Thurgh verray God, that is omnipotent,
Were doon in abstinence and in preyere. 115
Looketh the Bible, and ther ye may it leere.

Looke, Attilla, the grete conquerour,
Deide in his sleep, with shame and dishonour,
Bledinge ay at his nose in dronkenesse.
A capitain sholde live in sobrenesse. 120
And over al this, aviseth you right wel
What was comaunded unto Lamuel—
Nat Samuel, but Lamuel, seye I—
Redeth the Bible, and finde it expresly
Of win-yeving to hem that han justise. 125
Namoore of this, for it may wel suffise.

And now that I have spoken of glotonye,
Now wol I you deffenden hasardrye.
Hasard is verray mooder of lesinges,
And of deceite, and cursed forsweringes, 130
Blaspheme of Crist, manslaughtre, and wast also
Of catel and of time; and forthermo,
It is repreeve and contrarye of honour
For to ben holde a commune hasardour.
And ever the hyer he is of estaat, 135
The moore is he yholden desolaat.
If that a prince useth hasardrye,
In alle governaunce and policye
He is, as by commune opinioun,

---

111 *lordinges*, gentlemen; *o*, one   116 *looketh*, behold; *leere*, learn
121 *aviseth you*, reflect
125 *win-yeving*, serving of wine; *han justice*, administer the law
128 *deffenden*, prohibit; *hasardrye*, gambling
129 *mooder*, mother; *lesinges*, lies   132 *catel*, property
133 *repreeve*, disgrace

Yholde the lasse in reputacioun.   140
  Stilboun, that was a wis embassadour,
Was sent to Corinthe, in ful greet honour,
Fro Lacidomye, to make hire alliaunce.
And whan he cam, him happede, par chaunce,
That alle the gretteste that were of that lond,   145
Pleyinge atte hasard he hem fond.
For which, as soone as it mighte be,
He stal him hoom again to his contree,
And seide, "Ther wol I nat lese my name,
Ne I wol nat take on me so greet defame,   150
You for to allye unto none hasardours.
Sendeth othere wise embassadours;
For, by my trouthe, me were levere die
Than I you sholde to hasardours allye.
For ye, that been so glorious in honours,   155
Shul nat allyen you with hasardours
As by my wil, ne as by my tretee."
This wise philosophre, thus seide hee.
  Looke eek that to the king Demetrius
The king of Parthes, as the book seith us,   160
Sente him a paire of dees of gold in scorn,
For he hadde used hasard ther-biforn;
For which he heeld his glorye or his renoun
At no value or reputacioun.
Lordes may finden oother maner pley   165
Honest ynough to drive the day awey.
  Now wol I speke of othes false and grete
A word or two, as olde bookes trete.
Gret swering is a thing abhominable,
And fals swering is yet moore reprevable.   170
The heighe God forbad swering at al,

140 *lasse,* less   148 *stal him,* stole away
149 *lese,* lose   153 *trouthe,* troth
160 *Parthes,* the Parthians   161 *dees,* dice
170 *reprevable,* reprehensible

Witnesse on Mathew; but in special
Of swering seith the hooly Jeremye,
"Thou shalt swere sooth thine othes, and nat lie,
And swere in doom, and eek in rightwisnesse";   175
But idel swering is a cursednesse.
Bihoold and se that in the firste table
Of heighe Goddes heestes honurable,
How that the seconde heeste of him is this:
"Take nat my name in idel or amis."   180
Lo, rather he forbedeth swich swering
Than homicide or many a cursed thing;
I seye that, as by ordre, thus it stondeth;
This knoweth, that his heestes understondeth,
How that the seconde heeste of God is that.   185
And forther over, I wol thee telle al plat,
That vengeance shal nat parten from his hous
That of his othes is to outrageous.
"By Goddes precious herte," and "By his nailes,"
And "By the blood of Crist that is in Hailes,   190
Sevene is my chaunce, and thin is cink and treye!"
"By Goddes armes, if thou falsly pleye,
This daggere shal thurghout thin herte go!"—
This fruit cometh of the bicched bones two,
Forswering, ire, falsnesse, homicide.   195
Now, for the love of Crist, that for us dide,
Lete youre othes, bothe grete and smale.
But, sires, now wol I telle forth my tale.

    Thise riotoures thre of whiche I telle,
Longe erst er prime rong of any belle,   200
Were set hem in a taverne for to drinke,
And as they sat, they herde a belle clinke
Biforn a cors, was caried to his grave.

175 *doom,* equity   178 *heestes,* commandments
181 *rather,* sooner; *swich,* such   186 *forther over,* moreover; *plat,* flat
191 *cink and treye,* five and three   197 *lete,* leave
200 *erst er,* before; *prime,* 9 A.M.   203 *cors,* body

That oon of hem gan callen to his knave:
"Go bet," quod he, "and axe redily   205
What cors is this that passeth heer forby;
And looke that thou reporte his name weel."

   "Sire," quod this boy, "it nedeth never-a-deel;
It was me toold er ye cam heer two houres.
He was, pardee, an old felawe of youres;   210
And sodeinly he was yslain to-night,
Fordronke, as he sat on his bench upright.
Ther cam a privee theef, men clepeth Deeth,
That in this contree al the peple sleeth,
And with his spere he smoot his herte atwo,   215
And wente his wey withouten wordes mo.
He hath a thousand slain this pestilence.
And, maister, er ye come in his presence,
Me thinketh that it were necessarye
For to be war of swich an adversarye.   220
Beth redy for to meete him everemoore;
Thus taughte me my dame; I sey namoore."
"By seinte Marye!" seide this taverner
"The child seith sooth, for he hath slain this yeer,
Henne over a mile, withinne a greet village,   225
Bothe man and womman, child, and hine, and page;
I trowe his habitacioun be there.
To been avised greet wisdom it were,
Er that he dide a man a dishonour."

   "Ye, Goddes armes!" quod this riotour,   230
"Is it swich peril with him for to meete?
I shal him seke by wey and eek by strete,
I make avow to Goddes digne bones!

205 *bet,* ? quickly; *axe,* ask	208 *never-a-deel,* never a bit
211 *to-night,* last night	212 *fordronke,* dead drunk
213 *privee,* stealthy; *clepeth,* call	214 *sleeth,* slays
216 *mo,* more	225 *henne,* hence
226 *hine,* servant	227 *trowe,* believe
228 *avised,* wary	233 *digne,* honorable

Herkneth, felawes, we thre been al ones;
Lat ech of us holde up his hand til oother,   235
And ech of us bicomen otheres brother,
And we wol sleen this false traitour Deeth.
He shal be slain, he that so manye sleeth,
By Goddes dignitee, er it be night!"

    Togidres han thise thre hir trouthes plight   240
To live and dien ech of hem for oother,
As though he were his owene ybore brother.
And up they stirte, al dronken in this rage,
And forth they goon towardes that village
Of which the taverner hadde spoke biforn.   245
And many a grisly ooth thanne han they sworn,
And Cristes blessed body al torente—
Deeth shal be deed, if that they may him hente!

    Whan they han goon nat fully half a mile,
Right as they wolde han troden over a stile,   250
An oold man and a poure with hem mette.
This olde man ful mekely hem grette,
And seide thus, "Now, lordes, God you see!"

    The proudeste of thise riotoures three
Answerde again, "What, carl, with sory grace!   255
Why artou al forwrapped save thy face?
Why livestou so longe in so greet age?"

    This olde man gan looke in his visage,
And seide thus, "For I ne can nat finde
A man, though that I walked into Inde,   260
Neither in citee ne in no village,
That wolde chaunge his youthe for min age;
And therfore moot I han min age stille,
As longe time as it is Goddes wille.

234 *al ones,* i.e., all of one mind   235 *til,* to
240 *trouthes,* troths   242 *ybore,* born
243 *stirte,* jumped   247 *torente,* torn apart (with their oaths)
248 *hente,* catch   252 *grette,* greeted
255 *carl,* churl   256 *forwrapped,* wrapped up
259 *for,* because   263 *moot,* must

Ne Deeth, allas! ne wol nat han my lif.   265
Thus walke I, lik a resteless caitif,
And on the ground, which is my moodres gate,
I knokke with my staf, bothe erly and late,
And seye 'Leeve mooder, leet me in!
Lo how I vanisshe, flessh, and blood, and skin!   270
Allas! whan shul my bones been at reste?
Mooder, with you wolde I chaunge my cheste
That in my chambre longe time hath be,
Ye, for an heire clout to wrappe in me!'
But yet to me she wol nat do that grace,   275
For which ful pale and welked is my face.

    But, sires, to you it is no curteisye
To speken to an old man vileinye,
But he trespasse in word, or elles in dede.
In Hooly Writ ye may yourself wel rede: 280
'Agains an oold man, hoor upon his heed,
Ye sholde arise'; wherfore I yeve you reed,
Ne dooth unto an oold man noon harm now,
Namoore than that ye wolde men did to you
In age, if that ye so longe abide.   285
And God be with you, where ye go or ride!
I moot go thider as I have to go."

    "Nay, olde cherl, by God, thou shalt nat so,"
Seide this oother hasardour anon;
"Thou partest nat so lightly, by Seint John!   290
Thou spak right now of thilke traitour Deeth,
That in this contree alle oure freendes sleeth.
Have heer my trouthe, as thou art his espye,
Telle where he is, or thou shalt it abye,

266 *caitif,* captive   267 *moodres,* mother's
269 *leeve,* dear   274 *heire clout,* haircloth
276 *welked,* withered   279 *but,* unless
281 *agains,* in the presence of   282 *yeve,* give; *reed,* advice
286 *go,* walk   287 *moot,* must
291 *thilke,* that same   293 *espye,* spy
294 *abye,* pay for

By God, and by the hooly sacrement!   295
For soothly thou art oon of his assent
To sleen us yonge folk, thou false theef!"
    "Now, sires," quod he, "if that ye be so leef
To finde Deeth, turne up this croked wey,
For in that grove I lafte him, by my fey,   300
Under a tree, and there he wole abide;
Noght for youre boost he wole him no thing hide.
Se ye that ook? Right there ye shal him finde.
God save you, that boghte again mankinde,
And you amende!" Thus seide this olde man;   305
And everich of thise riotoures ran
Til he cam to that tree, and ther they founde
Of florins fine of gold ycoined rounde
Wel ny an eighte busshels, as hem thoughte.
No lenger thanne after Deeth they soughte,   310
But ech of hem so glad was of that sighte,
For that the florins been so faire and brighte,
That down they sette hem by this precious hoord.
The worste of hem, he spak the firste word.
    "Bretheren," quod he, "taak kep what that I seye;   315
My wit is greet, though that I bourde and pleye.
This tresor hath Fortune unto us yiven,
In mirthe and jolitee oure lif to liven,
And lightly as it comth, so wol we spende.
Ey! Goddes precious dignitee! who wende   320
To-day that we sholde han so faire a grace?
But mighte this gold be caried fro this place
Hoom to min hous, or elles unto youres—
For wel ye woot that al this gold is oures—
Thanne were we in heigh felicitee.   325

296 *assent,* party   298 *leef,* anxious
300 *lafte,* left; *fey,* faith   306 *everich,* each one
310 *lenger,* longer   315 *kep,* heed
316 *bourde,* joke   317 *yiven,* given
320 *wende,* would have supposed   324 *woot,* know

But trewely, by daye it may nat bee.
Men wolde seyn that we were theves stronge,
And for oure owene tresor doon us honge.
This tresor moste ycaried be by nighte
As wisely and as slyly as it mighte.   330
Wherfore I rede that cut among us alle
Be drawe, and lat se wher the cut wol falle;
And he that hath the cut with herte blithe
Shal renne to the town, and that ful swithe,
And bringe us breed and win ful prively.   335
And two of us shul kepen subtilly
This tresor wel; and if he wol nat tarye,
Whan it is night, we wol this tresor carye,
By oon assent, where as us thinketh best."
That oon of hem the cut broghte in his fest, 340
And bad hem drawe, and looke where it wol falle;
And it fil on the yongeste of hem alle,
And forth toward the town he wente anon.
And also soone as that he was gon,
That oon of hem spak thus unto that oother: 345
"Thou knowest wel thou art my sworen brother;
Thy profit wol I telle thee anon.
Thou woost wel that oure felawe is agon,
And heere is gold, and that ful greet plentee,
That shal departed been among us thre.   350
But nathelees, if I can shape it so
That it departed were among us two,
Hadde I nat doon a freendes torn to thee?"
    That oother answerde, "I noot how that may be.
He woot wel that the gold is with us tweye;   355

328 *doon us honge*, have us hanged   329 *moste*, must
331 *rede*, advise; *cut*, lot   334 *renne*, run; *swithe*, quickly
340 *fest*, fist   342 *fil*, fell
344 *also*, as   348 *woost*, know; *agon*, gone away
350 *departed*, divided   351 *nathelees*, nevertheless; *shape*, manage
353 *torn*, turn   354 *noot*, don't know
355 *twey*, two

What shal we doon? What shal we to him seye?"

"Shal it be conseil?" seide the firste shrewe,
"And I shal tellen in a wordes fewe
What we shal doon, and bringe it wel aboute."

"I graunte," quod that oother, "out of doute,   360
That, by my trouthe, I wol thee nat biwreye."

"Now," quod the firste, "thou woost wel we be tweye,
And two of us shul strenger be than oon.
Looke whan that he is set, that right anoon
Aris as though thou woldest with him pleye,   365
And I shal rive him thurgh the sides tweye
Whil that thou strogelest with him as in game,
And with thy daggere looke thou do the same;
And thanne shal al this gold departed be,
My deere freend, bitwixen me and thee.   370
Thanne may we bothe oure lustes all fulfille,
And pleye at dees right at oure owene wille."
And thus acorded been thise shrewes tweye
To sleen the thridde, as ye han herd me seye.

This yongeste, which that wente to the town,   375
Ful ofte in herte he rolleth up and down
The beautee of thise florins newe and brighte.
"O Lord!" quod he, "if so were that I mighte
Have al this tresor to myself allone,
Ther is no man that liveth under the trone   380
Of God that sholde live so murye as I!"
And atte laste the feend, oure enemy,
Putte in his thought that he sholde poison beye,
With which he mighte sleen his felawes tweye;
For-why the feend foond him in swich livinge   385
That he hadde leve him to sorwe bringe.
For this was outrely his fulle entente,

357 *conseil,* a secret; *shrewe,* villain   361 *biwreye,* expose
363 *strenger,* stronger   380 *trone,* throne
383 *beye,* buy   385 *forwhy,* because; *swich,* such
386 *leve,* permission   387 *outrely,* in sum

To sleen hem bothe, and nevere to repente.
And forth he gooth, no lenger wolde he tarye,
Into the town, unto a pothecarye,   390
And preyde him that he him wolde selle
Som poison, that he mighte his rattes quelle;
And eek ther was a polcat in his hawe,
That, as he seide, his capouns hadde yslawe,
And fain he wolde wreke him, if he mighte,   395
On vermin that destroyed him by nighte.

     The pothecarye answerde, "And thou shalt have
A thing that, also God my soule save,
In al this world ther is no creature,
That eten or dronken hath of this confiture   400
Noght but the montance of a corn of whete,
That he ne shal his lif anon forlete;
Ye, sterve he shal, and that in lasse while
Than thou wolt goon a paas nat but a mile,
This poisoun is so strong and violent."   405

     This cursed man hath in his hond yhent
This poisoun in a box, and sith he ran
Into the nexte strete unto a man,
And borwed him large botelles thre;
And in the two his poison poured he;   410
The thridde he kepte clene for his drinke.
For al the nyght he shoop him for to swinke
In caryinge of the gold out of that place.
And whan this riotour, with sory grace,
Hadde filled with win his grete botels thre,   415
To his felawes again repaireth he.

     What nedeth it to sermone of it moore?

---

392 *quelle,* kill   393 *hawe,* yard
394 *yslawe,* slain   395 *wreke him,* avenge himself
398 *also,* as   401 *montance,* amount
402 *forlete,* lose   403 *sterve,* die
404 *goon a paas,* take a walk   406 *yhent,* grasped
407 *sith,* afterward   409 *borwed,* borrowed from
412 *shoop him,* intended; *swinke,* work

For right as they hadde cast his deeth bifoore,
Right so they han him slain, and that anon.
And whan that this was doon, thus spak that oon: 420
"Now lat us sitte and drinke, and make us merye,
And afterward we wol his body berye."
And with that word it happed him, par cas,
To take the botel ther the poison was,
And drank, and yaf his felawe drinke also,   425
For which anon they storven bothe two.

   But certes, I suppose that Avicen
Wroot nevere in no canon, ne in no fen,
Mo wonder signes of empoisoning
Than hadde thise wrecches two, er hir ending.   430
Thus ended been thise homicides two,
And eek the false empoisonere also.

   O cursed sinne of alle cursednesse!
O traitours homicide, O wickednesse!
O glotonye, luxurye, and hasardrye!   435
Thou blasphemour of Crist with vileinye
And othes grete, of usage and of pride!
Allas! mankinde, how may it bitide
That to thy creatour, which that thee wroghte,
And with his precious herte-blood thee boghte,   440
Thou art so fals and so unkinde, allas?

   Now, goode men, God foryeve you youre trespas,
And ware you fro the sinne of avarice!
Min hooly pardoun may you alle warice,
So that ye offre nobles or sterlinges,   445
Or elles silver broches, spoones, ringes.
Boweth youre heed under this hooly bulle!
Cometh up, ye wives, offreth of youre wolle!

418 *cast*, devised   423 *par cas*, by chance
425 *yaf*, gave   426 *storven*, died
428 Avicenna's *Canons* were divided into sections called *fens*
429 *mo*, more   437 *usage*, habit
442 *foryeve*, forgive   443 *ware*, guard
444 *warice*, save   445 *so that*, if

Youre names I entre heer in my rolle anon:
Into the blisse of hevene shul ye gon.   450
I you assoille, by min heigh power,
You that wol offre, as clene and eek as cleer
As ye were born.—And lo, sires, thus I preche.
And Jesu Crist, that is oure soules leche,
So graunte you his pardoun to receive,   455
For that is best; I wol you nat deceive.

(Fragment VI, lines 463–918)

451 *assoile*, pardon   454 *leche*, physician

THE NUN'S PRIEST'S TALE

A povre widwe, somdeel stape in age
Was whilom dwelling in a narwe cotage,
Biside a grove, stondinge in a dale.
This widwe, of which I telle you my tale,
Sin thilke day that she was last a wif,   5
In pacience ladde a ful simple lif,
For litel was hir catel and hir rente.
By housbondrye of swich as God hire sente
She foond hirself and eek hir doghtren two.
Thre large sowes hadde she, and namo,   10
Three keen, and eek a sheep that highte Malle.
Ful sooty was hire bowr and eek hir halle,
In which she eet ful many a sklendre meel.
Of poinaunt sauce hir neded never a deel.
No deintee morsel passed thurgh hir throte;   15

1 *somdeel*, somewhat; *stape*, advanced
2 *whilom*, once upon a time; *narwe*, narrow   5 *sin*, since; *thilke*, that
6 *ladde*, led   7 *catel*, capital; *rente*, income
8 *housbondrye*, economy; *swich*, such   9 *foond*, provided for
10 *namo*, no more   11 *keen*, cows; *highte*, was named
13 *sklendre*, scanty   14 *poinaunt*, piquant; *deel*, bit

Hir diete was accordant to hir cote.
Repleccioun ne made hire nevere sik;
Attempree diete was al hir physik,
And exercise, and hertes suffisaunce.
The goute lette hire nothing for to daunce, 20
N'apoplexye shente nat hir heed.
No win ne drank she, neither whit ne reed;
Hir bord was served moost with whit and blak,
Milk and brown breed, in which she foond no lak,
Seind bacoun, and somtime an ey or tweye; 25
For she was, as it were, a maner deye.

A yeerd she hadde, enclosed al aboute
With stickes, and a drye dich withoute,
In which she hadde a cok, hight Chauntecleer.
In al the land of crowing nas his peer. 30
His vois was murier than the murye orgon
On messe-dayes that in the chirche gon.
Wel sikerer was his crowing in his logge
Than is a clocke or an abbey orlogge.
By nature he knew ech ascencioun 35
Of the equinoxial in thilke town;
For whan degrees fiftene weren ascended,
Thanne crew he, that it mighte nat been amended.
His coomb was redder than the fin coral,
And batailled as it were a castel wal; 40
His bile was blak, and as the jeet it shoon;
Lik asure were his legges and his toon;

---

16 *cote,* cottage   17 *repleccioun,* overeating
18 *attempree,* temperate   19 *suffisaunce,* sufficiency
20 *lette . . . daunce,* in no way hindered her from dancing
21 *shente,* hurt   23 *whit and blak,* i.e., milk and bread
24 *lak,* fault   25 *seind,* scorched, i.e., broiled; *ey,* egg; *tweye,* two
26 *maner deye,* sort of dairy maid   29 *hight,* named
30 *nas,* was not   32 *messe-dayes,* mass-days; *gon,* i.e., is played
33 *sikerer,* more reliable; *logge,* dwelling   34 *orlogge,* timepiece
38 *amended,* improved upon   40 *batailled,* battlemented
41 *bile,* bill; *jeet,* jet   42 *toon,* toes

His nailes whitter than the lilye flowr,
And lik the burned gold was his colour.
This gentil cok hadde in his governaunce   45
Sevene hennes for to doon al his plesaunce,
Whiche were his sustres and his paramours,
And wonder lik to him, as of colours;
Of whiche the faireste hewed on hir throte
Was cleped faire damoisele Pertelote.   50
Curteis she was, discreet, and debonaire,
And compaignable, and bar hirself so faire,
Sin thilke day that she was seven night oold,
That trewely she hath the herte in hoold
Of Chauntecleer, loken in every lith;   55
He loved hire so that wel was him therwith.
But swich a joye was it to here hem singe,
Whan that the brighte sonne gan to springe,
In sweete accord, "My lief is faren in londe!"
For thilke time, as I have understonde,   60
Beestes and briddes coude speke and singe.
    And so bifel that in a daweninge,
As Chauntecleer among his wives alle
Sat on his perche, that was in the halle,
And next him sat this faire Pertelote,   65
This Chauntecleer gan gronen in his throte,
As man that in his dreem is drecched soore.
And whan that Pertelote thus herde him roore,
She was agast, and seide, "Herte deere,
What eileth you, to grone in this manere?   70
Ye been a verray sleper; fy, for shame!"
    And he answerde, and seide thus: "Madame,

44 *burned,* burnished	49 *hewed,* colored
50 *cleped,* called	52 *bar,* bore
53 *sin,* since	54 *hoold,* keeping
55 *loken,* locked; *lith,* limb	57 *hem,* them
58 *springe,* rise   59 *my . . . londe,* my love has gone away
67 *drecched,* troubled	72 *agrief,* amiss

I pray you that ye take it nat agrief.
By God, me mette I was in swich meschief
Right now, that yet min herte is soore afright.   75
Now God" quod he, "my swevene recche aright,
And kepe my body out of foul prisoun!
Me mette how that I romed up and down
Withinne our yeerd, wheer as I saugh a beest
Was lik an hound, and wolde han maad areest   80
Upon my body, and wolde han had me deed.
His colour was bitwixe yelow and reed,
And tipped was his tail and bothe his eeris
With blak, unlik the remenant of his heeris;
His snoute smal, with glowinge eyen tweye.   85
Yet of his look for feere almoost I deye;
This caused me my groning, doutelees."

  "Avoy!" quod she, "fy on you, hertelees!
Allas!" quod she, "for, by that God above,
Now han ye lost min herte and al my love.   90
I can nat love a coward, by my feith!
For certes, what so any womman seith,
We alle desiren, if it mighte bee,
To han housbondes hardy, wise, and free,
And secree, and no nigard, ne no fool,   95
Ne him that is agast of every tool,
Ne noon avauntour, by that God above!
How dorste ye seyn, for shame, unto youre love
That any thing mighte make you aferd?
Have ye no mannes herte, and han a berd?   100
Allas! and conne ye been agast of swevenis?

---

73 *me mette*, I dreamed
76 *swevene*, dream; *recche aright*, interpret correctly, i.e., auspiciously
79 *saugh*, saw   80 *maad areest*, laid hold
81 *had me deed*, i.e., killed me   85 *tweye*, two
88 *avoy*, fie; *hertelees*, coward   94 *free*, generous
95 *secree*, discreet   96 *tool*, weapon
97 *avauntour*, braggart   98 *seyn*, say
101 *conne*, can; *swevenis*, dreams

Nothing, God woot, but vanitee in sweven is.
Swevenes engendren of replecciouns,
And ofte of fume and of complecciouns,
Whan humours been to habundant in a wight.   105
Certes this dreem, which ye han met tonight,
Cometh of the greete superfluitee
Of youre rede colera, pardee,
Which causeth folk to dreden in hir dremes
Of arwes, and of fir with rede lemes,   110
Of rede beestes, that they wol hem bite,
Of contek, and of whelpes, grete and lite;
Right as the humour of malencolye
Causeth ful many a man in sleep to crye
For feere of blake beres, or boles blake,   115
Or elles blake develes wole hem take.
Of othere humours coude I telle also
That werken many a man in sleep ful wo;
But I wol passe as lightly as I can.

　　Lo Catoun, which that was so wis a man,   120
Seide he nat thus, 'Ne do no fors of dremes?'
　　Now sire," quod she, "whan we flee fro the bemes,
For Goddes love, as taak som laxatif.
Up peril of my soule and of my lif,
I conseille you the beste, I wol nat lie,   125
That bothe of colere and of malencolye
Ye purge you; and for ye shal nat tarye,
Though in this town is noon apothecarye,
I shal myself to herbes techen you
That shul been for youre hele and for youre prow;   130

102 *woot,* knows
103 *engendren of,* have their origin in; *replecciouns,* overeating
104 *fume,* gas; *complecciouns,* (disturbances in) the balance of bodily
　　humors   105 *wight,* creature
106 *met,* dreamed   108 *colera,* bile
110 *arwes,* arrows; *lemes,* flames
112 *contek,* strife; *whelpes,* dogs; *lite,* little   115 *boles,* bulls
121 *ne . . . of,* pay no attention to   122 *flee,* fly
124 *up,* upon   130 *hele,* health; *prow,* benefit

And in oure yeerd tho herbes shal I finde
The whiche han of hire propretee by kinde
To purge you binethe and eek above.
Foryet nat this, for Goddes owene love!
Ye been ful colerik of compleccioun;　　135
Ware the sonne in his ascencioun
Ne finde you nat repleet of humours hoote.
And if it do, I dar wel leye a grote,
That ye shul have a fevere terciane,
Or an agu, that may be youre bane.　　140
A day or two ye shul have digestives
Of wormes, er ye take youre laxatives
Of lauriol, centaure, and fumetere,
Or elles of ellebor, that groweth there,
Of catapuce, or of gaitris beryis,　　145
Of herbe ive, growing in oure yeerd, ther mery is;
Pekke hem up right as they growe and ete hem in.
Be mirye, housbonde, for youre fader kin!
Dredeth no dreem, I can sey you namoore."
　　"Madame," quod he, "graunt mercy of youre
　　　loore.　　150
But nathelees, as touching daun Catoun,
That hath of wisdom swich a greet renoun,
Though that he bad no dremes for to drede,
By God, men may in olde bookes rede
Of many a man moore of auctorite　　155
Than evere Caton was, so moot I thee,
That al the revers seyn of this sentence,

131 *tho,* those　　　　　　　132 *hire,* their; *kinde,* nature
134 *foryet,* forget　　　　　　135 *colerik,* bilious
136 *ware,* beware that　　　　137 *hoote,* hot
138 *leye a grote,* bet a groat
139 *tercian,* occurring on alternate days　　140 *bane,* destruction
143–45: the recommended laxatives are: laureole, centaury, fumitory,
　　hellebore, catapuce, gaiter berries, and herb ivy
148 *fader,* father's　　　　150 *graunt mercy of,* many thanks for
151 *nathelees,* nevertheless; *daun,* master
156 *moot I thee,* may I thrive　　　157 *revers,* reverse

And han wel founden by experience
That dremes been significaciouns
As wel of joye as of tribulaciouns   160
That folk enduren in this lif present.
Ther nedeth make of this noon argument;
The verray preeve sheweth it in dede.

    Oon of the gretteste auctour that men rede
Seith thus; that whilom two felawes wente   165
On pilgrimage, in a ful good entente;
And happed so, they coomen in a town
Wher as ther was swich congregacioun
Of peple, and eek so streit of herbergage,
That they ne founde as muche as o cotage   170
In which they bothe mighte ylogged bee.
Wherfore they mosten of necessitee,
As for that night, departen compaignye;
And ech of hem gooth to his hostelrye,
And took his logging as it wolde falle.   175
That oon of hem was logged in a stalle,
Fer in a yeerd, with oxen of the plough;
That oother man was logged wel ynough,
As was his aventure or his fortune,
That us governeth alle as in commune.   180

    And so bifel that, longe er it were day,
This man mette in his bed, ther as he lay,
How that his felawe gan upon him calle,
And seide, 'Allas! for in an oxes stalle
This night I shal be mordred ther I lie.   185
Now help me, deere brother, or I die.
In alle haste com to me!' he saide.
This man out of his sleep for feere abraide;

163 *the verray preeve*, actual experience   165 *whilom*, once
168 *so strait of herbergage*, such inadequacy of lodging   170 *o*, one
172 *mosten*, must   177 *fer*, far
179 *aventure*, chance   182 *mette*, dreamed
183 *gan*, did
188 *abraide*, awoke

But whan that he was wakened of his sleep,
He turned him, and took of this no keep. 190
Him thoughte his dreem nas but a vanitee.
Thus twies in his sleping dremed hee;
And atte thridde time yet his felawe
Cam, as him thoughte, and seide, 'I am now slawe.
Bihoold my bloody woundes depe and wide! 195
Aris up erly in the morwe tide,
And at the west gate of the town,' quod he,
'A carte ful of dong ther shaltou se,
In which my body is hid ful prively;
Do thilke carte arresten boldely. 200
My gold caused my mordre, sooth to sayn.'
And tolde him every point how he was slain,
With a ful pitous face, pale of hewe.
And truste wel, his dreem he foond ful trewe,
For on the morwe, as soone as it was day, 205
To his felawes in he took the way;
And whan that he cam to this oxes stalle,
After his felawe he bigan to calle.

The hostiler answerede him anon,
And seide, 'Sire, your felawe is agon. 210
As soone as day he wente out of the town.'

This man gan fallen in suspecioun,
Remembringe on his dremes that he mette,
And forth he gooth—no lenger wolde he lette—
Unto the west gate of the town, and fond 215
A dong-carte, wente as it were to donge lond,
That was arrayed in that same wise
As ye han herd the dede man devise.
And with an hardy herte he gan to crye

190 *keep,* heed
194 *slawe,* slain
200 *do arresten,* have stopped
209 *hostiler,* innkeeper
213 *mette,* dreamed
218 *devise,* describe

191 *nas,* i.e., was nothing
196 *morwe tide,* morning
206 *in,* inn
210 *agon,* gone away
214 *lenger,* longer; *lette,* tarry

Vengeance and justice of this felonye.   220
'My felawe mordred is this same night,
And in this carte he lith gaping upright.
I crye out on the ministres,' quod he,
'That sholden kepe and reulen this citee.
Harrow! allas! heere lith my felawe slain!'   225
What sholde I moore unto this tale sayn?
The peple out sterte and caste the cart to grounde,
And in the middel of the dong they founde
The dede man, that mordred was al newe.

O blisful God, that art so just and trewe,   230
Lo, how that thou biwreyest mordre alway!
Mordre wol out, that se we day by day.
Mordre is so wlatsom and abhominable
To God, that is so just and resonable,
That he ne wol nat suffre it heled be,   235
Though it abide a yeer, or two, or thre.
Mordre wol out, this my conclusioun.
And right anon, ministres of that town
Han hent the carter and so soore him pined,
And eek the hostiler so soore engined,   240
That they biknewe hire wickednesse anon,
And were anhanged by the necke-bon.

Heere may men seen that dremes been to drede.
And certes in the same book I rede,
Right in the nexte chapitre after this—   245
I gabbe nat, so have I joye or blis—
Two men that wolde han passed over see,
For certein cause, into a fer contree,
If that the wind ne hadde been contrarye,
That made hem in a citee for to tarye   250

223 *lith*, lies; *upright*, flat	227 *sterte*, rushed
231 *biwreyest*, disclose	233 *wlatsom*, loathsome
235 *heled*, concealed	237 *this*, i.e., this is
239 *hent*, seized; *pined*, tortured	240 *engined*, racked
241 *biknewe*, confessed	242 *anhanged*, hanged
246 *gabbe*, lie	248 *fer*, far

That stood ful mirye upon an haven-side;
But on a day, again the even-tide,
The wind gan chaunge, and blew right as hem leste.
Jolif and glad they wente unto hir reste,
And casten hem ful erly for to saille.   255
But to that o man fil a greet mervaille:
That oon of hem, in sleping as he lay,
Him mette a wonder dreem again the day.
Him thoughte a man stood by his beddes side,
And him comanded that he sholde abide,   260
And seide him thus; 'If thou tomorwe wende,
Thou shalt be dreint; my tale is at an ende.'
He wook, and tolde his felawe what he mette,
And preyde him his viage for to lette;
As for that day, he preyde him to bide.   265
His felawe, that lay by his beddes side,
Gan for to laughe, and scorned him ful faste.
'No dreem,' quod he, 'may so min herte agaste
That I wol lette for to do my thinges.
I sette nat a straw by thy dreminges,   270
For swevenes been but vanitees and japes.
Men dreme alday of owles and of apes,
And eek of many a maze therwithal;
Men dreme of thing that nevere was ne shal.
But sith I see that thou wolt heere abide,   275
And thus forsleuthen wilfully thy tide,
God woot, it reweth me; and have good day!'

252 *again,* toward   253 *leste,* pleased
254 *hir,* their   255 *casten hem,* resolved
256 *o,* one; *fil,* befell
259 *him mette,* he dreamed; *wonder,* wonderful
262 *dreint,* drowned   263 *mette,* dreamed
264 *viage,* voyage; *lette,* delay
269 *lette . . . thinges,* delay getting my business done
271 *swevenes,* dreams; *japes,* frauds   272 *alday,* constantly
273 *maze,* delusion   274 *shal,* i.e., shall be
275 *sith,* since   276 *forsleuthen,* waste
277 *woot,* knows

And thus he took his leve, and wente his way.
But er that he hadde half his cours yseiled,
Noot I nat why, ne what mischaunce it eiled,   280
But casuelly the shippes botme rente,
And ship and man under the water wente
In sighte of othere shippes it biside,
That with hem seiled at the same tide.
And therfore, faire Pertelote so deere,   285
By swiche ensamples olde maystou leere
That no man sholde been to recchelees
Of dremes; for I seye thee, doutelees,
That many a dreem ful soore is for to drede.

Lo, in the lif of Seint Kenelm I rede,   290
That was Kenulphus sone, the noble king
Of Mercenrike, how Kenelm mette a thing.
A lite er he was mordred, on a day,
His mordre in his avisioun he say.
His norice him expouned every deel   295
His sweven, and bad him for to kepe him weel
For traisoun; but he nas but seven yeer oold,
And therfore litel tale hath he toold
Of any dreem, so hooly was his herte.
By God! I hadde levere than my sherte   300
That ye hadde rad his legende, as have I.

Dame Pertelote, I sey you trewely,
Marcrobeus, that writ the avisioun
In Affrike of the worthy Sipioun,
Affermeth dremes, and seith that they been   305
Warning of thinges that men after seen.

280 *noot I,* I don't know; *mischaunce it eiled,* was the trouble
281 *casuelly,* accidentally   286 *leere,* learn
287 *recchelees,* careless   292 *Mercenrike,* Mercia; *mette,* dreamed
293 *lite,* little   294 *avisioun,* dream; *say,* saw
295 *norice,* nurse; *deel,* bit   296 *sweven,* dream
297 *for,* against; *nas,* was not
298–99 *litel tale toold of,* set little store by   300 *sherte,* shirt
301 *rad,* read

And forthermoore, I pray you, looketh wel
In the Olde Testament, of Daniel,
If he heeld dremes any vanitee.
Reed eek of Joseph, and ther shul ye see   310
Wher dremes be somtime—I sey nat alle—
Warninge of thinges that shul after falle.
Looke of Egypte the king, daun Pharao,
His bakere and his butiller also,
Wher they ne felte noon effect in dremes.   315
Whoso wol seken actes of sondry remes
May rede of dremes many a wonder thing.
Lo Cresus, which that was of Lyde king,
Mette he nat that he sat upon a tree,
Which signified he sholde anhanged bee?   320
Lo heere Andromacha, Ectores wif,
That day that Ector sholde lese his lif,
She dremed on the same night biforn
How that the lif of Ector sholde be lorn,
If thilke day he wente into bataille.   325
She warned him, but it mighte nat availle;
He wente for to fighte natheles,
But he was slain anon of Achilles.
But thilke tale is al to longe to telle,
And eek it is ny day, I may nat dwelle.   330
Shortly I seye, as for conclusioun,
That I shal han of this avisioun
Adversitee; and I seye forthermoor,
That I ne telle of laxatives no stoor,
For they been venimous, I woot it weel;   335
I hem diffye, I love hem never a deel!

---

311 *wher,* whether   315 *wher,* whether
316 *remes,* realms   318 *Lyde,* Lydia
319 *mette,* dreamed   322 *lese,* lose
324 *lorn,* lost   326 *availle,* do any good
327 *natheles,* nevertheless   334 *telle stoor of,* set store by
336 *deel,* bit

Now let us speke of mirthe, and stinte al this.
Madame Pertelote, so have I blis,
Of o thing God hath sent me large grace;
For whan I se the beautee of youre face,   340
Ye been so scarlet reed aboute youre ÿen,
It maketh al my drede for to dien;
For al so siker as *In principio*,
Mulier est hominis confusio,—
Madame, the sentence of this Latin is,   345
'Womman is mannes joye and al his blis.'
For whan I feele a-night your softe side,
Al be it that I may nat on you ride,
For that oure perche is maad so narwe, allas!
I am so ful of joye and of solas,   350
That I diffye bothe sweven and dreem."
And with that word he fley down fro the beem,
For it was day, and eke his hennes alle,
And with a chuk he gan hem for to calle,
For he hadde founde a corn, lay in the yerd.   355
Real he was, he was namoore aferd.
He fethered Pertelote twenty time,
And trad hire eke as ofte, er it was prime.
He looketh as it were a grim leoun,
And on his toos he rometh up and down;   360
Him deigned nat to sette his foot to grounde.
He chucketh, whan he hath a corn yfounde,
And to him rennen thanne his wives alle.
Thus royal, as a prince is in his halle,
Leve I this Chauntecleer in his pasture,   365
And after wol I telle his aventure.

  Whan that the month in which the world bigan,

---

337 *stinte,* cease   339 *o,* one
341 *reed,* red; *yen,* eyes   343 *siker,* sure
345 *sentence,* meaning   350 *solas,* delight
352 *fley,* flew   356 *real,* regal
358 *trad,* trod; *prime,* 9 A.M.   362 *rennen,* run

That highte March, whan God first maked man,
Was compleet, and passed were also,
Sin March bigan, thritty dayes and two,   370
Bifel that Chauntecleer in al his pride,
His sevene wives walkinge by his side,
Caste up his eyen to the brighte sonne,
That in the signe of Taurus hadde yronne
Twenty degrees and oon, and somwhat moore,   375
And knew by kinde, and by noon oother loore,
That it was prime, and crew with blisful stevene.
"The sonne," he seide, "is clomben up on hevene
Fourty degrees and oon, and moore ywis.
Madame Pertelote, my worldes blis,   380
Herkneth thise blisful briddes how they singe,
And se the fresshe flowres how they springe,
Ful is min herte of revel and solas!"
But sodeinly him fil a sorweful cas,
For evere the latter ende of joye is wo.   385
God woot that worldly joye is soone ago;
And if a rethor coude faire endite,
He in a cronicle saufly mighte it write
As for a soverein notabilitee.
Now every wis man, lat him herkne me;   390
This storye is also trewe, I undertake,
As is the book of Launcelot de Lake,
That wommen holde in ful greet reverence.
Now wol I torne again to my sentence.

A col-fox, ful of sly iniquitee,   395
That in the grove hadde woned yeres three,

368 *highte,* is called   370 *sin,* since
376 *by kinde,* instinctively   378 *stevene,* voice
379 *ywis,* indeed   383 *solas,* delight
384 *fil,* befell; *cas,* chance   386 *woot,* knows; *ago,* passed
387 *rethor,* rhetorician   388 *saufly,* safely
391 *also,* as   394 *sentence,* main point
395 *col-fox,* fox with black markings   396 *woned,* dwelt

By heigh imaginacioun forncast,
The same night thurghout the hegges brast
Into the yerd ther Chauntecleer the faire
Was wont, and eek his wives, to repaire;   400
And in a bed of wortes stille he lay,
Til it was passed undren of the day,
Waitinge his time on Chauntecleer to falle,
As gladly doon thise homicides alle
That in await liggen to mordre men.   405
O false mordrour, lurkinge in thy den!
O newe Scariot, newe Genilon,
False dissimulour, o Greek Sinon,
That broghtest Troye al outrely to sorwe!
O Chauntecleer, acursed be that morwe   410
That thou into that yerd flaugh fro the bemes!
Thou were ful wel ywarned by thy dremes
That thilke day was perilous to thee;
But what that God forwoot moot nedes bee,
After the opinioun of certein clerkis.   415
Witnesse on him that any parfit clerk is,
That in scole is greet altercacioun
In this mateere, and greet disputisoun,
And hath been of an hundred thousand men.
But I ne can nat bulte it to the bren,   420
As can the hooly doctour Augustin,
Or Boece, or the Bisshop Bradwardin,
Wheither that Goddes worthy forwiting
Streineth me nedely for to doon a thing,—

397 *heigh imaginacioun,* i.e., divine planning; *forncast,* predestined
398 *hegges,* hedges; *brast,* broke   401 *wortes,* weeds
402 *undren,* mid-morning   405 *liggen,* lie
407 *Scariot,* Iscariot   409 *al outrely,* utterly
410 *morwe,* morning   411 *flaugh,* flew
414 *forwoot,* foreknows; *moot,* must   416 *parfit,* skilled
420 *bulte,* sift; *bren,* husks   422 *Boece,* Boethius
423 *forwiting,* foreknowledge
424 *streineth,* constrains; *nedely,* necessarily

"Nedely" clepe I simple necessitee;   425
Or elles, if free chois be graunted me
To do that same thing, or do it noght,
Though God forwoot it er that it was wroght;
Or if his witing streineth never a deel
But by necessitee condicioneel.   430
I wol nat han to do of swich mateere;
My tale is of a cok, as ye may heere,
That tok his conseil of his wif, with sorwe,
To walken in the yerd upon that morwe
That he hadde met that dreem that I you tolde.   435
Wommennes conseils been ful ofte colde;
Wommannes conseil broghte us first to wo,
And made Adam fro Paradis to go,
Ther as he was ful mirye and wel at ese.
But for I noot to whom it might displese,   440
If I conseil of wommen wolde blame,
Passe over, for I seide it in my game.
Rede auctours, where they trete of swich mateere,
And what they seyn of wommen ye may heere.
Thise been the cockes wordes, and nat mine;   445
I can noon harm of no womman divine.

    Faire in the soond, to bathe hire mirily,
Lith Pertelote, and alle hire sustres by,
Again the sonne, and Chauntecleer so free
Soong murier than the mermaide in the see;   450
For Physiologus seith sikerly
How that they singen wel and mirily.
And so bifel that, as he caste his ÿe
Among the wortes on a boterflye,

425 *clepe*, call   429 *witing*, knowledge; *deel*, bit
435 *met*, dreamed   440 *noot*, don't know
442 *game*, sport   446 *divine*, guess
447 *soond*, sand   448 *lith*, lies
449 *again*, in   450 *soong*, sang
451 *sikerly*, positively   453 *ÿe*, eye

He was war of this fox, that lay ful lowe.   455
Nothinge ne liste him thanne for to crowe,
But cride anon, "Cok! cok!" and up he sterte
As man that was affrayed in his herte.
For natureely a beest desireth flee
Fro his contrarye, if he may it see,   460
Though he never erst hadde sein it with his ÿe.
    This Chauntecleer, whan he gan him espye,
He wolde han fled, but that the fox anon
Seide, "Gentil sire, allas! wher wol ye gon?
Be ye affrayed of me that am youre freend?   465
Now, certes, I were worse than a feend,
If I to you wolde harm or vileinye!
I am nat come youre conseil for t'espye,
But trewely, the cause of my cominge
Was oonly for to herkne how that ye singe.   470
For trewely, ye have as mirye a stevene
As any aungel hath that is in hevene.
Therwith ye han in musik moore feelinge
Than hadde Boece, or any that can singe.
My lord youre fader—God his soule blesse!—   475
And eek youre mooder, of hire gentillesse,
Han in min hous ybeen to my greet ese;
And certes, sire, ful fain wolde I you plese.
But for men speke of singing, I wol seye,
So moote I brouke wel mine eyen tweye,   480
Save you, I herde nevere man so singe
As dide your fader in the morweninge.
Certes, it was of herte, al that he song.
And for to make his vois the moore strong,
He wolde so peine him that with bothe his ÿen   485

456 *liste,* pleased   457 *sterte,* started
461 *sein,* seen   462 *can,* did
468 *conseil,* secrets   471 *stevene,* voice
480 *moote,* may; *brouke,* enjoy the use of; *tweye,* two
483 *of herte,* heartfelt   485 *peine,* exert; *ÿen,* eyes

He moste winke, so loude he wolde cryen,
And stonden on his tiptoon therwithal,
And strecche forth his necke long and smal.
And eek he was of swich discrecioun
That ther nas no man in no regioun   490
That him in song or wisedom mighte passe.
I have wel rad in "Daun Burnel the Asse,"
Among his vers, how that ther was a cok,
For that a preestes sone yaf him a knok
Upon his leg whil he was yong and nice,   495
He made him for to lese his benefice.
But certein, ther nis no comparisoun
Bitwixe the wisedom and discrecioun
Of youre fader and of his subtiltee.
Now singeth, sire, for seinte charitee;   500
Lat se, conne ye youre fader countrefete?"

     This Chauntecleer his winges gan to bete,
As man that coude his traisoun nat espye,
So was he ravisshed with his flaterye.

     Allas! ye lordes, many a fals flatour   505
Is in youre courtes, and many a losengeour,
That plesen you wel moore, by my feith,
Than he that soothfastnesse unto you seith.
Redeth Ecclesiaste of flaterye;
Beth war, ye lordes, of hir trecherye.   510

     This Chauntecleer stood hye upon his toos,
Strecchinge his necke, and heeld his eyen cloos,
And gan to crowe loude for the nones.
And daun Russell the fox stirte up atones,

486 *moste,* must   490 *nas,* was not
492 *rad,* read; *Daun Burnel,* Master Burnellus   494 *yaf,* gave
495 *nice,* foolish   496 *lese,* lose
497 *nis,* is not   501 *conne,* can; *countrefete,* imitate
505 *flatour,* flatterer   506 *losengeour,* deceiver
509 *Ecclesiaste,* Ecclesiasticus   510 *hir,* their
513 *for the nones,* for the nonce, a phrase here having little meaning
514 *stirte,* jumped; *atones,* at once

And by the gargat hente Chauntecleer, 515
And on his bak toward the wode him beer,
For yet ne was ther no man that him sewed.

O destinee, that mayst nat been eschewed!
Allas, that Chauntecleer fleigh fro the bemes!
Allas, his wif ne roghte nat of dremes! 520
And on a Friday fil al this meschaunce.

O Venus, that art goddesse of plesaunce,
Sin that thy servant was this Chauntecleer,
And in thy service dide al his poweer,
Moore for delit than world to multiplye, 525
Why woldestou suffre him on thy day to die?

O Gaufred, deere maister soverain,
That whan thy worthy king Richard was slain
With shot, compleinedest his deeth so soore,
Why ne hadde I now thy sentence and thy loore 530
The Friday for to chide, as diden ye?
For on a Friday, soothly, slain was he.
Thanne wolde I shewe you how that I coude pleine
For Chauntecleres drede and for his peine.

Certes, swich cry ne lamentacion, 535
Was nevere of ladies maad whan Ilion
Was wonne, and Pyrrus with his streite swerd,
Whan he hadde hent king Priam by the berd,
And slain him, as seith us *Eneidos,*
As maden alle the hennes in the clos, 540
Whan they had sein of Chauntecleer the sighte.
But sovereinly dame Pertelote shrighte,
Ful louder than dide Hasdrubales wif,

---

515 *gargat,* throat; *hente,* seized   516 *beer,* bore
517 *sewed,* pursued   519 *fleigh,* flew
520 *roghte nat of,* set no store by   521 *fil,* befell
523 *sin,* since   525 *delit,* delight
527 *Gaufred,* Geoffrey (of Vinsauf)   530 *sentence,* intelligence
533 *pleine,* complain   537 *streite,* drawn
538 *hent,* seized   540 *clos,* yard
541 *sein,* seen   542 *sovereinly,* splendidly; *shrighte,* shrieked

Whan that hir housbonde hadde lost his lif,
And that the Romains hadde brend Cartage.   545
She was so ful of torment and of rage
That wilfully into the fir she sterte,
And brende hirselven with a stedefast herte.

    O woful hennes, right so criden ye,
As, whan that Nero brende the citee   550
Of Rome, criden senatoures wives
For that hir husbondes losten alle hir lives;
Withouten gilt this Nero hath hem slain.
Now wole I turne to my tale again.

    This sely widwe and eek hir doghtres two   555
Herden thise hennes crye and maken wo,
And out at dores stirten they anon,
And sien the fox toward the grove gon,
And bar upon his bak the cok away,
And criden, "Out! harrow! and weilaway!   560
Ha! ha! the fox!" and after him they ran,
And eek with staves many another man.
Ran Colle oure dogge, and Talbot, and Gerland,
And Malkin, with a distaf in hir hand;
Ran cow and calf, and eek the verray hogges,   565
So fered for the berking of the dogges
And shouting of the men and wommen eeke,
They ronne so hem thoughte hir herte breeke.
They yolleden as feendes doon in helle;
The dokes criden as men wolde hem quelle;   570
The gees for feere flowen over the trees;
Out of the hive cam the swarm of bees.
So hidous was the noise, a, *benedicitee!*

545 *brend,* burned	547 *sterte,* leaped
548 *brende,* burned	555 *sely,* poor
557 *stirten,* rushed	558 *sien,* saw
566 *fered,* terrified	568 *ronne,* ran; *breeke,* would break
569 *yolleden,* yelled	570 *dokes,* ducks; *quelle,* kill
571 *flowen,* flew	

Certes, he Jacke Straw and his meinee
Ne made nevere shoutes half so shrille,   575
Whan that they wolden any Fleming kille,
As thilke day was maad upon the fox.
Of bras they broghten bemes, and of box,
Of horn, of boon, in whiche they blewe and pouped,
And therwithal they skriked and they houped.   580
It semed as that hevene sholde falle.

    Now, goode men, I prey you herkneth alle:
Lo, how Fortune turneth sodeinly
The hope and pride eek of hir enemy!
This cok, that lay upon the foxes bak,   585
In al his drede unto the fox he spak,
And seide, "Sire, if that I were as ye,
Yet sholde I seyn, as wis God helpe me,
'Turneth again, ye proude cherles alle!
A verray pestilence upon you falle!   590
Now am I come unto the wodes side;
Maugree youre heed, the cok shal heere abide.
I wol him ete, in feith, and that anon!'"

    The fox answerde, "In feith, it shal be don."
And as he spak that word, al sodeinly   595
This cok brak from his mouth deliverly,
And heighe upon a tree he fleigh anon.
And whan the fox saugh that the cok was gon,
    "Allas!" quod he, "O Chauntecleer, allas!
I have to you," quod he, "ydoon trespas,   600
In as muche as I maked you aferd
Whan I you hente and broghte out of the yerd.
But, sire, I dide it in no wicke entente.

---

574 *meinee*, followers   578 *bemes*, trumpets; *box*, boxwood
579 *boon*, bone; *pouped*, tooted
580 *skriked*, shrieked; *houped*, whooped   588 *wis*, surely
592 *maugree youre heed*, despite your head, i.e., despite whatever you
    try to do   596 *brak*, broke; *deliverly*, nimbly
597 *fleigh*, flew   598 *saugh*, saw
602 *hente*, seized   603 *wicke*, wicked

Com down, and I shal telle you what I mente;
I shal seye sooth to you, God help me so!"   605
    "Nay thanne," quod he, "I shrewe us bothe two.
And first I shrewe myself, bothe blood and bones,
If thou bigile me ofter than ones.
Thou shalt namoore, thurgh thy flaterye,
Do me to singe and winke with min ÿe;   610
For he that winketh, whan he sholde see,
Al wilfully, God lat him nevere thee!"
    "Nay," quod the fox, "but God yeve him meschaunce,
That is so undiscreet of governaunce
That jangleth whan he sholde holde his pees."   615
    Lo, swich it is for to be recchelees
And necligent, and truste on flaterye.
    But ye that holden this tale a folye,
As of a fox, or of a cok and hen,
Taketh the moralite, goode men.   620
For seint Paul seith that al that writen is,
To oure doctrine it is ywrite, ywis;
Taketh the fruit, and lat the chaf be stille.
Now, goode God, if that it be thy wille,
As seith my lord, so make us alle goode men,   625
And bringe us to his heighe blisse! Amen.

            (Fragment VII, lines 2821–3446)

---

606 *shrewe,* beshrew   610 *do,* cause
612 *thee,* thrive   613 *yeve,* give
614 *governaunce,* management   616 *recchelees,* careless
622 *ywis,* indeed   623 *lat,* let

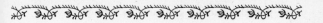

John Lydgate

(1370?–1451?)

A Lover's New Year's Gift

In honnour of this heghe fest, of custume yere by
    yere,
  Is first for to remembre me upon my lady dere.
For nowe upon this first day I wil my chois renuwe,
All the whiles that I live to hir to be truwe,
    Bothe to serve and love hir best with al min hert
      entier.   5

For I have maked min avowe, in verray sothefastnesse,
To be hir faithful truwe man, withoute doublenesse,
    Whersoever that I be, outher fer or ner.

Hit voideth al min hevinesse, bothe in thought and ded,
Whane that I remembre me upon hir goodelihed,   10
    Because she is so wommanly, bothe of port and chere.

And as I stoode myself alloone, upon the Nuwe Yere
    night,
I prayed unto the frosty moone, with hir pale light,
    To go and recomaunde me unto my lady dere.

And erly on the nexst morowe, kneling in my cloos,   15
I prayed eke the shene sonne, the houre whane he
    aroos,

1 *heghe,* high	**8** *outher,* either; *fer,* far
9 *hit,* it	**10** *goodelihed,* goodliness
11 *port and chere,* bearing and behavior	**15** *cloos,* i.e., chamber
16 *shene,* shining	

225

To gon also and sey the same in his bemis clere.

But tho ther came a cloudy thought, and gan min hert
assaile,
And saide me, howe my service ther me shoulde not
availe,
Til my lady mercilesse me had brought on beer.   20

Hit is ful hard to grave in steel and in a flint also,
And yit men may smite fire of hem bothe two,
But I may of hir hert of steel mercye noon requere.

Tho came gode hope ageine and gan min hert adawe,
And of min hevy stormy thought apeese wel the
wawe,   25
And so the skies of dispeire began to wexen clere.

And yit ageine for hevinesse I gan me to compleine,
That she was so fer away, min hertes soveraine,
Which to spek of wommanhed hath in this world no
peer.

And whanne I thenke verraily upon hir wommanhed, 30
And therwithal recorde also hir hevenly godelihed,
I se she is so fer fro me, allas, and I am here.

For she passeth of beaute Isaude and Eleine,
I sey in sothe as thenketh me, for me list not feine,
And yonge, fresshe Polyxene with hir eyen cler.   35

She passeth eke of desport Dido of Cartage,
Adrean and Medea by favour of visage,
And eke alle thoo that ever I sawe in any coost ap-
pere.

18 *tho,* then; *gan,* did   20 *beer,* bier
21 *hit,* it   22 *hem,* them
24 *adawe,* revive   25 *wawe,* wave
30 *thenke,* think   31 *recorde,* recall
34 *thenketh,* seems to; *me list not feine,* I do not please to pretend
38 *thoo,* those

Penalapee was in hir time moost famous of fairnesse,
And Ester was ycalled eke mirour of gentilesse,   40
   But yit noon of hem everichoon is like my lady dere.

Iff I shal reherce also Gresildes pacience,
My lady hath, I dare wel sey, more passing eloquence
   To reherse by and by hir vertus alle yfeere.

I had lever a looke alloone withouten any more   45
Of hir goodely eyen twoo min haromes to restore,
   Thanne have alle other at my wille, I recche not who
   hit here.

I have no thing to given hir at this gladde time,
But min hert undeparted, nowe this firste prime,
   The which this day I sende hir al hooly and entier. 50

And this litel simple gifft I prey hir nought refuse,
The whiche thoughe hit but simple be, but God wil me
   excuse,
   For yif she toke hit not aright, I shulde hit bye to
   dere.

Who giveth his hert he graunteth al his goodes in substaunce,
And unto hir I gif hit al withoute repentaunce,   55
   And that I am hir truwest man therby she may hit
   lere.

Now go forthe, hert, and be right glad with hir to abide,
And wait upon hir day or night, wher that she go or
   ride,
   And looke thou part not away, I charge, in no maner.

---

41 *hem everichoon*, them all
44 *by and by*, one after the other; *yfeere*, together
46 *haromes*, harms   47 *recche . . . here*, care not who hears it
49 *undeparted*, unshared; *firste prime*, i.e., first hour of the year
50 *hooly*, wholly   53 *yif*, if; *bye*, buy; *to*, too
56 *lere*, learn   58 *go*, walk

And thoughe thou sojourne ever ther, hit shal not coste
    gret   60
For constreint of the wintur colde ner sunne with his het,
    For despense of the vitaile shal nought be to deer.

Go nowe forthe, thou litel songe, upon my message,
And sey howe that I give hir hole with the surplusage,
    Hert, body, and al my good, and my service in
    fere.   65

Lat no wawes ne no winde lettin thy passage,
Ne stormes of the salte see, ne no rockes rage;
    The streemes of hir hevenly looke shul alle thy sor-
    owes steer.

Go forthe in hast, thou litel songe, and no lenger tarye,
Now upon the first day of this Januarye,   70
    And conferme fully up my choise ay from yere to
    yere.

61 *ner,* nor	62 *despense,* expense
63 *message,* errand	64 *hole,* whole
65 *in fere,* together	66 *wawes,* waves; *lettin,* hinder
68 *streemes,* beams; *steer,* check	69 *hast,* haste

FROM *Court of Sapience*

[*Lament*]

Farewell Mercy, farewell thy piteous grace,
So wellawey, that Vengeaunce shall prevaile,
Farewell the beamid light of hevins place,
Unto mankinde thou mayst nomore availe,
The pure derknes of hell thee doth assaile,   5
O light in vaine, the clips hath thee incluse,
Man was thy lord, now man is thy refuse.

6 *clips,* eclipse; *incluse,* closed up

O Seraphin, yeve up thine armony!
O Cherubin, thy glory do away!
O ye Thronis, late be all melody!   10
Youre Ierarchy disteined is for ay!
Youre Maisteresse see in what aray
She lith in soune, ylorene with debate!
Farewell, farewell, pure houshold desolate!

O souverain mighty Dominaciounes,   15
O ye Virtutes and ye Potestates,
O Principatis with all youre hevenly sounes,
Archaungell, Aungell, o thries thre Estates,
Youre spouse, Dame Pease, overset is with debates!
Now may ye wepe, and Ierarchies thre,   20
Youre Ordres nine may nat restorid be.

Farewell ye all! Dame Mercy lith in soune;
For Sothfastnes accusid hath mankinde,
And Rightwisnes, that shold do all reasoune,
Hath dampnid him as crewell and unkinde.   25
Mercy ne Pease for theim no grace may finde;
Natwithstanding jugement may have no sute
Because of pease but hit be execute.

Wo worth debate that never may have pease!
Wo worth penaunce that asketh no pite!   30
Wo worth vengeaunce that mercy may nat cease!
Wo worth jugement that hath noon equite!
Wo worth that trewthe that hath no charite!
Wo worth that juge that may none gilty save!
And wo worth right that may no favour have!   35

(Lines 435–69)

8 *yeve,* give   10 *late be,* leave off
11 *Ierarchy,* hierarchy; *disteined,* dimmed
13 *lith in soune,* lies in swoon; *ylorene,* destroyed
16 *Potestates,* Powers   17 *Principatis,* Principalities; *sounes,* sounds
19 *overset,* overcome   23 *Sothfastnes,* Truth
25 *dampnid,* condemned   27 *sute,* sanction
28: i.e., unless it be executed in the interests of peace
29 *wo worth,* i.e., woe to   31 *cease,* cause to cease

FROM *The Dance of Death*

[*The Dance*]

Death to the Ser-
geant.

Come forthe, sire sergeaunt, with your
    stately mace:
Make no defence ne no rebellioun.
Not may availe to grucche in this cace,
Though ye be deinous of condicioun;
For nouther peele ne proteccioun   5
May you fraunchise to do nature wronge,
For ther is noon so sturdy champioun,
Though he be mighty, another is as
    stronge.

The Sergeant an-
swers.

How dar this dethe sette on me areste
That am the kinges chosen officere,   10
Which yesterday bothe este and weste
Min office dede ful surquedous of chere?
But now this day I am arested here,
And may not fle, though I had hit
    sworne.
Eche man is lothe to die, ferre and
    nere,   15
That hath not lerned for to die aforne.

Death to the
Monk.

Sire monke also, with youre blake abite,
Ye may no lenger holde here sojoure.
Ther is no thinge that may you here re-
    spite,

---

3 *not,* naught; *grucche,* grumble   4 *deinous,* haughty
5 *nouther,* neither; *peele,* appeal   6 *fraunchise,* emprivilege
12 *dede,* did; *surquedous of chere,* arrogant of manner
14 *sworne,* i.e., sworn the contrary   16 *aforne,* before
17 *abite,* habit   18 *lenger,* longer; *sojoure,* sojourn

Ayein my might, you for to do socoure. 20
Ye mote accounte touching youre la-
　　boure,
How ye have spente hit in dede, worde,
　　and thought.
To erthe and asshes turneth every flowre:
The life of man is but a thinge of nought.

The Monk an-
swers.

I had levere in the cloistre be   25
Atte my boke, and studye my service,
Whiche is a place contemplatif to se,
But I have spente my life in many vise
Liche as a fole, dissolute and nice:
God of his mercy graunte me repent-
　　aunce.   30
Be chere outewarde harde is to device:
Al ben not mery whiche that men seen
　　daunce.

Death to the
Usurer.

Thou userere, loke up and beholde:
Unto winninge thou settest al thy peine,
Whose covetise wexeth never colde,   35
Thy gredy thruste so sore thee dothe con-
　　streine.
But thou shalt never thy desire atteine:
Such an etik thin herte frete shal,
That but of pite God his honde refreine,
Oo parilous stroke shal make thee lese
　　al.   40

The Usurer an-
swers.

Now me behoveth sodeinly to dey,
Which is to me grete peine and grete
　　grevaunce.

20 *ayein,* against
　　　　　　　　　　　　　　　　　　21 *mote,* must
22 *hit,* it   29 *liche,* like; *nice,* wanton
31: i.e., by outward expression it is hard to discern
35 *covetise,* avarice   36 *thruste,* thirst
38 *etik,* hectic fever; *frete,* gnaw   39 *refreine,* hold back
40 *oo,* one; *lese,* lose   41 *behoveth,* it is necessary

Socoure to finde I see no maner weye,
Of golde ne silver be no chevisshaunce.
Dethe thrugh his haste abitte no purvi-
  aunce   45
Of folkes blinde, that can not loke welle:
Ful ofte happeth be kinde or fatal
  chaunce
Somme have feire yyen that seen never a
  dele.

The Poor Man to   Usure to God is ful grete offence,
the Usurer.
And in His sight a grete abusioun. 50
The pore borweth par cas for indigence:
The riche lent be fals collucioun,
Only for lucre in his entencioun.
Dethe shal hem bothe to accomptes fette
To make rekenninge be computa-
  cioun: 55
No man is quitte that is behinde of dette.

Death to the   Maister of physik, whiche on youre urine
Physician.
So loke and gase and stare ayenne the
  sunne,
For al youre crafte and studye of medi-
  cine,
Al the practik and science that ye
  cunne,   60
Youre lives cours so ferforthe is yrunne,
Ayeine my might youre crafte may not
  endure,

---

44 *be no chevisshaunce*, by no money-lending
45 *abitte*, awaits; *purviaunce*, preparations
47 *be kinde*, by nature   48 *yyen*, eyes; *dele*, bit
50 *abusioun*, violation   51 *par cas*, perchance
52 *lent*, lends; *collucioun*, fraud 54 *hem*, them; *fette*, fetch
55 *be*, by   60 *cunne*, know
61 *ferforthe*, far

For al the golde that ye therby have
    wonne:
Good leche is he that can himself recure.

Ful long agon that I unto phesike   65
Sette my witte and my diligence,
In speculatif and also in practike,
To gete a name thurgh min excellence,
To finde oute ayens pestilence
Preservatifes to staunche hit and to
    fine: 70
But I dar saye, shortly in sentence,
Ayens dethe is worth no medicine.

Ye that be jentel, so fresshe and amerous,
Of yeres yonge, flowring in youre grene
    age,
Lusty fre of herte and eke desirous,   75
Ful of devises and chaunge in youre cor-
    age,
Plesaunt of porte, of loke, and of visage,
But al shal turne into asshes dede,
For al beaute is but a feinte image,
Which steleth away or folkes can take
    hede.   80

Allas, allas, I can now no socoure
Ayeins dethe for myselfe provide;
Adieu, of youthe the lusty fressh flowre;
Adieu, veinglorye of beute and of pride;
Adieu, al servise of the god Cupide;   85

---

64 *leche,* doctor; *recure,* heal
67: i.e., in theoretical and in practical medicine
70 *hit,* it; *fine,* bring to end   72 *worth,* effective
76 *devises,* fancies; *corage,* heart   80 *or,* ere

Adieu, my ladies so fresshe, so wel-be-
        seine;
For ayeine dethe no thinge may abide,
And windes grete gon downe with litel
        reine.

Come forthe, maistresse, of yeres yonge
        and grene,
Which holde youreself of beaute sov-
        ereine;   90
As feire as ye was sum time Pollycene,
Penelope and the quene Eleine;
Yitte on this daunce they wenten bothe
        tweine,
And so shul ye for al youre straunge-
        nesse:
Though daunger longe in love hathe lad
        youre reine,   95
Arested is youre chaunge of doublenesse.

O cruel dethe, that sparest noon astate,
To olde and yonge thou arte indefferente.
To my beaute thou haste yseide checke-
        mate,
So hasty is thy mortal jugemente;   100
For in my youthe this was min entente,
To my service many a man to a lured:
But she is a fole, shortly in sentemente,
That in her beaute is to moche assured.

Sire advocate, shorte process for to
        make,   105
Ye mote come plete afore the hye Juge;

86 *wel-beseine,* good-looking
94 *straungenesse,* coldness 95 *daunger,* coyness; *lad,* led; *reine,* reign
96 *chaunge of doubleness,* trading in duplicity   102 *to a,* to have
105 *processe,* summons   106 *mote,* must; *plete,* plead

Many a quarel ye have undurtake,
And for lucre to do folke refuge;
But my fraunchise is so large and huge
That counceile noon availe may but
    truth: 110
He scapeth wisely of dethe the grete del-
    uge
Tofore the dome who is not teinte with
    slouth.

The Man of Law Of right and resoun be natures lawe
answers.
I càn not put ayen dethe no defence,
Ne be no sleight me kepe ne with-
    drawe,   115
For al my witte and my grete prudence,
To make appele from his dredeful sen-
    tence;
No thing in erthe may a man preserve,
Ayeine his might to make no resistence:
God quiteth al men liche as they de-
    serve.   120

Death to the Maister joroure, whiche that atte assise
Juror.
And atte shires, questes doste embrace,
Departist londe like to thy devise,
And who moste gaf moste stode in thy
    grace;
The pore man loste londe and place; 125
For golde thou coudest folke disherite,

108 *do refuge,* give aid   109 *fraunchise,* jurisdiction
111 *scapeth,* escapes; *wisely,* surely
112: i.e., who is not seized with sloth before the judgment
113 *be,* by   115 *sleight,* trick
120 *quiteth,* requites; *liche,* like
121 *joroure,* juryman; *atte assise,* at assizes
122 *shires,* shire courts; *questes doste embrace,* undertake inquests
123 *departist,* apportion; *devise,* fancy   124 *gaf,* gave

But now lete see with thy teinte face
Tofore the Juge howe thou cannest thee
    quite.

The Juror an-
swers.

Somme time I was cleped in my cuntre
The belle-wedir, and that was not a
    lite;   130
Not loved but drad of hye and lowe de-
    gre,
For whom me liste be crafte I coude en-
    dite,
And hange the trewe and the thief re-
    spite.
Al the cuntre be my worde was lad,
But I dar sey, shortly for to write,   135
Of my dethe many a man is glad.

Death to the
Minstrel.

O thou minstral, that cannest so note and
    pipe
Unto folkes for to do pleasaunce,
By the right honde anoone I shal thee
    gripe,
With these other to go upon my
    daunce.   140
Ther is no scape nouther avoidaunce,
On no side to contrarye my sentence,
For in music be crafte and accordaunce
Who maister is shall shew his science.

The Minstrel an-
swers.

This newe daunce is to me so
    straunge,   145
Wonder diverse and passingly contrarye;

127 *teinte*, painted   128 *quite*, acquit
129 *cleped*, called
130 *belle-wedir*, bellwether; *a lite*, i.e., wide of the mark
131 *drad*, feared   132 *be*, by; *endite*, indict
134 *be*, by; *lad*, led   137 *note*, sing
141 *scape*, escape   143 *be*, by; *accordaunce*, harmony

The dredful foting dothe so ofte
    chaunge,
And the mesures so ofte sithes varye,
Whiche now to me is no thing necessarye
Yif hit were so that I might asterte: 150
But many a man, yif I shal not tarye,
Ofte daunceth, but no thinge of herte.

              (Lines 361–512)

---

148 *sithes,* times   150 *yif,* if; *hit,* it; *asterte,* escape
151 *yif,* if; *tarye,* i.e., hesitate to speak
152 *of herte,* at his own desire

Thomas Hoccleve

(1370?–1450?)

FROM *The Regimen of Princes*

[Prologue]

*Heere beginnith the Book how
Princis sholden be governid.*

Musing upon the restles bisinesse
  Which that this troubly world hath ay on honde,
That othir thing than fruit of bittirnesse
  Ne yeldeth nought, as I can undirstonde,
    At Chestre inne, right fast be the stronde,   5
      As I lay in my bed upon a night,
      Thought me bereft of sleep with force and might.

And many a day and night that wicked hine
  Hadde beforn vexid my poore goost
So grevously, that of anguish and pine   10
  No richere man was nougher in no coost;
    This dar I seyn, may no wight make his boost
      That he with Thought was bettir than I aqueinted,
      For to the deth it wel nigh hath me feinted.

Bisily in my minde I gan revolve   15
  The welthe onsure of everye creature,
How lightly that Fortune it can dissolve,

5 *fast,* close; *be the stronde,* by the riverbank   8 *hine,* thrall
9 *goost,* spirit   10 *pine,* torment
11 *nougher,* nowhere; *coost,* region   14 *feinted,* enfeebled
15 *gan,* did   16 *onsure,* unsure

Whan that hir list that it no lenger dure;
And of the brotilnesse of hire nature,
  My tremling hert so grete gastnesse hadde,   20
  That my spiritis were of my life sadde.

Me fel to minde how that, not long ago,
  Fortunes strok down threst estaat royal
Into mischeef; and I took heed also
  Of many anothir lord that had a fall;   25
  In mene estaat eek sikernesse at all
    Ne saw I noon; but I sey atte laste,
    Wher seurte, for to abide, hir caste.

In poore estaat sche pight hir paviloun,
  To covere hire from the stroke of descending;   30
For that sche kneew no lowere discencion,
  Save oonly deth, fro which no wight living
  Defendin him may; and thus, in my musing,
    I destitut was of joye and good hope,
    And to min ese no thing coude I groope.   35

For right as blive ran it in my thought,
  Though I be poore, yet somwhat leese I may;
Than deemed I that seurete would nought
  With me abide, it is nought to hir pay,
  Ther to sojurne as sche descende may;   40
    And thus unsikir of my smal lifloode,
    Thought leid on me full many an hevy loode.

I thought eek, if I into povert creepe,
  Than am I entred into sikirnesse;

18 *list*, pleases; *no lenger dure*, no longer endure
19 *brotilnesse*, fickleness   20 *tremling*, trembling; *gastnesse*, terror
23 *threst*, thrust   26 *mene*, middle; *sikernesse*, security
27 *sey*, saw   28 *seurte*, security; *hir caste*, placed herself
29 *pight*, erected   35 *groope*, find by groping
36 *blive*, quickly   37 *leese*, lose
39 *pay*, profit   41 *unsikir*, unsure; *lifloode*, livelihood
43 *povert*, poverty   44 *sikirnesse*, security

But swich seurete might I ay waile and weepe,   45
  For poverte breedeth nought but hevinesse.
Allas! wher is this worldis stabilnesse?
    Heer up, heer down; heer honour, heer repreef;
    Now hool, now seek; now bounte, now mischeef.

And whan I hadde rolled up and down   50
  This worldes stormy wawes in my minde,
I seey weel povert was exclusion
  Of all weelfare regning in mankinde;
  And how in bookes thus I writen finde,
    "The werste kinde of wrecchednesse is,   55
    A man to have been weelfull or this."

"Allas!" thoghte I, "what sikirnesse is that
  To live ay seur of greef and of nuisaunce?
What schal I do? best is I strive nat
  Againe the pais of Fortunes balaunce;   60
  For wele I wote, that hir brotel constaunce,
    A wight no while suffer can sojurne
    In a plit." Thus nat wiste I how to torne.

For whan a man weneth stond most constant,
  Than is he nexte to his overthrowing;   65
So flitting is sche, and so variant,
  Ther is no trust upon hir fair laughing;
  After glad looke sche schapith hir to sting;
    I was adrad so of hir gerinesse,
    That my lif was but a dedly gladnesse.   70

45 *swich*, such   47 *stabilnesse*, stability
48 *repreef*, disgrace   49 *hool*, hale; *seek*, sick
51 *wawes*, waves   52 *seey*, saw
56 *weelfull*, prosperous; *or*, ere   58 *seur*, sure
60 *againe*, against; *pais*, weight
61 *wote*, know; *brotel constaunce*, brittle constancy
62–63 *a wight . . . a plit*, can permit a man to remain no time in
  one condition   63 *wiste*, knew; *torne*, turn
64 *weneth*, supposes to   66 *flitting*, shifty
68 *shapith hir*, prepares herself
69 *adrad*, adread; *gerinesse*, capriciousness

Thus ilke night I walwid to and fro,
  Seking Reste; but certeinly sche
Apeerid noght, for Thoght, my crewel fo,
  Chaced hadde hir and slepe away fro me;
  And for I schulde not alone be,   75
    Again my luste, Wach profrid his servise,
    And I admittid him in hevy wise.

So long a night ne felde I never non,
  As was that same to my jugement;
Whoso that thoghty is, is wo-begon;   80
  The thoghtful wight is vessel of turment,
  Ther nis no greef to him equipolent;
    He graveth deppest of seekenesses alle;
    Ful wo is him that in swich thoght is falle.

What wight that inly pensif is, I trowe,   85
  His moste desire is to be solitarye;
That this is soth, in my persone I knowe,
  For evere whil that fretinge adversarye
  Min herte made to him tributarye,
    In soukinge of the fresschest of my blod,   90
    To sorwe soole, methoght it dide me good.

For the nature of hevinesse is this:
  If it habounde gretly in a wight,
The place eschewit he wher as joye is,
  For joye and he not mowe accorde aright;   95
  As discordant as day is unto night,
    And honour adversarye is unto schame,
    Is hevinesse so to joye and game.

---

71 *ilke,* every; *walwid,* tossed   76 *luste,* desire; *Wach,* waking
78 *felde,* felt   82 *nis no,* is no; *equipolent,* equal
83: i.e., he digs deepest of all sicknesses   88 *fretinge,* gnawing
90 *soukinge,* sucking   91 *to sorwe soole,* alone with sorrow
93 *habounde,* abound   95 *mowe,* may
97 *and honour,* and as honour

When to the thoghtful wight is tolde a tale,
  He heerith it as thogh he thennes were;   100
His hevy thoghtes him so plucke and hale
  Hider and thedir, and him greve and dere,
  That his eres availe him not a pere;
    He understondeth no thing what men seye,
    So ben his wittes fer gon hem to pleye.   105

The smert of thoght I by experience
  Knowe as wel as any man doth livinge;
His frosty swoot and firy hote fervence,
  And troubly dremes, drempt al in wakinge,
  My maized heed sleepless han of conninge   110
    And wit dispoilid, and so me bejapid,
    That after deth ful often have I gapid.

(Lines 1–112)

---

101 *hale*, pull   102 *hider and thedir*, hither and thither; *dere*, hurt
103 *pere*, pear   105 *fer gon . . . pleye*, gone far to sport themselves
108 *frosty swoot*, cold sweat; *fervence*, burning
110 *maized*, addled; *heed*, head; *conninge*, intelligence
110–11 *han . . . dispoilid*, have despoiled   111 *bejapid*, tricked
112 *gapid*, longed

Anonymous

The Second Shepherds' Play

(*The Towneley Mysteries*, 13)

Scene I—A moor

Enter Coll alone.

COLL. Lord, what these weders ar cold, and I am ill
        happid;
  I am nerehande dold, so long have I nappid;
  My legis thay fold, my fingers ar chappid.
  It is not as I wold, for I am al lappid
     In sorow,   5
     In stormes and tempest,
     Now in the eest, now in the west.
     Wo is him has never rest
        Midday nor morow.

  Bot we sely husbandis that walkis on the
        moore,   10
  In faith we are nerehandis outt of the doore.
  No wonder, as it standis, if we be poore,
  For the tilthe of oure landis lyis falow as the
        floore,
     As ye ken.
     We are so hamid,   15
     Fortaxed and ramid,

1 *what . . . cold,* how cold these storms are; *happid,* covered
2 *dold,* numb   3 *fold,* give way
10 *sely husbandis,* poor farmers   13 *tilthe,* i.e., arable part
14 *ken,* know   15 *hamid,* hamstrung
16: i.e., overtaxed and beaten down

We ar made hand-tamid
    With thise gentlery-men.

Thus thay refe us oure rest; oure Lady theim
        wary!
These men that ar lord-fest, thay cause the
        ploghe tary.   20
That men say is for the best, we finde it contrary.
Thus ar husbandis opprest in pointe to miscary.
        On life,
    Thus hold thay us hunder,
    Thus thay bring us in blonder;   25
    It were greatte wonder
        And ever shuld we thrife.

Ther shall com a swaine as proude as a po;
He must borow my waine, my ploghe also;
Then I am full faine to graunt or he go.   30
Thus lif we in paine, anger, and wo,
        By night and day;
    He must have if he lang it,
    If I shuld forgang it;
    I were better be hangid   35
        Then oones say him nay.

For may he gett a paint-slefe, or a broche, now-
        on-dayes,
Wo is him that him grefe, or onis againe says.
Dar no man him reprefe, what mastry he mays,

17–18 *made hand-tamid . . . gentlery men,* subjugated by these high-
    born men   19 *refe us,* deprive us of; *wary,* curse
20 *lord-fest,* i.e., attached to lords' households   24 *hunder,* under
25 *blonder,* trouble   27 *and,* if
28 *po,* peacock   30 *or,* ere
33 *lang,* wants   34: i.e., even if I have to go without it
37 *for may . . . paint-slefe,* for if a fellow can get himself an em-
    broidered sleeve (i.e., some position in a lord's household)
38 *grefe,* grieve; *againe says,* gainsays
39 *reprefe,* reprove; *what . . . he mays,* no matter what force he uses

And yit may no man lefe oone word that he
        says,   40
    No letter.
He can make purveance
With boste and bragance,
And all is thrugh mantenance
    Of men that are gretter.   45

It dos me good, as I walk thus by min oone,
Of this warld for to talk in maner of mone.
To my shepe will I stalk, and herkin anone,
Ther abide on a balk, or sitt on a stone,
    Full sone;   50
For I trowe, perdé,
Trew men if thay be,
We gett more compané
    Or it be none.

Enter Gib, who does not see Coll.

GIB. Benste and Dominus, what may this bemene? 55
Why fares this warld thus oft have we not sene?
Lord, thise winds ar spitus, and the weders full
        kene,
And the frostis so hidus they water min eene,
    No ly.
Now in dry, now in wete,   60
Now in snaw, now in slete,
When my shone fres to my fete,
    It is not all esy.

40 *lefe*, believe   42 *make purveance*, get provisions
43 *bragance*, bragging
44 *thrugh mantenance of*, because of protection by
45 *gretter*, greater   46 *by min oone*, by myself
47 *warld*, world; *mone*, complaint   49 *balk*, mound
50: i.e., straightway   51 *trowe*, believe
54: i.e., before it is noon   55 *benste*, bless us; *bemene*, mean
57 *spitus*, cruel   58 *eene*, eyes
61 *snaw*, snow   62 *shone*, shoes

Bot as far as I ken, or yit as I go,
We sely wedmen dre mekill wo;   65
We have sorow then and then, it fallis oft so.
Sely Capile, oure hen, both to and fro
    She cakils.
  Bot begin she to crok,
  To grone or to clok,   70
  Wo is him oure cok,
    For he is in the shakils.

These men that ar wed have not all thare will:
When they ar full hard sted thay sigh full still;
God wate thay are led full hard and full ill;   75
In bower nor in bed thay say noght thertill.
    This tide
  My parte have I fun;
  I know my lesson;
  Wo is him that is bun,   80
    For he must abide.

Bot now late in oure lifis—a mervell to me,
That I think my hart rifis sich wonders to see,
What that destany drifis it shuld so be—
Som men will have two wifis, and some men
    thre   85
    In store!
  Som ar wo that has any,
  Bot so far can I,
  Wo is him that has many,
    For he felis sore.   90

64 *go*, walk   65: i.e., we poor married men suffer much woe
66 *then and then*, constantly   70 *clok*, cluck
72 *shakils*, shackles   74 *sted*, situated; *still*, constantly
75 *wate*, knows   76 *thertill*, thereagainst
77 *tide*, time   78 *fun*, found
80 *bun*, bound   82 *lifis*, lives
83 *rifis*, splits; *sich*, such   84 *what*, how; *drifis*, drives
88 *can*, know   90 *felis*, feels

Bot yong men of-wowing, for God that you
       boght,

Be well war of weding and think in youre thoght:
"Had I wist" is a thing it servis of noght.

Mekill still mourning has weding home broght,
     And grefis   95
   With many a sharp showre,
   For thou may cach in an oure
   That shall savour fulle soure
     As long as thou liffis.

For, as ever red I pistill, I have oone to my
       fere   100
As sharp as a thistill, as rugh as a brere;
She is browid like a bristill, with a soure-loten
     chere;
Had she oones wett hir whistill she couth sing
     full clere
     Hir Pater Noster.
   She is as greatt as a whall,   105
   She has a galon of gall:
   By Him that died for us all,
     I wald I had rin to I had lost hir.

COLL.   Gib, looke over the raw! Full defly ye stand!

                            Arising.

GIB.   Yee, the devill in thy maw so tariand!   110
    Sagh thou awre of Daw?

COLL.   Yee, on a ley land

---

91 *of-wowing,* a-wooing   92 *war,* wary
93 *wist,* known   94 *mekill still,* much constant
96 *showre,* fight   97 *oure,* hour
100 *pistill,* epistle; *fere,* mate   101 *brere,* briar
102 *bristill,* hog's bristle; *soure-loten chere,* sour-looking face
103 *couth,* could   105 *whall,* whale
108 *wald,* would; *rin to,* run till   109 *raw,* hedgerow; *defly,* dully
110: i.e., ? may the Devil take your tardy guts
111 *sagh,* saw; *awre,* anywhere; *ley,* pasture
112 *hard,* heard; *blaw,* blow

Hard I him blaw. He commis here at hand,
    Not far.
  Stand still.

GIB.   Qwhy?

COLL. For he commis, hope I.   115

GIB. He will make us both a ly
    Bot if we be war.

Enter Daw, who does not see the others.

DAW. Cristis crosse me spede and Sant Nicholas!
    Therof had I nede; it is wars then it was,
    Whoso couthe take hede and lett the warld
        pas.   120
    It is ever in drede and brekill as glas,
      And slithis.
      This warld foure never so,
      With mervels mo and mo,
      Now in wele, now in wo,   125
        And all thing writhis.

  Was never sin Noe floode sich floodis sene,
  Windis and rainis so rude and stormes so kene:
  Som stamerd, som stod in doute, as I wene.
  Now God turne all to good! I say as I mene. 130
      For ponder:
    These floodis so thay drowne,
    Both in feldis and in towne,
    And beris all downe,
      And that is a wonder.   135

  We that walk on the nightis, oure catell to kepe,
  We se sodan sightis, when othere men slepe.

115 *hope,* think   117 *bot if,* unless
119 *wars,* worse   121 *brekill,* brittle
122 *slithis,* slips   123 *foure,* fared
124 *mo,* more   126 *writhis,* i.e., changes
127 *sin,* since   129 *wene,* suppose
137 *sodan,* unexpected

He sees the others, but does not address them.

    Yit methink my hart lightis, I se shrewis pepe.

    Ye ar two tall wightis. I will giff my shepe

        A turne.   140

      Bot full ill have I ment:

      As I walk on this bent

      I may lightly repent,

        My toes if I spurne.

    A, sir, God you save, and master mine!   145

                  Addressing the others.

    A drink fain wold I have, and somwhat to dine.

COLL. Cristis curs, my knave, thou art a ledir hine!

GIB. What, the boy list rave! Abide unto sine

      We have made it.

      Ill thrift on thy pate!   150

      Though the shrew cam late

      Yit is he in state

        To dine, if he had it.

DAW. Sich servandis as I, that swettis and swinkis,

    Etis oure brede full dry, and that me

        forthinkis.   155

    We ar oft wete and wery when master-men

        winkis,

    Yit commis full lately both diners and drinkis.

      Bot naitely

    Both oure dame and oure sire,

    When we have rin in the mire,   160

    Thay can nip at oure hire,

      And pay us full lately.

---

138 *shrewis pepe,* rascals are watching   140 *ment,* planned
141 *bent,* field   142 *lightly,* quickly
143 *spurne,* stub   147 *ledir hine,* worthless servant
148 *list rave,* feels like raving; *unto sine,* until after
154 *servandis,* servants; *swinkis,* work   155 *forthinkis,* distresses
156 *winkis,* sleep   158 *naitely,* profitably
160 *rin,* run   161 *nip at,* i.e., deduct from

Bot here my trouth, master, for the fare that ye
make
I shall do therafter: wirk as I take.
I shall do a litill, sir, and emang ever laike,   165
For yit lay my soper never on my stomake
    In feldis.
    Wherto shuld I threpe?
    With my staf can I lepe,
    And men say, "Light chepe   170
    Letherly foryeldis."

COLL. Thou were an ill lad to ride on wowing
    With a man that had bot litill of spending.
GIB. Peasse, boy, I bad, no more jangling,
    Or I shall make thee full rad, by the hevens
    king,   175
    With thy gaudis.
    Wher ar oure shepe, boy? We scorne.
DAW.   Sir, this same day at morne
    I thaim left in the corne,
    When thay rang Laudis.   180

Thay have pasture good, thay can not go wrong.
COLL. That is right. By the roode, thise nightis ar long;
    Yit I wold, or we yode, oone gaf us a song.
GIB. So I thoght as I stode, to mirth us emong.
DAW.   I grauntt.   185
COLL. Lett me sing the tenory.
GIB. And I the trible so hye.

163 *trouth*, pledge; *fare . . . make*, i.e., the sort of food you serve
164 *wirk . . . take*, i.e., work as I am paid
165 *emang ever laike*, meanwhile always sport   168 *threpe*, haggle
170–71 *light . . . foryeldis*, A cheap bargain repays badly
172–73: i.e., a lad like you would eat up all a poor master's money
175 *rad*, frightened   176 *gaudis*, tricks
177 *scorne*, ? behave foolishly
180 *Laudis*, the earliest service of the day
183 *or we yode*, ere we went; *gaf*, gave
184 *emong*, meanwhile

DAW.   Then the mene fallis to me.
          Lett se how you chauntt.   *They sing.*

Enter Mak, wearing a cloak over his clothes, soliloquizing.

MAK.   Now, Lord, for thy names seven, that made both
          mone and starnes,   190
    Well mo then I can neven, thy will, Lorde, of me
          tharnes.
    I am all uneven—that moves oft my harnes.
    Now wold God I were in heven, for ther wepe no
          barnes
          So still.

COLL.   Who is that pipis so poore?   195
MAK.   Wold God ye wist how I foore!   *Aside.*
    Lo, a man that walkis on the moore,   *Aloud.*
    And has not all his will.

GIB.   Mak, where has thou gon? Tell us tithing.
DAW.   Is he commen? Then ilkon take hede to his
          thing.   200
          Snatches cloak from Mak.
MAK.   What! ich be a yoman, I tell you, of the king,
          Pretending not to know them.
    The self and the same, sond from a greatt lording,
          And sich.
          Fy on you! Goth hence,
          Out of my presence,   205
          I must have reverence.
          Why, who be ich?

188 *mene*, middle part   190 *starnes*, stars
191 *mo*, more; *neven*, name; *tharnes*, fails
192 *uneven*, at odds; *harnes*, brains
          194 *still*, incessantly
196 *wist*, knew; *foore*, fared   199 *tithing*, news
200 *ilkon*, every one; *thing*, property   201 *ich*, I
202 *sond*, messenger

COLL. Why make ye it so quaint? Mak, ye do wrang.

GIB. Bot Mak, list ye saint? I trow that ye lang.

DAW. I trow the shrew can paint, the devill might
             him hang!   210

MAK. Ich shall make complaint and make you all to
             thwang,
      At a worde,
    And tell evin how ye doth.

COLL.   Bot Mak, is that sothe?
    Now take outt that sothren tothe,   215
      And sett in a torde!

GIB. Mak, the devill in youre ee! A stroke wold I lene
             you.

DAW. Mak, know ye not me? By God, I couthe tene
             you.

MAK. God looke you all thre! Methoght I had sene you
            As if recognizing them.
    Ye ar a faire compané.

COLL.   Can ye now mene you?   220

GIB.   Shrew, jape!
    Thus late as thou gos,
    What will men suppos?
    And thou has an ill nois
      Of steling of shepe.   225

MAK. And I am trew as stele, all men wate;
    Bot a sekenes I fele that haldis me full hate:
    My belly faris not wele, it is out of astate.

208 *make . . . quaint,* i.e., do you pretend to be a stranger
209 *list ye saint,* do you want to act like a saint; *lang,* long to
210 *paint,* i.e., play a part
211 *make . . . thwang,* have you all bound
215 *sothren tothe,* southern tooth, i.e., the southern dialect Mak has
    assumed   216 *torde,* turd
217 *ee,* eye; *lene,* lend   219 *couthe tene,* could grieve
220 *mene you,* remember   221: i.e., curse you, rascal
224 *nois,* reputation   226 *wate,* know
227 *sekenes,* sickness; *haldis,* keeps; *hate,* hot

DAW.   Seldom lyis the devill dede by the gate.

MAK.   Therfor   230
            Full sore am I and ill
            If I stande stone-still.
            I ete not an nedill
               This moneth and more.

COLL.   How fares thy wiff? By my hoode, how faris
               sho?   235

MAK.   Lyis waltering, by the roode, by the fire, lo!
        And a house full of brude; she drinkis well, to.
        Ill spede othere good that she will do!
               Bot sho
            Etis as fast as she can;   240
            And ilk yere that commis to man
            She bringis furth a lakan,
               And som yeres two.

        Bot were I not more gracius and richere be far,
        I were eten outt of house and of harbar.   245
        Yit is she a foull douse, if ye com nar;
        Ther is none that trowse nor knowis a war
               Than ken I.
            Now will ye se what I profer:
            To gif all in my cofer   250
            To-morne at next to offer
               Hir hed-maspenny.

GIB.   I wote so forwakid is none in this shire.
        I wold slepe if I takid les to my hire.

229 *dede,* dead; *gate,* path   233 *nedill,* i.e., bit
235 *sho,* she   236 *waltering,* wallowing
237 *brude,* children   238: i.e., that's all she will do
241 *ilk,* every   242 *lakan,* baby
244 *gracius,* prosperous; *be,* by   245 *harbar,* i.e., home
246 *douse,* darling; *nar,* near, i.e., to the truth
247 *trowse,* imagines; *war,* worse   251 *to-morne at next,* tomorrow
252: i.e., the mass-penny for her departed spirit
253 *forwakid,* worn out from waking

DAW. I am cold and nakid and wold have a fire.   255

COLL. I am wery, forrakid, and run in the mire:
  Wake thou!

GIB.   Nay, I will lig downe by,
  For I must slepe truly.

DAW.   As good a mans son was I   260
    As any of you.

Bot Mak, com heder, betwene shall thou lig
    downe.

MAK. Then might I lett you bedene of that ye wold
    roune,
    No drede.

  Fro my top to my too,   265
        Saying his prayers.

  Manus tuas commendo,
  Pontio Pilato.
  Crist-crosse me spede!

Now were time for a man that lackis what he
    wold   *Rising while the rest sleep.*
To stalk prevely than unto a fold,   270
And neemly to wirk than, and be not to bold,
For he might aby the bargain if it were told
    At the ending.
  Now were time for to rele,
  Bot he nedis good counsele   275
  That fain wold fare wele,
    And has bot litill spending.

Bot aboute you a cercill, as rounde as a mone,
        He puts a charm on the sleepers.

255 *if*, even if; *les*, less   256 *forrakid*, exhausted from walking
258 *lig*, lie   262 *heder*, hither
263: i.e., then I might hinder you if you wanted to whisper together
264 *no drede*, doubtless   270 *prevely*, secretly
271 *neemly*, nimbly   272 *aby*, pay for
274 *rele*, run riot   278 *mone*, moon

To I have done that I will, till that it be none,
That ye lig stone-still to that I have done;   280
And I shall say thertill of good wordis a fone:
    On hight,
    Over youre hedis my hand I lift.
    Outt go youre een! fordo your sight!
    Bot yit I must make better shift   285
        And it be right.

Lord, what thay slepe hard! That may ye all here.
Was I never a shepard, bot now will I lere;
If the flok be scard, yit shall I nip nere.
How! Drawes hederward! Now mendis oure
        chere   290
    From sorow.
    A fatt shepe, I dar say!
    A good flese, dar I lay!
    Eftquite when I may,
        Bot this will I borow.   295

Exit with sheep.

279 *to,* until; *that I,* what I   280 *to,* until
281 *thertill,* thereto; *fone,* few
284 *een,* eyes; *fordo,* rendered powerless   286 *and,* if
287 *here,* hear   288 *lere,* learn
289 *scard,* scared   293 *lay,* bet
294 *eftquite,* repay

Scene II—Mak's house

Mak speaks outside the door.

MAK. How, Gill, art thou in? Gett us som light.
GILL. Who makis sich din this time of the night?
    I am sett for to spin, I hope not I might
    Rise a penny to win, I shrew them on hight.
        So faris   5

3 *I hope . . . might,* I don't think I could
4 *shrew,* curse; *on hight,* aloud

A huswiff that has bene
To be rasid thus betwene.
Here may no note be sene
     For sich small charis.

MAK. Good wiff, open the hek! Ses thou not what I
               bring?   10

GILL. I may thole thee dray the snek. A, com in, my
               sweting!   *Opening*.

MAK. Yee, thou thar not rek of my long standing!
                                               He enters.

GILL. By the nakid nek art thou like for to hing.
                                              Seeing sheep.

MAK.   Do way!
     I am worthy my mete,   15
     For in a straite can I gett
     More then thay that swinke and swette
          All the long day.

     Thus it fell to my lott, Gill, I had sich grace.

GILL. It were a foull blott to be hanged for the case. 20

MAK. I have scapid, Jelott, oft as hard a glase.

GILL. "Bot so long gos the pott to the water," men says,
               "At last
     Comis it home broken."

MAK. Well knowe I the token,   25
     Bot let it never be spoken!
          Bot com and help fast.

     I wold he were slain, I list well ete;
     This twelmonthe was I not so fain of oone shepe-
               mete.

6–7: i.e., a housewife who has to endure being made to get up at
    intervals   8 *note*, completed work
9 *charis*, chores   10 *hek*, door
11 *thole thee . . . snek*, permit you to draw the latch
12 *thar*, need; *rek of*, care about
16 *straite*, pinch   13 *hing*, hang
                                                  17 *swinke*, work
21 *scapid*, escaped; *glase*, blow

GILL. Com thay or he be slain and here the shepe
      blete—   30

MAK. Then might I be tane. That were a cold swette!
      Go spar
  The gate doore.

GILL.   Yis, Mak.
  For and thay com at thy bak—

MAK.   Then might I by, for all the pak,   35
    The devill of the war.

GILL. A good bourde have I spied, sin thou can none:
Here shall we him hide to thay be gone,
In my credill. Abide! Lett me alone,
And I shall lig beside in childbed and grone. 40

MAK.   Thou red,
    And I shall say thou was light
    Of a knave-childe this night.

GILL.   Now well is me day bright
      That ever was I bred.   45

This is a good gise and a fair cast,
Yit a womans avise helpis at the last.

I wote never who spise; agane go thou fast.

MAK. Bot I com or thay rise, els blawes a cold blast.
    I will go slepe.   50
  Yit slepis all this meneye,
  And I shall go stalk prevely,
    As it had never bene I
      That caried thare shepe.

---

30 *or*, ere   31 *tane*, taken
32 *spar*, fasten   33 *gate*, street
34 *and*, if
35 *by*, pay; *for . . . pak*, because of all the pack (of pursuers)
36 *war*, worse   37: a good trick have I found, since you know none
38 *to*, until   40 *lig*, lie
41 *red*, put things in order   42 *light*, lightened
43 *knave-child*, manchild   44: i.e., it was a good day
46 *gise*, method; *cast*, trick   48 *wote*, know; *spise*, spies
49 *or*, ere
                              51 *meneye*, company

Scene III—The moor

Coll, Gib, Daw, and Mak are awaking

COLL.   *Resurrex a mortruis!* have hald my hand!
    Judas carnas dominus! I may not well stand.
    My fote slepes, by Jesus, and I walter fastand.
    I thoght that we laid us full nere Ingland.

GIB.   A, ye!   5
    Lord, what I have slept wele!
    As fresh as an ele!
    As light I me fele
    As lefe on a tre!

DAW.   Benste be herin! So my body quakis   10
    My hart is outt of skin, what so it makis.
    Who makis all this din? So my browes blakis,
    To the dowore will I win. Harke, felows, wakis!
      We were foure.
      See ye awre of Mak now?   15
COLL.   We were up or thou.
GIB.   Man, I gif God avowe
      Yit yede he nawre.

DAW.   Methoght he was lapt in a wolfe-skin.
COLL.   So are many hapt now, namely within.   20
DAW.   When we had long napt, methoght with a gin
    A fatt shepe he trapt, bot he made no din.
GIB.   Be still.

1 *hald,* hold   3 *walter,* lie; *fastand,* fasting
7 *ele,* eel   10 *benste,* blessing
11 *what . . . makis,* whatever causes it
12 *browes blakis,* ? face pales
13 *dowore,* burrow (? the shepherds' sleeping place); *win,* go
15 *awre,* anywhere   16 *or,* ere
17 *gif,* give   18 *yede,* went; *nawre,* nowhere
20 *hapt,* covered; *namely,* especially   21 *gin,* snare

Thy dreme makis thee woode.

It is bot fantom, by the roode.   25

COLL.   Now God turne all to good,

     If it be His will.

GIB.   Rise, Mak, for shame! Thou ligis right lang.

MAK.   Now Cristis holy name be us emang!

What is this? For Sant Jame, I may not well

       gang.   30

I trow I be the same. A, my nek has ligen wrang.

     Enoghe!   *One of them twists his neck.*

Mekill thank! Sin yistereven,

Now, by Sant Strevin,

I was flaid with a swevin,   35

     My hart out of sloghe.

I thoght Gill began to crok and travell full sad,

Wel ner at the first cok, of a yong lad

For to mend oure flok. Then be I never glad:

I have tow on my rok more then ever I had.   40

     A, my heede!

A house full of yong tharmes!

The devill knok outt thare harnes!

Wo is him has many barnes,

     And therto litill brede.   45

I must go home, by youre lefe, to Gill, as I

       thoght.

I pray you looke my slefe, that I stele noght.

I am loth you to grefe or from you take oght.

                     Exit.

---

24 *woode,* crazy	28 *ligis,* lie; *lang,* long
30 *gang,* walk	31 *ligen,* lain
33 *mekill,* much; *sin,* since	35 *flaid,* frightened; *swevin,* dream
36 *out of sloghe,* out of my skin	37 *sad,* constantly
40 *tow on my rok,* flax on my distaff	42 *tharmes,* guts
43 *harnes,* brains	46 *lefe,* leave
47 *slefe,* sleeve	

DAW. Go forth, ill might thou chefe! Now wold I we
        soght
              This morne   50
        That we had all oure store.

COLL. Bot I will go before.
        Let us mete.

GIB.   Whore?

DAW.   At the crokid thorne.

49 *chefe*, prosper   53 *whore*, where

Scene IV—Mak's house

Mak speaks outside the door.

MAK. Undo this doore! Who is here? How long shall I
        stand?

GILL. Who makis sich a bere? Now walk in the
        weniand.

MAK. A, Gill, what chere? It is I, Mak, youre husbande.

GILL. Then may we se here the devill in a bande,
        Sir Gile!   5
                      She opens, and he enters.
        Lo, he commis with a lote
        As he were holden in the throte.
        I may not sit at my note
        A handlang while.

MAK. Will ye here what fare she makis to gett hir a
        glose?   10
        And dos noght bot laikis and clowse hir toose?

GILL. Why, who wanders? Who wakis? Who commis?
        Who gose?

2 *bere*, outcry; *weniand*, the waning of the moon (an unlucky time)
6 *lote*, noise   8 *note*, work
9 *handlang*, i.e., short   10 *glose*, excuse
11 *laikis*, sports; *clowse*, scratches

Who brewis? Who bakis? What makis me thus
   hose?
   And than
It is reuthe to beholde,   15
Now in hote, now in colde.
Full wofull is the householde
  That wantis a woman.

Bot what ende has thou made with the hirdis,
   Mak?

MAK. The last worde that thay saide when I turnid
   my bak,   20
Thay wold looke that thay hade thare shepe all
   the pak.
I hope thay will nott be well paide when thay
   thare shepe lak,
   Perde!
Bot howso the gam gose,
To me thay will suppose,   25
And make a foull noise,
  And cry outt apon me.

Bot thou must do as thou hight.

GILL.   I accorde me thertill.
I shall swedill him right in my credill.
If it were gretter slight, yit couthe I help till. 30
I will lig downe stright; com hap me.

MAK.   I will.

GILL. Behinde
Com Coll and his maroo
That will nip us full naroo.

---

13 *hose*, hoarse   15 *reuthe*, pity
19 *hirdis*, herdsmen   22 *hope*, think; *paide*, pleased
24 *gam gose*, game goes   25 *suppose*, suspect
28 *hight*, promised   29 *swedill*, swaddle
30 *slight*, trick; *till*, to it 31 *stright*, straightway; *hap*, cover
33 *maroo*, mate   34 *naroo*, narrowly

MAK.   Bot I may cry out "Haroo!"   35
                  The shepe if thay finde.

GILL.   Harken ay when thay call; thay will com onone.
          Com and make redy all, and sing by thin oone;
          Sing lullay thou shall, for I must grone,
          And cry outt by the wall on Mary and John   40
              For sore.
              Sing lullay on fast
              When thou heris at the last,
              And bot I play a fals cast
              Trust me no more.   45

37 *onone*, anon   38 *by thin oone*, by yourself
39 *lullay*, lullaby   44 *bot*, unless; *cast*, trick

Scene V—*The moor*

Enter Coll, Gib, and Daw.

DAW.   A, Coll, goode morne, why slepis thou nott?
COLL.   Alas that ever was I borne! We have a foull blott:
          A fat wedir have we lorne.
DAW.   Mary, Godis forbott!
GIB.   Who shuld do us that scorne? That were a foull
                  spott.
COLL.   Som shrewe.   5
              I have soght with my dogis
              All Horbery shrogis,
              And of fiftene hogis
              Fond I bot oone ewe.

DAW.   Now trow me, if ye will, by Sant Thomas of
                  Kent,   10
          Aither Mak or Gill was at that assent.

3 *wedir*, wether; *lorne*, lost; *Godis forbott*, God forbid
7 *shrogis*, bushes   8 *hogis*, young sheep
9 *fond*, found   11 *assent*, i.e., conspiracy

COLL. Peasse, man, be still! I sagh when he went.
      Thou sclanders him ill, thou aght to repent
          Goode spede.

GIB.   Now as ever might I the,   15
      If I shuld evin here de,
      I wold say it were he
          That did that same dede.

DAW. Go we theder, I rede, and rin on oure feete.
      Shall I nevere ete brede the sothe to I weet.   20
COLL. Nor drink in my heede, with him till I mete.
GIB.   I will rest in no stede till that I him grete,
          My brothere.
      Oone I will hight:
      Till I se him in sight   25
      Shall I never slepe one night
         Ther I do anothere.

12 *sagh,* saw   13 *aght,* ought
15 *the,* prosper   16 *de,* die
19 *theder,* thither; *rede,* advise; *rin,* run
20 *sothe to I weet,* truth until I know
24 *oone . . . hight,* one thing I will promise

Scene VI—Mak's house

Mak and Gill within, she in bed, he singing. Enter Coll, Gib, and Daw outside the door.

DAW. Will ye here how thay hak? Oure sire list crone.
COLL. Hard I never none crak so clere out of tone.
      Call on him.
GIB.   Mak! Undo your doore sone!
MAK. Who is that spak, as it were none,
         On loft?   5
      Who is that, I say?

1 *hak,* bellow; *list crone,* feels like crooning
2 *hard,* heard; *crak,* i.e., song; *tone,* tune   4 *spak,* spoke; *none,* noon
5 *on loft,* aloud

DAW. Goode felowse, were it day.

MAK. As far as ye may,
   Good, spekis soft

Over a seke woman's heede, that is at mal-
   leasse: 10
I had lever be dede or she had any diseasse.

GILL. Go to anothere stede, I may not well queasse.
Ich fote that ye trede gos thorow my nese.
   So, hee!

COLL. Tell us, Mak, if ye may,   15
   How fare ye, I say?

MAK. Bot ar ye in this towne today?
   Now how fare ye?

Ye have rin in the mire and ar wete yit.
I shall make you a fire if ye will sit.   20
A nores wold I hire—think ye on yit?
Well quitt is my hire, my dreme this is itt
   A seson.
I have barnes, if ye knew,
   Well mo then enewe;   25
Bot we must drink as we brew,
   And that is bot reson.

I wold ye dinid or ye yode. Methink that ye
   swette.

GIB. Nay, nauther mendis oure mode drinke nor
   mette.

MAK. Why, sir, ailis you oght bot goode?

DAW.   Yee, oure shepe that we gett 30

9 *good,* good men   10 *seke,* sick
11 *or,* ere; *disease,* disturbance   12 *queasse,* breathe
13 *ich,* each; *nese,* nose   14 *hee,* scat
21 *nores,* nurse; *think ye on,* can you think of one   23 *A,* in
25 *mo,* more; *enewe,* enough   28 *or ye yede,* before you went
29 *nauther,* neither; *mode,* anger
30 *ailis you . . . goode,* is there anything the matter with you; *gett,*
 keep

Ar stollin as thay yode; oure los is grette.

MAK. Sirs, drinkis!
Had I bene thore
Som shuld have boght it full sore.

COLL. Mary, som men trowes that ye wore,   35
And that us forthinkis.

GIB. Mak, som men trowis that it shuld be ye.

DAW. Aither ye or youre spouse, so say we.

MAK. Now if ye have suspouse to Gill or to me,
Com and ripe oure house, and then may
ye se   40
Who had hir,
If I any shepe fott,
Aither cow or stott.
And Gill my wife rose nott
Here sin she laide hir.   45

As I am true and lele, to God here I pray
That this be the first mele that I shall ete this day.

COLL. Mak, as have I sele, avise thee, I say:
He lernid timely to stele that couth not say nay.

GILL. I swelt!   50
Outt, thefis, fro my wonis!
Ye com to rob us for the nonis.

MAK. Here ye not how she gronis?
Youre hartis shuld melt.

GILL. Outt, thefis, fro my barne! Negh him not
thor!   55

---

31 *yode*, walked; *los*, loss	33 *thore*, there
35 *wore*, were	36 *forthinkis*, disturbs
39 *suspouse*, suspicion	40 *ripe*, search
42 *fott*, fetched	43 *stott*, heifer
45 *sin*, since	46 *lele*, trustworthy
48 *sele*, happiness; *avise thee*, take thought	50 *swelt*, die
51 *thefis*, thieves; *wonis*, dwelling	52 *nonis*, nonce
55 *barne*, child; *negh*, approach; *thor*, there	

MAK. Wist ye how she had farne, youre hartis wold be
        sore.

Ye do wrang, I you warne, that thus commis
        before

To a woman that has farne—bot I say no more.

GILL.   A, my medill!

I pray to God so milde,   60

If ever I you begild,

That I ete this childe

    That ligis in this credill.

MAK. Peasse, woman, for Godis pain, and cry not so!

Thou spillis thy braine and makis me full wo.   65

GIB. I trow oure shepe be slain. What finde ye two?

DAW. All wirk we in vain; as well may we go.

      Bot hatters,

I can finde no flesh,

Hard nor nesh,   70

Salt nor fresh,

    Bot two tome platers.

Quik catell bot this, tame nor wilde,

None, as have I blis, as loude as he smilde.

                 Approaching the cradle.

GILL. No, so God me blis, and gif me joy of my
        childe!   75

COLL. We have merkid amis. I hold us begild.

GIB.   Sir, don!

Sir—oure Lady him save!—

Is youre child a knave?

MAK.   Any lord might him have,   80

---

56 *wist*, knew; *farne*, fared   57 *wrang*, wrong
59 *medill*, middle   65 *spillis*, spoil
68: i.e., except for clothes   70 *nesh*, soft
72 *tome*, empty   73 *quik catell*, livestock
74 *as loude . . . smilde*, ever smelled as bad as he
76 *merkid*, aimed   77 *don*, thoroughly
79 *knave*, boy

This child, to his son.

When he wakins he kippis, that joy is to se.

DAW. In good time to his hippis, and in selé.

Bot who was his gossippis, so sone redé?

MAK. So fare fall thare lippis—

COLL.   Hark now, a le.   85

Aside.

MAK.   So God thaim thank,

            Parkin, and Gibon Waller, I say,

            And gentill John Horne, in good fay,

            He made all the garray

               With the greatt shank.   90

GIB. Mak, frendis will we be, for we ar all oone.

MAK. We? Now I hald for me, for mendis gett I none.

      Farewell all thre, all glad were ye gone.

DAW. Faire wordis may ther be, bot luf is ther none

        This yere.   95

The shepherds start to leave.

COLL. Gaf ye the child anything?

GIB. I trowe not oone farthing.

DAW.   Fast againe will I fling.

        Abide ye me here.

      Mak, take it no grefe if I com to thy barne.   100

Returning into the room.

MAK. Nay, thou dos me greatt reprefe, and foull has thou farne.

DAW. The child will it not grefe, that litill day-starne.

---

82 *kippis*, kicks   83 *selé*, ? innocence
84 *gossippis*, godparents; *redé*, ready   85 *le*, lie
86 *fay*, faith   89 *garray*, commotion
89–90: obscure.
92: We? Now I'll keep by myself, for I get no apology
93 *all glad . . . gone*, i.e., I'd be glad if you were all gone
94 *luf*, love   96 *gaf*, gave
98 *fling*, dash   101 *reprefe*, shame; *farne*, behaved
102 *grefe*, grieve; *day-starne*, day-star

Mak, with youre lefe, let me gif youre barne
    Bot sixpence.   *Approaching the cradle.*

MAK.   Nay, do way, he slepis.   105
DAW.   Methink he pepis.
MAK.   When he wakins he wepis.
    I pray you go hence,

DAW.   Gif me lefe him to kis, and lift up the cloutt.
    What the devill is this? He has a long
        snoute.   110
                    Seeing the sheep.

COLL.   He is merkid amis, we wate ill aboute.
                    Joining Daw.

GIB.   Ill-spon weft, ywis, ay commis foull oute.
                    Joining them.

    Ay, so!
    He is like to oure shepe!
DAW.   How, Gib, may I pepe?   115
COLL.   I trow kinde will crepe
    Where it may not go.

GIB.   This was a quaintt gaude and a fair cast.
    It was a hee fraude.
DAW.   Yee, sirs, wast.
    Lett bren this bawde and bind hir fast.   120
    A fals scaude hang at the last:
        So shall thou.
    Will ye se how thay swedill
    His foure fete in the medill?

---

106 *pepis*, i.e., his eyes are open   109 *cloutt*, cloth
111 *merkid*, fashioned; *we wate . . . aboute*, i.e., we know some
    mischief has been at work
112: An ill-spun web, indeed, always comes out badly
116–17 i.e., I think nature will creep where it can't walk
118 *quaintt gaude*, curious trick; *cast*, dodge
119 *hee*, high; *wast*, it was
121 *scaud*, scold   120 *bren*, burn
                                              123 *swedill*, swaddle

      Sagh I never in a credill   125
        A hornid lad or now.

MAK. Peasse bid I! What, lett be youre fare!
      I am he that him gatt, and yond woman him
          bare.

COLL. What devill shall he hatt? Mak? Lo, Gib, Makis
          aire!

GIB. Lett be all that; now God gif him care;   130
      I sagh.

GILL.   A pratty child is he
      As sittis on a wamans kne,
      A dillydowne, perde,
         To gar a man laghe.   135

DAW. I know him by the eeremarke—that is a good
         tokin.

MAK. I tell you, sirs, hark! his nose was brokin.
      Sithen told me a clark that he was forspoken.

COLL. This is a fals wark. I wold fain be wrokin.
         Gett wepin.   140

GILL.   He was takin with an elfe—
      I saw it myself—
      When the clok stroke twelf
         He was forshapin.

GIB. Ye two ar well feft sam in a stede.   145

DAW. Sin thay mantein thare theft, let do thaim to dede.

MAK. If I trespas eft, gird of my heede.
      With you will I be left.

COLL.   Sirs, do my reede:

> For this trespas
> We will nauther ban ne flite,   150
> Fight nor chite,
> Bot have done as tite,
> And cast him in canvas.

They toss Mak in a blanket.

150: We will neither curse nor wrangle   151 *chite,* chide
152 *tite,* quickly

Scene VII—*The moor*

Enter Coll, Gib, and Daw.

COLL.   Lord, what I am sore, in point for to brist!
      In faith I may no more; therfor will I rist.

GIB.   As a shepe of seven score he weid in my fist.
      For to slepe aywhore methink that I list.

DAW.   Now I pray you   5
      Lig downe on this grene.

COLL.   On these thefis yit I mene.

DAW.   Wherto shuld ye tene?
      Do as I say you.

Enter an Angel, who sings Gloria in Excelsis *and then addresses the shepherds.*

ANGEL.   Rise, hirdmen hend, for now is He borne   10
      That shall take fro the Fend that Adam had
           lorne;
      That warloo to shend, this night is He borne.
      God is made youre frend now at this morne
          He behestis.

---

1 *what,* how; *brist,* burst   2 *rist,* rest
3 *weid,* weighed   4 *aywhore,* anywhere
7 *mene,* think   8 *tene,* grieve
10 *hend,* gentle   11 *lorne,* lost
12 *warloo to shende,* devil to confound   14 *behestis,* promises

       At Bedlem go se,   15
       Ther ligis that fre
       In a crib full poorely,
          Betwix two bestis.   *Exit.*

COLL.   This was a quaint stevin as ever yit I hard.
       It is a mervell to nevin thus to be scard.   20
GIB.   Of Godis Son of hevin he spak upward.
       All the wod on a levin methoght that he gard
          Appere.
DAW.   He spake of a barne
       In Bedlem, I you warne.   25
COLL.   That betokins yond starne.
       Let us seke him there.

GIB.   Say, what was his song? Hard ye not how he
          crakt it,
       Thre brefes to a long?
DAW.   Yee, Mary, he hakt it.
       Was no crochett wrong, nor nothing that
          lakt it.   30
COLL.   For to sing us emong, right as he knakt it,
          I can.
GIB.   Let se how ye crone!
       Can ye bark at the mone?
DAW.   Hold youre tonges! Have done!   35
COLL.   Hark after, than!

GIB.   To Bedlem he bad that we shuld gang.
       I am full fard that we tary to lang.
DAW.   Be mery and not sad: of mirth is oure sang.

15 *Bedlem,* Bethlehem   16 *fre,* noble one
19 *quaint stevin,* fine voice; *hard,* heard
20 *nevin,* name; *scard,* scared   22 *levin,* light; *gard,* made
26 *starne,* star   28 *crakt it,* sang it out
29 *thre . . . long,* three shorts to a long; *hakt it,* bellowed it
30 *crochett,* note   31 *knakt it,* trilled
32: I know how
38 *fard,* afraid; *lang,* long   37 *gang,* go

Everlasting glad to mede may we fang.   40

COLL.   Withoutt noise,
Hy we theder forthy;
If we be wete and wery,
To that child and that lady,
        We have it not to lose.   45

GIB.   We finde by the prophecy—let be youre din!—
Of David and Isay and mo then I min,
Thay prophecied by clergy that in a virgin
Shuld He light and ly, to sloken oure sin
        And slake it,   50
Save oure kinde from wo,
For Isay said so:
Ecce virgo
        Concipiet a child that is nakid.

DAW.   Full glad may we be, and abide that day,   55
That lufly to se, that all mightis may.
Lord, well were me, for ones and for ay,
Might I knele on my kne, som word for to say
        To that childe.
Bot the angell said   60
In a crib wos he laide,
He was poorly araid,
        Both mene and milde.

COLL.   Patriarkes that has bene, and prophetis beforne,
That desirid to have sene this childe that is
        borne,   65
Thay ar gone full clene; that have thay lorne.

---

40 *to mede,* for reward; *fang,* take   42: Let's hurry there therefore
47 *mo then I min,* more than I recall   48 *clergy,* learning
49 *sloken,* quench   51 *oure kinde,* i.e., mankind
56 *lufly to se,* lovely one to behold; *all mightis may,* is all-powerful
61 *wos,* was   63 *mene,* lowly
66 *that . . . lorne,* i.e., they have lost that chance

We shall se Him, I wene, or it be morne,
    To tokin.
When I se Him and fele,
Then wot I full wele   70
It is true as stele
    That prophetis have spokin:

To so poore as we ar that he wold appere,
First find and declare by his messingere.

GIB.   Go we now, let us fare, the place is us nere.   75

DAW.   I am redy and yare, go we in fere
    To that bright.
    Lord, if thy willes be—
    We ar lewde all thre—
    Thou grauntt us somkins gle   80
      To comfort thy wight.

---

67 *or*, ere   68 *to tokin*, as a sign
76 *yare*, prepared; *in fere*, together   77 *bright*, bright one
79 *lewde*, ignorant   80 *somkins gle*, some sort of cheer

Scene VIII—A stable in Bethlehem

COLL.   Haill, comly and clene! Haill, yong child!
Haill, Maker, as I mene, of a maidin so milde!
Thou hast warid, I wene, the warlo so wilde;
The fals giler of tene, now gos he begilde.
    Lo, He meris,   5
    Lo, He laghis, my sweting!
    A wel faire meting!
    I have holden my heting:
      Have a bob of cheris.

---

2 *of*, i.e., come of   3 *warid*, put a curse upon; *warlo*, devil
4 *giler*, beguiler; *tene*, grief   5 *meris*, is merry
8 *heting*, promise   9 *bob*, bunch

GIB.   Haill, sufferan Savioure! For Thou has us
        soght,   10
    Haill, frely fode and flowre that all thing has
        wroght!
    Haill, full of favoure, that made al of noght!
    Haill! I knele and I cowre. A bird have I broght
        To my barne.
        Haill, litill tine mop!   15
        Of oure crede Thou art crop.
        I wold drink on thy cop,
        Litill daystarne.

DAW.   Haill, derling dere, full of Godhede!
    I prey Thee be nere when that I have nede.   20
    Haill, swete is thy chere! My hart wold blede
    To se Thee sitt here in so poore wede,
        With no pennis.
        Haill! Put furth thy dall!
        I bring Thee bot a ball: 25
        Have and play Thee withall,
        And go to the tenis.

MARY.   The Fader of heven, God omnipotent,
    That sett all on seven, his Son has He sent.
    My name couth He neven, and light or He
        went.   30
    I conceivid Him full even thrugh might, as
        He ment,
        And now is He borne.
        He kepe you fro wo!
        I shall pray Him so;

10 *sufferan,* sovereign
11 *frely fode,* noble child
15 *tine mop,* tiny baby
17 *cop,* cup
24 *dall,* hand
29 *sett . . . seven,* i.e., created everything
30 *couth,* did; *neven,* name; *light,* alighted; *or,* ere
31 *ment,* intended

13 *cowre,* crouch
16 *crop,* head
21 *chere,* face
27 *tenis,* tennis

> Tell furth as ye go,   35
> And min on this morne.

COLL.   Farewell, lady, so faire to beholde,
       With thy childe on thy kne!

GIB.   But He ligis full cold.
       Lord, well is me; now we go, Thou behold.

DAW.   Forsothe, allredy it semis to be told   40
       Full oft.

COLL.   What grace we have fun!

GIB.   Com furth, now ar we won!

DAW.   To sing ar we bun,
       Let take on loft.   45

                         They sing.

---

36 *min on*, remember   42 *fun*, found
43 *won*, redeemed   44 *bun*, bound
45: Let's raise our voices

King James I of Scotland

(1394–1437)

FROM *The King's Quair (The King's Book)*

[*He Sees His Beloved*]

Bewailing in my chamber thus allone,
   Despeired of all joye and remedye,
Fortirit of my thoght, and wo-begone,
   Unto the window gan I walk in hye,
   To se the warld and folk that went forby;   5
As for the time, though I of mirthis fude
Might have no more, to luke it did me gude.

Now was there maid fast by the towris wall
   A gardin faire, and in the corneris set
Ane herbere grene:—with wandis long and small   10
   Railit about; and so with treis set
   Was all the place, and hawthorn hegis knet,
That lif was none walking there forby,
That might within scarce ony wight aspye.

So thik the bewis and the leves grene   15
   Beschadit all the aleyes that there were,
And middis every herbere might be sene
   The scharpe grene swete jenepere,

3 *fortirit of,* tired out by   4 *hye,* haste
6 *fude,* food   7 *luke,* look
8 *maid,* made; *fast,* close   10 *ane,* a; *herbere,* lawn; *wandis,* palings
11 *treis,* trees   12 *hegis knet,* hedges entwined
13 *lif,* person   15 *bewis,* boughs
16 *beschadit,* shaded; *aleyes,* paths   17 *middis,* amidst
18 *jenepere,* juniper

Growing so faire with branchis here and there,
That, as it semit to a lif without,   20
The bewis spred the herbere all about;

And on the smalle grene twistis sat
    The litill swete nightingale, and song
So loud and clere the ympnis consecrat
    Of lufis use, now soft, now loud among,   25
    That all the garding and the wallis rong
Right of thaire song, and of the copill next
Off thaire swete armony, and lo the text:

CANTUS

"Worschippe, ye that loveris bene, this May,
    For of your blisse the calendis are begonne,   30
And sing with us, away, winter away!
    Cum somer, cum, the swete sesoun and sonne!
    Awake for schame! that have your hevinnis wonne,
And amorously lift up your hedis all,
Thank Lufe that list you to his mercy call."   35

Qwhen thay this song had song a litill thrawe,
    Thay stent a qwhile, and therewith unaffraid,
As I beheld and cest min eyne alawe,
    From beugh to beugh thay hippit and thay playd,
    And freschly in thaire birdis kind arrayd   40
Thaire fetheris new, and fret thame in the sonne,
    And thankit Lufe, that had thaire makis wonne.

This was the plane ditee of thaire note,
    And therwithall unto myself I thoght,

22 *twistis*, twigs   23 *song*, sang
24 *ympnis*, hymns   25 *lufis*, love's; *among*, in turn
27 *right of*, with; *copill*, couplet   33 *hevinnis*, heavens
35 *Lufe that list*, Love whom it pleases   36 *thrawe*, space
37 *stent*, ceased   38 *cest*, cast; *alawe*, downwards
39 *beugh*, bough; *hippit*, hopped
40 *thaire birdis kind*, their birds' way   41 *fret*, preened
42 *thaire makis wonne*, won their mates for them
43 *plane*, entire; *note*, song

"Qwhat lif is this that makis birdis dote?   45
   Qwhat may this be, how cummith it of ought?
   Qwhat nedith it to be so dere ybought?
It is nothing, trowe I, bot feinit chere,
And that men list to counterfeten chere."

Eft wald I think; "O Lord, qwhat may this be,   50
   That Lufe is of so noble might and kinde,
Lufing his folk, and swich prosperitee
   Is it of him, as we in bukis find?
   May he oure hertes setten and unbind?
Hath he upon oure hertis swich maistrye?   55
Or all this is bot feinit fantasye?

"For gif he be of so grete excellence,
   That he of every wight hath cure and charge,
Qwhat have I gilt to him or doon offense,
   That I am thrall, and birdis gone at large,   60
   Sen him to serve he might set my corage?
And gif he be noght so, than may I seyne,
Qwhat makis folk to jangill of him in veine?

"Can I noght elles find, but gif that he
   Be lord, and as a god may live and regne,   65
To bind and louse, and maken thrallis free,
   Than wold I pray his blisful grace benigne,
   To hable me unto his service digne;
And evermore for to be one of tho
Him trewly for to serve in wele and wo."   70

48 *trowe*, believe; *feinit chere*, feigned behavior
49 *list*, please; *conterfeten*, imitate; *chere*, cheer   50 *eft*, again
51 *kinde*, nature   52 *lufing*, loving; *swich*, such
53 *bukis*, books   54 *setten*, fix
55 *maistrye*, dominion   57 *gif*, if
58 *cure*, care   59 *qwhat*, in what; *gilt to*, wronged
60 *gone*, go   61 *sen*, since; *set my corage*, direct my heart
63 *jangill*, babble   64 *but gif*, except
66 *louse*, loosen   68 *hable*, fit; *digne*, honorable
69 *tho*, those   70 *wele*, weal

And therewith cest I down min eye ageine,
   Qwhare as I sawe, walking under the towre,
Full secretly, new cummin hir to pleyne,
   The fairest or the freschest yonge flowre
   That ever I sawe, methoght, before that houre, 75
For qwhich sodain abate, anone astert
The blude of all my body to my hert.

And though I stude abaisit tho a lite,
   No wonder was; forqwhy my wittis all
Were so overcome with plesance and delite, 80
   Onely throu latting of min eyen fall,
   That sudainly my hert became hir thrall
For ever, of free will; for of manace
There was no takin in hir swete face.

And in my hede I drewe right hastily, 85
   And eftsones I lent it forth ageine,
And sawe hir walk, that verray womanly,
   With no wight mo, bot onely wommen tweine.
   Than gan I studye in myself, and seyne,
"A, swete, ar ye a warldly creature, 90
Or hevinly thing in likenesse of nature?

"Or ar ye god Cupidis owin princesse,
   And cummin are to louse me out of band?
Or ar ye verray Nature the goddesse,
   That have depainted with your hevinly hand 95
   This gardin full of flowris, as they stand?
Qwhat sall I think, allace! qwhat reverence
Sall I minister to your excellence?

---

73 *pleyne*, play   76 *abate*, subsided; *astert*, started up
77 *blude*, blood   78 *abaisit*, abashed; *tho a lite*, then a little
80 *forqwhy*, because   83 *manace*, menace
84 *takin*, sign   86 *lent*, leaned
87 *womanly*, i.e., womanly one   88 *wight mo*, other person
90 *warldly*, worldly   93 *louse*, loose

"Gif ye a goddesse be, and that ye like
 To do me paine, I may it noght astert; 100
Gif ye be warldly wight, that dooth me sike,
 Qwhy lest God mak you so, my derrest hert,
 To do a sely prisoner thus smert,
That lufis you all, and wote of noght but wo?
And therefor, mercy, swete! sen it is so." 105

Qwhen I a litill thrawe had maid my moon,
 Bewailling min infortune and my chance,
Unknawing how or qwhat was best to doon,
 So ferre yfallin into lufis dance,
 That sodeinly my wit, my contenance, 110
My hert, my will, my nature, and my mind,
Was changit clene right in another kind.

Off hir array the forme gif I sall write
 Toward, hir goldin haire and rich atire
In fret-wise couchit were with perllis qwhite 115
 And grete balas leming as the fire,
 With mony ane emerant and faire saphire;
And on hir hede a chaplet fresch of hewe,
Of plumis partit rede, and qwhite, and blewe;

Full of quaking spangis bright as gold, 120
 Forgit of schap like to the amorettis,
So new, so fresch, so plesant to behold,

99 *gif,* if
100 *astert,* escape
101 *dooth me sike,* makes me sigh
102 *lest,* does it please
103 *do,* cause; *sely,* poor
104 *lufis,* loves; *wote,* knows
105 *sen,* since
106 *thrawe,* while; *moon,* moan
107 *infortune,* bad fortune
109 *ferre,* far
113 *gif,* if
114 *toward,* fittingly
115 *in fret-wise,* i.e., with interlacing design; *couchit,* overlaid
116 *balas leming,* rubies gleaming
119 *plumis partit,* separate feathers
120 *quaking spangis,* trembling spangles
121 *forgit,* fashioned; *amorettis,* love-knots

The plumis eke like to the flowre-jonettis,
  And othir of schap like to the round crokettis,
And, above all this, there was, wele I wote,   125
Beautee eneuch to mak a world to dote.

About hir nek, qwhite as the fire-amaille,
  A gudely cheine of smale orfeverye,
Qwhareby there hang a ruby, without faille,
  Like to ane herte schapin verily,   130
  That, as a sperk of lowe, so wantonely
Semit birning upon hir qwhite throte:
Now gif there was gud partye, God it wote!

And forto walk that fresche Mayes morowe,
  Ane huke sche had upon hir tissew qwhite,   135
That gudeliare had noght bene sene toforowe,
  As I suppose; and girt sche was a lite.
  Thus halfling louse for haste, to swich delite
It was to see hir youth in gudelihede,
That for rudenes to speke thereof I drede.   140

In hir was youth, beautee, with humble aport,
  Bountee, richesse, and wommanly facture,
(God better wote than my pen can report)
  Wisedome, largesse, estate, and conning sure.
  In every point so guidit hir mesure,   145

123 *flowre-jonettis,* marigolds 124 *schap,* shape; *crokettis,* curled buds
125 *wote,* know   126 *eneuch,* enough
127 *fire-amaille,* fire enamel
128 *gudely,* goodly; *orfeverye,* workmanship   129 *faille,* flaw
131 *lowe,* flame   133 *gif,* if; *partye,* contrast of color; *wote,* knows
135 *huke,* cloak; *tissew,* dress
136 *gudeliare,* goodlier; *toforowe,* before
137 *girt . . . lite,* she was loosely girded
138 *halfling louse,* half loose   139 *gudelihede,* excellence
141 *aport,* bearing   142 *facture,* feature
144 *conning,* intelligence
145 *so guidit hir mesure,* measure so guided her

In word, in dede, in schap, in contenance,
That nature might no more hir childe avance.

Throu qwhich anone I knew and understude
    Wele, that sche was a warldly creature;
On qwhom to rest min eye, so mich gude   150
    It did my wofull hert, I you assure,
    That it was to me joye without mesure;
And, at the last, my luke unto the hevin
I threwe furthwith, and said thir versis sevin.

"O Venus clere! of goddis stellifyit!   155
    To qwhom I yelde homage and sacrifise,
Fro this day forth your grace be magnifyit,
    That me ressavit have in swich a wise,
    To live under your law and do servise;
Now help me furth, and for your mercy lede   160
My hert to rest, that deis nere for drede."

Qwhen I with gude entent this orisoun
    Thus endit had, I stint a litill stound;
And eft min eye full pitously adowne
    I cest, behalding to hir litill hound,   165
    That with his bellis playit on the ground;
Than wold I say, and sigh therewith a lite,
"A! wele were him that now were in thy plite!"

Anothir qwhile the litill nightingale,
    That sat apon the twiggis, wold I chide,   170
And say right thus, "Qwhare are thy notis smale,
    That thou of love has song this morowe-tide?
    Seis thou noght hire that sittis thee beside?

147 *avance*, improve   150 *mich*, much
153 *luke*, look   154 *thir*, these
155 *goddis*, gods; *stellifyit*, become a star   158 *ressavit*, received
161 *deis*, dies   163 *stint*, ceased; *stound*, while
164 *eft*, again   167 *a lite*, a little
168 *plite*, position   173 *seis*, see

For Venus sake, the blisfull goddesse clere,
Sing on agane, and mak my lady chere.   175

"And eke I pray, for all the paines grete,
    That for the love of Proigne thy sister dere,
Thou sufferit qwhilom, qwhen thy brestis wete
    Were, with the teres of thine eyen clere
    All bludy ronne; that pitee was to here   180
The crueltee of that unknightly dede,
Qwhare was fro thee bereft thy maidenhede,

"Lift up thine hert, and sing with gude entent;
    And in thy notis swete the tresone telle,
That to thy sister trewe and innocent   185
    Was kithit by hir husband false and fell;
    For qwhois gilt, as it is worthy wel,
Chide thir husbandis that are false, I say,
And bid thame mend, in the twenty devil way.

"O litill wrecch, allace! mayst thou noght se   190
    Qwho commith yond? Is it now time to wring?
Qwhat sory thoght is fallin upon thee?
    Opin thy throte; hastou no lest to sing?
    Allace! sen thou of resone had feling,
Now swete bird, say ones to me 'pepe':   195
I dee for wo; methink thou ginnis slepe.

"Hastou no minde of lufe? Qwhare is thy make?
    Or artou seke, or smit with jelousye?
Or is sche dede, or hath sche thee forsake?
    Qwhat is the cause of thy malancolye,   200
    That thou no more list maken melodye?

178 *qwhilom*, once   180 *bludy ronne*, i.e., covered with blood
186 *kithit*, shown   187 *qwhois*, whose
188 *thir*, these   189 *in the . . . way*, i.e., by the twenty devils
191 *wring*, lament   193 *lest*, desire
194 *sen*, since   196 *dee*, die; *ginnis*, begin
197 *make*, mate   198 *seke*, sick
201 *here*, i.e., here is

Sluggart, for schame! lo here thy goldin houre,
That worth were hale all thy livis laboure!

"Gif thou suld sing wele ever in thy live,
   Here is, in fay, the time, and eke the space: 205
Qwhat wostou than? sum bird may cum and strive
   In song with thee, the maistry to purchace.
   Suld thou than cesse, it were grete schame, allace!
And here, to win gree happily for ever,
Here is the time to sing, or ellis never."   210

I thoght eke thus, gif I my handis clap,
   Or gif I cast, than wil sche flee away;
And gif I hald my pes, than will sche nap;
   And gif I crye, sche wate noght qwhat I say;
   Thus qwhat is best, wate I nought be this day: 215
"Bot blawe, wind, blawe, and do the levis schake,
That sum twig may wag, and make hir wake."

With that anone right sche toke up a sang,
   Qwhare come anone mo birdis and alight;
Bot than, to here the mirth was thame amang,   220
   Over that to, to see the swete sicht
   Off hir image, my spirit was so light,
Methoght I flawe for joye without arest,
So were my wittis boundin all to fest.

And to the notis of the philomene,   225
   Qwhilkis sche sang, the ditee there I maid
Direct to hire that was my hertis quene,

202 *hale*, wholly   204 *gif*, if
205 *fay*, faith   206 *wostou*, desire you
207 *the maistry to purchace*, to gain the victory   209 *gree*, triumph
211 *gif*, if   212 *cast*, i.e., throw something
214 *wate*, knows   215 *be*, by
216 *do*, make   219 *mo*, more
221 *to*, too   223 *flawe*, flew; *arest*, stopping
224 *boundin . . . fest*, ? springing all to feast
225 *philomene*, nightingale   226 *qwhilkis*, which
226 *ditee*, verses

Withoutin qwhom no songis may me glade;
   And to that sanct, there walking in the schade,
My bedis thus, with humble hert entere,   230
Devotly than I said on this manere.

"Qwhen sall your mercy rew upon your man,
   Qwhois service is yit uncouth unto you?
Sen, qwhen ye go, ther is noght ellis than
   Bot, 'Hert! qwhere as the body may noght throu,   235
   Folow thy hevin! Qwho suld be glad bot thou,
That swich a gide to folow has undertake?
Were it throu hell, the way thou noght forsake!' "

And after this, the birdis everichone
   Tuke up anothir sang full loud and clere,   240
And with a voce said, "Wele is us begone,
   That with oure makis are togider here;
   We proine and play without dout and dangere,
All clothit in a soite full fresche and newe,
In Luifis service besy, glad, and trewe.   245

"And ye, fresche May, ay mercifull to bridis,
   Now welcum be ye, flowre of monethis all;
For noght onely your grace upon us bidis,
   Bot all the warld to witnes this we call,
   That strowit hath so plainly over all   250
With newe fresche swete and tender grene,
Oure lif, oure lust, oure governoure, oure quene."

This was thair song, as semit me full heye,
   With full mony uncouth swete note and schill,

---

229 *sanct,* saint   230 *bedis,* prayers; *entere,* entire
233 *yit,* yet; *uncouth,* unknown   234 *sen,* since; *than,* then
235 *throu,* i.e., get through   239 *everichone,* every one
240 *tuke,* took
241 *a,* one; *wele . . . begone,* we are happily situated
242 *makis,* mates   243 *proine,* preen
244 *soite,* suit   245 *Luifis,* Love's
246 *bridis,* birds   250 *strowit,* strewn; *plainly,* fully
253 *heye,* loud   254 *uncouth,* unusual; *schill,* shrill

And therewithall that faire upward hir eye   255
Wold cast amang, as it was Goddis will,
    Qwhare I might se, standing allane full still
The faire facture that nature, for maistrye,
In hir visage wroght had full lufingly.

And, qwhen sche walkit had a litill thrawe   260
    Under the swete grene bewis bent,
Hir faire fresche face, as qwhite as snawe,
    Scho turnit has, and furth hir wayis went;
    Bot tho began min axis and turment,
To sene hir part, and folowe I na might;   265
Methoght the day was turnit into night.

(Lines 204–469)

---

256 *amang*, now and then   257 *allane*, alone
258 *facture*, feature; *for maistrye*, i.e., to prove her skill
264 *tho*, then; *axis*, qualms

Robert Henryson

(c.1425–c.1506)

FROM *The Testament of Cresseid*

[*The Assembly of the Gods*]

As custome was, the pepill far and neir,
  Befoir the none, unto the tempill went
With sacrifice, devoit in thair maneir.
  But still Cresseid, hevye in hir intent,
  Into the kirk wald not hirself present,   5
For giving of the pepill ony deming
Of hir expuls fra Diomeid the king;

Bot past into ane secreit orature,
  Qwhair scho micht weip hir wofull desteny.
Behind hir bak scho cloisit fast the dure,   10
  And on hir kneis bair fell down in hy;
  Upon Venus and Cupide angerly
Scho cryit out, and said on this same wise,
"Allace, that ever I maid you sacrifice!

"Ye gave me anis ane devine responsaill   15
  That I suld be the flowr of luif in Troy,
Now am I maid ane unworthye outwaill,
  And all in cair translatit is my joy.

2 *none,* noon   3 *devoit,* devout
4 *intent,* i.e., heart   6 *deming,* suspicion
7 *expuls,* expulsion   8 *ane,* a; *orature,* oratory
9 *scho,* she   10 *dure,* door
11 *hy,* haste   15 *anis,* once; *responsaill,* oracular response
16 *luif,* love   17 *maid,* made; *outwaill,* outcast

287

Qwha sall me gide? Qwha sall me now convoy,
Sen I fra Diomeid, and nobill Troilus,   20
Am clene excludit, as abject odious?

"O fals Cupide, is nane to wite bot thou,
    And thy mother, of lufe the blind goddes!
Ye causit me alwayis understand and trow
    The seid of lufe was sawin in my face,   25
    And ay grew grene throw your supplye and grace.
Bot now, allace, that seid with froist is slane,
And I fra luifferis left, and all forlane."

Qwhen this was said, down in ane extasye,
    Ravischit in spreit, intill ane dreame scho fell,   30
And be apperance hard, qwhair scho did ly,
    Cupide the king ringand ane silver bell,
    Qwhilk men micht heir fra hevin unto hell;
At qwhais sound befoir Cupide appeiris
The sevin Planetis, discending fra thair spheiris,   35

Qwhilk hes power of all thing generabill
    To reull and steir be thair greit influence,
Wedder and wind, and coursis variabill.
    And first of all, Saturne gave his sentence,
    Qwhilk gave to Cupide litill reverence,   40
Bot, as ane busteous churle on his maneir,
Come crabitlye, with auster luik and cheir.

19 *qwha,* who   20 *sen,* since
21 *abject,* a cast-off   22 *nane to wite,* none to blame
23 *lufe,* love   24 *trow,* believe
25 *seid,* seed; *sawin,* sown   26 *supplye,* support
27 *froist,* frost   28 *luifferis,* lovers; *forlane,* laid aside
30 *spreit,* spirit; *intill,* into
31 *be apperance,* by an apparition; *hard,* she heard
32 *ringand,* ringing   33 *qwhilk,* which
34 *qwhais,* whose   36 *hes,* have; *generabill,* created by generation
37 *steir,* govern; *be,* by   38 *wedder,* weather
39 *sentence,* opinion   41 *busteous,* rude
42 *crabitlye,* sullenly; *luik,* look; *cheir,* countenance

His face fronsit, his lire was like the leid,
 His teith chatterit and cheverit with the chin,
His ene droupit, how sonkin in his heid,   45
 Out of his nois the meldrop fast can rin,
 With lippis bla, and cheikis leine and thin,
The ice-schoklis that fra his hair down hang
Was wonder greit, and as ane speir als lang.

Atovir his belt his liart lokkis lay   50
 Felterit unfair, ovirfret with froistis hoir;
His garmound and hus gite full gay of gray;
 His widderit weid fra him the wind out woir,
 Ane busteous bow within his hand he boir;
Under his girdill ane flasche of felloun flanis,   55
Fedderit with ice, and heidit with hailstanis.

Than Juppiter richt fair and amiabill,
 God of the starnis in the firmament,
And nureis to all thing generabill,
 Fra his father Saturne far different,   60
 With burelye face, and browis bricht and brent,
Upon his heid ane garland, wonder gay,
Of flowris fair, as it had bene in May.

His voice was cleir, as cristall wer his ene,
 As goldin wire sa glitterand was his hair,   65
His garmound and his gite full gay of grene,
 With golden listis gilt on everye gair;

43 *fronsit*, wrinkled; *lire*, flesh; *leid*, lead 44 *cheverit*, shivered
45 *ene*, eyes; *droupit*, lowered; *how*, hollow
46 *nois*, nose; *meldrop*, mucus; *can rin*, did run   47 *bla*, livid
48 *ice-schoklis*, icicles   49 *als*, as; *lang*, long
50 *atovir*, above; *liart*, gray
51 *felterit*, tangled; *ovirfret*, covered; *hoir*, hoar
52 *garmound*, garment; *gite*, mantle
53 *widderit weid*, ragged clothes; *out woir*, blew out 54 *boir*, bore
55 *flasche . . . flanis*, sheaf of murderous arrows
56 *fedderit*, feathered; *heidit*, headed   58 *starnis*, stars
59 *nureis*, nurse   61 *burelye*, stately; *brent*, unwrinkled
65 *glitterand*, glittering   67 *listis*, borders; *gair*, gore

Ane burelye brand about his middill bair;
In his richt hand he had ane groundin speir,
Of his father the wraith fra us to weir.   70

Nixt efter him come Mars, the god of ire,
    Of strife, debait, and all dissensioun,
To chide and fecht, als feirs as ony fire;
    In hard harnes, heumound, and habirgeoun;
    And on his hanche ane roustye fell fachioun,   75
And in his hand he had ane roustye sword;
Writhing his face with mony angrye word.

Schaikand his sword, befoir Cupide he come
    With reid visage and grislye glowrand ene;
And at his mouth ane bullar stude of fome,   80
    Like to ane bair qwhetting his tuskis kene,
    Richt tuilyeour-like, but temperance in tene;
Ane horne he blew with mony bosteous brag,
Qwhilk all this warld with weir hes maid to wag.

Than fair Phebus, lanterne and lamp of licht   85
    Of man and beist, baith frute and flourisching,
Tender nureis and banischer of nicht,
    And of the warld causing, be his moving
    And influence, life in all eirdlye thing,
Without comfort of qwhome, of force to nocht   90
Must all ga die that in this warld is wrocht.

As king royall he raid upon his chair,
    The qwhilk Phaeton gidit sumtime unricht,

68 *burelye,* stout; *brand,* sword   69 *groundin,* whetted
70 *wraith,* wrath; *weir,* ward off   73 *fecht,* fight; *als,* as
74 *heumound,* helmet   75 *fachioun,* falchion
78 *schaikand,* shaking   79 *ene,* eyes
80 *bullar,* bubble; *stude,* stood   81 *bair,* boar
82 *tuilyeour-like,* brawler-like; *but,* without; *tene,* anger
83 *brag,* blast   84 *weir,* war
86 *baith,* both   87 *nureis,* nurse
88 *be,* by   89 *eirdlye,* earthly
91 *ga,* go   92 *raid,* rode; *chair,* chariot
93 *sumtime,* once upon a time

The brichtness of his face, qwhen it was bair,
   Nane micht behald for peirsing of his sicht: 95
   This goldin cart with firye bemes bricht
Four yokkit steidis full different of hew,
But bait or tiring, throu the spheiris drew.

The first was soir, with mane als reid as rois,
   Callit Eoye into the Orient;   100
The secund steid to name hecht Ethios,
   Qwhitlye and paill, and sum deill ascendent;
   The thrid Peros, right hait and richt fervent;
The feird was blak, and callit Phlegonye,
Qwhilk rollis Phebus down into the sey.   105

Venus was thair present, that goddess gay,
   Her sonnis querrel for to defend, and mak
Hir awin complaint, cled in ane nice array,
   The ane half grene, the uther half sabill blak,
   Qwhite hair as gold, kemmit and sched abak,   110
Bot in hir face semit greit variance,
Qwhiles perfite treuth, and qwhiles inconstance.

Under smiling scho was dissimulait,
   Provocative with blenkis amorous,
And suddanely changit and alterait,   115
   Angrye as ony serpent vennemous,
   Richt pungitive with wordis odious:
Thus variant scho was, qwha list tak keip,
With ane eye lauch, and with the uther weip.

In taikning that all fleschelye paramour 120
    Qwhilk Venus hes in reull and governance,
Is sum time sweit, sum time bitter and sour,
    Richt unstabill, and full of variance,
    Mingit with cairfull joy and fals plesance,
Now hait, now cauld, now blyith, now full of wo, 125
Now grene as leif, now widderit and ago.

With buik in hand than come Mercurius,
    Richt eloquent and full of rethorye,
With polite termis and delicious,
    With pen and ink to report all reddye, 130
    Setting sangis and singand merilye.
His hude was reid, heklit atovir his crown,
Like to ane poeit of the auld fassoun.

Boxis he bair, with fine electuairis,
    And sugerit syropis for digestioun, 135
Spicis belangand to the pothecairis,
    With mony hailsum sweit confectioun,
    Doctour in physick, cled in ane scarlot gown,
And furrit weill, as sic ane aucht to be,
Honest and gude, and not ane word culd lie. 140

Nixt efter him come Lady Cynthia,
    The last of all, and swiftest in hir spheir,
Of colour blak, buskit with hornis twa,
    And in the nicht scho listis best appeir;
    Haw as the leid, of colour nathing cleir; 145

120 *taikning*, sign   124 *mingit*, mingled
126 *ago*, passed by   127 *buik*, book
128 *rethorye*, rhetoric   129 *polite*, polished
131 *setting*, writing down
132 *hude*, hood; *heklit*, fringed; *atovir*, over   133 *fassoun*, fashion
134 *electuairis*, medicines   136 *belangand*, appropriate
137 *hailsum*, wholesome
139 *furrit weill*, well lined with fur; *sic ane*, such a one; *aucht*, ought
143 *buskit*, arrayed; *twa*, two   145 *haw*, dull

For all hir licht scho borowis at hir brother
Titan, for of hirself scho hes nane uther.

Hir gite was gray, and full of spottis blak;
   And on hir breist ane churle paintit full evin,
Beirand ane bunche of thornis on his bak,   150
   Qwhilk for his thift micht clim na nar the hevin.
   Thus qwhen they gadderit war thir goddes sevin,
Mercurius they cheisit with ane assent
To be foirspeikar in the parliament.

Qwha had bene thair, and liken for to heir   155
   His facound toung and termis exquisite,
Of rethorick the prettick he micht leir,
   In breif sermone ane pregnant sentence write:
   Befoir Cupide veiling his cap a lite,
Speiris the caus of that vocatioun;   160
And he anone schew his intentioun.

"Lo," quod Cupide, "qwha will blaspheme the name
   Of his awin god, outher in word or deid,
To all goddis he dois baith lak and schame,
   And suld have bitter panis to his meid;   165
   I say this by yone wretchit Cresseid,
The qwhilk throu me was sum time flowr of lufe,
Me and my mother starklye can reprufe;

"Saying of hir greit infelecitye
   I was the caus and my mother Venus;   170
Ane blind goddes hir cald, that micht not se,

146 *at*, from   147 *nane uther*, no other
150 *beirand*, bearing   151 *thift*, theft; *clim na nar*, climb no nearer
152 *gadderit*, gathered; *thir*, these   153 *cheisit*, chose
154 *foirspeikar*, chairman   156 *facound*, eloquent
157 *prettick*, practice; *leir*, learn
158 *brief sermone*, few words; *sentence*, matter
159 *veiling*, doffing; *a lite*, a little
160 *speiris*, asks; *vocation*, convocation   164 *lak*, reproach
165 *panis*, pains; *meid*, reward   168 *can*, did

With sclander and defame injurious:
Thus hir leving unclene and lecherous
Scho wald returne on me and on my mother,
To qwhome I schew my grace abone all uther.   175

"And sen ye ar all sevin deificait,
    Participant of devine sapience,
This greit injure done to our hye estait
    Methink with pane we suld mak recompence;
    Was never to goddes done sic violence.   180
As weill for you as for myself I say,
Thairfoir ga help to revenge, I you pray."

Mercurius to Cupide gave answeir,
    And said, "Schir King, my counsall is that ye
Refer you to the hyest planeit heir,   185
    And tak to him the lawest of degre,
    The pane of Cresseid for to modifye:
As God Saturne, with him tak Cynthia."
"I am content," quod he, "to tak thay twa."

Than thus proceidit Saturne and the Mone,   190
    Qwhen thay the mater ripelye had degest,
For the dispite to Cupide scho had done,
    And to Venus oppin and manifest,
    In all hir life with pane to be opprest,
And torment sair, with seiknes incurabill,   195
And to all lovers be abhominabill.

This dulefull sentence Saturne tuik on hand,
    And passit down qwhair cairfull Cresseid lay,
And on hir heid he laid ane frostye wand;

172 *defame*, libel   173 *leving*, life
175 *schew*, showed; *abone*, above   176 *sen*, since; *deificait*, deified
179 *pane*, pain   181 *weill*, well
184 *Schir*, sir   186 *lawest*, lowest
187 *modifye*, determine   189 *thay twa*, those two
190 *degest*, digested   195 *sair*, sore; *seiknes*, sickness
197 *dulefull*, doleful; *tuik*, took

Than lawfullye on this wise can he say: 200
"Thy greit fairnes, and all thy beutye gay,
Thy wantoun blude, and eik thy goldin hair,
Heir I exclude fra thee for evermair.

"I change thy mirth into melancholy,
Qwhilk is the mother of all pensivenes;   205
Thy moisture and thy heit in cald and dry;
Thine insolence, thy play and wantones
To greit diseis; thy pomp and thy riches
In mortall neid; and greit penuritye
Thou suffer sall; and as ane beggar die."   210

O cruell Saturne! fraward and angrye,
Hard is thy dome, and to malitious:
On fair Cresseid qwhy hes thou na mercye,
Qwhilk was sa sweit, gentill, and amourous?
Withdraw thy sentence, and be gracious   215
As thou was never; so schawis thou thy deid,
Ane wraikfull sentence gevin on fair Cresseid.

Than Cynthia, qwhen Saturne past away,
Out of hir seit discendit down belive,
And red ane bill on Cresseid qwhair scho lay,   220
Contening this sentence diffinitive:
"Fra heit of bodye I thee now deprive,
And to thy seiknes sal be na recure,
But in dolour thy dayis to indure.

"Thy cristall ene minglit with blude I mak;   225
Thy voice sa cleir, unplesand, hoir, and hace;
Thy lustye lire ovirspred with spottis blak,

---

200 *can*, did
206 *heit in cald*, heat into cold
212 *dome*, sentence
217 *wraikfull*, vengeful
220 *bill*, statement
225 *ene*, eyes
227 *lustye lire*, pleasing flesh

202 *blude*, blood
211 *fraward*, malevolent
216 *deid*, deed
219 *belive*, quickly
223 *recure*, remedy
226 *hoir*, i.e., rough; *hace*, hoarse

And lumpis haw appeirand in thy face;
  Qwhair thou cummis, ilk man sall fle the place;
This sall thou go begging fra hous to hous,   230
With cop and clapper like ane lazarous."

This doolye dreame, this uglye visioun
  Brocht to ane end, Cresseid fra it awoik,
And all that court and convocatioun
  Vanischit away. Than rais scho up and tuik   235
  Ane poleist glas, and hir schaddow culd luik;
And qwhen scho saw hir face sa deformait,
Gif scho in hart was wa aneuch, God wait!

(Lines 113–350)

228 *haw*, dull   229 *ilk*, each
230 *this*, thus   231 *cop*, cup; *lazarous*, leper
232 *doolye*, doleful   236 *schaddow*, reflection; *culd*, did
238 *gif*, whether; *wa*, woe; *aneuch*, enough; *wait*, knows

Robin and Makin

Robene sat on gud grene hill,
  Kepand a flok of fe;
Mirry Makine said him till,
  "Robene, thou rew on me;
I haif thee luvit loud and still   5
  Thir yeiris two or thre;
My dule in dern bot gif thou dill,
  Doutless but dreid I de."

Robene answerit, "Be the rude,
  Nathing of lufe I knaw,   10

2 *fe*, cattle   3 *him till*, to him
5 *haif*, have   6 *thir*, these
7 *dule*, grief; *dern*, secret; *bot gif*, unless; *dill*, soothe
8 *but dreid*, without doubt; *de*, die   9 *be the rude*, by the cross

Bot keipis my scheip undir yone wud;
    Lo qwhair thay raik on raw.
Qwhat hes marrit thee in thy mude,
    Makine, to me thou schaw;
Or qwhat is lufe, or to be lude?   15
    Fane wald I leir that law."

"At luvis lair gife thou will leir,
    Tak thair ane a, b, c:
Be heind, courtass, and fair of feir,
    Wise, hardy, and fre;   20
So that no denger do thee deir,
    Qwhat dule in dern thou dre;
Preiss thee with pane at all poweir,
    Be patient and prevye."

Robene answerit hir agane,   25
    "I wait nocht qwhat is luve;
But I haif mervell in certane
    Qwhat makis thee this wanrufe:
The weddir is fair, and I am fane;
    My scheip gois haill aboif: 30
And we wald play us in this plane,
    Thay wald us baith reproif."

"Robene, tak tent unto my taill,
    And wirk all as I reid,
And thou sall haif my hairt all haill,   35
    Eik and my madenheid.

11 *wud*, wood   12 *raik on raw*, walk in rows
13 *hes marrit*, has harmed; *mude*, heart   15 *lude*, loved
16 *fane*, gladly; *leir*, learn   17 *lair*, lore; *gife*, if
19 *heind*, gracious; *feir*, behavior   20 *fre*, generous
21 *denger*, coyness; *deir*, vex
22: whatever grief you suffer in secret
23 *preiss thee*, urge yourself on; *pane*, pains; *at all poweir*, i.e., as hard as you can   24 *prevye*, secretive
26 *wait*, know   28 *wanrufe*, unrest
30 *gois haill aboif*, walk sound above   31 *and*, if; *plane*, plain
32 *baith*, both; *reproif*, reprove   33 *tak tent*, pay heed; *taill*, tale
34 *reid*, advise   35 *haill*, whole

Sen God sendis bute for baill,
    And for murning remeid,
I dern with thee bot gif I daill,
    Doutles I am bot deid."   40

"Makine, tomorne this ilk a tide,
    And ye will meit me heir,
Peraventure my scheip ma gang besid,
    Qwhill we haif liggit full neir;
But maugre haif I and I bid   45
    Fra thay begin to steir—
Qwhat lyis on hairt I will nocht hid:
    Makin, than mak gud cheir."

"Robene, thou reivis me roif and rest;
    I luve bot thee allone."   50
"Makine, adeu, the sone gois west,
    The day is neir hand gone."
"Robene, in dule I am so drest
    That lufe wil be my bone."
"Ga lufe, Makine, qwhairevir thou list,   55
    For lemman I lue none."

"Robene, I stand in sic a styll,
    I sicht, and that full sair."
"Makine, I haif bene heir this qwhile:
    At hame God gif I wair."   60
"My huny, Robene, talk ane qwhile,

---

37 *sen*, since; *bute*, comfort; *baill*, ill   38: and remedy for mourning
39: in secret with thee unless I deal   40 *deid*, dead
41 *tomorne*, tomorrow; *ilk a tide*, same time   42 *and*, if
43 *ma gang besid*, may walk close at hand
44 *qwhill*, until; *liggit*, lain
45 *maugre*, ill will; *and I bid*, if I remain
46: from the time that they begin to move about
49 *reivis me*, deprive me of; *roif*, peace
53 *dule*, grief; *drest*, placed   54 *bone*, destruction
56: for mistress love I none   57 *sic a styll*, such a condition
58 *sicht*, sigh; *sair*, sore   60 *gif*, grant

Gif thou will do na mair."
"Makine, sum uthir man begile,
    For hamewart I will fair."

Robene on his wayis went,   65
    Als licht as leif of tre;
Maukin murnit in hir intent,
    And trowd him nevir to se.
Robene braid attour the bent;
    Than Maukine cryit on hye,   70
"Now ma thou sing, for I am schent!
    Qwhat alis lufe at me?"

Maukine went hame withouttin faill;
    Full wery eftir couth weip.
Than Robene in a ful fair daill   75
    Assemblit all his scheip.
Be that sum pairte of Maukinis aill
    Out throu his hairt coud creip:
He fallowit hir fast thair till assaill,
    And till hir tuke gude keip.   80

"Abid, abid, thou fair Makine,
    A word for ony thing;
For all my luve it sal be thine,
    Withouttin depairting.
All haill thy harte for till haif mine   85
    Is all my cuvating;
My scheip tomorne qwhill houris nine
    Will neid of no keping."

62 *gif*, if   66 *als*, as
68 *trowd*, thought   69 *braid . . . bent*, started over the moor
70 *on hye*, aloud   71 *ma*, may; *schent*, ruined
72 *alis*, ails   74 *eftir couth weip*, afterwards did weep
75 *daill*, dale   77 *be that*, by that time; *aill*, trouble
78 *coud*, did   79 *fallowit*, followed; *assaill*, assault
80 *keip*, heed   84 *depairting*, sharing
86: to have thy heart all mine   86 *cuvating*, desire
87 *qwhill*, until

"Robene, thou hes hard soung and say,
　　In gestis and storeys auld,   90
'The man that will nocht qwhen he may
　　Sall haif nocht qwhen he wald.'
I pray to Jesu every day
　　Mot eik thair cairis cauld,
That first preiss with thee to play,   95
　　Be firth, forrest, or fauld."

"Makine, the nicht is soft and dry,
　　The wedder is warme and fair,
And the grene woid richt neir us by
　　To walk attour allqwhair;   100
Thair ma na janglour us espy,
　　That is to lufe contrair;
Thairin, Makine, bath ye and I
　　Unsene we ma repair."

"Robene, that warld is all away   105
　　And quit brocht till ane end,
And nevir agane thairto perfay
　　Sall it be as thou wend;
For of my pane thou maid it play,
　　And all in vane I spend;   110
As thou hes done, sa sall I say,
　　Murne on, I think to mend."

"Maukine, the houp of all my heill,
　　My hairt on thee is sett,
And evirmair to thee be leill,   115

89 *hes hard,* have heard   90 *gestis,* tales
94 *mot eik,* that He might increase; *cauld,* fatal
95 *preiss,* attempt   96: by wood, forest, or fold
100: to walk everywhere about   101 *ma,* may; *janglour,* tatler
103 *bath,* both   106 *quit,* quite
107 *perfay,* by faith   108 *wend,* supposed
109: for you made sport of my pain
110 *spend,* i.e., expended my pain
112 *think to mend,* intend to feel better
113 *houp . . . heill,* hope of all my health   115 *leill,* true

Qwhill I may leif but lett;
Nevir to faill, as utheris feill,
  Qwhat grace that evir I gett."
"Robene, with thee I will nocht deill;
  Adeu, for thus we mett." 120

Malkine went hame blith anneuche,
  Attour the holttis hair;
Robene murnit, and Makine leuche;
  Scho sang, he sichit sair;
And so left him, baith wo and weuche, 125
  In dolour and in cair,
Kepand his hird under a huche,
  Amangis the holtis hair.

116: while I may live without hindrance   119 *deill,* deal
121 *anneuche,* enough   122 *attour,* over; *hair,* hoar
123 *leuche,* laughed   124 *scho,* she; *sichit,* sighed
125 *weuche,* harm   127 *huche,* cliff

William Dunbar

(1460?–1520?)

Lament for the Makers

QWHEN HE WES SEK

I that in heill wes and gladnes,
Am trublit now with gret seiknes,
And feblit with infermitie;
   Timor mortis conturbat me.

Our plesance heir is all vaneglory,   5
This fals warld is bot transitory,
The flesche is brukle, the Fend is sle;
   Timor mortis conturbat me.

The stait of man dois change and vary,
Now sound, now seik, now blith, now sary,   10
Now dansand mery, now like to dee;
   Timor mortis conturbat me.

No stait in erd heir standis sickir;
As with the wind wavis the wickir,
Wavis this warldis vanite;   15
   Timor mortis conturbat me.

1 *heill*, health; *wes*, was   2 *seikness*, sickness
3 *feblit*, enfeebled   5 *heir*, here
6 *warld*, world   7 *brukle*, brittle; *Fend is sle*, Fiend is sly
9 *stait*, state   10 *seik*, sick; *sary*, sorry
11 *dansand*, dancing; *dee*, die   13 *erd*, earth; *sickir*, secure
14 *wickir*, twig

On to the ded gois all Estatis,
Princis, Prelotis, and Potestatis,
Baith riche and pur of al degre;
    Timor mortis conturbat me.   20

He takis the knichtis into feild,
Anarmit under helme and scheild;
Victour he is at all melle;
    Timor mortis conturbat me.

That strang unmercifull tyrand   25
Takis, on the moderis breist soukand,
The bab full of benignite;
    Timor mortis conturbat me.

He takis the campion in the stour,
The capitane closit in the towr,   30
The lady in bowr full of beute;
    Timor mortis conturbat me.

He spairis no lord for his piscence,
Na clerk for his intelligence;
His awfull strak may no man fle;   35
    Timor mortis conturbat me.

Art-magicianis, and astrologgis,
Rethoris, logicianis, and theologgis,
Thame helpis no conclusionis sle;
    Timor mortis conturbat me.   40

In medicine the most practicianis,
Lechis, surrigianis, and physicianis,

17 *the ded,* death   18 *Potestatis,* potentates
19 *baith,* both; *pur,* poor   21 *into,* in
23 *melle,* fight   25 *strang,* strong
26 *moderis,* mother's; *soukand,* sucking
29 *campion,* champion; *stour,* battle   30 *capitane,* castellan
33 *piscence,* puissance   34 *na,* no
35 *strak,* stroke   37 *art-magicianis,* magicians
38 *rethoris,* rhetoricians   39 *sle,* clever
41 *most practicianis,* most skilled of practicioners   42 *lechis,* doctors

Thameself fra ded may not supple;
Timor mortis conturbat me.

I se that makaris amang the laif   45
Playis heir ther pageant, sine gois to graif;
Sparit is nocht ther faculte;
Timor mortis conturbat me.

He hes done petuously devour
The noble Chaucer, of makaris flowr,   50
The Monk of Bery, and Gower, all thre;
Timor mortis conturbat me.

The gude Sir Hew of Eglintoun,
And eik Heriot, and Wintoun,
He hes tane out of this cuntre;   55
Timor mortis conturbat me.

That scorpion fell hes done infek
Maister Johne Clerk, and James Afflek,
Fra balat-making and tragidie;
Timor mortis conturbat me.   60

Holland and Barbour he hes berevit;
Allace! that he nocht with us levit
Schir Mungo Lokert of the Le;
Timor mortis conturbat me.

Clerk of Tranent eik he hes tane,   65
That maid the Anteris of Gawane;
Schir Gilbert Hay endit hes he;
Timor mortis conturbat me.

---

43 *fra ded*, from death; *supple*, deliver   45 *makaris*, poets; *laif*, rest
46 *sine*, then; *graif*, grave   47 *faculte*, profession
49: he has piteously devoured   54 *eik*, also
55 *hes tane*, has taken   57 *hes done infek*, has poisoned
61 *berevit*, taken away   62 *nocht*, not; *levit*, left
63 *schir*, sir   66 *maid*, i.e., wrote; *Anteris*, Adventures

He hes Blind Hary and Sandy Traill
Slaine with his schowr of mortall haill,   70
Qwhilk Patrik Johnestoun might nocht fle;
   Timor mortis conturbat me.

He hes reft Merseir his endite,
That did in luf so lifly write,
So schort, so quik, of sentence hye;   75
   Timor mortis conturbat me.

He hes tane Roull of Aberdene,
And gentill Roull of Corstorphin;
Two bettir fallowis did no man se;
   Timor mortis conturbat me.   80

In Dumfermeline he hes done roune
With Maister Robert Henrysoun;
Schir Johne the Ros enbrast hes he;
   Timor mortis conturbat me.

And he hes now tane, last of aw,   85
Gud gentill Stobo and Quintine Schaw,
Of qwham all wichtis hes pete:
   Timor mortis conturbat me.

Gud Maister Walter Kennedy
In point of dede lyis veraly,   90
Gret reuth it wer that so suld be;
   Timor mortis conturbat me.

Sen he hes all my brether tane,
He will nocht lat me lif alane,

---

71 *qwhilk,* which   73: he has deprived **Mercer** of his writing
74 *luf,* love; *lifly,* spiritedly   75 *of sentence hye,* noble of sentiment
81 *hes done roune,* has whispered   85 *aw,* all
87: of whom all creatures have pity   90 *dede,* death; *lyis,* lies
91 *reuth,* pity   93 *sen,* since; *brether,* brothers
94: he will not let me live alone

On forse I man his nixt pray be;   95
   Timor mortis conturbat me.

Sen for the deid remeid is none,
Best is that we for dede dispone,
Eftir our deid that lif may we;
   Timor mortis conturbat me.   100

95: perforce I must his next prey be
97 *the deid,* death; *remeid,* remedy
98 *for dede dispone,* dispose ourselves for death   99 *lif,* live

FROM *The Book of the Two Married Women and the Widow*

[*The Widow Speaks*]

Deid is now that divour and dollin in erd:
With him deit all my dule and my drery thoghtis;
Now done is my dolly night, my day is upsprungin,
Adeu dolour, adeu! my dainte now beginis:
Now am I a wedow, ywis, and weill am at ese;   5
I weip as I were woful, but wel is me for ever;
I busk as I wer bailfull, bot blith is my hert;
My mouth it makis murning, and my mind lauchis;
My clokis thay ar caerfull in colour of sabill,
Bot courtly and right curius my corse is therundir: 10
I drup with a ded luke in my dule habit,
As with manis daill I had done for dayis of my lif.
   Qwhen that I go to the kirk, cled in cair weid,

1: Dead is now that bankrupt and buried in earth
2 *deit,* died; *dule,* grief   3 *dolly,* doleful
4 *dainte,* delight   5 *ywis,* indeed; *weill,* well
7 *busk,* dress; *bailfull,* baleful   8 *lauchis,* laughs
10 *curius,* well-made; *corse,* body
11 *drup,* droop; *luke,* look; *dule,* dismal
12 *manis daill,* dealing with men   13 *cair,* a sort of cloth

As foxe in a lambis fleise fenye I my cheir;
Than lay I furght my bright buke one breid one my
    kne,   15
With mony lusty letter ellumminit with gold;
And drawis my clok forthwart our my face qwhit,
That I may spy, unaspyit, a space me beside:
Full oft I blenk by my buke, and blinis of devotioun,
To se qwhat berne is best brand or bredest in schul-
    deris,   20
Or forgeit is maist forcely to furnise a bancat
In Venus chalmer, valieandly, withoutin vane ruse:
And, as the new mone all pale, oppressit with change,
Kithis qwhilis her cleir face through cluddis of sable,
So keik I through my clokis, and castis kind lukis   25
To knichtis, and to cleirkis, and cortly personis.

    Qwhen frendis of my husbandis behaldis me one fer,
I haif a watter spunge for wa, within my wide clokis,
Than wring I it full wiely and wetis my chekis,
With that watteris min ene and welteris downe teris. 30
Than say thay all, that sittis about, "Se ye nought, al-
    lace!
Yone lustlese led so lelely scho luffit hir husband:
Yone is a pete to enprent in a princis hert,
That sic a perle of plesance suld yond pane dre!"
I sane me as I war ane sanct, and semis ane angell; 35

14 *fenye I my cheir,* I disguise my real appearance
15 *furght,* forth; *buke,* book; *one breid,* open   16 *lusty,* pleasant
17 *forthwart,* forward; *qwhit,* white
19 *blenk by,* look away from; *blinis of,* leave off
20 *berne,* man; *brand,* brawned; *bredest,* broadest
21 *forgeit,* fashioned; *maist forcely,* most vigorously; *furnise a bancat,*
    furnish a banquet   22 *chalmer,* chamber; *ruse,* boast
24 *kithis qwhilis,* shows at times; *cluddis,* clouds   25 *keik,* peep
27 *behaldis,* behold; *one fer,* from afar   28 *haif,* have; *wa,* woe
30 *ene,* eyes; *welteris,* pour
32 *led,* person; *lelely,* faithfully; *scho luffit,* she loved
33 *pete,* pet; *enprent,* imprint
34 *sic,* such; *pane dre,* pain suffer
35 *sane me,* cross myself; *ane sanct,* a saint

At langage of lichory I leit as I war crabit:
I sich, without sair hert or seiknes in body;
According to my sable weid I mon haif sad maneris,
Or thay will se all the suth; for certis, we wemen
We set us all far the sight to sile men of treuth: 40
We dule for na evill deid, sa it be derne haldin.

Wise wemen has wayis and wonderfull gidingis
With gret engine to bejaip ther jolius husbandis;
And quietly, with sic craft, convoyis our materis
That, under Crist, no creatur kennis of our doingis.   45
But folk a cury may muscuke, that knawledge wantis,
And has na colouris for to cover thair awne kindly fautis;
As dois thir damisellis, for derne dotit lufe,
That dogonis haldis in dainte and delis with thaim so
          lang,
Qwhill all the cuntre knaw ther kindnes and faith: 50
Faith has a fair name, bot falsheid faris bettir:
Fy one hir that can nought feine, her fame for to saif!
Yit am I wise in sic werk and wes all my time;
Thoght I want wit in warldines, I wilis haif in luf,
As ony happy woman has that is of hye blude: 55
Hutit be the halok las a hunder yeir of eild!

I have ane secrete servand, richt sobir of his toung,

---

36 *lichory*, lechery; *leit*, act; *crabit*, angry
37 *sich*, sigh; *sair*, sore; *seiknes*, sickness   38 *mon haif*, must have
39 *suth*, sooth
40: we are careful to blind men from the sight of truth
41 *dule*, grieve; *deid*, deed; *sa it . . . haldin*, as long as it is kept dark
42 *gidingis*, i.e., shifts   43 *engine*, device; *bejaip*, fool; *jolius*, jealous
44 *convoyis our materis*, arrange our affairs   45 *kennis*, knows
46: but folk who lack knowledge may miscook a dish
47 *colouris*, camouflages; *awne kindly fautis*, own natural faults
48 *thir*, these; *derne . . . lufe*, secret doting love
49: who hold rascals in delight, and deal with them so long
50 *qwhill*, until   52 *feine*, pretend; *saif*, save
53 *wes*, i.e., have been
54 *thoght*, though; *warldines*, worldliness; *wilis . . . luf*, have wiles
    in love   55 *blude*, blood
56: ? hooted be the ignorant lass a hundred years of age
57 *sobir*, discreet

That me supportis of sic nedis, qwhen I a sine mak:
Thoght he be simpill to the sicht, he has a tong sickir;
Full mony semeliar sege wer service dois mak: 60
Thoght I haif cair, under cloke, the cleir day qwhill
    night,
Yit haif I solace, under serk, qwhill the sone rise.

    Yit am I haldin a haly wif our all the haill schire,
I am sa peteouse to the pur, qwhen ther is personis
    mony.
In passing of pilgrimage I pride me full mekle, 65
Mair for the prese of peple na ony perdoun wining.

    Bot yit methink the best bourd, qwhen baronis and
    knichtis,
And othir bachilleris, blith bluming in youth,
And all my luffaris lele, my lugeing persewis,
And fillis me wine wantonly with weilfair and joy: 70
Sum rounis; and sum ralyeis; and sum redis ballatis;
Sum raiffis furght rudly with riatus speche;
Sum plenis, and sum prayis; sum prasis my beute,
Sum kissis me; sum clappis me; sum kindnes me proferis;
Sum cerffis to me curtasly; sum me the cop giffis; 75
Sum stalwardly steppis ben, with a stout curage,
And a stif standand thing staiffis in my neiff;
And mony blenkis ben our, that but full fer sittis,
That may, for the thik thrang, nought thrif as thay wald.

---

58 *sine*, sign
59 *sickir*, safe
60 *semeliar sege*, seemlier man; *wer*, worse
61 *qwhill*, until
62 *serk*, skirt   63 *haldin*, held; *haly*, holy; *our*, over; *haill*, whole
64 *pur*, poor; *personis mony*, i.e., many people watching
65 *mekle*, much
66 *mair*, more; *prese*, praise; *na*, than; *perdoun*, pardon
67 *bourd*, fun   68 *bluming*, blooming
69 *luffaris lele*, true lovers; *my lugeing persewis*, visit my lodging
70 *fillis me wine*, i.e., feast me   71 *rounis*, whisper; *ralyeis*, jest
72 *raiffis furght*, rave on; *riatus*, riotous   73 *plenis*, complain
74 *clappis*, embrace
75 *cerffis to*, carve for; *curtasly*, curteously; *cop*, cup; *giffis*, give
76 *ben*, close; *curage*, heart   77 *staiffis*, pushes; *neiff*, fist
78: And many who sit far at the other end of the room look over at
  my end   79 *thrang*, throng; *thrif*, thrive

Bot, with my fair calling, I comfort thaim all: 80
For he that sittis me nixt, I nip on his finger;
I serf him on the tothir side on the samin fasson;
And he that behind me sittis, I hard on him lene;
And him befor, with my fut fast on his I stramp;
And to the bernis far but sweit blenkis I cast: 85
To every man in speciall speke I sum wordis
So wisly and so womanly, qwhill warmis ther hertis.

Thar is no liffand leid so law of degre
That sall me luf unluffit, I am so loik-hertit;
And gif his lust so be lent into my lire qwhit,   90
That he be lost or with me lig, his lif sall nocht danger.
I am so mercifull in mind, and menis all wichtis,
My sely saull salbe saif, qwhen sa bot all jugis.
Ladyis leir thir lessonis and be no lassis fundin:
This is the legeand of my lif, thought Latine it be
      nane.   95

(Lines 410–504)

80 *calling*, greeting   82 *serf*, serve; *samin fasson*, same way
84 *fut*, foot; *stramp*, trample
85 *bernis far but*, men sitting far away; *blenkis*, looks
87 *qwhill*, until   88 *liffand leid*, living man; *law*, low
89 *luf unluffit*, love unloved; *loik-hertit*, warm-hearted
90 *gif*, if; *lent*, inclined; *lire qwhit*, white flesh
91 *lig*, lie; *danger*, be endangered
92 *menis all wichtis*, comfort all creatures
93 *sely saull*, poor soul; *qwhen . . . jugis*, ? the meaning is apparently:
    when God judges all   94 *leir*, learn; *thir*, these; *fundin*, found
95 *thought*, though; *nane*, none

FROM *The Golden Targe*

[*The Poet's Dream*]

Right as the stern of day begouth to schine,
Qwhen gone to bed war Vesper and Lucine,
      I raise and by a rosere did me rest;

1 *right*, just; *stern*, star; *begouth*, began   2 *war*, were
3 *raise*, rose; *rosere*, rosebush

Up sprang the goldin candill matutine,
With clere depurit bemes cristalline,   5
    Glading the mery fowlis in thair nest;
    Or Phebus was in purpur cape revest
Up raise the lark, the hevins menstrale fine
    In May, intill a morrow mirthfullest.

Full angellike thir birdis sang thair houris   10
Within thair courtins grene, into thair bowris,
    Apparalit qwhite and red with blomes swete;
Anamalit was the felde with all colouris,
The perly droppis schake in silvir schowris,
    Qwhill all in balme did branch and levis flete;   15
    To part fra Phebus did Aurora grete,
Hir cristall teris I saw hing on the flowris,
    Qwhilk he for lufe all drank up with his hete.

For mirth of May, with skippis and with hoppis,
The birdis sang upon the tender croppis,   20
    With curiouse note, as Venus chapell clerkis:
The rosis yong, new spreding of thair knopis,
War powderit bricht with hevinly beryall droppis,
    Throu bemes rede birning as ruby sperkis;
    The skies rang for schouting of the larkis,   25
The purpur hevin, ourscailit in silvir sloppis,
    Ourgilt the treis, branchis, lef, and barkis.

Downe throu the rice a rivir ran with stremis,
So lustily again thay likand lemis,

---

5 *depurit*, purified   7 *or*, ere; *revest*, clothed
9 *intill*, into; *morow*, morning   10 *thir*, these
11 *into*, in   13 *anamalit*, enameled
15 *qwhill*, until; *flete*, float   16 *grete*, weep
17 *hing*, hang   18 *qwhilk*, which; *lufe*, love
20 *croppis*, treetops   22 *knopis*, buds
23 *beryall*, beryl
26 *ourscailit*, scaled over; *sloppis*, mantles (i.e., clouds)
27 *ourgilt*, overgilt   28 *rice*, branches
29 *lustily*, pleasantly; *thay*, those; *likand lemis*, pleasing gleams

That all the lake as lamp did leme of licht,   30
Qwhilk schadowit all about with twinkling glemis;
That bewis bathit war in secund bemis
    Throu the reflex of Phebus visage bricht;
    On every side the hegies raise on hicht,
The bank was grene, the bruke was full of bremis,   35
    The stanneris clere as stern in frosty nicht.

The cristall air, the sapher firmament,
The ruby skies of the orient,
    Cest beriall bemes on emerant bewis grene;
The rosy garth depaint and redolent,   40
With purpur, azure, gold, and goulis gent
    Arayed was, by dame Flora the quene,
    So nobily, that joy was for to sene;
The roch again the rivir resplendent
    As low enluminit all the leves schene.   45

Qwhat throu the mery foulis armony,
And throu the riveris soune richt ran me by,
    On Florais mantill I slepit as I lay,
Qwhare sone into my dremes fantasy
I saw approch, again the orient sky,   50
    A saill, als qwhite as blossum upon spray,
    With merse of gold, bricht as the stern of day,
Qwhilk tendit to the land full lustily,
    As falcoune swift desirouse of hir pray.

And hard on burd unto the blomit medis,   55
Among the grene rispis and the redis,

---

30 *lake,* stream; *leme,* gleam   32 *bewis,* boughs; *secund,* reflected
34 *hegies,* hedges   35 *bruke,* brook; *bremis,* carp
36 *stanneris,* beach pebbles   39 *cest,* cast
40 *garth,* garden; *dapaint,* painted   41 *goulis gent,* soft gules
44 *roch,* cliff   45 *low,* flame; *schene,* resplendent
47 *soune,* sound   51 *als,* as
52 *merse,* mast-top; *stern,* star   55 *hard on burd unto,* close alongside
56 *rispis,* sedge

Arrivit sche, qwhar fro anone thare landis
Ane hundreth ladies, lusty into wedis,
Als fresch as flowris that in May up spredis,
    In kirtillis grene, withoutin kell or bandis: 60
    Thair bricht hairis hang gletering on the strandis
In tressis clere, wippit with goldin thredis;
    With pappis qwhite, and midlis small as wandis.

Discrive I wald, bot qwho could wele endite
How all the feldis with thay lilies qwhite   65
    Depaint war bricht, qwhilk to the hevin did glete:
Noucht thou, Omer, als fair as thou coud write
For all thine ornate stylis so perfite;
    Nor yit thou, Tullius, qwhois lippis swete
    Off rethorike did into termes flete: 70
Your aureate tongis both bene all to lite,
    For to compile that paradise complete.

Thare saw I Nature and Venus, quene and quene,
The fresch Aurora, and lady Flora schene,
    Juno, Appollo, and Proserpina,   75
Diane the goddesse chaste of woddis grene,
My lady Cleo, that help of makaris bene,
    Thetes, Pallas, and prudent Minerva,
    Fair feinit Fortune, and lemand Lucina,
Thir michty quenis in crownis micht be sene,   80
    With bemis blith, bricht as Lucifera.

There saw I May, of mirthfull monethis quene,
Betwix Aprile and June, her sistir schene,
    Within the garding walking up and down,

58 *hundreth,* hundred; *lusty into,* gay as to   60 *kell,* hairnet
62 *wippit,* bound around   63 *pappis,* breasts
65 *thay,* those   66 *glete,* shine
69 *qwhois,* whose   70 *into termes flete,* abound in figures
71 *lite,* small   74 *schene,* fair
76 *woddis,* woods   77 *makaris,* poets
79 *feinit,* disguised; *lemand,* gleaming   80 *thir,* these

Qwham of the fowlis gladdith al bedene;   85
Scho was full tender in hir yeris grene.
    Thare saw I Nature present hir a gowne
    Rich to behald and nobil of renowne,
Off eviry hew under the hevin that bene
    Depaint, and broud be gude proporcioun.   90

Full lustily thir ladies all in fere
Enterit within this park of most plesere,
    Qwhare that I lay ourhelit with levis ronk;
The mery fowlis, blisfullest of chere,
Salust Nature, methoucht, on thair manere,   95
    And eviry blome on branch, and eke on bonk,
    Opnit and spred thair balmy levis donk,
Full low enclining to thair Quene so clere,
    Qwham of thair nobill norising thay thonk.

Sine to dame Flora, on the samin wise,   100
Thay saluse, and thay thank a thousand sise;
    And to dame Venus, lufis michty quene,
Thay sang ballettis in lufe, as was the gise,
With amourouse notis lusty to devise,
    As thay that had lufe in thair hertis grene;   105
    Thair hony throtis, opnit fro the splene,
With werblis swete did perse the hevinly skies,
    Qwhill loud resounit the firmament serene.

Ane othir court thare saw I consequent,
Cupide the king, with bow in hand ybent,   110
    And dredefull arowis grundin scharp and square;
Thare saw I Mars, the god armipotent,

85 *qwham of*, of whom; *bedene*, together   86 *scho*, she
90 *broud*, embroidered; *be*, in   91 *in fere*, together
93 *ourhelit*, covered over; *ronk*, luxuriant   95 *salust*, saluted
99 *norising*, nourishing,   100 *sine*, after; *samin*, same
101 *sise*, times   102 *lufis*, love's
103 *gise*, fashion   104 *lusty to devise*, pleasant to contrive
106 *splene*, i.e., heart   108 *qwhill*, until
109 *consequent*, thereafter

Awfull and sterne, strong and corpolent;
  Thare saw I crabbit Saturn ald and haire,
  His luke was like for to perturb the aire;   115
Thare was Mercurius, wise and eloquent,
  Of rethorike that fand the flowris faire;

Thare was the god of gardingis, Priapus;
Thare was the god of wildernes, Phanus;
  And Janus, god of entree delitable;   120
Thare was the god of fludis, Neptunus;
Thare was the god of windis, Eolus,
  With variand luke, richt like a lord unstable;
  Thare was Bacus the gladder of the table;
Thare was Pluto, the elrich incubus,   125
  In cloke of grene, his court usit no sable.

And eviry one of thir, in grene arayit,
On harp or lute full merily thay playit,
  And sang ballettis with michty notis clere:
Ladies to dance full sobirly assayit;   130
Endlang the lusty rivir so thay mayit,
  Thair observance richt hevinly was to here;
  Than crap I throu the levis, and drew nere,
Qwhare that I was richt sudainly affrayit,
  All throu a luke, qwhilk I have boucht full dere.   135

And schortly for to speke, be lufis quene
I was aspyit; scho bad hir archearis kene
  Go me arrest; and thay no time delayit;
Than ladies fair lete fall thair mantillis grene,
With bowis big in tressit hairis schene,   140
  All sudainly thay had a felde arayit;

114 *crabbit,* sullen; *haire,* hoar   115 *luke,* look
117 *fand,* devised   125 *elrich,* hideous
127 *thir,* these   130 *assayit,* ventured
131 *endlang,* along; *mayit,* celebrated May   133 *crap,* crept
135 *boucht,* paid for   136 *be,* by
137 *scho,* she   141 *arayit,* prepared for battle

And yit richt gretly was I noucht affrayit,
The party was so pleasand for to sene:
   A wonder lusty bickir me assayit.

And first of all, with bow in hand ybent,   145
Come dame Beautee, richt as scho wald me schent;
   Sine folowit all hir dameselis yfere,
With mony diverse awfull instrument,
Unto the pres; Fair Having with hir went,
   Fine Portrature, Plesance, and Lusty Chere.   150
   Than come Resoun, with schelde of gold so clere;
In plate and maille, as Mars armipotent,
   Defendit me that nobil chevallere.

Sine tender Youth come with hir virgins ying,
Grene Innocence, and schamefull Abaising,   155
   And quaking Drede, with humble Obedience;
The Goldin Targe harmit thay no thing;
Curage in thame was noucht begonne to spring;
   Full sore thay dred to done a violence:
   Swete Womanhede I saw cum in presence,   160
Of artilye a warld sche did in bring,
   Servit with ladies full of reverence.

Sche led with hir Nurture and Lawlines,
Contenence, Pacience, Gude Fame, and Stedfastness,
   Discrecioun, Gentrise, and Considerance,   165
Levefell Company, and Honest Besines,
Benigne Luke, Milde Chere, and Sobirnes:
   All thir bure ganyeis to do me grevance;
   But Resoun bure the Targe with sic constance,

---

143 *party*, i.e., opposing army
144 *lusty bicker*, pleasing skirmish; *assayit*, assailed
146 *schent*, destroy   147 *sine*, after; *yfere*, together
149 *pres*, melee   150 *Lusty Chere*, Pleasant Demeanor
154 *ying*, young   155 *Abaising*, Dismay
161 *artilye*, artillery; *warld*, world   163 *Lawliness*, Lowliness
165 *Gentrise*, Gentleness   166 *Levefull*, lawful
167 *Luke*, look   168 *thir bure ganyeis,* these bore crossbows
169 *sic*, such

Thair scharp assayes micht do no dures   170
　　To me, for all thair awfull ordinance.

Unto the pres persewit Hye Degree,
Hir folowit ay Estate, and Dignitee,
　　Comparisoun, Honour, and Noble Array,
Will, Wantonnes, Renown, and Libertee,   175
Richesse, Fredome, and eke Nobilitee:
　　Wit ye thay did thair baner hye display;
　　A cloud of arowis as haile schowr lousit thay.
And schot, qwhill wastit was thair artilye,
　　Sine went abak reboitit of thair pray.   180

Qwhen Venus had persavit this rebute,
Dissimilance scho bad go mak persute,
　　At all powere to perse the Goldin Targe;
And scho, that was of doubilnes the rute,
Askit hir choise of archeris in refute.   185
　　Venus the best bad hir go wale at large;
　　Scho tuke Presence, plicht ankers of the barge,
And Fair Calling, that wele a flain coud schute,
　　And Cherising for to complete hir charge.

Dame Hamelines scho tuke in company,   190
That hardy was and hende in archery,
　　And broucht dame Beautee to the felde again;
With all the choise of Venus chevalry
Thay come and bickerit unabaisitly:
　　The schowr of arowis rappit on as rain;   195
　　Perilouse Presence, that mony sire has slaine,

170 *dures*, violence　　　　　　　176 *Fredome*, Generosity
177 *wit*, know　　　　　　　　　　178 *lousit*, loosed
179 *qwhill*, until　　　　　　　　　180 *reboitit*, repulsed
181 *persavit*, perceived; *rebute*, repulse
182 *Dissimilance*, Dissembling　183 *at all powere*, with all her might
184 *doubilnes*, duplicity; *rute*, root　　　185 *in refute*, under shelter
186 *wale*, choose　　　　　　187 *plicht ankers*, ? sheet anchor
189 *flain*, arrow　　　　　　　　190 *Hamelines*, Intimacy
191 *hende*, skilful　　194 *bickerit unabaisitly*, fought undismayed
195 *rappit*, struck

The bataill broucht on bordour hard us by;
  The salt was all the sarar, suth to sayn.

Thik was the schote of grundin dartis kene;
Bot Resoun, with the Scheld of Gold so schene,   200
  Warly defendit, qwhosoevir assayit;
The awfull stowre he manly did sustene,
Qwhill Presence cest a pulder in his ene,
  And than as drunkin man he all forwayit:
  Qwhen he was blind, the fule with him thay
    playit,   205
And banist him among the bewis grene;
  That sory sicht me sudainly affrayit.

Than was I woundit to the deth wele nere,
And yoldin as a wofull prisonnere
  To lady Beautee in a moment space;   210
Methoucht scho semit lustiar of chere,
Efter that Resoun tint had his eyne clere,
  Than of before, and lufliare of face:
  Qwhy was thou blindit, Resoun? qwhy, allace!
And gert ane hell my paradise appere,   215
  And mercy seme, qwhare that I fand no grace.

Dissimulance was besy me to sile,
And Fair Calling did oft apon me smile,
  And Cherising me fed with wordis fair;
New Acquaintance enbracit me a qwhile,   220
And favourit me, qwhill men micht go a mile,
  Sine tuk hir leve, I saw hir nevir mare:

198 *salt*, assault; *sarar*, bitterer   199 *grundin*, whetted
200 *warly*, cautiously   202 *stoure*, battle
203 *qwhill*, until; *cest . . . ene*, cast a powder in his eye
204 *forwayit*, staggered   205 *fule*, fool
206 *banist*, banished   209 *yoldin*, yielded
211 *lustiar of chere*, pleasanter of face   212 *tint*, lost
215 *gert*, made   216 *seme*, i.e., seem to be; *fand*, found
217 *sile*, beguile   222 *mare*, more

Than saw I Dangere toward me repair;
I coud eschew hir presence be no wile.
   On side scho lukit with ane fremit fare,   225

And at the last departing coud hir dresse,
And me deliverit unto Hevinesse
   For to remaine, and scho in cure me tuke.
Be this the Lord of Windis, with wodenes,
God Eolus, his bugill blew, I gesse,   230
   That with the blast the levis all to-schuke;
   And sudainly, in the space of a luke,
All was hine went, thare was bot wildernes,
   Thare was no more bot birdis, bank, and bruke.

In twinkling of ane eye to schip thay went,   235
And swith up saile unto the top thay stent,
   And with swift course atour the flude thay frak;
Thay firit gunnis with powder violent,
Till that the reke raise to the firmament,
   The rochis all resounit with the rak;   240
   For reirde it semit that the rainbow brak;
With spirit affraide apon my fete I sprent,
   Amang the clewis so carefull was the crak.

And as I did awake of my sweving,
The joyfull birdis merily did sing   245
   For mirth of Phebus tendir bemes schene;
Swete war the vapouris, soft the morowing,
Halesum the vale, depaint with flowris ying;

---

223 *Dangere,* Coyness   224 *be,* by
225 *fremit fare,* unfriendly demeanor
226 *departing . . . dresse,* ? she made ready to depart
228 *cure,* care   229 *be this,* by this time; *wodenes,* frenzy
231 *to-schuke,* quaked   233 *hine,* hence
236 *swith,* quickly; *stent,* stretched   237 *atour,* over; *frak,* sped
239 *reke,* smoke   240 *rak,* shock
241 *reirde,* noise   242 *sprent,* leaped
243 *clewis,* valleys; *carefull,* awful   244 *sweving,* sleep
248 *halesum,* wholesome

The air attemperit, sobir, and amene;
  In qwhite and rede was all the felde besene,   250
Throu Naturis nobil fresch anamaling,
  In mirthfull May, of eviry moneth Quene.

(Lines 1–252)

249 *amene*, pleasant   250 *besene*, arrayed

On the Resurrection of Christ

Done is a battell on the dragon blak,
Our campioun Christ confoundit hes his force;
The yettis of hell ar brokin with a crak,
The signe triumphall rasit is of the croce,
The divillis trimmillis with hiddouss voce,   5
The saulis ar borrowit and to the bliss can go,
Christ with his blud our ransonis dois indoce:
Surrexit Dominus de sepulchro.

Dungin is the deidly dragon Lucifer,
The crewall serpent with the mortall stang;   10
The auld kene tegir with his teith on char,
Qwhilk in a wait hes line for us so lang,
Thinking to grip us in his clowss strang;
The mercifull Lord wald nocht that it wer so,
He maid him for to felye of that fang: 15
Surrexit Dominus de sepulchro.

He for our saik that sufferit to be slane,
And lik a lamb in sacrifice wes dicht,

2 *campioun*, champion; *hes*, has   3 *yettis*, gates
4 *rasit*, raised; *croce*, cross   5 *trimmillis*, tremble; *voce*, voice
6 *borrowit*, redeemed
7 *our ransonis . . . indoce*, is effecting our ransoms
9 *dungin*, beaten down   10 *stang*, sting
11 *tegir*, tiger; *on char*, ajar
12 *qwhilk*, which; *in a wait*, in ambush; *line*, lain
15 *maid*, made; *felye*, fail; *fang*, prey   18 *wes dicht*, was offered up

Is lik a lione rissin up agane,
And as giane raxit him on hicht;   20
Sprungin is Aurora radius and bricht,
On loft is gone the glorius Appollo,
The blisfull day departit fro the nicht:
Surrexit Dominus de sepulchro.

The grit victour agane is rissin on hicht,   25
That for our querrell to the deth wes woundit;
The sone that wox all paill now schinis bricht,
And dirkness clerit, our faith is now refoundit;
The knell of mercy fra the hevin is soundit,
The Cristin ar deliverit of thair wo,   30
The Jowis and thair errour ar confoundit:
Surrexit Dominus de sepulchro.

The fo is chasit, the battell is done ceiss,
The presone brokin, the jevellouris fleit and flemit;
The weir is gone, confermit is the peiss,   35
The fetteris lousit and the dungeoun temit,
The ransoun maid, the presoneris redemit;
The feild is win, ourcumin is the fo,
Dispulit of the tresur that he yemit:
Surrexit Dominus de sepulchro.   40

20 *giane,* giant; *raxit him,* stretched himself   21 *radius,* radiant
23 *departit,* separated   25 *grit,* great
30 *Cristin,* Christians   33 *done ceis,* brought to end
34 *jevellouris,* jailers; *fleit and flemit,* put to flight and banished
35 *weir,* war   36 *lousit,* loosened; *temit,* emptied
38 *win,* won; *ourcumin,* overcome   39 *dispulit,* despoiled; *yemit,* kept

Gavin Douglas

(1474?–1522)

FROM King Hart

[Hart's Castle]

King Hart, into his cumlye castell strang
Closit about with craft and meikill ure,
So semlye wes he set his folk amang,
That he no dout had of misaventure:
So proudlye wes he polist, plane and pure, 5
With youthheid and his lustye levis grene;
So fair, so fresche, so liklye to endure,
And als so blith as bird in simmer schene.

For wes he never yit with schowris schot,
Nor yit ourrun with rouk, or ony raine; 10
In all his lusty lecam nocht ane spot,
Na never had experience into paine,
Bot alway into liking, nocht to laine;
Onlye to love, and verrye gentilnes,
He was inclinit cleinlye to remane, 15
And wonn under the wing of wantounes.

So strang this King him thocht his castell stude,
With mony towre and turat crownit hye:

1 *strang*, strong   2 *meikill ure*, great labor
4 *dout*, fear   5 *polist*, polished; *plane*, smooth
8 *als so*, as; *schene*, fair   9 *schot*, assailed
10 *ourrun*, overrun; *rouk*, mist   11 *lecam*, body; *ane*, one
13 *liking*, pleasure; *nocht to laine*, to hide nothing
15 *cleinlye*, i.e., permanently   16 *wonn*, dwell
17 *stude*, stood

About the wall thair ran ane water wude,
Blak, stinkand, sour, and salt as is the sey,   20
That on the wallis wiskit, gre by gre,
Boldning to ryis the castell to confound;
Bot thay within maid sa grit melody,
That for thair reird thay micht nocht heir the sound.

(Stanzas 1, 2, 10)

19 *wude,* raging   20 *stinkand,* stinking
21 *wiskit,* lapped; *gre,* step   22 *boldning,* swelling; *ryis,* rise
23 *sa grit,* so great   24 *reird,* noise

FROM *The Palace of Honor*

[*Nightmare*]

My ravist spreit in that desart terribill,
Approchit neir that uglye flude horribill,
Like till Cochyte the river infernall,
With vile water qwhilk maid a hiddious trubil,
Rinnand overheid, blude reid, and impossibill   5
That it had been a river naturall;
With brayis bair, raif rochis like to fall,
Qwhairon na gers nor herbis wer visibill,
Bot swappis brint with blastis boriall.

This laithlye flude rumland as thonder routit,   10
In qwhome the fisch yelland as elvis schoutit,
Thair yelpis wilde my heiring all fordeifit,

1 *ravist spreit,* ravished spirit   2 *flude,* flood
3 *Cochyte,* Cocytus   4 *qwhilk,* which; *trubil,* disturbance
5 *rinnand overheid,* running precipitously
7 *brayis,* banks; *raif rockis,* cleft rocks   8 *gers,* grass
9 *swappis brint,* sedge burnt
10 *laithlye,* loathsome; *rumland,* rumbling; *routit,* roared
11 *yelland,* yelling   12 *fordeifit,* deafened

Thay grim monstures my spreits abhorrit and doutit.
Not throu the soil bot muskane treis sproutit,
Combust, barrant, unblomit and unleifit,   15
Auld rottin runtis qwhairin na sap was leifit,
Moch, all waist, widderit with granis moutit,
A ganand den, qwhair murtherars men reifit.

    Qwhairfoir myselvin was richt sair agast,
This wildernes abhominabill and waist,   20
(In qwhome nathing was nature comfortand)
Was dark as rock, the qwhilk the sey upcast.
The qwhissilling wind blew mony bitter blast,
Runtis rattillit and uneith michte I stand.
Out throu the wod I crap on fute and hand,   25
The river stank, the treis clatterit fast.
The soil was nocht bot marres, slike, and sand.

    And not but caus my spreitis wer abaisit,
All solitair in that desert arraisit,
"Allace," I said, "is nane uther remeid?   30
Cruell Fortoun, qwhy hes thou me betraisit?
Qwhy hes thou thus my fatall end compassit?
Allace, allace, sall I thus sone be deid
In this desert, and wait nane uther reid,
Bot be devoirit with sum beist ravenous?   35
I weip, I waill, I plene, I cry, I pleid,
Inconstant warld and qwheill contrarious.

13 *thay,* those; *doutit,* feared
14 *not throu,* naught through; *muskane,* rotten
15 *combust,* burnt; *barrant,* barren
16 *auld,* old; *runtis,* stumps; *leifit,* left
17 *moch,* moist; *widderit,* withered; *granis moutit,* mouldy branches
18 *ganand,* gaping; *reifit,* robbed   19 *sair,* sore
22 *sey,* sea   24 *uneith,* scarcely
25 *crap,* crept   27 *marres,* swamp; *slike,* slime
28 *not but caus,* because; *abaisit,* abashed   29 *arraisit,* snatched away
30 *is . . . remeid,* is there no other remedy   31 *betraisit,* betrayed
32 *compassit,* contrived   34 *wait . . . reid,* expect no other aid
36 *plene,* complain   37 *qwheill,* (Fortune's) wheel

"Thy transitorye plesance qwhat availlis?
Now thair, now heir, now hye and now devaillis,
Now to, now fra, now law, now magnifyis, 40
Now hait, now cauld, now lauchis, now bewaillis,
Now seik, now haill, now werye, now not aillis,
Now gude, now evill, now weitis, and now dryis,
Now thou promittis, and richt now thou denyis,
Now wo, now weill, now firme, now frivolous, 45
Now gam, now gram, now lowis, now defyis,
Inconstant warld and qwheill contrarious.

"Ha, qwha suld have affiance in thy blis?
Ha, qwha suld have firme esperance in this,
Qwhilk is, allace, sa freuch and variant? 50
Certes, nane; sum hes no wicht? surelye yis.
Than has myself bene giltye? ye, ywis.
Thairfoir, allace, sall danger thus me dant?
Qwhidder is become sa sone this duillye hant?
And ver translait in winter furious? 55
Thus I bewaill my faitis repugnant,
Inconstant warld and qwheill contrarious."

(Part I, lines 10–67)

39 *devaillis,* descends   40 *law,* low
41 *hait,* hot; *lauchis,* laughs   42 *seik,* sick; *not aillis,* naught ails
43 *weitis,* wets   44 *promittis,* promises
45 *weill,* weal
46 *gam,* sport; *gram,* grief; *lowis,* permits; *defyis,* rejects
48 *qwha,* who; *affiance,* trust   49 *esperance,* hope
50 *freuch,* frail   51 *sum hes no wicht,* has no creature some (hope)
52 *ywis,* indeed
54 *qwhidder,* to what end; *become,* i.e., come; *duillye hant,* dolefu
haunt   55 *ver,* spring; *translait,* transformed

Stephen Hawes

(1474–1523)

FROM *The Pastime of Pleasure*

[*Dame Music*]

And so to a chambre full solacious
Dame Musike wente with La Bell Pucell.
All of jasper with stones precious
The rofe was wrought curiously and well;
The windowes glased mervailously to tell;   5
With clothe of tissue in the richest maner
The walles were hanged hye and circuler.

There sate dame Musike with all her minstralsy,
As taboures, trumpettes, with pipes melodious,
Sakbuttes, organs, and the recorder swetely,   10
Harpes, lutes, and crowddes right delicious,
Symphans, doussemers, with claricymbales glorious,
Rebeckes, claricordes, eche in their degre,
Dide sitte aboute their ladyes mageste.

Before dame Musike I dide knele adowne,   15
Sayenge to her, "O faire lady pleasaunt,
Your prudence reineth most hye in renowne,
For you be ever right concordant
With perfite reason, whiche is not variaunt:

1 *solacious*, delightful   2 *La Bell Pucell*, the Fair Maiden
10 *sakbuttes*, bass trumpets   11 *crowddes*, fiddles
12 *symphans*, instruments in general; *doussemers*, dulcimers; *claricymbales*, clavicymbals
bales, clavicymbals   13 *claricordes*, clavichords
17 *reineth*, reigns   19 *perfite*, perfect

I beseche your grace with all my diligence   20
To instructe me in your noble science."

"It is," she saide, "right gretely prouffitable,
For musike doth sette in all unite
The discorde thinges which are variable,
And devoideth mischefe and grete iniquite;   25
Where lacketh musicke there is no pleinte,
For musike is concorde and also peace:
Nothinge without musike maye well encreace.

The seven sciences in one monacorde
Eche upon other do full well depende;   30
Musike hath them so set in concorde
That all in one maye right well extende;
All perfite reason they do so comprehende
That they are waye and perfite doctrine
To the joye above, whiche is celestine.   35

And yet also the perfite physike,
Which appertaineth well to the body,
Doth well resemble unto the musike;
Whan the inwarde intrailes tourneth contrary,
That nature cannot werke directly,   40
Than doth phesike the partes interiall
In ordre set to their originall."   (Lines 1520–61)

And musike selfe it is melodious
To rejoyce the eeres and confort the braine,
Sharpinge the wittes with sounde solacious,   45
Devoidinge bad thoughtes which dide remaine;
It gladdeth the herte also well certaine,
Lengthe the life with dulcet armony;
It is good recreacion after study."

24 *discorde,* discordant   25 *devoideth,* expels
26 *pleinte,* plenty   29 *monacorde,* harmony
35 *celestine,* celestial   41 *interiall,* internal
45 *solacious,* delightful   48 *lengthe,* lengthens

She commaunded her minstrelles right anone to play 50
Mamours, the swete and the gentill daunce;
With La Bell Pucell that was faire and gaye
She me recommaunded with all pleasaunce
To daunce true mesures without variaunce.
O Lorde God, how glad than was I, 55
So for to daunce with my swete lady.

By her propre hande soft as ony silke
With due obeisaunce I dide her than take.
Her skinne was white as whalles bone or milke;
My thought was ravisshed; I might not aslake 60
My brenninge hert: she the fire dide make.
These daunces truely Musike hath me tought:
To lute or daunce but it availed nought.

For the fire kindled and waxed more and more;
The dauncinge blewe it with her beaute clere; 65
My hert sekened and began waxe sore:
A minute six houres, and six houres a yere,
I thought it was, so hevy was my chere;
But yet for to cover my great love aright,
The outwarde countenance I made gladde and light. 70

(Lines 1576–1603)

51 *Mamours*, "My Love"   53 *recommaunded*, advised
57 *propre*, own   58 *obeisaunce*, deference
61 *brenninge*, burning   66 *sekened*, sickened

[*The Seven Deadly Sins*]

A KNIGHT SPEAKS

The good dame Mercy with dame Charite
My body buried full right humbly
In a faire temple of olde antiquite,
Where was for me a *Dirige* devoutely,

And with many a Masse full right solempnely;   5
And over my grave to be in memory
Remembraunce made this litill epitaphy:

"O erthe, on erthe it is a wonders cace
That thou arte blinde and will not thee knowe;
Though upon erthe thou hast thy dwellinge place,   10
Yet erthe at laste muste nedes thee overthrowe.
Thou thinkest thee to be none erthe, I trowe,
For if thou didest thou woldest than apply
To forsake pleasure and to lerne to dy.

PRIDE

O erthe, of erthe why arte thou so proude?   15
Now what thou arte call to remembraunce;
Open thine eres unto my songe aloude!
Is not thy beaute, strength, and puissaunce,
Though it be cladde with clothes of pleasaunce,
Very erthe and also wormes fode,   20
Whan, erthe, to erthe shall to-tourne the blode?

WRATH

And, erthe, with erthe why arte thou so wrothe?
Remembre thee that it vaileth right nought;
For thou mayst thinke of a perfite trothe,
If with the erthe thou hast a quarell sought: 25
Amiddes the erthe there is a place ywrought,
Whan erthe to erthe is torned proprely,
Thee for thy sinne to punisshe wonderly.

ENVY

And, erthe, for erthe why hast thou envy,
And thee, erthe, upon erthe to be more prosperous   30

---

8 *wonders cace*, wonderful condition   13 *apply*, i.e., employ yourself
21 *to erthe . . . blode*, when the blood shall turn to earth
23 *vaileth*, avails   24 *perfite trothe*, perfect truth

Than thou thyselfe fretinge thee inwardly?
It is a sinne right foule and vicious,
And unto God also full odious:
Thou thinkest, I trowe, there is no punisshemente
Ordeined for sinne by egall jugemente.   35

SLOTH

Towarde heven to folowe on the way
Thou arte full slowe and thinkest nothinge
That thy nature dooth full sore decay,
And dethe right fast is to thee cominge.
God graunte thee mercy, but no time enlonginge;   40
Whan thou hast time, take time and space:
Whan time is past, lost is the time of grace.

AVARICE

And whan erthe to erthe is nexte to reverte,
And nature lowe in the laste age,
Of erthely treasure erthe doth set his herte,   45
Insaciatly upon covetise to rage;
He thinketh not his life shall asuage;
His good is his god, with his grete riches:
He thinketh not for to leve it, doutles.

GLUTTONY

The pomped carkes with fode delicious   50
Erthe often fedeth with corrupte glotony,
And nothinge with werkes vertuous.
The soule doth fede right well ententifly;
But without mesure full inordinatly
The body liveth and will not remembre   55
How erthe to erthe must his strength surrendre.

---

31 *fretinge*, gnawing   35 *egall*, equal
41 *time enlonging*, prolongation of time   43 *nexte*, i.e., about
45 *of*, on   47 *asuage*, diminish
50 *pomped*, pampered; *carkes*, carcass   53 *ententifly*, heedfully

LECHERY

The vile carkes set upon a fire
Dooth often haunte the sinne of lechery,
Fulfillinge the foule carnall desire:
Thus erthe with erthe is corrupte mervailously,   60
And erthe on erthe will nothinge purifye,
Till erthe to erthe be nere subverted,
For erthe with erthe is so perverted."

THE KNIGHT

O mortall folke, you may beholde and se
How I lie here, sometime a mighty knight;   65
The ende of joye and all prosperite
Is dethe at last through his course and might:
After the day there cometh the derke night,
For though the day be never so longe,
At last the belles ringeth to evensonge.   70

And myselfe called La Graunde Amoure,
Sekinge adventure in the worldly glory,
For to attaine the riches and honoure,
Dide thinke full litell that I sholde here ly,
Till dethe dide marke me full right prively.   75
Lo, what I am and whereto you must:
Like as I am so shall you be all dust.

Than in your minde inwardely dispise
The brittle worlde so full of doublenes,
With the vile flesshe, and right soone arise   80
Out of your slepe of mortall hevines.
Subdue the devill with grace and mekenes,
That after your life, fraile and transitory,
You may than live in joye perdurably.

(Lines 5411–94)

57 *upon a*, on   62 *subverted*, overthrown
75 *marke . . . right*, hit me squarely   76 *must*, i.e., must go
84 *perdurably*, everlastingly

[*Time and Eternity*]

"Withouten Time is no erthely thinge,
Nature, fortune, or yet dame Sapience,
Hardines, clergy, or yet lerninge,
Past, future, or yet in presence:
Wherfore I am of more hye preeminence, 5
As cause of fame, honoure, and clergy;
They can nothinge without me magnify.

Do not I, Time, cause nature to augment?
Do not I, Time, cause nature to decay?
Do not I, Time, cause man to be present? 10
Do not I, Time, take his life away?
Do not I, Time, cause dethe take his say?
Do not I, Time, passe his youth and age?
Do not I, Time, every thinge asuage?

In time Troye the cite was edefied; 15
By time also was the distruccion.
Nothinge without time can be fortefied;
No erthely joye nor tribulacion
Without time is for to suffre passion;
The time of erthe was our distruccion, 20
And the time of erthe was our redempcion.

Adam of erthe, sone of virginite,
And Eve by God of Adam create,
These two the worlde dampned in certainte,
By disobedience so foule and viciate, 25
And all other that frome them generate,
Till peace and mercy made right to encline
Out of the lion to entre the virgine.

3 *clergy*, science 12 *take his say*, taste his food
14 *asuage*, decrease 15 *edefied*, built
19: i.e., may be experienced without time 24 *dampned*, damned
25 *viciate*, depraved

Like as the worlde was distroyed totally
By the virgins sone, so it semed well   30
A virgins sone to redeme it piteously,
Whose hye godheed in the chosen vessell
Forty wekes naturally dide dwell,
Nature takinge as the hye God of Kinde:
In the virgin He dide suche nature finde.   35

Thus withoute nature, nature wonderly
In a virgin pure openly hath wrought;
To the God of Nature nothinge truely
Impossible is, for He made of nought
Nature first, whiche naturinge hath tought   40
Naturately right naturate to make:
Why may not He than the pure nature take

By his Godhede of the virgin Mary?
His electe moder and arke of testament,
Of holy chirche the blessid luminary,   45
After the birthe of her sone excellent
Virgin she was yet alway permanent,
Disnullinge the sectes of false idolatry,
And castinge downe the fatall heresy.

Thus whan I, Time, in every nacion   50
Reigned in rest and also in peace,
And Octavian in his dominacion
Thorough the worlde and the peopled preace
Lettres had sent, his honoure to encreace,
Of all the nombre for to be certaine   55
For to obey him as their soveraine,

In whose time God toke His nativite,
For to redeme us with His precious blode

34: assuming human nature as the high God of Nature
40–41 *whiche naturinge . . . to make,* ? (nature) which has taught
  the creative power by means of creation to make things created
48 *disnullinge,* destroying   53 *preace,* throng

Frome the devilles bonde of grete iniquite;
His herte was perst, hanginge on the rood—   60
Was not this time unto man right good?
Shall not I, Time, evermore abide
Till that in Libra, at the dredefull tide

Of the day of dome, than in the balaunce,
Almighty God shall be just and egall   65
To every persone withouten doubtaunce?
Eche as they dide deserve in generall,
Some to have joye, some paine eternall.
Than I am past, I may no lenger be,
And after me is Dame Eternite."   70

And thus as Time made his conclusion,
Eternite in a faire white vesture
To the temple came with hole affeccion,
And on her hede a diademe right pure,
With thre crownes of precious treasure.   75
"Eternite," she saide, "I am, nowe doubtles
Of heven quene and of hell empres.

First God made heven His propre habitacle;
Though that His power be in every place,
In eterne heven is His tabernacle;   80
Time is there in no maner of cace;
Time renneth alwaye his ende to enbrace.
Now I myselfe shall have none endinge,
And my Maker had no beginninge.

In heven and hell I am continually,   85
Withouten ende to be inextinguissible,
As evermore to reigne full rially;
Of every thinge I am invincible:

63 *Libra*, the Scales (astrological); *tide*, time
64 *balaunce*, scales (of justice)
73 *hole*, whole
87 *rially*, royally

69 *lenger*, longer
82 *renneth*, runs

Man of my power shall be intelligible
Whan the soule shall rise against the body   90
To have jugemente to live eternally,

In heven or hell, as he dothe deserve.
Who that loveth God above every thinge
All his commaundementes he will then observe,
And spende his time in vertuous livinge;   95
Idlenes will evermore be eschewinge,
Eternall joye he shall then attaine,
After his laboure and his besy paine.

O mortall folke, revolve in your minde
That worldly joye and fraile prosperite,   100
What is it like but a blaste of winde,
For you therof can have no certainte:
It is now so full of mutabilite.
Set not your minde upon worldly welthe,
But evermore regarde your soules helthe.   105

Whan erthe in erth hath tane his corrupte taste,
Than to repente it is for you to late;
Whan you have time, spende it nothinge in waste;
Time past with vertue must enter the gate
Of joye and blisse, with min hye estate,   110
Withoute time for to be everlastinge,
Whiche God graunte us at our last endinge."

Now blissed lady of the helthe eternall,
The quene of comforte and of hevenly glorye,
Pray to thy swete sone whiche is infinall   115
To give me grace to winne the victory
Of the devill, the worlde, and of my body,
And that I may myselfe well apply,
Thy sone and thee to laude and magnify.

                        (Lines 5677–5795)

96 *will*, i.e., will he   106 *tane*, taken
113 *blissid*, blessed   115 *infinall*, infinite

Anonymous

Everyman
(1510)

DRAMATIS PERSONÆ

God	Knowledge
Everyman	Confession
Death	Beauty
Fellowship	Strength
Kindred	Discretion
Cousin	Five Wits
Goods	Messenger
Good Deeds	Angel

Doctor

Here Beginneth a Treatise how the hye Fader of Heven sendeth Dethe to somon every Creature to come and give Acounte of their lives in this Worlde, and is in Maner of a Morall Playe.

Enter Messenger.

MESSENGER. I pray you all give your audience,
And here this mater with reverence,
By figure a morall playe.
"The Somoninge of Everyman" called it is,
That of our lives and endinge shewes   5
How transitory we be all daye.
This mater is wonder precious;
But the entent of it is more gracious,

---

3 *by figure*, in form   4 *somoninge*, summoning
6 *all daye*, always

And swete to bere awaye.

The story saith:—Man, in the beginninge   10
Loke well, and take good heed to the endinge,
Be you never so gay!
Ye thinke sinne in the beginninge full swete,
Whiche in the ende causeth the soule to wepe
Whan the body lieth in claye.   15
Here shall you se how Felawship, and Jolite,
Bothe Strengthe, Pleasure, and Beaute,
Will fade from thee as flowre in Maye;
For ye shall here how our Heven Kinge
Calleth Everyman to a generall rekeninge.   20
Give audience, and here what he doth saye.   *Exit.*
Enter God.

GOD. I perceive, here in my majeste,
How that all creatures be to me unkinde,
Livinge without drede in worldely prosperite.
Of ghostly sight the people be so blinde,   25
Drowned in sinne, they know me not for their God.
In worldely riches is all their minde;
They fere not my rightwisnes, the sharpe rod;
My lawe that I shewed whan I for them died
They forgete clene, and shedinge of my blode rede;   30
I hanged bytwene two, it can not be denied;
To gete them life I suffred to be deed;
I heled their fete, with thornes hurt was my heed.
I coude do no more than I dide, truely;
And nowe I se the people do clene forsake me.   35
They use the seven deedly sinnes dampnable,
As pride, coveitise, wrathe, and lechery
Now in the worlde be made commendable;
And thus they leve of aungelles the hevenly company.

---

25 *ghostly*, spiritual
28: they fear not the severe rod of my righteousness   32 *deed*, dead
36 *dampnable*, damnable   37 *coveitise*, avarice

Every man liveth so after his owne pleasure,   40
And yet of their life they be nothinge sure.
I se the more that I them forbere
The worse they be fro yere to yere;
All that liveth appaireth faste.
Therfore I will, in all the haste,   45
Have a rekeninge of every mannes persone;
For, and I leve the people thus alone
In their life and wicked tempestes,
Verily they will become moche worse than beestes;
For now one wolde by envy another up ete;   50
Charite they do all clene forgete.
I hoped well that every man
In my glory shulde make his mansion;
And therto I had them all electe.
But now I se, like traitours dejecte,   55
They thanke me not for the pleasure that I to them ment,
Nor yet for their beinge that I them have lent.
I profered the people grete multitude of mercy,
And fewe there be that asketh it hertly.
They be so combred with worldly riches   60
That nedes on them I must do justice,
On every man livinge without fere.
Where arte thou Deth, thou mighty messengere?
Enter Death.
DEATH. Almighty God, I am here at your will,
Your commaundement to fulfill.   65
GOD. Go thou to Everyman,
And shewe him, in my name,
A pilgrimage he must on him take,
Which he in no wise may escape;
And that he bringe with him a sure rekeninge,   70

44 *appaireth,* deteriorates   47 *and,* if
55 *dejecte,* abased   59 *hertly,* heartily
60 *combred,* encumbered

Without delay or ony taryenge.

DEATH. Lorde, I will in the worlde go renne over all,
And cruelly out-serche bothe grete and small. *Exit God.*
Every man will I beset that liveth beestly
Out of Goddes lawes, and dredeth not foly.					75
He that loveth richesse I will strike with my darte,
His sight to blinde, and fro heven to departe—
Excepte that almes dedes be his good frende—
In hell for to dwell, worlde without ende.

Loo, yonder I se Everyman walkinge.					80
Full litell he thinketh on my cominge;
His minde is on flesshely lustes, and his treasure;
And grete paine it shall cause him to endure
Before the Lorde, hevene Kinge.

Enter Everyman.

Everyman, stande still! Whider arte thou goinge					85
Thus gaily? Hast thou thy maker forgete?

EVERYMAN. Why askest thou?
Woldest thou wete?

DEATH. Ye, sir; I will shewe you:
In grete hast I am sende to thee					90
Fro God out of his majeste.

EVERYMAN. What! sente to me?

DEATH. Ye, certainly.
Thoughe thou have forgete him here,
He thinketh on thee in the hevenly spere,					95
As, or we departe, thou shalte knowe!

EVERYMAN. What desireth God of me?

DEATH. That shall I shewe thee:
A rekeninge he will nedes have
Without ony lenger respite.					100

---

72 *renne*, run						77 *departe*, separate
85 *whider*, whither						88 *wete*, know
90 *hast*, haste						95 *spere*, sphere
96 *or*, ere; *departe*, separate						100 *lenger*, longer

EVERYMAN. To give a rekeninge longer laiser I crave.
This blinde mater troubleth my witte.

DEATH. On thee thou must take a longe journey;
Therfore thy boke of counte with thee thou bringe,
For turne againe thou can not by no waye.　　　105
And loke thou be sure of thy rekeninge,
For before God thou shalte answere and shewe
Thy many badde dedes, and good but a fewe,
How thou hast spente thy life, and in what wise,
Before the Chefe Lorde of paradise.　　　110
Have ado that we were in that waye,
For wete thou well thou shalte make none attournay.

EVERYMAN. Full unredy I am suche rekeninge to give.
I knowe thee not. What messenger arte thou?

DEATH. I am Dethe, that no man dredeth;　　　115
For every man I rest, and no man spareth;
For it is Goddes commaundement
That all to me sholde be obedient.

EVERYMAN. O Deth! thou comest whan I had thee leest
in minde!
In thy power it lieth me to save;　　　120
Yet of my good wil I give thee, if thou wil be kinde;
Ye, a thousande pounde shalte thou have,
And differre this mater till an other daye.

DEATH. Everyman, it may not be, by no waye!
I set not by golde, silver, nor richesse,　　　125
Ne by pope, emperour, kinge, duke, ne princes;
For, and I wolde receive giftes grete,
All the worlde I might gete;
But my custome is clene contrary.

---

101 *laiser*, leisure　　　　　　102 *blinde*, unanticipated
104 *counte*, accounts
111: i.e., let's get started on this business at once
112 *wete*, know; *none*, no one; *attournay*, your attorney
115: i.e., who dreads no man　　　116 *rest*, arrest
123 *and differre*, if you defer　　　125 *set not by*, care naught for
127 *and*, if

I give thee no respite. Come hens, and not tary!   130
EVERYMAN. Alas! shall I have no lenger respite?
I may saye Deth geveth no warninge!
To thinke on thee it maketh my herte seke,
For all unredy is my boke of rekeninge.
But twelve yere and I might have a bidinge,   135
My countinge-boke I wolde make so clere
That my rekeninge I sholde not nede to fere.
Wherfore, Deth, I praye thee, for Goddes mercy,
Spare me till I be provided of remedy!
DEATH. Thee availeth not to crye, wepe, and praye;   140
But hast thee lightly that thou were gone that journaye!
And preve thy frendes, if thou can;
For wete thou well the tide abideth no man;
And in the worlde eche livinge creature
For Adams sinne must die of nature.   145
EVERYMAN. Dethe, if I sholde this pilgrimage take,
And my rekeninge suerly make,
Shewe me, for Saint Charite,
Sholde I not come againe shortly?
DEATH. No, Everyman; and thou be ones there,   150
Thou mayst never more come here,
Trust me verily.
EVERYMAN. O gracious God in the hye sete celestiall,
Have mercy on me in this moost nede!
Shall I have no company fro this vale terestriall   155
Of mine acqueintaunce that way me to lede?
DEATH. Ye, if ony be so hardy
That wolde go with thee and bere thee company.
Hye thee that thou were gone to Goddes magnificence,
Thy rekeninge to give before his presence.   160

130 *hens*, hence   132 *geveth*, gives
133 *seke*, sick   135 *and*, if
141 *hast*, haste   142 *preve*, prove
143 *wete*, know   145 *of nature*, naturally
150 *and*, if   159 *hye*, haste

What! wenest thou thy live is given thee,
And thy worldely gooddes also?

EVERYMAN. I had wende so, verile.

DEATH. Nay, nay; it was but lende thee;
For, as soone as thou arte go,   165
Another a while shall have it, and than go therfro,
Even as thou hast done.
Everyman, thou arte made! Thou hast thy wittes five,
And here on erthe will not amende thy live;
For sodeinly I do come.   170

EVERYMAN. O wretched caitife! wheder shall I flee
That I might scape this endles sorowe?
Now, gentill Deth, spare me till to-morowe,
That I may amende me
With good advisement.   175

DEATH. Naye; therto I will not consent,
Nor no man will I respite;
But to the herte sodeinly I shall smite
Without ony advisement.
And now out of thy sight I will me hy.   180
Se thou make thee redy shortely,
For thou mayst saye this is the daye
That no man livinge may scape awaye.   *Exit Death.*

EVERYMAN. Alas! I may well wepe with sighes depe!
Now have I no maner of company   185
To helpe me in my journey and me to kepe;
And also my writinge is full unredy.
How shall I do now for to excuse me?
I wolde to God I had never be gete!
To my soule a full grete profite it had be;   190
For now I fere paines huge and grete.
The time passeth. Lorde, helpe, that all wrought!

161 *wenest*, suppose   163 *wende*, supposed
168 *made*, mad   171 *wheder*, whither
172 *scape*, escape   175 *advisement*, i.e., preparations
186 *kepe*, guard   189 *gete*, begotten

For though I mourne it availeth nought;
The day passeth, and is almoost ago.
I wote not well what for to do.   195
To whome were I best my complaint to make?
What and I to Felawship therof spake,
And shewed him of this sodeine chaunce?
For in him is all mine affiaunce,
We have in the worlde so many a daye   200
Be good frendes in sporte and playe.
I se him yonder certainely.
I trust that he will bere me company,
Therfore to him will I speke to ese my sorowe.
Well mette, good Felawship! and good morowe!   205
Enter Fellowship.
FELLOWSHIP. Everyman, good morowe, by this daye!
Sir, why lokest thou so piteously?
If ony thinge be amisse, I praye thee me saye,
That I may helpe to remedy.
EVERYMAN. Ye, good Felawship, ye;   210
I am in greate jeoparde.
FELLOWSHIP. My true frende, shewe to me your minde;
I will not forsake thee to my lives ende
In the waye of good company.
EVERYMAN. That was well spoken, and lovingly!   215
FELLOWSHIP. Sir, I must nedes knowe your hevinesse;
I have pite to se you in ony distresse.
If ony have you wronged, ye shall revenged be,
Thoughe I on the grounde be slaine for thee,
Though that I knowe before that I sholde die!   220
EVERYMAN. Verily, Felawship, gramercy.
FELLOWSHIP. Tusshe! by thy thankes I set not a strawe!
Shewe me your grefe, and saye no more.
EVERYMAN. If I my herte sholde to you breke,

194 *ago,* gone   195 *wote,* know
197 *and,* if   199 *affiaunce,* trust
224 *breke,* disclose

And than you to tourne your minde fro me   225
And wolde not me comforte whan ye here me speke,
Than sholde I ten times sorier be.

FELLOWSHIP. Sir, I saye as I will do, indede.

EVERYMAN. Than be you a good frende at nede!
I have founde you true here before.   230

FELLOWSHIP. And so ye shall evermore;
For, in faith, and thou go to hell
I will not forsake thee by the waye.

EVERYMAN. Ye speke like a good frende! I bileve you
well.
I shall deserve it, and I may.   235

FELLOWSHIP. I speke of no deservinge, by this daye!
For he that will saye, and nothinge do,
Is not worthy with good company to go.
Therfore shewe me the grefe of your minde,
As to your frende mooste lovinge and kinde.   240

EVERYMAN. I shall shewe you how it is:
Commaunded I am to go a journaye—
A longe waye, harde, and daungerous—
And give a straite counte, without delaye,
Before the hye Juge, Adonay.   245
Wherfore, I pray you, bere me company,
As ye have promised, in this journaye.

FELLOWSHIP. That is mater indede! Promise is duty;
But, and I sholde take suche a viage on me,
I knowe it well, it shulde be to my paine.   250
Also it maketh me aferde, certaine.
But let us take counsell here, as well as we can;
For your wordes wolde fere a stronge man.

EVERYMAN. Why, ye said if I had nede
Ye wolde me never forsake, quicke ne deed,   255

232 *and,* if   235 *deserve,* repay
244 *straite counte,* strict accounting   245 *Adonay,* i.e., God
249 *and,* if; *viage,* voyage   253 *fere,* frighten
255 *deed,* dead

Thoughe it were to hell, truely.

FELLOWSHIP. So I said, certainely!

But suche pleasures be set aside, the sothe to saye.

And also, if we toke suche a journaye,

Whan sholde we againe come? 260

EVERYMAN. Naye, never againe, till the daye of dome!

FELLOWSHIP. In faith! than will not I come there!

Who hath you these tidinges brought?

EVERYMAN. Indede, Deth was with me here.

FELLOWSHIP. Now, by God, that all hathe bought, 265

If Dethe were the messenger,

For no man that is livinge to-daye

I will not go that lothe journaye—

Not for the fader that bigate me!

EVERYMAN. Ye promised otherwise, parde. 270

FELLOWSHIP. I wote well I said so, truely.

And yet, if thou wilte ete, and drinke, and make good
    chere,

Or haunt to women the lusty company,

I wolde not forsake you while the daye is clere,

Truste me, verily. 275

EVERYMAN. Ye, therto ye wolde be redy!

To go to mirthe, solas, and playe;

Your minde to Folye will soner apply,

Than to bere me company in my longe journaye.

FELLOWSHIP. Now, in good faith, I will not that
    waye. 280

But and thou will murder, or ony man kill,

In that I will helpe thee with a good will.

EVERYMAN. O, that is a simple advise, indede.

Gentill felaw, helpe me in my necessite!

We have loved longe, and now I nede; 285

---

268 *lothe,* loathsome   269 *bigate,* begot
273: or frequent the lusty company of women   277 *solas,* delight
281 *and,* if   283 *simple,* foolish

And now, gentill Felawship, remember me!

FELLOWSHIP. Wheder ye have loved me or no,

By Saint John, I will not with thee go!

EVERYMAN. Yet, I pray thee, take the labour, and do so
　　moche for me

To bringe me forwarde, for Saint Charite,　　　　　290

And comforte me till I come without the towne.

FELLOWSHIP. Nay, and thou wolde give me a newe
　　gowne,

I will not a fote with thee go!

But, and thou had taried, I wolde not have lefte thee so.

And as now God spede thee in thy journaye!　　　295

For from thee I will departe as fast as I maye.

EVERYMAN. Wheder awaye, Felawship? Will thou for-
　　sake me?

FELLOWSHIP. Ye, by my faye! To God I betake thee.

EVERYMAN. Farewell, good Felawship! for thee my herte
　　is sore.

Adeue for ever! I shall se thee no more!　　　　　300

FELLOWSHIP. In faith, Everyman, fare well now at the
　　ende!

For you I will remember that partinge is mourninge.

　　　　　　　　　　　　　　　Exit Fellowship.

EVERYMAN. Alacke! shall we this departe indede

(A, Lady helpe!) without ony more comforte?

Lo, Felawship forsaketh me in my moost nede.　　　305

For helpe in this worlde wheder shall I resorte?

Felawship here before with me wolde mery make,

And now litell sorowe for me dooth he take.

It is said, "In prosperite men frendes may finde.

Whiche in adversite be full unkinde."　　　　　　　310

Now wheder for socoure shall I flee,

287 *wheder,* whether
290 *bringe me forwarde,* i.e., escort me for a little way　　292 *and,* if
294 *and,* if　　　　　　　　　　　　　　297 *wheder,* whither
298 *faye,* faith; *betake,* commend　　303 *this,* thus; *departe,* separate

Sith that Felawship hath forsaken me?
To my kinnesmen I will, truely,
Prayenge them to helpe me in my necessite.
I bileve that they will do so,   315
For kinde will crepe where it may not go.
I will go saye, for yonder I se them,
Where be ye now my frendes and kinnesmen.
Enter Kindred and Cousin.
KINDRED. Here be we now at your commaundement.
Cosin, I praye you shewe us your entent   320
In ony wise, and not spare.
COUSIN. Ye, Everyman, and to us declare
If ye be disposed to go ony whider;
For, wete you well, we will live and die togider.
KINDRED. In welth and wo we will with you holde, 325
For over his kinne a man may be bolde.
EVERYMAN. Gramercy, my frendes and kinnesmen
    kinde.
Now shall I shewe you the grefe of my minde.
I was commaunded by a messenger
That is a hye kinges chefe officer;   330
He bad me go a pilgrimage, to my paine;
And I knowe well I shall never come againe:
Also I must give a rekeninge straite,
For I have a grete enemy that hath me in waite,
Whiche entendeth me for to hinder.   335
KINDRED. What acounte is that whiche ye must render?
That wolde I knowe.
EVERYMAN. Of all my workes I must shewe
How I have lived, and my dayes spent;
Also of ill dedes that I have used   340
In my time sith life was me lent,

312 *sith*, since   316: for "kin will creep where it cannot walk"
317 *saye*, make trial   318 *where*, whether
323 *ony whider*, anywhere   324 *wete*, know
334 *in waite*, under observation   341 *sith*, since

And of all vertues that I have refused.
Therfore, I praye you, go thider with me
To helpe to make min accounte, for Saint Charite.
COUSIN. What! to go thider? Is that the mater?   345
Nay, Everyman, I had lever fast brede and water
All this five yere and more.
EVERYMAN. Alas, that ever I was bore!
For now shall I never be mery,
If that you forsake me.   350
KINDRED. A, sir, what! ye be a mery man!
Take good herte to you, and make no mone.
But one thinge, I warne you, by Saint Anne—
As for me, ye shall go alone!
EVERYMAN. My Cosin, will you not with me go?   355
COUSIN. No, by Our Lady! I have the crampe in
    my to.
Trust not to me; for, so God me spede,
I will deceive you in your moost nede.
KINDRED. It availeth you not us to tise.
Ye shall have my maide with all my herte;   360
She loveth to go to feestes, there to be nise,
And to daunce, and abrode to sterte:
I will give her leve to helpe you in that journey,
If that you and she may agree.
EVERYMAN. Now, shewe me the very effecte of your
    minde;   365
Will you go with me, or abide behinde?
KINDRED. Abide behinde? ye, that will I, and I maye!
Therfore farewell till another daye.   *Exit Kindred.*
EVERYMAN. Howe sholde I be mery or gladde?
For faire promises men to me make,   370
But whan I have moost nede they me forsake.

---

345 *fast*, i.e., fast on   348 *bore*, born
352 *mone*, moan   359 *tise*, entice
361 *nise*, wanton   362 *sterte*, move
367 *and*, if

I am deceived; that maketh me sadde.

COUSIN. Cosin Everyman, farewell now;
For verily I will not go with you.
Also of mine owne an unredy rekeninge   375
I have to accounte; therfore I make taryenge.
Now God kepe thee, for now I go.   *Exit Cousin.*

EVERYMAN. A Jesus! is all come hereto?
Lo, faire wordes maketh fooles faine;
They promise, and nothinge will do certaine.   380
My kinnesmen promised me faithfully
For to abide with me stedfastly;
And now fast awaye do they flee.
Even so Felawship promised me.
What frende were best me of to provide?   385
I lose my time here longer to abide;
Yet in my minde a thinge there is:
All my life I have loved riches;
If that my good now helpe me might
He wolde make my herte full light.   390
I will speke to him in this distresse.
Where arte thou, my Gooddes and riches?

GOODS [*within*]. Who calleth me? Everyman? What!
    hast thou haste?
I lie here in corners, trussed and piled so hye,
And in chestes I am locked so fast,   395
Also sacked in bagges. Thou mayst se with thin eye
I can not stire in packes lowe where I lie.
What wolde ye have? lightly me saye.

EVERYMAN. Come hider, Good, in al the hast thou may;
For of counseill I must desire thee.   400
Enter Goods.

GOODS. Sir, and ye in the worlde have sorowe or
    adversite,

387 *a,* one   389 *good,* goods
393 *what,* why   398 *lightly,* quickly
401 *and,* if

That can I helpe you to remedy shortly.

EVERYMAN. It is another disease that greveth me;
In this worlde it is not, I tell thee so;
I am sent for an other way to go,   405
To give a straite counte generall
Before the hyest Jupiter of all;
And all my life I have had joye and pleasure in thee,
Therfore, I pray thee, go with me;
For, paraventure, thou mayst before God Almighty   410
My rekeninge helpe to clene and purifye;
For it is said ever amonge
That money maketh all right that is wronge.

GOODS. Nay, Everyman; I singe an other songe!
I folowe no man in suche viages;   415
For, and I wente with thee,
Thou sholdes fare moche the worse for me;
For because on me thou did set thy minde,
Thy rekeninge I have made blotted and blinde,
That thine accounte thou can not make truly—   420
And that hast thou for the love of me!

EVERYMAN. That wolde greve me full sore,
Whan I sholde come to that ferefull answere.
Up, let us go thider togider.

GOODS. Nay, not so! I am to britell; I may not en-
    dure.   425
I will folowe no man one fote, be ye sure.

EVERYMAN. Alas! I have thee loved, and had grete
    pleasure
All my life-dayes on good and treasure.

GOODS. That is to thy dampnacion, without lesinge!
For my love is contrary to the love everlastinge.   430
But if thou had me loved moderately duringe

As to the poore to give parte of me,
Than sholdest thou not in this dolour be,
Nor in this grete sorowe and care.
EVERYMAN. Lo! now was I deceived or I was ware;   435
And all I may wite mispendinge of time.
GOODS. What! wenest thou that I am thine?
EVERYMAN. I had went so.
GOODS. Naye, Everyman; I saye no.
As for a while I was lente thee;   440
A season thou hast had me in prosperite.
My condicion is mannes soule to kill;
If I save one, a thousande I do spill.
Wenest thou that I will folowe thee?
Nay, fro this worlde, not verile.   445
EVERYMAN. I had wende otherwise.
GOODS. Therfore to thy soule Good is a thefe;
For whan thou arte deed, this is my gise—
Another to deceive in this same wise
As I have done thee, and all to his soules reprefe. 450
EVERYMAN. O false Good! cursed thou be,
Thou traitour to God, that hast deceived me
And caught me in thy snare!
GOODS. Mary! thou brought thyselfe in care!
Wherof I am gladde.   455
I must nedes laugh; I can not be sadde.
EVERYMAN. A, Good! thou hast had longe my hertely
    love;
I gave thee that which sholde be the Lordes above.
But wilte thou not go with me indede?
I praye thee trouth to saye.   460
GOODS. No, so God me spede!
Therfore farewell, and have good daye!   *Exit Goods.*

435 *or,* ere   436 *wite,* blame on
438 *went,* supposed   443 *spill,* ruin
446 *wende,* supposed   448 *gise,* fashion
450 *reprefe,* shame

EVERYMAN. O, to whome shall I make my mone
For to go with me in that hevy journaye?
First Felawship said he wolde with me gone—   465
His wordes were very plesaunte and gaye;
But afterwarde he lefte me alone.
Than spake I to my kinnesmen, all in despaire,
And also they gave me wordes faire—
They lacked no faire spekinge!   470
But all forsake me in the endinge.
Than wente I to my Goodes, that I loved best,
In hope to have comforte; but there had I leest,
For my Goodes sharpely did me tell
That he bringeth many into hell.   475
Than of myselfe I was ashamed;
And so I am worthy to be blamed.
Thus may I well myselfe hate.
Of whom shall I now counseill take?
I thinke that I shall never spede   480
Till that I go to my Good Dede.
But, alas! she is so weke
That she can nother go nor speke.
Yet will I venter on her now.
My Good Dedes, where be you?   485
Good Deeds speaks from the ground.
GOOD DEEDS. Here I lie, colde in the grounde.
Thy sinnes hath me sore bounde,
That I can not stere.
EVERYMAN. O Good Dedes! I stande in fere!
I must you pray of counseill,   490
For helpe now sholde come right well.
GOOD DEEDS. Everyman, I have understandinge
That ye be somoned acounte to make
Before Missias, of Jherusalem Kinge;

473 *leest,* least   483 *go,* walk
484 *venter,* gamble   488 *stere,* stir
493 *somoned,* summoned   494 *Missias,* Messiah

And you do by me, that journay with you will I take. 495

EVERYMAN. Therfore I come to you my moone to make.

I praye you that ye will go with me.

GOOD DEEDS. I wolde full faine, but I can not stande, verily.

EVERYMAN. Why, is there ony thinge on you fall?

GOOD DEEDS. Ye, sir, I may thanke you of all! 500

If ye had parfitely chered me,

Your boke of counte full redy had be.

Good Deeds shows him his book of account.

Loke the bokes of your workes and dedes eke,

Ase how they lie under the fete

To your soules hevines. 505

EVERYMAN. Our Lorde Jesus helpe me!

For one letter here I can not se.

GOOD DEEDS. There is a blinde rekeninge in time of distres!

EVERYMAN. Good Dedes, I praye you helpe me in this nede,

Or elles I am for ever dampned indede! 510

Therfore helpe me to make rekeninge

Before the Redemer of all thinge,

That Kinge is, and was, and ever shall.

GOOD DEEDS. Everyman, I am sory of your fall;

And faine wolde I helpe you, and I were able. 515

EVERYMAN. Good Dedes, your counseill I pray you give me.

GOOD DEEDS. That shall I do verily.

Thoughe that on my fete I may not go,

I have a sister that shall with you also,

Called Knowlege, whiche shall with you abide 520

To helpe you to make that dredefull rekeninge.

---

495 *and,* if; *by me,* i.e., by my advice   496 *moone,* moan
501 *parfitely,* perfectly   504 *ase,* as
508 *blinde,* illegible   515 *and,* if

Enter Knowledge.

KNOWLEDGE. Everyman, I will go with thee, and be thy
　　gide,

In thy moost nede to go by thy side.

EVERYMAN. In good condicion I am now in every
　　thinge,

And am hole content with this good thinge,　　　　525

Thanked be God my creature!

GOOD DEEDS. And whan she hath brought you there

Where thou shalte hele thee of thy smarte,

Than go you with your rekeninge and your Good Dedes
　　togider

For to make you joyfull at herte　　　　　　　　530

Before the Blessid Trinite.

EVERYMAN. My Good Dedes, gramercy!

I am well content, certainly,

With your wordes swete.

KNOWLEDGE. Now go we togider lovingly　　　　535

To Confession, that clensing rivere.

EVERYMAN. For joy I wepe! I wolde we were there!

But, I pray you, give me cognicion

Where dwelleth that holy man, Confession?

KNOWLEDGE. In the house of salvacion;　　　　540

We shall finde him in that place,

That shall us comforte, by Goddes grace.

Knowledge leads Everyman to Confession.

Lo, this is Confession. Knele downe, and aske mercy;

For he is in good conceite with God Almighty.

EVERYMAN [*kneeling*]. O glorious fountaine, that all
　　unclennes doth clarify,　　　　　　　　　　　545

Wasshe fro me the spottes of vice unclene,

That on me no sinne may be sene.

I come, with Knowlege, for my redempcion,

---

525 *hole*, wholly　　　　　　　　　526 *creature*, creator
538 *cognicion*, knowledge　　　　　　544 *conceite*, esteem

Redempte with herte and full contricion;
For I am commaunded a pilgrimage to take,   550
And grete accountes before God to make.
Now I praye you, Shrifte, moder of salvacion,
Helpe my Good Dedes for my piteous exclamacion.

CONFESSION. I knowe your sorowe well, Everyman.
Bicause with Knowlege ye come to me,   555
I will you comforte as well as I can;
And a precious jewell I will give thee,
Called penaunce, voider of adversite;
Therwith shall your body chastised be
With abstinence, and perseveraunce in Goddes serv-
    ice.   560
Here shall you receive that scourge of me,
Whiche is penaunce stronge that ye must endure
To remembre thy Saviour was scourged for thee
With sharpe scourges, and suffred it paciently;
So must thou, or thou scape that painful pilgrimage. 565
Knowlege, kepe him in this viage,
And by that time Good Dedes will be with thee.
But in ony wise be seker of mercy,
For your time draweth fast; and ye will saved be,
Aske God mercy, and he will graunte truely.   570
Whan with the scourge of penaunce man doth him
    binde,
The oile of forgivenes than shall he finde.

EVERYMAN. Thanked be God for his gracious werke!
For now I will my penaunce begin;
This hath rejoised and lighted my herte,   575
Though the knottes be painfull and harde within.

KNOWLEDGE. Everyman, loke your penaunce that ye ful-
    fill,

549 *redempte*, redeemed   552 *moder*, mother
558 *voider*, expeller   565 *or*, ere
566 *kepe*, guard   568 *seker*, confident
569 *and*, if

What paine that ever it to you be;
And Knowlege shall give you counseill at will
How your accounte ye shall make clerely.   580
EVERYMAN. O eternal God! O hevenly figure!
O way of rightwisnes! O goodly vision!
Whiche descended downe in a virgin pure
Because he wolde every man redeme,
Whiche Adam forfaited by his disobedience!   585
O blessid Godheed! electe and hye devine!
Forgive my grevous offence.
Here I crye thee mercy in this presence.
O ghostly treasure! O raunsomer and redemer!
Of all the worlde hope and conduiter!   590
Mirrour of joye! foundatour of mercy,
Whiche enlumineth heven and erth therby!
Here my clamorous complaint, though it late be.
Receive my prayers, of thy benignitye.
Though I be a sinner moost abhominable,   595
Yet let my name be writen in Moises table.
O Mary! praye to the Maker of all thinge
Me for to helpe at my endinge,
And save me fro the power of my enemy;
For Deth assaileth me strongly.   600
And, Lady, that I may by meane of thy prayer
Of your Sones glory to be partinere
By the meanes of his passion, I it crave.
I beseche you helpe my soule to save.
Knowlege, give me the scourge of penaunce.   605
My flesshe therwith shall give aqueintaunce.
I will now begin, if God give me grace.
KNOWLEDGE. Everyman, God give you time and space!
Thus I bequeth you in the handes of our Saviour.
Now may you make your rekeninge sure.   610
EVERYMAN. In the name of the Holy Trinite

590 *conduiter*, guide   591 *foundatour*, founder

My body sore punisshid shall be.
Take this, body, for the sinne of the flesshe!
Also thou delitest to go gay and fresshe,
And in the way of dampnacion thou did me
    bringe, 615
Therfore suffre now strokes of punisshinge!
Now of penaunce I will wade the water clere,
To save me from purgatory, that sharpe fire.
GOOD DEEDS. I thanke God, now I can walke and go,
And am delivered of my sikenesse and wo. 620
Therfore with Everyman I will go, and not spare;
His good workes I will helpe him to declare.
KNOWLEDGE. Now, Everyman, be mery and glad!
Your Good Dedes cometh now, ye may not be sad.
Now is your Good Dedes hole and sounde, 625
Goinge upright upon the grounde.
EVERYMAN. My herte is light, and shalbe evermore.
Now will I smite faster than I dide before.
GOOD DEEDS. Everyman, pilgrime, my speciall frende,
Blessid be thou without ende! 630
For thee is preparate the eternall glory!
Ye have me made hole and sounde,
Therfore I will bide by thee in every stounde.
EVERYMAN. Welcome, my Good Dedes! Now I here thy
    voice
I wepe for very swetenes of love. 635
KNOWLEDGE. Be no more sad, but ever rejoice;
God seeth thy livinge in his trone above.
Put on this garment to thy behove,
Whiche is wette with your teres,
Or elles before God you may it misse, 640
Whan ye to your journeys ende come shall.

614 *also,* as
626 *goinge,* walking
633 *stounde,* trial
638 *behove,* advantage

625 *hole,* hale
631 *preparate,* prepared
637 *trone,* throne

EVERYMAN. Gentill Knowlege, what do ye it call?

KNOWLEDGE. It is a garmente of sorowe;

Fro paine it will you borowe;

Contricion it is   645

That getteth forgivenes,

He pleaseth God passinge well.

GOOD DEEDS. Everyman, will you were it for your hele?

EVERYMAN. Now blessid be Jesu, Maryes sone,

For now have I on true contricion.   650

And lette us go now without taryenge.

Good Dedes, have we clere our rekeninge?

GOOD DEEDS. Ye, indede, I have it here.

EVERYMAN. Than I trust we nede not fere.

Now, frendes, let us not parte in twaine.   655

KNOWLEDGE. Nay, Everyman, that will we not, certaine.

GOOD DEEDS. Yet must thou led with thee

Thre persones of grete might.

EVERYMAN. Who sholde they be?

GOOD DEEDS. Discrecion and Strength they hight,   660

And thy Beaute may not abide behinde.

KNOWLEDGE. Also ye must call to minde

Your Five Wittes as for your counseilours.

GOOD DEEDS. You must have them redy at all houres.

EVERYMAN. Howe shall I gette them hider?   665

KNOWLEDGE. You must call them all togider,

And they will here you incontinent.

EVERYMAN. My frendes, come hider and be present,

Discrecion, Strengthe, my Five Wittes, and Beaute!

Enter Discretion, Strength, Five Wits, and Beauty.

BEAUTY. Here at your will we be all redy.   670

What will ye that we sholde do?

GOOD DEEDS. That ye wolde with Everyman go

---

644 *borowe,* redeem   648 *hele,* health
660 *hight,* are named   665 *hider,* hither
667 *incontinent,* immediately

And helpe him in his pilgrimage.

Advise you; will ye with him or not in that viage?

STRENGTH. We will bringe him all thider, 675

To his helpe and comforte, ye may beleve me.

DISCRETION. So will we go with him all togider.

EVERYMAN. Almighty God, loved might thou be!

I give thee laude that I have hider brought

Strength, Discrecion, Beaute and Five Wittes. Lacke I
nought. 680

And my Good Dedes, with Knowlege clere,

All be in my company at my will here.

I desire no more to my besines.

STRENGTH. And I, Strength, will by you stande in distres,

Though thou wolde in bataile fight on the grounde. 685

FIVE WITS. And though it were thrugh the worlde
rounde,

We will not departe for swete ne soure.

BEAUTY. No more will I, unto dethes houre,

Whatsoever therof befall.

DISCRETION. Everyman, advise you first of all; 690

Go with a good advisement and deliberacion.

We all give you vertuous monicion

That all shall be well.

EVERYMAN. My frendes, harken what I will tell—

I praye God rewarde you in his heven spere— 695

Now herken all that be here,

For I will make my testament

Here before you all present:

In almes halfe my good I will give with my handes
twaine

In the way of charite with good entent, 700

---

674 *advise you,* take thought   678 *loved,* praised
691 *advisement,* preparation   692 *monicion,* forewarning
695 *spere,* sphere

And the other halfe still shall remaine,
I queth to be retourned there it ought to be.
This I do in despite of the fende of hell,
To go quite out of his perell
Ever after and this daye.   705

KNOWLEDGE. Everyman, herken what I saye:
Go to Presthode, I you advise,
And receive of him, in ony wise,
The holy sacrament and ointement togider;
Than shortly se ye tourne againe hider;   710
We will all abide you here.

FIVE WITS. Ye, Everyman, hye you that ye redy were.
There is no emperour, kinge, duke, ne baron,
That of God hath commicion
As hath the leest preest in the worlde beinge;   715
For of the blessid sacramentes pure and benigne
He bereth the keyes, and therof hath the cure
For mannes redempcion—it is ever sure—
Whiche God for our soules medicine
Gave us out of his herte with grete paine,   720
Here in this transitory life for thee and me.
The blessid sacramentes seven there be—
Baptim, confirmacion, with preesthode good,
And the sacrament of Goddes precious flesshe and blod,
Mariage, the holy extreme unccion, and penaunce.   725
These seven be good to have in remembraunce,
Gracious sacramentes of hye devinite.

EVERYMAN. Faine wolde I receive that holy body,
And mekely to my ghostly fader I will go.

FIVE WITS. Everyman, that is the best that ye can
      do.   730
God will you to salvacion bringe,

701 *queth,* bequeath   704 *quite,* quit
712 *hye,* haste   715 *leest,* least
717 *cure,* care   729 *ghostly fader,* spiritual father

For preesthode excedeth all other thinge:
To us holy scripture they do teche,
And converteth man fro sinne heven to reche;
God hath to them more power given   735
Than to ony aungell that is in heven.
With five wordes he may consecrate
Goddes body in flesshe and blode to make,
And handeleth his Maker bytwine his handes.
The preest bindeth and unbindeth all bandes,   740
Both in erthe and in heven.
Thou ministres all the sacramentes seven;
Though we kisse thy fete, thou were worthy;
Thou arte surgion that cureth sinne deedly;
No remedy we finde under God   745
But all onely preesthode.
Everyman, God gave preests that dignite
And setteth them in his stede amonge us to be.
Thus be they above aungelles in degree.

                                    Exit Everyman.
KNOWLEDGE. If preestes be good, it is so, suerly.   750
But whan Jesu hanged on the crosse with grete smarte,
There he gave out of his blessid herte
The same sacrament in grete tourment.
He solde them not to us, that Lorde omnipotent;
Therefore Saint Peter the Apostell dothe saye   755
That Jesus curse hath all they
Whiche God their Saviour do by or sell,
Or they for ony money do take or tell.
Sinfull preests giveth the sinners example bad;
Their children sitteth by other mennes fires, I have
      harde;   760
And some haunteth womens company
With unclene life, as lustes of lechery.

---

742 *ministres,* administer   **758 tell,** count out
760 *harde,* heard

These be with sinne made blinde.

FIVE WITS. I trust to God no suche may we finde.

Therfore let us preesthode honour, 765
And folowe their doctrine for our soules socoure.
We be their shepe, and they shepeherdes be,
By whome we all be kepte in suerte.
Peas! for yonder I se Everyman come,
Whiche hath made true satisfaccion. 770

GOOD DEEDS. Methinke it is he indede.

Re-enter Everyman.

EVERYMAN. Now Jesu be your alder spede!
I have received the sacrament for my redempcion,
And than mine extreme unccion.
Blessid be all they that counseiled me to take it! 775
And now, frendes, let us go without longer respite.
I thanke God that ye have taried so longe.
Now set eche of you on this rodde your honde,
An shortely folowe me.
I go before there I wolde be. God be our gide! 780

STRENGTH. Everyman, we will not fro you go
Till ye have done this viage longe.

DISCRETION. I, Discrecion, will bide by you also.

KNOWLEDGE. And though this pilgrimage be never so stronge,
I will never parte you fro. 785

STRENGTH. Everyman, I will be as sure by thee
As ever I dide by Judas Machabee.

EVERYMAN. Alas! I am so faint I may not stande!
My limmes under me doth folde!
Frendes, let us not tourne againe to this lande, 790
Not for all the worldes golde;
For into this cave must I crepe

768 *suerte*, security
772 *your alder spede*, the source of prosperity for you all
780 *there*, where   784 *stronge*, grievous
787 *dide*, did

And tourne to erth, and there to slepe.

BEAUTY. What! into this grave? Alas!

EVERYMAN. Ye, there shall ye consume, more and
    lesse. 795

BEAUTY. And what! sholde I smoder here?

EVERYMAN. Ye, by my faith, and never more appere.
In this worlde live no more we shall,
But in heven before the hyest Lorde of all.

BEAUTY. I crosse out all this! Adeue, by Saint
    John! 800
I take my tappe in my lappe, and am gone.

EVERYMAN. What, Beaute! whider will ye?

BEAUTY. Peas! I am defe. I loke not behinde me,
Not and thou woldest give me all the golde in thy chest!
                      Exit Beauty.

EVERYMAN. Alas! wherto may I truste? 805
Beaute gothe fast awaye fro me!
She promised with me to live and die.

STRENGTH. Everyman, I will thee also forsake and
    denye.
Thy game liketh me not at all.

EVERYMAN. Why than, ye will forsake me all? 810
Swete Strength, tary a litell space.

STRENGTH. Nay, sir, by the rode of grace!
I will hye me from thee fast,
Though thou wepe to thy herte to-brast.

EVERYMAN. Ye wolde ever bide by me, ye said. 815

STRENGTH. Ye, I have you ferre ynoughe conveide!
Ye be olde ynoughe, I understande,
Your pilgrimage to take on hande.
I repent me that I hider came.

---

795 *consume*, decay   796 *smoder*, smother
801 *take . . . lappe*, i.e., tuck the loose ends of my belt into my
    pocket   804 *and*, if
809 *liketh*, pleases   812 *rode*, rood
814 *to*, until; *to-brast*, break   816 *ferre*, far

EVERYMAN. Strength, you to displease I am to
    blame,   820
Yet promise is dette, this ye well wot.
STRENGTH. In faith, I care not!
Thou arte but a foole to complaine.
You spende your speche, and wast your braine.
Go, thrist thee into the grounde!   825

Exit Strength.

EVERYMAN. I had wende surer I shulde you have
    founde.
He that trusteth in his Strength
She him deceiveth at the length.
Bothe Strength and Beaute forsaketh me;
Yet they promised me faire and lovingly.   830
DISCRETION. Everyman, I will after Strength be gone.
As for me, I will leve you alone.
EVERYMAN. Why Discrecion! will ye forsake me?
DISCRETION. Ye, in faith, I will go fro thee;
For whan Strength goth before   835
I folowe after ever more.
EVERYMAN. Yet, I pray thee, for the love of the Trinite,
Loke in my grave ones piteously.
DISCRETION. Nay, so nye will I not come.
Fare well everichone!   840

Exit Discretion.

EVERYMAN. O, all thinge faileth, save God alone—
Beaute, Strength, and Discrecion;
For whan Deth bloweth his blast
They all renne fro me full fast.
FIVE WITS. Everyman, my leve now of thee I take.   845
I will folowe the other, for here I thee forsake.
EVERYMAN. Alas! than may I waile and wepe,

---

821 *wot,* know
825 *thrist,* thrust
840 *everichone,* everyone

824 *wast,* waste
826 *wende,* supposed
844 *renne,* run

For I toke you for my best frende.

FIVE WITS. I will no lenger thee kepe.

Now farewell, and there an ende! 850

Exit Five Wits.

EVERYMAN. O Jesu, helpe! All hath forsaken me!

GOOD DEEDS. Nay, Everyman; I will bide with thee.

I will not forsake thee indede;

Thou shalte finde me a good frende at nede.

EVERYMAN. Gramercy, Good Dedes! Now may I
true frendes se. 855

They have forsaken me, everichone;

I loved them better than my Good Dedes alone.

Knowlege, will ye forsake me also?

KNOWLEDGE. Ye, Everyman, whan ye to Deth shall go;

But not yet, for no maner of daunger. 860

EVERYMAN. Gramercy, Knowlege, with all my herte!

KNOWLEDGE. Nay, yet I will not from hens departe

Till I se where ye shall become.

EVERYMAN. Methinke, alas, that I must be gone

To make my rekeninge, and my dettes paye; 865

For I se my time is nye spent awaye.

Take example, all ye that this do here or se,

How they that I loved best do forsake me,

Excepte my Good Dedes that bideth truely.

GOOD DEEDS. All erthly thinges is but vanite. 870

Beaute, Strength, and Discrecion do man forsake,

Folisshe frendes, and kinnesmen, that faire spake,—

All fleeth save Good Dedes, and that am I.

EVERYMAN. Have mercy on me, God moost mighty,

And stande by me, thou moder and maide, Holy
Mary! 875

GOOD DEEDS. Fere not; I will speke for thee.

EVERYMAN. Here I crye God mercy!

GOOD DEEDS. Shorte oure ende, and minisshe our paine.

862 *hens,* hence   863 *where . . . become,* what shall become of you

Let us go, and never come againe.

EVERYMAN. Into thy handes, Lorde, my soule I com-
mende.   880
Receive it, Lorde, that it be not lost.
As thou me boughtest, so me defende,
And save me from the fendes boost.
That I may appere with that blessid hoost
That shall be saved at the day of dome.   885
In manus tuas, of mightes moost
For ever, *commendo spiritum meum!*
Everyman and Good Deeds descend into the grave.

KNOWLEDGE. Now hath he suffred that we all shall
endure.
The Good Dedes shall make all sure.
Now hath he made endinge.   890
Methinketh that I here aungelles singe,
And make grete joy and melody
Where Everymannes soule received shall be.

ANGEL [*within*]. Come excellente electe spouse to Jesu!
Here above thou shalte go,   895
Bicause of thy singuler vertue.
Now the soule is taken the body fro,
Thy rekeninge is crystall clere.
Now shalte thou into the hevenly spere;
Unto the whiche all ye shall come   900
That liveth well before the daye of dome.
Enter Doctor.

DOCTOR. This memoriall men may have in minde.
Ye herers, take it of worth, olde and yonge!
And forsake Pride, for he deceiveth you in the ende.
And remembre Beaute, Five Wittes, Strength, and Dis-
crecion,   905

878 *shorte,* shorten; *minisshe,* diminish
886 *of mightes moost,* i.e., most mighty One   899 *spere,* sphere
903 *take,* i.e., judge

They all at the last do every man forsake,
Save his good dedes there dothe he take—
But beware, for and they be small
Before God he hath no helpe at all,
None excuse may be there for every man. 910
Alas, how shall he do, than?
For, after dethe, amendes may no man make;
For than mercy and pite doth him forsake.
If his rekeninge be not clere whan he doth come
God will saye: *"Ite, maledicti, in ignem eternum!"* 915
And he that hath his accounte hole and sounde,
Hye in heven he shall be crownde.
Unto whiche place God bringe us all thider,
That we may live body and soule togider.
Therto helpe, the Trinite! 920
Amen, saye ye, for Saint Charite.

907 *save*, unless   908 *and*, if
916 *hole*, whole

John Skelton

(1460?–1529)

The auncient acquaintance, madam

The auncient acquaintance, madam, betwen us twain,
   The familiarite, the formar daliaunce,
Causith me that I can not myself refraine
   But that I must write for my pleasaunt pastaunce:
   Remembring your passing goodly countenaunce,   5
Your goodly port, your beuteous visage,
Ye may be countid comfort of all corage.

Of all your feturs favorable to make tru discripcion,
   I am insufficient to make such enterprise;
For thus dare I say, without contradiccion,   10
   That dame Melanippe was never half so wise:
   Yet so it is that a rumer beginnith for to rise,
How in good horsmen ye set your hole delight,
And have forgoten your old trew loving knight.

With bound and rebound, bounsingly take up   15
   His jentill curtoil, and set nought by small naggis!
Spur up at the hinder girth, with, gup, morell, gup!
   With, jaist ye, jenet of Spaine, for your taill waggis!
   Ye cast all your corage uppon such courtly haggis.

4 *pastaunce*, pastime   7 *all corage*, every heart
8 *feturs favorable*, fair features   13 *hole*, whole
15–26: There are puns throughout these verses
16 *curtoil*, dock-tailed horse
17–18 *gup, jaist*, words of command to horses; *morell, jenet*, types of
   horse   19 *corage*, heart; *haggis*, ? effeminate fellows

Have in sergeaunt ferrour, mine horse behinde is
    bare;   20
He rideth well the horse, but he rideth better the mare.

Ware, ware, the mare winsith with her wanton hele!
    She kikith with her kalkins and keilith with a clench;
She goith wide behinde, and hewith never a dele:
    Ware galling in the widders, ware of that
        wrenche!   25
    It is perlous for a horseman to dig in the trenche.
This grevith your husband, that right jentill knight,
And so with youre servantis he fersly doth fight.

So fersly he fitith, his minde is so fell,
    That he drivith them downe with dintes on ther day-
        wach;   30
He bresith their brainpannis and makith them to swell,
    Theire browis all to-brokin, such clappis they cach;
    Whose jalausy malicious makith them to lepe the
        hach;
By their conusaunce knowing how they serve a wily py:
Ask all your neibours whether that I ly.   35

It can be no counsell that is cried at the cros:
    For your jentill husband sorowfull am I;
How be it, he is not furst hath had a los:
    Advertising you, madame, to warke more secretly,
    Let not all the world make an outcry;   40
Play faire play, madame, and loke ye play clene,
Or ells with gret shame your game wilbe sene.

---

20 *ferrour,* farrier   22 *winsith,* kicks
23 *keilith,* ? kills; *clench,* clinch-nail
24 *hewith,* strikes one foot against the other; *dele,* bit
25 *widders,* withers; *wrenche,* jerk   26 *perlous,* perilous
30 *day-wach,* i.e., day shift   31 *bresith,* bruises
32 *browis all to-brokens,* foreheads all split; *clappis,* blows
33 *hach,* door   35 *conusaunce,* i.e., livery; *py,* magpie
36 *counsell,* secret   39 *advertising,* admonishing; *warke,* work

Lullay, Lullay

With, Lullay, lullay, like a childe,
Thou slepist to long, thou art begilde.

"My darling dere, my daisy flowre,
  Let me," quod he, "ly in your lap."
"Ly still" quod she, "my paramoure,   5
  Ly still hardely, and take a nap."
  His hed was hevy, such was his hap,
All drowsy dreming, drownd in slepe,
That of his love he toke no kepe,
       With, Hey, lullay, etc.

With ba, ba, ba, and bas, bas, bas,   10
  She cherished him both cheke and chin,
That he wist never where he was;
  He had forgoten all dedely sin.
  He wantid wit her love to win:
He trusted her payment, and lost all his pay: 15
She left him sleping, and stale away.

The rivers routh, the waters wan;
  She sparid not to wete her fete;
She wadid over, she found a man
  That halsid her hartely and kist her swete: 20
  Thus after her cold she cought a hete.
"My lefe," she said, "routith in his bed;
Ywis he hath an hevy hed."

6 *hardely,* confidently	9 *kepe,* heed
10 *ba,* kiss	12 *wist,* knew
16 *stale,* stole	17 *routh,* rough
20 *halsid,* hugged	22 *lefe,* beloved; *routith,* snores

What dremist thou, drunchard, drousy pate!
    Thy lust and liking is from thee gone;   25
Thou blinkerd blowboll, thou wakist to late,
    Behold, thou lieste, luggard, alone!
    Well may thou sigh, well may thou grone,
To dele with her so cowardly:
Ywis, poule-hachet, she blerid thine i.   30

23 *ywis*, indeed   25 *lust and liking*, delight and pleasure
26 *blinkerd blowboll*, shut-eye blow-bowl   27 *luggard*, sluggard
30 *poule-hachet*, ? hatchet-face; *blerid thine i*, bleared your eye, i.e.,
    deceived you

Philip Sparrow

I. PLACEBO

Pla-ce-bo,
Who is there, who?
Di-le-xi,
Dame Margery;
Fa, re, mi, mi,   5
Wherefore and why, why?
For the soule of Philip Sparowe,
That was late slain at Carowe,
Among the Nones Blake,
For that swete soules sake,   10
And for all sparowes soules,
Set in our bederolles,
Pater noster qui,
With an *Ave Mari,*
And with the corner of a Crede,   15
The more shalbe your mede.
    When I remember again

9 *Nones Blake*, Black Nuns   12 *bederolles*, prayer lists

How my Philip was slain,
Never halfe the paine
Was betwene you twaine,   20
Pyramus and Thesbe,
As than befell to me:
I wept and I wailed,
The tearis downe hailed;
But nothinge it availed   25
To call Philip againe,
Whom Gib our cat hath slaine.

   Gib, I saye, our cat
Worrowid her on that
Which I loved best: 30
It can not be exprest
My sorowfull hevinesse,
But all without redresse;
For within that stounde,
Halfe slumbringe, in a sounde   35
I fell downe to the grounde.

   Unneth I cest mine eyes
Towarde the cloudy skies:
But whan I dide beholde
My sparow dead and colde,   40
No creatuer but that wolde
Have rewed upon me,
To behold and se
What hevinesse did me pange;
Wherewith my handes I wrange,   45
That my senaws cracked,
As though I had ben racked,
So pained and so strained,
That no life wellnye remained.

29 *worrowid her,* crammed herself   34 *stounde,* time
35 *sounde,* swoon   37 *unneth,* with difficulty; *cest,* cast
45 *wrange,* wrung   46 *senaws,* sinews

I sighed and I sobbed,   50
For that I was robbed
Of my sparowes life.
O maiden, widow, and wife,
Of what estate ye be,
Of hye or lowe degre,   55
Great sorowe than ye might se,
And lerne to wepe at me!
Such paines did me frete,
That mine hert did bete,
My visage pale and dead,   60
Wanne, and blewe as lead;
The panges of hatefull death
Wellnye had stopped my breath.

    Heu, heu, me,
That I am wo for thee!   65
Ad Dominum, cum tribularer, clamavi:
Of God nothinge els crave I
But Phillipes soule to kepe
From the marees deepe
Of Acherontes well,   70
That is a flode of hell;
And from the great Pluto,
The prince of endles wo;
And from foule Alecto,
With visage blacke and blo;   75
And from Medusa, that mare,
That like a fende doth stare;
And from Megeras edders,
For rufflinge of Phillips fethers,
And from her firy sparklinges,   80
For burninge of his winges;

58 *frete*, gnaw   61 *blewe*, dull
69 *marees*, swamp   75 *blo*, livid
76 *mare*, hag   78 *edders*, adders

And from the smokes soure
Of Proserpinas bowre;
And from the dennes darke,
Wher Cerberus doth barke,   85
Whom Theseus did afraye,
Whom Hercules did outraye,
As famous poetes say;
From that hell hounde,
That lieth in cheines bounde,   90
With gastly hedes thre,
To Jupiter pray we
That Phillip preserved may be!
Amen, say ye with me!
    Do-mi-nus,   95
Helpe nowe, swete Jesus!
Levavi oculos meos in montes:
Wolde God I had Zenophontes,
Or Socrates the wise,
To shew me their devise,   100
Moderatly to take
This sorow that I make
For Phillip Sparowes sake!
So fervently I shake,
I fele my body quake;   105
So urgently I am brought
Into carefull thought.
Like Andromach, Hectors wife,
Was wery of her life,
Whan she had lost her joye,   110
Noble Hector of Troye;
In like maner also
Encreaseth my dedly wo,
For my sparowe is go.

87 *outraye,* vanquish   100 *devise,* scheme

It was so prety a fole,   115
It wold sit on a stole,
And lerned after my scole
For to kepe his cut,
With, Phillip, kepe your cut!

It had a velvet cap,   120
And wold sit upon my lap,
And seke after small wormes,
And somtime white bred crommes;
And many times and ofte
Betwene my brestes softe   125
It wolde lie and rest;
It was propre and prest.

Somtime he wolde gaspe
Whan he sawe a waspe;
A fly or a gnat,   130
He wolde flye at that;
And pritely he wold pant
Whan he saw an ant;
Lord, how he wolde pry
After the butterfly!   135
Lorde, how he wolde hop
After the gressop!
And whan I said, Phip, Phip,
Than he wold lepe and skip,
And take me by the lip.   140
Alas, it will me slo,
That Phillip is gone me fro!
    Si in-i-qui-ta-tes,
Alas, I was evill at ease!
De pro-fun-dis cla-ma-vi,   145

115 *fole,* fool   118 *cut,* distance
123 *crommes,* crumbs   127: it was neat and keen
132 *pritely,* prettily   137 *gressop,* grasshopper
141 *slo,* slay

Whan I sawe my sparowe die!
  Nowe, after my dome,
Dame Sulpicia at Rome,
Whose name registred was
For ever in tables of bras,   150
Because that she did pas
In poesy to endite,
And eloquently to write,
Though she wolde pretende
My sparowe to commende,   155
I trowe she coude not amende
Reportinge the vertues all
Of my sparowe royall.
  For it wold come and go,
And fly so to and fro;   160
And on me it wolde lepe
Whan I was aslepe,
And his fethers shake,
Wherewith he wolde make
Me often for to wake,   165
And for to take him in
Upon my naked skin;
God wot, we thought no sin:
What though he crept so lowe?
It was no hurt, I trowe,   170
He did nothinge, perde,
But sit upon my kne:
Phillip, though he were nise,
In him it was no vise;
Phillip had leve to go   175
To pike my litell too;
Phillip might be bolde

147 *dome*, opinion
154 *pretende*, attempt
168 *wot*, knows
176 *pike*, peck

151 *pas*, surpass
156 *trowe*, think; *amende*, i.e., exaggerate
173 *nise*, wanton

And do what he wolde;
Phillip wolde seke and take
All the flees blake 180
That he coulde there espye
With his wanton eye.

 O-pe-ra,
La, soll, fa, fa,
Confitebor tibi, Domine, in toto corde meo. 185
Alas, I wold ride and go
A thousand mile of grounde!
If any such might be found,
It were worth an hundreth pound
Of kinge Cresus golde, 190
Or of Attalus the olde,
The riche prince of Pargame,
Who so list the story to se.
Cadmus, that his sister sought,
And he shold be bought 195
For golde and fee,
He shuld over the see,
To wete if he coulde bringe
Any of the ofspringe,
Or any of the blode. 200
But whoso understode
Of Medeas arte,
I wolde I had a parte
Of her crafty magike!
My sparowe than shuld be quicke 205
With a charme or twaine,
And playe with me againe.
But all this is in vaine
Thus for to complaine.

---

186 *go,* walk   193 *list,* pleases
195 *and,* if; *he,* i.e., the sparrow   196 *fee,* property
198 *wete,* know

I toke my sampler ones,   210
Of purpose, for the nones,
To sowe with stitchis of silke
My sparow white as milke,
That by representacion
Of his image and facion,   215
To me it might importe
Some pleasure and comforte
For my solas and sporte:
But whan I was sowing his beke,
Methought, my sparow did speke,   220
And opened his prety bill,
Sayinge, Maid, ye are in will
Againe me for to kill,
Ye pricke me in the head!
With that my nedle waxed red,   225
Methought, of Phillips blode;
Mine hear right upstode,
And was in suche a fray,
My speche was taken away.
I cest downe that there was,   230
And said, Alas, alas,
How commeth this to pas?
My fingers, dead and colde,
Coude not my sampler holde;
My nedle and threde   235
I threwe away for drede.
The best now that I maye,
Is for his soule to pray:
A *porta inferi*,
Good Lorde, have mercy   240
Upon my sparowes soule,

211 *nones*, occasion   215 *facion*, appearance
216 *importe*, convey   218 *solas*, delight
227 *hear*, hair   228 *fray*, fright
230: I threw down what I'd done

Writen in my bederoule!
   Au-di-vi vo-cem,
Japhet, Cam, and Sem,
Ma-gni-fi-cat,   245
Shewe me the right path
To the hilles of Armony,
Wherfore the birdes yet cry
Of your fathers bote,
That was sometime aflote,   250
And nowe they lie and rote;
Let some poetes write
Deucalions flode it hight:
But as verely as ye be
The naturall sonnes thre   255
Of Noe the patriarke,
That made that great arke,
Wherin he had apes and owles,
Beestes, birdes, and fowles,
That if ye can finde   260
Any of my sparowes kinde,
God sende the soule good rest!
I wolde have yet a nest
As pretty and as prest
As my sparowe was.   265
But my sparowe did pas
All sparowes of the wode
That were sins Noes flode,
Was never none so good;
Kinge Philip of Macedony   270
Had no such Philip as I,
No, no, sir, hardely.
   That vengeaunce I aske and crye,

---

242 *bederoule,* prayer-list   247 *Armony,* Armenia
251 *rote,* rot   253 *hight,* is called
263 *nest,* brood   264 *prest,* alert
266 *pas,* surpass   272 *hardely,* certainly

By way of exclamacion,
On all the hole nacion　　　　　　　　275
Of cattes wilde and tame;
God send them sorowe and shame!
That cat specially
That slew so cruelly
My litell prety sparowe　　　　　　　280
That I brought up at Carowe.

　　O cat of carlishe kinde,
The finde was in thy minde
Whan thou my birde untwinde!
I wold thou haddest ben blinde!　　　285
The leopardes savage,
The lions in their rage,
Might catche thee in their pawes,
And gnawe thee in their jawes!
The serpentes of Lybany　　　　　　290
Might stinge thee venimously!
The dragones with their tonges
Might poison thy liver and longes!
The manticors of the montaines
Might fede them on thy braines!　　　295
　　Melanchates, that hounde
That plucked Aceteon to the grounde,
Gave him his mortall wounde,
Chaunged to a dere,
The story doth appere,　　　　　　　300
Was chaunged to an harte:
So thou, foule cat that thou arte,
The selfe same hounde
Might thee confounde,
That his owne lord bote,　　　　　　305

275 _hole_, whole
283 _finde_, fiend
293 _longes_, lungs
305 _bote_, bit

282 _carlishe_, churlish; _kinde_, nature
284 _untwinde_, destroyed
294 _manticors_, a fabulous monster

Might bite asondre thy throte!
　Of Inde the gredy gripes
Might tere out all thy tripes!
Of Arcady the beares
Might plucke awaye thine eares!　310
The wilde wolfe Lycaon
Bite asondre thy backe bone!
Of Ethna the brenninge hill,
That day and night brenneth stil,
Set in thy taile a blase,　315
That all the world may gase
And wonder upon thee,
From Occian the greate se
Unto the Iles of Orchady,
From Tillbery fery　320
To the plaine of Salisbery!
So traiterously my birde to kill
That never ought thee evill will!
　Was never birde in cage
More gentle of corage　325
In doinge his homage
Unto his soveraine.
Alas, I say againe,
Deth hath departed us twaine!
The false cat hath thee slaine:　330
Farewell, Phillip, adeu!
Our Lorde thy soule reskeu!
Farewell without restore,
Farewell for evermore!
　And it were a Jewe,　335
It wolde make one rew,
To se my sorow new.

307 *gripes*, griffins　　　　　308 *tripes*, guts
313 *brenninge*, burning　　　　　323 *ought*, bore
325 *corage*, heart　　　329 *departed*, separated
335 *and*, if

These vilanous false cattes
Were made for mise and rattes,
And not for birdes smale.   340
Alas, my face waxeth pale,
Tellinge this piteius tale,
How my birde so faire,
That was wont to repaire,
And go in at my spaire,   345
And crepe in at my gore
Of my gowne before,
Flickeringe with his winges!
Alas, my hert it stinges,
Remembringe pretty thinges!   350
Alas, mine hert it sleth
My Phillippes dolefull deth,
Whan I remembre it,
How pretely it wolde sit,
Many times and ofte,   355
Upon my finger aloft!
I played with him tittel tattill,
And fed him with my spattil,
With his bill betwene my lippes;
It was my prety Phippes!   360
Many a prety kusse
Had I of his swete musse;
And now the cause is thus,
That he is slaine me fro,
To my great paine and wo.   365
    Of fortune this the chaunce
Standeth on variaunce:
Oft time after pleasaunce
Trouble and grevaunce;
No man can be sure   370

345–46 *spaire, gore,* openings in a garment   351 *sleth,* slays
358 *spattil,* spittle   361 *kusse,* kiss
362 *musse,* mouth

Allway to have pleasure:
As well perceive ye maye
How my disport and play
From me was taken away
By Gib, our cat savage,   375
That in a furious rage
Caught Phillip by the head,
And slew him there starke dead.
    Kyrie, eleison,
      Christe, eleison,   380
    Kyrie, eleison!
For Philip Sparowes soule,
Set in our bederolle,
Let us now whisper
A *Pater noster.*   385
    Lauda, anima mea, Dominum!
To wepe with me loke that ye come,
All maner of birdes in your kind;
Se none be left behinde.
To morninge loke that ye fall   390
With dolorous songes funerall,
Some to singe, and some to say,
Some to wepe, and some to pray,
Every birde in his laye.
The goldfinche, the wagtaile;   395
The janglinge jay to raile,
The fleckid pye to chatter
Of this dolorous mater;
And robin redbrest,
He shall be the preest   400
The requiem masse to singe,
Softly warbelinge,
With helpe of the red sparow,

390 *morninge,* mourning   394 *laye,* tune
397 *pye,* magpie   400 *preest,* priest
403 *red sparow,* reed sparrow

And the chattringe swallow,
This herse for to halow;   405
The larke with his longe to;
The spinke, and the martinet also;
The shovelar with his brode bek;
The doterell, that folishe pek,
And also the mad coote,   410
With a balde face to toote;
The feldefare, and the snite;
The crowe, and the kite;
The ravin, called Rolfe,
His plaine songe to solfe;   415
The partriche, the quaile;
The plover with us to waile;
The woodhacke, that singeth "chur"
Horsly, as he had the mur;
The lusty chaunting nightingale;   420
The popingay to tell her tale,
That toteth oft in a glasse,
Shal rede the Gospell at masse;
The mavis with her whistell
Shal rede there the pistell.   425
But with a large and a longe
To kepe just plaine songe,
Our chaunters shalbe the cuckoue,
The culver, the stockedowue,
With "puwit" the lapwing,   430
The versicles shall sing.
    The bitter with his "bumpe,"

406 *to*, toe   407 *spinke*, finch
408 *shovelar*, spoonbill   409 *pek*, dolt
411 *toote*, peer at   412 *snite*, snipe
415 *solfe*, sing   418 *woodhacke*, woodpecker
419 *mur*, catarrh   422 *toteth*, peers
425 *pistell*, epistle   426 *large . . . longe*, long and short note
428 *cuckoue*, cuckoo   429 *stockedowue*, stockdove
432 *bitter*, bittern

The crane with his trumpe,
The swan of Menander,
The gose and the gander, 435
The ducke and the drake,
Shall watche at this wake;
The pecocke so proude,
Because his voice is loude,
And hath a glorious taile, 440
He shall sing the graile;
The owle, that is so foule,
Must helpe us to howle;
The heron so gaunte,
And the cormoraunte, 445
With the fesaunte,
And the gaglinge gaunte,
And the churlisshe chough;
The route and the rough;
The barnacle, the bussarde, 450
With the wilde mallarde;
The divendop to slepe;
The water hen to wepe;
The puffin and the tele
Money they shall dele 455
To poore folke at large,
That shall be their charge;
The semewe and the titmose;
The wodcocke with the longe nose;
The threstil with her warbling; 460
The starling with her brabling;
The roke, with the ospraye
That putteth fisshes to a fraye;

433 *trumpe,* trumpet 441 *graile,* Gradual
447 *gaglinge gaunte,* gabbling gannet
449 *route,* a type of goose; *rough,* sandpiper 452 *divendrop,* dabchick
455 *dele,* distribute 458 *semewe,* seamew
460 *threstil,* throstle 462 *roke,* rook
463 *fraye,* fright

And the denty curlewe,
With the turtill most trew.   465
    At this *Placebo*
We may not well forgo
The countringe of the coe:
The storke also,
That maketh his nest   470
In chimneyes to rest;
Within those walles
No broken galles
May there abide
Of cokoldry side,   475
Or els philosophy
Maketh a great lie.
    The estrige, that will eate
An horshowe so great,
In the stede of meate,   480
Such fervent heat
His stomacke doth freat;
He can not well fly,
Nor singe tunably,
Yet at a braide   485
He hath well assaide
To solfe above ela,
Fa, lorell, fa, fa;
Ne quando
Male cantando,   490
The best that we can,
To make him our belman,
And let him ring the bellis;
He can do nothing ellis.

464 *denty*, dainty
468 *countringe*, accompaniment-singing; *coe*, jackdaw
473 *galls*, blisters   475: i.e., pertaining to cuckoldry
478 *estrige*, ostrich   479 *horshowe*, horseshoe
482 *freat*, gnaw   485: Yet for a whim
487: to sing above high C   488 *lorell*, loafer

Chaunteclere, our coke,   495
Must tell what is of the clocke
By the astrology
That he hath naturally
Conceived and cought,
And was never tought   500
By Albumazer
The astronomer,
Nor by Ptholomy
Prince of astronomy,
Nor yet by Haly;   505
And yet he croweth daily
And nightly the tides
That no man abides,
With Partlot his hen,
Whom now and then   510
Hee pluckth by the hede
Whan he doth her trede.

The birde of Araby,
That potencially
May never die,   515
And yet there is none
But one alone;
A phenex it is
This herse that must blis
With armaticke gummes   520
That cost great summes,
The way of thurification
To make a fumigation,
Swete of reflare,
And redolent of eire,   525
This corse for to sence

---

507 *tides,* times   519 *blis,* bless
524 *reflare,* odor   525 *eire,* smell
526: the corpse to cense

With greate reverence,
As patriarke or pope
In a blacke cope;
Whiles he senseth the herse,   530
He shall singe the verse,
Libera me,
In de, la, soll, re,
Softly bemole
For my sparowes soule.   535
Plinny sheweth all
In his story naturall
What he doth finde
Of the phenix kinde;
Of whose incineracion   540
There riseth a new creacion
Of the same facion
Without alteracion,
Saving that olde age
Is turned into corage   545
Of fresshe youth againe;
This matter trew and plaine,
Plaine matter indede,
Who so list to rede.

But for the egle doth flye   550
Hyest in the skye,
He shall be the sedeane,
The quere to demeane,
As provost principall,
To teach them their ordinall;   555
Also the noble faucon,
With the gerfaucon,

530 *senseth,* censes
542 *facion,* fashion
552 *sedeane,* subdean
555 *ordinall,* service book
534 *bemole,* i.e., sing the flat part
545 *corage,* heartiness
553: to manage the choir
556 *faucon,* falcon

The tarsell gentill,
They shall morne soft and still
In their amisse of gray;   560
The sacre with them shall say
Dirige for Phillippes soule;
The goshauke shall have a role
The queresters to controll;
The lanners and the marlions   565
Shall stand in their morning gownes;
The hobby and the muskette
The sensers and the crosse shall fet;
The kestrell in all this warke
Shall be holy water clarke.   570

   And now the darke cloudy night
Chaseth away Phebus bright,
Taking his course toward the west,
God sende my sparoes sole good rest!
Requiem aeternam dona eis, Domine!   575
Fa, fa, fa, mi, re, re,
A por-ta in-fe-ri,
Fa, fa, fa, mi, mi.
   Credo videre bona Domini,
I pray God Phillip to heven may fly!   580
Domine, exaudi orationem meam!
To heven he shall, from heven he cam!
   Do-mi-nus vo-bis-cum!
Of al good prayers God send him sum!
   Oremus   585
  Deus, cui proprium est misereri et parcere,

558 *tarsell*, tercel   559 *morne*, mourn
560 *amisse*, amice   561 *sacre*, a type of falcon
564 *queresters*, choristers   565 *lanners, marlions*, types of falcon
566 *morning*, mourning
567 *hobby*, a type of falcon; *muskette*, sparrowhawk
568 *sensers*, censers; *fet*, fetch   569 *warke*, work
570 *clarke*, clerk   574 *sparoes*, sparrow's

On Phillips soule have pite!
For he was a prety cocke,
And came of a gentill stocke,
And wrapt in a maidenes smocke,   590
And cherisshed full daintely,
Till cruell fate made him to dy:
Alas, for dolefull desteny!
But whereto shuld I
Lenger morne or crye?   595
To Jupiter I call,
Of heven emperiall,
That Phillip may fly
Above the starry sky,
To treade the prety wren,   600
That is our Ladyes hen:
Amen, amen, amen!
   Yet one thinge is behinde,
That now commeth to minde;
An epitaphe I wold have   605
For Phillippes grave:
But for I am a maide,
Timerous, halfe afraide,
That never yet asayde
Of Eliconis well,   610
Where the Muses dwell;
Though I can rede and spell,
Recounte, reporte, and tell
Of the Tales of Caunterbury,
Some sad stories, some mery;   615
As Palamon and Arcet,
Duke Theseus, and Partelet;
And of the Wife of Bath,
That worketh moch scath
Whan her tale is tolde   620

595 *lenger*, longer   619: who does much harm

Amonge huswives bolde,
How she controlde
Her husbandes as she wolde,
And them to despise
In the homiliest wise,   625
Bringe other wives in thought
Their husbandes to set at nought:
And though that rede have I
Of Gawen and sir Guy,
And tell can a great pece   630
Of the Golden Flece,
How Jason it wan,
Like a valiaunt man;
Of Arturs rounde table,
With his knightes commendable,   635
And dame Gaynour, his quene,
Was somwhat wanton, I wene;
How sir Launcelote de Lake
Many a spere brake
For his ladyes sake;   640
Of Tristram, and kinge Marke,
And al the hole warke
Of Bele Isold his wife,
For whom was moch strife;
Some say she was light,   645
And made her husband knight
Of the comine hall,
That cuckoldes men call;
And of sir Lybius,
Named Disconius;   650
Of Quater Filz Amund,
And how they were sommonde

---

630 *pece*, piece   632 *wan*, won
636 *Gaynour*, Guinevere   637 *wene*, think
642 *hole warke*, whole business   647 *comine*, common

To Rome, to Charlemaine,
Upon a great paine,
And how they rode eche one   655
On Bayarde Mountalbon;
Men se him now and then
In the forest of Arden:
What though I can frame
The stories by name   660
Of Judas Machabeus,
And of Cesar Julious;
And of the love betwene
Paris and Viene;
And of the duke Hanniball,   665
That made the Romaines all
Fordrede and to quake;
How Scipion did wake
The citye of Cartage,
Which by his unmerciful rage   670
He bete downe to the grounde:
And though I can expounde
Of Hector of Troye,
That was all their joye,
Whom Achilles slew,   675
Wherfore all Troy did rew;
And of the love so hote
That made Troilus to dote
Upon faire Cresside,
And what they wrote and said,   680
And of their wanton willes
Pandaer bare the billes
From one to the other;
His maisters love to further,
Somtime a precious thing,   685

667 *fordrede,* terrified   668 *wake,* keep watch on
682: Pandarus bore the letters

An ouche, or els a ring;
From her to him again
Somtime a prety chain,
Or a bracelet of her here,
Prayd Troilus for to were   690
That token for her sake;
How hartely he did it take,
And moche therof did make;
And all that was in vaine,
For she did but faine;   695
The story telleth plaine,
He coulde not optaine,
Though his father were a king,
Yet there was a thing
That made the male to wring;   700
She made him to sing
The song of lovers lay;
Musing night and day,
Mourning all alone,
Comfort had he none,   705
For she was quite gone;
Thus in conclusion,
She brought him in abusion;
In ernest and in game
She was moch to blame;   710
Disparaged is her fame,
And blemisshed is her name,
In maner half with shame;
Troilus also hath lost
On her moch love and cost,   715
And now must kis the post;

---

686 *ouche*, trinket   689 *here*, hair
690 *were*, wear   695 *faine*, feign
697 *optaine*, succeed   700: i.e., that caused him trouble
702 *lay*, law   708 *abusion*, deceit
714 *kis the post*, i.e., be disappointed

Pandara, that went betwene,
Hath won nothing, I wene,
But light for somer grene;
Yet for a speciall laud   720
He is named Troilus bawd,
Of that name he is sure
Whiles the world shall dure:
   Though I remembre the fable
Of Penelope most stable,   725
To her husband most trew,
Yet long time she ne knew
Whether he were on live or ded;
Her wit stood her in sted,
That she was true and just   730
For any bodely lust
To Ulixes her make,
And never wold him forsake:
   Of Marcus Marcellus
A proces I could tell us;   735
And of Anteocus;
And of Josephus
De Antiquitatibus;
And of Mardocheus,
And of great Assuerus,   740
And of Vesca his queene,
Whom he forsoke with teene,
And of Hester his other wife,
With whom he ledd a plesaunt life;
Of king Alexander;   745
And of king Evander;
And of Porcena the great,
That made the Romains to sweat.
   Though I have enrold

719: i.e., nothing useful   723 *dure*, endure
731 *bodely*, bodily   732 *make*, mate
735 *proces*, account   742 *teene*, anger

A thousand new and old   750
Of these historious tales,
To fill bougets and males
With bokes that I have red,
Yet I am nothing sped,
And can but litell skill   755
Of Ovid or Virgill,
Or of Plutharke,
Or Frauncis Petrarke,
Alcheus or Sapho,
Or such other poetes mo,   760
As Linus and Homerus,
Euphorion and Theocritus,
Anacreon and Arion,
Sophocles and Philemon,
Pindarus and Simonides,   765
Philistion and Phorocides;
These poetes of aunciente,
They ar to diffuse for me:
   For, as I tofore have said,
I am but a yong maid,   770
And cannot in effect
My style as yet direct
With English wordes elect:
Our naturall tong is rude,
And hard to be ennewde   775
With pullisshed termes lusty;
Our language is so rusty,
So cankered, and so full
Of frowardes, and so dull,
That if I wolde apply   780

752 *bougets and males,* pouches and bags   754 *sped,* i.e., versed
755: and have but little knowledge   760 *mo,* more
767 *aunciente,* antiquity   768 *diffuse,* obscure
769 *tofore,* before   775 *ennewde,* colored
776: with polished pleasing terms   779 *frowardes,* awkwardnesses

To write ornatly,
I wot not where to find
Termes to serve my minde.

   Gowers English is olde,
And of no value told;   785
His mater is worth gold,
And worthy to be enrold.

   In Chauser I am sped,
His tales I have red:
His mater is delectable,   790
Solacious, and commendable;
His English well alowed,
So as it is emprowed,
For as it is enployd,
There is no English void,   795
At those dayes moch commended,
And now men wold have amended
His English, whereat they barke,
And mar all they warke:
Chaucer, that famus clerke,   800
His termes were not darke,
But plesaunt, easy, and plaine;
No worde he wrote in vaine.

   Also Johnn Lydgate
Writeth after an hyer rate;   805
It is diffuse to finde
The sentence of his minde,
Yet writeth he in his kind,
No man that can amend
Those maters that he hath pende;   810
Yet some men finde a faute,

782 *wot*, know   785 *told*, accounted
791 *solacious*, delightful   792 *alowed*, approved
793 *emprowed*, used (by him)   795: ? there is no fault in his English
799 *warke*, work on   805 *hyer rate*, more exalted style
806 *diffuse*, i.e., difficult   807 *sentence*, meaning
811 *faute*, fault

And say he writeth to haute.
    Wherfore hold me excused
If I have not well perused;
Mine Englissh halfe abused,   815
Though it be refused,
In worth I shall it take,
And fewer wordes make.
    But, for my sparowes sake,
Yet as a woman may,   820
My wit I shall assay
An epitaphe to wright
In Latine plaine and light,
Wherof the elegy
Foloweth by and by: 825
Flos volucrum formose, vale!
Philippe, sub isto
Marmore iam recubas,
Qui mihi carus eras.
Semper erunt nitido   830
Radiantia sidera caelo;
Impressusque meo
Pectore semper eris.
Per me laurigerum
Britonum Skeltonida vatem   835
Haec cecinisse licet
Ficta sub imagine texta.
Cuius eris volucris,
Praestanti corpore virgo:
Candida Nais erat,   840
Formosior ista Joanna est;
Docta Corinna fuit,
Sed magis ista sapit.
    Bien men sovient.

---

812 *to haute,* too exaltedly   817 *in worth,* in good part
822 *wright,* write

II. COMMENDATIONS

Beati im-ma-cu-la-ti in via,
O gloriosa femina!
Now mine hole imaginacion
And studious meditacion
Is to take this commendacion   5
In this consideracion;
And under pacient tolleracion
Of that most goodly maid
That *Placebo* hath said,
And for her sparow prayd   10
In lamentable wise,
Now will I enterprise,
Thorow the grace divine
Of the Muses nine,
Her beautye to commende,   15
If Arethusa will send
Me enfluence to endite,
And with my pen to write;
If Apollo will promise
Melodiously to it devise   20
His tunable harpe stringes
With armony that singes
Of princes and of kinges
And of all pleasaunt thinges,
Of lust and of delight,   25
Thorow his godly might;
To whom be the laude ascribed
That my pen hath enbibed
With the aureat droppes,
As verely my hope is,   30

3 *hole*, whole   28 *enbibed*, absorbed

Of Thagus, that golden flod,
That passeth all erthly good;
And as that flode doth pas
Al floodes that ever was
With his golden sandes,   35
Who so that understandes
Cosmography, and the stremis
And the floodes in straunge remes,
Right so she doth excede
All other of whom we rede,   40
Whose fame by me shall sprede
Into Perce and Mede,
From Britons Albion
To the Towre of Babylon.

 I trust it is no shame,   45
And no man will me blame,
Though I regester her name
In the courte of Fame;
For this most goodly flowre,
This blossome of fresshe coulour,   50
So Jupiter me socour,
She florissheth new and new
In beute and vertew:
Hac claritate gemina
O gloriosa femina,   55
Retribue servo tuo, vivifica me!
Labia mea laudabunt te.

 But enforsed am I
Openly to ascry,
And to make an outcry
Against odious Envy,   60
That evermore wil ly,

---

38 *remes,* realms   52 *new and new,* ever anew
59 *ascry,* exclaim

And say cursedly;
With his ledder ey,
And chekes dry;   65
With visage wan,
As swarte as tan;
His bones crake,
Leane as a rake;
His gummes rusty   70
Are full unlusty;
His herte withall
Bitter as gall;
His liver, his longe
With anger is wronge;   75
His serpentes tonge
That many one hath stonge;
He frowneth ever;
He laugheth never,
Even nor morow,   80
But other mennes sorow
Causeth him to grin
And rejoice therin;
No slepe can him catch,
But ever doth watch,   85
He is so bete
With malice, and frete
With angre and ire,
His foule desire
Will suffre no slepe   90
In his hed to crepe;
His foule semblaunt
All displesaunte;

64 *ledder*, evil   67 *tan*, tanbark
68 *crake*, creak   71 *lusty*, unpleasant
74 *longe*, lung   75 *wronge*, wrung
80: evening or morning   85 *watch*, wake
86 *bete*, beaten   87 *frete*, gnawed
92 *semblaunt*, appearance

Whan other ar glad,
Than is he sad;   95
Frantike and mad;
His tong never still
For to say ill,
Writhing and wringing,
Biting and stinging;   100
And thus this elf
Consumeth himself,
Himself doth slo
With paine and wo.
This fals Envy   105
Saith that I
Use great folly
For to endite,
And for to write,
And spend my time   110
In prose and rime,
For to expres
The noblenes
Of my maistres,
That causeth me   115
Studious to be
To make a relation
Of her commendation;
And there againe
Envy doth complaine,   120
And hath disdaine;
But yet certaine
I will be plaine,
And my style dres
To this prosses.   125

103 *slo*, slay   114 *maistres*, mistress
119 *againe*, against
125 *prosses*, argument

Now Phebus me ken
To sharpe my pen,
And lede my fist
As him best list,
That I may say   130
Honour alway
Of womankind!
Trouth doth me bind
And loyalte
Ever to be   135
Their true bedell,
To write and tell
How women excell
In noblenes;
As my maistres,   140
Of whom I think
With pen and ink
For to compile
Some goodly style;
For this most goodly flowre, etc.   145
Hac claritate gemina
O gloriosa femina,
Legem pone mihi, domina, in viam iustificationum tu-
    arum!
Quemadmodum desiderat cervus ad fontes aquarum.

How shall I report   150
All the goodly sort
Of her fetures clere,
That hath non erthly pere?
Her favour of her face
Ennewed all with grace,   155
Confort, pleasure, and solace,

126 *ken*, teach   129: as it pleases him best
133 *trouth*, faith   136 *bedell*, herald
153 *pere*, peer   155 *ennewed*, tinted

Mine hert doth so enbrace,
And so hath ravished me
Her to behold and se,
That in wordes plaine   160
I cannot me refraine
To loke on her againe:
Alas, what shuld I faine?
It wer a plesaunt paine
With her aye to remaine.   165
Her eyen gray and stepe
Causeth mine hert to lepe;
With her browes bent
She may well represent
Faire Lucres, as I wene,   170
Or els faire Polexene,
Or els Caliope,
Or els Penolope;
For this most goodly flowre, etc.
Hac claritate gemina   175
O gloriosa femina,
Memor esto verbi tui servo tuo!
Servus tuus sum ego.

  The Indy saphire blew
Her vaines doth ennew;   180
The orient perle so clere,
The whitnesse of her lere;
The lusty ruby ruddes
Resemble the rose buddes;
Her lippes soft and mery   185
Emblomed like the chery,
It were an hevenly blisse
Her sugred mouth to kisse.

163 *what*, why; *faine*, feign   166 *stepe*, prominent
180 *ennew*, color   182 *lere*, face
183 *ruddes*, cheeks   186 *enblomed*, blooming

Her beautye to augment,
Dame Nature hath her lent   190
A warte upon her cheke,
Who so list to seke
In her visage a scar,
That semith from afar
Like to the radiant star,   195
All with favour fret,
So properly it is set:
She is the violet,
The daisy delectable,
The columbine commendable,   200
The jelofer amiable:
For this most goodly flowre, etc.
Hac claritate gemina
O gloriosa femina,
Bonitatem fecisti cum servo tuo, domina, 205
Et ex praecordiis sonant praeconia!

And whan I perceived
Her wart and conceived,
It cannot be denayd
But it was well convayd,   210
And set so womanly,
And nothinge wantonly,
But right conveniently,
And full congruently,
As Nature cold devise,   215
In most goodly wise;
Who so list beholde,
It makethe lovers bolde
To her to sewe for grace,
Her favoure to purchase;   220

196 *fret*, adorned   201 *jelofer*, gillyflower
208 *conceived*, observed   209 *denayd*, denied
210 *convayd*, borne   219 *sewe*, sue

The scer upon her chin,
Enhached on her faire skin,
Whiter than the swan,
It would make any man
To forget deadly sin   225
Her favour to win;
For this most goodly flowre, etc.
Hac claritate gemina
O gloriosa femina,
Defecit in salutatione tua anima mea;   230
Quid petis filio, mater dulcissima? babae!

   Soft, and make no din,
For now I will begin
To have in remembraunce
Her goodly daliaunce,   235
And her goodly pastaunce:
So sad and so demure,
Behavinge her so sure,
With wordes of pleasure
She wold make to the lure   240
And any man convert
To give her his hole hert.
She made me sore amased
Upon her whan I gased,
Me thought min hert was crased,   245
My eyne were so dased;
For this most goodly flowre, etc.
Hac claritate gemina
O gloriosa femina,
Quomodo dilexi legem tuam, domina!   250
Recedant vetera, nova sint omnia.

---

221 *scer*, scar   222 *enhached*, inlaid
236 *pastaunce*, pastime   237 *sad*, sober
240: i.e., she would tempt   242 *hole*, whole
245 *crased*, crushed

And to amende her tale,
Whan she list to avale,
And with her fingers smale,
And handes soft as silke,   255
Whiter than the milke,
That are so quickely vained,
Wherwith my hand she strained,
Lorde, how I was pained!
Unneth I me refrained,   260
How she me had reclaimed,
And me to her retained,
Enbrasinge therwithall
Her goodly middell small
With sides longe and streite;   265
To tell you what conceite
I had than in a trice,
The matter were to nise,
And yet there was no vice,
Nor yet no villany,   270
But only fantasy;
For this most goodly flowre, etc.
Hac claritate gemina
O gloriosa femina,
Iniquos odio habui!   275
Non calumnientur me superbi.

But whereto shulde I note
How often did I tote
Upon her prety fote?
It raised mine hert rote   280
To se her treade the grounde
With heles short and rounde.

---

252 *her tale*, the account of her   253 *avale*, humble herself
257 *quickely*, lively   258 *strained*, pressed
260 *unneth*, scarcely   261 *reclaimed*, tamed
266 *conceite*, idea   268 *nise*, delicate
278 *tote*, peer   280 *raisid*, excited; *rote*, root

She is plainly expresse
Egeria, the goddesse,
And like to her image, 285
Emportured with corage,
A lovers pilgrimage;
Ther is no beest savage,
Ne no tiger so wood,
But she wolde chaunge his mood, 290
Such relucent grace
Is formed in her face;
For this most goodly flowre, etc.
Hac claritate gemina
O gloriosa femina, 295
Mirabilia testimonia tua!
Sicut novellae plantationes in iuventute sua.

So goodly as she dresses,
So properly she presses
The bright golden tresses 300
Of her heer so fine,
Like Phebus beames shine.
Wherto shuld I disclose
The garteringe of her hose?
It is for to suppose 305
How that she can were
Gorgiously her gere;
Her fresshe habilementes
With other implementes
To serve for all ententes, 310
Like dame Flora, quene
Of lusty somer grene;
For this most goodly flowre, etc.
Hac claritate gemina
O gloriosa femina, 315

286 *emportured,* portrayed; *corage,* spirit   289 *wood,* raging
301 *heer,* hair

Clamavi in toto corde, exaudi me!
Misericordia tua magna est super me.

Her kirtell so goodly lased,
And under that is brased
Such plasures that I may   320
Neither write nor say;
Yet though I write not with inke,
No man can let me thinke,
For thought hath liberte,
Thought is franke and fre;   325
To thinke a mery thought
It cost me litell nor nought.
Wolde God mine homely style
Were pullisshed with the file
Of Ciceros eloquence,   330
To prase her excellence!
For this most goodly flowre, etc.
Hac claritate gemina
O gloriosa femina,
Principes persecuti sunt me gratis!   335
Omnibus consideratis,
Paradisus voluptatis
Haec virgo est dulcissima.

My pen it is unable,
My hand it is unstable,
My reson rude and dull   340
To praise her at the full;
Goodly maistres Jane,
Sobre, demure Diane;
Jane this maistres hight   345
The lode star of delight,
Dame Venus of all pleasure,

319 *brased,* girt   323: no one can keep me from thinking
329 *pullisshed,* polished   345 *hight,* is named

The well of worldly treasure;
She doth excede and pas
In prudence dame Pallas;   350
For this most goodly flowre, etc.
Hac claritate gemina
O gloriosa femina!

   Requiem aeternam dona eis, Domine!
With this psalme, *Domine, probasti me,*   355
Shall saile over the see,
With *Tibi, Domine, commendamus,*
On pilgrimage to saint Jamis,
For shrimpes, and for pranis,
And for stalkinge cranis;   360
And where my pen hath offendid,
I pray you it may be amendid
By discrete consideracion
Of your wise reformacion;
I have not offended, I trust,   365
If it be sadly discust.
It were no gentle gise
This treatise to despise
Because I have written and said
Honour of this faire maid;   370
Wherefore shulde I be blamed,
That I Jane have named,
And famously proclamed?
She is worthy to be enrolde
With letters of golde.   375
        Car elle vault.
Per me laurigerum Britonum Skeltonida vatem
Laudibus eximiis merito haec redimita puella est:
Formosam cecini, qua non formosior ulla est;

---

359 *pranis*, prawns   366 *sadly*, soberly
367 *gise*, fashion

Formosam potius quam commendaret Homerus.   380
Sic iuvat interdum rigidos recreare labores,
Nec minus hoc titulo tersa Minerva mea est.
          Rien que plaisere.

THUS ENDETH THE BOKE OF PHILIP SPAROW,
AND HERE FOLOWETH AN ADICION
MADE BY MAISTER SKELTON

          The gise now a dayes
          Of some janglinge jayes
          Is to discommende
          That they cannot amend,
          Though they wold spend   5
          All the wittes they have.
          . What aile them to deprave
          Phillip Sparowes grave?
          His *Dirige*, her Commendacion
          Can be no derogacion,   10
          But mirth and consolacion
          Made by protestacion,
          No man to miscontent
          With Phillippes enterement.
          Alas, that goodly maid,   15
          Why shuld she be afraide?
          Why shuld she take shame
          That her goodly name,
          Honorably reported,
          Sholde be set and sorted,   20
          To be matriculate
          With ladies of estate?
          I conjure thee, Phillip Sparow,

4 *that*, what   14 *enterement*, interment
20 *set and sorted*, placed and assigned   21 *matriculate*, registered

By Hercules that hell did harow,
And with a venemous arow   25
Slew of the Epidaures
One of the Centaures,
Or Onocentaures,
Or Hipocentaures;
By whose might and maine   30
An hart was slaine
With hornes twaine
Of glittering gold;
And the appels of gold
Of Hesperides withhold,   35
And with a dragon kept
That never more slept,
By marciall strength
He wan at length;
And slew Geryon   40
With three bodies in one;
With mighty corage
Adauntid the rage
Of a lion savage;
Of Diomedes stable   45
He brought out a rable
Of coursers and rounses
With leapes and bounses;
And with mighty lugging,
Wrestling and tugging,   50
He plucked the bull
By the horned skull,
And offred to Cornucopia;
And so forth *per cetera*:
    Also by Ecates bower   55

38 *marciall*, martial   39 *wan*, won
42 *corage*, heart   46 *rable*, rabble
47 *rounses*, horses

In Plutos gastly tower;
   By the ugly Eumenides,
That never have rest nor ease;
   By the venemous serpent,
That in hell is never brent,   60
In Lerna the Grekes fen,
That was engendred then;
   By Chemeras flames,
And all the dedly names
Of infernall posty,   65
Where soules frye and rosty;
   By the Stygiall flood,
And the streames wood
Of Cocytus botumles well;
   By the feryman of hell,   70
Caron with his beerd hore,
That roweth with a rude ore
And with his frounsid fore top
Gideth his bote with a prop:
   I conjure Philip, and call   75
In the name of king Saul;
Primo Regum expresse,
He bad the Phytonesse
To witchcraft her to dresse,
And by her abusions,   80
And dampnable illusions
Of marveilus conclusions,
And by her supersticions,
And wonderfull conditions,
She raised up in that stede   85
Samuell that was dede;
But whether it were so,

---

60 *brent,* burned   65 *posty,* power
66 *rosty,* roast   68 *wood,* raging
73 *frounsid fore top,* wrinkled forehead   79 *dresse,* apply
80 *abusions,* deceits   81 *dampnable,* damnable

He were *idem in numero*,
The selfe same Samuell,
How be it to Saull did he tell   90
The Philistinis shuld him ascry,
And the next day he shuld die,
I will my selfe discharge
To lettred men at large:
   But, Philip, I conjure thee   95
Now by these names thre,
Diana in the woodes grene,
Luna that so bright doth shene,
Procerpina in hell,
That thou shortly tell,   100
And shew now unto me
What the cause may be
Of this perplexite!

Inferias, Philippe, tuas Scroupe pulchra Joanna
Instanter petiit: cur nostri carminis illam   105
Nunc pudet? est sero; minor est infamia vero.

   Than suche as have disdained
And of this worke complained,
I pray God they be pained
No worse than is contained   110
In verses two or thre
That folowe as you may se.

Luride, cur, livor, volucris pia funera damnas?
Talia te rapiant rapiunt quae fata volucrem!
   Est tamen invidia mors tibi continua.   115

---

91 *ascry,* challenge to fight
98 *shene,* shine

from *Speak, Parrot*

Lectoribus auctor recipit opusculi huius auxesim.
Crescet in immensum me vivo pagina praesens;
Hinc mea dicetur Skeltonidis aurea fama.

[*Parrot's Soliloquy*]

PARROT

My name is Parrot, a bird of paradise,
   By nature devised of a wonderous kinde,   5
Dientely dieted with divers dilicate spice,
   Til Euphrates, that flode, driveth me into Inde;
   Where men of that countrey by fortune me find,
And send me to greate ladies of estate:
Than Parot must have an almon or a date;

A cage curiously carven, with silver pin,   10
   Properly painted, to be my covertoure;
A mirrour of glasse, that I may toote therin;
   These maidens ful mekely with many a divers flowre
   Freshly they dresse and make swete my bowre,
With, Speke, Parrot, I pray you, full curtesly they
     say;   15
Parrot is a goodly bird, a prety popagey:

With my becke bent, my littil wanton eye,
   My fedders freshe as is the emraude grene,
About my neck a circulet like the riche rubye,
   My littill leggis, my feet both fete and clene,   20

6 *dientely,* daintily	12 *toote,* gaze
16 *popagey,* popinjay	17 *becke bent,* curved beak
18 *fedders,* feathers; *emraude,* emerald	20 *fete,* neat

I am a minion to wait uppon a quene;
My proper Parrot, my littil prety foole;
With ladies I lerne, and go with them to scole.

Hagh, ha, ha, Parrot, ye can laugh pretily!
    Parrot hath not dined of al this long day: 25
Like your pus cate, Parrot can mute and cry
    In Lattin, in Ebrew, Araby, and Caldey;
    In Greke tong Parrot can bothe speke and say,
As Percius, that poet, doth reporte of me,
Quis expedivit psittaco suum chaire?   30

Douse French of Parrise Parrot can lerne,
    Pronounsinge my purpose after my properte,
With, *Perliez bien,* Parrot, *ou perlez rien;*
    With Douch, with Spanish, my tong can agre;
    In English to God Parrot can supple,   35
Crist save King Henry the VIII, our royall king,
The red rose in honour to florish and springe!

With Katerine incomparable, our riall quene also,
    That pereles pomegarnet, Christ save her noble grace!
Parrot, *saves hablar Castiliano,*   40
    With *fidasso de cosso* in Turkey and in Trace;
    Vis consilii expers, as techith me Horace,
Mole ruit sua, whose dictes ar pregnaunte,
Soventez fois, Parrot, *en sovenaunte.*

My lady maistres, dame Philology,   45
    Gave me a gifte in my nest whan I laye,
To lerne all language, and it to spake aptely:
    Now *pandez mory,* wax franticke, some men saye;
    Phroneses for Freneses may not holde her way.

---

22 *proper,* excellent   26 *pus cate,* pussycat; *mute,* mew
31 *douse,* soft   32 *after my properte,* according to my character
35 *supple,* pray   38 *riall,* royal
39 *pereles,* peerless; *pomegarnet,* pomegranate   43 *dictes,* sayings
45 *maistres,* mistress

An almon now for Parrot, dilicatly drest;   50
In *Salve festa dies, toto* their doth best.

Moderata iuvant, but *toto* doth excede;
    Discression is moder of noble vertues all;
Miden agan in Greke tonge we rede;
    But reason and wit wantith their provinciall   55
    When wilfulnes is vicar generall.
Haec res acu tangitur, Parrot, *par ma foy:*
Ticez vous, Parrot, *tenez vous coye.*

Besy, besy, besy, and besines againe!
    Que pensez voz, Parrot? what meneth this besi-
        nes?   60
Vitulus in Oreb troubled Arons braine,
    Melchisedeck mercifull made Moloc merciles;
    To wise is no vertue, to medling, to restles;
In mesure is tresure, *cum sensu maturato;*
Ne tropo sanno, ne tropo mato.   65

Aram was fired with Caldies fier called Ur;
    Jobab was brought up in the lande of Hus;
The linage of Lot toke supporte of Assur;
    Jereboseth is Ebrue, who list the cause discus.
    Peace, Parrot, ye prate, as ye were *ebrius:*   70
Houst thee, *Liver God van Hemrick, ic seg;*
In Popering grew peres, whan Parrot was an eg.

What is this to purpose? Over in a whinny Meg!
    Hop Lobin of Loudeon wald have e bit of bred;
The jebet of Baldock was made for Jack Leg;   75
    An arrow unfethered and without an hed,

---

50 *drest,* prepared   53 *moder,* mother
55 *provinciall,* synod   63 *to,* too
71 *houst,* hush   72 *peres,* pears
73 *over . . . Meg,* ? the first line of a ballad
74 *e, a:* this is also probably a phrase from a ballad
75 *jebet,* gibbet

A bagpipe without blowinge standeth in no sted:
Some run to far before, some run to far behinde,
Some be to churlisshe, and some be to kinde.

Ic dien serveth for the erstrich fether,   80
   Ic dien is the language of the land of Beme;
In Affric tongue *byrsa* is a thonge of lether;
   In Palestina there is Jerusalem.
   Colostrum now for Parot, white bred and swete
     creme!
Our Thomasen she doth trip, our Jenet she doth
     shaile: 85
Parrot hath a blacke beard and a faire grene taile.

Morishe mine owne shelfe, the costermonger saith;
   Fate, fate, fate, ye Irish waterlag;
In flattring fables men finde but littil faith:
   But *moveatur terra*, let the world wag;   90
   Let sir Wrigwrag wrastell with sir Delarag;
Every man after his maner of wayes,
Paube une arver, so the Welche man sayes.

Suche shredis of sentence, strowed in the shop
   Of auncient Aristippus and such other mo,   95
I gader togither and close in my crop,
   Of my wanton conseit, *unde depromo*
   Dilemmata docta in paedagogio
Sacro vatum, whereof to you I breke:
I pray you, let Parot have liberte to speke.   100

But ware the cat, Parot, ware the fals cat!
   With, Who is there? a maid? nay, nay, I trow:

78 *to*, too   80 *erstrich*, ostrich
81 *Beme*, Bohemia   85 *shaile*, limp
87 *Morishe*, Morris; *shelfe*, self   88 *fate*, ? cask; *waterlag*, water-carter
94 *sentence*, sense   95 *mo*, more
96 *gader*, gather   97 *conseit*, i.e., thoughts
99 *breke*, impart

Ware riat, Parrot, ware riot, ware that!
  Mete, mete for Parrot, mete, I say, how!
    Thus divers of language by lerning I grow: 105
With, Bas me, swete Parrot, bas me, swete swete;
To dwell among ladies Parrot is mete.

Parrot, Parrot, Parrot, praty popigay!
  With my beke I can pike my littel praty too;
My delight is solas, pleasure, disporte, and pley;   110
  Like a wanton, whan I will, I rele to and froo:
    Parot can say, *Caesar, ave,* also;
But Parrot hath no favour to Esebon:
Above all other birdis, set Parrot alone.

Ulula, Esebon, for Jeromy doth wepe!   115
  Sion is in sadnes, Rachell ruly doth loke;
Madionita Jetro, our Moises kepith his shepe;
  Gedeon is gon, that Zalmane undertoke,
    Oreb *et* Zeb, of *Judicum* rede the boke;
Now Geball, Amon, and Amaloch,—harke, harke!   120
Parrot pretendith to be a bibill clarke.

O Esebon, Esebon! to thee is cum againe
  Seon, the regent *Amorraeorum,*
And Og, that fat hog of Basan, doth retaine,
  The crafty *coistronus Cananaeorum;*   125
    And *asylum,* whilom *refugium miserorum,*
Non fanum, sed profanum, standith in littill sted:
Ulula, Esebon, for Jepte is starke ded!

Esebon, Marybon, Wheston next Barnet;
  A trim tram for an horse-mill it were a nise
        thing;   130

---

106 *bas,* kiss	108 *praty,* pretty
109 *pike,* peck	110 *solas,* amusement
111 *rele,* prance	116 *ruly,* ruefully
121 *pretendith,* professes; *bibill clarke,* Bible clerk	126 *whilom,* once
130 *tram,* cart shaft; *nise,* foolish	

Deintes for dammoisels, chaffer far fet:
   Bo-ho doth bark wel, but Hough-ho he rulith the
      ring;
   From Scarpary to Tartary renown therin doth spring,
With, He said, and we said, ich wot now what ich wot,
Quod magnus est dominus Judas Scariot.   135

Tholomye and Haly were cunning and wise
   In the volvell, in the quadrant, and in the astroloby,
To pronosticate truly the chaunce of fortunis dise;
   Som trete of their tirikis, som of astrology,
   Som *pseudo-propheta* with chiromancy: 140
If fortune be frendly, and grace be the guide,
Honoure with renowne will ren on that side.

          Monon calon agaton
          Quod Parato
          In Graeco.   145

Let Parrot, I pray you, have liberte to prate,
   For *aurea lingua Graeca* ought to be magnified,
If it were cond perfitely, and after the rate
   As *lingua Latina* in scole matter occupied;
   But our Grekis their Greke so well have applied,   150
That they cannot say in Greke, ridinge by the way,
How, hosteler, fetche my hors a botell of hay!

Neither frame a sylogisme in *phrisesomorum,*
   Formaliter et Graece, cum medio termino:
Our Grekis ye walow in the washbol *Argolicorum;*   155
   For though ye can tell in Greke what is *phormio,*
   Yet ye seke out your Greke in *Capricornio;*

131 *deintes,* dainties; *chaffer far fet,* merchandise fetched from afar
134 *ich wot,* I know   137 *volvell,* volvellum
138 *dise,* dice   139 *tirikis,* ? obscure
142 *ren,* run   144 *quod,* quoth
148 *cond,* studied; *perfitely,* skilfully; *after the rate,* in proportion
152 *botell,* bundle   155 *washbol,* washtub

For they scrape out good scripture, and set in a gall,
Ye go about to amende, and ye mare all.

Some argue *secundum quid ad simpliciter,*   160
    And yet he wolde be rekenid *pro Areopagita;*
And some make distinctions *multipliciter,*
    Whether *ita* were before *non,* or *non* before *ita,*
    Nether wise nor wel lernid, but like *hermaphrodita:*
Set *sophia* aside, for every Jack Raker   165
And every mad medler must now be a maker.

In Academia Parrot dare no probleme kepe;
    For *Graece fari* so occupieth the chaire,
That *Latinum fari* may fall to rest and slepe,
    And *syllogisari* was drowned at Sturbridge faire;   170
    Trivials and quatrivials so sore now they appaire,
That Parrot the popagay hath pitye to beholde
How the rest of good lerning is roufled up and trold.

Albertus de modo significandi,
    And *Donatus* be driven out of scole;   175
Prisians hed broken now handy dandy,
    And *Inter didascolos* is rekened for a fole;
    Alexander, a gander of Menanders pole,
With *Da Conciles,* is cast out of the gate,
And *Da Rationales* dare not shew his pate.   180

Plauti in his comedies a child shall now reherse,
    And medill with Quintilian in his Declamacions,
That Pety Caton can scantly construe a verse,
    With *Aveto in Graeco,* and such solempne salutacions,

158 *gall,* sore spot   159 *mare,* mar
166 *maker,* poet
170 *trivials and quatrivials,* i.e., divisions of the liberal arts; *appaire,*
    decay   173 *roufled up,* confused; *trold,* knocked down
176 *Prisians,* Priscian's   177 *fole,* fool
178 *pole,* pool   182 *medill,* meddle
183 *Pety Cato,* Little Cato, a textbook; *scantly,* hardly

Can scantly the tensis of his conjugacions;   185
Settinge their mindis so moche of eloquens,
That of their scole maters lost is the hole sentens.

Now a nutmeg, a nutmeg, *cum garyophyllo,*
    For Parrot to pike upon, his braine for to stable,
Swete sinamum stickis and *pleris cum musco!*   190
    In Paradice, that place of pleasure perdurable,
    The progeny of Parrottis were faire and favorable;
Now *in valle* Ebron Parrot is faine to fede:
Cristecrosse and saint Nicholas, Parrot, be your good
    spede!

The mirrour that I tote in, *quasi diaphanum,*   195
    Vel quasi speculum, in aenigmate,
Elencticum, or elss *enthymematicum,*
    For logicions to loke on, somewhat *sophistice:*
    Retoricions and oratours in freshe humanite,
Support Parrot, I pray you, with your suffrage
    ornate,   200
Of *confuse tantum* avoidinge the chekmate.

But of that supposicion that callid is arte
    Confuse distributive, as Parrot hath devised,
Let every man after his merit take his parte,
    For in this processe Parrot nothing hath surmised,   205
    No matter pretendid, nor nothing enterprised,
But that *metaphora, allegoria* with all,
Shall be his protection, his pavis, and his wall.

For Parot is no churlish chough, nor no flekid pye,
    Parrot is no pendugum, that men call a carling,   210

185 *can,* knows   187 *hole sentens,* whole meaning
189 *pike,* peck   190 *sinamum,* cinnamon
191 *perdurable,* everlasting   195 *tote,* gaze
199 *humanite,* learning   200 *suffrage,* support
202 *sopposicion,* basis for argument
205 *processe,* i.e., field; *surmised,* alleged   206 *pretendid,* undertaken
208 *pavis,* shield   209 *pye,* magpie

Parrot is no woodecocke, nor no butterfly,
   Parrot is no stamering stare, that men call a starling;
   But Parot is my owne dere harte and my dere derling;
Melpomene, that faire maide, she burneshed his beke:
I pray you, let Parrot have liberte to speke.   215

Parrot is a faire bird for a lady;
   God of his goodnes him framed and wrought;
When Parrot is ded, she dothe not putrefy:
   Ye, all thing mortall shall torne unto nought,
   Except mannes soule, that Christ so dere bought;   220
That never may die, nor never die shall:
Make moche of Parrot, the popegay riall.

For that pereles prince that Parrot did create,
   He made you of nothinge by his magistye:
Point well this probleme that Parrot doth prate,   225
   And remembre amonge how Parrot and ye
   Shall lepe from this life, as mery as we be;
Pompe, pride, honour, riches, and worldly lust,
Parrot saith plainly, shall tourne all to dust.

       Thus Parrot dothe pray you   230
         With hert most tender,
       To rekin with this recule now,
         And it to remember.

Psittacus, ecce, cano, nec sunt mea carmina Phoebo
   Digna scio, tamen est plena camena deo.   235

     Secundum Skeltonida famigeratum,
     In Piereorum catalogo numeratum.

Itaque consolamini invicem in verbis istis, etc.
Candidi lectores, callide callete; vestrum fovete Psitta-
        cum, etc.

                       (Lines 1–239)

210 *pendugum,* ? penguin; *carling,* ? witch   212 *stare,* starling
222 *riall,* royal   226 *amonge,* meanwhile
232 *recule,* collection of verses

FROM *The Garland of Laurel*

TO MISTRESS ISABELL PENNELL

By saint Mary, my lady,
Your mammy and your dady
Brought forth a godely baby!
   My maiden Isabell,
Reflaring rosabell,   5
The flagrant camamell;
   The ruddy rosary,
The soveraine rosemary,
The praty strawbery;
   The columbine, the nepte,   10
The jeloffer well set,
The propre violet;
   Enuwid your coloure
Is like the dasy flowre
After the Aprill showre;   15
   Sterre of the morow gray,
The blossom on the spray,
The fresshest flowre of May;
   Maidenly demure,
Of womanhode the lure;   20
Wherfore I make you sure,
   It were an hevenly helth,
It were an endeles welth,
A life for God himselfe,

5: redolent rose   6: the ardent camomile
7 *rosary*, rosebush   9 *praty*, pretty
10 *nepte*, catnip   11 *jeloffer*, gillyflower
12 *propre*, excellent   13 *enuwid*, tinted
16 *sterre*, star; *morow*, morning

To here this nightingale,   25
Amonge the birdes smale,
Warbelinge in the vale,
Dug, dug,
Jug, jug,
Good yere and good luk,   30
With chuk, chuk, chuk, chuk!

(Lines 973–1003)

II. TO MISTRESS MARGARET HUSSEY

Mirry Margaret,
As midsomer flowre,
Jentill as faucoun
Or hawke of the towre;
  With solace and gladnes,   5
Moche mirthe and no madnes,
All good and no badnes,
So joyously,
So maidenly,
So womanly   10
Her demening
In every thinge,
Far, far passinge
That I can endight,
Or suffice to wright   15
Of mirry Margarete,
As midsomer flowre,
Jentill as facoun
Or hawke of the towre;
  As pacient and as still,   20
And as full of good will,

---

3 *faucoun,* falcon   5 *solace,* delight
6 *moche,* much   11 *demening,* demeanor
14 *endight,* endite   15 *wright,* write

As faire Ysaphill;
Coliaunder,
Swete pomaunder,
Good Cassaunder;   25
Stedfast of thought,
Wele made, wele wrought;
Far may be sought
Erst that ye can finde
So corteise, so kinde   30
As mirry Margarete,
This midsomer flowre,
Jentill as faucoun
Or hawke of the towre.

(*Lines 1004–1037*)

Anonymous Lyrics and Songs

Westron winde, when will thou blow?

Westron winde, when will thou blow,
The smalle raine downe can raine?
Crist, if my love wer in my armis,
And I in my bed againe.

Benedicite, what dremid I this night?

Benedicite, what dremid I this night?
Methought the worlde was turnid up-so-downe:
The son, the moone had lost ther force and light;
The see also drownid both towre and towne;
Yett more mervell how that I hard the soune   5
Of onis voice saying, "Bere in thy mind
Thy lady hath forgoten to be kind."

To complaine me, alas, why shulde I so?
For my complaint it did me nevir good,
But by constraint now must I shew my woo   10
To her only which is min ÿes fode,
Trusting sum time that she will chaunge her mode,
And lett me not allway be guerdonless,
Sith for my trouth she nedith no wittness.

5 *soune,* sound   6 *onis,* one's
11 *ijes fode,* eyes' food   14 *sith,* since; *trouth,* fidelity

426

Alas, it is I that wote nott what to say, 15
Forwhy I stond as he that is abusid;
Ther as I trusted, I was late cast away,
And no cause gevin to be so refusid.
But pite it is that trust shulde be misusid
Other by colour or by fals semblaunce; 20
Wher that is usid can be no suraunce.
I am he that hath you daily servid,
Thow I be litill in your remembraunce,
And mervell I have sith I not deservid
To be put oute of your good governaunce. 25

15 *wote,* know   16 *forwhy,* because; *abusid,* mistreated
20 *other,* either; *colour,* pretext
21 *is usid,* i.e., occurs; *suraunce,* confidence

Who shall have my faire lady?

Who shall have my faire lady?
Who shall have my faire lady?
Who but I, who but I, who but I?
Under the levis grene!

The fairest man 5
That best love can,
Dandirly, dandirly,
Dandirly, dan,
Under the levis grene.

The maidens came

The maidens came
When I was in my mothers bower.
I hade all that I wolde.

The baily berith the bell away,
The lilly, the rose, the rose I lay,   5
The silver is whit, red is the golde,
The robes thay lay in fold;
The baily berith the bell away,
The lilly, the rose, the rose I lay;
And through the glasse window   10
Shines the sone.
How shuld I love and I so young?
The baily berith the bell away,
The lilly, the rose, the rose I lay.

For to report it were now tedius: 15
We will therfor now sing no more
Of the games joyus.
Right mighty and famus
  Elizabeth, our quen princis,
  Prepotent and eke victorius,   20
  Vertuos and bening,
  Lett us pray all
  To Christ Eternall,
  Which is the hevenly King,
After ther liff grant them   25
A place eternally to sing. Amen.

4: The bailiff carries the prize away   21 *bening*, benign

A Lyke-Wake Dirge

This ae nighte, this ae nighte,
  Every night and alle,
Fire, and sleete, and candle lighte,
  And Christe receive thye saule.

When thou from hence away are paste,
  Every night and alle,
To Whinny-muir thou comest at laste,
  And Christe receive thye saule.

If ever thou gavest hosen and shoon,
  Every night and alle,
Sit thee down and put them on,
  And Christe receive thye saule.

If hosen and shoon thou ne'er gavest nane,
  Every night and alle,
The whinnes shall pricke thee to the bare bane,
  And Christe receive thye saule.

From Whinny-muir when thou mayst passe,
  Every night and alle,
To Brigg o' Dread thou comest at laste,
  And Christe receive thye saule.

From Brigg o' Dread when thou mayst passe,
  Every night and alle,
To purgatory fire thou comest at laste,
  And Christe receive thye saule.

If ever thou gavest meat or drink
  Every night and alle,
The fire shall never make thee shrinke,
  And Christe receive thye saule.

If meate or drinke thou never gavest nane,
  Every night and alle,
The fire will burn thee to the bare bane,
  And Christe receive thye saule.

This ae nighte, this ae nighte,
  Every night and alle,
Fire, and sleete, and candle lighte,
  And Christe receive thye saule.

To-morrow shall be my dancing day

To-morrow shall be my dancing day,
　　I would my true love did so chance
To see the legend of my play,
　　To call my true love to my dance.
Sing, oh! my love, oh! my love, my love, my love,
This have I done for my true love.

Then was I born of a Virgin pure,
　　Of her I took fleshly substance;
Thus was I knit to man's nature,
　　To call my true love to my dance.
Sing, oh! etc.

In a manger laid and wrapp'd I was,
　　So very poor, this was my chance,
Betwixt an ox and a silly poor ass,
　　To call my true love to my dance.

Then afterwards baptized I was,
　　The Holy Ghost on me did glance,
My Father's voice heard from above,
　　To call my true love to my dance.

Into the desert I was led,
　　Where I fasted without substance;
The Devil bade me make stones my bread,
　　To have me break my true love's dance.

The Jews on me they made great suit,
　　And with me made great variance,
Because they lov'd darkness rather than light,
　　To call my true love to my dance.

For thirty pence Judas me sold,
　His covetousness for to advance;
Mark whom I kiss, the same do hold,
　The same is he shall lead the dance.

Before Pilate the Jews me brought,
　Where Barabbas had deliverance,
They scourg'd me and set me at nought,
　Judged me to die to lead the dance.

Then on the cross hanged I was,
　Where a spear to my heart did glance;
There issued forth both water and blood,
　To call my true love to my dance.

Then down to Hell I took my way
　For my true love's deliverance,
And rose again on the third day
　Up to my true love and the dance.

Then up to Heaven I did ascend,
　Where now I dwell in sure substance,
On the right hand of God, that man
　May come unto the general dance.

(*As printed in Sandys' Christmas Carols, London, 1833*)

Anonymous Ballads

The Wife of Usher's Well

There lived a wife at Usher's Well,
    And a wealthy wife was she;
She had three stout and stalwart sons,
    And sent them oer the sea.

They hadna been a week from her,
    A week but barely ane,
Whan word came to the carlin wife
    That her three sons were gane.

They hadna been a week from her,
    A week but barely three,
Whan word came to the carlin wife
    That her sons she'd never see.

"I wish the wind may never cease,
    Nor fashes in the flood,
Till my three sons come hame to me,
    In earthly flesh and blood."

It fell about the Martinmass,
    When nights are lang and mirk,
The carlin wife's three sons came hame,
    And their hats were o the birk.

It neither grew in syke nor ditch,
    Nor yet in ony sheugh;
But at the gates o Paradise,
    That birk grew fair eneugh.

"Blow up the fire, my maidens,
    Bring water from the well;
For a' my house shall feast this night,
    Since my three sons are well."

And she has made to them a bed,
    She's made it large and wide,
And she's taen her mantle her about,
    Sat down at the bed-side.

Up then crew the red, red cock,
    And up and crew the gray;
The eldest to the youngest said,
    " 'T is time we were away."

The cock he hadna crawd but once,
    And clappd his wings at a',
When the youngest to the eldest said,
    "Brother, we must awa.

"The cock doth craw, the day doth daw;
    The channerin worm doth chide;
Gin we be mist out o our place,
    A sair pain we maun bide.

"Fare ye weel, my mother dear!
    Fareweel to barn and byre!
And fare ye weel, the bonny lass
    That kindles my mother's fire!"

Edward

"Why dois your brand sae drap wi bluid,
        Edward, Edward,
Why dois your brand sae drap wi bluid,

And why sae sad gang yee O?"
"O I hae killed my hauke sae guid,
        Mither, mither,
O I hae killed my hauke sae guid,
   And I had nae mair bot hee O."

"Your haukis bluid was nevir sae reid,
        Edward, Edward,
Your haukis bluid was nevir sae reid,
   My deir son I tell thee O."
"O I hae killed my reid-roan steid,
        Mither, mither,
O I hae killed my reid-roan steid,
   That erst was sae fair and frie O."

"Your steid was auld, and ye hae gat mair,
        Edward, Edward,
Your steid was auld, and ye hae gat mair,
   Sum other dule ye drie O."
"O I hae killed my fadir deir,
        Mither, mither,
O I hae killed my fadir deir,
   Alas, and wae is mee O!"

"And whatten penance wul ye drie for that,
        Edward, Edward?
And whatten penance will ye drie for that?
   My deir son, now tell me O."
"Ile set my feit in yonder boat,
        Mither, mither,
Ile set my feit in yonder boat,
   And Ile fare ovir the sea O."

"And what wul ye doe wi your towirs and your ha,
        Edward, Edward?
And what wul ye doe wi your towirs and your ha,
   That were sae fair to see O?"

"Ile let thame stand tul they doun fa,
  Mither, mither,
Ile let thame stand tul they doun fa,
  For here nevir mair maun I bee O."

"And what wul ye leive to your bairns and your wife,
  Edward, Edward?
And what wul ye leive to your bairns and your wife,
  Whan ye gang ovir the sea O?"
"The warldis room, late them beg thrae life,
  Mither, mither,
The warldis room, late them beg thrae life,
  For thame nevir mair wul I see O."

"And what wul ye leive to your ain mither deir,
  Edward, Edward?
And what wul ye leive to your ain mither deir?
  My deir son, now tell me O."
"The curse of hell frae me sall ye beir,
  Mither, mither,
The curse of hell frae me sall ye beir,
  Sic counseils ye gave to me O."

The Unquiet Grave

"The wind doth blow today, my love,
  And a few small drops of rain;
I never had but one true-love,
  In cold grave she was lain.

"I'll do as much for my true-love
  As any young man may;
I'll sit and mourn all at her grave
  For a twelvemonth and a day."

The twelvemonth and a day being up,
   The dead began to speak:
"Oh who sits weeping on my grave,
   And will not let me sleep?"

"'Tis I, my love, sits on your grave,
   And will not let you sleep;
For I crave one kiss of your clay-cold lips,
   And that is all I seek."

"You crave one kiss of my clay-cold lips;
   But my breath smells earthy strong;
If you have one kiss of my clay-cold lips,
   Your time will not be long.

"'Tis down in yonder garden green,
   Love, where we used to walk,
The finest flower that e'er was seen
   Is withered to a stalk.

"The stalk is withered dry, my love,
   So will our hearts decay;
So make yourself content, my love,
   Till God calls you away."

Sir Patrick Spens

The king sits in Dumferling toune,
   Drinking the blude-reid wine:
"O whar will I get guid sailor,
   To sail this schip of mine."

Up and spak an eldern knicht,
   Sat at the kings richt kne:

"Sir Patrick Spens is the best sailor
   That sails upon the se."

The king has written a braid letter,
   And signd it wi his hand,
And sent it to Sir Patrick Spens,
   Was walking on the sand.

The first line that Sir Patrick red,
   A loud lauch lauched he;
The next line that Sir Patrick red,
   The teir blinded his ee.

"O wha is this has don this deid,
   This ill deid don to me,
To send me out this time o' the yeir,
   To sail upon the se!

"Mak hast, mak haste, my mirry men all,
   Our guid schip sails the morne":
"O say na sae, my master deir,
   For I feir a deadlie storme.

"Late late yestreen I saw the new moone,
   Wi the auld moone in hir arme,
And I feir, I feir, my deir master,
   That we will cum to harme."

O our Scots nobles wer richt laith
   To weet their cork-heild schoone:
Bot lang owre a' the play wer playd,
   Thair hats they swam aboone.

O lang, lang may their ladies sit,
   Wi thair fans into their hand,
Or eir they se Sir Patrick Spens
   Cum sailing to the land.

O lang, lang may the ladies stand,
   Wi thair gold kems in thair hair,
Waiting for thair ain deir lords,
   For they'll se thame na mair.

Haf owre, haf owre to Aberdour,
   It's fiftie fadom deip,
And thair lies guid Sir Patrick Spens,
   Wi the Scots lords at his feit.

The Three Ravens

There were three ravens sat on a tree
   Downe a downe, hay down, hay downe
There were three ravens sat on a tree,
   With a downe
There were three ravens sat on a tree,
They were as blacke as they might be.
   With a downe derrie, derrie, derrie, downe, downe

The one of them said to his mate,
"Where shall we our breakefast take?"

"Downe in yonder greene field,
There lies a knight slain under his shield.

"His hounds they lie downe at his feete,
So well they can their master keepe.

"His haukes they flie so eagerly,
There's no fowle dare him come nie."

Downe there comes a fallow doe,
As great with yong as she might goe.

She lift up his bloudy hed,
And kist his wounds that were so red.

She got him up upon her backe,
And carried him to earthen lake.

She buried him before the prime,
She was dead herselfe ere even-song time.

God send every gentleman,
Such haukes, such hounds, and such a leman.

The Laily Worm and the Machrel
of the Sea

"I was bat seven year alld
  Fan my mider she did dee,
My father marrëd the ae warst woman
  The wardle did ever see.

"For she has made me the lailly worm
  That lays att the fitt of the tree,
An o my sister Meassry
  The machrel of the sea.

"An every Saterday att noon
  The machrl comes to me,
An she takes my laylë head,
  An lays it on her knee,
An keames it we a silver kemm,
  An washes it in the sea.

"Seven knights ha I slain
  Sane I lay att the fitt of the tree;
An ye war na my ain father,
  The eight an ye sud be."

"Sing on your song, ye laily worm,
  That ye sung to me";

"I never sung that song
But fatt I wad sing to ye.

"I was but seven year aull
Fan my mider she did dee,
My father marrëd the a warst woman
The wardle did ever see.

"She changed me to the layely worm
That layes att the fitt of the tree,
An my sister Messry
To the makrell of the sea.

"And every Saterday att noon
The machrell comes to me,
An she takes my layly head,
An layes it on her knee,
An kames it weth a siller kame,
An washes it in the sea.

"Seven knights ha I slain
San I lay att the fitt of the tree;
An ye war na my ain father,
The eight ye sud be."

He sent for his lady
As fast as sen cod he:
"Far is my son,
That ye sent fra me,
And my daughter,
Lady Messry?"

"Yer son is att our king's court,
Sarving for meatt an fee,
And yer daughter is att our quin's court,
A mary suit an free."

"Ye lee, ye ill woman,
Sa loud as I hear ye lea,

For my son is the layelly worm
    That lays at the fitt of the tree,
An my daughter Messry
    The machrell of the sea."

She has tain a silver wan
    An gine him stroks three,
An he started up the bravest knight
    Your eyes did ever see.

She has tane a small horn
    An loud an shill blue she,
An a' the fish came her tell but the proud machrell,
    An she stood by the sea:
"Ye shaped me ance an unshemly shape,
    An ye's never mare shape me."

He has sent to the wood
    For hathorn an fun,
An he has tane that gay lady,
    An ther he did her burne.

The Riddling Knight

There were three sisters fair and bright,
    Jennifer gentle and rosemaree,
And they three loved one valiant knight.
    As the dew flies over the mulberry tree.

The eldest sister let him in,
And barred the door with a silver pin.

The second sister made his bed,
And placed soft pillows under his head.

The youngest sister, fair and bright,
Was resolved for to wed with this valiant knight.

"And if you can answer questions three,
O then, fair maid, I will marry with thee.

"What is louder than an horn,
And what is sharper than a thorn?"

"Thunder is louder than an horn,
And hunger is sharper than a thorn."

"What is broader than the way,
And what is deeper than the sea?"

"Love is broader than the way,
And hell is deeper than the sea."

.   .   .

"And now, fair maid, I will marry with thee."

Sir Thomas Wyatt

(1503?–1542)

Who so list to hount

Who so list to hount, I knowe where is an hynde,
 But as for me, helas, I may no more:
 The vayne travaill hath weried me so sore.
 I ame of theim that farthest commeth behinde;
Yet may I by no meanes my weried mynde
 Drawe from the Diere: but as she fleeth afore,
Faynting I folowe. I leve of therefore,
 Sins in a nett I seke to hold the wynde.
Who list her hount, I put him owte of dowbte,
 As well as I may spend his tyme in vain:
 And, graven with Diamonds, in letters plain
There is written her faier neck rounde abowte:
 Noli me tangere, for Cesars I ame;
 And wylde for to hold, though I seme tame.

The Lover Compareth His State to a Shippe in Perilous Storme Tossed on the Sea

My galy charged with forgetfulnes
 Thorrough sharpe sees in wynter nyghtes doeth pas
 Twene Rock and Rock; and eke myn ennemy, Alas,
 That is my lorde, sterith with cruelnes;

443

And every owre a thought in redines,
  As tho that deth were light in suche a case.
  An endles wynd doeth tere the sayll apase
  Of forced sightes and trusty ferefulnes.
A rayn of teris, a clowde of derk disdain,
  Hath done the wered cordes great hinderaunce;
  Wrethed with errour and eke with ignoraunce.
The starres be hid that led me to this pain;
  Drowned is reason that should me consort,
  And I remain dispering of the port.

The Lover Sheweth How He Is Forsaken of Such as He Sometime Enjoyed

They fle from me that sometyme did me seke
  With naked fote stalking in my chambre.
I have sene theim gentill tame and meke
  That nowe are wyld and do not remembre
  That sometyme they put theimself in daunger
To take bred at my hand; and nowe they raunge
Besely seking with a continuell chaunge.

Thancked be fortune, it hath ben othrewise
  Twenty tymes better; but ons in speciall,
In thyn arraye after a pleasaunt gyse,
  When her lose gowne from her shoulders did fall,
  And she me caught in her armes long and small;
Therewithall swetely did me kysse,
And softely saide, *dere hert, howe like you this?*

It was no dreme: I lay brode waking.
  But all is torned thorough my gentilnes
Into a straunge fasshion of forsaking;

And I have leve to goo of her goodenes,
And she also to use new fangilnes.
But syns that I so kyndely ame served,
I would fain knowe what she hath deserved.

Ys yt possyble

Ys yt possyble
That so hye debate,
So sharpe, so sore, and off suche rate,
Shuld end so sone and was begone so late?
Is it possyble?

Ys yt possyble
So cruell intent,
So hastly hete and so sone spent,
Ffrom love to hate, and thens ffor to Relent?
Is it possyble?

Ys yt possible
That eny may fynde
Within on hert so dyverse mynd,
To change or torne as wether and wynd?
Is it possyble?

Is it possyble
To spye yt in an Iye
That tornys as oft as chance on dy?
The trothe whereoff can eny try?
Is it possyble?

It is possyble
Ffor to torne so oft,
To bryng that lowyste that wasse most aloft,

And to fall hyest yet to lyght sofft:
    It is possyble.

All ys possyble,
    Who so lyst beleve;
Trust therefore fyrst, and after preve:
As men wedd ladyes by lycence and leve,
    All ys possyble.

What shulde I saye

What shulde I saye
    Sins faithe is dede,
And truthe awaye
    From you ys fled?
    Shulde I be led
With doblenesse?
Naye, naye, mistresse!

I promiside you
    And you promisid me
To be as true
    As I wolde bee;
    But sins I se
Your doble herte,
Farewell my perte!

Though for to take
    Yt ys not my minde
But to forsake—
    I am not blind—
    And as I finde
So will I truste.
Farewell, unjuste!

Can ye saye naye?
But you saide
That I allwaye
Shulde be obeide;
And thus betraide
Or that I wiste—
Fare well, unkiste!

The Lover Complayneth the Unkindness of His Love

My lute awake! perfourme the last
Labor that thou and I shall wast,
  And end that I have now begon;
For when this song is sung and past,
  My lute be still, for I have done.

As to be herd where ere is none,
As lede to grave in marbill stone,
  My song may perse her hert as sone;
Should we then sigh, or syng, or mone?
  No, no, my lute, for I have done.

The Rokkes do not so cruelly
Repulse the waves continuelly,
  As she my suyte and affection,
So that I ame past remedy:
  Whereby my lute and I have done.

Prowd of the spoyll that thou hast gott
Of simple hertes thorough loves shot,
  By whome, unkynd, thou hast theim wone,
Thinck not he haith his bow forgot,
  All tho my lute and I have done.

Vengeaunce shall fall on thy disdain,
That makest but game on ernest pain;
   Thinck not alone under the sonne
Unquyt to cause thy lovers plain,
   All tho my lute and I have done.

Perchaunce the lye wethered and old,
The wynter nyghtes that are so cold,
   Playnyng in vain unto the mone;
Thy wisshes then dare not be told;
   Care then who lyst, for I have done.

And then may chaunce the to repent
The tyme that thou hast lost and spent
   To cause thy lovers sigh and swoune;
Then shalt thou knowe beaultie but lent,
   And wisshe and want as I have done.

Now cesse, my lute, this is the last
Labour that thou and I shall wast,
   And ended is that we begon;
Now is the song boeth sung and past:
   My lute be still, for I have done.

What no, perdy

What no, perdy, ye may be sure!
Thinck not to make me to your lure,
   With wordes and chere so contrarieng,
   Swete and sowre contrewaing;
To much it were still to endure.
Trouth is trayed where craft is in ure;
But though ye have had my hertes cure,
   Trow ye I dote withoute ending?
     What no, perdy!

Though that with pain I do procure
For to forgett that ons was pure,
   Within my hert shall still that thing,
   Unstable, unsure, and wavering,
Be in my mynde withoute recure?
     What no, perdy!

Perdye I saide yt not

Perdye I saide yt not
   Nor never thought to do,
As well as I ye wott
   I have no powre thereto;
And if I ded, the lott
   That first ded me enchaine
Do never slake the knott
   But strayt it to my payne.

And if I ded, eche thing
   That maye do harme or woo
Contynuallye maye wring
   My herte whereso I goo;
Reporte maye always ring
   Of shame of me for aye,
Yf yn my herte ded spring
   The worde that ye doo saye.

Yf I saide so, eche sterre
   That is yn heven above
Maye frowne on me to marre
   The hope I have yn love;
And if I ded, suche warre
   As they brought unto Troye

Bring all my lyf afarre
   From all this luste and joye.

And if I ded so saye,
   The bewtye that me bounde
Encresse from daye to daye
   More cruell to my wounde,
With all the mone that maye
   To playnte maye torne my song;
My lif maye sone dekaye
   Without redresse bye wrong.

Yf I be clere fro thought,
   Whye do ye then complaine?
Then ys this thing but sought
   To torne me to more payne.
Then that that ye have wrought
   Ye must yt now redresse;
Of right therefore ye ought
   Such Rigor to represse.

And as I have deservid,
   So graunte me nowe my hire;
Ye kno I never swervid,
   Ye never fownd me lyre.
For Rachell have I servid,
   (For Lya carid I never)
And her I have Reservid
   Within my herte for ever.

Deme as ye list uppon goode cause

Deme as ye list uppon goode cause
   I maye and think of this or that,
But what or whye my self best knowes,

Wherebye I thinck and fere not;
But there unto I maye well think
   The doubtefull sentence of this clause:
I wolde yt ware not as I think,
   I wolde I thought yt ware not.

Ffor if I thought yt ware not soo,
   Though yt ware so yt greved me not;
Unto my thought yt ware as tho
   I harkenid tho I here not.
At that I see I cannot wynk,
   Nor from mye thought so let it goo:
I wolde yt ware not as I think,
   I wolde I thought yt ware not.

Lo how my thought might make me free
   Of that perchaunce that nedeth nott;
Perchaunce no doubte the drede I see,
   I shrink at that I bere not;
But in my harte this worde shall sink
   Unto the proffe may better be:
I wolde yt ware not as I think,
   I wolde I thought yt ware not.

Yf yt be not, shewe no cause whye
   I shoulde so think, then care I not;
For I shall soo my self applie
   To bee that I apere not;
That is as one that shall not shrink
   To be your owne untill I dye:
And if yt be not as I think,
   Lyke wyse to think yt is not.

Stond who so list upon the Slipper toppe

Stond who so list upon the Slipper toppe
　Of courtes estates, and lett me heare rejoyce;
And use me quyet without lett or stoppe,
　　Unknowen in courte, that hath suche brackishe joyes:
　　　In hidden place, so lett my dayes forthe passe,
　　That when my yeares be done, withouten noyse,
　　　I may dye aged after the common trace.
For hym death greep' the right hard by the croppe
　　　That is moche knowen of other; and of him self alas,
　　　Doth dye unknowen, dazed with dreadfull face.

Satire I

Myne owne John Poynz, sins ye delight to know
　The cause why that homeward I me drawe,
　　And fle the presse of courtes wher soo they goo,
Rather then to lyve thrall, under the awe
　Of lordly lokes, wrappid within my cloke,
　　To will and lust learning to set a lawe;
It is not for becawse I skorne or moke
　The powar of them, to whome fortune hath lent
　Change over us, of Right, to strike the stroke:
But true it is that I have allwais ment
　Lesse to estime them then the common sort,
　Of outward thinges that juge in their intent,
Withowt regarde what dothe inwarde resort.
　I grawnt sumtime that of glorye the fyar

Dothe touche my hart: me lyst not to report
Blame by honour and honour to desyar.
But how may I this honour now atayne
That cannot dy the coloure blak a lyer?
My Poynz, I cannot frame me tune to fayne,
To cloke the trothe for praisse withowt desart,
Of them that lyst all vice for to retayne.
I cannot honour them that settes their part
With Venus and Baccus all theire lyf long;
Nor holld my pece of them allthoo I smart.
I cannot crowche nor knelle to do so grete a wrong,
To worship them, lyke gode on erthe alone,
That ar as wollffes thes sely lambes among.
I cannot with my wordes complayne and mone,
And suffer nought; nor smart wythout complaynt,
Nor torne the worde that from my mouthe is gone.
I cannot speke and loke lyke a saynct,
Use wiles for witt and make deceyt a pleasure,
And call crafft counsell, for proffet styll to paint.
I cannot wrest the law to fill the coffer
With innocent blode to fede my sellff fat,
And doo most hurt where most hellp I offer.
I am not he that can alow the state
Off highe Cesar and dam Cato to dye,
That with his dethe dyd skape owt off the gate
From Cesares handes (if Lyve do not lye)
And wolld not lyve whar lyberty was lost:
So did his hert the commonn wele aplye.
I am not he suche eloquence to boste,
To make the crow singing as the swane,
Nor call the lyon of cowarde bestes the moste
That cannot take a mows as the cat can:
And he that dithe for hunger of the golld
Call him Alessaundre; and say that Pan
Passithe Apollo in muske manyfolld;

Praysse Syr Thopas for a nobyll talle,
   And skorne the story that the knyght tolld.
Praise him for counceill that is droncke of ale;
   Grynee when he laugheth that bereth all the swaye,
   Frowne when he frowneth and grone when he is pale;
On othres lust to hang boeth nyght and daye:
   None of these pyntes would ever frame in me;
   My wit is nought—I cannot lerne the waye.
And much the lesse of thinges that greater be,
   That asken helpe of colours of devise
   To joyne the mene with eche extremitie,
With the neryst vertue to cloke always the vise:
   And as to pourpose like wise it shall fall,
   To presse the vertue that it may not rise;
As dronkenes good felloweshippe to call;
   The frendly ffoo with his dowble face
   Say he is gentill and courtois therewithall;
And say that Favell hath a goodly grace
   In eloquence; and crueltie to name
   Zele of justice and chaunge in tyme and place;
And he that suffreth offence withoute blame
   Call him pitefull; and him true and playn
   That raileth rekles to every mans shame.
Say he is rude that cannot lye and fayn;
   The letcher a lover; and tirannye
   To be the right of a prynces reigne.
I cannot, I. No, no, it will not be.
   This is the cause that I could never yet
   Hang on their slevis that way as thou maist se
A chippe of chaunce more then a pownde of witt.
   This maketh me at home to hounte and to hawke
   And in fowle weder at my booke to sitt.
In frost and snowe then with my bow to stawke,
   No man doeth marke where so I ride or goo;
   In lusty lees at libertie I walke,

And of these newes I fele nor wele nor woo,
   Sauf that a clogg doeth hang yet at my hele:
   No force for that for it is ordered so,
That I may lepe boeth hedge and dike full well.
   I ame not now in Ffraunce to judge the wyne,
   With saffry sauce the delicates to fele;
Nor yet in Spaigne where oon must him inclyne
   Rather then to be, owtewerdly to seme.
   I meddill not with wittes that be so fyne,
No Fflaunders chiere letteth not my sight to deme
   Of black and white, nor taketh my wit awaye
   With bestylnes, they beeste do so esteme;
Nor I ame not where Christe is geven in pray
   For mony, poison and traison at Rome,
   A commune practise used nyght and daie:
But here I ame in Kent and Christendome
   Emong the muses where I rede and ryme;
   Where if thou list, my Poynz, for to come,
Thou shalt be judge how I do spend my tyme.

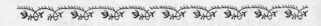

Thomas, Lord Vaux

(1510–1556)

The Aged Lover Renounceth Love

I lothe that I did love,
In youth that I thought swete:
As time requires for my behove
Me thinkes they are not mete,
  My lustes they do me leave,
  My fansies all be fledde:
And tract of time begins to weave,
Gray heares upon my hedde.

  For age with stelyng steppes,
Hath clawed me with his cowche:
And lusty life away she leapes,
As there had bene none such.
  My muse dothe not delight
  Me as she did before:
My hand and pen are not in plight,
As they have bene of yore.

  For reason me denies,
This youthly idle rime:
And day by day to me she cryes,
Leave of these toyes in time.
  The wrincles in my brow,
  The furrowes in my face:
Say limpyng age will hedge him now,
Where youth must geve him place.

  The harbinger of death,

456

To me I see him ride:
The cough, the colde, the gaspyng breath,
Do thee bid me to provide.

A pikeax and a spade,
And eke a shrowdyng shete,
A house of claye for to be made,
For such a gest most mete.

Me thinkes I heare the clarke,
That knols the careful knell:
And bids me leave my wofull warke,
Er nature me compell.

My kepers knit the knot,
That youth did laugh to scorne:
Of me that clene shalbe forgot,
As I had not ben borne.

Thus must I youth geve up,
Whose badge I long did weare:
To them I yelde the wanton cup
That better may it beare.

Loe here the bared scull,
By whose balde signe I know:
That stoupyng age away shall pull,
Which youthfull yeres did sowe.

For beauty with her bande
These croked cares hath wrought:
And shipped me into the lande,
From whence I first was brought.

And ye that bide behinde,
Have ye none other trust:
As ye of claye were cast by kinde,
So shall ye waste to dust.

Henry Howard, Earl of Surrey

(1517?–1547)

Translation from the Aeneid

It was then night; the sounde and quiet slepe
Had through the earth the weried bodyes caught;
The woodes, the ragyng seas were falne to rest;
When that the starres had halfe their course declined;
The feldes whist, beastes, and fowles of divers hue,
And what so that in the brode lakes remainde,
Or yet among the bushy thickes of bryar,
Laide downe to slepe by silence of the night,
Gan swage their cares, mindlesse of travels past.
Not so the spirite of this Phenician,
Unhappy she, that on no slepe could chance,
Nor yet nightes rest enter in eye or brest;
Her cares redoble; love doth rise and rage againe,
And overflowes with swellyng stormes of wrath.

(Book IV, 702–715)

Complaint That His Ladie After She Knew of His Love Kept Her Face Alway Hidden from Him

I never sawe my Ladye laye apart
Her cornet blacke, in colde nor yet in heate,
Sith first she knew my griefe was growen so great,

458

Which other fansies driveth from my hart
That to my selfe I do the thought reserve,
The which unwares did wounde my wofull brest:
But on her face mine eyes mought never rest,
Yet, sins she knew I did her love and serve
Her golden tresses cladde alway with blacke,
Her smilynge lokes that hid thus evermore,
And that restraines whiche I desire so sore.
So dothe this cornet governe me alacke:
In somer, sunne: in winters breath, a frost:
Wherby the light of her faire lokes I lost.

Thomas Sackville, Earl of Dorset

(1536–1608)

The Complaint
of Henrie Duke of Buckinghame

INDUCTION

The wrathfull winter proching on apace
With blustering blasts had all ybared
    the treen,
And old *Saturnus* with his frostie face
With chilling cold had pearst the tender
    grene;
The mantels reant wherin enwrapped
    bene
The gladsome groves that now laie over-
    thrown
The tapettes torne and everie blome
    downe blowen.

The soile that erst so semelie was to sene
Was all bereved of her bewties hewe,
And sote freshe floures wherwith the
    Somers Queene
Had clad the earth now *Boreas* blastes
    doune blewe,
And small fowles flocking in their song
    did rewe

460

The winters wrathe wherwith eache thing
 defaste
In wofull wise bewaild the Somer paste.

Hawthorne had lost his motleie liverie,
The naked twigs were shivering all for
 colde
And, dropping doune the teares abun-
 dantlie,
Each thing me thought with wepinge eie
 me tolde
The cruell seasonne, bidding me with-
 holde
Me selfe wythin for I was gotten out
In to the meades wheras I walkt about.

When lo the night with mistie mantels
 spred
Gan darke the daie and dimme the azure
 skies,
And *Venus Hermes* in her message sped
To blooddie *Mars* to will hym not to ryse
While she her selfe approcht in spedie
 wyse,
And *Virgo* hiding her disdainfull breast
With *Thetis* now had laied her doune to
 reast.

While *Scorpio* dreding *Sagittaries* darte,
Whose bowe prest beant in fight the
 stringe had slipt,
Downe slidde in to the *Ocean* aparte,
The *Beare* that in the yrishe seas had dipt
His grislie fote with spede from thence
 he whipt,
For *Thetis* hasting from the *Virgins* bed

Pursued the *Beare* that er she came was
    fled.

And *Phæton* now, nere reaching to his
    race
With glistening beames, gold streaming
    wher they bent,
Was prest to enter in his resting place;
Eritheus that in the cart furst went
Had even now atteind his jornies stent
And fast declininge hid awaie his hed,
While *Titan* couched him in his purper
    bed.

And pale *Cinthea,* with her borrowed
    light
Beginninge to supplie her brothers place,
Was past *Meridiem* syx grees in my sight
When that the stars fraught in the
    heavens face
With twinckeling light shone on the earth
    apace
That, while they brought about the
    nightes chare,
The darke had dimd the daie er I was
    ware.

And sorrowing I to se the somer flowres,
The livelie grene, the lustie leas forlorne,
The sturdie trees so shattred with the
    showres,
The feldes so fade that florisht so beforne,
It taught me well all earthlie thing is
    borne
To die the death for nought long time
    may last,
The somers bewtie yeldes to winters blast.

Then loking upward to the hevens beames
With nightes stars beset in everie wheare
Which erst so glistend with the golden streames
That cherful *Phoebus* spred doune from his spheare,
Beholding darke oppresse the daie so neare,
The soden sight resorted to my minde
The sundrie chaunges here in earth we finde;

That, musing on this worldlie welthe in thought
That comes and goes more faster than we se
The flickering flame that with the fire is wrought,
My busie traunce presented unto me
Such falles of peres as in this realme had be
That oft I wisht their falles had bene descrive
To warne the rest that fortune left alive.

Sorowe apereth unto me.

And strait furth stalking with a doubled pace
For that I sawe the night draw on so fast
In black all clad, there fell before my face
A piteous wight that woe had all forwast;
Furth from her eien the cristall teares out brast,
And, sighing sore, her handes she wrang and fold,
Tare all her heare that ruth was to behold.

Her bodie small forwitherd and forspente
As is the stalke that somers drought op-
prest,
Her welked face wyth wofull teares be-
sprente,
Her colour pale and, as yt semd her best,
In wo and plaint reposed was her rest,
And as the stone that drops of water
weares
So dented weare her cheakes wyth fall of
teares.

Her eien holow and drownd in teares
aflote,
Wherwith wyth lokes thrown up full pit-
ouslie
Her forceles handes together oft she
smote,
With dolfull shrekes that eckowede in the
skie
Whos plaint such sighes did strait accom-
panie,
That in my dome was never man did se
A wight not half so wobegon as she.

I stode agast beholding all her plight,
Twene dreade and dolour so distraind in
hart
That while my heare upstarted with the
sight
The teares out stremde for sorow of her
smart
But when I saw no end that cold apart
The dedlie dole which she so sore did
make

With dolfull voice then thus to her I
    spake:

Unwrap thie woes what ever wight thou
    be
And stint betime to spill thie self with
    plaint,
Tel who thow art and whence, for wel I
    se
Thow canst not dure with sorow thus at-
    taint.
And with that word of Sorowe all forfaint
She loked up and prostrate as she laie,
Wyth pitous sound lo thus she gan to
    saie:

Alas I wretche whom thus thow seest dis-
    traind
With wasting woes that never shall
    aslake,
Sorowe I am in endles tormentes pained
Amonge the *Furies* in th' infernall lake
Wher *Pluto* god of hell so grislie blacke
Doth hold his trone and *Lethes* dedlie tast
Doth reave remembrance of ech thing for
    past.

Whence come I am the drerie destenie
And luckles lot for to bemone of those
Whom fortune in this maze of miserie
Of wretched chaunce right woful mir-
    rhours chose,
That, when thow seest how lightlie they
    did lose
Their pompe, their power and that they
    thought most sure,

Thow maist sone deame no earthlie joy
    may dure.

Whos rufull voice no soner had outbraied
Thes wofull wordes wherwith she
    sorowed so
But out alas she shrekt and never staied,
Fell doune and all to dasht her self for
    wo;
The cold pale drede my lims gan overgoe
And I so sorowed at her sorowes eft
That what with greif and feare my wittes
    weare reft.

I stretcht me self and strait my hart re-
    vives
That drede and dolour erst did so appale,
Lyke him that with the fervent fever
    strives
When sicknes sekes his castell helth to
    scale,
With gatherd sprites so forst I feare tavale
And, rering her with anguishe all fordoon,
My sprites returnd and thus I then be-
    goon.

O sorrow, alas, syth sorow is thy name
And that to the this drere doth wel per-
    tain,
In vain it were to seke to cesse the same
But as a man him self with sorrow slain,
So I alas to comfort the in paine
That here in sorow art forsonke so depe
That at thie sight I can but sighe and
    wepe.

I had no soner spoken of a syke
But that the stormes so rumbled in her
    brest
As *Eolus* cold never rore the lyke,
And showres dounrained from her eien so
    fast
That all bedreint the place till at the last
Well eased they the dolour of her minde
As rage of rain doth swage the stormy
    wind.

For furth she paced in her terfull tale:
Come, Come (quod she), and se what I
    shall show,
Come here the plaining and the bitter
    bale
Of worthie men unworthelie orethrowe,
Come thow and se them rewing all arowe;
They were but shades that erst in mind
    thow rold,
Come, Come with me, thine eien shall
    them beholde.

What could thes wordes but make me
    more agast
To here her tell wheron I mused while
    ere,
So was I mazed therwith till at the last,
Beating upon her wordes and what they
    weare,
All sodenlie well lessened was my feare
For to my mind returned how she telde
Both what she was, and wher her woon
    she helde.

Wherbie I knew that she a goddesse was
And therwythall resortede to my minde
My thought that late presented me the
      glas
Of brittell state of cares that here we
      finde
Of thousand woes to selie man assignde,
And how she now bad me come and be-
      hold
To se with eie that erst in thought I rold.

Flat doune I fell and with all reverence
Gan worship her, perceaving now that
      she
A goddesse seant by godlie providence
In earthlie shape thus pered unto me
To waile and rew this worldes uncertein-
      tie,
And while I thus honnord her godheds
      might
With plaining voice thes wordes to me
      she shright:

I shall the guide furst to the grislie lake
And thence unto the blisfull place of rest,
And thow shalt se and here the plaint
      they make
That whilome here bare swinge above
      the best;
This shalt thow se, but grete is the unrest
That thow must bide before thow canst
      attaine
Unto the place wher is this hugie plain.

And with thes wordes as I upraised stode
And gan to folow her that strait furth
      paced,

Er I was ware in to a mightie wood
We now were come wher, hand in hand
   imbraced,
She led the waie and through the thick
   so traced
As but I had bene guided by her might
Yt was no waie for anie mortall wight.

But lo while thus amid the desart darke
We passed on with steppes and pace un-
   mete
A rumbling rore confusd with howle and
   barke
Of dogs shoke all the grownd under our
   fete
And stroke the din within our eares so
   depe
As halfe distraught unto the ground I fell,
Besought returne and not to visite hell.

But she furthwith uplifting me apace
Removd my drede and with a stedfast
   mind
Bade me come on for here was now the
   place,
The place wher we our travels end shold
   find;
Therwith I rose and to the place assighnd
Astound I stalke, when strait we proched
   nere
This dredfull place that you will dred to
   here.

The descripcion
of helle.

An hidous hole al vast withouten shape
Of endles depthe orewhelmd with ragged
   stone,

With ouglie mouthe and grislie jawes
    doth gape
And to our sight confoundes it self in one;
Here enterd we and yeading furth anon
A horrible lothlie lake we might discerne
As black as pitche that cleped is *Averne*.

A dedlie gulphe wher nought but rub-
    byshe growes,
With fowle black swelth that in thickend
    lumpes lies
Which up in thaier such stinking vapours
    throwes
That over ther may flie no fowle but dies
Chokt with the pestilent savours that
    arise;
Hither we came whence furth we stil did
    pace
In dredfull feare amid this dredfull place.

And furst within the porche and jawes of
    hell

Remorce of conscience.

Sate depe remorce of conscience, all be-
    sprent
With teares, and to her self oft wold she
    tell
Her wretchedness and, cursing, never
    stent
To sobbe and sighe but ever thus lament
With thoughtfull care as she that all in
    vain
Wold weare and wast continuewallie in
    paine.

Her eies unstedfast rolling here and there
Whirld on ech place as place that venge-
    ance brought,

So was her mind continuewallie in feare,
Tost and tormented with the tedious
thought
Of thos detested crimes which she had
wrought,
With dredfull chere and lokes throwen to
the skie,
Wishing for dethe and yet she cold not
die.

And next within the entrie of this lake
Sate fell revenge gnashing her tethe for
yre
Revenge. And sekes all meanes how she may
vengeance take,
Never in rest till she have her desyre,
But frettes within so far furth with the
fire
Of wreking flames as now determde is
she
To die the death or by deathe venged to
be.

And fast by her pale maladie was plast
Sore sicke in bed; her colour all forgone
Maladie. Bereft of stomacke savour and of tast,
Ne cold she broke no mete but brothes
alone,
Her brethe corrupt, her kepers everie one
Abhorring her, her sicknes past recure,
Detesting phisick and all phisickes cure.

And next in order sad old age we fownde,
His beard all hore, his eien holowe and
blind,
Wyth drouping chere still poringe on the
grounde

As on the place wher nature him as-
　　sighnd.
To rest when that the susters had untwind
His vitall thred and ended with their
　　kniefe
The fleating course of fast declininge
　　liefe.

Ther herd we him with broken and
　　holow pleint
Rew with him self his end approching
　　fast
And all fornought his wretched mind tor-
　　ment
With swete remembraunce of his pleas-
　　ures past
And fresh delightes of lustie youth for-
　　wast,
Recompting which how wold he sobbe
　　and syke
And to be younge againe of Jove beseke.

But and the cruell fates so fixed be
That time forpast can not returne againe,
This one request of Jove yet praied he
That in such witherd plight and
　　wretched pain
As eld accompanied with his lothsome
　　traine
Had brought on him all weare it woe and
　　greife
He might a while yet linger furth his liefe

And not so sone descend in to the pit
Wher deth whan he the mortall corps
　　hath slain

With rechles hand in grave doth cover yt
Therafter never to enjoie againe
The gladsom light but in the ground
　　ylaien
In depth of darknes wast and were to
　　nought
As he had never in the world ben
　　brought.

But who had sene him sobbing how he
　　stode
Unto him self, and how he wold bemone
His youth forpast, as though it did him
　　good
To talke of youth all were his youth for-
　　gon,
He wold have musd and merveld much
　　wheron
This wretched age liefe shold desire so
　　faine
And knowes full wel lief doth but length
　　his pain.

Crokebackt he was, toth shaken and
　　bleare eied,
Went on thre fete and somtimes crept on
　　fower.
With old lame bones that ratled by his
　　side,
His scalpe all pild and he with eld forlore,
His witherd fist still knocking at dethes
　　dore,
Fumbling and drivling as he drawes his
　　breathe,
For brief the shape and messenger of
　　deathe.

Next saw we drede all trembling how he
  shoke
Wyth fete uncerten profferd here and
  there,
Benomd of spech and with a gastlie loke

Dreade.

Sercht everie place all pale and ded for
  feare,
His cap born up with staring of his heare,
Stoonde and amazde at his own shade for
  dreede
And fering greter daungers then was
  nede.

But (o) the dolfull sight that then we se
We turnd our loke and on the other syde

Famine.

A grislie shape of famine mought we se
With gredie lokes and gapinge mouth
  that cried
And rored for meate as she shold ther
  have died,
Her bodie thin and bare as anie bone
Wherto was left nought but the cace
  alone,

And that alas was gnawen in everie
  wheare,
All ful of holes that I ne mought refraine
From teares to se how she her armes
  wold teare
And with her tethe gnashe on the bones
  in vain,
When all fornought she fain wold so
  sustaine
Her starven corpse that rather semde a
  shade
Then anie substaunce of a creature made.

Grete was her force whom stone wall
    could not staie,
Her tering nailes snatching at all she saw,
With gaping jawes that by no meanes
    may
Be satisfied from hunger of her maw
But etes her self as she that hath no law,
Gnawing alas her karcas all in vain,
Wher you may compt ech sinew bone
    and vain.

On her while we thus firmelie fixt our eies
That bled for ruthe of such a drerie sight,
Lo sodenlie she shreked in so huge wise
As made the erth to shiver with the might,
Wherwith a dart we sawe how it did light
Right on her brest and therwithall pale
    dethe
Enthrillinge it to reave her of her brethe.

And by and by a dum ded corps we sawe,
Heavie and cold, the shape of deth aright

Deathe

That dauntes all erthlie cretures to his
    lawe,
Against whos force in vain it is to fight;
Ne peres, ne princes nor no mortall wight
Ne rules ne realmes cities ne strongest
    towre
But all perforce must yeld unto his power.

His dart anon out of the corpse he toke
And in his hand a dredfull sight to se
With grete triumphe eftsons the same he
    shoke
That most of all my feares affraied me;

His bodie dight with nought but bones
    perde,
The naked shape of man ther saw I plain
All save the fleshe the sinew and the vain.

Whan dethe had thus adrad us with his
    dart
And shewed him self as next in order set,
With trembling lims softlie we gan de-
    part
Til in our eies another sight we met
When from my hart a sighe furtwith I fet
Rewing alas upon the wofull plight.
Of povertie that next aperd in sight.

His face was leane and somdeale pind
    awaie
And eke his handes consumd unto the
    bone
Povertie   But what his bodie was I can not saie,
For on the same I thinke sure he had on
A thousand patches peced one by one,
With staf in hand, and scrippe on shol-
    ders cast,
His cheif defence ageinst the winters
    blast.

His fode for most was wild frute of the
    tre
Unles somtime some croms fel to his
    share,
Which in his wallet long god wot kept he
As on the which ful deintlie wold he fare;
His drink the running streame, his cup
    the bare

Of his palm closde, his bed the hard cold
    ground;
To this pore lief was povertie ybound.

Whos wretched state when we had wel
    beheld
With tender ruth on him and on his feres,

Labour.   In thoughtfull cares furth then our pace
    we held
And by and by another shape aperes
Of busie labour brushing up the breres,
His knockles knobd, his fleshe depe
    dented in
With tawed handes and hard ytanned
    skin.

The morow graie no soner hath begoon
To sprede his light even peping in our
    eies
When he is up and to his work yroon,
But let the night his misti mantels rise
And with foule dark never so much dis-
    guise
The fair bright daie, yet cesses he no
    while
But hath his candels to prolong his toile.

By him lay heavie slepe the cousin of
    dethe,
Flat on the ground and stil as ani stone,

Slepe.   A verie corpse save yelding furth a breth;
Small kepe toke he whom fortune
    frowned on
Or whom she lifted up in to the trone
Of high renowne, but as a living deth
So ded alive of liefe he drew the breth.

The bodies rest, the quiet of the harte,
The travals ese, the stil nightes fere was
  he
And of our liefe in erth the better part,
Rever of sight and yet in whom we se
Things oft that tide and oft that never
  be,
Without respect esteming equallie
King *Cresus* pomp and *Irus* povertie.

Warre

Lastlie stode warre in glittering armes
  yclad,
With visage grim sterne lokes and black-
  lie hued;
In his right hand a naked sword he had
That to the hiltes was all with blood
  imbrued
And in his left that kinges and kingdomes
  rewed
Famine and fire he held, and therwithall
He rased townes and threw doune towres
  and all.

Cities he sackt and relmes that whilome
  flowred
In honnor glorie and rule above the best
He overwhelmed and all their fame devoured,
Consumde, destroied, wasted and never
  cest
Til he their welth their name and al
  oprest,
His face forhewd with woundes, and by
  his syde
Their hong his targe with gashes depe
  and wide.

In midst of which depainted ther we found

Warres Targe and what was painted therin.

Dedlie debate all full of snakie here

That with a blooddie fillet was ybound,

Out brething nought but discord everie wher,

And round about were portraied here and there

Darius king of Percia whome Alexander conquered.

The hugie hostes *Darius* and his power,

His kinges, princes, his peres, and all his flowre

Whom grete *Macedo* vanquisht ther in fight

With depe slaughter despoiling all his pride,

Perst through his relmes and daunted al his might;

Hannibals victory at Cannas.

Duke *Hannibal* beheld I ther beside,

In *Cannas* feld victour how he did ride,

And wofull Romans that in vain withstode

And Consull *Paulus* covered all in blood.

The fight at Trasimene and Trebie wher Hanibal was victor in both. The last battel between Scipio and Hanibal wher Scipio was victour.

Yet saw I more the fight at *Trasimene*

And *Trebeie* feld and eke whan *Hannibal*

And worthi *Scipio* last in armes wer sene

Before *Carthago* gate to trie for all

The worldes empire to whom it shold befall,

The Civile wars of Pompei and Caesar.

Pompeie I saw and Caesar clad in armes,

Their hostes alied and all their civile harmes,

With Conquerors handes forbathd in their owne blood,

And *Caesar* weeping over *Pompeies* hed;

The Crueltie of Scilla and Marius

Yet saw I *Scilla* and *Marius* wher they
stood,

Their grete crueltie and the depe bloodshed

Of frends; *Cirus* I saw and his host ded,

Cirus slain by the quene Tomiris

And how the quene with gret despite
hath flonge

His hed in blood of them she overcome.

Xerxes king of Percia put to flight in Grece by

Xerxes the Percian king, yet saw I there

With his huge host that drank the rivers
drie,

Dismounted hils and made the vales
uprere,

His host and all yet saw I slain perdie,

Thebes raced by Tirus sacked by Alexander

Thebes I saw all raced how it did lie

In heapes of stones, and *Tirus* put to
spoile

With wals and towers flat evened with
the soyle.

Troie destroied by the Grecians

But *Troie* alas, me thought above them all

It made mine eies in vearie teres consume

When I beheld the woful werd befall

That by the wrathfull wil of gods was
come,

And *Joves* unmoved sentence and for-
dome

On *Priam* king and on his town so bent,

I cold not lin but I must ther lament,

And that the more, syth destenie was so
sterne

As force perforce ther mought no force
availe

But she must fall and by her fall we
    learne
That cities, towres, welth, world, and all
    shal quaile,
No manhod might nor nothing mought
    prevaile;
All were ther prest, full mainie a prince
    and pere
And mainie a knight that sold his dethe
    ful dere.

Not worthie *Hector* worthiest of them all
Her hope, her joie, his force was now for
    nought;
O *Troie Troie*, ther is no bote but bale,
The hugie horse within thy walles is
    brought,
Thy turrets fall, thie knightes that whil-
    ome fought
In armes amid the feld ar slain in bed,
Thie gods defild, and all thine honnour
    ded.

The flames upspring and cruellie they
    crepe
From wall to ruf til all to cinders wast,
Some fire the houses wher the wretches
    slepe,
Some rush in here, some roon in ther as
    fast,
In everie wher or sword or fire they tast;
The walles ar torne, the towres whurld to
    ground,
Ther is no mischeif but may ther be
    found.

Cassandra

Cassandra yet ther saw I how they haled
From *Pallas* hous with spercled tresse
    undoon,
Her wrestes fast bound and with grekes
    rout empaled,

Priam slain by Pirrhus.

And *Priam* eke in vain how he did roon
To armes, whom Pirrhus with despite
    hath doon
To cruell dethe and bathd him in the
    baine
Of his soons blood before the Aulter
    slaine.

But how can I descrive this dolful sight
That in the sheld so livelike fair did shine
Syth in this world I think was never
    wight
Could have set furth the half not half so
    fine;
I can no more but tel how ther is sene
Fair *Ilium* fall in burning red gledes
    doune,
And from the soyle gulf *Troie Neptunus*
    towne.

Here from, when scarce I could mine eyes
    withdrawe
That fyld with teares as doth the spring-
    ing well,
We passed on so far furth til we sawe
Rude *Achæron* a lothsome lake to tell
That boyles and bubles swelth as black
    as hell,
Wher grislie Charon at their fixed tide
Still ferreies ghostes unto the farther syde.

The aged god no soner sorowe spied
But hasting call unto the bank apace
With holow call unto the rout he cried
To swarve apart and geve the goddes
    place;
Strait it was doom when to the shore we
    pace
Wher hand in hand as we then linked
    fast
Within the bote we ar together plast

And furth we launce full fraughted to the
    brinke
Wher with th' unwonted weight the rustic
    kele
Began to crack as if the same shold sinke,
We stroke up mast and saile that in a
    while
We fet the shore wher scarcelie we had
    while
For to arive but that we herd anon
A thresound bark confounded all in one.

We had not long furthpast but that we
    saw
Cerberus   Black *Cerberus* the hidous hound of hell,
With bristels reard and with a thre
    mouthed jaw,
Fordinning the aier with his horrible yell
Out of the depe dark cave wher he did
    dwell;
The goddesse strait he knew and by and
    by
He peaced and couch while that we
    passed by.

The hugie plaine wher at the princes weare. And al estates that died in adversitie

Thens come we to the horrour and the
   hell
The large kingdomes and the dredfull
   raigne
Of *Pluto* in his trone wher he did dwell,
The wide wast places and the hugie plain,
The wailinges, shreks, the sundrie sortes
   of pain,
The sighes, the sobbes, the depe and ded-
   lie grone,
Earth, aier, and all resounding plaint and
   mone.

Here pewled the babes and here the
   maides unwed
With folded handes·their sorie chaunce
   bewailed,
Here wept the giltles slain and lovers ded
That slew them selves when nothing els
   availd;
A thousand sortes of sorowes here that
   wailed
With sighes and teres, sobbes, shrekes an
   all yfeere
That oh alas it was a hell to here.

We staied us strait and with a rufull feare
Beheld this heavie sight, while from mine
   eies
The vapord teares dounstilled here and
   there,
And sorowe eke in far more wofull wise
Toke on with plaint, upheaving to the
   skies
Her wretched handes, that with her crie
   the rout

Gan all in heapes to swarme us round
about.

Lo here quod sorow princes of renowne
That whilome sate on top of fortunes
whele
Now laied full low lyke wretches
whurled doune,
Even with on frown that staied but with
a smile,
And now behold the thing that thow er
while
Saw onlie in thought, and what thow now
shalt here
Recompt the same to kesar, king, and
pere.

George Gascoigne

(1542?–1577)

I could not though I would

I could not though I would: good Lady say not so,
Since one good word of your good wil might soone re-
  dresse my wo
Where would is free before, there could can never fayle:
For profe, you see how gallies passe where ships can
  beare no sayle.
The weary mariner when skies are overcast,
By ready will doth guyde his skill and wins the haven
  at last.
The prety byrd that sings with pricke against hir brest,
Doth make a vertue of hir need to watch when others
  rest.
And true the proverbe is, which you have layed apart,
There is no hap can seeme to hard unto a willing hart.
Then lovely Lady myne, you say not as you should,
In doubtful termes to aunswer thus: I could not thogh
  I would.
Yes, yes, full well you know, your can is quicke and
  good:
And wilfull will is eke too swift to shed my giltlesse
  blood.
But if good will were bent as prest as power is,
Such will would quickly find the skill to mend that is
  amisse.
Wherfore if you desire to see my true love spilt,

Commaund and I will slea my self, that yours may be
   the gilt.
But if you have no power to say your servaunt nay,
Write thus: I may not as I would, yet must I as I may.

And if I did what then?

And if I did what then?
Are you agreev'd therfore?
The Sea hath fishe for every man,
And what would you have more?

Thus did my Mistresse once,
Amaze my mind with doubt:
And popt a question for the nonce,
To beat my braynes about.

Wherto I thus replied,
Eche fisherman can wishe,
That all the Sea at every tyde,
Were his alone to fishe.

And so did I (in vaine),
But since it may not be:
Let such fishe there as find the gaine,
And leave the losse for me.

And with such lucke and losse,
I will content my selfe:
Till tydes of turning time may tosse,
Such fishers on the shelfe.

And when they sticke on sands,
That every man may see:
Then will I laugh and clappe my hands,
As they do now at mee.

My worthy Lord, I pray you

My worthy Lord, I pray you wonder not
To see your wodman shoote so ofte awrie,
Nor that he stands amased like a sot,
And lets the harmlesse deare (unhurt) go by.
Or if he strike a doe which is but carren,
Laugh not good Lord, but favoure such a fault,
Take well in worth, he wold faine hit the barren,
But though his harte be good, his happe is naught:
And therefore now I crave your Lordships leave,
To tell you playne what is the cause of this:
First if it please your honour to perceive,
What makes your wodman shoote so ofte amisse,
Beleeve me L. the case is nothing strange,
He shootes awrie almost at every marke,
His eyes have bene so used for to raunge,
That now God knowes they be both dimme and darke.
For proofe he beares the note of follie nowe,
Who shotte sometimes to hit Philosophie,
And aske you why? forsooth I make avow,
Bycause his wanton wittes went all awrie.
Next that, he shot to be a man of lawe,
And spent some time with learned Litleton,
Yet in the end, he proved but a dawe,
For lawe was darke and he had quickly done.
Then could he wish Fitzharbert such a braine,
As *Tully* had, to write the law by arte,
So that with pleasure, or with litle paine,
He might perhaps, have caught a trewants parte.
But all to late, he most mislikte the thing,
Which most might helpe to guide his arrow streight,
He winked wrong, and so let slippe the string,

Which cast him wide, for all his queint conceit.
From thence he shotte to catch a courtly grace,
And thought even there to wield the world at will,
But out alas he much mistooke the place,
And shot awrie at every rover still.

The blasing baits which drawe the gazing eye,
Unfethered there his first affection,
No wonder then although he shot awrie,
Wanting the fethers of discretion.

Yet more than them, the marks of dignitie,
He much mistooke and shot the wronger way,
Thinking the purse of prodigalite,
Had bene best meane to purchase such a pray.

He thought the flattring face which fleareth still,
Had bene full fraught with all fidelitie,
And that such words as courtiers use at will,
Could not have varied from the veritie.

But when his bonet buttened with gold,
His comelie cape begarded all with gay,
His bumbast hose, with linings manifold,
His knit silke stocks and all his queint aray,

Had pickt his purse of all the Peter pence,
Which might have paide for his promotion,
Then (all to late) he found that light expence,
Had quite quencht out the courts devotion.

So that since then the tast of miserie,
Hath bene always full bitter in his bit,
And why? forsooth bicause he shot awrie,
Mistaking still the markes which others hit.

But now behold what marke the man doth find,
He shootes to be a souldier in his age,
Mistrusting all the vertues of the minde,
He trusts the power of his personage.

As though long limmes led by a lusty hart,
Might yet suffice to make him rich againe,

But flussing fraies have taught him such a parte,
That now he thinks the warres yeld no such gaine.
And sure I feare, unlesse your lordship deigne,
To traine him yet into some better trade,
It will be long before he hit the veine,
Wherby he may a richer man be made.
He cannot climbe as other catchers can,
To leade a change before himselfe be led,
He cannot spoile the simple sakeles man,
Which is content to feede him with his bread.
He cannot pinch the painefull souldiers pay,
And sheare him out his share in ragged sheetes,
He cannot stop to take a gredy pray
Upon his fellowes groveling in the streetes.
He cannot pull the spoile from such as pill,
And seeme full angrie at such foule offence,
Although the gayne content his greedie will,
Under the cloake of contrarie pretence:
And nowe adayes, the man that shootes not so,
Maye shoote amisse, even as your Woodman dothe:
But then you marvell why I lette them go,
And never shoote, but saye farewell forsooth:
Alas my Lorde, whyle I doe muze hereon,
And call to mynde my youthfull yeares myspente,
They give mee suche a boane to gnawe upon,
That all my senses are in silence pente.
My mynde is rapte in contemplation,
Wherein my dazeled eyes onely beholde,
The blacke houre of my constellation,
Whyche framed mee so lucklesse on the molde:
Yet therewithall I can not but confesse,
That vayne presumption makes my heart to swell,
For thus I thinke, not all the worlde (I guesse),
Shootes bet than I, nay some shootes not so well.
In *Aristotle* somewhere did I learne,

To guyde my manners all by comelynesse,
And *Tullie* taught me somewhat to discerne
Betweene sweete speeche and barbarous rudenesse.
Olde *Parkyns, Rastall,* and *Dan Bractens* bookes,
Did lende mee somewhat of the lawlesse Lawe,
The craftie Courtyers with their guylefull lookes,
Muste needes put some experience in my mawe:
Yet can not these with manye maystries mo,
Make me shoote streyght at any gaynfull pricke,
Where some that never handled such a bow,
Can hit the white, or touch it neare the quicke,
Who can nor speake, nor write in pleasant wise,
Nor leade their life by *Aristotles* rule,
Nor argue well on questions that arise,
Nor pleade a case more than my Lord Maiors mule,
Yet can they hit the marks that I do misse,
And winne the meane which may the man mainteine,
Nowe when my mynde dothe mumble upon this,
No wonder then although I pyne for payne:
And whyles myne eyes beholde this mirroure thus,
The hearde goeth by, and farewell gentle does:
So that your lordship quickely may discusse
What blyndes myne eyes so ofte (as I suppose).
But since my Muse can to my Lorde reherse
What makes me misse, and why I doe not shoote,
Let me imagine in this woorthlesse verse:
If right before mee, at my standings foote
There stoode a Doe, and I shoulde strike hir deade,
And then shee prove a carrion carkas too,
What figure might I fynde within my head,
To scuse the rage which rulde mee so to doo?
Some myghte interprete by playne paraphrase,
That lacke of skill or fortune ledde the chaunce,
But I muste otherwyse expounde the case,
I saye *Jehova* did this Doe advaunce,

And made hir bolde to stande before mee so,
Till I had thrust myne arrowe to hir harte,
That by the sodaine of hir overthrowe,
I myght endevour to amende my parte,
And turne myne eyes that they no more beholde,
Suche guylefull markes as seeme more than they be:
And though they glister outwardely lyke golde,
Are inwardly but brasse, as men may see:
And when I see the milke hang in hir teate,
Me thinkes it sayth, olde babe nowe learne to sucke,
Who in thy youthe couldst never learne the feate
To hitte the whytes whiche live with all good lucke.
Thus have I tolde my Lorde, (God graunt in season)
A tedious tale in rime, but little reason.

Gascoigne's Lullabie

Sing lullabie, as women do,
Wherewith to bring their babes to rest,
And lullabie can I sing to
As womanly as can the best.
With lullabie they still the childe,
And if I be not much beguilde,
Full many wanton babes have I
Which must be stilld with lullabie.

First lullaby my youthfull yeares,
It is now time to go to bed,
For crooked age and hoarie heares,
Have wonne the haven within my head:
With Lullabye then youth be still,
With Lullabye content thy will,
Since courage quayles, and commes behynde,
Goe sleepe, and so beguyle thy mynde.

Next Lullaybye my gazing eyes,
Whiche woonted were to glaunce apace:
For every glasse maye nowe suffise,
To shewe the furrowes in my face:
With Lullabye then wynke a whyle,
With Lullabye youre lookes beguyle:
Lette no fayre face, nor beautie bryghte
Entice you efte with vayne delyght.

And Lullabye my wanton will,
Lette reasons rule nowe reigne thy thought,
Since all too late I fynde by skill,
Howe deare I have thy fansies bought:
With Lullabye now take thyne ease,
With Lullabye thy doubtes appease:
For trust to this, if thou be still,
My bodie shall obey thy will.

Eke Lullabye my loving boye,
My little Robyn take thy rest,
Since Age is colde, and nothyng coye,
Keepe close thy coyne, for so is beste:
With Lullabye bee thou content,
With Lullabye thy lustes relente,
Lette others paye whiche have mo pence,
Thou arte to poore for suche expense.

Thus Lullabie my youth, myne eyes,
My will, my ware, and all that was,
I can no mo delayes devise,
But welcome payne, lette pleasure passe:
With Lullabye nowe take your leave,
With Lullabye youre dreames deceyve,
And when you rise with waking eye,
Remembre *Gascoignes* Lullabye.

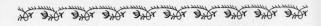

Sir Edward Dyer

(c. 1540–1607)

Wher one would be

Wher one would be ther not to be,
  What is a greater paine;
Or what more greife ther not to be,
  Wher thou wouldest be full faine?

Longe time semes shorte when thou art there
  Where thou wouldest gladly be:
Arte thou not there wher thou wouldest be,
  Then eche day semeth three.

Unrippe but that with threede is sowen,
  How lothe it dothe departe;
Much lother then must needes be puld
  The bodie from the hearte.

Then doe thou haste thee to the stafe,
  With speede thy threde untwine;
Eche lovings harte would see his frynde,
  And soe woulde I doe mine.

The lowest trees have topps

The lowest trees have topps, the ante her gall,
The flie her spleene, the little sparke his heat:
The slender hears cast shadows, though but small,

494

And bees have stinges, although they be not great;
  Seas have their sourse, and soe have shallow springes:
  And Love is Love, in beggers and in Kinges.

Wher waters smothest ronne, ther deepest are the
      foords,
The diall stirrs, yet none perceives it moove;
The firmest fayth is fownd in fewest woordes,
The turtles doe not singe, and yet they love;
  True heartes have ears and eyes, no tongues to
      speake:
  They heare and see, and sigh, and then they breake.

My mynde to me a kyngdome is

My mynde to me a kyngdome is,
Such perfect joy therin I fynde,
That it excells all other blisse
That worlde afords or growes by kynde:
  Though muche I wante which moste would have,
  Yet still my mynde forbides to crave.

No princely pompe, no wealthy store,
Nor force to wine the victorye,
No wilye witt to salve a sore,
No shape to feade a lovinge eye;
  To none of these I yealde as thrall:
  For why? my minde dothe serve for all.

I see how plenty suffers ofte,
And hastye clymers sone do fall:
I see that those whiche are alofte
Myshapp dothe threaten moste of all:
  They get with toylle, they keepe with feare:
  Such cares my mynde coulde never beare.

Contente I live, this is my staye:
I seeke no more than may suffyse,
I presse to beare no haughtie swaye;
Look, what I lack my mynde suppliese:
    Lo, thus I tryumphe lyke a kynge,
    Content with that my mynde doth bringe.

Some have to muche, yet still do crave,
I little have, and seeke no more:
They are but poore, though muche they have,
And I am ryche with lytle store:
    They poore, I ryche; they begg, I geve:
    They lacke, I leave; they pyne, I lyve.

I laugh not at an others loss,
I grudge not at an others gaine:
No wordly waves my mynde can toss,
My state at one dothe still remayne:
    I feare no foe, I fawne no freende,
    I lothe not lyfe, nor dread no ende.

Some waye theyre pleasure by theyre luste,
Their wisdom by theyre rage of will:
Theire treasure is theire only truste,
A cloked crafte theyre store of skyll:
    But all the pleasure that I fynde
    Is to mayntayne a quiet mynde.

My wealthe is healthe and perfecte ease,
My conscience cleere my chiefe defense:
I neither seeke by brybes to please,
Nor by deserte to breede offence:
    Thus do I lyve, thus will I dye;
    Would all did so, as well as I.

Sir Philip Sidney

(1554–1586)

FROM *Arcadia*

LOVED I AM, AND YET
COMPLAINE OF LOVE

Loved I am, and yet complaine of Love:
As loving not, accus'd, in Love I die.
When pittie most I crave I cruell prove:
Still seeking Love, love found as much I flie.
  Burnt in my selfe, I muse at others fire:
What I call wrong, I doo the same, and more:
Bard of my will, I have beyond desire:
I waile for want, and yet am chokte with store.
    This is thy worke, thou God for ever blinde:
Though thousands old, a Boy entit'led still.
Thus children doo the silly birds they finde,
With stroking hurt, and too much cramming kill.
  Yet this much Love, O Love, I crave of thee:
  Let me be lov'd, or else not loved be.

MY TRUE LOVE HATH MY HART

My true love hath my hart, and I have his,
By just exchange, one for the other giv'ne.
I holde his deare, and myne he cannot misse:
There never was a better bargaine driv'ne.

His hart in me, keepes me and him in one,
My hart in him, his thoughts and senses guides:
He loves my hart, for once it was his owne:
I cherish his, because in me it bides.

His hart his wound receaved from my sight:
My hart was wounded, with his wounded hart,
For as from me, on him his hurt did light,
So still me thought in me his hurt did smart:
    Both equall hurt, in this change sought our blisse:
    My true love hath my hart and I have his.

GET HENCE FOULE GRIEFE

Get hence foule Griefe, the canker of the minde:
Farewell Complaint, the misers only pleasure:
Away vayne Cares, by which fewe men do finde
                Their sought-for treasure.

Ye helplesse Sighes, blowe out your breath to nought,
Teares, drowne your selves, for woe (your cause) is
    wasted,
Thought, thinke to ende, too long the frute of thought
                My minde hath tasted.

But thou, sure Hope, tickle my leaping heart.
Comfort, step thou in place of wonted sadnes.
Fore-felt Desire, begin to savour parts
                Of comming gladnes.

Let voice of Sighes into cleare musike runne,
    let your Teares with gazing now be mended,
     of Thought, true pleasure be begunne,
                And never ended.

O SWEET WOODS

O sweet woods the delight of solitarines!
O how much I do like your solitarines!
Where mans mind hath a freed consideration
Of goodnes to receive lovely direction.
Where senses do behold th' order of heav'nly hoste,
And wise thoughts do behold what the creator is:
Contemplation here holdeth his only seate:
Bownded with no limitts, borne with a wing of hope
Clymes even unto the starres, Nature is under it.
Nought disturbs thy quiet, all to thy service yeelds
Each sight draws on a thought, thought mother of
        science,
Sweet birds kindly do graunt harmony unto thee,
Faire trees shade is enough fortification,
Nor danger to thy selfe if be not in thy selfe.

O sweete woods the delight of solitarines!
O how much I do like your solitarines!
Here nor treason is hidd, vailed in innocence,
Nor envies snaky ey, finds any harbor here,
Nor flatterers venomous insinuations,
Nor comming humorists puddled opinions,
Nor courteous ruin of proffered usury,
Nor time pratled away, cradle of ignorance,
Nor causeless duty, nor comber of arrogance,
Nor trifling title of vanity dazleth us,
Nor golden manacles, stand for a paradise,
Here wrongs name is unheard: slander a monster is
Keepe thy sprite from abuse, here no abuse doth haunte.
What man grafts in a tree dissimulation?

O sweete woods the delight of solitarines!
O how well I do like your solitarines!

Yet deare soile, if a soule closed in a mansion
As sweete as violetts, faire as lilly is,
Streight as Cedar, a voice staines the Cannary birds,
Whose shade safely doth hold, danger avoideth her:
Such wisedome, that in her lives speculation:
Such goodnes that in her simplicitie triumphs:
Where envies snaky ey, winketh or els dyeth,
Slander wants a pretext, flattery gone beyond:
Oh! if such a one have bent, to a lonely life,
Her stepps gladd we receave, gladd we receave her eys.
    And thinke not she doth hurt our solitarines,
    For such company decks such solitarines.

DOUBLE SESTINE

STREPHON

You Gote-heard Gods, that love the grassie mountaines,
You Nimphes that haunt the springs in pleasant vallies,
You Satyrs joyde with free and quiet forrests,
Vouchsafe your silent eares to playning musique,
Which to my woes gives still an early morning:
And drawes the dolor on till wery evening.

KLAIUS

O *Mercurie,* foregoer to the evening,
O heavenlie huntresse of the savage mountaines,
O lovelie starre, entitled of the morning,
While that my voice doth fill these wofull vallies,
Vouchsafe your silent eares to plaining musique,
Which oft hath *Echo* tir'd in secrete forrests.

STREPHON

I that was once free-burges of the forrests,
Where shade from Sunne, and sports I sought at eve-
    ning,

I that was once esteem'd for pleasant musique,
Am banisht now among the monstrous mountaines
Of huge despaire, and foule afflictions vallies,
Am growne a shrich-owle to my selfe each morning.

KLAIUS

I that was once delighted every morning,
Hunting the wilde inhabiters of forrests,
I that was once the musique of these vallies,
So darkened am, that all my day is evening,
Hart-broken so, that molehilles seeme high mountaines,
And fill the vales with cries in steed of musique.

STREPHON

Long since alas, my deadly Swannish musique
Hath made it selfe a crier of the morning,
And hath with wailing strength climb'd highest
   mountaines:
Long since my thoughts more desert be then forrests:
Long since I see my joyes come to their evening,
And state throwen downe to over-troden vallies.

KLAIUS

Long since the happie dwellers of these vallies,
Have praide me leave my strange exclaiming musique,
Which troubles their dayes works, and joyes of evening:
Long since I hate the night, more hate the morning:
Long since my thoughts chase me like beasts in forrests,
And make me wishe my selfe layd under mountaines.

STREPHON

Me seemes I see the high and stately mountaines,
Transforme themselves to lowe dejected vallies:
Me seemes I heare in these ill-changed forrests,
The Nightingales doo learne of Owles their musique:
Me seemes I feele the comfort of the morning
Turnde to the mortall serene of an evening.

KLAIUS

Me seemes I see a filthie clowdie evening,
As soon as Sunne begins to clime the mountaines:
Me seemes I feele a noysome sent, the morning
When I doo smell the flowers of these vallies:
Me seemes I heare, when I doo heare sweete musique,
The dreadfull cries of murdred men in forrests.

STREPHON

I wish to fire the trees of all these forrests;
I give the Sunne a last farewell each evening;
I curse the fidling finders out of Musicke:
With envie I doo hate the loftie mountaines;
And with despite despise the humble vallies:
I doo detest night, evening, day, and morning.

KLAIUS

Curse to my selfe my prayer is, the morning:
My fire is more, then can be made with forrests;
My state more base, then are the basest vallies:
I wish no evenings more to see, each evening;
Shamed I have my selfe in sight of mountaines,
And stoppe mine eares, lest I growe mad with Musicke.

STREPHON

For she, whose parts maintainde a perfect musique,
Whose beautie shin'de more then the blushing morning,
Who much did passe in state the stately mountaines,
In straightnes past the Cedars of the forrests,
Hath cast me wretch into eternall evening,
By taking her two Sunnes from these darke vallies.

KLAIUS

For she, to whom compar'd, the Alpes are vallies,
She, whose lest word brings from the spheares their
　　musique,
At whose approach the Sunne rose in the evening,

Who, where she went, bare in her forhead morning,
Is gone, is gone from these our spyled forrests,
Turning to desarts our best pastur'de mountaines.

STREPHON AND KLAIUS

These mountaines witnesse shall, so shall these vallies,
These forrests eke, made wretched by our musique,
Our morning hymne is this, and song at evening.

FROM *Astrophel and Stella*

WITH HOW SAD STEPS, Ô MOONE

With how sad steps, ô Moone, thou climb'st the skies,
  How silently, and with how wanne a face,
  What may it be, that even in heav'nly place
  That busie archer his sharpe arrowes tries?

Sure if that long with *Love* acquainted eyes
  Can judge of *Love*, thou feel'st a Lovers case;
  I reade it in thy lookes, thy languisht grace
  To me that feele the like, thy state descries.

Then ev'n of fellowship, ô Moone, tell me,
  Is constant *Love* deem'd there but want of wit?
  Are Beauties there as proud as here they be?

Do they above love to be lov'd, and yet
  Those Lovers scorne whom that *Love* doth possesse?
  Do they call *Vertue* there ungratefulnesse?

WHAT HAVE I THUS BETRAYED
MY LIBERTIE?

What have I thus betrayed my libertie?
  Can those blacke beames such burning markes en-
    grave
  In my free side? or am I borne a slave,
  Whose necke becomes such yoke of tyranny?

Or want I sense to feele my miserie?
  Or spirite, disdaine of such disdaine to have?
  Who for long faith, tho dayly helpe I crave,
  May get no almes but scorne of beggerie.

Vertue awake, Beautie but beautie is,
  I may, I must, I can, I will do
  Leave following that, which it is gaine to misse,

Let her go: soft, but here she comes, go to,
  Unkind, I love you not: O me, that eye
  Doth make my heart give to my tongue the lie.

IF ORPHEUS VOYCE HAD FORCE

If *Orpheus* voyce had force to breathe such musickes
    love
Through pores of senceless trees, as it could make them
    move:
If stones good measure daunc'd the *Theban* walles to
    build,
To cadence of the tunes, *Amphyons* lyre did yeeld,
More cause a like effect at leastwise bringeth:
O stones, ô trees, learne hearing, *Stella* singeth.

If Love might sweet'n so a boy of shepheard brood,
To make a Lyzard dull to taste Loves daintie food;

If Eagle fierce could so in *Grecian* Maid delight,
As his light was to her eyes, her death his endlesse night:
Earth gave that Love heav'n I trow Love refineth:
O beasts, ô birds, looke, love, lo, *Stella* shineth.

The birds, beasts, stones and trees feele this, and feeling,
    love;
And if the trees, nor stones stirre not the same to prove,
Nor beasts, nor birds do come into this blessed gaze,
Know, that small Love is quicke, and great Love doth
    amaze:
They are amaz'd, but you with reason armed,
O eyes, ô eares of men, how are you charmed!

WHO IS IT THAT THIS DARKE NIGHT

    Who is it that this darke night,
    Underneath my window playneth?
    It is one who from thy sight,
    Being (ah) exild, disdayneth
    Every other vulgar light.

    Why alas, and are you he?
    Be not yet those fancies changed?
    Deere when you find change in me,
    Though from me you be estranged,
    Let my chaunge to ruine be.

    Well, in absence this will dy,
    Leave to see, and leave to wonder:
    Absence sure will helpe, if I
    Can learne, how my selfe to sunder
    From what in my hart doth ly.

    But time will these thoughts remove:
    Time doth worke what no man knoweth,

Time doth as the subject prove,
With time still the affection groweth
In the faithfull Turtle dove.

What if you new beauties see,
Will not they stir new affection?
I will thinke thy pictures be,
(Imagelike of Saints perfection)
Poorely counterfeting thee.

But your reasons purest light,
Bids you leave such minds to nourish?
Deere, do reason no such spite,
Never doth thy beauty florish
More, then in my reasons sight.

But the wrongs love beares, will make
Love at length leave undertaking;
No the more fooles it do shake,
In a ground of so firme making,
Deeper still they drive the stake.

Peace, I thinke that some give eare:
Come no more, least I get anger.
Blisse, I will my blisse forbeare,
Fearing (sweete) you to endanger,
But my soule shall harbour there.

Well, be gone, be gone I say,
Lest that *Argus* eyes perceive you,
O unjust fortunes sway,
Which can make me thus to leave you,
And from lowts to run away.

In wonted walkes

In wonted walkes, since wonted fancies change,
　　Some cause there is, which of strange cause doth rise:
　　For in each thing wherto mine eye doth range,
　　Part of my paine me seemes engraved lyes.

The Rockes which were of constant mind, the marke
　　In clyming steepe, now hard refusall show:
　　The shading woods seeme now my Sunne to darke,
　　And stately hilles disdaine to looke so low.

The restfull Caves now restlesse visions give,
　　In Dales I see each way a hard assent:
　　Like late mowne meades, late cut from joy I live.
　　Alas sweete Brookes do in my teares augment:
　　　　Rockes, woods, hilles, caves, dales, meads, brookes,
　　　　　　answere me,
　　　　Infected mindes infect each thing they see.

If I could thinke how these my thoughts to leave,
　　Or thinking still my thoughts might have good end:
　　If rebell sence would reasons law receave;
　　Or reason foyld would not in vaine contend:
　　　　Then might I thinke what thoughts were best to
　　　　　　thinke:
　　　　Then might I wisely swimme or gladly sinke.

If either you would change your cruell hart,
　　Or cruell (still) time did your beautie staine:
　　If from my soule this love would once depart,
　　Or for my love some love I might obtaine,
　　　　Then might I hope a change or ease of minde,
　　　　By your good helpe, or in my selfe to finde.

But since my thoughts in thinking still are spent,
   With reasons strife, by senses overthrowne,
   You fairer still, and still more cruell bent,
   I loving still a love that loveth none,
      I yeeld and strive, I kisse and curse the paine:
      Thought, reason, sense, time, you, and I, maintaine.

Who hath his fancie pleased

Who hath his fancie pleased,
   With fruits of happie sight,
   Let here his eyes be raised
   On natures sweetest light.
A light which doth dissever,
   And yet unite the eyes,
   A light which dying never,
   Is cause the looker dyes.

She never dies but lasteth
   In life of lovers hart,
   He ever dies that wasteth
   In love, his chiefest part.
Thus is her life still guarded,
   In never dying faith:
   Thus is his death rewarded,
   Since she lives in his death.

Looke then and dye, the pleasure
   Doth answere well the paine:
   Small losse of mortall treasure,
   Who may immortall gaine.
Immortall be her graces,
   Immortall is her minde:

> They fit for heavenly places,
> This heaven in it doth binde.

But eyes these beauties see not,
  Nor sence that grace descryes:
  Yet eyes deprived be not,
  From sight of her faire eyes:
Which as of inward glorie
  They are the outward seale:
So may they live still sorie
  Which die not in that weale.

But who hath fancies pleased,
  With fruits of happie sight,
  Let here his eyes be raysed
  On natures sweetest light.

When to my deadlie pleasure

When to my deadlie pleasure,
When to my livelie torment,
Ladie mine eyes remained,
Joyned alas to your beames.

With violence of heav'nly
Beautie tied, to vertue,
Reason abasht retyred,
Gladly my senses yeelded.

Gladly my senses yeelding,
Thus to betray my harts fort,
Left me devoid of all life.

They to the beamie Sunnes went,
Where by the death of all deaths,
Finde to what harme they hastned.

Like to the silly *Sylvan*,
Burn'd by the light he best liked,
When with a fire he first met.

Yet, yet a life to their death,
Lady you have reserved,
Lady the life of all love.

For though my sense be from me,
And I be dead who want sense,
Yet do we both live in you.

Turned anew by your meanes,
Unto the flowre that ay turnes,
As you, alas, my Sunne bends.

Thus do I fall to rise thus,
Thus do I dye to live thus,
Changed to a change, I change not.

Thus may I not be from you:
Thus be my senses on you:
Thus what I thinke is of you:
Thus what I seeke is in you:
    All what I am, it is you.

Fulke Greville,
Lord Brooke

(1554–1628)

FROM *Caelica*

Fye foolish Earth, thinke you the heaven wants glory,
Because your shadowes doe your selfe be-night?
All's darke unto the blind, let them be sory,
The heavens in themselves are ever bright.

Fye fond desire, thinke you that Love wants glory,
Because your shadowes doe your selfe benight?
The hopes and feares of lust, may make men sorie,
But *love still in her selfe finds her delight.*

Then Earth stand fast, the skye that you benight
Will turne againe, and so restore your glory;
Desire be steady, hope is your delight,
An orbe wherein no creature can be sorie;
   Love being plac'd above these *middle* regions.
   Where every passion warres it selfe with legions.

                              (xvi)

      Absence, the noble truce
      Of *Cupids* warre:
      Where though desires want use,
      They honoured are.
      Thou art the just protection,

511

Of prodigall affection,
Have thou the praise;
When bankrupt *Cupid* braveth,
Thy mines his credit saveth,
With sweet delayes.

Of wounds which presence makes
With Beauties shot,
Absence the anguish slakes,
But healeth not:
Absence records the Stories,
Wherein Desire glories,
Although she burne;
She cherisheth the spirits
Where Constancy inherits
And passions mourne.

Absence, like dainty Clouds,
On glorious-bright,
Natures weake senses shrowds,
From harming light.
Absence maintaines the treasure
Of pleasure unto pleasure,
Sparing with praise;
Absence doth nurse the fire,
Which starves and feeds desire
With sweet delayes.

Presence to every part
Of Beauty tyes,
Where Wonder rules the Heart
There Pleasure dyes:
Presence plagues minde and senses
With modesties defences,
Absence is free:
Thoughts doe in absence venter

On *Cupids* shadowed center,
They winke and see.

But Thoughts be not so brave,
With absent joy;
For you with that you have
Your selfe destroy:
The absence which you glory,
Is that which makes you sory,
And burne in vaine:
For Thought is not the weapon,
Wherewith *thoughts-ease* men cheapen,
Absence is paine.

(xlv)

All my senses, like Beacons flame,
Gave *Alarum* to desire
To take armes in Cynthia's name,
And set all my thoughts on fire:
Furies wit perswaded me,
Happy love was hazards heire,
Cupid did best shoot and see
In the night where smooth is faire;
Up I start beleeving well
To see if *Cynthia* were awake;
Wonders I saw, who can tell?
And thus unto my selfe I spake;
Sweet God *Cupid* where am I,
That by pale *Diana's* light:
Such rich beauties doe espie,
As harme our senses with delight?
Am I borne up to the skyes?
See where *Jove* and *Venus* shine,
Shewing in her heavenly eyes
That desire is divine:

Looke where lyes the Milken way,
Way unto that dainty throne,
Where while all the Gods would play,
Vulcan thinkes to dwell alone.
I gave reynes to this conceipt,
Hope went on the wheele of lust:
Phansies scales are false of weight,
Thoughts take thought that goe of trust,
I stept forth to touch the skye,
I a God by *Cupid* dreames,
Cynthia who did naked lye,
Runnes away like silver streames;
Leaving hollow banks behind,
Who can neither forward move,
Nor if rivers be unkind,
Turne away or leave to love.
There stand I, like *Articke* pole,
Where *Sol* passeth o're the *line*,
Mourning my benighted soule,
Which so loseth light divine.
There stand I like Men that preach
From the Execution place,
At their death content to teach
All the world with their disgrace:
He that lets his *Cynthia* lye,
Naked on a bed of play,
To say prayers ere she dye,
Teacheth time to runne away:
Let no Love-desiring heart,
In the Starres goe seeke his fate,
Love is onely Natures art,
Wonder hinders Love and Hate.
  None can well behold with eyes,
  But what underneath him lies.

                                            (lvi)

Who Grace, for *Zenith* had, from which no shadowes
  grow,
Who hath seene Joy of all his hopes, and end of all his
  woe,
Whose Love belov'd hath beene the crowne of his de-
  sire,
Who hath seene sorrowes glories burnt, in sweet affec-
  tions fire:
If from this heavenly state, which soules with soules
  unites,
He be falne downe into the darke despaired warre of
  sprites;
Let him lament with me, for none doth glorie know,
That hath not beene above himselfe, and thence falne
  downe to woe:
But if there be one hope left in his languish'd heart,
In feare of worse, if wish of ease, if horrour may depart,
He playes with his complaints, he is no mate for me,
Whose love is lost, whose hopes are fled, whose feares
  for ever be.
Yet not those happy feares which shew Desire her death
Teaching with use a peace in woe, and in despaire a
  faith:
No, no, my feares kill not, but make uncured wounds,
Where joy and peace doe issue out, and onely paine
  abounds.
Unpossible are helpe, reward and hope to me,
Yet while unpossible they are, they easie seeme to be.
Most easie seemes remorse, despaire and deathe to me,
Yet while they passing easie seeme, unpossible they be.
So neither can I leave my hopes that doe deceive
Nor can I trust mine owne despaire, and nothing else
  receive.

Thus be unhappy men, blest to be more accurst;

Neere to the glories of the Sunne, clouds with most horrour burst.

Like Ghosts raised out of graves, who live not, though they goe,

Whose walking feare to others is, and to themselves a woe:

So is my life by her whose love to me is dead,

On whose worth my despaire yet walks, and my desire is fed;

I swallow downe the baite, which carries downe my death;

I cannot put love from my heart, while life drawes in my breath;

My Winter is within which withereth my joy;

My Knowledge, seate of Civill warre, where friends and foes destroy,

And my Desires are Wheeles, whereon my heart is borne,

With endlesse turning of themselves, still living to be torne.

My Thoughts are Eagles food, ordayned to be a prey

To worth; and being still consum'd, yet never to decay.

My Memorie, where once my heart laid up the store

Of helpe, of joy, of spirits wealth to multiply them more;

Is now become the Tombe wherein all these lye slaine,

My helpe, my joy, my spirits wealth all sacrific'd to paine.

In Paradise I once did live; and taste the tree,

Which shadowed was from all the world, in joy to shadow me.

The tree hath lost his fruit, or I have lost my seate,

My soule both blacke with shadow is, and over-burnt with heat:

Truth here for triumph serves, to shew her power is
    great,
Whom no desert can overcome, nor no distresse intreat.
Time past layes up my joy; and time to come my griefe,
She ever must be my *desire*, and never my *reliefe*.
Wrong, her Lieutenant is; my wounded Thoughts are
    they,
Who have no power to keepe the field, nor will to runne
    away.
O ruefull Constancy, and where is Change so base,
As it may be compar'd with thee in scorne, and in dis-
    grace?
Like as the Kings forlorne, depos'd from their estate,
Yet cannot choose but love the Crowne, although new
    Kings they hate;
If they doe plead their right, nay, if they onely live,
Offences to the Crowne alike their Good and Ill shall
    give;
So (I would I were not) because I may complaine,
And cannot choose but love my Wrongs, and joy to
    Wish in vaine;
This faith condemneth me, my right doth rumor move,
I may not know the cause I fell, nor yet without cause
    love.
Then Love where is reward, at least where is the fame
Of them that being, beare thy crosse, and being not, thy
    name?
The worlds example I, a Fable every where,
A Well from whence the springs are dried, a Tree that
    doth not beare:
I like the Bird in cage at first with cunning caught,
And in my bondage for delight with greater cunning
    taught.
Now owners humour dyes, I neither loved nor fed,
Nor freed am, till in the cage forgotten I be dead.

The Ship of *Greece*, the Streames and she be not the
    same

They were, although Ship, Streames and she still beare
    their antique name.

The Wood which was, is worne, those waves are runne
    away,

Yet still a Ship, and still a Streame, still running to a
    Sea.

She lov'd, and still she loves, but doth not still love me,

To all except my selfe yet is, as she was wont to be.

O, my once happy thoughts, the heaven where grace
    did dwell,

My Saint hath turn'd away her face, and made that
    heaven my hell.

A hell, for so is that from whence no soules returne,

Where, while our spirits are sacrific'd, they waste not
    though they burne.

Since then this is my state, and nothing worse than this,

Behold the mappe of death-like life exil'd from lovely
    blisse,

Alone among the world, strange with my friends to be,

Shewing my fall to them that scorne, see not or will not
    see.

My Heart a wildernesse, my studies only feare,

And as in shadowes of curst death, a prospect of de-
    spaire.

My Exercise, must be my horrours to repeat,

My Peace, Joy, End, and Sacrifice her dead Love to
    intreat.

My Food, the time that was; the time to come, my Fast;

For Drinke, the barren thirst I feele of glories that are
    past;

Sighs and salt teares my Bath; Reason, my Looking-
    glasse,

To shew me *he most wretched is, that once most happy
    was.*
Forlorne desires my Clocke to tell me every day,
That time hath stolne Love, Life, and All but my dis-
    tresse away.
For Musicke heavy sighes, my Walke an inward woe.
Which like a shadow ever shall before my body goe;
And I my selfe am he, that doth with none compare,
Except in woes and lacke of worth; whose states more
    wretched are.
Let no man aske my name, nor what else I should be;
For *Greiv-Ill*, paine, forlorne estate doe best decipher me.

(lxxxiii)

When as Mans life, the light of humane lust,
In socket of his earthly lanthorne burnes,
That all this glory unto ashes must,
And generation to corruption turnes;
    Then fond desires that onely feare their end,
    Doe vainely wish for life, but to amend.

But when this life is from the body fled,
To see it selfe in that *eternall Glasse*,
Where time doth end, and thoughts accuse the dead,
Where all to come, is one with all that was;
    Then living men aske how he left his breath,
    That while he lived never thought of death.

(lxxxvii)

Three things there be in Mans opinion deare,
Fame, many *Friends*, and *Fortunes* dignities:
False visions all, which in our sense appeare,
To sanctifie desire's Idolatries.

For what is Fortune, but a wat'ry glasse?
Whose chrystall forehead wants a steely backe,
Where raine and stormes beare all away that was,
Whose shape alike both depths and shallowes wracke.

Fame againe, which from blinding power takes light,
Both *Caesars* shadow is, and *Cato's* friend.
The child of humour, not allyed to right,
Living by oft exchange of winged end.

And many *Friends,* false strength of feeble mind,
Betraying equals, as true slaves to might;
Like *Ecchoes* still send voyces down the wind,
But never in adversity finde right.

Then Man, though vertue of extremities,
The middle be, and so hath two to one,
By Place and Nature constant enemies,
And against both these no strength but her owne,
   Yet quit thou for her, Friends, Fame, Fortunes throne;
   Divils, there many be, and Gods but one.

(cv)

Syon lyes waste, and thy *Jerusalem,*
O Lord, is falne to utter desolation,
Against thy Prophets, and thy holy men,
The sinne hath wrought a fatall combination,
   Prophan'd thy name, thy worship overthrowne,
   And made thee living Lord, a God unknowne.

Thy powerfull lawes, thy wonders of creation,
Thy Word incarnate, glorious heaven, darke hell,
Lye shadowed under Mans degeneration,
Thy Christ still crucifi'd for doing well,
   Impiety, O Lord, sits on thy throne,
   Which makes thee living Light, a God unknown.

Mans superstition hath thy truths entomb'd,
His Atheisme againe her pomps defaceth,
That sensuall unsatiable vaste wombe
Of thy seene Church, thy unseene Church disgraceth;
 There lives no truth with them that seem thine own,
 Which makes thee living Lord, a God unknowne.

Yet unto thee, Lord, (mirrour of transgression)
Wee, who for earthly Idols, have forsaken
Thy heavenly Image (sinlesse pure impression)
And so in nets of vanity lye taken,
 All desolate implore that to thine owne,
 Lord, thou no longer live a God unknowne.

Yet Lord let *Israels* plagues not be eternall,
Nor sinne for ever cloud thy sacred Mountaines,
Nor with false flames spirituall but infernall,
Dry up thy mercies ever springing fountaines,
 Rather, sweet *Jesus*, fill up time and come,
 To yeeld the sinne her everlasting doome.

(cix)

FROM *Mustapha*

CHORUS SACERDOTUM

Oh wearisome Condition of Humanity!
Borne under one Law, to another bound:
Vainely begot, and yet forbidden vanity,
Created sicke, commanded to be sound:
What meaneth Nature by these diverse Lawes?
Passion and Reason, selfe-division cause:
Is it the marke, or Majesty of Power
To make offences that it may forgive?

Nature herselfe, doth her owne selfe defloure,
To hate those errors she her selfe doth give.
For how should man thinke that, he may not doe
If Nature did not faile, and punish too?
Tyrant to others, to her selfe unjust,
Onely commands things difficult and hard.
Forbids us all things, which it knowes is lust,
Makes easie paines, unpossible reward.
If Nature did not take delight in blood,
She would have made more easie waies to good.
We that are bound by vowes, and by Promotion,
With pompe of holy Sacrifice and rites,
To teach beleefe in good and still devotion,
To preach of Heavens wonders, and delights:
Yet when each of us, in his owne heart lookes,
He findes the God there, farre unlike his Bookes.

Edmund Spenser

(1552?–1599)

FROM *The Shepheardes Calender*

APRILL

ÆGLOGA QUARTA

ARGUMENT

This Æglogue is purposely intended to the honor and prayse of our most gracious sovereigne, Queene Elizabeth. The speakers herein be Hobbinoll and Thenott, two shepheardes: the which Hobbinoll, being before mentioned greatly to have loved Colin, is here set forth more largely, complayning him of that boyes great misadventure in love, whereby his mynd was alienate and withdrawen not onely from him, who moste loved him, but also from all former delightes and studies, as- well in pleasaunt pyping as conning ryming and singing, and other his laudable exercises. Whereby he taketh occasion, for proofe of his more excellencie and skill in poetrie, to recorde a songe which the sayd Colin sometime made in honor of her Majestie, whom abruptely he termeth Elysa.

THENOT. Tell me, good Hobbinoll, what garres thee
    greete?
  What! hath some wolfe thy tender lambes ytorne?
Or is thy bagpype broke, that soundes so sweete?
  Or art thou of thy loved lasse forlorne?

Or bene thine eyes attempred to the yeare,
  Quenching the gasping furrowes thirst with rayne?

523

Like April shoure, so stremes the trickling teares
  Adowne thy cheeke, to quenche thy thristye payne.

HOBBINOLL. Nor thys, nor that, so muche doeth make
    me mourne,
  But for the ladde whome long I lovd so deare
Nowe loves a lasse that all his love doth scorne:
  He, plongd in payne, his tressed locks dooth teare.

Shepheards delights he dooth them all forsweare,
  Hys pleasaunt pipe, whych made us meriment,
He wylfully hath broke, and doth forbeare
  His wonted songs, wherein he all outwent.

THENOT. What is he for a ladde you so lament?
  Ys love such pinching payne to them that prove?
And hath he skill to make so excellent,
  Yet hath so little skill to brydle love?

HOBBINOLL. Colin thou kenst, the southerne shepheardes
    boye:
  Him Love hath wounded with a deadly darte.
Whilome on him was all my care and joye,
  Forcing with gyfts to winne his wanton heart.

But now from me hys madding mynd is starte,
  And woes the widdowes daughter of the glenne:
So nowe fayre Rosalind hath bredde hys smart,
  So now his frend is chaunged for a frenne.

THENOT. But if hys ditties bene so trimly dight,
  I praye thee, Hobbinoll, recorde some one,
The whiles our flockes doe graze about in sight,
  And we close shrowded in thys shade alone.

HOBBINOLL. Contented I: then will I singe his laye
  Of fayre Elisa, queene of shepheardes all;

Which once he made, as by a spring he laye,
   And tuned it unto the waters fall.

"Ye dayntye Nymphs, that in this blessed brooke
   Doe bathe your brest,
Forsake your watry bowres, and hether looke,
   At my request.
And eke you Virgins that on Parnasse dwell,
Whence floweth Helicon, the learned well,
    Helpe me to blaze
    Her worthy praise
Which in her sexe doth all excell.

"Of fayre Elisa be your silver song,
   That blessed wight:
The flowre of virgins, may shee florish long
   In princely plight.
For shee is Syrinx daughter without spotte,
Which Pan, the shepheards god, of her begot:
    So sprong her grace
    Of heavenly race,
No mortall blemishe may her blotte.

"See, where she sits upon the grassie greene,
   (O seemely sight!)
Yclad in scarlot, like a mayden queene,
   And ermines white.
Upon her head a cremosin coronet,
With damaske roses and daffadillies set:
    Bayleaves betweene,
    And primroses greene,
Embellish the sweete violet.

"Tell me, have ye seene her angelick face,
   Like Phœbe fayre?
Her heavenly haveour, her princely grace,
   Can you well compare?

The redde rose medled with the white yfere,
In either cheeke depeincten lively chere.
   Her modest eye,
   Her majestie,
Where have you seene the like, but there?

"I sawe Phœbus thrust out his golden hedde,
   Upon her to gaze:
But when he sawe how broade her beames did spredde,
   It did him amaze.
He blusht to see another sunne belowe,
Ne durst againe his fyrye face out showe:
   Let him, if he dare,
   His brightnesse compare
With hers, to have the overthrowe.

"Shewe thy selfe, Cynthia, with thy silver rayes,
   And be not abasht:
When shee the beames of her beauty displayes,
   O how art thou dasht!
But I will not match her with Latonaes seede;
Such follie great sorow to Niobe did breede:
   Now she is a stone,
   And makes a dayly mone,
Warning all other to take heede.

"Pan may be proud, that ever he begot
   Such a bellibone,
And Syrinx rejoyse, that ever was her lot
   To beare such an one.
Soone as my younglings cryen for the dam,
To her will I offer a milkwhite lamb:
   Shee is my goddesse plaine,
   And I her shepherds swayne,
Albee forswonck and forswatt I am.

"I see Calliope speede her to the place,
   Where my goddesse shines,

And after her the other Muses trace,
    With their violines.
Bene they not bay braunches which they doe beare,
All for Elisa in her hand to weare?
    So sweetely they play,
    And sing all the way,
That it a heaven is to heare.

"Lo, how finely the Graces can it foote
    To the instrument:
They dauncen deffly, and singen soote,
    In their meriment.
Wants not a fourth Grace, to make the daunce even?
Let that rowme to my Lady be yeven:
    She shalbe a Grace,
    To fyll the fourth place,
And reigne with the rest in heaven.

"And whither rennes this bevie of ladies bright,
    Raunged in a rowe?
They bene all Ladyes of the Lake behight,
    That unto her goe.
Chloris, that is the chiefest nymph of al,
Of olive braunches beares a coronall:
    Olives bene for peace,
    When wars doe surcease:
Such for a princesse bene principall.

"Ye shepheards daughters, that dwell on the greene,
    Hye you there apace:
Let none come there, but that virgins bene,
    To adorne her grace.
And when you come whereas shee is in place,
See that your rudenesse doe not you disgrace:
    Binde your fillets faste,
    And gird in your waste,
For more finesse, with a tawdrie lace.

"Bring hether the pincke and purple cullambine,
   With gelliflowres;
Bring coronations, and sops in wine,
   Worne of paramoures;
Strowe me the ground with daffadowndillies,
And cowslips, and kingcups, and loved lillies:
   The pretie pawnce,
   And the chevisaunce,
Shall match with the fayre flowre delice.

"Now ryse up, Elisa, decked as thou art,
   In royall aray;
And now ye daintie damsells may depart
   Echeone her way.
I feare I have troubled your troupes to longe:
Let Dame Eliza thanke you for her song:
   And if you come hether
   When damsines I gether,
I will part them all you among."

THENOT. And was thilk same song of Colins owne mak-
      ing?
   Ah, foolish boy, that is with love yblent!
Great pittie is, he be in such taking,
   For naught caren, that bene so lewdly bent.

HOBBINOLL. Sicker, I hold him for a greater fon,
   That loves the thing he cannot purchase.
But let us homeward, for night draweth on,
   And twincling starres the daylight hence chase.

THENOTS EMBLEME
O quam te memorem, virgo?

HOBBINOLS EMBLEME
O dea certe!

NOVEMBER

ÆGLOGA UNDECIMA

ARGUMENT

In this xi. Æglogue he bewayleth the death of some mayden of greate bloud, whom he calleth Dido. The personage is secrete, and to me altogether unknowne, albe of him selfe I often required the same. This Æglogue is made in imitation of Marot his song, which he made upon the death of Loys the Frenche Queene: but farre passing his reache, and in myne opinion all other the Eglogues of this booke.

THENOT. Colin, my deare, when shall it please thee sing,
As thou were wont, songs of some jouisaunce?
Thy Muse to long slombreth in sorrowing,
Lulled a sleepe through loves misgovernaunce:
Now somewhat sing whose endles sovenaunce
Emong the shepeheards swaines may aye remaine,
Whether thee list thy loved lasse advaunce,
Or honor Pan with hymnes of higher vaine.
COLIN. Thenot, now nis the time of merimake,
Nor Pan to herye, nor with love to playe:
Sike myrth in May is meetest for to make,
Or summer shade, under the cocked haye.
But nowe sadde winter welked hath the day,
And Phœbus, weary of his yerely taske,
Ystabled hath his steedes in lowlye laye,
And taken up his ynne in Fishes haske.
Thilke sollein season sadder plight doth aske,
And loatheth sike delightes as thou doest prayse:
The mornefull Muse in myrth now list ne maske,
As shee was wont in youngth and sommer dayes.
But if thou algate lust light virelayes,
And looser songs of love, to underfong,

Who but thy selfe deserves sike Poetes prayse?
Relieve thy oaten pypes that sleepen long.
THENOT. The nightingale is sovereigne of song,
Before him sits the titmose silent bee:
And I, unfitte to thrust in skilfull throng,
Should Colin make judge of my fooleree.
Nay, better learne of hem that learned bee,
And han be watered at the Muses well:
The kindlye dewe drops from the higher tree,
And wets the little plants that lowly dwell.
But if sadde winters wrathe, and season chill,
Accorde not with thy Muses meriment,
To sadder times thou mayst attune thy quill,
And sing of sorrowe and deathes dreeriment:
For deade is Dido, dead, alas! and drent,
Dido, the greate shepehearde his daughter sheene:
The fayrest may she was that ever went,
Her like shee has not left behinde I weene.
And if thou wilt bewayle my wofull tene,
I shall thee give yond cosset for thy payne:
And if thy rymes as rownd and rufull bene
As those that did thy Rosalind complayne,
Much greater gyfts for guerdon thou shalt gayne
Then kidde or cosset, which I thee bynempt.
Then up, I say, thou jolly shepeheard swayne,
Let not my small demaund be so contempt.
COLIN. Thenot, to that I choose thou doest me tempt:
But ah! to well I wote my humble vaine,
And howe my rymes bene rugged and unkempt:
Yet, as I conne, my conning I will strayne.

Up, then, Melpomene, thou mournefulst Muse of nyne!
Such cause of mourning never hadst afore:
Up, grieslie ghostes! and up my rufull ryme!
Matter of myrth now shalt thou have no more:

For dead shee is that myrth thee made of yore.
  Dido, my deare, alas! is dead,
  Dead, and lyeth wrapt in lead:
    O heavie herse!
Let streaming teares be poured out in store:
    O carefull verse!

Shepheards, that by your flocks on Kentish downes
    abyde,
Waile ye this wofull waste of Natures warke:
Waile we the wight whose presence was our pryde:
Waile we the wight whose absence is our carke.
The sonne of all the world is dimme and darke:
  The earth now lacks her wonted light,
  And all we dwell in deadly night:
    O heavie herse!
Breake we our pypes, that shrild as lowde as larke:
    O carefull verse!

Why doe we longer live, (ah, why live we so long?)
Whose better dayes death hath shut up in woe?
The fayrest floure our gyrlond all emong
Is faded quite, and into dust ygoe.
Sing now, ye shepheards daughters, sing no moe
  The songs that Colin made in her prayse,
  But into weeping turne your wanton layes:
    O heavie herse!
Now is time to die. Nay, time was long ygoe:
    O carefull verse!

Whence is it that the flouret of the field doth fade,
And lyeth buried long in winters bale:
Yet soone as spring his mantle doth display,
It floureth fresh, as it should never fayle?
But thing on earth that is of most availe,
  As vertues braunch and beauties budde,

Reliven not for any good.
O heavie herse!
The braunch once dead, the budde eke needes must
    quaile:
O carefull verse!

She, while she was, (that was, a woful word to sayne!)
For beauties prayse and plesaunce had no pere:
So well she couth the shepherds entertayne
With cakes and cracknells and such country chere.
Ne would she scorne the simple shepheards swaine,
    For she would cal hem often heame,
    And give hem curds and clouted creame.
    O heavie herse!
Als Colin Cloute she would not once disdayne.
    O carefull verse!

But nowe sike happy cheere is turnd to heavie chaunce,
Such pleasaunce now displast by dolors dint:
All musick sleepes where Death doth leade the daunce,
And shepherds wonted solace is extinct.
The blew in black, the greene in gray, is tinct;
    The gaudie girlonds deck her grave,
    The faded flowres her corse embrave.
    O heavie herse!
Morne nowe, my Muse, now morne with teares besprint.
    O carefull verse!

O thou greate shepheard, Lobbin, how great is thy griefe!
Where bene the nosegayes that she dight for thee?
The coloured chaplets, wrought with a chiefe,
The knotted rushringes, and gilte rosemaree?
For shee deemed nothing too deere for thee.
    Ah! they bene all yclad in clay,
    One bitter blast blewe all away.
    O heavie herse!

Thereof nought remaynes but the memoree.
O carefull verse!

Ay me! that dreerie Death should strike so mortall
   stroke,
That can undoe Dame Natures kindly course:
The faded lockes fall from the loftie oke,
The flouds do gasp, for dryed is theyr sourse,
And flouds of teares flowe in theyr stead perforse.
   The mantled medowes mourne,
   Theyr sondry colours tourne.
   O heavie herse!
The heavens doe melt in teares without remorse.
   O carefull verse!

The feeble flocks in field refuse their former foode,
And hang theyr heads, as they would learne to
   weepe:
The beasts in forest wayle as they were woode,
Except the wolves, that chase the wandring sheepe,
Now she is gon that safely did hem keepe.
   The turtle, on the bared braunch,
   Laments the wound that Death did launch.
   O heavie herse!
And Philomele her song with teares doth steepe.
   O carefull verse!

The water nymphs, that wont with her to sing and
   daunce,
And for her girlond olive braunches beare,
Now balefull boughes of cypres doen advaunce:
The Muses, that were wont greene bayes to weare,
Now bringen bitter eldre braunches seare:
   The Fatall Sisters eke repent
   Her vitall threde so soone was spent
   O heavie herse!

Morne now, my Muse, now morne with heavie cheare.
  O carefull verse!

O trustlesse state of earthly things, and slipper hope
Of mortal men, that swincke and sweate for nought,
And shooting wide, doe misse the marked scope:
Now have I learnd, (a lesson derely bought)
That nys on earth assuraunce to be sought:
  For what might be in earthlie mould,
  That did her buried body hould.
  O heavie herse!
Yet saw I on the beare when it was brought.
  O carefull verse!

But maugre Death, and dreaded sisters deadly spight,
And gates of Hel, and fyrie furies forse,
She hath the bonds broke of eternall night,
Her soule unbodied of the burdenous corpse.
Why then weepes Lobbin so without remorse?
  O Lobb! thy losse no longer lament;
  Dido nis dead, but into heaven hent.
  O happye herse!
Cease now, my Muse, now cease thy sorrowes sourse:
  O joyfull verse!

Why wayle we then? why weary we the gods with
    playnts,
As if some evill were to her betight?
She raignes a goddesse now emong the saintes,
That whilome was the saynt of shepheards light:
And is enstalled nowe in heavens hight.
  I see thee, blessed soule, I see,
  Walke in Elisian fields so free.
  O happy herse!
Might I once come to thee! O that I might!
  O joyfull verse!

Unwise and wretched men, to weete whats good or ill,
Wee deeme of death as doome of ill desert:
But knewe we, fooles, what it us bringes until,
Dye would we dayly, once it to expert.
No daunger there the shepheard can astert:
 Fayre fieldes and pleasaunt layes there bene,
 The fields ay fresh, the grasse ay greene:
 O happy herse!
Make hast, ye shepheards, thether to revert:
 O joyfull verse!

Dido is gone afore (whose turne shall be the next?)
There lives shee with the blessed gods in blisse,
There drincks she nectar with ambrosia mixt,
And joyes enjoyes that mortall men doe misse.
The honor now of highest gods she is,
 That whilome was poore shepheards pryde,
 While here on earth she did abyde.
 O happy herse!
Ceasse now, my song, my woe now wasted is.
 O joyfull verse!

THENOT. Ay, francke shepheard, how bene thy verses
 meint
With doolful pleasaunce, so as I ne wotte
Whether rejoyce or weepe for great constrainte!
Thyne be the cossette, well hast thow it gotte.
Up, Colin, up, ynough thou morned hast:
Now gynnes to mizzle, hye we homeward fast.

     COLINS EMBLEME
     La mort ny mord.

FROM *Amoretti*

The soverayne beauty which I doo admyre,
Witnesse the world how worthy to be prayzed;
The light wherof hath kindled heavenly fyre
In my fraile spirit, by her from basenesse raysed:
That being now with her huge brightnesse dazed,
Base thing I can no more endure to view;
But looking still on her, I stand amazed
At wondrous sight of so celestiall hew.
So when my toung would speake her praises dew,
It stopped is with thoughts astonishment;
And when my pen would write her titles true,
It ravisht is with fancies wonderment.
Yet in my hart I then both speake and write
The wonder that my wit cannot endite.

(iii)

Lyke as a huntsman after weary chace,
Seeing the game from him escapt away,
Sits downe to rest him in some shady place,
With panting hounds beguiled of their pray:
So after long pursuit and vaine assay,
When I all weary had the chace forsooke,
The gentle deare returnd the selfe-same way,
Thinking to quench her thirst at the next brooke.
There she beholding me with mylder looke,
Sought not to fly, but fearelesse still did bide:
Till I in hand her yet halfe trembling tooke,
And with her owne goodwill hir fyrmely tyde.
Strange thing me seemd to see a beast so wyld,
So goodly wonne with her owne will beguyld.

(lxvii)

Epithalamion

Ye learned sisters, which have oftentimes
Beene to me ayding, others to adorne,
Whom ye thought worthy of your gracefull rymes,
That even the greatest did not greatly scorne
To heare theyr names sung in your simple layes,
But joyed in theyr praise;
And when ye list your owne mishaps to mourne,
Which death, or love, or fortunes wreck did rayse,
Your string could soone to sadder tenor turne,
And teach the woods and waters to lament
Your dolefull dreriment:
Now lay those sorrowfull complaints aside,
And having all your heads with girland crownd,
Helpe me mine owne loves prayses to resound;
Ne let the same of any be envide:
So Orpheus did for his owne bride,
So I unto my selfe alone will sing,
The woods shall to me answer, and my eccho ring.

Early, before the worlds light giving lampe
His golden beame upon the hils doth spred,
Having disperst the nights unchearefull dampe,
Doe ye awake, and, with fresh lusty hed,
Go to the bowre of my beloved love,
My truest turtle dove:
Bid her awake; for Hymen is awake,
And long since ready forth his maske to move,
With his bright tead that flames with many a flake,
And many a bachelor to waite on him,
In theyr fresh garments trim.

Bid her awake therefore and soone her dight,
For lo the wished day is come at last,
That shall for al the paynes and sorrowes past,
Pay to her usury of long delight:
And whylest she doth her dight,
Doe ye to her of joy and solace sing,
That all the woods may answer and your eccho ring.

Bring with you all the Nymphes that you can heare
Both of the rivers and the forrests greene:
And of the sea that neighbours to her neare,
Al with gay girlands goodly wel beseene.
And let them also with them bring in hand
Another gay girland
For my fayre love of lillyes and of roses,
Bound truelove wize with a blew silke riband.
And let them make great store of bridale poses,
And let them eeke bring store of others flowers
To deck the bridale bowers.
And let the ground whereas her foot shall tread,
For feare the stones her tender foot should wrong
Be strewed with fragrant flowers all along,
And diapred lyke the discolored mead.
Which done, doe at her chamber dore awayt,
For she will waken strayt,
The whiles doe ye this song unto her sing,
The woods shall to you answer and your Eccho ring.

Ye Nymphes of Mulla which with careful heed,
The silver scaly trouts doe tend full well,
And greedy pikes which use therein to feed,
(Those trouts and pikes all others doo excell)
And ye likewise which keepe the rushy lake,
Where none doo fishes take,
Bynd up the locks the which hang scatterd light,
And in his waters which your mirror make,

Behold your faces as the christall bright,
That when you come whereas my love doth lie,
No blemish she may spie.
And eke ye lightfoot mayds which keepe the deere,
That on the hoary mountayne use to towre,
And the wylde wolves, which seeke them to devoure,
With your steele darts doo chace from comming neer,
Be also present heere,
To helpe to decke her, and to help to sing,
That all the woods may answer, and your eccho ring.

Wake now, my love, awake! for it is time:
The rosy Morne long since left Tithones bed,
All ready to her silver coche to clyme,
And Phœbus gins to shew his glorious hed.
Hark how the cheerefull birds do chaunt theyr laies,
And carroll of loves praise!
The merry larke hir mattins sings aloft,
The thrush replyes, the mavis descant playes,
The ouzell shrills, the ruddock warbles soft,
So goodly all agree, with sweet consent,
To this dayes merriment.
Ah! my deere love, why doe ye sleepe thus long,
When meeter were that ye should now awake,
T' awayt the comming of your joyous make,
And hearken to the birds love-learned song,
The deawy leaves among?
For they of joy and pleasance to you sing,
That all the woods them answer, and theyr eccho ring.

My love is now awake out of her dreame,
And her fayre eyes, like stars that dimmed were
With darksome cloud, now shew theyr goodly beams
More bright then Hesperus his head doth rere.
Come now, ye damzels, daughters of delight,
Helpe quickly her to dight.

But first come ye, fayre Houres, which were begot,
In Joves sweet paradice, of Day and Night,
Which doe the seasons of the year allot,
And al that ever in this world is fayre
Do make and still repayre.
And ye three handmayds of the Cyprian Queene,
The which doe still adorne her beauties pride,
Helpe to addorne my beautifullest bride:
And as ye her array, still throw betweene
Some graces to be seene:
And as ye use to Venus, to her sing,
The whiles the woods shal answer, and your eccho ring.

Now is my love all ready forth to come:
Let all the virgins therefore well awayt,
And ye fresh boyes, that tend upon her groome,
Prepare your selves, for he is comming strayt.
Set all your things in seemely good aray,
Fit for so joyfull day,
The joyfulst day that ever sunne did see.
•Faire Sun, shew forth thy favourable ray,
And let thy lifull heat not fervent be,
For feare of burning her sunshyny face,
Her beauty to disgrace.
O fayrest Phœbus, father of the Muse,
If ever I did honour thee aright,
Or sing the thing that mote thy mind delight,
Doe not thy servants simple boone refuse,
But let this day, let this one day be myne,
Let all the rest be thine.
Then I thy soverayne prayses loud wil sing,
That all the woods shal answer, and theyr eccho ring.

Harke how the minstrels gin to shrill aloud
Their merry musick that resounds from far,

The pipe, the tabor, and the trembling croud,
That well agree withouten breach or jar.
But most of all the damzels doe delite,
When they their tymbrels smyte,
And thereunto doe daunce and carrol sweet,
That all the sences they doe ravish quite,
The whyles the boyes run up and downe the street,
Crying aloud with strong confused noyce,
As if it were one voyce.
"Hymen, Iö Hymen, Hymen," they do shout,
That even to the heavens theyr shouting shrill
Doth reach, and all the firmament doth fill;
To which the people, standing all about,
As in approvance doe thereto applaud,
And loud advaunce her laud,
And evermore they "Hymen, Hymen" sing,
That al the woods them answer, and theyr eecho ring.

Loe! where she comes along with portly pace,
Lyke Phœbe, from her chamber of the east,
Arysing forth to run her mighty race,
Clad all in white, that seemes a virgin best.
So well it her beseemes, that ye would weene
Some angell she had beene.
Her long loose yellow locks lyke golden wyre,
Sprinckled with perle, and perling flowres atweene,
Doe lyke a golden mantle her attyre,
And being crowned with a girland greene,
Seeme lyke some mayden queene.
Her modest eyes, abashed to behold
So many gazers as on her do stare,
Upon the lowly ground affixed are;
Ne dare lift up her countenance too bold,
But blush to heare her prayses sung so loud,

So farre from being proud.
Nathlesse doe ye still loud her prayses sing,
That all the woods may answer, and your eccho ring.

Tell me, ye merchants daughters, did ye see
So fayre a creature in your towne before,
So sweet, so lovely, and so mild as she,
Adornd with beautyes grace and vertues store?
Her goodly eyes lyke saphyres shining bright,
Her forehead yvory white,
Her cheekes lyke apples which the sun hath rudded,
Her lips lyke cherryes charming men to byte,
Her brest like to a bowle of creame uncrudded,
Her paps lyke lyllies budded,
Her snowie necke lyke to a marble towre,
And all her body like a pallace fayre,
Ascending uppe, with many a stately stayre,
To honors seat and chastities sweet bowre.
Why stand ye still, ye virgins, in amaze,
Upon her so to gaze,
Whiles ye forget your former lay to sing,
To which the woods did answer, and your eccho ring?

But if ye saw that which no eyes can see,
The inward beauty of her lively spright,
Garnisht with heavenly guifts of high degree,
Much more then would ye wonder at that sight,
And stand astonisht lyke to those which red
Medusaes mazeful hed.
There dwels sweet Love, and constant Chastity,
Unspotted Fayth, and comely Womanhood,
Regard of Honour, and mild Modesty;
There Vertue raynes as queene in royal throne,
And giveth lawes alone,
The which the base affections doe obay,
And yeeld theyr services unto her will;

Ne thought of thing uncomely ever may
Thereto approch to tempt her mind to ill.
Had ye once seene these her celestial threasures,
And unrevealed pleasures,
Then would ye wonder, and her prayses sing,
That al the woods should answer, and your echo ring.

Open the temple gates unto my love,
Open them wide that she may enter in,
And all the postes adorne as doth behove,
And all the pillours deck with girlands trim,
For to receyve this saynt with honour dew,
That commeth in to you.
With trembling steps and humble reverence,
She commeth in before th' Almighties vew:
Of her, ye virgins, learne obedience,
When so ye come into those holy places,
To humble your proud faces.
Bring her up to th' high altar, that she may
The sacred ceremonies there partake,
The which do endlesse matrimony make;
And let the roring organs loudly play
The praises of the Lord in lively notes,
The whiles with hollow throates
The choristers the joyous antheme sing,
That al the woods may answere, and their eccho ring.

Behold, whiles she before the altar stands,
Hearing the holy priest that to her speakes,
And blesseth her with his two happy hands,
How the red roses flush up in her cheekes,
And the pure snow with goodly vermill stayne,
Like crimsin dyde in grayne:
That even th' angels, which continually
About the sacred altare doe remaine,
Forget their service and about her fly,

Ofte peeping in her face, that seemes more fayre,
The more they on it stare.
But her sad eyes, still fastened on the ground,
Are governed with goodly modesty,
That suffers not one looke to glaunce awry,
Which may let in a little thought unsownd.
Why blush ye, love, to give to me your hand,
The pledge of all our band?
Sing, ye sweet angels, Alleluya sing,
That all the woods may answere, and your eccho ring.

Now al is done; bring home the bride againe,
Bring home the triumph of our victory,
Bring home with you the glory of her gaine,
With joyaunce bring her and with jollity.
Never had man more joyfull day then this,
Whom heaven would heape with blis.
Make feast therefore now all this live long day;
This day for ever to me holy is;
Poure out the wine without restraint or stay,
Poure not by cups, but by the belly full,
Poure out to all that wull,
And sprinkle all the postes and wals with wine,
That they may sweat, and drunken be withall.
Crowne ye God Bacchus with a coronall,
And Hymen also crowne with wreathes of vine;
And let the Graces daunce unto the rest,
For they can doo it best:
The whiles the maydens doe theyr carroll sing,
To which the woods shal answer, and theyr eccho ring.

Ring ye the bels, ye yong men of the towne,
And leave your wonted labors for this day:
This day is holy; doe ye write it downe,
That ye for ever it remember may.
This day the sunne is in his chiefest hight,

With Barnaby the bright,
From whence declining daily by degrees,
He somewhat loseth of his heat and light,
When once the Crab behind his back he sees.
But for this time it ill ordained was,
To chose the longest day in all the yeare,
And shortest night, when longest fitter weare:
Yet never day so long, but late would passe.
Ring ye the bels, to make it weare away,
And bonefiers make all day,
And daunce about them, and about them sing:
That all the woods may answer, and your eccho ring.

Ah! when will this long weary day have end,
And lende me leave to come unto my love?
How slowly do the houres theyr numbers spend!
How slowly does sad Time his feathers move!
Hast thee, O fayrest planet, to thy home
Within the westerne fome:
Thy tyred steedes long since have need of rest.
Long though it be, at last I see it gloome,
And the bright evening star with golden creast
Appeare out of the east.
Fayre childe of beauty, glorious lampe of love,
That all the host of heaven in rankes doost lead,
And guydest lovers through the nightes dread,
How chearefully thou lookest from above,
And seemst to laugh atweene thy twinkling light,
As joying in the sight
Of these glad many, which for joy doe sing,
That all the woods them answer, and their echo ring!

Now ceasse, ye damsels, your delights forepast;
Enough is it that all the day was youres:
Now day is doen, and night is nighing fast:
Now bring the bryde into the brydall boures.

The night is come, now soone her disaray,
And in her bed her lay;
Lay her in lillies and in violets,
And silken courteins over her display,
And odourd sheetes, and Arras coverlets.
Behold how goodly my faire love does ly,
In proud humility!
Like unto Maia, when as Jove her tooke
In Tempe, lying on the flowry gras,
Twixt sleepe and wake, after she weary was
With bathing in the Acidalian brooke.
Now it is night, ye damsels may be gon,
And leave my love alone,
And leave likewise your former lay to sing:
The woods no more shal answere, nor your echo ring.

Now welcome, night! thou night so long expected.
That long daies labour doest at last defray,
And all my cares, which cruell Love collected,
Hast sumd in one, and cancelled for aye:
Spread thy broad wing over my love and me,
That no man may us see,
And in thy sable mantle us enwrap,
From feare of perrill and foule horror free.
Let no false treason seeke us to entrap,
Nor any dread disquiet once annoy
The safety of our joy:
But let the night be calme and quietsome,
Without tempestuous storms or sad afray:
Lyke as when Jove with fayre Alcmena lay,
When he begot the great Tirynthian groome:
Or lyke as when he with thy selfe did lie,
And begot Majesty.
And let the mayds and yongmen cease to sing:
Ne let the woods them answer, nor theyr eccho ring

Let no lamenting cryes, nor dolefull teares,
Be heard all night within, nor yet without:
Ne let false whispers, breeding hidden feares,
Breake gentle sleepe with misconceived dout.
Let no deluding dreames, nor dreadful sights,
Make sudden sad affrights;
Ne let house-fyres, nor lightnings helplesse harmes,
Ne let the Pouke, nor other evill sprights,
Ne let mischivous witches with theyr charmes,
Ne let hob goblins, names whose sense we see not,
Fray us with things that be not.
Let not the shriech oule, nor the storke be heard,
Nor the night raven that still deadly yels,
Nor damned ghosts cald up with mighty spels,
Nor griesly vultures make us once affeard:
Ne let th' unpleasant quyre of frogs still croking
Make us to wish theyr choking.
Let none of these theyr drery accents sing;
Ne let the woods them answer, nor theyr eccho ring.

But let stil Silence trew night watches keepe,
That sacred Peace may in assurance rayne,
And tymely Sleep, when it is tyme to sleepe,
May poure his limbs forth on your pleasant playne,
The whiles an hundred little winged loves,
Like divers fethered doves,
Shall fly and flutter round about our bed,
And in the secret darke, that none reproves,
Their pretty stealthes shall worke, and snares shal spread
To filch away sweet snatches of delight,
Conceald through covert night.
Ye sonnes of Venus, play your sports at will:
For greedy Pleasure, carelesse of your toyes,
Thinks more upon her paradise of joyes,
Then what ye do, albe it good or ill.

All night therefore attend your merry play,
For it will soone be day:
Now none doth hinder you, that say or sing,
Ne will the woods now answer, nor your eccho ring.

Who is the same which at my window peepes?
Or whose is that faire face that shines so bright?
Is it not Cinthia, she that never sleepes,
But walkes about high heaven al the night?
O fayrest goddesse, do thou not envy
My love with me to spy:
For thou likewise didst love, though now unthought,
And for a fleece of woll, which privily
The Latmian shephard once unto thee brought,
His pleasures with thee wrought.
Therefore to us be favorable now;
And sith of wemens labours thou hast charge,
And generation goodly dost enlarge,
Encline thy will t' effect our wishfull vow,
And the chast wombe informe with timely seed,
That may our comfort breed:
Till which we cease our hopefull hap to sing,
Ne let the woods us answere, nor our eccho ring.

And thou, great Juno, which with awful might
The lawes of wedlock still dost patronize,
And the religion of the faith first plight
With sacred rites hast taught to solemnize,
And eeke for comfort often called art
Of women in their smart,
Eternally bind thou this lovely band,
And all thy blessings unto us impart.
And thou, glad Genius, in whose gentle hand
The bridale bowre and geniall bed remaine,
Without blemish or staine,
And the sweet pleasures of theyr loves delight

With secret ayde doest succour and supply,
Till they bring forth the fruitfull progeny,
Send us the timely fruit of this same night.
And thou, fayre Hebe, and thou, Hymen free,
Grant that it may so be.
Til which we cease your further prayse to sing,
Ne any woods shal answer, nor your eccho ring.

And ye high heavens, the temple of the gods,
In which a thousand torches flaming bright
Doe burne, that to us wretched earthly clods
In dreadful darknesse lend desired light,
And all ye powers which in the same remayne,
More then we men can fayne,
Poure out your blessing on us plentiously,
And happy influence upon us raine,
That we may raise a large posterity,
Which from the earth, which they may long possesse
With lasting happinesse,
Up to your haughty pallaces may mount,
And for the guerdon of theyr glorious merit,
May heavenly tabernacles there inherit,
Of blessed saints for to increase the count.
So let us rest, sweet love, in hope of this,
And cease till then our tymely joyes to sing:
The woods no more us answer, nor our eccho ring.

Song, made in lieu of many ornaments
With which my love should duly have bene dect,
Which cutting off through hasty accidents,
Ye would not stay your dew time to expect,
But promist both to recompens,
Be unto her a goodly ornament,
And for short time an endlesse moniment.

Iambicum Trimetrum

Unhappie Verse, the witnesse of my unhappie state,
   Make thy selfe fluttring wings of thy fast flying
   Thought, and fly forth unto my love, whersoever she
      be:

Whether lying reastlesse in heavy bedde, or else
   Sitting so cheerelesse at the cheerfull boorde, or else
   Playing alone carelesse on hir heavenlie virginals.

If in bed, tell hir, that my eyes can take no reste:
   If at boorde, tell hir, that my mouth can eate no
      meate:
   If at hir virginals, tel hir, I can heare no mirth.

Asked why? say: Waking love suffereth no sleepe:
   Say, that raging love dothe appall the weake
      stomacke:
   Say, that lamenting love marreth the musicall.

Tell hir, that hir pleasures were wonte to lull me asleepe:
   Tell hir, that hir beautie was wonte to feede mine
      eyes:
   Tell hir, that hir sweete tongue was wonte to make me
      mirth.

Nowe doe I nightly waste, wanting my kindely reste:
   Nowe doe I dayly starve, wanting my lively foode:
   Nowe doe I alwayes dye, wanting thy timely mirth.

Aid if I waste, who will bewaile my heavy chaunce?
   And if I starve, who will record my cursed end?
   And if I dye, who will saye: *This was Immerito?*

FROM *The Faerie Queene*

[*The Cave of Mammon*]

Guyon findes Mamon in a delve,
　　Sunning his threasure hore:
Is by him tempted, and led downe,
　　To see his secrete store.

As pilot well expert in perilous wave,
That to a stedfast starre his course hath bent,
When foggy mistes or cloudy tempests have
The faithfull light of that faire lampe yblent,
And cover'd heaven with hideous dreriment,
Upon his card and compas firmes his eye,
The maysters of his long experiment,
And to them does the steddy helme apply,
Bidding his winged vessell fairely forward fly:

So Guyon, having lost his trustie guyde,
Late left beyond that Ydle Lake, proceedes
Yet on his way, of none accompanyde;
And evermore himselfe with comfort feedes
Of his owne vertues and praise-worthie deedes.
So long he yode, yet no adventure found,
Which Fame of her shrill trompet worthy reedes:
For still he traveild through wide wastfull ground,
That nought but desert wildernesse shewed all around.

At last he came unto a gloomy glade,
Cover'd with boughes and shrubs from heavens light,
Whereas he sitting found in secret shade
An uncouth, salvage, and uncivile wight,

Of griesly hew and fowle ill favour'd sight;
His face with smoke was tand, and eies were bleard,
His head and beard with sout were ill bedight,
His cole-blacke hands did seeme to have ben seard
In smythes fire-spitting forge, and nayles like clawes
    appeard.

His yron cote, all overgrowne with rust,
Was underneath enveloped with gold,
Whose glistring glosse, darkned with filthy dust,
Well yet appeared to have beene of old
A worke of rich entayle and curious mould,
Woven with antickes and wyld ymagery:
And in his lap a masse of coyne he told,
And turned upside downe, to feede his eye
And covetous desire with his huge threasury.

And round about him lay on every side
Great heapes of gold, that never could be spent:
Of which some were rude owre, not purifide
Of Mulcibers devouring element;
Some others were new driven, and distent
Into great ingowes, and to wedges square;
Some in round plates withouten moniment:
But most were stampt, and in their metal bare
The antique shapes of kings and kesars straung and
    rare.

Soone as he Guyon saw, in great affright
And haste he rose, for to remove aside
Those pretious hils from straungers envious sight,
And downe them poured through an hole full wide
Into the hollow earth, them there to hide.
But Guyon, lightly to him leaping, stayd
His hand, that trembled as one terrifyde;
And though him selfe were at the sight dismayd,
Yet him perforce restraynd, and to him doubtfull sayd:

"What art thou, man, (if man at all thou art)
That here in desert hast thine habitaunce,
And these rich heapes of welth doest hide apart
From the worldes eye, and from her right usaunce?"
Thereat, with staring eyes fixed askaunce,
In great disdaine, he answerd: "Hardy Elfe,
That darest vew my direfull countenaunce,
I read thee rash and heedlesse of thy selfe,
To trouble my still seate, and heapes of pretious pelfe.

"God of the world and worldlings I me call,
Great Mammon, greatest god below the skye,
That of my plenty poure out unto all,
And unto none my graces do envye:
Riches, renowme, and principality,
Honour, estate, and all this worldes good,
For which men swinck and sweat incessantly,
Fro me do flow into an ample flood,
And in the hollow earth have their eternall brood.

"Wherefore, if me thou deigne to serve and sew,
At thy commaund, lo! all these mountaines bee;
Or if to thy great mind, or greedy vew,
All these may not suffise, there shall to thee
Ten times so much be nombred francke and free."
"Mammon," said he, "thy godheads vaunt is vaine,
And idle offers of thy golden fee;
To them that covet such eye-glutting gaine
Proffer thy giftes, and fitter servaunts entertaine.

"Me ill besits, that in derdoing armes
And honours suit my vowed daies do spend,
Unto thy bounteous baytes and pleasing charmes,
With which weake men thou witchest, to attend:
Regard of worldly mucke doth fowly blend
And low abase the high heroicke spright,

That joyes for crownes and kingdomes to contend;
Faire shields, gay steedes, bright armes be my delight:
Those be the riches fit for an advent'rous knight."

"Vaine glorious Elfe," saide he, "doest not thou weet,
That money can thy wantes at will supply?
Sheilds, steeds, and armes, and all things for thee meet
It can purvay in twinckling of an eye;
And crownes and kingdomes to thee multiply.
Doe not I kings create, and throw the crowne
Sometimes to him that low in dust doth ly?
And him that raignd into his rowme thrust downe,
And whom I lust do heape with glory and renowne?"

"All otherwise," saide he, "I riches read,
And deeme them roote of all disquietnesse;
First got with guile, and then preserv'd with dread,
And after spent with pride and lavishnesse,
Leaving behind them griefe and heavinesse.
Infinite mischiefes of them doe arize,
Strife and debate, bloodshed and bitternesse,
Outrageous wrong and hellish covetize,
That noble heart, as great dishonour, doth despize.

"Ne thine be kingdomes, ne the scepters thine;
But realmes and rulers thou doest both confound,
And loyall truth to treason doest incline:
Witnesse the guiltlesse blood pourd oft on ground,
The crowned often slaine, the slayer cround,
The sacred diademe in peeces rent,
And purple robe gored with many a wound;
Castles surprizd, great citties sackt and brent:
So mak'st thou kings, and gaynest wrongfull govern-
     ment.

"Long were to tell the troublous stormes, that tosse
The private state, and make the life unsweet:

Who swelling sayles in Caspian sea doth crosse,
And in frayle wood on Adrian gulf doth fleet,
Doth not, I weene, so many evils meet."
Then Mammon, wexing wroth, "And why then," sayd,
"Are mortall men so fond and undiscreet,
So evill thing to seeke unto their ayd,
And having not, complaine, and having it, upbrayd?"

"Indeede," quoth he, "through fowle intemperaunce,
Frayle men are oft captiv'd to covetise:
But would they thinke, with how small allowaunce
Untroubled nature doth her selfe suffise,
Such superfluities they would despise,
Which with sad cares empeach our native joyes:
At the well head the purest streames arise:
But mucky filth his braunching armes annoyes,
And with uncomely weedes the gentle wave accloyes.

"The antique world, in his first flowring youth,
Fownd no defect in his Creators grace,
But with glad thankes, and unreproved truth,
The guifts of soveraine bounty did embrace:
Like angels life was then mens happy cace:
But later ages pride, like corn-fed steed,
Abusd her plenty and fat swolne encreace
To all licentious lust, and gan exceed
The measure of her meane, and naturall first need.

"Then gan a cursed hand the quiet wombe
Of his great grandmother with steele to wound,
And the hid treasures in her sacred tombe
With sacriledge to dig. Therein he fownd
Fountaines of gold and silver to abownd,
Of which the matter of his huge desire
And pompous pride eftsoones he did compownd;
Then avarice gan through his velnes inspire
His greedy flames, and kindled life-devouring fire."

"Sonne," said he then, "lett be thy bitter scorne,
And leave the rudenesse of that antique age
To them that liv'd therin in state forlorne.
Thou, that doest live in later times, must wage
Thy workes for wealth, and life for gold engage.
If then thee list my offred grace to use,
Take what thou please of all this surplusage;
If thee list not, leave have thou to refuse:
But thing refused doe not afterward accuse."

"Me list not," said the Elfin knight, "receave
Thing offred, till I know it well be gott;
Ne wote I, but thou didst these goods bereave
From rightfull owner by unrighteous lott,
Or that blood guiltinesse or guile them blott."
"Perdy," quoth he, "yet never eie did vew,
Ne tong did tell, ne hand these handled not;
But safe I have them kept in secret mew
From hevens sight, and powre of al which them pour-
    sew."

"What secret place," quoth he, "can safely hold
So huge a masse, and hide from heavens eie?
Or where hast thou thy wonne, that so much gold
Thou canst preserve from wrong and robbery?"
"Come thou," quoth he, "and see." So by and by,
Through that thick covert he him led, and fownd
A darkesome way, which no man could descry,
That deep descended through the hollow grownd,
And was with dread and horror compassed arownd.

At length they came into a larger space,
That stretcht it selfe into an ample playne,
Through which a beaten broad high way did trace,
That streight did lead to Plutoes griesly rayne:
By that wayes side there sate infernall Payne,

And fast beside him sat tumultuous Strife:
The one in hand an yron whip did strayne,
The other brandished a bloody knife,
And both did gnash their teeth, and both did threten
   life.

On th'other side, in one consort, there sate
Cruell Revenge, and rancorous Despight,
Disloyall Treason, and hart-burning Hate;
But gnawing Gealosy, out of their sight
Sitting alone, his bitter lips did bight;
And trembling Feare still to and fro did fly,
And found no place, wher safe he shroud him might;
Lamenting Sorrow did in darknes lye;
And Shame his ugly face did hide from living eye.

And over them sad Horror with grim hew
Did alwaies sore, beating his yron wings;
And after him owles and night-ravens flew,
The hatefull messengers of heavy things,
Of death and dolor telling sad tidings;
Whiles sad Celeno, sitting on a clifte,
A song of bale and bitter sorrow sings,
That hart of flint a sonder could have rifte:
Which having ended, after him she flyeth swifte.

All these before the gates of Pluto lay;
By whom they passing, spake unto them nought.
But th' Elfin knight with wonder all the way
Did feed his eyes, and fild his inner thought.
At last him to a litle dore he brought,
That to the gate of hell, which gaped wide,
Was next adjoyning, ne them parted ought:
Betwixt them both was but a litle stride,
That did the house of Richesse from hellmouth divide.

Before the dore sat selfe-consuming Care,
Day and night keeping wary watch and ward,
For feare least Force or Fraud should unaware
Breake in, and spoile the treasure there in gard:
Ne would he suffer Sleepe once thetherward
Approch, albe his drowsy den were next;
For next to Death is Sleepe to be compard:
Therefore his house is unto his annext:
Here Sleep, ther Richesse, and helgate them both be-
    twext.

So soone as Mammon there arrivd, the dore
To him did open and affoorded way;
Him followed eke Sir Guyon evermore,
Ne darkenesse him, ne daunger might dismay.
Soone as he entred was, the dore streight way
Did shutt, and from behind it forth there lept
An ugly feend, more fowle then dismall day,
The which with monstrous stalke behind him stept,
And ever as he went, dew watch upon him kept.

Well hoped hee, ere long that hardy guest,
If ever covetous hand, or lustfull eye,
Or lips he layd on thing that likte him best,
Or ever sleepe his eiestrings did untye,
Should be his pray. And therefore still on hye
He over him did hold his cruell clawes,
Threatning with greedy gripe to doe him dye,
And rend in peeces with his ravenous pawes,
If ever he transgrest the fatall Stygian lawes.

That houses forme within was rude and strong,
Lyke an huge cave, hewne out of rocky clifte,
From whose rough vaut the ragged breaches hong,
Embost with massy gold of glorious guifte,

And with rich metall loaded every rifte,
That heavy ruine they did seeme to threatt;
And over them Arachne high did lifte
Her cunning web, and spred her subtile nett,
Enwrapped in fowle smoke and clouds more black then
    jett.

Both roofe, and floore, and walls were all of gold,
But overgrowne with dust and old decay,
And hid in darkenes, that none could behold
The hew thereof: for vew of cherefull day
Did never in that house it selfe display,
But a faint shadow of uncertein light;
Such as a lamp, whose life does fade away;
Or as the moone, cloathed with clowdy night,
Does shew to him that walkes in feare and sad affright.

In all that rowme was nothing to be seene,
But huge great yron chests and coffers strong,
All bard with double bends, that none could weene
Them to efforce by violence or wrong:
On every side they placed were along.
But all the grownd with sculs was scattered,
And dead mens bones, which round about were flong;
Whose lives, it seemed, whilome there were shed,
And their vile carcases now left unburied.

They forward passe, ne Guyon yet spoke word,
Till that they came unto an yron dore,
Which to them opened of his owne accord,
And shewd of richesse such exceeding store,
As eie of man did never see before,
Ne ever could within one place be fownd,
Though all the wealth, which is, or was of yore,
Could gathered be through all the world arownd,
And that above were added to that under grownd.

The charge thereof unto a covetous spright
Commaunded was, who thereby did attend,
And warily awaited day and night,
From other covetous feends it to defend,
Who it to rob and ransacke did intend.
Then Mammon, turning to that warriour, said:
"Loe here the worldes blis! loe here the end,
To which al men doe ayme, rich to be made!
Such grace now to be happy is before thee laid."

"Certes," sayd he, "I n'ill thine offred grace,
Ne to be made so happy doe intend:
Another blis before mine eyes I place,
Another happines, another end.
To them that list, these base regardes I lend:
But I in armes, and in atchievements brave,
Do rather choose my flitting houres to spend,
And to be lord of those that riches have,
Then them to have my selfe, and be their servile
    sclave."

Thereat the feend his gnashing teeth did grate,
And griev'd, so long to lacke his greedie pray;
For well he weened that so glorious bayte
Would tempt his guest to take thereof assay:
Had he so doen, he had him snatcht away,
More light then culver in the faulcons fist.
Eternall God thee save from such decay!
But whenas Mammon saw his purpose mist,
Him to entrap unwares another way he wist.

Thence forward he him ledd, and shortly brought
Unto another rowme, whose dore forthright
To him did open, as it had beene taught:
Therein an hundred raunges weren pight,
And hundred fournaces all burning bright:

By every fournace many feendes did byde,
Deformed creatures, horrible in sight;
And every feend his busie paines applyde,
To melt the golden metall, ready to be tryde.

One with great bellowes gathered filling ayre,
And with forst wind the fewell did inflame;
Another did the dying bronds repayre
With yron tongs, and sprinckled ofte the same
With liquid waves, fiers Vulcans rage to tame,
Who, maystring them, renewd his former heat;
Some scumd the drosse, that from the metall came,
Some stird the molten owre with ladles great;
And every one did swincke, and every one did sweat.

But when an earthly wight they present saw,
Glistring in armes and battailous aray,
From their whot work they did themselves withdraw
To wonder at the sight: for, till that day,
They never creature saw, that cam that way.
Their staring eyes, sparckling with fervent fyre,
And ugly shapes did nigh the man dismay,
That, were it not for shame, he would retyre;
Till that him thus bespake their soveraine lord and syre:

"Behold, thou Faeries sonne, with mortall eye,
That living eye before did never see:
The thing that thou didst crave so earnestly
To weet, whence all the wealth late shewd by mee
Proceeded, lo! now is reveald to thee.
Here is the fountaine of the worldes good:
Now therefore, if thou wilt enriched bee,
Avise thee well, and chaunge thy wilfull mood;
Least thou perhaps hereafter wish, and be withstood."

"Suffise it then, thou Money God," quote hee,
"That all thine ydle offers I refuse.

All that I need I have; what needeth mee
To covet more then I have cause to use?
With such vaine shewes thy worldlinges vyle abuse:
But give me leave to follow mine emprise."
Mammon was much displeased, yet no'te he chuse
But beare the rigour of his bold mesprise,
And thence him forward ledd, him further to entise.

He brought him through a darksom narrow strayt,
To a broad gate, all built of beaten gold:
The gate was open, but therein did wayt
A sturdie villein, stryding stiffe and bold,
As if that Highest God defy he would:
In his right hand an yron club he held,
But he himselfe was all of golden mould,
Yet had both life and sence, and well could weld
That cursed weapon, when his cruell foes he queld.

Disdayne he called was, and did disdayne
To be so cald, and who so did him call:
Sterne was his looke, and full of stomacke vayne,
His portaunce terrible, and stature tall,
Far passing th' hight of men terrestriall,
Like an huge gyant of the Titans race;
That made him scorne all creatures great and small,
And with his pride all others powre deface:
More fitt emongst black fiendes then men to have his
    place.

Soone as those glitterand armes he did espye,
That with their brightnesse made that darknes light,
His harmefull club he gan to hurtle hye,
And threaten batteill to the Faery knight;
Who likewise gan himselfe to batteill dight,
Till Mammon did his hasty hand withhold,
And counseld him abstaine from perilous fight:

For nothing might abash the villein bold,
Ne mortall steele emperce his miscreated mould.

So having him with reason pacifyde,
And the fiers carle commaunding to forbeare,
He brought him in. The rowme was large and wyde,
As it some gyeld or solemne temple weare:
Many great golden pillours did upbeare
The massy roofe, and riches huge sustayne,
And every pillour decked was full deare
With crownes, and diademes, and titles vaine,
Which mortall princes wore, whiles they on earth did
  rayne.

A route of people there assembled were,
Of every sort and nation under skye,
Which with great uprore preaced to draw nere
To th' upper part, where was advaunced hye
A stately siege of soveraine majestye;
And thereon satt a woman gorgeous gay,
And richly cladd in robes of royaltye,
That never earthly prince in such aray
His glory did enhaunce and pompous pryde display.

Her face right wondrous faire did seeme to bee,
That her broad beauties beam great brightnes threw
Through the dim shade, that all men might it see:
Yet was not that same her owne native hew,
But wrought by art and counterfetted shew,
Thereby more lovers unto her to call;
Nath'lesse most hevenly faire in deed and vew
She by creation was, till she did fall;
Thenceforth she sought for helps to cloke her crime
  withall.

There as in glistring glory she did sitt,
She held a great gold chaine ylincked well,

Whose upper end to highest heven was knitt,
And lower part did reach to lowest hell;
And all that preace did rownd about her swell,
To catchen hold of that long chaine, thereby
To climbe aloft, and others to excell:
That was Ambition, rash desire to sty,
And every linck thereof a step of dignity.

Some thought to raise themselves to high degree
By riches and unrighteous reward;
Some by close shouldring, some by flatteree;
Others through friendes, others for base regard;
And all by wrong waies for themselves prepard.
Those that were up themselves, kept others low,
Those that were low themselves, held others hard,
Ne suffred them to ryse or greater grow,
But every one did strive his fellow downe to throw.

Which whenas Guyon saw, he gan inquire,
What meant that preace about that ladies throne,
And what she was that did so high aspyre.
Him Mammon answered: "That goodly one,
Whom all that folke with such contention
Doe flock about, my deare, my daughter is:
Honour and dignitie from her alone
Derived are, and all this worldes blis,
For which ye men doe strive: few gett, but many mis.

"And fayre Philotime she rightly hight,
The fairest wight that wonneth under skye,
But that this darksom neather world her light
Doth dim with horror and deformity,
Worthie of heven and hye felicitie,
From whence the gods have her for envy thrust:
But sith thou hast found favour in mine eye,
Thy spouse I will her make, if that thou lust,
That she may thee advance for works and merits just."

"Gramercy, Mammon," said the gentle knight,
"For so great grace and offred high estate,
But I, that am fraile flesh and earthly wight,
Unworthy match for such immortall mate
My selfe well wote, and mine unequall fate:
And were I not, yet is my trouth yplight,
And love avowd to other lady late,
That to remove the same I have no might:
To chaunge love causelesse is reproch to warlike
    knight."

Mammon emmoved was with inward wrath;
Yet, forcing it to fayne, him forth thence ledd,
Through griesly shadowes by a beaten path,
Into a gardin goodly garnished
With hearbs and fruits, whose kinds mote not be redd:
Not such as earth out of her fruitfull woomb
Throwes forth to men, sweet and well savored,
But direful deadly black, both leafe and bloom,
Fitt to adorne the dead and deck the drery toombe.

There mournfull cypresse grew in greatest store,
And trees of bitter gall, and heben sad,
Dead sleeping poppy, and black hellebore,
Cold coloquintida, and tetra mad,
Mortall samnitis, and cicuta bad,
With which th' unjust Atheniens made to dy
Wise Socrates, who thereof quaffing glad,
Pourd out his life and last philosophy
To the fayre Critias, his dearest belamy.

The Gardin of Proserpina this hight;
And in the midst thereof a silver seat,
With a thick arber goodly overdight,
In which she often usd from open heat
Her selfe to shroud, and pleasures to entreat.

Next thereunto did grow a goodly tree,
With braunches broad dispredd and body great,
Clothed with leaves, that none the wood mote see,
And loaden all with fruit as thick as it might bee.

Their fruit were golden apples glistring bright,
That goodly was their glory to be behold;
On earth like never grew, ne living wight
Like ever saw, but they from hence were sold;
For those, which Hercules with conquest bold
Got from great Atlas daughters, hence began,
And, planted there, did bring forth fruit of gold;
And those with which th' Eubœan young man wan
Swift Atalanta, when through craft he her out ran.

Here also sprong that goodly golden fruit,
With which Acontius got his lover trew,
Whom he had long time sought with fruitlesse suit:
Here eke that famous golden apple grew,
The which emongst the gods false Ate threw;
For which th' Idæan ladies disagreed,
Till partiall Paris dempt it Venus dew,
And had of her fayre Helen for his meed,
That many noble Greekes and Trojans made to bleed.

The warlike Elfe much wondred at this tree,
So fayre and great, that shadowed all the ground,
And his broad braunches, laden with rich fee,
Did stretch themselves without the utmost bound
Of this great gardin, compast with a mound:
Which over-hanging, they themselves did steepe
In a blacke flood, which flow'd about it round;
That is the river of Cocytus deepe,
In which full many soules do endlesse wayle and weepe.

Which to behold, he clomb up to the bancke,
And, looking downe, saw many damned wightes,

In those sad waves, which direfull deadly stancke,
Plonged continually of cruell sprightes,
That with their piteous cryes, and yelling shrightes,
They made the further shore resounden wide.
Emongst the rest of those same ruefull sightes,
One cursed creature he by chaunce espide,
That drenched lay full deepe, under the garden side.

Deepe was he drenched to the upmost chin,
Yet gaped still, as coveting to drinke
Of the cold liquor which he waded in,
And stretching forth his hand, did often thinke
To reach the fruit which grew upon the brincke:
But both the fruit from hand, and flood from mouth,
Did fly abacke, and made him vainely swincke:
The whiles he sterv'd with hunger and with drouth,
He daily dyde, yet never throughly dyen couth.

The knight, him seeing labour so in vaine,
Askt who he was, and what he ment thereby:
Who, groning deepe, thus answered him againe:
"Most cursed of all creatures under skye,
Lo! Tantalus, I here tormented lye:
Of whom high Jove wont whylome feasted bee,
Lo! here I now for want of food doe dye:
But if that thou be such as I thee see,
Of grace I pray thee, give to eat and drinke to mee."

"Nay, nay, thou greedy Tantalus," quoth he,
"Abide the fortune of thy present fate,
And unto all that live in high degree
Ensample be of mind intemperate,
To teach them how to use their present state."
Then gan the cursed wretch alowd to cry,
Accusing highest Jove and gods ingrate,
And eke blaspheming heaven bitterly,
As authour of unjustice, there to let him dye.

He lookt a litle further, and espyde
Another wretch, whose carcas deepe was drent
Within the river, which the same did hyde:
But both his handes, most filthy feculent,
Above the water were on high extent,
And faynd to wash themselves incessantly;
Yet nothing cleaner were for such intent,
But rather fowler seemed to the eye;
So lost his labour vaine and ydle industry.

The knight, him calling, asked who he was;
Who, lifting up his head, him answered thus:
"I Pilate am, the falsest judge, alas!
And most unjust; that, by unrighteous
And wicked doome, to Jewes despiteous
Delivered up the Lord of Life to dye,
And did acquite a murdrer felonous:
The whiles my handes I washt in purity,
The whiles my soule was soyld with fowle iniquity."

Infinite moe, tormented in like paine,
He there beheld, too long here to be told:
Ne Mammon would there let him long remayne,
For terrour of the tortures manifold,
In which the damned soules he did behold,
But roughly him bespake: "Thou fearefull foole,
Why takest not of that same fruite of gold,
Ne sittest downe on that same silver stoole,
To rest thy weary person in the shadow coole?"

All which he did, to do him deadly fall
In frayle intemperaunce through sinfull bayt;
To which if he inclyned had at all,
That dreadfull feend, which did behinde him wayt,
Would him have rent in thousand peeces strayt:
But he was wary wise in all his way,

And well perceived his deceiptfull sleight,
Ne suffred lust his safety to betray;
So goodly did beguile the guyler of his pray.

And now he has so long remained theare,
That vitall powres gan wexe both weake and wan,
For want of food and sleepe, which two upbeare,
Like mightie pillours, this frayle life of man,
That none without the same enduren can.
For now three dayes of men were full outwrought,
Since he this hardy enterprize began:
Forthy great Mammon fayrely he besought,
Into the world to guyde him backe, as he him brought.

The god, though loth, yet was constraynd t' obay,
For, lenger time then that, no living wight
Below the earth might suffred be to stay:
So backe againe him brought to living light.
But all so soone as his enfeebled spright
Gan sucke this vitall ayre into his brest,
As overcome with too exceeding might,
The life did flit away out of her nest,
And all his sences were with deadly fit opprest.

(Book II, canto vii entire)

[*The Bower of Bliss*]

Guyon by palmers governaunce
    Passing through perilles great,
Doth overthrow the Bowre of Blis,
    And Acrasy defeat.

Now ginnes this goodly frame of Temperaunce
Fayrely to rise, and her adorned hed
To pricke of highest prayse forth to advaunce,
Formerly grounded and fast setteled

On firme foundation of true bountyhed:
And that brave knight, that for this vertue fightes,
Now comes to point of that same perilous sted,
Where Pleasure dwelles in sensuall delights,
Mongst thousand dangers, and ten thousand magick
   mights.

Two dayes now in that sea he sayled has,
Ne ever land beheld, ne living wight,
Ne ought save perill, still as he did pas:
Tho, when appeared the third morrow bright,
Upon the waves to spred her trembling light,
An hideous roring far away they heard,
That all their sences filled with affright,
And streight they saw the raging surges reard
Up to the skyes, that them of drowning made affeard.

Said then the boteman, "Palmer, stere aright,
And keepe an even course; for yonder way
We needes must pas (God doe us well acquight!)
That is the Gulfe of Greedinesse, they say,
That deepe engorgeth all this worldes pray;
Which having swallowd up excessively,
He soone in vomit up againe doth lay,
And belcheth forth his superfluity,
That all the seas for feare doe seeme away to fly.

"On thother syde an hideous rock is pight
Of mightie magnes stone, whose craggie clift
Depending from on high, dreadfull to sight,
Over the waves his rugged armes doth lift,
And threatneth downe to throw his ragged rift
On whoso cometh nigh; yet nigh it drawes
All passengers, that none from it can shift:
For whiles they fly that gulfes devouring jawes,
They on this rock are rent, and sunck in helples wawes."

Forward they passe, and strongly he them rowes,
Untill they nigh unto that gulfe arryve,
Where streame more violent and greedy growes:
Then he with all his puisaunce doth stryve
To strike his oares, and mightily doth dryve
The hollow vessell through the threatfull wave,
Which, gaping wide, to swallow them alyve
In th' huge abysse of his engulfing grave,
Doth rore at them in vaine, and with great terrour rave.

They, passing by, that grisely mouth did see,
Sucking the seas into his entralles deepe,
That seemd more horrible then hell to bee,
Or that darke dreadfull hole of Tartare steepe,
Through which the damned ghosts doen often creep
Backe to the world, bad livers to torment:
But nought that falles into this direfull deepe,
Ne that approcheth nigh the wyde descent,
May backe retourne, but is condemned to be drent.

On thother side they saw that perilous rocke,
Threatning it selfe on them to ruinate,
On whose sharp cliftes the ribs of vessels broke,
And shivered ships, which had beene wrecked late,
Yet stuck, with carcases exanimate
Of such, as having all their substance spent
In wanton joyes and lustes intemperate,
Did afterwardes make shipwrack violent,
Both of their life, and fame for ever fowly blent.

Forthy this hight the Rock of vile Reproch,
A daungerous and detestable place,
To which nor fish nor fowle did once approch,
But yelling meawes, with seagulles hoars and bace,
And cormoyraunts, with birds of ravenous race,
Which still sat wayting on that wastfull clift

For spoile of wretches, whose unhappy cace,
After lost credit and consumed thrift,
At last them driven hath to this despairefull drift.

The palmer, seeing them in safetie past,
Thus saide: "Behold th' ensamples in our sightes
Of lustfull luxurie and thriftlesse wast:
What now is left of miserable wightes,
Which spent their looser daies in leud delightes,
But shame and sad reproch, here to be red
By these rent reliques, speaking their ill plightes?
Let all that live, hereby be counselled
To shunne Rock of Reproch, and it as death to dread."

So forth they rowed, and that ferryman
With his stiffe oares did brush the sea so strong,
That the hoare waters from his frigot ran,
And the light bubles daunced all along,
Whiles the salt brine out of the billowes sprong.
At last far off they many islandes spy,
On every side floting the floodes emong:
Then said the knight: "Lo! I the land descry;
Therefore, old syre, thy course doe thereunto apply."

"That may not bee," said then the ferryman,
"Least wee unweeting hap to be fordonne:
For those same islands, seeming now and than,
Are not firme land, nor any certein wonne,
But stragling plots, which to and fro doe ronne
In the wide waters: therefore are they hight
The Wandring Islands. Therefore doe them shonne;
For they have ofte drawne many a wandring wight
Into most deadly daunger and distressed plight.

"Yet well they seeme to him, that farre doth vew,
Both faire and fruitfull, and the grownd dispred
With grassy greene of delectable hew,

And the tall trees with leaves appareled,
Are deckt with blossoms dyde in white and red,
That mote the passengers thereto allure;
But whosoever once hath fastened
His foot thereon, may never it recure,
But wandreth ever more uncertein and unsure.

"As th' isle of Delos whylome, men report,
Amid th' Aegæan sea long time did stray,
Ne made for shipping any certeine port,
Till that Latona traveiling that way,
Flying from Junoes wrath and hard assay,
Of her fayre twins was there delivered,
Which afterwards did rule the night and day;
Thenceforth it firmely was established,
And for Apolloes honor highly herried."

They to him hearken, as beseemeth meete,
And passe on forward: so their way does ly,
That one of those same islands, which doe fleet
In the wide sea, they needes must passen by,
Which seemd so sweet and pleasaunt to the eye,
That it would tempt a man to touchen there:
Upon the banck they sitting did espy
A daintie damsell, dressing of her heare,
By whom a little skippet floting did appeare.

She, them espying, loud to them gan call,
Bidding them nigher draw unto the shore;
For she had cause to busie them withall;
And therewith lowdly laught; but nathemore
Would they once turne, but kept on as afore:
Which when she saw, she left her lockes undight,
And running to her boat withouten ore,
From the departing land it launched light,
And after them did drive with all her power and might.

Whom overtaking, she in merry sort
Them gan to bord, and purpose diversly,
Now faining dalliaunce and wanton sport,
Now throwing forth lewd wordes immodestly;
Till that the palmer gan full bitterly
Her to rebuke, for being loose and light:
Which not abiding, but more scornfully
Scoffing at him that did her justly wite,
She turnd her bote about, and from them rowed quite.

That was the wanton Phœdria, which late
Did ferry him over the Idle Lake:
Whom nought regarding, they kept on their gate,
And all her vaine allurements did forsake;
When them the wary boteman thus bespake:
"Here now behoveth us well to avyse,
And of our safety good heede to take;
For here before a perlous passage lyes,
Where many mermayds haunt, making false melodies.

"But by the way there is a great quicksand,
And a whirlepoole of hidden jeopardy:
Therefore, sir palmer, keepe an even hand;
For twixt them both the narrow way doth ly."
Scarse had he saide, when hard at hand they spy
That quicksand nigh with water covered;
But by the checked wave they did descry
It plaine, and by the sea discoloured:
It called was the Quickesand of Unthriftyhed.

They, passing by, a goodly ship did see,
Laden from far with precious merchandize,
And bravely furnished as ship might bee,
Which through great disaventure, or mesprize,
Her selfe had ronne into that hazardize;
Whose mariners and merchants, with much toyle,

Labour'd in vaine to have recur'd their prize,
And the rich wares to save from pitteous spoyle;
But neither toyle nor traveill might her backe recoyle.

On th' other side they see that perilous poole,
That called was the Whirlepoole of Decay,
In which full many had with haplesse doole
Beene suncke, of whom no memorie did stay:
Whose circled waters rapt with whirling sway,
Like to a restlesse wheele, still ronning round,
Did covet, as they passed by that way,
To draw their bote within the utmost bound
Of his wide labyrinth, and then to have them dround.

But th' heedfull boteman strongly forth did stretch
His brawnie armes, and all his bodie straine,
That th' utmost sandy breach they shortly fetch,
Whiles the dredd daunger does behind remaine.
Suddeine they see from midst of all the maine
The surging waters like a mountaine rise,
And the great sea, puft up with proud disdaine,
To swell above the measure of his guise,
As threatning to devoure all that his powre despise.

The waves come rolling, and the billowes rore
Outragiously, as they enraged were,
Or wrathfull Neptune did them drive before
His whirling charet, for exceeding feare;
For not one puffe of winde there did appeare;
That all the three thereat woxe much afrayd,
Unweeting what such horrour straunge did reare.
Eftsoones they saw an hideous hoast arrayd
Of huge sea monsters, such as living sence dismayd.

Most ugly shapes and horrible aspects,
Such as Dame Nature selfe mote feare to see,

Or shame that ever should so fowle defects
From her most cunning hand escaped bee;
All dreadfull pourtraicts of deformitee:
Spring-headed hydres, and sea-shouldring whales,
Great whirlpooles, which all fishes make to flee,
Bright scolopendraes, arm'd with silver scales,
Mighty monoceros with immeasured tayles,

The dreadfull fish, that hath deserv'd the name
Of Death, and like him lookes in dreadfull hew,
The griesly wasserman, that makes his game
The flying ships with swiftnes to pursew,
The horrible sea-satyre, that doth shew
His fearefull face in time of greatest storme,
Huge ziffius, whom mariners eschew
No lesse then rockes, (as travellers informe,)
And greedy rosmarines with visages deforme.

All these, and thousand thousands many more,
And more deformed monsters thousand fold,
With dreadfull noise and hollow rombling rore,
Came rushing, in the fomy waves enrold,
Which seem'd to fly for feare them to behold:
Ne wonder, if these did the knight appall;
For all, that here on earth we dreadfull hold,
Be but as bugs to fearen babes withall,
Compared to the creatures in the seas entrall.

"Feare nought," then saide the palmer well aviz'd;
"For these same monsters are not these in deed,
But are into these fearefull shapes disguiz'd
By that same wicked witch, to worke us dreed,
And draw from on this journey to proceed."
Tho, lifting up his vertuous staffe on hye,
He smote the sea, which calmed was with speed,
And all the dreadfull armie fast gan flye
Into great Tethys bosome, where they hidden lye.

Quit from that danger, forth their course they kept,
And as they went they heard a ruefull cry
Of one that wayld and pittifully wept,
That through the sea the resounding plaints did fly:
At last they in an island did espy
A seemely maiden, sitting by the shore,
That with great sorrow and sad agony
Seemed some great misfortune to deplore,
And lowd to them for succour called evermore.

Which Guyon hearing, streight his palmer bad
To stere the bote towards that dolefull mayd,
That he might know and ease her sorrow sad:
Who, him avizing better, to him sayd:
"Faire sir, be not displeasd if disobayd:
For ill it were to hearken to her cry;
For she is inly nothing ill apayd,
But onely womanish fine forgery,
Your stubborne hart t' affect with fraile infirmity.

"To which when she your courage hath inclind
Through foolish pitty, then her guilefull bayt
She will embosome deeper in your mind,
And for your ruine at the last awayt."
The knight was ruled, and the boteman strayt
Held on his course with stayed stedfastnesse,
Ne ever shroncke, ne ever sought to bayt
His tyred armes for toylesome wearinesse,
But with his oares did sweepe the watry wildernesse.

And now they nigh approched to the sted,
Where as those mermayds dwelt: it was a still
And calmy bay, on th' one side sheltered
With the brode shadow of an hoarie hill,
On th' other side an high rocke toured still,
That twixt them both a pleasaunt port they made,

And did like an halfe theatre fulfill:
There those five sisters had continuall trade,
And usd to bath themselves in that deceiptfull shade.

They were faire ladies, till they fondly striv'd
With th' Heliconian maides for maystery;
Of whom they over-comen, were depriv'd
Of their proud beautie, and th' one moyity
Transformd to fish, for their bold surquedry;
But th' upper halfe their hew retayned still,
And their sweet skill in wonted melody;
Which ever after they abusd to ill,
T' allure weake traveillers, whom gotten they did kill.

So now to Guyon, as he passed by,
Their pleasaunt tunes they sweetly thus applyde:
"O thou fayre sonne of gentle Faery,
That art in mightie armes most magnifyde
Above all knights that ever batteill tryde,
O turne thy rudder hetherward a while:
Here may thy storme-bett vessell safely ryde;
This is the port of rest from troublous toyle,
The worldes sweet in from paine and wearisome
    turmoyle."

With that the rolling sea, resounding soft,
In his big base them fitly answered,
And on the rocke the waves breaking aloft,
A solemne meane unto them measured,
The whiles sweet Zephyrus lowd whisteled
His treble, a straunge kinde of harmony;
Which Guyons senses softly tickeled,
That he the boteman bad row easily,
And let him heare some part of their rare melody.

But him the palmer from that vanity
With temperate advice discounselled,

That they it past, and shortly gan descry
The land, to which their course they leveled;
When suddeinly a grosse fog over spred
With his dull vapour all that desert has,
And heavens chearefull face enveloped,
That all things one, and one as nothing was,
And this great universe seemd one confused mas.

Thereat they greatly were dismayd, ne wist
How to direct theyr way in darkenes wide,
But feard to wander in that wastefull mist,
For tombling into mischiefe unespide:
Worse is the daunger hidden then descride.
Suddeinly an innumerable flight
Of harmefull fowles, about them fluttering, cride,
And with their wicked wings them ofte did smight,
And sore annoyed, groping in that griesly night.

Even all the nation of unfortunate
And fatall birds about them flocked were,
Such as by nature men abhorre and hate;
The ill-faste owle, deaths dreadfull messengere,
The hoars night-raven, trump of dolefull drere,
The lether-winged batt, dayes enimy,
The ruefull strich, still waiting on the bere.
The whistler shrill, that who so heares doth dy,
The hellish harpyes, prophets of sad destiny.

All those, and all that els does horror breed,
About them flew, and fild their sayles with feare:
Yet stayd they not, but forward did proceed,
Whiles th' one did row, and th' other stifly steare;
Till that at last the weather gan to cleare,
And the faire land it selfe did playnly sheow.
Said then the palmer: "Lo where does appeare
The sacred soile where all our perills grow;

Therfore, sir knight, your ready arms about you
 throw."

He hearkned, and his armes about him tooke,
The whiles the nimble bote so well her sped,
That with her crooked keele the land she strooke.
Then forth the noble Guyon sallied,
And his sage palmer, that him governed;
But th' other by his bote behind did stay.
They marched fayrly forth, of nought ydred,
Both firmely armd for every hard assay,
With constancy and care, gainst daunger and dismay.

Ere long they heard an hideous bellowing
Of many beasts, that roard outrageously,
As if that hungers poynt or Venus sting
Had them enraged with fell surquedry;
Yet nought they feard, but past on hardily,
Untill they came in vew of those wilde beasts:
Who all attonce, gaping full greedily,
And rearing fercely their upstarting crests,
Ran towards, to devoure those unexpected guests.

But soone as they approcht with deadly threat,
The palmer over them his staffe upheld,
His mighty staffe, that could all charmes defeat:
Eftesoones their stubborne corages were queld,
And high advaunced crests downe meekely feld;
Instead of fraying, they them selves did feare,
And trembled, as them passing they beheld:
Such wondrous powre did in that staffe appeare,
All monsters to subdew to him that did it beare.

Of that same wood it fram'd was cunningly,
Of which Caduceus whilome was made,
Caduceus, the rod of Mercury,
With which he wonts the Stygian realmes invade,

Through ghastly horror and eternall shade;
Th' infernall feends with it he can asswage,
And Orcus tame, whome nothing can persuade,
And rule the Furyes, when they most doe rage:
Such vertue in his staffe had eke this palmer sage.

Thence passing forth, they shortly doe arryve
Whereas the Bowre of Blisse was situate;
A place pickt out by choyce of best alyve,
That Natures worke by art can imitate:
In which what ever in this worldly state
Is sweete, and pleasing unto living sense,
Or that may dayntest fantasy aggrate,
Was poured forth with plentifull dispence,
And made there to abound with lavish affluence.

Goodly it was enclosed rownd about,
As well their entred guestes to keep within,
As those unruly beasts to hold without;
Yet was the fence thereof but weake and thin;
Nought feard theyr force, that fortilage to win,
But wisedomes powre, and temperaunces might,
By which the mightiest things efforced bin:
And eke the gate was wrought of substaunce light,
Rather for pleasure then for battery or fight.

Yt framed was of precious yvory,
That seemd a worke of admirable witt;
And therein all the famous history
Of Jason and Medæa was ywritt;
Her mighty charmes, her furious loving fitt,
His goodly conquest of the golden fleece,
His falsed fayth, and love too lightly flitt,
The wondred Argo, which in venturous peece
First through the Euxine seas bore all the flowr of
  Greece.

Ye might have seene the frothy billowes fry
Under the ship, as thorough them she went,
That seemd the waves were into yvory,
Or yvory into the waves were sent;
And otherwhere the snowy substaunce sprent
With vermell, like the boyes blood therein shed,
A piteous spectacle did represent;
And otherwhiles with gold besprinkeled,
Yt seemd thenchaunted flame, which did Creusa wed.

All this and more might in that goodly gate
Be red; that ever open stood to all
Which thether came: but in the porch there sate
A comely personage of stature tall,
And semblaunce pleasing, more then naturall,
That traveilers to him seemd to entize;
His looser garment to the ground did fall,
And flew about his heeles in wanton wize,
Not fitt for speedy pace or manly exercize.

They in that place him Genius did call:
Not that celestiall powre, to whom the care
Of life, and generation of all
That lives, perteines in charge particulare,
Who wondrous things concerning our welfare,
And straunge phantomes, doth lett us ofte forsee,
And ofte of secret ill bids us beware:
That is our selfe, whom though we doe not see,
Yet each doth in him selfe it well perceive to bee.

Therefore a god him sage antiquity
Did wisely make, and good Agdistes call:
But this same was to that quite contrary,
The foe of life, that good envyes to all,
That secretly doth us procure to fall,
Through guilefull semblants, which he makes us see.

He of this gardin had the governall,
And Pleasures porter was devizd to bee,
Holding a staffe in hand for more formalitee.

With diverse flowres he daintily was deckt,
And strowed rownd about, and by his side
A mighty mazer bowle of wine was sett,
As if it had to him bene sacrifide;
Wherewith all new-come guests he gratyfide:
So did he eke Sir Guyon passing by:
But he his ydle curtesie defide,
And overthrew his bowle disdainfully,
And broke his staffe, with which he charmed semblants
  sly.

Thus being entred, they behold arownd
A large and spacious plaine, on every side
Strowed with pleasauns, whose fayre grassy grownd
Mantled with greene, and goodly beautifide
With all the ornaments of Floraes pride,
Wherewith her mother Art, as halfe in scorne
Of niggard Nature, like a pompous bride
Did decke her, and too lavishly adorne,
When forth from virgin bowre she comes in th' early
  morne.

Thereto the heavens alwayes joviall,
Lookte on them lovely, still in stedfast state,
Ne suffred storme nor frost on them to fall,
Their tender buds or leaves to violate,
Nor scorching heat, nor cold intemperate,
T' afflict the creatures which therein did dwell,
But the milde ayre with season moderate
Gently attempred, and disposd so well,
That still it breathed forth sweet spirit and holesom
  smell.

More sweet and holesome then the pleasaunt hill
Of Rhodope, on which the nimphe that bore
A gyaunt babe her selfe for griefe did kill;
Or the Thessalian Tempe, where of yore
Fayre Daphne Phœbus hart with love did gore;
Or Ida, where the gods lov'd to repayre,
When ever they their heavenly bowres forlore;
Or sweet Parnasse, the haunt of Muses fayre;
Or Eden selfe, if ought with Eden mote compayre.

Much wondred Guyon at the fayre aspect
Of that sweet place, yet suffred no delight
To sincke into his sence, nor mind affect,
But passed forth, and lookt still forward right,
Brydling his will, and maystering his might:
Till that he came unto another gate,
No gate, but like one, being goodly dight
With bowes and braunches, which did broad dilate
Their clasping armes, in wanton wreathings intricate:

So fashioned a porch with rare device,
Archt over head with an embracing vine,
Whose bounches, hanging downe, seemd to entice
All passers by to taste their lushious wine,
And did them selves into their hands incline,
As freely offering to be gathered:
Some deepe empurpled as the hyacine,
Some as the rubine laughing sweetely red,
Some like faire emeraudes, not yet well ripened.

And them amongst, some were of burnisht gold,
So made by art, to beautify the rest,
Which did themselves emongst the leaves enfold,
As lurking from the vew of covetous guest,
That the weake boughes, with so rich load opprest,
Did bow adowne, as overburdened.

Under that porch a comely dame did rest,
Clad in fayre weedes, but fowle disordered,
And garments loose, that seemd unmeet for womanhed.

In her left hand a cup of gold she held,
And with her right the riper fruit did reach,
Whose sappy liquor, that with fulnesse sweld,
Into her cup she scruzd, with daintie breach
Of her fine fingers, without fowle empeach,
That so faire winepresse made the wine more sweet:
Thereof she usd to give to drinke to each,
Whom passing by she happened to meet:
It was her guise, all straungers goodly so to greet.

So she to Guyon offred it to tast,
Who, taking it out of her tender hond,
The cup to ground did violently cast,
That all in peeces it was broken fond,
And with the liquor stained all the lond:
Whereat Excesse exceedingly was wroth,
Yet no'te the same amend, ne yet withstond,
But suffered him to passe, all were she loth;
Who, nought regarding her displeasure, forward goth.

There the most daintie paradise on ground
It selfe doth offer to his sober eye,
In which all pleasures plenteously abownd,
And none does others happinesse envye:
The painted flowres, the trees upshooting hye,
The dales for shade, the hilles for breathing space,
The trembling groves, the christall running by;
And that which all faire workes doth most aggrace,
The art, which all that wrought, appeared in no place.

One would have thought, (so cunningly the rude
And scorned partes were mingled with the fine,)
That Nature had for wantonesse ensude

Art, and that Art at Nature did repine;
So striving each th' other to undermine,
Each did the others worke more beautify;
So diff'ring both in willes agreed in fine:
So all agreed through sweete diversity,
This gardin to adorne with all variety.

And in the midst of all a fountaine stood,
Of richest substance that on earth might bee,
So pure and shiny that the silver flood
Through every channell running one might see:
Most goodly it with curious ymageree
Was overwrought, and shapes of naked boyes,
Of which some seemd with lively jollitee
To fly about playing their wanton toyes,
Whylest others did them selves embay in liquid joyes.

And over all, of purest gold was spred
A trayle of yvie in his native hew:
For the rich metall was so coloured,
That wight, who did not well avis'd it vew,
Would surely deeme it to bee yvie trew:
Low his lascivious armes adown did creepe,
That themselves dipping in the silver dew,
Their fleecy flowres they tenderly did steepe,
Which drops of christall seemd for wantones to weep.

Infinit streames continually did well
Out of this fountaine, sweet and faire to see,
The which into an ample laver fell,
And shortly grew to so great quantitie,
That like a litle lake it seemd to bee;
Whose depth exceeded not three cubits hight,
That through the waves one might the bottom see,
All pav'd beneath with jaspar shining bright,
That seemd the fountaine in that sea did sayle upright.

And all the margent round about was sett
With shady laurell trees, thence to defend
The sunny beames, which on the billowes bett,
And those which therein bathed mote offend.
As Guyon hapned by the same to wend,
Two naked damzelles he therein espyde,
Which, therein bathing, seemed to contend
And wrestle wantonly, ne car'd to hyde
Their dainty partes from vew of any which them eyd.

Sometimes the one would lift the other quight
Above the waters, and then downe againe
Her plong, as over maystered by might,
Where both awhile would covered remaine,
And each the other from to rise restraine;
The whiles their snowy limbes, as through a vele,
So through the christall waves appeared plaine:
Then suddeinly both would themselves unhele,
And th' amarous sweet spoiles to greedy eyes revele.

As that faire starre, the messenger of morne,
His deawy face out of the sea doth reare,
Or as the Cyprian goddesse, newly borne
Of th' oceans fruitfull froth, did first appeare,
Such seemed they, and so their yellow heare
Christalline humor dropped downe apace.
Whom such when Guyon saw, he drew him neare,
And somewhat gan relent his earnest pace;
His stubborne brest gan secret pleasaunce to embrace.

The wanton maidens, him espying, stood
Gazing a while at his unwonted guise;
Then th' one her selfe low ducked in the flood,
Abasht that her a straunger did avise:
But thother rather higher did arise,
And her two lilly paps aloft displayd,

And all, that might his melting hart entyse
To her delights, she unto him bewrayd:
The rest, hidd underneath, him more desirous made.

With that the other likewise up arose,
And her faire lockes, which formerly were bownd
Up in one knott, she low adowne did lose:
Which, flowing long and thick, her cloth'd arownd,
And th' yvorie in golden mantle gownd:
So that faire spectacle from him was reft,
Yet that which reft it no lesse faire was fownd:
So hidd in lockes and waves from lookers theft,
Nought but her lovely face she for his looking left.

Withall she laughed, and she blusht withall,
That blushing to her laughter gave more grace,
And laughter to her blushing, as did fall.
Now when they spyde the knight to slacke his pace,
Them to behold, and in his sparkling face
The secrete signes of kindled lust appeare,
Their wanton meriments they did encreace,
And to him beckned to approch more neare,
And shewd him many sights, that corage cold could
    reare.

On which when gazing him the palmer saw,
He much rebukt those wandring eyes of his,
And, counseld well, him forward thence did draw.
Now are they come nigh to the Bowre of Blis,
Of her fond favorites so nam'd amis:
When thus the palmer: "Now, sir, well avise;
For here the end of all our traveill is:
Here wonnes Acrasia, whom we must surprise,
Els she will slip away, and all our drift despise."

Eftsoones they heard a most melodious sound,
Of all that mote delight a daintie eare,

Such as attonce might not on living ground,
Save in this paradise, be heard elswhere:
Right hard it was for wight which did it heare,
To read what manner musicke that mote bee:
For all that pleasing is to living eare
Was there consorted in one harmonee;
Birdes, voices, instruments, windes, waters, all agree.

The joyous birdes, shrouded in chearefull shade,
Their notes unto the voice attempred sweet:
Th' angelicall soft trembling voyces made
To th' instruments divine respondence meet:
The silver sounding instruments did meet
With the base murmure of the waters fall;
The waters fall with difference discreet,
Now soft, now loud, unto the wind did call:
The gentle warbling wind low answered to all.

There, whence that musick seemed heard to bee,
Was the faire witch, her selfe now solacing
With a new lover, whom, through sorceree
And witchcraft, she from farre did thether bring:
There she had him now laid a slombering,
In secret shade after long wanton joyes:
Whilst round about them pleasauntly did sing
Many faire ladies and lascivious boyes,
That ever mixt their song with light licentious toyes.

And all that while, right over him she hong,
With her false eyes fast fixed in his sight,
As seeking medicine whence she was stong,
Or greedily depasturing delight:
And oft inclining downe, with kisses light,
For feare of waking him, his lips bedewd,
And through his humid eyes did sucke his spright,
Quite molten into lust and pleasure lewd;
Wherewith she sighed soft, as if his case she rewd.

The whiles some one did chaunt this lovely lay:—
"Ah! see, who so fayre thing doest faine to see,
In springing flowre the image of thy day;
Ah! see the virgin rose, how sweetly shee
Doth first peepe foorth with bashfull modestee,
That fairer seemes, the lesse ye see her may;
Lo! see soone after, how more bold and free
Her bared bosome she doth broad display;
Lo! see soone after, how she fades and falls away.

So passeth, in the passing of a day,
Of mortall life the leafe, the bud, the flowre,
Ne more doth florish after first decay,
That earst was sought to deck both bed and bowre
Of many a lady, and many a paramowre:
Gather therefore the rose, whilest yet is prime,
For soone comes age, that will her pride deflowre:
Gather the rose of love, whilest yet is time,
Whilest loving thou mayst loved be with equall crime."

He ceast, and then gan all the quire of birdes
Their diverse notes t' attune unto his lay,
As in approvaunce of his pleasing wordes.
The constant payre heard all that he did say,
Yet swarved not, but kept their forward way,
Through many covert groves and thickets close,
In which they creeping did at last display
That wanton lady, with her lover lose,
Whose sleepie head she in her lap did soft dispose.

Upon a bed of roses she was layd,
As faint through heat, or dight to pleasant sin,
And was arayd, or rather disarayd,
All in a vele of silke and silver thin,
That hid no whit her alablaster skin,
But rather shewd more white, if more might bee:

More subtile web Arachne cannot spin,
Nor the fine nets, which oft we woven see
Of scorched deaw, do not in th' ayre more lightly flee.

Her snowy brest was bare to ready spoyle
Of hungry eies, which n'ote therewith be fild;
And yet through languour of her late sweet toyle,
Few drops, more cleare then nectar, forth distild,
That like pure orient perles adowne it trild;
And her faire eyes, sweet smyling in delight,
Moystened their fierie beames, with which she thrild
Fraile harts, yet quenched not, like starry light,
Which, sparckling on the silent waves, does seeme more
    bright.

The young man, sleeping by her, seemd to be
Some goodly swayne of honorable place,
That certes it great pitty was to see
Him his nobility so fowle deface:
A sweet regard and amiable grace,
Mixed with manly sternesse, did appeare,
Yet sleeping, in his well proportiond face,
And on his tender lips the downy heare
Did now but freshly spring, and silken blossoms beare.

His warlike armes, the ydle instruments
Of sleeping praise, were hong upon a tree,
And his brave shield, full of old moniments,
Was fowly ra'st, that none the signes might see;
Ne for them, ne for honour, cared hee,
Ne ought that did to his advauncement tend,
But in lewd loves, and wastfull luxuree,
His dayes, his goods, his bodie he did spend:
O horrible enchantment, that him so did blend!

The noble Elfe and carefull palmer drew
So nigh them, minding nought but lustfull game,

That suddein forth they on them rusht, and threw
A subtile net, which only for that same
The skilfull palmer formally did frame:
So held them under fast, the whiles the rest
Fled all away for feare of fowler shame.
The faire enchauntresse, so unwares opprest,
Tryde all her arts and all her sleights, thence out to
    wrest.

And eke her lover strove: but all in vaine;
For that same net so cunningly was wound,
That neither guile nor force might it distraine.
They tooke them both, and both them strongly bound
In captive bandes, which there they readie found:
But her in chaines of adamant he tyde;
For nothing else might keepe her safe and sound;
But Verdant (so he hight) he soone untyde,
And counsell sage in steed thereof to him applyde.

But all those pleasaunt bowres and pallace brave
Guyon broke downe, with rigour pittilesse;
Ne ought their goodly workmanship might save
Them from the tempest of his wrathfulnesse,
But that their blisse he turn'd to balefulnesse:
Their groves he feld, their gardins did deface,
Their arbers spoyle, their cabinets suppresse,
Their banket houses burne, their buildings race,
And, of the fayrest late, now made the fowlest place.

Then led they her away, and eke that knight
They with them led, both sorrowfull and sad:
The way they came, the same retourn'd they right,
Till they arrived where they lately had
Charm'd those wild-beasts, that rag'd with furie mad:
Which, now awaking, fierce at them gan fly,
As in their mistresse reskew, whom they lad;

But them the palmer soone did pacify.
Then Guyon askt, what meant those beastes which there
   did ly.

Sayd he: "These seeming beasts are men indeed,
Whom this enchauntresse hath transformed thus,
Whylome her lovers, which her lustes did feed,
Now turned into figures hideous,
According to their mindes like monstruous."
"Sad end," quoth he, "of life intemperate,
And mournefull meed of joyes delicious!
But, palmer, if it mote thee so aggrate,
Let them returned be unto their former state."

Streight way he with his vertuous staffe them strooke,
And streight of beastes they comely men became;
Yet being men they did unmanly looke,
And stared ghastly, some for inward shame,
And some for wrath, to see their captive dame:
But one above the rest in speciall,
That had an hog beene late, hight Grylle by name,
Repyned greatly, and did him miscall,
That had from hoggish forme him brought to naturall.

Saide Guyon: "See the mind of beastly man,
That hath so soone forgot the excellence
Of his creation, when he life began,
That now he chooseth, with vile difference,
To be a beast, and lacke intelligence."
To whom the palmer thus: "The donghill kinde
Delightes in filth and fowle incontinence:
Let Gryll be Gryll, and have his hoggish minde;
But let us hence depart, whilest wether serves and
   winde."

                  (Book II, canto xii entire)

[The Garden of Adonis]

Shee brought her to her joyous paradize,
Wher most she wonnes, when she on earth does dwell:
So faire a place as Nature can devize:
Whether in Paphos, or Cytheron hill,
Or it in Gnidus bee, I wote not well;
But well I wote by triall, that this same
All other pleasaunt places doth excell,
And called is by her lost lovers name,
The Gardin of Adonis, far renowmd by fame.

In that same gardin all the goodly flowres,
Wherewith Dame Nature doth her beautify,
And decks the girlonds of her paramoures,
Are fetcht: there is the first seminary
Of all things that are borne to live and dye,
According to their kynds. Long worke it were,
Here to account the endlesse progeny
Of all the weeds that bud and blossome there;
But so much as doth need must needs be counted here.

It sited was in fruitfull soyle of old,
And girt in with two walls on either side,
The one of yron, the other of bright gold,
That none might thorough breake, nor overstride:
And double gates it had, which opened wide,
By which both in and out men moten pas;
Th' one faire and fresh, the other old and dride:
Old Genius the porter of them was,
Old Genius, the which a double nature has.

He letteth in, he letteth out to wend,
All that to come into the world desire:

A thousand thousand naked babes attend
About him day and night, which doe require
That he with fleshly weeds would them attire:
Such as him list, such as eternall Fate
Ordained hath, he clothes with sinfull mire,
And sendeth forth to live in mortall state,
Till they agayn returne backe by the hinder gate.

After that they againe retourned beene,
They in that gardin planted bee agayne,
And grow afresh, as they had never seene
Fleshly corruption nor mortall payne.
Some thousand yeares so doen they there remayne,
And then of him are clad with other hew,
Or sent into the chaungefull world agayne,
Till thether they retourne, where first they grew:
So like a wheele arownd they ronne from old to new.

Ne needs there gardiner to sett or sow,
To plant or prune: for of their owne accord
All things, as they created were, doe grow,
And yet remember well the mighty word,
Which first was spoken by th' Almighty Lord,
That bad them to increase and multiply:
Ne doe they need with water of the ford
Or of the clouds to moysten their roots dry;
For in themselves eternall moisture they imply.

Infinite shapes of creatures there are bred,
And uncouth formes, which none yet ever knew;
And every sort is in a sondry bed
Sett by it selfe, and ranckt in comely rew:
Some fitt for reasonable sowles t' indew,
Some made for beasts, some made for birds to weare,
And all the fruitfull spawne of fishes hew

In endlesse rancks along enraunged were,
That seemd the ocean could not containe them there.

Daily they grow, and daily forth are sent
Into the world, it to replenish more;
Yet is the stocke not lessened nor spent,
But still remaines in everlasting store,
As it at first created was of yore:
For in the wide wombe of the world there lyes,
In hatefull darknes and in deepe horrore,
An huge eternal chaos, which supplyes
The substaunces of Natures fruitfull progenyes.

All things from thence doe their first being fetch,
And borrow matter whereof they are made,
Which, whenas forme and feature it does ketch,
Becomes a body, and doth then invade
The state of life out of the griesly shade.
That substaunce is eterne, and bideth so,
Ne when the life decayes, and forme does fade,
Doth it consume and into nothing goe,
But chaunged is, and often altred to and froe.

The substaunce is not chaungd nor altered,
But th' only forme and outward fashion;
For every substaunce is conditioned
To chaunge her hew, and sondry formes to don,
Meet for her temper and complexion:
For formes are variable, and decay
By course of kinde and by occasion;
And that faire flowre of beautie fades away,
As doth the lilly fresh before the sunny ray.

Great enimy to it, and to all the rest,
That in the Gardin of Adonis springs,
Is wicked Tyme, who, with his scyth addrest,
Does mow the flowring herbes and goodly things,

And all their glory to the ground downe flings,
Where they do wither and are fowly mard:
He flyes about, and with his flaggy winges
Beates downe both leaves and buds without regard,
Ne ever pitty may relent his malice hard.

Yet pitty often did the gods relent,
To see so faire thinges mard and spoiled quight:
And their great mother Venus did lament
The losse of her deare brood, her deare delight:
Her hart was pierst with pitty at the sight,
When walking through the gardin them she saw,
Yet no'te she find redresse for such despight:
For all that lives is subject to that law:
All things decay in time, and to their end doe draw.

But were it not, that Time their troubler is,
All that in this delightfull gardin growes
Should happy bee, and have immortall blis:
For here all plenty and all pleasure flowes,
And sweete Love gentle fitts emongst them throwes,
Without fell rancor or fond gealosy:
Franckly each paramor his leman knowes,
Each bird his mate, ne any does envy
Their goodly meriment and gay felicity.

There is continuall spring, and harvest there
Continuall, both meeting at one tyme:
For both the boughes doe laughing blossoms beare,
And with fresh colours decke the wanton pryme,
And eke attonce the heavy trees they clyme,
Which seeme to labour under their fruites lode:
The whiles the joyous birdes make their pastyme
Emongst the shady leaves, their sweet abode,
And their trew loves without suspition tell abrode.

Right in the middest of that paradise
There stood a stately mount, on whose round top
A gloomy grove of mirtle trees did rise,
Whose shady boughes sharp steele did never lop,
Nor wicked beastes their tender buds did crop,
But like a girlond compassed the hight,
And from their fruitfull sydes sweet gum did drop,
That all the ground, with pretious deaw bedight,
Threw forth most dainty odours, and most sweet delight.

And in the thickest covert of that shade
There was a pleasaunt arber, not by art,
But of the trees owne inclination made,
Which knitting their rancke braunches part to part,
With wanton yvie twyne entrayld athwart,
And eglantine and caprifole emong,
Fashiond above within their inmost part,
That nether Phoebus beams could through them throng,
Nor Aeolus sharp blast could worke them any wrong.

And all about grew every sort of flowre,
To which sad lovers were transformde of yore;
Fresh Hyacinthus, Phœbus paramoure
And dearest love,
Foolish Narcisse, that likes the watry shore,
Sad Amaranthus, made a flowre but late,
Sad Amaranthus, in whose purple gore
Me seemes I see Amintas wretched fate,
To whom sweet poets verse hath given endlesse date.

There wont fayre Venus often to enjoy
Her deare Adonis joyous company,
And reape sweet pleasure of the wanton boy:
There yet, some say, in secret he does ly,
Lapped in flowres and pretious spycery,
By her hid from the world, and from the skill

Of Stygian gods, which doe her love envy;
But she her selfe, when ever that she will,
Possesseth him, and of his sweetnesse takes her fill.

And sooth, it seemes, they say: for he may not
For ever dye, and ever buried bee
In balefull night, where all thinges are forgot;
All be he subject to mortalitie,
Yet is eterne in mutabilitie,
And by succession made perpetuall,
Transformed oft, and chaunged diverslie:
For him the father of all formes they call;
Therfore needs mote he live, that living gives to all.

There now he liveth in eternall blis,
Joying his goddesse, and of her enjoyd:
Ne feareth he henceforth that foe of his,
Which with his cruell tuske him deadly cloyd:
For that wilde bore, the which him once annoyd,
She firmely hath emprisoned for ay,
That her sweet love his malice mote avoyd,
In a strong rocky cave, which is, they say,
Hewen underneath that mount, that none him losen
    may.

There now he lives in everlasting joy,
With many of the gods in company,
Which thether haunt, and with the winged boy
Sporting him selfe in safe felicity:
Who, when he hath with spoiles and cruelty
Ransackt the world, and in the wofull harts
Of many wretches set his triumphes hye,
Thether resortes, and laying his sad dartes
Asyde, with faire Adonis playes his wanton partes.

(*Book III, canto vi, stanzas 29–49*)

[*The Masque of Cupid*]

The noble mayd, still standing, all this vewd,
And merveild at his straunge intendiment:
With that a joyous fellowship issewd
Of minstrales, making goodly meriment,
With wanton bardes, and rymers impudent,
All which together song full chearefully
A lay of loves delight, with sweet concent:
After whom marcht a jolly company,
In manner of a maske, enranged orderly.

The whiles a most delitious harmony
In full straunge notes was sweetly heard to sound,
That the rare sweetnesse of the melody
The feeble sences wholy did confound,
And the frayle soule in deepe delight nigh drownd:
And when it ceast, shrill trompets lowd did bray,
That their report did far away rebound,
And when they ceast, it gan againe to play,
The whiles the maskers marched forth in trim aray.

The first was Fansy, like a lovely boy,
Of rare aspect and beautie without peare,
Matchable ether to that ympe of Troy,
Whom Jove did love and chose his cup to beare,
Or that same daintie lad, which was so deare
To great Alcides, that, when as he dyde,
He wailed womanlike with many a teare,
And every wood and every valley wyde
He fild with Hylas name; the nymphes eke Hylas cryde.

His garment nether was of silke nor say,
But paynted plumes, in goodly order dight,

Like as the sunburnt Indians do aray
Their tawney bodies, in their proudest plight:
As those same plumes, so seemd he vaine and light,
That by his gate might easily appeare;
For still he far'd as dauncing in delight,
And in his hand a windy fan did beare,
That in the ydle ayre he mov'd still here and theare.

And him beside marcht amorous Desyre,
Who seemd of ryper yeares then th' other swayne,
Yet was that other swayne this elders syre,
And gave him being, commune to them twayne:
His garment was disguysed very vayne,
And his embrodered bonet sat awry;
Twixt both his hands few sparks he close did strayne,
Which still he blew, and kindled busily,
That soone they life conceiv'd, and forth in flames did
    fly.

Next after him went Doubt, who was yclad
In a discolour'd cote of straunge disguyse,
That at his backe a brode capuccio had,
And sleeves dependaunt Albanese-wyse:
He lookt askew with his mistrustfull eyes,
And nycely trode, as thornes lay in his way,
Or that the flore to shrinke he did avyse,
And on a broken reed he still did stay
His feeble steps, which shrunck when hard thereon he
    lay.

With him went Daunger, cloth'd in ragged weed,
Made of beares skin, that him more dreadfull made,
Yet his owne face was dreadfull, ne did need
Straunge horrour to deforme his griesly shade:
A net in th' one hand, and a rusty blade
In th' other was, this Mischiefe, that Mishap;

With th' one his foes he threatned to invade,
With th' other he his friends ment to enwrap:
For whom he could not kill he practizd to entrap.

Next him was Feare, all arm'd from top to toe,
Yet thought himselfe not safe enough thereby,
But feard each shadow moving too or froe,
And his owne armes when glittering he did spy,
Or clashing heard, he fast away did fly,
As ashes pale of hew, and wingyheeld;
And evermore on Daunger fixt his eye,
Gainst whom he alwayes bent a brasen shield,
Which his right hand unarmed fearefully did wield.

With him went Hope in rancke, a handsome mayd,
Of chearefull looke and lovely to behold;
In silken samite she was light arayd,
And her fayre lockes were woven up in gold;
She alway smyld, and in her hand did hold
An holy water sprinckle, dipt in deowe,
With which she sprinckled favours manifold
On whom she list, and did great liking sheowe,
Great liking unto many, but true love to feowe.

And after them Dissemblaunce and Suspect
Marcht in one rancke, yet an unequall paire:
For she was gentle and of milde aspect,
Courteous to all and seeming debonaire,
Goodly adorned and exceeding faire:
Yet was that all but paynted and pourloynd,
And her bright browes were deckt with borrowed haire:
Her deeds were forged, and her words false coynd,
And alwaies in her hand two clewes of silke she twynd.

But he was fowle, ill favoured, and grim,
Under his eiebrowes looking still askaunce;
And ever as Dissemblaunce laught on him,

He lowrd on her with daungerous eyeglaunce,
Shewing his nature in his countenaunce;
His rolling eies did never rest in place,
But walkte each where, for feare of hid mischaunce;
Holding a lattis still before his face,
Through which he stil did peep, as forward he did pace.

Next him went Griefe and Fury matcht yfere;
Griefe all in sable sorrowfully clad,
Downe hanging his dull head, with heavy chere,
Yet inly being more then seeming sad:
A paire of pincers in his hand he had,
With which he pinched people to the hart,
That from thenceforth a wretched life they ladd,
In wilfull languor and consuming smart,
Dying each day with inward wounds of dolours dart.

But Fury was full ill appareiled
In rags, that naked nigh she did appeare,
With ghastly looks and dreadfull drerihed;
For from her backe her garments she did teare,
And from her head ofte rent her snarled heare:
In her right hand a firebrand shee did tosse
About her head, still roming here and there;
As a dismayed deare in chace embost,
Forgetfull of his safety, hath his right way lost.

After them went Displeasure and Pleasaunce,
He looking lompish and full sullein sad,
And hanging downe his heavy countenaunce;
She chearfull fresh and full of joyaunce glad,
As if no sorrow she ne felt ne drad;
That evill matched paire they seemd to bee:
An angry waspe th' one in a viall had,
Th' other in hers an hony-laden bee.
Thus marched these six couples forth in faire degree.

After all these there marcht a most faire dame,
Led of two grysie villeins, th' one Despight,
The other cleped Cruelty by name:
She, dolefull lady, like a dreary spright
Cald by strong charmes out of eternall night,
Had deathes owne ymage figurd in her face,
Full of sad signes, fearfull to living sight,
Yet in that horror shewd a seemely grace,
And with her feeble feete did move a comely pace.

Her brest all naked, as nett yvory,
Without adorne of gold or silver bright,
Wherewith the craftesman wonts it beautify,
Of her dew honour was despoyled quight,
And a wide wound therein (O ruefull sight!)
Entrenched deep with knyfe accursed keene,
Yet freshly bleeding forth her fainting spright,
(The worke of cruell hand) was to be seene,
That dyde in sanguine red her skin all snowy cleene.

At that wide orifice her trembling hart
Was drawne forth, and in silver basin layd,
Quite through transfixed with a deadly dart,
And in her blood yet steeming fresh embayd:
And those two villeins, which her steps upstayd,
When her weake feete could scarcely her sustaine,
And fading vitall powers gan to fade,
Her forward still with torture did constraine,
And evermore encreased her consuming paine.

Next after her, the Winged God him selfe
Came riding on a lion ravenous,
Taught to obay the menage of that elfe,
That man and beast with powre imperious
Subdeweth to his kingdome tyrannous:
His blindfold eies he bad a while unbinde,

That his proud spoile of that same dolorous
Faire dame he might behold in perfect kinde,
Which seene, he much rejoyced in his cruell minde.

Of which ful prowd, him selfe up rearing hye,
He looked round about with sterne disdayne,
And did survay his goodly company:
And marshalling the evill ordered trayne,
With that the darts which his right hand did straine
Full dreadfully he shooke, that all did quake,
And clapt on hye his coulourd winges twaine,
That all his many it affraide did make:
Tho, blinding him againe, his way he forth did take.

Behinde him was Reproch, Repentaunce, Shame;
Reproch the first, Shame next, Repent behinde:
Repentaunce feeble, sorowfull, and lame;
Reproch despightful, carelesse, and unkinde;
Shame most ill favourd, bestiall, and blinde:
Shame lowrd, Repentaunce sigh'd, Reproch did scould;
Reproch sharpe stings, Repentaunce whips entwinde,
Shame burning brond-yrons in her hand did hold:
All three to each unlike, yet all made in one mould.

And after them a rude confused rout
Of persons flockt, whose names is hard to read:
Emongst them was sterne Strife, and Anger stout,
Unquiet Care, and fond Unthriftyhead,
Lewd Losse of Time, and Sorrow seeming dead,
Inconstant Chaunge, and false Disloyalty,
Consuming Riotise, and guilty Dread
Of Heavenly Vengeaunce, faint Infirmity,
Vile Poverty, and lastly Death with Infamy.

(Book III, canto xii, stanzas 5–25)

[Dame Nature]

Then forth issewed (great goddesse) great Dame Na-
    ture,
With goodly port and gracious majesty,
Being far greater and more tall of stature
Then any of the gods or powers on hie:
Yet certes by her face and physnomy,
Whether she man or woman inly were,
That could not any creature well descry:
For, with a veile that wimpled every where,
Her head and face was hid, that mote to none appeare.

That, some doe say, was so by skill devized,
To hide the terror of her uncouth hew
From mortall eyes, that should be sore agrized;
For that her face did like a lion shew,
That eye of wight could not indure to view:
But others tell that it so beautious was,
And round about such beames of splendor threw,
That it the sunne a thousand times did pass,
Ne could be seene, but like an image in a glass.

That well may seemen true: for well I weene
That this same day, when she on Arlo sat,
Her garment was so bright and wondrous sheene,
That my fraile wit cannot devize to what
It to compare, nor finde like stuffe to that:
As those three sacred saints, though else most wise,
Yet on Mount Thabor quite their wits forgat,
When they their glorious Lord in strange disguise
Transfigur'd sawe; his garments so did daze their eyes.

In a fayre plaine upon an equall hill
She placed was in a pavilion;
Not such as craftes-men by their idle skill
Are wont for princes states to fashion:
But th' Earth her self, of her owne motion,
Out of her fruitfull bosome made to growe
Most dainty trees, that, shooting up anon,
Did seeme to bow their bloosming heads full lowe,
For homage unto her, and like a throne did shew.

So hard it is for any living wight
All her array and vestiments to tell,
That old Dan Geffrey (in whose gentle spright,
The pure well head of poesie did dwell)
In his *Foules Parley* durst not with it mel,
But it transferd to Alane, who he thought
Had in his *Plaint of Kinde* describ'd it well:
Which who will read set forth so as it ought,
Go seek he out that Alane where he may be sought.

And all the earth far underneath her feete
Was dight with flowres, that voluntary grew
Out of the ground, and sent forth odours sweet;
Tenne thousand mores of sundry sent and hew,
That might delight the smell, or please the view;
The which the nymphes from all the brooks thereby
Had gathered, which they at her foot-stoole threw;
That richer seem'd then any tapestry,
That princes bowres adorne with painted imagery.

And Mole himselfe, to honour her the more,
Did deck himself in freshest faire attire,
And his high head, that seemeth alwaies hore
With hardned frosts of former winters ire,
He with an oaken girlond now did tire,
As if the love of some new nymph late seene

Had in him kindled youthfull fresh desire,
And made him change his gray attire to greene:
Ah, gentle Mole! such joyance hath thee well beseene.

Was never so great joyance since the day
That all the gods whylome assembled were
On Hæmus hill in their divine array,
To celebrate the solemne bridall cheare
Twixt Peleus and Dame Thetis pointed there;
Where Phœbus self, that god of poets hight,
They say did sing the spousall hymne full cleere,
That all the gods were ravisht with delight
Of his celestiall song, and musicks wondrous might.

This great grandmother of all creatures bred,
Great Nature, ever young yet full of eld,
Still mooving, yet unmoved from her sted,
Unseene of any, yet of all beheld,
Thus sitting in her throne, as I have teld,
Before her came Dame Mutabilitie;
And being lowe before her presence feld,
With meek obaysance and humilitie,
Thus gan her plaintif plea, with words to amplifie:

"To thee, O greatest goddesse, onely great,
An humble suppliant loe! I lowely fly,
Seeking for right, which I of thee entreat,
Who right to all dost deale indifferently,
Damning all wrong and tortious injurie,
Which any of thy creatures doe to other
(Oppressing them with power, unequally)
Sith of them all thou art the equall mother,
And knittest each to each, as brother unto brother.

"To thee therefore of this same Jove I plaine,
And of his fellow gods that faine to be,
That challenge to themselves the whole worlds raign;

Of which the greatest part is due to me,
And heaven it selfe by heritage in fee:
For heaven and earth I both alike do deeme,
Sith heaven and earth are both alike to thee;
And gods no more then men thou doest esteeme:
For even the gods to thee, as men to gods, do seeme.

"Then weigh, O soveraigne goddesse, by what right
These gods do claime the worlds whole soverainty,
And that is onely dew unto thy might
Arrogate to themselves ambitiously:
As for the gods owne principality,
Which Jove usurpes unjustly, that to be
My heritage, Jove's self cannot deny,
From my great grandsire Titan unto mee
Deriv'd by dew descent; as is well knowen to thee.

"Yet mauger Jove, and all his gods beside,
I doe possesse the worlds most regiment;
As, if ye please it into parts divide,
And every parts inholders to convent,
Shall to your eyes appeare incontinent.
And first, the Earth (great mother of us all)
That only seems unmov'd and permanent,
And unto Mutability not thrall,
Yet is she chang'd in part, and eeke in generall.

"For all that from her springs, and is ybredde,
How-ever fayre it flourish for a time,
Yet see we soone decay; and, being dead,
To turne again unto their earthly slime:
Yet, out of their decay and mortall crime,
We daily see new creatures to arize,
And of their winter spring another prime,
Unlike in forme, and chang'd by strange disguise;
So turne they still about, and change in restlesse wise."

(Book VII, canto vii, stanzas 5–18)

[*Mutability*]

When these were past, thus gan the Titanesse:
"Lo! mighty mother, now be judge, and say
Whether in all thy creatures more or lesse
Change doth not raign and beare the greatest sway:
For who sees not that Time on all doth pray?
But times do change and move continually:
So nothing here long standeth in one stay:
Wherefore, this lower world who can deny
But to be subject still to Mutabilitie?"

Then thus gan Jove: "Right true it is, that these,
And all things else that under heaven dwell,
Are chaung'd of Time, who doth them all disseise
Of being: but who is it (to me tell)
That Time himselfe doth move and still compell
To keep his course? Is not that namely wee,
Which poure that vertue from our heavenly cell
That moves them all, and makes them changed be?
So them we gods doe rule, and in them also thee."

To whom thus Mutability: "The things
Which we see not how they are mov'd and swayd
Ye may attribute to your selves as kings,
And say they by your secret powre are made:
But what we see not, who shall us perswade?
But were they so, as ye them faine to be,
Mov'd by your might, and ordred by your ayde;
Yet what if I can prove, that even yee
Your selves are likewise chang'd, and subject unto mee?

"And first, concerning her that is the first,
Even you, faire Cynthia, whom so much ye make
Joves dearest darling; she was bred and nurst

On Cynthus hill, whence she her name did take:
Then is she mortall borne, how-so ye crake;
Besides, her face and countenance every day
We changed see, and sundry forms partake,
Now hornd, now round, now bright, now brown and
    gray;
So that *as changefull as the moone* men use to say.

"Next Mercury, who though he lesse appeare
To change his hew, and alwayes seeme as one,
Yet he his course doth altar every yeare,
And is of late far out of order gone:
So Venus eeke, that goodly paragone,
Though faire all night, yet is she darke all day;
And Phœbus self, who lightsome is alone,
Yet is he oft eclipsed by the way,
And fills the darkned world with terror and dismay.

"Now Mars, that valiant man, is changed most:
For he some times so far runs out of square,
That he his way doth seem quite to have lost,
And cleane without his usuall sphere to fare;
That even these star-gazers stonisht are
At sight thereof, and damne their lying bookes:
So likewise grim Sir Saturne oft doth spare
His sterne aspect, and calme his crabbed lookes:
So many turning cranks these have, so many crookes.

"But you, Dan Jove, that only constant are,
And king of all the rest, as ye do clame,
Are you not subject eeke to this misfare?
Then let me aske you this withouten blame:
Where were ye borne? Some say in Crete by name,
Others in Thebes, and others other-where;
But wheresoever they comment the same,

They all consent that ye begotten were
And borne here in this world, ne other can appeare.

"Then are ye mortall borne, and thrall to me,
Unlesse the kingdome of the sky yee make
Immortall and unchangeable to be:
Besides, that power and vertue which ye spake,
That ye here worke, doth many changes take,
And your owne natures change: for each of you,
That vertue have, or this or that to make,
Is checkt and changed from his nature trew,
By others opposition or obliquid view.

"Besides, the sundry motions of your spheares,
So sundry waies and fashions as clerkes faine,
Some in short space, and some in longer yeares;
What is the same but alteration plaine?
Onely the starrie skie doth still remaine:
Yet do the starres and signes therein still move,
And even it self is mov'd, as wizards saine.
But all that moveth doth mutation love:
Therefore both you and them to me I subject prove.

"Then since within this wide great universe
Nothing doth firme and permanent appeare,
But all things tost and turned by transverse:
What then should let, but I aloft should reare
My trophee, and from all the triumph beare?
Now judge then (O thou greatest goddesse trew!)
According as thy selfe doest see and heare,
And unto me addoom that is my dew;
That is the rule of all, all being rul'd by you."

So having ended, silence long ensewed;
Ne Nature to or fro spake for a space,
But, with firme eyes affixt, the ground still viewed.

Meane while, all creatures, looking in her face,
Expecting th' end of this so doubtfull case,
Did hang in long suspence what would ensew,
To whether side should fall the soveraigne place:
At length, she, looking up with chearefull view,
The silence brake, and gave her doome in speeches few:

"I well consider all that ye have sayd,
And find that all things stedfastnes doe hate
And changed be: yet being rightly wayd,
They are not changed from their first estate;
But by their change their being doe dilate:
And turning to themselves at length againe,
Doe worke their owne perfection so by fate:
Then over them Change doth not rule and raigne;
But they raigne over Change, and doe their states main-
        taine.

"Cease therefore, daughter, further to aspire,
And thee content thus to be rul'd by me:
For thy decay thou seekst by thy desire:
But time shall come that all shall changed bee,
And from thenceforth none no more change shall see."
So was the Titaness put downe and whist,
And Jove confirm'd in his imperiall see.
Then was that whole assembly quite dismist,
And Natur's selfe did vanish, whither no man wist.

When I bethinke me on that speech whyleare
Of Mutability, and well it way,
Me seemes, that though she all unworthy were
Of the heav'ns rule, yet, very sooth to say,
In all things else she beares the greatest sway:
Which makes me loath this state of life so tickle,
And love of things so vaine to cast away;
Whose flowring pride, so fading and so fickle,

Short Time shall soon cut down with his consuming
 sickle.

Then gin I thinke on that which Nature sayd,
Of that same time when no more change shall be,
But stedfast rest of all things, firmely stayd
Upon the pillours of eternity,
That is contrayr to Mutabilitie:
For all that moveth doth in change delight:
But thence-forth all shall rest eternally
With Him that is the God of Sabaoth hight:
O that great Sabbaoth God graunt me that Sabaoths
 sight!

(Book VII, canto vii, stanzas 47–end; canto viii entire)

Index of Titles and First Lines